NEIGHBORHOOD CHALLENGE

NEIGHBORHOOD CHALLENGE
The European Union and Its Neighbors

Edited by

BEZEN BALAMİR-COŞKUN
&
BİRGÜL DEMİRTAŞ- COŞKUN

Universal Publishers
Boca Raton

Neighborhood Challenge: The European Union and Its Neighbors

Copyright © 2009 Bezen Balamir-Coşkun & Birgül Demirtaş-Coşkun
All rights reserved.

No part of this book may be reproduced or transmitted in any form or by any means, electronic or mechanical, including photocopying, recording, or by any information storage and retrieval system, without written permission from the publisher.

Universal Publishers
Boca Raton, Florida • USA
2009

ISBN-10: 1-59942-968-3
ISBN-13: 978-1-59942-968-7

www.universal-publishers.com

Library of Congress Cataloging-in-Publication Data

Neighborhood challenge : European Union and its neighbors / Bezen Balamir-Coskun & Birgül Demirtas-Coskun (eds.).
　p. cm.
　Includes bibliographical references.
　ISBN 978-1-59942-968-7 (pbk. : alk. paper)
　1. European Union. 2. European Union countries--Foreign relations. I. Balamir-Coskun, Bezen, 1973- II. Demirtas-Coskun, Birgül.
　JN30.N435 2008
　341.242'2--dc22
　　　　　　　　　　　　2008026575

To our children

Zeynepnaz & Eren

Acknowledgements

First of all, we wish to thank all the contributors to this volume for their dedication and commitment. We are grateful they all delivered their manuscripts on time and dealt with editorial comments in the most professional and prompt way. It has been a pleasure working with them all. Thanks are also due to Zülfe Eyles and Amy Day who helped us by proofreading the chapters. Their contribution to this volume must be acknowledged and praised.

We are also grateful to each of our colleagues who read and commented on our drafts. Last but not least, we would like to offer our special thanks to Loughborough University Centre for Studies of International Governance for their financial and administrative support for our preliminary workshop.

We are indebted to Jeff Young, our publisher, for his constant support and encouragement from the beginning to the very end of this book.

We also would like to thank our families who provided an endless support during all our academic endeavors. Special thanks go to our children to whom we dedicate this book.

It is a great pleasure to acknowledge the deepened friendships created through the joint efforts put into the creation of this volume.

Editors
Bezen Balamir-Coşkun and Birgül Demirtaş-Coşkun

Contents

Notes on Contributors	xiii
Abbreviations	xix
Introduction	23
Birgül DEMİRTAŞ-COŞKUN	

Part I Western Balkans

1 The EU in the Western Balkans: Setting the Foundations of a Cohesive Strategy?   31
Vasilis MARGARAS

2 Of Cops and Robbers: European Union Policy on the Problem of Organized Crime in Bosnia Herzegovina   47
Ana E. JUNCOS

3 EU's Kosovo Policy: Multiple Challenges, Challenging Answers?   69
Birgül DEMİRTAŞ-COŞKUN

Part II Middle East

4 Greater Middle East and North Africa Project and EU Policy   95
İdris BAL

5 The Involvement of the European Union in the Middle East Peace Process   119
Umut UZER

6 The Euro-Mediterranean Partnership – On Good Intentions, Shopping Lists and à la carte Menus   145
Zuhal YEŞİLYURT-GÜNDÜZ

7 Limited Possibilities: Defining the Interaction Between the EU and the GCC   165
Christian KOCH

8 Europe's Role in Iran's Quest for Nuclear Power   187
Mustafa KİBAROĞLU

Part III Russia and the CIS

9 The South Caucasus in the European Periphery 211
Vít STŘÍTECKÝ

10 EU Policy Toward Central Asia 231
Yelda DEMİRAĞ

11 Inner-Caspian Neighborhood Challenge for the EU: Significance and Characteristics of an Emerging Energy Hub 253
Mert BİLGİN

12 Opportunities and Challenges for Cooperation in the Black Sea Region: The EU and the BSEC 273
Emel G. OKTAY

13 EU Security Involvement in the Greater Black Sea Area: A Romanian Perspective 293
Christina ROMILA

14 European Union's Neighborhood Relations with Eastern Europe and Russia: Values, Interests and Future Challenges for EU Foreign Policy 313
Giselle BOSSE

15 The EU Policies Toward the Ukraine 329
Sergiy GLEBOV

16 The European Union and Uzbekistan Since Independence 353
Havva KÖK

Part IV Turkey: Bridge to Neighborhood?

17 Linking Turkey's EU Accession Process and the ENP Regional Initiative: Necessary Cross-Border Cooperation with South Caucasus 379
Burcu GÜLTEKİN-PUNSMANN

18 Turkey Between the Middle East and the EU:
Boundaries and Bridges 397
Bezen BALAMİR-COŞKUN

Conclusion
The EU's Neighborhood Challenge 413
Bezen BALAMİR-COŞKUN

Index 417

Notes on Contributors

İdris Bal studied Political Science at Istanbul University between 1985-1989. He continued his studies in the Politics Department of Nottingham University, UK. He received his MA in International Relations in September 1992 after which he transferred to the Department of Middle Eastern Studies at Manchester University for research toward a Ph.D. He received his Ph.D. degree in 1998. He was promoted and appointed as Assistant Professor in 1998. He was the deputy editor of Journal of Police Sciences (Polis Bilimleri Dergisi) between 2001 and 2003. Fulbright has awarded him a scholarship and he studied in Center for Middle Eastern Studies, Harvard University in the term 2003-2004. In 2005, he was appointed to the Directorship of Policy Center in Ankara. He gained the degree of Associate Professorship in 2004. He has five published books and several national and international articles.

Bezen Balamir-Coşkun received her PhD in Politics, International Relations and European Studies from Loughborough University. Coskun's research fields include the Middle East, security region building in the Middle East and Middle East policies of the EU and Turkey. Coskun has several articles, book chapters and research papers on Middle East security, the EU's Middle East policy and Turkey's Middle East policy. Recently her article entitled *Analysing Desecuritisations: Problems and Prospects in Israeli-Palestinian Reconciliation* has won 2007 Routledge Global Change, Peace & Security Essay Competition.

Mert Bilgin received his PhD degrees in Political Science from Middle East Technical University and in Socio-Economy of Development from *L'École des Hautes Études en Sciences Sociales*. Currently he is an associate professor of International Relations at Bahçeşehir University, Istanbul. His research interests include political economy of hydrocarbons, sustainable development and sustainability modelling.

Giselle Bosse is an assistant professor at Maastricht University, the Netherlands. She holds an MA degree from the College of Europe (Natolin) in Warsaw, Poland and has conducted PhD research at the University of Aberystwyth, UK. Her research and publications focus on EU external relations and in particular, the European Neighbourhood Policy (ENP) and the Eastern Partnership (EaP). She is specifically interested in the role of "values" in the EU's policies, as well as the mechanisms through which the EU attempts to project its norms and rules to neighboring states (external governance, shifting "boundaries of order," partnership, conditionality). She is currently co-coordinating a 3-year research project on "Europeanizing or securitizing the 'outsiders'? Assessing the EU's partnership building approach with Eastern Europe" funded by the UK government's Economic and Social Research Council (RES-061-25-0001).

Yelda Demirağ graduated from the Department of History of Middle East Technical University. She received her Master's degree from Hacettepe University and PhD from Gazi University, Ankara. She works as an assistant professor at the Department of Political Science and International Relations at Başkent University since 2001. Dr. Demirağ, who published several articles in leading academic journals and edited a book, mainly focuses her work on Central Asia and Caucasia and on the nineteenth and early twentieth century Ottoman modernization and diplomacy.

Birgül Demirtaş-Coşkun received her Ph.D. from Free University Berlin in 2005. She is working as lecturer at the Department of Political Science and International Relations, Başkent University, Ankara, Turkey. She is also the assistant editor of the refereed journal *Uluslararası İlişkiler (International Relations)*, which is published by Turkish International Relations Council. She owns publications on Turkish foreign policy, Balkans and European Union. She is also the author of the following books: *Turkey, Germany and the Wars in Yugoslavia: A Search for Reconstruction of State Identities?* (Berlin: Logos Verlag, 2006), *The Vlachs: A Forgotten Minority in the Balkans* (London: Frank Cass, 2001) and *Bulgaristan'la Yeni Dönem: Soğuk Savaş Sonrası Ankara-Sofya İlişkileri (New Period with Bulgaria: Relations between Ankara and Sofia in Post-Cold War Era*, published by ASAM, Ankara, 2001). She is the editor of the book entitled *Türkiye-Yunanistan: Eski Sorunlar, Yeni Arayışlar (Turkey-Greece: Old Problems, New Approaches*, Ankara: ASAM, 2002) and co-editor of: *Balkan Diplomasisi (Balkan Diplomacy*, Ankara: ASAM, 2001).

Sergiy V. Glebov is an associate professor at the Department of International Relations and Leading Research Fellow at the Center for International Studies, Odessa Mechnikov National University. He is *kandydat politicheskih nayk* (equivalent to Ph.D. in Political Science and International Relations). He carried out researches and gave lectures in fields of foreign and security policy of the Ukraine, European and Euro-Atlantic security, international relations in the Black Sea-Caspian region, foreign policy of Russia, NATO-the Ukraine, and EU-the Ukraine relations. In 2000/2001 he was a visiting scholar at the Center for European Studies, University of Exeter (Exeter, UK) and at Columbia University, Harriman Institute (New-York City, U.S.) in 2003. His recent publications include: "Eastern concerns" of the "Big Mediterranean": Europeanization, the Black Sea region and the Ukraine," Florence, Italy, 2005; "War on Terror" and "Asymmetric" Response of International Terrorism," Odessa, 2006; "The Black Sea-

Caspian Security: GUAM," Kyiv, 2006; "the Ukraine's Foreign Policy Role: New Potential Opportunities," Odessa, 2007.

Burcu Gültekin-Punsmann holds a PhD from the Institut d'Etudes Politiques de Paris (Sciences-Po Paris). She is a Research Associate at the Center for European Studies at the *Middle East Technical University* in Ankara and the Turkey project manager of the *Caucasus Business and Development Network (CBDN)* project run by the London-based international NGO *International Alert*, which seeks to explore economy-related peacebuilding opportunities in Southern Caucasus region and will lay the foundation for a community of business people to engage in cross-conflict dialogue and economic cooperation. She has worked as a consultant for the European Parliament Directorate General External Policies of the Union. Former NATO Manfred Wörner research fellow for the preparation of a report entitled: *"Prospects for Regional Cooperation on NATO's South-Eastern Border, Developing a Turkish-Russian Cooperation in South Caucasus,"* she is currently acting as the principal investigator of the NATO-financed project, *"Bridging Perceptions of Security, Integrating the Black Sea Region,"* which involves researchers from Romania, Moldova, Georgia, Russia, and Turkey. Her current research is about the European Neighborhood Policy, energy security, cross-border cooperation, and conflict resolution.

Ana E. Juncos is a Lecturer in European Politics at the Department of Politics, University of Bristol. She was formerly a Post-Doctoral Research Fellow at the University of Bath, where she worked on a project about the "EU's Global Role," in cooperation with the Federal Trust and funded by the James Madison Trust. She holds a PhD in Politics, International Relations, and European Studies from Loughborough University. Her doctoral research, partly funded by Riksbankens Jubileumsfond through the European Foreign and Security Policy Studies Programme, focused on the coherence and effectiveness of the EU's Foreign and Security Policy in Bosnia.

Mustafa Kibaroğlu received his PhD in International Relations at Bilkent University in Ankara (1996) with his doctoral dissertation entitled: *"The Nuclear Non-proliferation Regime at the Crossroads: Strengthening or Uncertainty."* Dr. Kibaroglu joined the Department of International Relations at Bilkent University in Ankara in 1997 where he teaches courses on WMD proliferation, strategy, arms control & disarmament, Middle East Security, and Turkish foreign policy. He was awarded the Associate Professor title in October 2003. Dr. Kibaroglu spent his sabbatical leave during the 2004-2005 academic year at the Belfer Center for Science and International Affairs at Harvard University's Kennedy School of Government in Cambridge,

Massachusetts, U.S.. Dr. Kibaroglu has published chapters in edited books and articles in academic journals such as *Security Dialogue*, *The Nonproliferation Review*, *The Bulletin of the Atomic Scientists*, *Middle East Quarterly*, *The Middle East Journal*, *Brown Journal of World Affairs*, *European Security*, and *Middle Eastern Studies*. He also wrote op-eds, which appeared in the U.S. in *Defense News* as well as in Turkish dailies such as *Milliyet*, *Radikal*, *Cumhuriyet*, *Aksam* and *The Turkish Daily News*.

Christian Koch is the Director of International Studies at the Gulf Research Center located in Dubai, UAE. Prior, he worked as Head of the Strategic Studies Section at the Emirates Center for Strategic Studies and Research, Abu Dhabi. Dr. Koch received his PhD from the University of Erlangen-Nürnberg, Germany and also studied at the American University in Washington, D.C. and the University of South Carolina. He is the editor of *Unfulfilled Potential: Exploring the GCC-EU Relationship* (Dubai: Gulf Research Center, 2004), the *Gulf Yearbook* (2005 to 2007 editions), and co-editor of *Gulf Security in the Twenty-First Century* (Abu Dhabi: ECSSR, 1997) and *A Window of Opportunity: Europe, Gulf Security and the Aftermath of the Iraq War* (Dubai: Gulf Research Center, 2005). He is also a regular contributor to edited volumes, magazines and newspapers as well as for Jane's Sentinel Publications on Gulf issues. He is a member of the advisory board of the German Orient Foundation since January 2007.

Havva Kök is an assistant professor at the Department of International Relations, Hacettepe University in Ankara, and has held this position since 2004. From 2000 to 2003, she served as an advisor to the State Minister of Turkey responsible for Eurasian affairs at the Prime Ministry in Ankara. She graduated from Ankara University, Faculty of Politial Sciences in 1987. She received her first M.A. degree from Intitut Europeen des Hautes Etudes Internationales in 1990 in Nice, France. Her thesis was entitled, "Les obstacles politiques dans l'entreé de la Turquie a la Communauté europenne." She received her second M.A. degree in 1995 (thesis entitled, "Democratisation of Russian Foreign Policy") and her Ph.D. degree in 2000 (dissertaton entitled, "The Effects of Caspian Oil Pipeline on Russian Foreign Policy in the Caucasus") from the Department of Politics, Leeds University, UK. Currently, she is completing an Advanced MA Degree in Peace and Conflict Studies at European Peace University, Austria. She is the author of several publications touching on Eurasian politics, Turkish foreign policy, nonviolence and peace education. Her areas of interest are peace and conflict studies and international ethics, as well as Russia, Central Asia, and the Caucasus.

Contributors

Vasilis Margaras is a Visiting Researcher at the Centre for European Policy Studies in Brussels and he received his Ph.D from Loughborough University. He is working on an ESDP project regarding values and beliefs of EU member states manifested in their foreign policies. His main research interests are related to fields of foreign affairs, security and defense, and comparative European politics. Vasilis previously worked as a Visiting Lecturer/Researcher Assistant at Wolverhampton University and is the Chairman of the UACES Student Forum. He also previously worked as a researcher/campaign manager for Members of the European Parliament and other politicians in Spain, Greece and the UK. Vasilis has been granted a Young Faces Scholarship (2007-8) and would like to thank the Compagnia di San Paolo for all their valuable support.

Emel G. Oktay is an associate professor of international relations at Hacettepe University, Ankara. She completed her MA in the Department of European and International Studies at Reading University, England as a Jean Monnet Scholar. After receiving her PhD from Bilkent University, Ankara in 1999, she worked at the Foreign Relations Directorate of Undersecretariat for Defense Industries, Turkish Ministry of National Defense until September 2001. She was also the senior researcher and department head of Balkan and Cyprus Studies at the Eurasian Center for Strategic Studies (ASAM) between 2001 and 2003. She has a book titled "The Wars of Yugoslav Dissolution and Britain's Role in Shaping Western Policy" published by the Center for Strategic Research (SAM) in Ankara and has published several articles in national and international journals on Balkan and Black Sea Politics. She was a senior researcher at Netherlands Institute of International Relations in the Hague, Clingendael European Studies Program between 2005-2007.

Christina Romila is currently a PhD student at the Romanian National Defence University. She graduated the Faculty of Political Sciences of Bucharest, Romania and holds a MA degree in International Relations and Crisis Management.

Vít Střitecký is a research fellow at the Institute of International Relations and a PhD candidate in IR at Charles University, Prague. He is also currently doing a postgraduate research degree in international security at the School of IR, University of St. Andrews, Scotland. He holds a MA in IR from Charles and has also studied at Uppsala University, Sweden and Tbilisi State University, Georgia. His major interests include EU external policies, security developments in the South Caucasus, and theories of IR, security, conflict studies, and terrorism.

Contributors

Umut Uzer is a Postdoctoral fellow at the Center for Middle Eastern Studies, Harvard University. Previously he worked as assistant professor of International Relations at the Department of International Relations, Atılım University, Ankara, Turkey. He received his Bachelor's degree in International Relations from Bilkent University and his Master of Science degree in International Relations from the Middle East Technical University, Ankara, Turkey. He obtained his PhD from the Politics Department at the University of Virginia, U.S. Dr. Uzer's research deals with the impact of nationalism and state identity on foreign policy behavior. Empirically, he studied Cyprus, Azerbaijan and other neighboring regions of Turkey and Turkey's interest in their political and cultural affairs. He also researched the Arab-Israeli conflict and prospects for its resolution. He has articles published in *The Journal of South Asian and Middle Eastern Studies*, *Journal of Muslim Minority Affairs*, and *Perceptions*. Umut Uzer is currently working on a biography of the Turkish Cypriot leader, Rauf Denktaş.

Zuhal Yeşilyurt Gündüz received her PhD in Political Science at Bonn University in 2000 with her doctoral dissertation on *"Die Türkei und die Europaeische Union: Chancen und Grenzen der Integration"* (*"Turkey and the European Union: Chances and Limits of Integration"*), which was also published as a book in Germany. She joined Baskent University in 2001 where she gives lectures on International Relations, European Union, Turkey – EU integration, and Sociology. She has also published a book in Germany on *"Die Demokratisierung ist weiblich...Die türkische Frauenbewegung und ihr Beitrag zur Demokratisierung der Türkei"* (*"Democratization is female...The Turkish Women's Movement and its Contribution to the Democratization of Turkey"*) and has articles published in academic journals like *Ankara Review of European Studies, Auslandsinformationen, Internationale Politik, International Policy Analysis, Perceptions – Journal of International Affairs, WeltTrends, Zeitschrift für Türkeistudien – Journal for Studies on Turkey*.

Abbreviations

ADB	Asian Development Bank
AEOI	Atomic Energy Organization of Iran
AHDR	Arab Human Development Reports
AKP	Justice and Development Party (*Adalet ve Kalkınma Partisi*)
AKT	Azerbaijan, Kazakhstan and Turkmenistan
BBC	British Broadcasting Corporation
BSEC	Black Sea Economic Cooperation
BSTDB	Black Sea Trade and Development Bank
BTC	Baku-Tbilisi-Ceyhan Oil Pipeline
BTE	Baku-Tbilisi-Erzurum Gas Pipeline
CAP	Common Agricultural Policy
CARDS	Community Assistance for Reconstruction, Development and Stabilization
CBC	Cross-Border Cooperation
CEECs	Central and Eastern European Countries
CEO	Chief Executive Officer
CFSP	Common Foreign and Security Policy
CIS	Commonwealth of Independent States
CMFA	Council of Ministers of Foreign Affairs
CNPC	Chinese National Petroleum Company
CP	Communist Party
CPC	Caspian Pipeline Consortium
CS	Common Strategy
CSCE	Conference on Security and Cooperation in Europe
CSO	Committee of Senior Officials
DANBLAS	Danube-Black Sea Environmental Task Force
DG	Directorate General
EAD	Euro-Arab Dialogue
EAGGF	European Agricultural Guidance and Guarantee Fund
EBRD	European Bank for Reconstruction and Development
EC	European Community
EEC	European Economic Community
EIB	European Investment Bank
EIDHR	European Initiative for Democracy and Human Rights
EMP	Euro-Mediterranean Partnership
ENP	European Neighborhood Policy
ENPI	European Neighborhood and Partnership Instrument
EPC	European Political Cooperation
EPE	Energy Policy for Europe
ERDF	European Regional Development Fund
ESDP	European Security and Defense Policy

ESS	European Security Strategy
EU	European Union
EUBAM	European Union Border Assistance Mission
EUFOR	European Union Force
EUPM	European Union Police Mission
EURATOM	European Atomic Energy Community
EUROJUST	European Judicial Cooperation Unit
EUROPOL	European Police Office
EUSR	European Union Special Representative
FDI	Foreign Direct Investment
FRONTEX	European Agency for the Management of Operational Cooperation at the External Borders of the Members of the European Union (*Frontières Extérieures*)
FTA	Free Trade Agreement
FYROM	Former Yugoslav Republic of Macedonia
G-7	Group of Seven
G-8	Group of Eight
GAERC	General Affairs and External Relations Council
GBSA	Greater Black Sea Area
GCC	Gulf Cooperation Council
GDP	Gross Domestic Product
GKU	German Kraftwerk Union
GUAM	Georgia, the Ukraine, Azerbaijan, and Moldova
HDZ	Croat Democratic Union (*Hrvatska Demokratska Zajednica*)
IAEA	International Atomic Energy Agency
ICAO	International Civil Aviation Organization
ICBSS	International Center for Black Sea Studies
ICG	International Crisis Group
ICR	International Civilian Representative
ICTY	International Criminal Tribunal for the Former Yugoslavia
IDB	Islam Development Bank
IDP	Internally Displaced Persons
IISS	International Institute for Strategic Studies
IMF	International Monetary Fund
IMU	Islamic Movement of Uzbekistan
INFCE	International Nuclear Fuel Cycle Evaluation
INOGATE	Interstate Oil and Gas Transport to Europe
IPA	Instrument for Pre-Accession Assistance
IPTF	International Police Task Force
ISAF	International Security Assistance Force
IWPR	Institute for War and Peace Reporting
JHA	Justice and Home Affairs
KFOR	Kosovo Force

Abbreviations

KGB	Committee for State Security (*Komityet Gosudarstvennoy Bezopasnosti*)
LEU	Low Enriched Uranium
LMFBR	Light Metal Fast Breeder Reactors
LWR	Light Water Reactors
MEDA	Mediterranean European Development Action
MFO	Multinational Force
NAP	New Azerbaijan Party
NATO	North Atlantic Treaty Organization
NGO	Non-Governmental Organization
NIS	Newly Independent States
NNWS	Non-Nuclear Weapons State
NPT	The Treaty on the Non-Proliferation of Nuclear Weapons
NSG	Nuclear Suppliers Group
OAPEC	Organization of Arab Petroleum Exporting Countries
OBNOVA	European Community Emergency Support Program for the Western Balkans
OSCE	Organization for Security and Cooperation in Europe
PA	Palestinian Authority
PABSEC	Parliamentary Assembly of the Black Sea Economic Cooperation
PDF	Project Development Fund
PERMIS	Permanent International Secretariat
PHARE	Poland and Hungary: Assistance to the Restructuring of the Economy
PM	Prime Minister
PNA	Palestinian National Authority
PCA	Partnership and Cooperation Agreement
PLO	Palestinian Liberation Organization
RFE/RL	Radio Free Europe/Radio Liberty
SAA	Stabilization and Association Agreement
SABIC	Saudi Basic Industries Corporation
SAP	Stabilization and Association Process
SBS	State Border Service
SECI	Southeast European Co-operative Initiative
SIPA	State Investigation and Protection Agency
TACIS	Technical Assistance to the Commonwealth of Independent States
TAIEX	Technical Assistance and Information Exchange
TRACECA	Transport Corridor Europe-Caucasus-Asia
TIM	Temporary International Mechanism
UÇK	Liberation Army of Kosovo (*Ushtria Clirimtare e Kosoves*)
UK	United Kingdom
UN	United Nations

Abbreviations

UNDP	United Nations Development Program
UNIFIL	United Nations Interim Force in Lebanon
UNMIK	United Nations Mission in Kosovo
UNSC	United Nations Security Council
US	United States
USSR	Union of Soviet Socialist Republics
VMRO	Democratic Party for Macedonian National Unity
WMD	Weapons of Mass Destruction
WTO	World Trade Organization
YES	Yalta European Strategy

Introduction

Birgül Demirtaş-Coşkun

Laying the foundation for a conflict-free European continent was a primary goal of the European integration in the 1950s. During the two world wars that broke out in the first half of the twentieth century, it was witnessed how rivalries and enmities among European powers could cause turmoil throughout the world. It was then seen that any great instability stemming from Europe would not remain limited to the region itself; rather it has the potential to spread to other regions and to pull the prominent powers into the conflict directly. This showed that without creating a peaceful ground for Europe, providing peace in the world would not be possible. For this reason, the U.S. was one of the greatest supporters of the European integration project. Taking lessons from the two world wars, the Washington administration encouraged European countries to initiate a regional integration based on common political and financial grounds.

As the European integration process began to bear fruit, member countries started to understand that providing peace and stability only in Europe was not possible without also securing peace in other parts of the world. Under the pressure of the Cold War era that carried serious risks of a nuclear war, European countries felt themselves insecure in the absence of security precautions. Under these circumstances, the Conference on Security and Cooperation in Europe has been an important turning point for the European integration. Thereby, member countries gave support for strengthening the *détente* between superpowers which they also found important for their own security. While aiming to create a Europe free from conflict and wars in the late 1940s and early 1950s, the European countries also realized the significance of providing a more secure environment in the rest of the world. As it became clear for other countries that the establishment of a firmly secure and peaceful Europe was very important for global security, the now increasingly integrated European countries also admitted that stability and peace in other countries were also very important for their own security. As a result of this, the importance of the multilateral security and cooperative relations started to be seen more clearly.

Apart from its attempts to tame two superpowers—the U.S. and the USSR—starting in the 1960s, the European Union launched regional cooperation initiatives. Why did the Union become so disposed to regional cooperation schemes? This was mainly because EU policymakers believed that regional cooperation could alleviate inter-state problems and pave the way for diplomatic methods as opposed to conflict and wars that may also have a negative effect on European security. The EU's strong belief in and support for regional cooperation also results from the fact that the Union is the fruit of cooperative attempts of continental countries and is regarded as a success story in many aspects. In this respect, Karen Smith names the Union's policy toward regional cooperation as a kind of "narcissism."[1] In other words, it can also be considered as an attempt to repeat its own example rules, set by itself, although being aware that repeating the same example is possibly much more limited. However, hope seems to exist that the longer the regional countries cooperate, the less probability there is for them to engage in a combat against each other. Regional cooperation initiatives are generally most successful when they act inclusively toward other countries in the region. The case of Central and Eastern European countries is the most recent example of this. In the aftermath of the Cold War era, the Union decided to prepare a regional approach for Central and Eastern Europe to which it extended the prospect of full membership in the foreseeable future. Therefore, reform processes in these countries moved ahead faster and the content of the reforms was very comprehensive. In that respect, comparing the impact of the regional cooperation toward Central and Eastern Europe with any other region would give us an idea about the avidity that the prospect of a full membership can trigger.

However, as the Union decided to enlarge toward former Warsaw Pact countries, it also recognized the need to dampen the current waves of enlargement. The enlargement forced the Union to review its foreign and security policies that stretch beyond the frontiers which brought a number of challenges to the EU's foreign and security policies. As a result of these challenges, the responsibility of engaging in the political and economic stabilization of neighborhood regions was deemed necessary by the EU.

The EU's engagement in its neighborhood, which is a broad geographical area from the Commonwealth of Independent States (CIS) to the Middle East and North Africa, presents a genuine challenge for foreign and security policies. In general, this broad neighborhood is divided into three regional groups: the Mediterranean, including many of the Middle East states, the Western Balkans, Russia, and other eastern neighbors.

Becoming aware of the fact the Union could not enlarge to encompass the whole of neighboring regions because of financial, political, historical, and social reasons, the EU prepared a new project called European Neighborhood Policy (ENP) which foresaw increasing cooperation toward the regions for which the Union did not intend to give the prospect of full membership. The main objective of the ENP is expressed in the Communication on the Commission Proposal for Action Plans under the ENP as "to share the benefits of the EU's 2004 enlargement with neighboring countries in strengthening stability, security and well-being for all concerned."[2] The policy offers privileged relationship with neighbors, which will be built on mutual commitment to common values within the fields of the rule of law, good governance, respect for human rights, and promotion of good neighborly relations. The commitments present certain aspects of the EU's external actions including combating against terrorism, proliferation of weapons of mass destruction, abidance by international law, and efforts to achieve conflict resolution.

The ENP was a sign of the fact that the Union believed the neighboring regions played an important role in European security. Declared in 2004 with the aim of establishing "a ring of friends around the borders of the new enlarged EU,"[3] the ENP intended to create bilateral cooperation schemes with neighbors in the east and south of Europe. For the time being, it is difficult to assess the impact of the ENP so far. It is, however, uncertain whether it could achieve the intended objectives under the present circumstances in which no accession prospect is provided.

This study will approach the concept of European neighborhood from a perspective that is different than the one depicted by the ENP. The study includes close and distant geographical neighbors of the Union that have considerable impact upon political and security affairs of Europe. In this regard, three geographical areas will be under consideration: Western Balkans, Middle East and former Soviet countries that are not yet members of the Union. Each of these areas has special relations with the EU that is peculiar to their geographical and political nature. While countries of Western Balkans, for example, are already enjoying the process of accession, countries of the Middle East, on the other hand, despite being part of an important previous regional initiative, Euro-Med, do not have any foreseeable prospect of membership. Former Soviet countries, on the other hand, are not expected to enter into accession negotiations in the short- or medium-term and some of them are not even part of the ENP. Among the countries mentioned above, only some of the Middle Eastern and former Soviet countries constitute a part of the ENP. This study outlines the EU neighborhood as the regions both in the close and distant neighboring areas that affect the EU's security and the regions that are affected by Union policies irrespective of whether they are included in the enlargement process or under the ENP project. Hence, this book views the concept of neighborhood from a wider perspective, since we believe that all these countries, no matter whether they are on the way to full membership or have concluded cooperation agreements under the ENP, are not yet part of the EU and do not have the prospect of accession, at least in the very short-term. Therefore, all of them can be grouped together under the concept of "neighbors" that have interaction with the Union, but are not full members yet.

The study will try to find answers for the following questions: What kind of impact has the EU exerted over its neighboring areas so far? What are the challenges and opportunities stemming from these neighboring areas? What are the perceptions of the EU, and the perceptions of the concerned country or region toward each other? How does the EU's evolving relationship with its broad neighborhood affect its global posture? How does the Union's impact differ from one region to another, or from one country to another, and what are the reasons for this differentiation?

Each part of the study includes two types of analysis: regional and country-based. While the region-focused analysis examines the type of relationship the Union conducts with that particular area, country-specific analysis concentrates on the Unions's attitude toward that particular country. Most of our authors are academics and some of them are decision-makers.

This book is divided into three main parts: Western Balkans, Middle East, and Russia and the CIS. These regions can be considered as the most important neighborhoods for the Union because of several different reasons. Western Balkans, have been in the process of accession since the end of the 1990s, proving that every conflict or disagreement in this region directly affects the security of the Union. Still being one of the most volatile regions, the Middle East is on the top of the agenda of all global actors, especially after the 9/11. Europe is dependent on the rich energy sources of the region and directly interested in Middle Eastern problems. Russia and the CIS comprise another vital region because of their underground resources and Russia's global role, mainly due to its membership with the United Nations Security Council.

The first part of the study deals with the EU's role in the Western Balkans. Vasilis Margaras presents a general picture of the Unions's policies toward the region by looking at its positive and negative features. He also presents some suggestions for the EU to improve its record. The second article looks at a more specific case in the region, which is the organized crime in Bosnia-Hercegovina and the approach of the Union toward this problem. The article written by Ana E. Juncos focuses on four tensions that stem from the present policies of the Union: tension over a hard-security approach and a developmental approach; tension over securitization and inclusive approach; tension over three-pillar structure of the Union and cross-pillar characteristics of the struggle against organized crime; and tension over securitization against organized crime and ownership principle. The last article in this part deals with a current topic related to the Kosovo issue and its repercussions in the EU. In her article, Birgül Demirtaş-Coşkun examines the EU's policy toward Kosovo from the beginning of the 1980s untill its declaration of independence. In her study, she tries to answer the following questions: Is there a consistent EU policy toward Kosovo throughout the post-Cold War years or is it marked by instable policies? How do the concepts of "state sovereignty" and "self-determination" relate to the EU's approach to the region in general, and the problem of Kosovo in particular? Because of its geographic location and recent history of ethnic clashes, Kosovo is important for the EU. Any regional conflict leads to a flow of refugees and also to an increase in activities of organized criminal groups. Therefore, it is worth analyzing European policies related to the Kosovo issue.

The second part is related to the EU's approach toward the Middle Eastern region. As a new Middle East is being planned in Washington after 9/11, the region is among the very forefront issues of the CFSP. The first article in this part deals with the approach of the Union toward the Greater Middle East Project designed and implemented by the U.S. Comparing the EU approach toward the region with that of the American approach, İdris Bal argues that, despite the fact the Union is one of the important supporters of the democratization of the region, it rejects the hard-security approach being implemented by the Washington administration.

Umut Uzer, on the other hand, analyzes how the Middle East peace process is perceived by the Union. His main argument is that the role of the EU in the peace process is rather auxiliary, since it did not have a substantial role in it from the beginning. A related subject is considered by Zuhal Yeşilyurt-Gündüz in her article entitled "The Euro-Mediterranean Partnership: On good intentions, shopping lists and à la carte menus." She examines the performance of the Euro-Med partnership in detail by analyzing it from a critical perspective. Additionally, she discusses whether the Union can be considered as a normative power with regard to its performance in the Barcelona Process that started the Euro-Mediterranean partnership. Christian Koch, on the other hand, discusses the nature of the relationship between the EU and Gulf Cooperation Council from the past up until present time. The article tries to shed light on the reasons that can be credited for the limited nature of this relationship.

Iran is another important actor in the Middle East, and the current controversy of a possible conflict between the U.S. and Iran poses a new challenge for the EU after the Iraqi case. In his article, Mustafa Kibaroğlu analyzes policies of European countries from past to present regarding the development of Iranian nuclear capabilities.

The last part is devoted to European policies toward CIS countries. Vit Stritecký looks at the EU's policies toward the South Caucasian countries and tries to make clear whether the Union has played a substantial role in finding a solution to the conflicts and disagreements in the region. In addition, Yelda Demirağ evaluates the ties between Europe and Central Asia by concentrating her research on the following questions: Does the EU have a significant influence on Central Asia? Does the Union play an effective role in the solution of conflicts affecting this region?

The importance of Caucasus and Central Asia for the Union must be understood not only because they are in Russia's backyard, but also because of their huge energy resources. In that respect, Mert Bilgin provides a new perspective in his study as to how the Union can combine its security approach with its energy needs.

The Black Sea region can be considered a new region that appeared on the stage after the end of the bipolar world. Two articles in this book deal with the EU's approach to this particular region. While Emel Oktay examines the fundamental problems and opportunities that the region presents to the Union, Christina Romila provides an analysis based on Romanian perspective regarding the EU's approach toward the Black Sea.

By examining European attitude toward Russia in order to understand whether the value-based approach is dominant or not, Giselle Bosse draws attention to a sensitive issue in the foreign policy of the EU. Whether European foreign policy is based on interests or values is another important matter of debate. Bosse discusses this important question by examining the EU's relations with Russia. Another important regional actor, the Ukraine, is the topic of an article written by Sergiy Glebov. He discusses how the Union approaches the Ukraine and whether it provides any accession perspective.

Havva Kök's article deals with issues related to Kazakhstan, an important country in Central Asia. She tries to answer the questions of how the Kazakhi-European Union relations develop and their perspectives to improve their ties.

The last part discusses the possible Turkish contribution for the EU's foreign policy regarding its relations with the Caucasus and the Middle East. Burcu Gültekin-Punsmann looks at the Caucasian dimension and Turkey's possible role in furthering relations between Caucasian countries and the Union. In addition, Bezen Balamir-Coşkun analyzes Turkey's relations with the West and the Middle East, and argues that these relations cannot be considered separately, but should be considered as complementary.

---

[1] Karen E. Smith, *European Union Foreign Policy in a Changing World* (Cambridge: Polity, 2003), p. 70.
[2] Commission Proposal: Action Plans Under the European Neighborhood Policy (ENP), (The European Commission Proposal, 2004, p. 795 final)
[3] ENP Web Site http://www.europa.eu.int/comm/world/enp/index_en.htm

PART I
WESTERN BALKANS

Chapter 1
The EU in the Western Balkans: Setting the Foundations of a Cohesive Strategy?*

Vasilis MARGARAS

In this paper, by analyzing positive and negative aspects of the EU's policies, we try to examine the general record of the EU in the Western Balkans. The term Western Balkans is used in this chapter to group the states that emerged from the dissolution of the former Republic of Yugoslavia, including Albania. Initially, we briefly introduce policies of the EU regarding the region and show positive aspects of these policies. Following these introductory explanations, to be able to make a fair and objective evaluation of achievements and limitations of EU's policies, we focus on problems that occur in practical applications caused by these policies. The aim of this chapter is not to provide a detailed list of all EU policy instruments, but rather to explain the contribution of these instruments in bringing the Western Balkans closer to the EU through the promotion of political, social and economic development. Finally, the chapter ends with suggestions on how the EU can become a more influential actor in the Western Balkans. In this chapter, we mainly intend to demonstrate that the EU, despite its extensive contribution to the security of the region, still has to do a lot more to become a dynamic policy actor in this particular area. The EU has to reconsider its Balkan strategy and it also has to find new innovative ways of policy engagement with the fragile countries of the Western Balkans.

EU Policies in the Western Balkans: a Short Description

The EU has been involved in Balkan affairs since the early 1990s. During the first years of the Balkan crisis, the action of the EU was characterized by fragmentation and weakness. However, as time went by, the EU became more interested in the Western Balkans and consolidated its position as one of the most important regional policy players. The European Union has been offering assistance (mainly through the ECHO, PHARE and OBNOVA programs) focusing on refugee programs and reconstruction. In 1999, the EU established the Stability Pact for South Eastern Europe, which can be seen as the first attempt to set a comprehensive conflict-prevention strategy for the region. The primary goal of the Pact was to provide a framework to stimulate regional cooperation and expedite the integration into institutional European structures. The Pact focuses on three main themes - issues of democratization and human rights, economic reconstruction (including cooperation, development matters) and security issues.[1]

The EU has also been influential throughout the establishment of the Stabilization and Association Process (SAP). The SAP seeks to promote stability within the region while also facilitating closer association with the EU. One of the key elements of the SAP for countries that attained a sufficient political, economic and administrative capacity, is the establishment of formal a contractual relationship with the EU in the form of the Stabilization and Association Agreement (SAA). The SAP is designed to help each country progress at its own pace toward greater European integration. It supports the Western Balkan countries' development and preparations for their future EU memberships by combining three main instruments: the SAA, autonomous trade measures and substantial financial assistance. Also, promoting regional cooperation among Western Balkan states is a cornerstone for the SAP.[2]

The CARDS program (Community Assistance for Reconstruction, Development and Stabilization) is an important SAP instrument which was formed in 2000. It is the EU's main instrument of financial assistance to the Western Balkans, covering specifically Croatia, Bosnia-Herzegovina, Serbia, Montenegro, FYROM, and Albania. Reconstructing these countries, providing democratic stabilization, establishing reconciliation among them, returning refugees, attaining institutional and legislative development including harmonization with the EU norms in order to underpin democracy and the rule of law in the region, protecting human rights and promoting measures that will strengthen the civil society are among the objectives of this program. Achieving sustainable economic development through well-established open markets and promoting closer relations and regional cooperation among the countries of the region can also be listed among the goals of the CARDS initiative.[3] As a result of the Community's reform of external aid, the CARDS program was replaced by the new Instrument for Pre-Accession Assistance (IPA) in 2007. The major objective of IPA is to streamline all pre-accession assistance in a single framework and to unite both candidate and potential candidate countries under the same regulation, and, thereby, assist them in achieving progressive alignment with the standards and policies of the EU.

Since 2001, EU priorities gradually shifted from post-war reconstruction, to institutional capacity-building and economic development. As a result of this policy change, the main focal point of the EU's policies moved toward strengthening the Western Balkan states so they are able to fulfil their responsibilities as states, including adopting and accomplishing their internal reforms. Development of state-level public administration and institutions, economic reforms, customs and taxation, policing, justice, and border management are the key areas affected by this policy shift. Furthermore, in May 2003, the Commission proposed to enrich EU policy toward the region with elements taken from the enlargement process, thus to reinforce the ultimate goal of extending EU membership to the Western Balkans. The Thessaloniki Summit Declaration of June 2003 further cemented the process of rapprochement between the EU and the Western Balkans.[4] After the door of the EU was opened to Western Balkans states, the EU carried out relations with Western Balkan states at different paces due to their varied situations. For instance, the EU-Croatia relationship has run more smoothly as the country is now economically and politically more prosperous than other Balkan states. The relationship with the Union of Serbia and Montenegro, however, remained problematic due to a number of internal problems that plunged the country in continuous crises. The EU-Albanian and the EU-FYROM relationships, on the other hand, have improved significantly. However, the bad economic state of these two countries mentioned above puts a limit on the degree to which integration can be achieved. What is more, although the EU-Bosnian relationship has significantly progressed, it still lacks dynamism due to the critical condition of the state of Bosnia Herzegovina which is still a very fragmented entity.

The Positive Impact of the Policies of the EU

The 1990s were a difficult decade for the whole Balkan Peninsula. However, not all was gloom and doom in the Balkans. Greece has been a stable member of the EU since 1981, following Slovenia, which joined the EU in 2004. Romania and Bulgaria also joined in 2007. Croatia and FYROM showed a strong determination to follow suit. The positive opinion of the Commission on the Croatian application for EU membership sent a clear message to the Western Balkan countries outside the EU. This message can be summarized with this order: 'Implement the reforms and you will be accepted in the big European family.' Furthermore, there have been talks regarding the extension of the SAA with Bosnia Herzegovina, which allows a degree of optimism regarding Bosnian prospects of rapprochement with the EU.

The EU management of the Western Balkans' portfolio is now directed by the Enlargement Directorate which attributes a greater importance to the countries of the Western Balkans. This gesture of the EU is a positive step, as it stresses the message of integration. The perspective of EU membership linked to the step by step implementation of the SAP has become the major source of the EU's influence in the region.[5] Even in the most divided states such as Bosnia Herzegovina, the prospect of EU membership can also unite people who have been previously engaged in a civil war. According to the former High Representative in Bosnia Herzegovina, Wolfgang Petritsch: 'Europe is the one idea shared unanimously by all the citizens of the country. Serbs, Croats and Bosniacs are alike; they all want to become citizens of the EU.'[6] In addition, the EU's key role in the Ohrid Agreement and the

Belgrade agreement of 2002, which founded the Union of Serbia and Montenegro, demonstrates that the EU has become active in the state-building process and in shaping the status quo of the region. In this respect, the EU re-empowered the weak Balkan states, first by recognizing them as negotiable entities, and second, by reserving them a place in the future of the EU.

Much of the EU's actions on the Balkans have caused a positive impact in bringing the fragile entities of the Western Balkans closer to the EU's norms and policies. Along with the rest of the western world, the EU was influential in putting an end to the war in former Yugoslavia and stopping the massive atrocities that were committed in the early and late 1990s. In addition, in terms of security, the EU has become an important actor in the region as it took over the police and military missions in Bosnia Herzegovina. These missions are influential in maintaining order in the country. Previously, the EU was influential in other security initiatives. For instance, the EU was vital in brokering the 2001 Ohrid Agreement between the two main ethnic groups in FYROM, thus preserving the fragile peace. In general, the peace-enforcing measures (such as the EU's support for the return of the refugees in the Western Balkans) have paid off as life slowly returns back to normal.

In his following statement, Stefan Lehne, the Director of the Balkans, Eastern Europe and South–East Europe Directorate in the Council Secretariat, mentions that a new consensus on Balkan policy has been established, which hence leads to unified EU positions: 'All EU member states had learned lessons from the experience of the early 1990s. At that time there had been little expertise of the Balkans in most European foreign ministries. The initial division had therefore been rather the result of historical reflexes based on past alliances with various parties in the region than a genuine clash of interests. In the course of the intensive work on Balkan issues throughout the 1990s the EU had developed a common analysis. The shared interest in the stabilization of the region gradually came to the fore. There was now sufficient agreement on the objectives to develop a more ambitious policy.'[7] The consensus of EU member states regarding the future of the Balkans led to a partial filling of the 'expectations-capability' gap from which the EU was suffering in the early 1990s.[8] In the case of the Balkans, the EU has been transformed from a weak policy actor to a more influential player. It has assumed the main responsibility of maintaining the Balkans as a peaceful and integrated region. It is crucial to say that this assumption of responsibility comes at a time when the U.S. is focusing in other parts of the world, which leaves a security vacuum in the Balkans.

The EU can at least take credit for the fact that it tries to promote peace, stability and economic regeneration in one of the most troubled corners of our planet. Furthermore, the EU has expanded its role in the Western Balkans by shifting its resources from reconstruction to strengthening of the Western Balkan states by encouraging further adoption of the EU 'acquis.' In addition, the European Partnerships opened up new ways of increasing the interaction between the EU and the Western Balkans by promoting an economic policy dialogue, practicing twinning and monitoring exercises and granting these countries the right of participating in EU programs. One should also mention that the EU has been the main trading partner with all Western Balkan countries. Many trade preferential regimes secure the entrance of Western Balkan goods in the EU market, which encourages the development of the regional economy. In addition, due to the number of programs developed, the Western Balkans has managed to benefit from an inflow of resources, donations and expertise that the EU coordinated in the region.

In general, the EU has acted as a form of consensus-building role by bringing conflicting sides together, as regional cooperation is now an explicit condition for the advancement toward EU integration. This is due to the particular 'normative' power of the EU which serves as a magnet for all players involved in the conflict who carry the prospect of joining the Community. According to Rupnik: 'one thing is certain: the only way to obtain important concessions on all sides is the promise of a more important gain, which can only be membership of the EU.'[9] Indeed, regional normalization of state relationships, improvement of minority rights and other 'painful' constitutional amendments can only be attained within the context of the EU. Furthermore, the influence of the EU does not end up in its 'soft' policy elements. The EU-led operations of Concordia/Proxima/EUFOR/EUPM in FYROM and Bosnia Herzegovina had a positive impact on maintaining security in areas which had been torn apart by ethnic hatred. These operations have been very successful, thus reinforcing the view that the EU could take over more demanding missions and play the role of an influential security provider. Therefore, the EU further consolidated its position in the area by getting involved in new peacekeeping operations in Kosovo.

The Western Balkans Today: Still not a Rosy Picture

The EU should naturally take credit for the good actions it has performed in the Western Balkans. This progress, however, is not an excuse for complacency. The Europeans bear a huge share of responsibility for what happened in the Balkans in the early 1990s. One must not forget that the delay of the coming of 'the hour of Europe' that the Luxembourg PM Jacques Poos promised in 1992 cost thousands of civilian lives.[10] In addition, although the EU action in the Balkans has changed significantly, there is still considerable room for improvement.

In many parts of the Western Balkans, there is a superficially stable climate which carries positive aspects along with negative ones. While positive aspects come from signals indicating that the massive atrocities between different ethnicities are ending, negative aspects, on the other hand, are emanating from those problems swept beneath the carpet without being solved. In this case, the EU and the rest of the Western World should face the realities of the Balkans in the post-conflict period and deal with them more comprehensively. Meanwhile, the end of atrocities neither means that all issues have been resolved, nor that the future of the Balkans will indefinitely be secure and peaceful. The critical situation that the Western Balkan states are in can create a breeding ground for further ethno-nationalist tendencies as well as more social and ethnic unrest. The assassination of Serbian Prime Minister Zoran Djindjic in March 2003, as well as the 2004 ethnic killings in Kosovo, combined with parallel ethnic tensions in FYROM, demonstrates that there are still important hotbeds of restlessness in the area.

The challenges awaiting the Western Balkans are indeed great. Commenting on the future of Bosnia Herzegovina, former High Representative Wolfgang Petritsch states that the country faces a 'triple transition challenge': from war to peace, from communism to democracy and market economy and from dependency to self-sustainability.[11] These three challenges also account for most of the Western Balkans.

First of all, economies of the Western Balkan states are still in a bad situation. Although a certain level of economic growth has been recorded, one has to be cautious with statistics, as most of the increase is due to the very low starting levels where much of the Western Balkans struggled to reach pre-communist levels of growth.[12] A high deficit in the balance of trade demonstrates that most of the Western Balkan countries are not capable of getting any advantages from trade liberalization that the EU is keenly promoting.[13] Furthermore, remittance amounts from emigrant workers in Western Europe, an important income source for the Western Balkan countries, are in decline. Economic reforms, with the exception of Croatia, are slow and the flow of new foreign direct investment is not satisfactory. Corruption is endemic both in the civil service and in the wider economic scope. In addition, the elites of the Titoist/Hotza regime are the dominant actors in the post-communist economies, which do not allow new economic forces to appear. Furthermore, in certain parts of the Balkans, ethnicity is an obstacle in front of economic growth. For instance, in Bosnia Herzegovina, there are three different economies within one state; each is shaped according to the ethnic borders of each community.

In addition, building the regional infrastructure that has been damaged during the wars in the 1990s requires further assistance. Although international assistance partially helped rebuild war-torn infrastructures (houses, schools, clinics, roads, etc.), efforts for re-igniting the regional economy have so far been insufficient. The international community provided generous aids during the first years of reconstruction; however, this is no longer the case. In terms of international aid, there is a 'donor fatigue' since major international donors now believe that the Western Balkans had their chance and other global locations require more immediate attention. However, while Western Balkan economies failed to be regenerated, a vicious circle of misery is continuing: failed economies generate high levels of unemployment and, in turn, the shortage of employment in the most troubled spots of the Balkans (e.g. Bosnia, Kosovo) drives some parts of the population toward black market trading and other illegal means. Continuous trends of underdevelopment and de-industrialization have forced the farming population of the Western Balkans to return to using primitive agricultural production methods in order to survive. Poverty rates and social disparities between rural and urban areas have increased in Albania, Bosnia and Serbia. As levels of poverty continue to rise, a big portion of the population is becoming impoverished. Consequently, the temptation of finding a 'political refuge' concealed under claims of extreme nationalism becomes a possible nightmare scenario.

Political instability brings about political extremism. Politics in the Western Balkans is characterized by volatile political parties, low participation, low electoral turn outs, and a lack of a strong notion of civil society. With the death of former war barons (Tudjman, Milosevic, Izetbegovic) the political scene of the Western Balkans desperately needs new political elites to take over. Although some new faces appear in post-conflict politics, there is still a high degree of embedded nationalism in all major political parties. For instance, the return of the 'patriotic' VMRO in FYROM, the power of ruling to be captured by the HDZ in Croatia and the strong performance of extreme nationalists in the recent Serbian Parliamentary elections, all demonstrate that mild and extreme forms of nationalism are still popular in the region. Nationalist rhetoric pose another problem to the process of EU integration, as the whole EU project is based on 'loosening' ethnic consciousness and on the construction of a common European identity. Furthermore, the policy of EU conditionality in issues of human rights, minority protection and regional cooperation will only work in practice if new policy elites take over and if the public feels ready to accept the EU's 'instructions' regarding human rights issues.

Furthermore, most Western Balkan states are still weak. Western Balkan countries are characterized by weak bureaucracies (e.g. Albania) or chaotic bureaucracies of multi-layered governance (e.g. Bosnia Herzegovina). Many institutions are only a few years old and have not yet reached a level of institutional maturity. For example, both Bosnia and Kosovo are international protectorates. In these two cases, the international presence has exacerbated the tendency of passivity and dependency on foreign institutions. For instance, according to Knaus and Cox, in the case of Bosnia, 'civil society finds it more productive to direct its lobbying activities toward the international community, and turn away from domestic politics. At the same time, Bosnian politicians are all very happy to allow international officials, who do not have to face election, to take the responsibility for difficult or unpopular decisions.'[14] Furthermore, too much power is concentrated in the hands of the High Representative who has been dismissing politicians and civil servants from their posts. Although this seems the only solution in the short-term, it is detrimental in the long-run as it does not allow local people to reach decisions on local issues. The international community plays a similar role in Kosovo. The EU needs to take the initiative so that an allocation of power to the people of Bosnia and Kosovo is implemented in the near future. In a post-modern world,[15] imposing solutions in a neo-colonial style will simply not solve the problems. Local people have to face the problems themselves and take the whole responsibility in their own hands.

Furthermore, although the EU carries good intentions, they are usually lost in a conundrum of international bureaucracy. The vast number of parallel projects, the great number of NGOs and international players involved in the region make it more difficult for the EU to achieve full coordination. For instance, the UN still has a role to play in its standard peace-keeping tasks like policing, judicial duties and civil affairs, including basic public services, while the OSCE has responsibility for institution-building in services related to human resources, democratization and governance, human rights, holding elections, and EU reconstruction, including regional reconstruction and economic stabilization.[16] In addition, EU projects that are conducted parallel to national projects have often been deficit in coordination.[17] The consequence of this process of multi-layered international bureaucracies is the creation of 'a fragmented, multi-headed monster with disastrous incapacity for implementation.'[18]

The commitment and energy spent by the EU for the region is not sufficient to activate a full reform process in the Western Balkans. In the past, the EU and the international actors focused more on stabilization, reconstruction, returning refugees, and implementing peace. Today, however, the EU's policies regarding the region are concentrated more on institutional, economic and social reinforcement. Although this is the correct strategy, it still can be seen as 'too little too late' and requires further consolidation. Furthermore, other 'soft' security issues must also be taken into account when it comes to EU policy planning in the area. Environment, health and education are policy fields in which the EU has to invest heavily if it really cares about the wellbeing of the citizens of the region.

In addition, in terms of education, the number of children in schools is falling.[19] The reform of education is vital for creating hearts and minds of future citizens. Education, so far, has served to promote irredentist ethnic images and to cultivate nationalism. The EU should support educational systems which work in favor of further reconciliation, and not ethnic separation. One should not forget that brain drainage is an increasing problem for the area. People who have acquired further education and professional experience prefer to stay abroad rather than returning to their homelands. While the younger generations consider the West an escape from the harsh realities of their everyday lives, a certain number of refugees prefer to stay in their host countries in search of a better life. Although the EU cannot solve the problem of unemployment on its own, it can still allocate some of its regional institutional posts to local people with a 'locals first' policy.

The EU should be very careful on how its resources are used. In this respect, already, different strategies that are specific to each Balkan country are being followed. However, because of the EU's candidature process and the conditionality of the SAP, a major portion of aids are being given to countries which are already steady on the EU track, such as Croatia, while many parts of the Balkans are qualified for the lowest level of EU assistance. Lehne suggests there is a problem with the allocation of EU resources: 'the most developed countries enjoy the most generous EU assistance, a situation that is questionable in terms of both fairness and the overall development of the region.'[20] Therefore, the process of partial Europeanization of the area is a risky strategy as it poses the danger of splitting the Balkans into a 'Europeanized' and a non-Europeanized zone, which can widen the gap between strong and weak Balkan states.

Another important issue regarding the role played by the EU in this region is the EU's policy toward Kosovo. According to Bugajski, the current Kosovo situation is problematic, since Pristina has limited tools at its disposal to implement international standards and it lacks a complete legitimacy, as it is seen as a weak proxy of the UN administration which looks illegitimate to the eyes of the Serbian minority.[21] In the case of Kosovo, it is not easy to predict what the status of the region will be in the future. However, the ongoing uncertainty makes it difficult for both local and international actors, as well as the EU, to plan a long-term strategy for the region.

Although the EU has managed to cover the conflicting opinions within the EU on deciding the future of the region, two main opinion groups can be seen. While the first group of EU states, led by the UK and France, claim that a partition between the Serbian and Albanian parts of Kosovo is necessary, the second group of states (Greece, Cyprus, Hungary, Slovakia, and Spain) are cautious about granting full autonomy for Kosovo.[22] Although the EU has accepted the Ahtisaari plan which supports Kosovo's independence, according to the countries in the latter bloc, such a decision may be lethal. They think that an independent, unstable Kosovo might worsen the already restless area by pumping the dreams of extreme nationalist Albanians who are still dreaming about a 'Great Albania.' Kosovo's independence might also trigger moves for further self-determination of the Albanian minority within FYROM. Furthermore, the breaking up of Kosovo from Serbia will signal a resurgence of ethno-nationalism and a bitter feeling against the EU within Serbia. When taking a side on the issue of Kosovo, the European leaders should weigh the pros and cons of Kosovo's independence carefully and calculate the domino effects as some scholars have gone as far as to claim that Kosovo is already used as a precedent for secession.[23] In the case where possible separatist movements may emerge, will the EU leaders be capable of refusing a possible recognition of independence for other Balkan multi-ethnic entities such as Republika Srpska and Vojvodina? Once secession begins, it is difficult to see where it will end. Therefore, there is always a risk that, by taking a brick out of the fragmented Balkans wall, the whole wall might collapse.

The EU has been brave enough to deal with the Kosovo problem by encouraging the two conflicting sides to work together to engage in mutual conversation under the auspices of EU Representative Wolfgang Ischinger. However, any solution to the Kosovo issue will not be a simple one. The EU should accept the consequences of its Kosovo policy, be ready for the worst scenario and plan how to deal with it. This is not an easy task as the EU is called to undertake more of the Kosovo security burden. From this point of view, certain issues are raised. Will the EU have the necessary resources to carry out this duty? Will a possible Kosovo mission curtail any other EU global missions due to the overstretching of resources of the EU? How will the EU manage to secure the safety of the Serbian minority in Kosovo? Will an independent Kosovo be able to secure its economic viability, which is a crucial pre-requisite for its security?

Furthermore, the status of Kosovo has become a burden for the bilateral relationship between the EU and Serbia. The EU-Serbian relationship has been undergoing a crisis for a long time as internal political developments in Serbia have gone against the demands of the EU, especially regarding the Serbian collaboration with the International Criminal Tribunal for the former Yugoslavia (ICTY). Since the 2004 Gymnich meeting, the EU foreign ministers decided to pursue a two-way process with Serbia and Montenegro.[24] Pro-independentist slogans during the Montenegro referendum regime have emphasized the fact that it would be easier for Montenegro to become an EU member if it stands on its own which reinforces the views of the separatists. On the other hand, the EU-Serbia talks were frozen just before the Montenegro referendum took place, which was a fact that reinforced the view claiming that Montenegro might stand a better chance on its own than by being a part of the Union of Serbia and Montenegro. Therefore, although the EU declares the 'inviolability of borders' on paper, the magnetism of EU integration has contributed to Montenegrin independence and has made Serbs cautious about the real aims of the EU regarding their own country.

Suggestions: an EU-Western Balkans Agenda for the Future

The EU's policy of Stabilization and Association has contributed to progress achieved throughout the region by promoting stability and by bringing the Western Balkan countries closer to the Union. However, the EU must become a more influential actor so it can provide better assistance to the Western Balkan countries in addressing their challenges. A cohesive and simplified Grand Plan prepared for the region is actually what the EU needs. However, the EU is suffering from fragmented bureaucratized mechanisms which make allocating aids to those in need more difficult. In order to simplify the bureaucracy, EU programs and initiatives should also be amalgamated into one major European project.

The idea of conditionality must remain as the cornerstone of EU policies. Opinion polls indicate a high support for Western Balkans to join in the European integration. However, the EU should be aware of the waves of enthusiasm in enlargement that cause provocations in the Balkans. While the EU should continue to encourage political trends, which bring the Balkans closer to the EU on one hand, it, on the other, should be clear on its responsibilities born by the EU rapprochement, in order to avoid causing further disappointment and giving of false expectations. The European Union must continue to stress the fact that the road to the EU is open only if the EU 'acquis' is implemented. An EU-Balkan relationship will only be successful if both parties have a clear view of the real challenges of the EU-Western Balkan rapprochement and the real responsibilities that such a relationship brings.

In addition, the EU must continue to promote policies providing further regional integration within the Western Balkans. For instance, creating a visa-free movement zone in the Western Balkans must become a priority in EU policy regarding the region. The countries of the Western Balkans should commit themselves to the idea of abolishing visa requirements for travelling between their countries through bilateral agreements. The commitment to fight against corruption and crime has become a cause of regional cooperation, since many illegal clans have numerous bases within and outside the country in which they are operating. With this in mind, the EU should take the lead in the fight against corruption and organized crime. Although the Western Balkan countries have made some progress in this field, continuation of efforts at all levels is crucial to advance the fight against crime in the area.

Meanwhile, all EU initiatives should be invigorated with active local participation. Related to this matter, former High Representative Petritsch mentioned the issue of local 'ownership.' This ownership is linked to the engagement of civil society in political life and contributes to the 'belonging' feeling of citizens.[25] So far, the international community has been influential in dictating rules and imposing decisions. However, it did not perform well in mingling with local actors and exhibiting strong patterns of cooperation. The idea of local 'belonging' should be put into practice by encouraging further participation of local actors into EU plans.[26] While talking about the future of Bosnia Herzegovina, the former High Representative for Bosnia added:

'The end result must not be a Western clone in the Balkans. Ideally, the end result should be a country that has found its own modern identity.'[27] The same argument is valid for EU actions in many other parts of the fragile Western Balkan states.

Furthermore, the spirit of 'Europeanization' can be further promoted by strengthening the relationship between the EU and bureaucracies of Western Balkan states. Europeanization will be complete only if Western Balkans have the opportunity to develop legal thinking and understanding of the principles that form the basis of Western democratic systems and the EU. This can only happen through continuous interaction between Balkan civil service sectors and EU institutions. Although this is already taking place, a more cohesive plan for institutional integration is necessary. More consulting committees should be created in order to engraft the importance of Europeanization in decision-makers' minds. This will contribute to better implementation of the EU's policies. For example, in order to deal with issues of underdevelopment, the EU, using its experience gained from the Social Fund, can also utilize local experts.[28] Another good initiative the EU can assume is to appropriately invite the SAP countries to align themselves with EU demarches, declarations and common positions on CFSP issues. Participation in coordination and briefing meetings organized by the EU for candidate and associated countries in capitals and headquarters of international organizations must also be considered as a necessary part of an appropriate strategy. Twinning practices, secondment of civil servants from EU Member States to work as advisers in beneficiary institutions and mutual exchange of personnel between the Balkan and EU civil services will also contribute to the modernization of the Balkan institutional structures. This process will also help the EU to better understand the problems and limitations of the Western Balkan structures.

Much has been said about the economic problems the Balkans are facing. In this matter, however, the human factor should also be taken into account. The policy goals of the Western Balkans should be anthropocentric. An effective Western Balkan policy should combine highly technocratic elements with effective policies, which must also consider human development indicators. In this respect, the UN Millennium Development Goals should be seen as a priority for the Western Balkans. In terms of education, for instance, through establishing a vibrant youth policy, granting scholarships and student exchanges between Western Balkan and European universities can be very advantageous. In addition, the EU should encourage the countries of the region to take concrete initiatives with the objective of revising history textbooks. The teaching of history, which is based on ethno nationalist patterns, only serves to perpetuate the ethnic problems. This is a unique opportunity for the EU to shape future Balkan developments, for rewriting history can be accepted by the conflicting partners only if this process is carried out under the auspices of the EU.

In addition, there is still a lack of solid political parties and social movements that will bring the Western Balkan countries closer to the EU. Without a new generation of politicians equipped with a clear, European vision, any reform the EU demands to be implemented will be doomed to fail. Forging of a new democratic political culture is necessary if the Western Balkans want to get fully integrated with the EU. Lehne provides a comparison of the EU-Central Eastern Europe relationship where the political elites were strongly oriented toward the EU.[29] As a result of elite Europeanization in Central and Eastern Europe, the enlargement process has been less difficult. This is not the case in the Western Balkans where much of the political scene is tempted by populist and nationalist choices. The European Parliament along with national parliaments and political groups can take the lead in promoting Democratic Party structures, citizenship involvement and the modernization of the national debates through policy-oriented discussions. EU integration does not end with economics; it has to be performed at many other levels as well. With its Brusselised NGOs, associations and political parties, the EU demos should make room for its Balkan counterparts and establish a network of mutually beneficial relationships. Without the creation of Europeanized demos in the Western Balkans, any kind of transformation will carry the risk of remaining only on paper. However, political encouragement of pro-EU actors is a delicate matter: How can one directly deal with national elites without being perceived as intervening in issues that are in the sphere of national sovereignty? Will further EU movement to make extremist elements illegitimate turn them into national martyrs in times of crisis? Therefore, any process of political EU involvement should be handled with care.

In addition, although much attention has been given on the question of Kosovo, the EU must not forget that the question of Serbia is also of vital importance for the future of the region. In its Feasibility Report on April 12, 2005, the European Commission concluded that Serbia and Montenegro are sufficiently prepared to negotiate a SAA with the EU. However, following a negative assessment on the state of cooperation of Serbia and Montenegro and the failure of Serbia to locate, arrest and transfer Ratko Mladić to the ICTY, the Commission decided on May 3, 2006 to call off negotiations. However, Serbia cannot continue to be the odd man out in Europe. Its vital geographic position in the center of the Balkans, as well as its links and influence on neighboring states, make it an influential player. Many EU economic programs and the effective regional cooperation process the EU envisages pass through Serbia. Without a stable Serbia, the idea of stable Balkans is an illusion. Therefore, a new and productive relationship is necessary for both the EU and Serbia.

Last but not least, EU member states must also realize that the commitment to the Western Balkans is long-term. A change in European mentality regarding the future of the region is important. Europeans must stop looking down on the Balkans and accept the fact that the region was always part of Europe. This constitutes a political challenge as, at present, there is not a favorable political climate for a future Western Balkan enlargement. Current trends of xenophobia and racism in Western Europe have benefitted parties which campaign on an anti-immigration and anti-EU ticket. EU politicians should be careful in their declarations and policies regarding the Western Balkans. They themselves have to cross the Rubicon of populism and demonstrate to the public that integration of Western Balkans into the EU would yield benefit for Europe in the long-term. This is not an easy task if one takes into account that the pro-enlargement feelings of the European public have cooled down. Although certain EU members suffer from enlargement fatigue, it would not be prudent for the EU to lose the momentum of Balkan modernization by letting the process of EU-Balkan rapprochement slow.

Conclusions

In the 1990s, the major preoccupation of the EU was to end the conflict in the Western Balkans. With the end of the crisis, the challenge has become twofold. Not only does the EU have to maintain order, it also has to consolidate peace by contributing to the empowerment of the Western Balkan states through social, infrastructural, political, and bureaucratic modernization. This is not an easy task. The problems and challenges that the international society faces while trying to reconstruct war-torn nations can be tremendous. Within this context, although many comments have been made about the gap between the EU's capabilities and its expectations, it is also evident that in this part of the world (as in many others) even a superpower such as the U.S. could not completely solve post-war problems. However, the depth of these problems should not make the EU surrender to a wave of fatalism. After all, the fatalist idea that the Balkans are there to destruct themselves is part of the wider problem emanating from people's mentalities in the area. Nevertheless, there is still room for optimism as a considerable progress was achieved by the EU by reclaiming the lost policy space of the early 1990s. However, in order to be a more successful policy player, the EU must also invent new ways to deal with Western Balkan issues.

---

* The author would like to thank the Compagnia di San Paolo, the Volkswagen Stiftung Foundation and the Riksbankens Jubileumsfond Foundation for their valuable support.
[1] For Further details regarding the aims of the Stability Pact for South Eastern Europe, visit the official Stability Pact webpage: http://www.stabilitypact.org/
[2] Stability Pact for South Eastern Europe http://www.stabilitypact.org/about/default.asp

[3] European Commission, 'CARDS' http://ec.europa.eu/enlargement/financial_assistance/cards/index_en.htm
[4] European Commission, EU-Western Balkans Declaration, Thessaloniki, Greece, 21 June 2003, http://ec.europa.eu/enlargement/enlargement_process/accession_process/how_does_a_country_join_the_eu/sap/thessaloniki_summit_en.htm
[5] Stephan Lehne, "Has the 'Hour of Europe' Come at Last? The EU's Strategy for the Balkans," *The Western Balkans: Moving On*, (Paris: Institute for Security Studies, Chaillot Paper, No. 70, 2004), p. 114
[6] Wolfgang Petritsch and Christophe Solioz, 'The Interview: the Fate of Bosnia and Herzegovina: an Exclusive Interview of Christophe Solioz with Wolfgang Petritsch,' *Journal of Southern Europe and the Balkans*, vol. no. 5 (3) (2003), p. 362
[7] Lehne 2004: p. 112
[8] Christopher Hill, "The Capability-Expectations Gap, or Conceptualizing Europe's International Role," *Journal of Common Market Studies*, vol. 31, no. 3, (1993), pp. 305-28.
[9] Jacques Rupnik, "The Demise of Balkan Nationalism? A Sceptical View," in Judy Batt, ed. *The Western Balkans: Moving On*, (Paris: Institute for Security Studies, Chaillot Paper, No. 70, 2004) p. 110
[10] Denis McShane, Europe's Hour: Come and Gone? Newsweek, August 2006, http://findarticles.com/p/articles/mi_kmnew/is_200608/ai_n16623146
[11] Petritsch 2003: 359
[12] Franz-Lothar Altmann and Eugene Whitlock, eds., *European and U.S. Policies in the Balkans*, (German Institute for International and Security Affairs, Berlin, 2004), p. 78
[13] Ibid., p. 71
[14] Gerard Knaus, and Marcus Cox, "Bosnia and Herzegovina: Europeanisation by Decree?" In Judy Batt, ed., in *The Western Balkans: Moving On*, (Paris: Institute for Security Studies, Chaillot Paper, No. 70, 2004), p. 59
[15] Robert Cooper. *The Post-Modern State and the World Order* (London: Demos, 2000)
[16] L.S. Woodward, "Transatlantic Harmony or Stable Kosovo?" in Franz-Lothar Altmann and Eugene Whitlock, eds, *European and U.S. Policies in the Balkans*, (Berlin: German Institute for International and Security Affairs, 2004) pp. 25-30.
[17] Lehne 2004: p. 118
[18] For instance Woodward provides the example of the directly opposing positions by the UN pillar and the EU pillar, publicly announced, on privatization of public sector firms, with resulting delays and confusion all around. (Woodward 2004: p. 27).
[19] Altmann 2004: pp. 77, 82
[20] Lehne 2004: p. 122
[21] Bugajski in Altmann: 2004: pp. 31-2
[22] EU divided over future status of Kosovo EU OBSERVER 29.11.2005 - 18:02 CET | By Mark Beunderman In Kosovo.net http://www.kosovo.net/ news/archive/2005/November_30/3.htmlBELGRADE, Oct 29, 2006
[23] According to IISS analyst Oksana Antonenko: 'the idea of Kosovan independence is taken as a precedent by other separatist states in South Caucasus which may have damaging implications for EU energy interests.' The breakaway Georgian regions of Abkhazia and South Ossetia and the Armenian-occupied Azerbaijan region, Nagorno-Karabakh, are using the Kosovan model to legitimise their own "de facto

states" Source: Andrew Rettman EUOBSERVER / BRUSSELS (24/02/06) - International Institute for Strategic Studies http://www.iiss.org/whats-new/iiss-in-the-press/february-2006/kosovo-issue-inflaming-separatism

[24] Ivan Vejvoda, "Serbia After Four Years of Transition," *The Western Balkans: Moving On*, (Paris: Institute for Security Studies, Chaillot Paper, No. 70, 2004), p.41

[25] Petritsch 2003: p. 360

[26] Ibid., p. 364

[27] Ibid., p. 366

[28] Judy Batt, *The Western Balkans: Moving On*, (Paris: Institute for Security Studies, Chaillot Paper, No. 70, 2004), p. 131

[29] Lehne 2004: p. 120

Chapter 2
Of Cops and Robbers:
European Union Policy on the Problem of Organized Crime in Bosnia and Herzegovina

Ana E. Juncos

> For a prince should have **two fears**: one **within**, on account of his subjects; the other **outside**, on account of external powers. From (For?) the latter one is defended with good arms and good friends; and if one has good arms, one will always have good friends (Niccolò Machiavelli, The Prince, XIX-2, emphasis added).

The Machiavellian concept of security clearly distinguished between internal (conspiracy) and external (foreign powers) threats. This perception was later reinforced with the development of the modern state, which led to the formation of two separate bodies (national police and national armies) to deal with two separate spheres of security. Following this traditional division, crime is regarded as an internal affair of the nation-state which should have at its disposal an entire machinery to discipline and punish.[1] However, globalization has made Machiavelli's distinction between internal and external security increasingly blurred. Criminals have been particularly successful at adapting to the challenges and exploiting the opportunities offered by this process. Crime has become global both in terms of scale and involvement, and criminals have taken advantage of the latest developments in communication technologies and the openness of international markets. In the European context, they have benefited from the establishment of the single market and freedom of movement within the borders of the European Union (EU). As a consequence, international cooperation and foreign policy tools are required more and more in order to equally respond to this phenomenon.

Among other things, organized crime has also become a subject of concern at the EU level because of the development of the EU's competencies in the area of Justice and Home Affairs (JHA) and organized crime has been identified as a key threat in the *European Security Strategy*.[2] As mentioned in the European Security Strategy, such an external threat requires an effective response from the Union. For its part, the Western Balkan region has been singled out in the European Security Strategy as it is one of the main nests of organized crime and, as a result, the EU's policies toward the region have placed the fight against organized crime among their top priorities.

Against this backdrop, with this contribution, we discuss the EU's approach against organized crime in the Balkans, particularly in Bosnia and Herzegovina (hereafter Bosnia). In this chapter, after briefly discussing the process of externalization of the EU's internal security policies and main features of organized crime, three theoretical approaches to understanding organized crime—utilitarian, constructivist and structuralist—are introduced. It is argued that these approaches are helpful in pinpointing four tensions that have arisen from the current EU strategy (or rather lack thereof). First is the tension between a hard, security-based approach resulting from the securitization of this phenomenon and a developmental approach that acknowledges the root causes of organized crime. Second, one can identify the tension between the securitization of this issue and the principle of ownership that is meant to be present in the EU's policies toward the region. Third, there is a contradiction between the securitization of the EU's neighborhood and the inclusive nature of the project epitomized by the EU's enlargement. Finally, a tension remains between the cross-pillar nature of the fight against organized crime and the pillarization of the EU's external action, including the fragmentation of the EU civil/military policies and instruments. Before moving to conceptualization of transnational organized crime, the following section provides an overview of the process of externalization of the EU's internal security policies.

The EU's Export of Security: The Externalization of the Third Pillar

The increasing interdependence in the security realm as a result of the globalization process has left an imprint in the development of the EU's internal and external policies. The exported/externalization of internal security[3] has resulted from the recognition that it is not possible anymore to maintain an artificial separation between the internal and external security, and they must be considered interlinked.[4] Having been organized in three pillars since the passing of the Maastricht Treaty (1992),[5] the pillarization of the EU soon appeared to be ill-adapted to deal with security issues like transnational organized crime, terrorism and immigration, all involving aspects from the three pillars. In many cases, the roots of these internal security threats can be found outside the EU borders and, therefore, to tackle these problems, an international cooperation is required as in the case of organized crime. Although organized crime was originally a competence of the third pillar (Justice and Home Affairs (JHA)), it was soon realized that criminal networks operated beyond EU borders and, in some cases, had an external origin. To deal with this problem, the EU made use of external policy tools such as international agreements or ESDP instruments (i.e.

police, rule of law and military operations) which usually fell under the second pillar realm, that of the Common Foreign and Security Policy (CFSP). As a result, what started as a mere internal policy, seeking the harmonization of judicial systems and the promotion of police and judicial cooperation, has now expanded beyond that, reaching areas traditionally under the CFSP. If the objective was to establish an 'area of freedom, security and justice,' the external face of internal security should also be incorporated into the equation.

In the Tampere European Council (1999), the EU leaders agreed that JHA ought to be 'integrated in the definition and implementation of other Union policies and activities.' As far as the external policies are concerned, the EU should mainstream JHA objectives, for example, in the agreements with third countries. More recently, in *Strategy for the external dimension of JHA*, it is stated that 'the EU should therefore make JHA a central priority in its external relations and ensure a coordinated and coherent approach.'[6] With this objective in mind, the EU has included clauses related to justice and home affairs in its agreements with third countries (e.g. Russia, the countries included in its European Neighborhood Policy or the Western Balkans). By doing so, the EU has exported the model of cooperation that had long been established among the member states based on the approximation of their criminal law and criminal procedures and the development of a regime of police and judicial cooperation to third countries in various degrees.[7] In the same vein, the EU has tried to foster a 'security partnership' with neighboring countries, based on mutual trust and common interests, in order to combat threats such as organized crime, terrorism and the challenge of migration.[8] Without doubt, the most successful strategy to export its security governance model has been the enlargement process that has allowed the EU to transfer the *acquis communautaire* to the candidate countries by offering, as a major incentive, the membership perspective. In sum, the EU is increasingly using its foreign policy instruments to deal with internal, security-related problems. Given the emphasis the EU has placed on issues such as transnational organized crime, it is high time for an assessment of the EU's role in this policy area.

Organized Crime: Definition and Theoretical Approaches

Organized crime, which is regarded here as a transnational criminal network,[9] is not a new phenomenon; on the contrary, it has always been present in Western societies in one way or another. The revived interest in organized crime is due to the reduction of military/nuclear threats after the Cold War,[10] as well as the new security agenda that emerged after the 9/11 attacks that are linked to organized terrorist actions. This term includes a broad range of illegal activities, such as drug trafficking, human trafficking and white slave trading, illegal immigration, fraud, money counterfeiting and laundering, illegal logging, smuggling of all weapons and other goods, and intellectual property theft.[11] Crime has gradually become a transnational phenomenon whose operations expand beyond the borders of a particular nation-state. Although some criminal organizations can have a national or ethnic basis (Albanians, Colombians, Russians), its transnational character comes from close links of their members with transnational networks of other criminal organizations.[12] Because of its transnational nature, states cannot fight against organized crime on their own or by traditional means; rather, a global and interdependent approach is required.

In the EU, both the external dimension and external origin of organized crime have been increasingly emphasized, symbolizing the blurred distinction between internal security and external policies. Moreover, it is a fact that organized crime is associated with a broad range of 'threats' from immigration to terrorism and that proliferation of weapons of mass destruction has increased the intractability and emergency character of this phenomenon.[13] According to the *European Security Strategy*: 'Europe is a prime target for organized crime. This internal threat to our security has an important external dimension: cross-border trafficking in drugs, women, illegal migrants, and weapons for a large part of the activities of criminal gangs. It can have links with terrorism.'[14]

However, even though organized crime has usually been depicted as an *external threat* coming from its neighborhood (for instance in the *European Security Strategy*), the Europol Reports show that the biggest threat for the EU comes from criminal groups *within* the EU: 'Indigenous organized crime groups from the European Union (EU), particularly those with extensive international networks, continue to represent the main threat to the EU.'[15]

Even though there has been an extensive use of the term "organized crime" in the political and academic discourse, there is no agreement on what this concept means, leading to different and sometimes clashing strategies.[16] According to Alice Hills, in the EU, 'organized crime remains ill-defined and its capabilities are not necessarily well-understood by EU enforcement agencies.'[17] Three main approaches to organized crime can be distinguished in the official and scholarly literature; utilitarian, structuralist and constructivist.[18]

From the utilitarian (rationalist) point of view, organized crime is seen as an activity carried out by individuals benefitting from the economic profit crime provides. When organized crime is conceptualized in this way, it can be combated by increasing the 'cost' associated with committing the crime, i.e. by increasing police and judicial measures or by reducing the demand. The EU's discourse has often adopted this utilitarian perspective. Organized crime has been conceptualized in terms of 'offer'/'demand' relationship and these illegal activities seen as 'criminal markets.'[19] At the ministerial Conference on organized crime in Southeastern Europe held in London (2002), Javier Solana referred to the offer/demand approach and argued that this was not only a problem that concerned the Balkan countries (offer), but that the cause of the problem had been found in EU countries (demand): '[t]he Western Balkans will remain the gateway of organized crime to Europe until the criminal networks are stopped from making their business in our countries.'[20]

On the other hand, the structuralist approach explains organized crime in terms of social structures and economic factors such as poverty or marginalization. From this perspective, one has to take into account the roots of the problems that cause illegal activities and emergence of black markets. Gender oppression can also explain a great deal about why young girls and women are one of the target groups of human trafficking. From this point of view, organized crime can be seen as:

> A safety net, that is, as a form of assistance and protection against economic shocks and other unpredictable events, particularly when states are weak and unstable and unable or unwilling to provide that protection. This is a particularly acute aspect of organized crime in southeast Europe currently because of the regime transition.[21]

Hence, the best way to 'fight' organized crime would be to focus on improving the socio-economic situation of the people involved in such activities[22] and reduce the oppressive structures that lead to the victimization of women. This part of the story has generally been absent from EU discourses, although some NGOs have drawn attention to the root causes of criminality.[23]

Another approach sees the threat of organized crime as something socially constructed, depending on who constructs which threat.[24] Threats are socially constructed by political actors who possess the power to legitimize a security discourse. From this perspective, what is considered 'normal' in a given society depends on discursive practices at work and is an expression of power relationships. This constructivist understanding of organized crime owes much to critical theory, the Copenhagen School and the concept of 'securitization.' This refers to the process whereby a problem is elevated from a level of normal political discussion to special category status. Security is considered as a 'speech act.'[25] By naming a certain development a security problem, the state claims a special right to intervene.[26]

Through securitization, an issue is framed as an existential threat, 'which calls for extraordinary measures beyond the routines and norms of everyday politics.'[27] It introduces images of friends and enemies, with reminiscences of the Schmittian idea of the politics of emergency.[28] This process can, therefore, prevent democratic control over it; instead, militarization, secrecy and urgency characterize its treatment. In the case of organized crime, discourses of political leaders, feature articles in the media, statistics, and communications by police and customs authorities abound in references to increasing dangers coming from organized crime. The intractability of the problem means that it must be framed as a matter for European security and that emergency measures can be applied.

Following a tendency toward securitization in the EU discourse, organized crime is often referred to as the 'enemy' and the fight against organized crime as a 'battle.' For example, in his speech at the London Conference, Solana affirmed that: 'the challenge is vast, and our enemies are resourceful [...] The battle against organized crime will only be won if we are determined and united.'[29] In the final statement of the Conference, it was said: 'It is an enemy we must defeat, or it will defeat us.'[30] This language has made securitization against organized crime possible, by portraying it as an existential threat that must be defeated by using any necessary means, even beyond normal politics. 'Desecuritizing' public discourses and unveiling hidden power relationships appears as the best strategy to counteract these securitizing processes of crime organizations.

The aim of this paper is to track the influence of these different conceptualizations of organized crime in the EU's discourse and praxis. In other words, does the EU see organized crime as a profit-driven phenomenon (as a rationalist approach would argue)? Has the EU's conception of organized crime in Bosnia resulted from a process of securitization of this issue and what have been the consequences of such a process? Does the EU take the structural causes of organized crime into account when designing its policies? Keeping these three approaches in mind, this issue can, therefore, be better understood. Such an analysis of the EU's strategy will help unveil existing contradictions in its policies against organized crime.

Organized Crime in the Western Balkans

The Balkans, a buffer zone between the West and the East, between developed countries and developing ones, is likely to be the target of transnational criminal groups as a transit area for illegal goods and people. According to the ESS, organized crime constitutes a major security challenge for the EU, and the Balkans is described as one of the main hubs of organized crime groups: '90percent of the heroin in Europe comes from poppies grown in Afghanistan [...] Most of it is distributed through Balkan criminal networks, which are also responsible for some 200,000 of the 700,000 women victims of the sex trade worldwide.'[31] In the Europol Reports, the Balkans are also portrayed as a key transit route for organized crime.[32]

Transnational criminal groups have benefitted from the conflicts in the region. The embargoes during the 1990s have propelled black market activities, which were usually carried out by warlords, war criminals and agents from the Former Yugoslavian security services. When the conflicts ended, most of these networks remained active throughout the Western Balkans. In most cases, these criminals are still protected by their local communities because of the role they played during the war.[33] Criminal networks have often been established across ethnic lines and across different countries within the region.[34] Ironically, regional cooperation has worked better among the gangs than among the Balkan states.[35]

On numerous occasions, the EU has expressed its concerns about the scale of this problem in the Balkans. According to Solana, organized crime is not only a threat to the Union, but also to the countries of the region and it could put the prospects of membership at risk.[36] The Declaration issued after the EU-Balkan summit in June 2003 stated that 'organized crime and corruption is a real obstacle to democratic stability, the rule of law, economic development, and development of civil society in the region, and is a source of grave concern to the EU. Combating it constitutes a major priority.'[37] With this objective in mind, the EU has deployed an impressive range of instruments in the region like the Europol, Eurojust, a Border Control Agency (Frontex), several ESDP missions and Commission activities, together with the activities of the EU member states. Despite the high involvement of the EU, and although organized crime has been on the political radar of the Union for some time now, the EU's strategy in the Western Balkans has been neither coherent nor effective. According to some NGOs, organized crime still continues to thrive in the region.[38] In a report of the 'Friends of the Presidency' in October 2004, it was acknowledged that:

- The EU has no agreed overarching strategy for tackling organized crime in the Western Balkans.
- The EU's approach to fighting organized crime in the Western Balkans is uncoordinated and compartmentalized.
- There remain serious weaknesses in the institutional capacities of the Western Balkan States to fight organized crime.'[39]

In 2006, to partially redress this situation, in an Action Paper, the EU identified the main short- and long-term priorities that deal with organized crime, corruption, illegal immigration, and terrorism. The Action Plan stated that organized crime 'originating from or linked to the Western Balkans endangers long-term political, economical and social development in the region and undermines the concept of the rule of law.'[40] The Action Paper recommends some measures to improve regional cooperation of law enforcement agencies, cooperation between different EU bodies at the operational level, donor coordination and specific measures in the fight against corruption, terrorism and illegal immigration, and border control. It is still too early to assess the impact of these measures on the EU's approach toward organized crime in the Balkans; however, given the seriousness of the problems affecting it (see sections below), these measures seem limited to say the least.[41] The analysis of the EU's anti-organized crime policies in Bosnia will serve to illustrate four tensions present in the current EU's strategy: (1) tension between hard and soft security policies deployed by the EU in the fight against organized crime; (2) tension between the securitization of organized crime and the need to foster local ownership of the reforms; (3) tension between the exclusive effects of securitization and the inclusive nature of the enlargement policy; and (4) problems resulting from the pillarization of the EU's external action and the cross-pillar nature of anti-organized crime policies.

EU's Approach Against Organized Crime in Bosnia

Since the signing of the Dayton Agreement, which established the two entities, the *Republika Srpska* and the Federation of Bosnia and Herzegovina (Croat-Muslim), the security situation in the country has shown some signs of improvement. Although it is not completely ruled out, ethnic violence among the armies of different entities is not likely to recommence. According to the defense reform that has been recently agreed upon, there will be a single Bosnian army in coming years. Today, the main challenge in front of Bosnia's stability seems, above all, to be political issues: A long-awaited agreement on the police reform and a new Constitution. Progress on the first issue is obtained by signing the Stabilization and Association Agreement with the EU that will bring it closer to the perspective of EU membership, which brought the disbandment of the Office of the High Representative. From the EU's perspective, Bosnia holds another issue that attracts full attention of the EU: transnational organized crime.

The geostrategic location of Bosnia does not alone explain the thriving of criminal groups in recent years. The dramatic events during the 1990s also added effects to this phenomenon. Paramilitary and criminal groups emerged from the collapse of the socialist regime and the ethnic conflict (1992-1995). The warring parties made use of these groups to finance the war through smuggling weapons and oil, extortion, kidnapping, and black market activities. War-profiteering activities flourished on both sides and continued after the formal ending of hostilities. Since then, every ethnic group has tried to control the police forces and security agencies under its territory and widespread corruption of the political, police and judicial system became an everyday phenomenon.[42] Police forces often turned a blind eye to or even participated in criminal activities.[43] The catastrophic economic situation in the post-war period also explains why high levels of illegal activities and organized crime have continued in Bosnia where such activities are even socially accepted.

The agreement signed in Dayton meant that the competency to deal with this issue is split among various police forces (overall, thirteen different police forces in the country), separate judicial systems and two different Ministries of the Interior, and that there is not authority at the state level in this respect. Criminals have benefitted from this fragmented system and moved across entity lines with impunity. The first efforts to overcome these problems came from the international community, the International Police Task Force (IPTF), and the High Representative. The IPTF carried out a certification process of Bosnian police forces and supported the creation of several law enforcement agencies at the state level. This responsibility was later taken over by the European Union Police Mission (EUPM). From being a mere protection agency, the newly created State Investigation and Protection Agency (SIPA) soon acquired more investigative powers to launch anti-organized crime investigations. Meanwhile, the State Border Service (SBS) was established in 2000 to manage Bosnia's borders and international airports.[44]

The involvement of the EU in Bosnia has been a very intense one since the beginning of the 1990s. The EC Monitoring Mission was launched in July 1991 to observe the cease-fire in Slovenia and then deployed to other countries in the region, including Bosnia, to monitor human rights and other security-related issues. In 2003, the EU decided to launch its first ever police mission in Bosnia. At the same time, Paddy Ashdown was appointed as the EU's Special Representative (EUSR). The main task of the EUSR was to facilitate coordination of various EU bodies in the country. For its part, the Commission retained various activities starting with the war in 1992 with the provision of humanitarian aid and later technical assistance to the country in the framework of the Stabilization and Association Process (SAP). Finally, in 2004 the EU launched EUFOR Althea with the main task of maintaining a safe and secure environment and supporting the implementation of the Dayton Agreement.

When we look at the relationship between the EU and Bosnia, we see that fighting against organized crime scored high. The Commission's financial assistance, funded through the CARDS program, was mainly devoted to training activities (twinnings), supply of equipment and databases and other technical assistance for institution-building. The fight against organized crime and corruption were among the strategic objectives of the first EUPM (2003-2005), which was operationalized through its program 'Public Order and Security.' For its part, the EUFOR's mandate identified the fight against organized crime as one of its supporting tasks. The EU has toughened this policy in the last two years. The new EUPM mandate (2006-2007) identified the fight against organized crime as one of its three key objectives and this mandate further extended for another two years.[45] In the same context, the EUSR's organization has been reinforced with an advisor on prosecutorial matters, a border expert, and a fraud and special finance advisor. Moreover, the issue continues to be among priorities in the Commission assistance in the field of policing for the financial framework 2007-2013.[46] The following sections analyze the EU's activities against organized crime in Bosnia in more detail, and expose several tensions resulting from the current approach.

The Securitization of Organized Crime: Hard Security vs. Developmental Policies

Two main features characterize the EU's approach against the organized crime in Bosnia. First, it has often adopted a utilitarian perspective that has considered this problem from a rationalist point of view, gauging cost *versus* benefits and highlighting the need for hard security policies (police and judicial measures) to adequately respond to this threat. Second, drawing on a constructivist perspective, one could argue that organized crime has been securitized, i.e., it has been portrayed as an existential threat to the EU. This can be said not only of this particular policy in Bosnia, but as mentioned earlier, it can be seen as a more general aspect in the EU's anti-organized crime policy. In Bosnia, organized crime has been described by the EU as a grave, major problem, not only for the EU, but also for the country itself. In its Progress Report, the Commission argued that 'organized crime remains the single main threat to Bosnia and Herzegovina in terms of security and stability.'[47] In another report, the Commission gave this blunt picture of the situation in Bosnia:

> Sophisticated crime networks take full advantage of differing definitions of crime, of fragmented State structures, of multiple jurisdictions, and investigative bodies. Clearly, crime fighting capacities do not match the sophistication of the criminal networks they (should) confront.[48]

However, according to some authors, organized crime is not perceived in the same way (as an existential threat) by the local population.[49] In contrast, Bosnians are more concerned with other issues such as the economic situation, petty crime or freedom of movement across Europe (visas).[50] Economic assistance and access to EU labor markets can be seen, from this perspective, as the best recipe to combat organized crime.[51] As it was put by a Bosnian official:

> The EU sees this region mostly as a political and security issue: the bodies that are today present in Bosnia are mostly dealing with security issues [...] They have to change their focus [...] The disparity in economic development and the lack of real

convergence between Bosnia and the rest of Europe, that is the real threat to stability in the region.[52]

And he added that if the EU really wanted to have an impact on Bosnia, 'they should be ready to talk about visas.'[53] The gap between the EU's perceptions and the Bosnian perceptions results (1) from a lack of an appropriate analysis of the situation in Bosnia and (2) the lack of a real dialogue between the two parties (see next section). Thus, in spite of the official claims made portraying organized crime as a 'megathreat' in Bosnia, there was no proper assessment of the impact of organized crime until 2006.[54] A report on the impact of organized crime was finally carried out by EUPM that year to provide a global picture of the problem in the country and enhanced advice to the local authorities.[55] Yet, in spite of having a better analysis of the situation, EU policies in Bosnia still focus on security aspects as opposed to a broader (socio-economic) understanding of the problem.

The securitization of organized crime has affected the strategy and instruments that are used to deal with it. It has usually led to the treatment of organized crime as a hard security issue that has to be confronted with border control, police and military instruments, and therefore, is consistent with utilitarian arguments. It follows from this kind of understanding of organized crime that in Bosnia the emphasis has been placed on the development of security and intelligence technologies (capacity-building) to improve cooperation with its EU counterparts, and to build a first line of defense for the EU borders.[56] In order to reform and strengthen the Bosnian judicial and policing system, the EU has provided technical assistance and twinning programs and has launched several ESDP missions. The relevant actors responsible for putting this approach into practice are security sector officials (legislatures, police, courts, intelligence services, ministries of the interior), rather than officials with an expertise in socio-economic problems.[57]

In general, the EU's approach has neglected the socio-economic conditions where criminal activities arise, conditions that explain the involvement of the population in such activities and even legitimized them in the eyes of the Bosnian population. Even if acknowledging the links between organized crime and the socio-economic situation, the Commission's projects against organized crime have so far concentrated on increasing institutional and intelligence capacities, whereas neglected other developmental issues, such as high unemployment and low wages. Only on few occasions, has the EU made known the need to tackle the underlying causes of the problem. For example, regarding migration and human trafficking, the Council stated that 'the EU must also work for more effective policy coherence between migration and development cooperation to address the structural causes (including conflicts) of the mobility of people.'[58] On the ground, several EU officials have underlined the socio-economic factors behind organized crime and have referred to the low salaries of the Bosnian police to explain corruption among police officers.[59] However, these concerns have not yet been integrated into EU policies. As mentioned by Athanassapoulou, 'crime control initiatives need to move away from the mindset of just cops and robbers, crooks and victims and address a whole range of problems including the basic question of how to stop poverty.'[60]

Securitization vs. Local Ownership

Allegedly, the principle of 'local ownership' guides the relations between the EU and third countries and constitutes one of the foundations of the process of enlargement. According to this principle, Bosnia should assume responsibility and participate on an equal footing in determining the pace and priorities in its relationships with the EU. Local ownership should not be limited to the Bosnian elites, but it should also refer to the concept of participatory democracy, incorporating civil society actors into the process. In this vein, the European Commission has often underlined that Bosnia should become a self-sustained state, capable of handling independently the process of integration in the EU without the interference of external actors (mainly referring to the intervention of the High Representative).[61] For its part, the aim of EUPM was 'to establish sustainable policing arrangements under Bosnia ownership in accordance with best European and international practice.'[62] In order to strengthen local ownership of the reforms, EUPM established a Police Steering Board at the level of the Police Commissioner/Director of Police, where projects of reform, for instance, to fight organized crime, were discussed and agreed. At the lower levels of the police hierarchy, EUPM advised on the creation of Project Implementation Boards that were created throughout Bosnia to develop projects at the local level. In this way, Bosnian police officers could offer solutions to organized crime.

However, civil society groups and the Bosnian population in general were kept out of these discussions. EUPM projects neither fully involved the citizens and non-governmental organizations nor gave them an active role in the policing of their communities.[63] Some EUPM projects failed because they did not take local circumstances into account, which was necessary. This approach undermined the effectiveness of the policies against organized crime. Commenting on this long-term approach and local ownership, one EUPM official stated:

> Our focus has been wrong; we should be looking at a more long-term development of management skills. We should be developing local ownership much more than we have. We should be developing sustainable improvement, rather than to pick up one or two things.[64]

Despite repeated claims by EU officials that the aim of EU activities in the country is to develop local ownership and increase local capacities, a real partnership and dialogue among equals has not yet crystallized. A top-down approach still characterizes the relations between the EU and Bosnia and in many cases, 'weak local capabilities' have justified an interventionist style on the part of the EU.[65] In the case of the EU police mission, the result has been 'a slippage from law-enforcement aid based on the notion of local ownership police reforms to the pursuit of Western crime-fighting objectives.'[66] For his part, a high-ranking Bosnian official from the Directorate for European Integration asked for a more equal relationship between EU institutions and Bosnian authorities (i.e. a real partnership) instead of the existing top-down structure. He did not want imposed policies without a proper understanding of the problems in the country: 'I expect real dialogue and partnership [...] Let's work together.'[67] In other words, there should be a more balanced approach between the objectives established in Brussels and local realities and needs. The process of securitization not only affects local ownership, but also leads to processes of exclusion, as is shown in the next section.

Exclusive Securitization vs. Inclusive Enlargement

The enlargement perspective for the countries of the Western Balkans is seen as the main tool to maintain peace and stability in the region and the strongest incentive behind the reforms.[68] In principle, the enlargement process should have an inclusive nature, like integrating these countries into the EU family. The securitization of organized crime has, however, served as an excuse to build new walls around the EU-27. Western Balkan countries have been portrayed as a nest of organized crime and, therefore, seen as 'the other.' The official picture of the region is still one of instability and criminality and reinforces the psychological and physical division between 'us' and 'the others;' a 'safe internal space' and a 'threatening external neighborhood.'[69] This barrier-building process is in real contradiction with the aims of the enlargement and creates animosities among EU citizens against people from the Western Balkan region. The *in/out* image is still very effective in mobilizing citizenship and propelling the process of building a *European fortress*. According to Monar, 'people from outside which actually or potentially endanger the safe inside must be kept outside or brought under appropriate control.'[70] This is the basis of the idea of 'Fortress Europe' that has been much criticized in recent years. More freedom for Europeans entails less freedom for foreigners.

The visa regime plays a fundamental role in controlling foreign populations and reducing potential threats such as terrorism or organized crime. Thus, in spite of being a potential candidate, the EU still applies strict visa regime against Bosnians.[71] Yet, this visa regime has several negative effects that have not been considered by EU authorities. First, it contributes to the stigmatization of the country and its citizens. It establishes a rigid distinction between us and others; and between wanted and unwanted immigrants, and thus supports the process of securitization. Furthermore, as argued by the ICG Report, the visa regime does not stop organized crime, and even encourages criminality (not to mention nationalism and radicalization) because those who cannot legally obtain a visa will be willing to get it by illegal means.[72] The consequences of the current policy for the Western Balkans were summarised by the ICG Report as follows:

> Current policies risk disenchanting the very political elite which counts on EU membership as the motivation for deep reform. Continued isolation and economic depression in the Western Balkans is a social time-bomb; a young and largely unemployed population isolated from other cultures is a recipe for disaster.[73]

Moreover, the securitization and isolation of the region carry the risk of decreasing the pace of reform. The EU has used enlargement as its attraction power, to export its judicial and police model to the candidate countries. Hence the 'potential candidate' countries like Bosnia have to adopt the *acquis communautaire* in the area of JHA as a precondition to join the EU.[74] This involves an intense reform process, and in most cases, a huge financial burden for these countries. However, it is seen as a crucial requirement for accession to preserve the internal security of the Union. As put by Alice Hills, 'a single external border is, after all, only as strong as its weakest link.'[75]

In the case of Bosnia, progress in this area has been considered essential if the country wants to get closer to the EU. One of the main conditions imposed by the EU refers to the restructuring of the police force. According to the EU, this reform will strengthen the effectiveness of the Bosnian police to fight organized crime. An initial agreement was reached at the end of 2005, largely as a result of pressures coming from the EU and the threat that the failure in agreeing to this reform would frustrate Bosnian hopes to join the EU one day. However, conditionality has already shown its limits in this case. For the last two years, local parties have been unable to agree on the implementation of the aforementioned reform. Apart from domestic turfs, the mixed signals following the Constitutional referendum and the message given by the visa regime that implies the Bosnian population is unwanted and 'a threat' for the EU did not help at all. As it is admitted by many, the power of attraction of the EU can only work as long as it offers credible incentives and so far, that has not been the case. Having realized some of these problems, the EU has recently moved to a policy of visa facilitation for specific groups of people such as businessmen or students, and bilateral agreements have been signed with each country of the region.[76] However, visa liberalization is still off the agenda. Apart from these problems, coherence has proven a challenge and has affected the implementation of the EU policies, an issue examined in the following section.

Pillarization of the EU vs. the Cross-pillar Nature of Organized Crime

The EU is considered to be well placed to address the multidimensional nature of organized crime due to the broad range of instruments at its disposal, from economic assistance to diplomatic tools, as well as the police force, rule of law and military operations. However, the existence of the three pillars makes it difficult for the EU to mobilize these instruments in a coherent and effective way. Coherence continues to be the cause of concern regarding the EU's external action. Thus, in the *Strategy for the external dimension of JHA*, it was expressed that horizontal and vertical coherence must be ensured, i.e. coherence between EU policies and coherence between the member states' policies and EU policies; specific measures to improve these EU policies were recommended.[77]

In practice, however, coherence has suffered from lack of agreement on conceptualizing organized crime in a better way, and finding the best strategies to deal with this problem. The pillarization of the EU has only added more problems. While the Commission has been eager to develop soft security policies and target long-term institution-building, the Council, on the other hand, has placed more emphasis on hard security policies and short-term crisis management through ESDP operations. These divergent approaches and different chains of command that every mission follows have also caused some trouble. In sum, the overall EU strategy in the fight against organized crime has been 'disorganized' to say the least.[78]

For instance, while EUPM, designed by the Council structures, aimed to satisfy urgent needs of Bosnian police forces in the fight against organized crime through mentoring, monitoring and inspecting, the Commission Delegation in Bosnia has focused more on long-term institutional-building projects such as: the creation of databases, and the provision of equipment and legal advice to harmonize legislation. As a result, the programs implemented in Bosnia did not always follow the same logic. EUPM officials complained that there was not always full cooperation in order to harmonize the projects launched by the Commission and the EUPM's projects, and that this affected the financing of EUPM's activities on some occasions. There were also problems due to the duplication of advisors (one co-located police officer coming from EUPM and one advisor from the Commission's twinning projects) to some Bosnian institutions.

The fragmentation of the EU's institutional structure also resulted in problems of coordination between civilian and military instruments. A case in point here was the clash between the approach implemented by EUPM and the short-term, military interventions carried out by EUFOR. From December 2004, several operations were launched by EUFOR in order to support local law enforcement agencies in the fight against illegal activities like weapons' smuggling, drug trafficking, human trafficking, and illegal logging. Whereas the EUPM's projects aimed at increasing the local capabilities in the fight against organized crime, EUFOR's participation in such organized operations undermined this approach. According to EUPM officials, EUFOR operations increased external dependence of the local police forces. By actively participating in these operations, EUFOR was actually doing the locals' job.[79]

These problems, however, have led to some changes in EU policies. First, a comprehensive strategy to tackle organized crime in the Western Balkans was considered. In a letter to the Council, the High Representative urged the Presidency to develop this strategy. According to Solana, the strategy 'should set priorities, so that the many bodies concerned can direct their activities toward a coherent set of goals.'[80] This strategy should ensure a coherent approach towards the region and effective communication and coordination between EU actors. As a result, a new regional approach and guidelines for ESDP operations activities in the fight against organized crime have recently been developed. Improvements have also taken place on the ground with a new agreement reached among the representatives of EUPM, EUFOR and the EUSR.[81] According to this agreement, the EU police mission will take the lead in policing aspects of organized crime, while EUFOR will provide the operational support when required. The implementation of these principles means that EUFOR's role in the combat against organized crime will be progressively reduced in general, and it has improved coordination between the different EU bodies on the ground.[82]

Conclusions

The analysis of the EU's strategy in the fight against organized crime has revealed some serious deficiencies affecting the general strategy and instruments used to tackle this phenomenon. From the theoretical perspectives discussed here, it is evident that some of these problems result from (1) the securitization of organized crime by the EU, (2) an excessive emphasis on security policies, in line with a utilitarian conception of crime and (3) the omission of the socio-economic dimension and its impact on organized crime. Thus, the EU has privileged police, military and border control instruments to 'fight' against organized crime, instead of implementing developmental policies to address the root causes and consequences of organized crime. A more developmental, long-term approach could remedy these shortcomings in the EU's strategy. For example, the EU could address some of these problems by providing more economic assistance or by widening its visa regime.[83]

It seems the greatest challenge for local ownership has come from the securitization of organized crime within the EU. The fact that organized crime has been framed as a vital threat means there is no room for dialogue with the locals and it has led to a very authoritarian approach, with the EU imposing its own security agenda on the locals. There has been little space for a real dialogue or mutual understanding in this relationship. Thus, even when organized crime is not among the main concerns of the Bosnian population, the EU's policies have made it one of its priorities. By contrast, the liberalization of the visa regime has not been on the EU's agenda. This typifies the non-egalitarian relationship between the EU and Bosnia when it comes to setting the priorities of the security agenda and the failure of the local ownership principle.

Third, the threat of organized crime still stigmatizes the Bosnians who are perceived as a malign 'other' or a threat. This perspective, led by subjective images and political imperatives, is not helping the country and is making integration into the EU increasingly difficult, in spite of the messages supporting the enlargement process. This may put an end to the reform process that this country is currently undergoing, particularly in the areas of policing and justice. As a Bosnian official warned, 'if the EU does not send clear messages supporting the next enlargement, this could also affect the effectiveness and the pace of reforms in this region.'[84]

Last, but by no means least, this chapter has illustrated several problems in ensuring coherent EU external action. To a certain extent, these problems have resulted from the pillarization of the EU's institutional setting and the different strategies put in place by the Commission/Council and the civilian/military ESDP operations. As mentioned before, in recent months there has been some progress in improving coordination among different EU organizations and instruments, but the transversal and multidimensional nature of organized crime means that these *ad hoc* measures will not be sufficient, and that changes in the EU's institutional structure such as those contained in the Reform Treaty are very much needed. To see whether this will be enough to ensure long-term coherence and effectiveness of the EU's external action or not, one will have to wait for the actual implementation of such reforms.

---

[1] Michel Foucault, *Discipline and punish: the birth of the prison* (New York, Vintage Books, 1995).

[2] European Council, *A Secure Europe in a Better World. European Security Strategy. Report presented by the High Representative for the CFSP to the Brussels European Council* (Brussels, 12 December 2003).

[3] Francesca Longo, "The export of the fight against organized crime policy model and the EU's international actorness," in Michèle Knodt and Sebatiaan Princen, *Understanding the European Union's External Relations* (London, New York, Routledge,

2003). Wyn Rees, "The External Face of Internal Security," in Christopher Hill and Michael Smith, *International Relations and the European Union* (Oxford, Oxford University Press, 2005).

[4] Benita Ferrero-Waldner, "The EU's role in protecting Europe's security," *Conference on "Protecting Europe: Policies for enhancing security in the European Union,"* Brussels, May 30, 2006.

[5] The Maastricht Treaty established three pillars: the first or communitarian pillar, mainly covering trade and internal economic activities; the second pillar involving foreign and security issues; and the third pillar for justice and home affairs.

[6] Council of the EU, *A Strategy for the External Dimension of JHA: Global Freedom, Security and Justice*, doc 15446/05, Brussels, December 6, 2005, p. 2.

[7] Longo, "The export of the fight against organized crime," pp. 159-162.

[8] Statewatch News Online, *Vienna Declaration on Security Partnership*, Vienna, May 5, 2006, www.statewatch.org/news/2006/may/01vienna-declaration.htm (accessed November 6, 2007).

[9] The UN Convention against Transnational Organized Crime defines organized criminal groups as 'a structuring group of three or more persons, existing for a long period of time and acting in concert with the aim of committing, one or more serious crimes or offences [...] in order to obtain, directly or indirectly, a financial or other material benefit' (quoted in Lucia Montanaro-Jankovski, "Good cops, bad mobs? EU policies to fight trans-national organized crime in the Western Balkans," *EPC Issue Paper*, No 40, (2005), p. 12.

[10] Rees, "The External Face of internal security," p. 208.

[11] Europol, *EU organized Crime Report. Public Version*, The Hague, October 25, 2005, www.europol.eu.int; Europol, *EU organized Crime Threat Assessment, 2006*, www.europol.eu.int/publications/organized crimeTA/organized crimeTA2006.pdf

[12] Longo, "The export of the fight against organized crime," p. 161.

[13] Rees, "The External Face of internal security," p. 209.

[14] European Council, *A Secure Europe in a Better World*, p. 4.

[15] Europol, *EU organized Crime Report*, p. 5. See also Europol, European Union organized Crime Report (Luxembourg: Office for Official Publications of the European Communities, 2003), p. 13.

[16] Felix Berenskoetter, "Under Construction: ESDP and the 'Fight Against organized Crime'," *Working Paper CHALLENGE*, July 5, 2006, http://www.sgir.org/archive/turin/uploads/Berenskoetter-ESDP%20and%20OC%20Berenskoetter.pdf (accessed November 6, 2007), p. 5.

[17] Alice Hills, "Border Security in the Balkans: Europe's gatekeepers," *Adelphi Papers*, Vol. 44, No. 371, (2004), p. 23.

[18] For more on utilitarian and constructivist approaches on organized crime, see Berenskoetter, "Under Construction".

[19] See, for example, Europol, *EU Organized Crime Report* and Europol, *EU organized Crime Threat Assessment*.

[20] Javier Solana, "Intervention by Javier Solana, EU High Representative for the Common Foreign and Security Policy," *London Conference on organized crime in South Eastern Europe*, London, November 25, 2002.

21 Susan Woodward, "Enhancing Cooperation against Transborder Crime in Southeast Europe: Is There an Emerging Epistemic Community?," *Southeast European and Black Sea Studies*, Vol. 4, No. 2 (2004), p. 231.
22 See, for instance, the contributions in *Southeast European and Black Sea Studies*, Vol. 4, No. 2 (2004).
23 Cornelius Frisendorf, "Sex Trafficking in Southeastern Europe Thrives, So Does the Effort to Combat It," *HumanTrafficking.org*, September 14, 2006, http://www.humantrafficking.org/updates/413 (accessed November 6, 2007).
24 Berenskoetter, "Under Construction," p. 4.
25 Barry Buzan, Wæver and Jaap de Wilde, *Security: A New Framework for Analysis*, (Boulder, Lynne Rienner, 1998).
26 Ibid., p. 26; Ole Wæver, "Securitization and Desecuritization," in Ron Lipschutz (ed.) *On Security*, (New York, Columbia University Press, 1995), p. 55.
27 Michael Williams, "Words, Images, Enemies: Securitization and International Politics," *International Studies Quarterly*, Vol. 47 (2003), p. 514.
28 Ibid.
29 Solana, "Intervention by Javier Solana".
30 Quoted in Michael Merlingen and Rasa Ostrauskaite, "Power/Knowledge in International Peacebuilding: The Case of the EU Police Mission in Bosnia," *Alternatives*, 30 (2005), pp. 311.
31 European Council, *A Secure Europe in a Better World*, p. 5.
32 Europol, *EU organized Crime Report* and Europol, *EU organized Crime Threat Assessment*.
33 Kari Osland, "The EU Police Mission in Bosnia and Herzegovina," *International Peacekeeping*, Vol. 11, No 3 (2004), p. 554.
34 Montanaro-Jankovski, "Good cops, bad mobs?," p. 12.
35 Misha Glenny, "Migration Policies of Western European Governments and the Fight Against organized Crime in SEE," *Southeast European and Black Sea Studies*, Vol. 4, No. 2 (2004), p. 251.
36 Solana, "Intervention by Javier Solana".
37 European Council, *EU-Western Balkans Summit Declaration*, Thessaloniki, June 21, 2003.
38 Frisendorf, "Sex Trafficking in Southeastern Europe."
39 Quoted in Council of the EU, *Action Oriented Paper on Improving Cooperation, on organized Crime, Corruption, Illegal Immigration and Counter-terrorism, between the EU, Western Balkans and relevant ENP countries*, doc 9272/06, Brussels, May 12, 2006, p. 4.
40 Ibid.
41 First assessments of the Action Paper's implementation by EU officials also seem to confirm this point (Interview with the author, June 2007).
42 Two members of the former tri-members Presidency have been accused of corruption charges, Mirko Sarovic, the former Bosnian Serb president and Dragan Covic, the Bosnian Croat President.
43 According to the Commission's 2003 Report: 'The particularly brutal form of organized crime associated with trafficking of women and children for sexual exploitation persists [in Bosnia], sometimes with the involvement of those meant to fight it' (European Commission, *Bosnia and Herzegovina. Stabilization and Association Report 2003*. COM (2003) 139 final, Brussels, March 26, 2003, p. 29).

44 Today, it constitutes one of the most modern border management agencies in the region. However, the SBS still requires more personnel and the establishment of an Integral Border Management system (Ministry of Security of BiH, *Report on Security in Bosnia and Herzegovina in 2004*, Sarajevo, April 2005, p. 29).
45 Interview with the author, Brussels, May 2007.
46 Interviews with the author, Brussels and Sarajevo, 2006.
47 European Commission, *Bosnia and Herzegovina. 2005 Progress Report*. COM 2005 561 final, Brussels, November 9, 2005, p. 64.
48 European Commission, *Bosnia and Herzegovina. Stabilization and Association Report*, p. 29.
49 Merlingen and Ostrauskaite, "Power/Knowledge in International Peacebuilding"; International Crisis Group, "EU Visas and the Western Balkans," *Europe Report* No. 168, November 29, 2005.
50 In the 2004 Report on Security in Bosnia produced by the Bosnian Ministry of Security, the term organized crime did not appear. Instead, the report referred to 'international smuggling channels' when discussing problems with human trafficking, drug trafficking or smuggling of cigarettes and other commodities. The report placed more emphasis on other type of security threats such as thefts, corporate criminality, refugee return or traffic security and highlighted the socio-economic consequences of transnational criminality for the local victims (e.g. lack of appropriate places to house the victims or for rehabilitation) (Ministry of Security of BiH, *Report on Security in Bosnia and Herzegovina in 2004*).
51 Glenny, "Migration Policies of Western European Governments."
52 Interview with the author, Sarajevo, June 2005.
53 Ibid.
54 Interview with the author, Sarajevo, July 2005. In a letter to the Council dated of 14 December 2005, Javier Solana recognized that 'we need a thorough assessment of the impact of organized crime in the Balkans' (Secretary General/High Representative, *Letter of the Secretary General/High Representative to the Presidency and the Members of European Council, S416/05*, December 14, 2005, p. 11).
55 Interview with the author, Brussels, June 2007.
56 Hills, "Border Security in the Balkans," p. 7.
57 Woodward, "Enhancing Cooperation against Transborder Crime," p. 227.
58 Council of the EU, *A Strategy for the External Dimension of JHA*, p. 4.
59 As one EUPM officer put it, 'there is a broad agreement that we need to reform the police, but the lower level, the station commander does not have an interest in European integration […] He needs to survive now, to get money now..' Interview with the author, London, January 2006.
60 Ekavi Athanassapoulou, "Introduction: Fighting organized crime in SEE," *Southeast European and Black Sea Studies*, Vol. 4, No. 2 (2004), p. 219.
61 Interviews with the author, Brussels and Sarajevo, 2005-2006.
62 Council of the EU, "Council Joint Action 2002/210/CFSP of 11 March 2002 on the European Union Police Mission," *Official Journal of the European Communities*, L70, 13 March, p. 1.
63 Maybe the only exception here is the establishment of a hotline called 'Krimo-Lovci' ('Crime-Catchers') that allowed citizens to make anonymous calls informing about possible crimes.

⁶⁴ Interview with the author, Sarajevo, April 2005.
⁶⁵ Interview with the author, Brussels, June 2007.
⁶⁶ Merlingen and Ostrauskaite, "Power/Knowledge in International Peacebuilding," p. 311.
⁶⁷ Interview with the author, Sarajevo, June 2005.
⁶⁸ The Feira European Council confirmed the European perspective of the Western Balkans in June 2000. The Brussels European Council of March 2003 reaffirmed that 'the future of the Western Balkans [lies] within the EU' and that '[t]he unification of Europe will not be complete until these countries join the European Union..'
⁶⁹ Rees, "The External Face of internal security."
⁷⁰ Jorg Monar, "Justice and Home Affairs in a Wider Europe: The Dynamics of Inclusion and Exclusion," *ESRC 'One Europe or Several?' Program Working Paper* 07/00 (2000), p. 5.
⁷¹ In March 2001, Bosnia, together with Albania, Macedonia and Serbia and Montenegro, was placed in the black list of the EU, i.e. those countries whose nationals should have a visa in order to cross the EU borders.
⁷² Glenny, "Migration Policies of Western European Governments;" International Crisis Group, "EU visas and the Western Balkans"; pp. 1-2.
⁷³ International Crisis Group, "EU visas and the Western Balkans," p. 10.
⁷⁴ According to the Schengen Protocol, Art. 8: 'Schengen Acquis and further measures taken by the institutions within its scope [...] must be accepted by all States candidates for admission..'
⁷⁵ Hills, "Border Security in the Balkans," p. 18.
⁷⁶ Progress in negotiations on visa facilitation have been however linked to negotiations on readmission agreements with the and to progress in reforms in different JHA areas.
⁷⁷ Council of the EU, *A Strategy for the External Dimension of JHA*, pp. 7-8.
⁷⁸ Montanaro-Jankovski, "Good cops, bad mobs?," p. 23.
⁷⁹ Interviews with the author, Sarajevo, 2005.
⁸⁰ General/High Representative, *Letter of the Secretary General/High Representative*.
⁸¹ EUPM, EUFOR, EUSR, *Guidelines for Increasing Cooperation between EUPM-EUFOR and EUSR*, September 2005, Sarajevo.
⁸² Interviews with the author, May-June 2007.
⁸³ European Stability Initiative, *Breaking out of the Balkan Ghetto: Why IPA should be changed*, ESI Report, Berlin-Brussels-Istanbul, June 1, 2005, www.esiweb.org; Glenny, "Migration Policies of Western European Governments."
⁸⁴ Interview with the author, Sarajevo, June 2005.

Chapter 3
EU's Kosovo Policy:
Multiple Challenges, Challenging Answers?*

Birgül Demirtaş-Coşkun

As the European Community (EC) went through a radical structural transformation in the 1990s due to both deepening and enlargement, the conflicts in the Western Balkans started to be considered as a test case for this changing Europe. Conflicts, wars and tensions that broke out in the former Yugoslavian territories, which disturbed the whole Europe, proved that the emerging new era following the end of the bipolar international politics was not going to be as peaceful as had been desired. The complexity of the problems of former Yugoslavia has effected the evolution of the European Union which has been, with the encouragement of the U.S., trying to be a regional actor by developing a more coherent approach to the issues of foreign affairs and security policies among its member states.

The rising tension between Serbs and Albanians in Kosovo[1] has been one of the most complicated problems among all the other regional conflicts. First of all, Kosovo is the place where the first signs of dissolution of the Federation of Yugoslavia emerged in demonstrations of Albanian youth at the beginning of the 1980s. However, until the violent attacks of the UÇK (*Ushtria Clirimtare e Kosoves* - Kosovo Liberation Army) occured in the second half of the 1990s, the disagreement did not attract the attention of the international community, including the EU. Second, the conflict had the potential to spread to neighboring countries as was argued by those who believed that a greater Albania was in the making.[2]

To be able to analyze whether the Union has adopted coherent and effective policies toward the Kosovo issue, in this study, we will focus on the EU's policies regarding this particular matter. Considering the major role the EU plays in conflicts in and around its territory, it is significant to understand the EU's attitude toward Kosovo from the 1990s, since the Kosovo problem includes many challenges for external actors emanating from its status within the former Yugoslavia and its relations with Albania. With the Kosovo problem being the most complicated, perhaps the most unsolvable issue in the region, it presents a kind of platform that can test the problem-solving ability, regional capacity and effectiveness the EU can exhibit in this region while playing its role to solve this dispute of the post-Cold War era. What is more, the case of Kosovo can also be regarded as an important step for the EU's evolution toward being "a global player"[3] since the Kosovo issue is not important in only regional politics, but also in international politics. Therefore, we might expect that if the EU plays a constructive role in the peaceful resolution of the Kosovo problem, this might encourage it to pursue a more active foreign and security policy toward global issues as well.

There are different approaches regarding the EU's evolving role in international politics: One approach emphasizes the normative/civilian features of the Union's foreign policy arguing that the Union mainly adopts non-military measures in its international politics. Second approach claims that the EU is on the way to becoming a superpower in the coming decades, for it has steadily increased its power over the time since its establishment after the Second World War. Last, but not least, approach claims that the Union is becoming a more powerful regional actor; however, it has neither the will nor the potential to become a global power. In this article, dwelling on this conceptual distinction, we will try to understand which approach more evidently explains the EU's attitude toward the Kosovo problem.

The study consists of the following parts: First, it presents the conceptual framework by shedding light on the different approaches mentioned above. Second, it has a brief analysis of the dynamics of the Kosovo issue. In the following part, it examines the EU's policies toward the Yugoslavian problems from Slovenia and Croatia to Bosnia. The fourth part tries to shed light on the Union's policies toward the Kosovo issue, both before and after the NATO operation in 1999. The fifth part deals with the EU's role in the negotiations that started in 2006 between Serbia and Kosovo Albanians under the guidance of the Contact Group. The main findings and arguments are summarized in the conclusion.

Conceptual Framework[4]

In one of George Modelski's studies entitled "The Long Cycle of Global Politics and the Nation-State," world powers or global powers[5] were defined as follows: "... world (or) global powers control (or substantially control) the global political system and hence also have the capacity to regulate other global processes (such as long-distance travel)."[6] Modelski, in the same work, explained that each world power experiences two phases that are called the ascending phase and the descending phase. In his view, each ascending phase consists of some parts that will lead to its destruction. At some point, some international problems may emerge from points where the existing world power could not solve them or from where some conflicts break out. In this case, some other actors can attempt to solve these problems. He argues that these events will lead to a global conflict that is followed by the emergence of a new global power. Based on his historical analysis, he calculates that the life of each world power is about a hundred years. He estimates that at that time, the world power was about to pass the ascending phase and enter the descending phase.[7] At the same time, he argues that it was only the nation states that could play the role of global power. Only nation states could conduct global operations, he states. He gives the example of city-states and empires in the past centuries claiming that they could not play global roles.[8]

Using the framework provided by William Fox, Christopher Hill defines the superpower as the one that has the power to shape the global politics according to its own wishes and decisions. Its influence is felt worldwide. It can deploy its forces anywhere in the world. It has a great sphere of influence. That means it has a huge economic and military power. At the same time, it has enough domestic resources to provide the necessary basis for its autonomy. According to this view, a superpower does not depend on any other actor economically or militarily. Since the Cold War era, the term "superpower" is associated with nuclear weapons as well. Beginning in the 1940s, all superpowers are supposed to own nuclear weapons.[9]

Combining both approaches, it can be stated that a superpower or world power is expected to extend its influence worldwide and also determine how the international system functions. But it must, first of all, have the will and the intention to play this kind of a role.

Meanwhile, the terms "economic giant and political dwarf" and "civilian power" approach were emphasized in the literature on the EU's role in world politics. Especially until the end of the Cold War era, the EU was not able to make any important progress in political integration, but was seen as an important economic power, more clearly, one of the three biggest economic powers in the world, with the other two being the U.S. and Japan. But its international role was perceived as limited to its economic power. In the political realm, however, it was not seen as a united actor, since member states preserved their full sovereignty in foreign policy and defense matters.

Hanns W. Maull explains the concept of civilian power the following way: 1) Its basic tool must be cooperation in its relations with other states or actors, 2) in order to realize its interests, it must use non-military measures, basically economic ones and 3) it must have the will to cede its sovereignty with the aim of making supranational arrangements.[10] In other words, it must accept "reciprocal dependence."[11] The civilian power approach was dominant, especially in the 1970's, which was the period when both superpowers did not refrain from using military instruments in their foreign policy. The U.S. was fighting in Vietnam and the USSR was using force in Czechoslovakia. The European emphasis on civilian power instruments, however, became a shelter for it to avoid any involvement in Vietnam.[12] At the time, the European youth was heavily interested in politics as seen in the protest movements.

In contrast, there were some scholars who argued that the EU had the potential, or was on the way to becoming a global power. Johan Galtung, in his books entitled *"The European Community: A Superpower in the Making,"* published in 1973, and *"Europe in the Making,"* published in 1989, argued that the EC would have the potential to be a colonial power once again.[13] He argued that, ever since its inception, the EU was enlarging its geographical space by integrating new, full and associate members, increasing the range of the subjects it was dealing with and also furthering its level of integration. Since most of the European countries had a colonial past, the possibility of the EU turning into a superpower should not be overlooked, according to Galtung's book.[14] There are also some more recent publications stating that the EU had the potential to become a superpower.[15]

A third group of studies, however, are focusing on the increasing role of the EU in world politics, after the dissolution of the Eastern Bloc, since the Union achieved more maneuvering space during that time. By accepting new members, it tried to deepen its integration on one hand, and on the other, it became enlarged. The successful realization of both processes was perceived as a great success on the part of the EU. These studies stress upon the increasing role of the EU in world affairs.[16] Another emphasized factor was the increasing expectations of other international actors from the Union. In the post-Cold War era, especially the U.S. wanted the EU to share more of the burden, particularly concerning the conflicts in the neighborhood of the EU. The EU itself seemed more confident in the wake of revolutionary changes as exemplified by the famous statement of Jacques Poos, the Foreign Minister of Luxembourg and then-term president of the European Community, that it was "the hour of Europe,"[17] referring to the solutions to the war in Yugoslavia in 1991. However, the EU realized that "its hour" was full of challenges and complexities.

In brief, there are three fundamental views about the position of the EU in international politics: First, the civilian power or normative power approach,[18] second, the possible superpower approach, and third, the approach of the EU's increasing power and capabilities. It should be emphasized that these do not have to be mutually exclusive categories as they intersect at certain common points.

Kosovo Issue

Kosovo was the first place in which the nationalities' problem in Yugoslavia broke out after the death of Tito.[19] It was one of the two autonomous provinces (the other was Vojvodina) within the country and consisted of an Albanian majority (90 percent) and a Serbian minority (10 percent). Although Tito granted important rights to Kosovo Albanians and recognized the status of Kosovo as an autonomous region in the 1974 Constitution, Kosovo Albanians were not content with this and asked to raise the region's political status to that of a republic. The rising tension in the province after the death of Tito was also related to the increasing amount of socio-economic problems and the rise of unemployment among Albanian youth. In 1981, university students in the capital, Pristina, started a protest demonstration against the Belgrade regime and declared their wish to separate Kosovo from the rest of Yugoslavia. The demonstration could only be suppressed by the police force. After Milosevic had seized leadership, the situation in Kosovo became even tenser. Milosevic's visit to Kosovo in 1989 on the 600th anniversary of the Ottoman conquest of the region became an important signal of the start of his nationalist policies. In his speech, he promised to protect the rights of Serbians in Kosovo and accused Albanians of violating the rights of the Serbian minority. In the same year, by a constitutional amendment, the Belgrade government lifted the autonomous status of Kosovo.[20] This move destroyed "the sensitive balance" in the country and started the process of dissolution of the Yugoslav state.[21] Thus, although the Albanian majority had not been content with the autonomous status, they had to face a new situation in which they lost even their previous rights. Albanian people did not accept the new situation and organized demonstrations which were suppressed by force and led to casualties and human rights violations.

Meanwhile, Milosevic launched new initiatives to rid the Albanians of their rights. He banned the use of Albanian language in schools and media and replaced it with Serbian language. Furthermore, thousands of Albanians were fired from their jobs just because of their nationality. Those measures increased the hatred and doubts of the Albanians toward the Belgrade government.

Developments in other regions of Yugoslavia affected the course of events in Kosovo as well. The increasing economic difficulties, as well as the danger of Serbian hegemony, started a process in which most of the republics and regions tried to find ways to go their own direction by declaring independence from the central state. In September 1991, a referendum on independence was carried out in the province that resulted in an overwhelming majority's positive votes. The Republic of Kosovo was proclaimed and afterward, Ibrahim Rugova was elected as the President. Rugova represented the moderate wing of the Kosovo Albanian political movement and favored use of non-military means to reach the aim of international recognition of the independence of the province. Under his leadership, Kosovo Albanians established a so-called shadow state in which they formed parallel structures by organizing the Albanian education system, health system etc. financed by the Albanian emigrants abroad. Thus, they showed that they did not recognize the new conditions implemented by force by the central state. In the meantime, due to the high rate of unemployment, some of the young Albanians migrated to the Western countries.[22] The Albanian majority in Kosovo hoped the international community would be aware of the serious problems in Kosovo in time and take necessary measures before it was too late. It represented a kind of Gandhian non-violent search for achieving independence and international recognition.

The Dayton Peace Agreement that put an end to the war in Bosnia did not help to solve the problem of Kosovo at all despite the fact that Kosovo has always been the "key problem" for the fate of Yugoslavia.[23] It was clear that Kosovo was a possible conflict region, but in spite of this well-known fact, it was left aside during the Dayton negotiations. It was not at all a coincident that the violent attacks by the Albanian underground organization UÇK began just in the aftermath of the Dayton Agreement.[24] Some groups in Kosovo drew a lesson from Dayton assuming that nobody would be interested in the case of Kosovo Albanians unless violence was used. According to them, use of violent means was inevitable to attract the attention of the international actors to the problem. Rugova's peaceful search for a solution that continued for about a decade did not yield any fruitful success and has not been able to deter the Serbian side from pursuing nationalist policies in the province. In this context, UÇK fulfilled the role of being a "mental vacuum" at the time.[25]

There is not much information about the exact date of formation of the UÇK; however the data available indicate that it was formed in the early 1990s. It recruited people from various sources like pro-communist movements, clans and former militant groups. In the beginning, Rugova did not admit the existence of such a group and argued that this was an invention of Serbian intelligence. UÇK started its attacks against Serbian security forces and Albanian "collaborators" in 1996. However, the conflict gained a new dimension with the attempted assassination of the rector of Pristina University who was known as an anti-Albanian. Meanwhile, Serbian police attacked three UÇK militants for the first time. UÇK increased its military strength through the banking crisis that took place in Albania in 1997. The chaotic situation that emerged as a result of the fall of the pyramid system provided an appropriate environment for the UÇK militants to get a large amount of weaponry. The conflict between UÇK militants and Serbian security forces intensified in a short period of time.[26] Serbian forces did not distinguish between militants and civilians during their operations. From 1998 forward, as the situation became more violent, international actors began to pay more attention to the problem.

Yugoslavian Wars and the EU

From the beginning, the process of dissolution of Yugoslavia led to a heated discussion among EU member countries regarding the European policy to be applied. The Yugoslavian wars were the first test case of the newly evolving Common Foreign and Security Policy (CFSP). The crux of the issue was based on the dilemma over respecting the right of territorial integrity or self-determination. Although some member states were favoring the first principle of international law, some argued for the priority of the second.

In addition, the wars in Bosnia constituted the first important foreign policy debate of the post-Cold War era. The order and stability of Europe in the "new world order" was put at stake.[27] During the Gulf Crisis of 1990 and 1991, Europe was criticized for not being a leading power, but instead was following American leadership. The U.S., on the other hand, had strategic interests in the Middle East, like oil. That was the reason that proved the idea deeming that it was natural for America to lead itself in the campaign against Saddam Hussein.

But the wars in Yugoslavia were totally different. They were in Europe's backyard.[28] They came out as a result of the end of the Cold War. There was the very optimism that Europe itself could solve this problem. America waited for two and a half years for Europe to take the initiative to find an effective solution to the conflict in Bosnia. At the time, European leaders believed they could stop the fight by peaceful means. According to Jacques Poos, the president of the European Council at the time, "the chance to intervene as mediators in the Yugoslav crisis was the hour of Europe... If one problem could be solved by the Europeans, it was the Yugoslav problem. It is a European country and it is not up to anyone else."[29]

For many observers as well, it was a European problem to be solved by the institutions of Europe.[30] It was the first chance for the EC to prove that it could settle a problem in its own backyard.[31] U.S.'s President Clinton stated then that Bosnian conflict lied at the heart of Europe and threatened to destabilize the entire continent. He added: "...There is the very real risk that it could spread beyond Bosnia and involve Europe's new democracies as well as our NATO allies."[32]

When the war first started in Slovenia and Croatia, there were very important events on the agenda of the Western governments. The unification of two Germanys was still being discussed. The Gulf War had just finished. The negotiations for the Maastricht Treaty were still going on which would determine the future of the EC. The Soviet Union was showing the signals of dissolution and the West did not know how to react to such a development. When all these matters came to an end, more or less in early 1992, the EC, with the insistence of Germany, decided to recognize the independence of Slovenia and Croatia. Even if this was seen as a courageous move on the part of the EC, it did not prevent the conflict from spreading to Bosnia.

From the very beginning of the conflict, Western governments were unsure about what procedure to follow in the situation. The idea of CFSP could not be implemented. They had some general principles as how to provide stability in the Balkans, to avoid setting a model for other parts of the former communist bloc, to maintain good relations with Russia...[33] They preferred to ignore the real aim of Serbian nationalist leader Slobodan Milosevic to create "Greater Serbia." The war was seen—or preferred to be seen—as the natural result of "ancient ethnic hatreds" and every party to the conflict was treated equally responsible.[34]

When the war started in Bosnia in April 1992, the public witnessed a wicked brutality in the Balkan Peninsula. In August of the same year, Western media, for the first time, discovered a Serb concentration camp in northern Bosnia. Following this news, public opinion in Western countries pressured the governments "to do something." Subsequently, a joint EC-UN Conference was convened in London, in which the parties were "kindly" asked to settle their disputes in a peaceful way. The warring parties certainly did not do so.[35]

In this conference two negotiators, Cyrus Vance representing the UN and Lord Owen representing the EC, were appointed to pursue peacemaking activities. They prepared a peace plan known as Vance-Owen plan in October 1992. It envisioned the division of Bosnia-Herzegovina into 7 to 10 largely autonomous cantons under a loose central government.[36] In January 1993, a second draft of the plan was made public, which assigned even ethnic labels to the cantons as Serbs, Croats and Muslims. This plan was criticized since such an obvious endorsement of the ethnic separation would only benefit the offender. The Serbs, with the belief that they could push further, rejected this plan.[37]

Meanwhile, the Democratic Party under the leadership of Bill Clinton won the election in November 1992. The new U.S. government developed a new strategy to end the war in Bosnia called "lift and strike." "Lift" meant to exempt Bosnian government from the arms embargo to enable them to buy arms to balance the Serbian side. "Strike" meant if Serbs violated UN resolutions, threat or use of air power would be considered. Warren Christopher, the U.S. Secretary of State at the time, explained this plan to his European counterparts during his visit in May 1993. Britain and France, however, firmly opposed the plan. In fact, this was not a surprise, because from the very beginning of the war they opposed any kind of intervention that involved the military.[38]

The Serbian attack on the market place in Sarajevo in February 1994 that led to the death of 68 people resulted in considerable change in the stance of the U.S. From then on, it became more involved in the negotiations and threatened Serbs with the use of air strikes to prevent the occupation of Sarajevo.[39]

After the attack, NATO planes started bombing Serbian targets. At the same time, it gave an ultimatum to the Serbs demanding a NATO-defined heavy weapons exclusion zone around Sarajevo which Serbs unwillingly accepted. The failure of previous diplomatic efforts of Western governments and the success of U.S.-initiated air strike campaigns proved that only military intervention could make the Serbian leadership accept the proposals. Otherwise they would continue their vicious attacks against Croats and Muslims.

Those who argued that the West, mainly European countries, made a big mistake by not considering the use or threat of armed force supported their ideas with the following reasons: First, they claimed that the existence of moral argument for a military intervention is ethically justified when domestic turmoil threatens regional or international security and when massive human rights violations occur. This has been the case with Yugoslavia.[40] Second, European governments recognized the independence of Bosnia in April 1992. From that time onward, it was not a domestic conflict anymore, but became an aggression exerted by one state against the other. That is why stopping the aggression by any entity was justified. Third, a strategic argument was presented which assured that the re-establishment of a lasting peace in Bosnia was significant for both regional and global security. The conflict had the risk of spreading to other Balkan countries. The fourth reason is defined as deterring potential ethnic cleansers. By not intervening militarily, the European governments did in fact encourage would-be-Milosevics all around the world.[41] Noel Malcolm states that the Western world's reaction to the Bosnian war has been a victory of diplomacy over foreign policy. He makes the distinction between two terms as such:

> The sign of successful diplomacy is that one party can come out of a meeting feeling that their interests have been respected. The sign of successful foreign policy is that one party can come out of the meeting knowing that its own interests have been advanced. Diplomacy seeks to assuage, to conciliate, to reassure... Foreign policy, on the other hand, has concrete aims: to make things happen...[42]

In fact, throughout history, the world has rarely witnessed so much peacemaking efforts despite so many casualties.[43] The Yugoslav experience has shown that resolutions and cease-fires do not have meaning when they are not backed by any other mechanisms.[44] In brief, beginning from the issue of the early recognition of Slovenia and Croatia to the Bosnian War, the foreign policy performance of the Union was not considered effective, since it did not seem to contribute to the solution of the conflict. It satisfied neither internal nor external expectations. Despite all hope, it was understood that "the hour of Europe" did not come yet and was actually still in the making.

Kosovo Issue and the EU

It was important that as soon as the recent conflict between Kosovo Albanians and Serbs ignited, Western countries immediately tried to develop active policies in order to prevent it from progressing any further. This time, Europe did not want to repeat Bosnia's mistakes and, in that sense, did not wish to allow the emergence of a second Bosnia on the European continent.[45] In this regard, Germany acted together with France in the framework of the Contact Group[46] in order to convince Milosevic to end the violence. In late November 1997, then German Foreign Minister Kinkel and his French counterpart Védrine in their joint letter demanded from Milosevic a dialogue with the Albanian side for a special status of Kosovo without any preconditions and accept the meditation of a third-party. In return, they promised him the "carrot" of improving relations with regional and international organizations. They stated that if Milosevic accepted those conditions, diplomatic relations between Belgrade and the EU could be established, its membership to the Organization for Security and Cooperation in Europe (OSCE) could be supported, the most favored nation status with the EU could be granted, and its integration process into the EU could be started.[47]

As members of the Contact Group, German and French ministers visited Belgrade in March 1998 and held talks with Milosevic leadership. The policy was again a mixture of carrots and sticks claiming that if the Serbian side would accept their conditions, they would be able to obtain substantial political and economic advantages. If not, they had to face new sanctions imposed by the Contact Group countries that could make life harder for Yugoslavia. Both ministers wanted Belgrade to stop all military operations, to withdraw the special police force from Kosovo, and to start a credible dialogue with the Kosovo Albanians. It can be argued that, being aware of Serbia's financial difficulties, by offering some new chances, they tried to convince Serbia to peacefully return to the international community. In this way, both ministers tried to show "the light at the end of the tunnel" to the Serbian government.[48]

An important initiative of the Contact Group was to bring the parties together for negotiations in Rambouillet in France in February 1999. Both parties were presented with a set of norms and principles which were expected to be agreed upon. During the Rambouillet negotiations, both Serbian and Albanian sides were asked to implement a ceasefire as soon as possible, to find a peaceful way of solving the conflict and to allow for a three-year interim period, to respect minorities, and carry out free and fair elections under the guidance of the OSCE.[49] The main goal of the negotiations was to provide the end of violence immediately and then work for a durable solution in a peaceful manner. In the end, although the Albanian side had to sign the agreement because of the international pressure, the Serbian side refrained from giving its approval since Serbian authorities believed the agreement could, in the long run, lead to an independent Kosovo.

Since all diplomatic initiatives failed to bring peace, NATO member countries decided to intervene militarily under the leadership of the U.S. When NATO launched its air strikes on March 24, 1999, the event had a historical importance for the European Union. Since the NATO intervention could not get the approval of the UN Security Council because of the Russian objection, the operation led to a sensitive discussion over whether an international intervention just on the basis of humanitarian concerns without the approval of the Security Council could be launched or not. Despite the continuing debates, nine out of 15 member countries participated in the NATO intervention called Operation Allied Force, namely the United Kingdom, France, Germany, Belgium, Netherlands, Spain, Portugal, Denmark, and Italy.

In addition, the operation had a historical importance for Germany since it was its first time taking part in a military campaign since the end of the Second World War. What is more, this operation was a military mission of the international community without any reservation and, from the beginning, it did not have the UN mandate. During the Bosnian War, taking part in monitoring sanctions and the no-fly zone, or deploying AWACS, carried important problems in Germany's internal politics. However, in the Kosovo intervention, such a controversy did not occur. on the first day, four German Tornados were involved in the strikes. Throughout the whole campaign, which lasted about two and a half months, 15 German combat aircrafts and hundreds of support troops were deployed in the NATO intervention.

Following the NATO intervention, Germany seized leadership of the European policy of the region. The German government held the upper hand in diplomatic initiatives by the proclamation of the Fischer Plan in April 1999, which stipulated the following six points: 1) ending all Serbian military actions in Kosovo, 2) withdrawing all troops from the region, 3) returning all refugees to their homelands, 4) defining a political solution based on the Rambouillet agreement, 5) despatching soldiers by the international community, and 6) giving Russia and the UN a greater role in order to reach a solution.[50]

The Fischer Plan was adopted by the G-8 Summit the following month. With the inclusion of Russia and the UN in the same framework, it represented an important initiative of Germany that, in fact, tried to find a balance between Russia and America. The Fischer Plan included both civilian and military instruments, the former supported by Moscow, the latter by Washington. The overall plan was welcomed by both the Russian and American governments.[51] While the NATO intervention continued, German decision-makerss began emphasizing the need to launch a comprehensive plan for the Balkan region that would include economic, political and security elements. As a result of this German influence, it has been acknowledged that only military means are not sufficient at all in generating permanent solutions to the problems of the region. A general plan was needed, which would comprise all the countries of the region and aim to cooperate in different realms. It should also give the countries of the region the opportunity to become part of the European integration if they fulfill certain conditions. In April 1999, Foreign Minister Fischer explained that they aimed to establish the "Stability Pact for the South Balkans."[52] The Pact was supposed to be based on the CSCE Act signed in Helsinki, and was to be composed of "security architecture" for all the countries and minorities of the region. Russia should also be part of the plan. According to this initiative, not only Kosovo, but also Bosnia, Macedonia, and Albania should be included in the plan. Second, Europe should contribute to the economic development of the region. The region must be economically supported by the EU for at least two decades. The third part of the plan was about the establishment of democratic and civil society institutions. Meanwhile, Schröder, then German Chancellor, also pointed out the need for the establishment of some sort of a Marshall plan for the region.[53] For Schröder, such a plan was necessary for long-term stabilization and the improvement of security, democratization and economic improvement. He emphasized that this was the duty of Europe and it could not escape it. The idea of a stability pact was also the product of the belief that there could not be long-term stability, if reaction to events is shown only after they occurred. Instead, a strategy should be developed to find the reasons for the conflict and try to eliminate them to prevent further conflicts from erupting.

As soon as the war ended in Kosovo in June 1999, a summit was organized in Cologne to implement the Stability Pact for Southeastern Europe with the participation of the regional countries (Albania, Bosnia-Hercegovina, Bulgaria, Croatia, Macedonia, Moldova, Romania, Serbia, and Montenegro), EU member states, the U.S., Russia, Turkey, Canada, Japan, Norway, Switzerland, and the international organizations UN, OSCE, IMF, European Bank for Reconstruction and Development, European Investment Bank, Council of Europe Development Bank, and some regional initiatives like BSEC and the Central European Initiative.[54] The pact was composed of three working tables: democratization and human rights; economic reconstruction, cooperation and development; and security issues. The European Commission and the World Bank were assigned the job of coordinating economic aid for the region. The Pact represented an important European initiative for the region.

European Policy Toward Western Balkans After the End of the Kosovo Operation

When a violent conflict on the European continent re-emerged as a result of the disagreement between Serbs and Kosovo Albanians, it became clear that post-Dayton policies of the West toward the region were not sufficient. We must also underline the fact that, despite all the international assistance and guidance, the case of Bosnia-Hercegovina did not give much hope for the future. This was mainly because the different ethnic groups in the region found it very difficult to implement the civilian items of the Dayton Peace Agreement. Although the question of Bosnia was not yet near any solution, the West then had to confront the Kosovo issue. As argued earlier, drawing lessons from the Bosnian War, the international community spent less time on diplomatic initiatives during the Kosovo conflict and, as soon as it was understood that the diplomacy did not bear fruit, military action was launched.

Meanwhile, the EU understood that different measures were needed for the region to gain a durable stability, security and inter-ethnic peace. The Kosovo conflict made the EU see more clearly that the security of the Balkans had a direct impact on EU member countries. The flow of thousands of refugees to EU countries and the increase in organized crime have been examples of these cases that influence European security in a rather direct way. In addition, each unsolved conflict was harming the international prestige and image of the Union; in other words, harming its soft power. Similarly, it was also obstructing the newly evolving Common Foreign and Security Policy.

The new measures taken by the Union to "debalkanize the Balkans,"[55] and similarly to prevent "the balkanization of Europe,"[56] had internal and external dimensions. With regard to the internal dimension, the EU tried to adapt its foreign and security policy to Balkan challenges. The Amsterdam Treaty was an example of how the EU acted to better its political integration. The Treaty put forward a new mechanism called constructive abstention that would allow member countries to abstain from voting instead of using their vetoes. Moreover, the use of qualified majority voting was extended, and the frequency of the cases where the unanimous voting was required was lessened. It also established some new mechanisms, like Policy Planning and Early Warning Unit, which followed the developments in the region and tried to uncover possible flashpoints. Another new feature of the Treaty was the establishment of the High Representative for the CFSP, the first of whom was Javier Solana. With these attempts, it was obvious the EU was trying to draw lessons from its failures and to improve its mechanisms and tools, and it was not discouraged by the heavy criticisms of other actors.

The Balkan wars especially sped up the process of achieving cooperation in matters of security. Experiencing that the EU could not play an active role for the solution of a conflict on its own continent, member states decided to think over the issue of their political integration. After the historical decisions taken by Britain and France in St. Malo concerning the relationship between NATO and the EU, the Helsinki Summit officially started European Security and Defence Policy (ESDP). At the Summit, a headline goal was that by the year 2003, the EU should develop a military force consisting of 60,000 soldiers that could be deployed within 60 days and should remain on the deployed site for one year. This force was supposed to carry out the Petersburg tasks which consisted of humanitarian and rescue tasks, peacekeeping and crisis management tasks, including peacemaking efforts.

After the establishment of the ESDP, the Union carried out military missions in Macedonia, the Democratic Republic of Congo and Georgia. Currently, it implements operations in Bosnia-Herzegovina, Palestine and Iraq. It has police missions in Macedonia and the Republic of Congo.[57] Some of the previous NATO operations in the Balkans are now taken over by the EU.[58] Hence, the EU started to replace the role of the NATO and the U.S. in this region. Although these EU missions cannot be considered as operations of great scale, they are, nevertheless, still important as they take place for the first time in the history of the Community.

So far, we have tried to analyze how the EU attempted to improve its internal dimension in order to cope with the Balkan challenges in a better way. In addition, we must also mention the efforts of the EU in developing its external policy toward the region. In the aftermath of the Kosovo conflict, two new mechanisms were developed: regionalism and conditionality.[59] The first one refers to the fact that the Union started developing a regional approach with the awareness that all the regional problems were connected to each other. The second one addresses the impact of the accession process on the candidate states, hence, argues for the inclusion of Balkan countries to the enlargement wave as soon as they meet necessary criteria. The Stability Pact for Southeastern Europe was an important sign that the Union would like to deal with the regional problems together. In addition, in June 2000, the Feira European Council stated that the countries of the Western Balkans had the potential to become candidate countries:

> The European Council confirms that its objective remains the fullest possible integration of the countries of the region into the political and economic mainstream of Europe through the Stabilization and Association process, political dialogue, liberalisation of trade and cooperation in Justice and Home Affairs. All the countries concerned are potential candidates for EU membership. The Union will support the Stabilization and Association process through technical and economic assistance. The Commission has already presented proposals to the Council to streamline and accelerate the procedures for disbursement of assistance and the early extension of asymmetrical industrial and agricultural trade benefits to the Balkan States.[60]

Thessaloniki Summit of 2003 is considered as a milestone in the EU's relations with the Western Balkan countries. It offered the regional states the perspective of membership:

The EU reiterates its unequivocal support to the European perspective of the Western Balkan countries. The future of the Balkans is within the European Union. The ongoing enlargement and the signing of the Treaty of Athens in April 2003 inspire and encourage the countries of the Western Balkans to follow the same successful path. Preparation for integration into European structures and ultimate membership into the European Union, through adoption of European standards, is now the big challenge ahead. The Croatian application for EU membership is currently under examination by the Commission. The speed of movement ahead lies in the hands of the countries of the region. The countries of the region fully share the objectives of economic and political union and look forward to joining a EU that is stronger in the pursuit of its essential objectives and more present in the world.[61]

Ever since the NATO intervention, the EU has tried to follow the developments regarding the Kosovo issue closely. In addition, it does not only follow, but also tries to effect the solution to the problem. In this regard, EU's contribution to the United Nations Mission in Kosovo (UNMIK) should be mentioned. The Union plays an important role in the Pillar IV of the UNMIK in which it tries to contribute to the economic plight of Kosovo.[62]

Although the Union seemed to oppose the idea of independence of Kosovo before the violent events of 1998 and 1999 took place,[63] in the aftermath of the NATO intervention, it appeared that the Union started accepting the idea that nothing in the status of Kosovo would be the same as it had been before. Therefore, although it officially accepted the "standards before the status" approach of the UNMIK, it, de facto, started to treat Kosovo differently from Yugoslavia. In December 2000, for example, the Union launched Autonomous Trade Measures for Kosovo separate from the Yugoslavian state. In addition, the EU provided Kosovo with a different customs status from Belgrade and its independence for trade negotiations was also taken for granted.[64] These policies can be interpreted as a shift from the "standards before status" approach to the "standards and status approach."[65]

The European perspective of Kosovo was underlined in a Communication from the Commission titled "A European Future for Kosovo," which was published in 2005. In this document, the EU emphasized its economic contribution for the development of Kosovo and it also made clear that while its neighbors were making progress toward the accession, it was important that Kosovo did not remain behind.[66]

In January 2006, the Union also adopted a European Partnership Document for Serbia and Montenegro, including Kosovo. In fact, the document was a part of the stabilization and association process and tried to bring the regional countries closer to the Union. The Provisional Institutions of Self Government in Kosovo prepared an action plan in order to realize the conditions stated in the European Partnership Document. Based upon this action plan, the EU and Kosovo authorities began meeting to discuss further developments. An annual progress report for Kosovo was prepared by the Union in 2005.[67]

The economic contributions of the Union to Kosovo have been immense. So far, the EU contributed the biggest amount for the Kosovo economy by supplying 1.8 billion euros. Most of the aid was provided in the framework of Community Assistance for Reconstruction, Development and Stabilization (CARDS).[68] It has not only been economic support, as the EU has provided most of the international help to Kosovo. The member countries also provided aid for most of the Kosovo Force (KFOR) soldiers.[69]

Status Negotiations and the EU

Reemergence of inter-ethnic violence in Kosovo in 2004 was considered an important sign of what would happen in the region if the stalemate conditions continued. The ambiguity regarding the status of Kosovo did not contribute to the consolidation of a stable Balkans. In contrast, the status vacuum seemed to strengthen the hand of the hardliners. But it was also remembered that Kosovo was seen as a time bomb[70] that could explode at any time and could start a regional fire. Therefore, in order to end the ambiguity over the status issue, a new process was started for Kosovo under the leaderhip of the United Nations.

Under the auspices of the UN Special Envoy for Status Talks, Martti Ahtisaari, Serbian and Kosovo Albanian sides started to come together in February 2006. The negotiations, in which Contact Group members also participated, lasted until March 2007 without yielding any positive result. Then, thanks to a German proposal, a new process was started in August 2007, with the mediation of the troika U.S., Russia and the EU.[71] This process continued for about four months; however, the result was not different from the previous initiative: failure.

Why did the international mediation attempts, including the EU member countries or the EU itself, always result in unambiguous failure? The reason has mainly been the radically and stubbornly opposing views of the Serbians and Kosovo Albanians. Although the Serbian side accepted to give wide autonomy to Kosovo, it has certainly been against any official independence of Kosovo. This position of Belgrade might be explained by various factors: First of all, the status of Kosovo in the 1974 Constitution of Yugoslavia was different from that of Bosnia-Hercegovina, Montenegro, the Republic of Macedonia, etc. Therefore, for Serbia, it might be much more difficult to accept Kosovan independence than Montenegro. The historical importance of the region for the Serbian people, where their religous roots lie in some historical Serbian churches, can also be taken as a second consideration.

When we look at the position of the EU during the negotiations, we see that it faced its historical problem for the common foreign policy: speaking with one voice. The Union tried to formulate "one" foreign policy toward the Kosovo issue. But it seemed there were different opinions among member countries. Although a majority of the member states saw independent Kosovo as a possibility, some countries like Greece, Greek Cyprus, Slovakia, Romania, and Spain, did not favor an independent Kosovo. But this time, the differences were not as sharp as they were during the independence of Slovenia and Croatia. Even the countries not favoring an independent Kosovo appeared not to be harboring any intention to block the CFSP process. The mechanisms of constructive abstention and enhanced cooperation can be used in order to protect both the CFSP and the individual autonomies of these states.[72]

Kosovo declared its independence on February 17, 2008. Although the majority of EU countries extended diplomatic recognition, the aforementioned member countries did not recognize it, mostly because of their internal problems. Kosovo declared its independence in accordance with the Ahtisaari Plan. Therefore, some call it not a declaration of independence but a "declaration of dependence."[73] The EU is going to play a major role by initiating International Civilian Representative (ICR) and ESDP missions. Hence, the EU will be the institution that supervises the conditional independence of Kosovo in the transition period. ICR shall be responsible for supervising the implementation of the possible Kosovo settlement and will have the right to abolish decisions and laws as well as dismiss public officials.[74] In addition, the ESDP Mission to Kosovo will be the biggest EU mission so far[75] and have responsibilities in the areas of "the rule of law, particularly in the fields of judiciary, policing, border controlling, customs, and correctional services."[76]

In addition, the independence of Kosovo seems to be another important item in the transatlantic relationship. While the U.S. has been the most vocal supporter of an independent Kosovo, the Union tries to act more carefully. There were some reports that the U.S. exerted pressure on the European countries to recognize Kosovo as soon as it declared independence.[77] The recognition reportedly led to the resignation of a Slovenian diplomat.[78]

EU's Role: On the Way to be a More Powerful Regional Power?

The case of Kosovo played an important role in the evolution of the European foreign and security policy. It was after the Kosovo conflict in 1998-1999 that the EU changed the general framework of its policies toward the Western Balkans. The outbreak of violence on the territory of Kosovo showed that without a comprehensive European approach, no stability could be achieved in the region.

This article tried to analyze the EU policies toward the Kosovo issue from a historical perspective. The main findings can be summarized as follows: The Union still suffers from the dilemma of territorial integrity versus self-determination. This dilemma has not been substantially solved since the beginning of the 1990s. However, one should note the development stemming from the discussion of the aforementioned dilemma seemed not to obstruct the formulation of a common foreign policy. The countries objecting Kosovo independence did not declare their reactions openly, probably in an effort not to harm the CFSP.

From the Kosovo example, we can say that the EU is on the way to becoming a more powerful regional actor. In the Kosovo case, almost all the important EU officials in foreign policy emphasize that it is the European matter, not anyone else's. It is for sure that the EU performance for the solution of the Kosovo conflict plays a role in the fate of the CFSP and ESDP. Kosovo's importance as a soft power for the EU could be compared only to Afghanistan operation's value for the fate of NATO.

Kosovo Albanian authorities try to assure the U.S. and EU officials that they will coordinate their activities with them and be careful not to act unilaterally on such a sensitive matter. Meanwhile, the election of Boris Tadic for the second term as Serbian President and the victory of his party in general elections can be seen as a boost for the Union's policies, since the incumbent president was seen as a pro-EU candidate.

Conclusion

The challenges that the EU faced in its Kosovo policy can be summarized as follows: First, the member states still diverge over the issue of whether to respect the right of territorial integrity or self-determination. Second, the EU does not want to repeat violent conflicts in its own backyard. Therefore, one of its priorities is the prevention of violence at any cost. The third challenge awaiting the EU is not to allow the resurrection of any nationalism, be it Albanian or Serbian. The EU's offer of an interim agreement to facilitate trade relations and ease the travel restrictions to Serbia just before the presidential elections can be seen as a proof of this. The fourth challenge is to prevent any unilateral movement from Serbian or Kosovar parts. In this context, the Union wants to establish itself as the main regional player with influence over regional countries. The fifth challenge is related to the global structuring of power, which means that the Union does not want any major disagreement to break out among global powers just because of the Kosovo issue.

In brief, the Union aims to continue its role as the main regional power in the case of Kosovo. To give the region a European perspective, the EU initiated new policies toward the Western Balkans in the aftermath of the NATO operation to Kosovo in 1999. Thanks to the Kosovo conflict, the member countries perceived that, unless a comprehensive plan for the region was developed, a possibility of conflict would always exist. In this paper, considering the issue of Kosovo, we claim that the EU is aiming to increase its regional role, and consequently, its power over the region. Therefore, as was the case in the 1990s, the Western Balkans, in general, and Kosovo, in particular, are the main test cases for the CFSP and ESDP.

---

* This article was finished in June 2008.
[1] Between Serbs and Albanians, there is a disagreement even over the name of Kosovo. Although Serbs prefer to name the region as Kosovo, in Albanian, it is named as Kosova. In this article, the name Kosovo is preferred just because it has become a conventional usage in most of the English literature.
[2] For a discussion of the Greater Albania issue please see Birgül Demirtaş Coşkun, "Arnavutluk'un Dış Politikası ve Balkanlar'da Arnavut Sorunu," in *Balkan Diplomasisi* ed. Ömer E. Lütem and Birgül Demirtaş-Coşkun (Ankara: ASAM, 2001) p. ??
[3] The Union is defined as "a global player" in the European Security Strategy, A Secure Europe in a Better World, Brussels, 12 December 2003.
[4] The conceptual framework used in this study is based on the following publication of the author: "EU's New Position in the International Order: From Regional to Global Power?" *Perceptions* XI, no. 1, (2006): pp. 49-75.
[5] In this study the concepts of "world power," "global power" and "superpower" are used interchangeably.
[6] George Modelski, "The Long Cycle of Global Politics and the Nation-State," *Comparative Studies in Society and History* 20, (1978): p. 216. For the Turkish translation of the article see George Modelski, "Küresel Politikanın Uzun Döngüsü ve Ulus Devlet," *Uluslararası İlişkiler* 2, no.7, (2005): pp. 3-30.
[7] Modelski, "The Long Cycle of Global Politics and the Nation-State," p. 235.
[8] Ibid., p. 230.
[9] Christopher Hill, "Superstate or Superpower? The future of the European Union in world politics," July 2002, http://www.lse.ac.uk/Depts/intrel/pdfs/EFPU-superpowerorsuperstate.pdf, p. 6-7.
[10] Hanns W. Maull, "Germany and Japan: The New Civilian Powers," *Foreign Affairs* 69, no.5, (1990): pp. 92-93. In his study, Maull applies the civilian power category to Germany and Japan.

[11] Lily Gardner Feldman, "The EC in the International Arena: A New Activism?" in *Europe and the United States, Competition and Cooperation in the 1990s*, ed. Glennon J. Harrison (New York: M. E. Sharpe, 1994), p. 146.
[12] Panos Tsakaloyannis, "The EC: from civilian power to military integration," in *The European Community and the Challenge of the Future*, ed. Juliet Lodge (London: Pinter Publishers, 1989), p. 243.
[13] Johan Galtung, *The European Community: A Superpower in the Making*, Oslo: International Peace Reserach Institute, 1973 quoted in Hill, "Superstate or Superpower? The future of the European Union in world politics," p. 5-6.
[14] Johan Galtung, *Europe in the Making* (New York, Crane Russak, 1989), p. 22.
[15] Tsakaloyannis, "The EC: from civilian power to military integration," pp. 241-255; Rockwell A. Schnabel and Francis X. Rocca, *The Next Superpower? The Rise of Europe and Its Challenge to the United States* (Lanham: Rowman&Littlefield Publishers, 2005).
[16] For example, see Richard G. Whitman, *From Civilian Power to Superpower? The International Identity of the European Union* (Hampshire: Palgrave, 1998), p. 108.
[17] Quoted in Hill, "Superstate or Superpower? The future of the European Union in world politics," p. 7.
[18] For an analytical comparison of the phrases "civilian power" and "normative power" please see Thomas Diez, "Constructing the Self and Changing Others: Reconsidering 'Normative Power Europe'," *Millennium* 33, no. 3, (2005): pp. 613-618.
[19] In writing this part the author benefitted from the relevant section in her Ph.D. dissertation "A Comparative Study of Turkish and German Foreign Policies toward the Conflicts in Yugoslavia: A Search for Reconstruction of State Identities?," Free University Berlin, 2005.
[20] Ramet, "War in the Balkans," pp. 83-84.
[21] Holm Sundhaussen, "Kosovo: Eine Konfliktgeschichte," in *Der Kosovo-Konflikt, Ursachen-Akteure-Verlauf*, ed. Konrad Clewing and Jens Reuter (München: Bayerische Landeszentrale für politische Bildungsarbeit, 2000), p. 83.
[22] Peter Schubert, "Kosovo und die albanische Frage," *WeltTrends*, no. 20 (Fall 1998): p. 121.
[23] Roland Schönfeld, "Die Rolle der EU beim Abschluss des Dayton-Vertrags und bei den Rambouillet-Verhandlungen," in *Frieden und Sicherheit in (Südost-) Europa: EU-Beitritt, Stabilitätspakt und europäische Sicherheits- und Verteidigungspolitik*, ed. Heinz-Jürgen Axt and Christoph Rohloff (München: Südosteuropa Gesellschaft, 2001), p. 127.
[24] Rafael Biermann, *Die Kosovo-Politik der internationalen Gemeinschaft vor Kriegsausbruch, Dramaturgie und Ursachen einer gescheiterten Konflikt-prävention*, Habilitation Thesis, Department of Political Science, Rheinische Friedrich-Wilhelms-Universität Bonn, 3 January 2004, p. 361.
[25] Ibid., p. 354.
[26] Concerning formation and development of the UÇK see Biermann, *Die Kosovo-Politik*, pp. 354-363.
[27] Robert W. Tucker and David C. Hendrickson, "America and Bosnia," *The National Interest*, no. 33, (1993): pp. 14-15.
[28] Mark Almond, *Europe's Backyard War: The War in the Balkans*, (London: Heinemann, 1994), p. 31.
[29] Quoted in Ibid., pp. 31-32.

30 Gregory L. Schulte, "Former Yugoslavia and the New NATO," *Survival* 39, no. 1 (1997), p. 19.
31 Alex Macleod, "French Policy Toward the War in the Former Yugoslavia: A Bid for International Relationship," *International Journal* 52, no. 2, (1997): p. 244.
32 Carpenter and Perlmutter, op cit, p. 53.
33 Noel Malcolm, "Bosnia and the West: A Study in Failure," *The National Interest* no. 39, (1995): p. 3.
34 Ibid., p. 4.
35 Ibid., p. 3
36 Nimet Beriker Atiyas, "Mediating Regional Conflicts and Negotiating Flexibility: Peace Efforts in Bosnia-Herzegovina," *ANNALS, AAPSS*, no. 542, (1995): pp. 192-193.
37 Malcolm, op cit, p. 8.
38 Dilek Eryılmaz, "*The U.S. and the Bosnian War: An Analytical Survey on the Formulation of U.S. Policy from the Yugoslav Dissolution to the Dayton Accords, 1991-1995,*" Unpublished Master's Thesis, Bilkent University, March 1997, pp. 40-45.
39 Ibid., pp. 58-59.
40 Stanley Hoffmann, "The Politics and Ethics of Military Intervention," *Survival* 37, no. 4, (1995-1996): p. 29.
41 Jane M.O. Sharp, "Intervention in Bosnia: The Case For," *The World Today* 49, no. 2, (1993): pp. 29-30.
42 Malcolm, op cit, p. 3.
43 Almond, op cit, p. 233.
44 Sharp, op cit, p. 31.
45 Marie-Janine Calic, "Die Jugoslawienpolitik des Westens seit Dayton," *Aus Politik und Zeitgeschichte*, B 34/99, (20 August 1999): p. 26.
46 The Contact Group was established in 1994 in order to give an end to the Bosnian War. It originally consisted of the following countries: United States, Russia, United Kingdom, Germany and France. Italy joined the Contact Group in 1996.
47 "Kinkel mahnt Belgrad wegen Kosovo-Politik," *Frankfurter Allgemeine Zeitung*, 29 December 1997.
48 "Kinkel und Védrine drohen Serbien mit neuen Sanktionen," *Süddeutsche Zeitung*, 19 March 1998. Concerning Kinkel and Védrine's visit to Belgrade also see "Einige verlieren die Nerven," Interview with Klaus Kinkel, *Der Spiegel*, no. 12, 16 March 1998, p. 180.
49 Calic, "Die Jugoslawienpolitik des Westens seit Dayton," p. 27.
50 Jeffrey Lantis, "The moral imperative of force: The evolution of German strategic culture in Kosovo," *Comparative Strategy* 21, no. 1 (2002): pp. 34-35.
51 William Drozdiak, "Russia and the G-7 draft Kosovo plan," *International Herald Tribune*, 7 May 1999; "Verdienstvolles Drängen im Lärm der Bomben," *Süddeutsche Zeitung*, 7 May 1999.
52 "Bundesregierung setzt verstärkt auf Diplomatie," *Süddeutsche Zeitung*, 7 April 1999.
53 "Erklärung der Bundesregierung zur aktuellen Lage im Kosovo," *Bulletin*, no. 16, 16 April 1999, p. 171.
54 Stability Pact for Southeastern Europe, Cologne, 10 June 1999, http://www.stabilitypact.org (Accessed 20 July 2004).

[55] Johannes Varwick, "Die EU nach dem Kosovo-Krieg: Ein überforderter Stabilitätsanker?" http://www.dgap.org/midcom-serveattachmentguid-b046b086cb 0211da98df1b279a0ce6cbe6cb/kosovarw.pdf, p. 1.
[56] Ibid., p. 2.
[57] The European Union web site http://ue.eu.int/showPage.asp?lang=en&id=268&mode=g&name
[58] Schnabel and Rocca, *The Next Superpower?* p. 63.
[59] Daniela Heimerl and Wim Van Meurs, "The Balkans between Paris and Berlin," *Southeast European and Black Sea Studies* 4, no. 3, (2004): p. 357.
[60] Santa Maria da Feira European Council 19 and 20 June 2000, Conclusions of the Presidency, http://www.europarl.europa.eu/summits/fei1_en.htm#V
[61] EU-Western Balkans Summit Declaration, Thessaloniki, 21 June 2003, http://ec.europa.eu/enlargement/enlargement_process/accession_process/how_does_a_country_join_the_eu/sap/thessaloniki_summit_en.htm
[62] http://www.euinkosovo.org/
[63] "Pressekonferenz des EU-Ratsvorsitzenden und britischen Außenministers," Robin Cook, nach einem informellen EU-Außenministertreffen am 13. März 1998 in Edinburgh über die Erörterung des ehemaligen Jugoslawiens," http://www.internationalepolitik.de/archiv/jahrgang1998/april98/pressekonferenz-des-eu-ratsvorsitzenden-und-britischen-aussenministers--robin-cook--nach-einem-informellen-eu-aussenministertreffen-am-13--marz-1998-in-edinburgh-uber-die-erorterung-des-ehemaligen-jugoslawiens.html
[64] Makro Klasnja, "The EU and Kosovo. Time to Rethink the Enlargement and Integration Policy," *Politics of Post-Communism*, Vol. 54, No. 4, July-August 2007, p. 17.
[65] Ibid., p. 22.
[66] Communication form the Commission, A European Future for Kosovo, Brussels, 20.4.2005.
[67] "Kosovo-EU Relations," http://ec.europa.eu/enlargement/serbia/kosovo/eu_kosovo_relations_en.htm
[68] Ibid.
[69] "Breaking the Kosovo Stalemate: Europe's Responsibility," International Crisis Group, Europe Report No: 185, 21 August 2007.
[70] Aristotle Tziampiris, "Kosovo's Future Sovereignty: A Role for the European Union," *Southeast European and Black Sea Studies* 5, no. 2, (2005): pp. 285-286.
[71] Tamás Szemlér et al., "The EU Presence in a Post-Status Kosovo Challenges and Opportunities," *Südosteuropa* 55, no. 2-3, (2007): p. 145.
[72] Ibid.
[73] Timothy Garton Ash, "This dependent independence is the least worst solution for Kosovo," *Guardian*, February 21, 2008.
[74] United Nations Security Council, Comprehensive Proposal for the Kosovo Status Settlement.
[75] Dušan Reljić, "Kosovo: Die EU am Zug," *SWP-Aktuell*, no. 38, (2007), p. 1.
[76] United Nations Security Council, Comprehensive Proposal for the Kosovo Status Settlement.
[77] Dan Bilefsky, "U.S. and Germany Plan to Recognize Kosovo," *The New York Times*, January 11, 2008.

[78] "Slovenian Diplomat Resigns in Furor over U.S. Links," RFE/RL Newsline 12, no. 20, Part II, 30 January 2008.

PART II
MIDDLE EAST

Chapter 4
Greater Middle East and North Africa Project and EU Policy

İdris Bal

After the dissolution of the USSR, the U.S. became the single super power of the post Cold War era. Nowadays, in order to maintain and strengthen her position, the U.S. is trying to safeguard global as well as regional balances. Furthermore, the U.S. attempts to manipulate the developments and shape a new world to strengthen her position.[1] In this regard, for the U.S., the Middle East is important for security as well as for economic reasons. Terrorism and radical movements are growing in the region and the U.S. regards these as important threats for her interests. On the other hand, the region is also extremely rich in hydrocarbon resources. The importance of the region encourages the U.S. to manipulate developments in the region and, if possible, shape the region. In this regard, successful U.S. administrations have placed the Greater Middle East Project in the forefront. The project has been discussed since the war broke out in Iraq in 2003 by different circles. Therefore, the main aim of this chapter is to focus on the Greater Middle East and North African Projects and the EU's reactions and policies regarding these projects and the Middle East. Within this context, first, the Greater Middle East and North African projects will be outlined. Then, the EU's related reactions and policies will be discussed.

What is the Greater Middle East Project?

There is no common definition of the Greater Middle East region. However, the term is usually used to refer to the Arab world, Israel, Turkey, Iran, Central Asia, and the Caucasus. Afghanistan and Pakistan are also included in the region by different circles as well. There are many different views on this term. First, the term was changed to the Greater Middle East and North African Project, and with this change, the North African region was also included as a target region. Then, the "New Middle East" term was used instead of the "Greater Middle East" by U.S. Secretary of State Condoleezza Rice, in June 2006, in Tel Aviv. However, there is not much difference in these terms. Secretary Rice said during a press conference that "What we are seeing here, in a sense, is the growing—the 'birth pangs'—of a

'New Middle East' and whatever we do we have to be certain that we're pushing forward to the New Middle East, not going back to the old one."[2]

The project was debated starting from early 1990s. Following the invasion of Iraq (2003), the U.S. has re-opened the project for discussion. On November 6, 2003, George W. Bush, Jr. declared that "...the U.S. has adopted a new policy, a forward strategy of freedom, in the Middle East."[3] Original documentation of the U.S. State Department was leaked in February 2004 to the Arab newspaper, al-Hayat. According to the documentation, the initiative was to cover 22 Arab nations plus Turkey, Israel, Pakistan, and Afghanistan. The document was actually modified and promulgated at the Sea Island, Georgia meeting of the G-8 in June 2004. "The GMEI was the third initiative to be launched by the U.S. since 9/11. In December 2002, a U.S. Middle East Partnership Initiative was launched and in February 2003, the U.S.-Middle East Free Trade Area."[4]

As Richard G. Lugar did, it is usually argued that:

> Today, we, in the West, face a major challenge. It is the threat of weapons of mass destruction, terrorism, failed states and instability that arises in major part from extremist organizations in the Greater Middle East. The terrorist ideology generated there has global reach. The region is the prime source of what I believe is the greatest single threat to modern civilization in the 21st century—that is, the nexus between terrorism and weapons of mass destruction. We must promote security and stability in this vast but troubled region, where demographics, religious extremism, autocratic governments, isolation, stagnant economic systems, and war have often overwhelmed the talents of its people and the wealth of its natural resources.[5]

However, there are of course other opinions about the project. It is usually believed that the project has different purposes that can be categorized as visible and invisible. For instance; Girdner argued that "the Greater Middle East Initiative for "democratization" is not about increasing freedom and democracy for the people in the region, but also about increasing freedom for Western capital and ensuring continued U.S. political control of the region."[6] Similarly, according to Achar, what the U.S. is desiring with the Greater Middle East Project is to strengthen her influence on Middle East oil resources and markets, and her tendency is to extend her network of military bases and facilities, all in the name of democratization.[7]

The Greater Middle East region poses a unique challenge and opportunity for the international community. The UNDP's Arab Human Development Reports summarize this situation as follows: the Middle East and Mediterranean regions suffer from three deficits: a deficit in freedom of political and civil liberties; a knowledge deficit in terms of education and access to information; and a gender deficit, as Arab women are clearly at a disadvantage in their societies."[8] The three "deficits" identified by the Arab authors of the 2002 and 2003 United Nations Arab Human Development Reports (AHDR) as mentioned above, freedom, knowledge, and women's empowerment, have contributed to conditions that threaten the national interests of all G-8 members. It is emphasized in the report that so long as the region's pool of politically and economically disenfranchised individuals grows, we will witness an increase in extremism, terrorism, international crime, and illegal migration. The statistics describing the current situation in the Greater Middle East are daunting.[9] For instance, about 65 million adult Arabs are illiterate; two thirds of those are women. It is important to note that illiteracy rates are much higher than in much poorer countries of the world.[10]

The Greater Middle East Project aims to build new economic, social and political structures that require a reconstructing process. This project is definitely dependent on the democratization program. Democratization is seen as remedy of anti-democratic political structures. It can also be regarded as a confession of "western" sins of the past that involved supporting dictatorships in the region. In this frame, political infrastructure is only now being built to run free elections and to function as a democratic system. Gaining public support is another important aim of this project. Therefore, during this process, non-governmental organizations, civil public leaders, media, and religious clerics are very crucial to opening new, healthy communication channels. So far, due to the widespread anti-Americanism and anti-westernization in the region, this has not been fully achieved.

Another aspect of the project underlines women rights. Women are encouraged to participate more in political and public life. An information society with institutional dimensions is desired. In this vein, it is a goal to reduce the ratio of illiterates by half until 2010 within this geography where approximately 800 million people live. In connection with this, there is a plan to train 100 thousand women teachers until 2008, grant schoolbooks, raise the quality of living by reforms and services like installing internet networks, and translating Western classics into the Arabic language.[11]

For the purpose of providing democratization and an economic development, there is a plan to establish commercial collaboration, both among the states of the region and international markets, and to implement a fund for the region similar to that Marshall Aid applied to post–World War II European countries. Also, a regional development bank is planned to be established to support both technological developments and a free trade zone to lay foundations for a liberal economic system.[12]

The Middle East is important for world politics, as well as for the U.S., for several reasons. Basically, the geo-strategic position of the region, its rich hydrocarbon reserves, scarcity of water, existence of believers of three major religions and several religious sects in the region, deficiency of democracy, and, as a reaction to this, rising radicalism, poverty and ignorance, existence of small, divided artificial nations, the Arab-Israeli problem, including: connections with international terrorism, drug trafficking, and failure to create a successful nationhood, are outstanding characteristics of the region and the same factors that make the region vital for global powers.[13] There are many comments regarding the importance of the Middle East, while the instability within the region has became a common knowledge all over the world. For instance, Hatipoğlu pointed out that;

> The Greater Middle East diversity makes it an exceptionally vibrant region in the world. However, a host of problems it faces makes it also very volatile. The latter can be briefly summarized as follows: political instability of the existing governments and state structures that has a potential to cause the disintegration and collapse of entire geopolitical systems with grave consequences for the whole world; Severe demographic pressure and massive out-migration (mainly to Europe) because of slow economic growth, rapid population growth, unemployment and poverty, income disparities and ethnic tensions; proliferation of Weapons and existence of multiple conflicts; the rise of politically radical, militant Islam generally perceived as a threat and a source of instability, etc. In addition to these, several other challenges to regional stability are also affecting the situation in the region where there are no appropriate economic integration schemes, no system of arms control or collective defense.[14]

For geo-strategic and geo-economic reasons, the Middle East occupies an important position on the world's political agenda. As Mackinder's and Spykman's thoughts suggest, the region is important as being a part of Rimland, control of which could neutralize the power of the Heartland.[15] One of the outstanding features of the Middle East is, despite the oil reserves discovered in the Caspian region and the Central Asia, its ability to still carry an overwhelming strategic importance. However, it is a fact that nearly two thirds (65.3percent) of the world's oil reserves is located in the Middle East and production costs are relatively low in this region. Moreover, more than one third (36.1percent) of the world's natural gas reserves is located in the Middle East, as well. Rich hydrocarbon resources are, therefore, enough to make the region a center of attraction in the world.[16] The EIA reports that North American oil imports from the Middle East and North Africa will increase from 3.3 MMBD (Million Barrels for day) in 2001 to 6.1 MMBD in

2025 and the exports to Western Europe will increase from 4.7 MMBD to 7.4 MMBD.[17]

Monitoring of petroleum and natural gas resources from production period to the distribution stage and controlling their prices are factors that affect global superiority. The U.S. needs 20 million barrels just for one day. Her domestic resources constitute approximately 7-8 million barrels. It is anticipated that the U.S.'s national oil resources will run out within 10-11 years and, therefore, energy, especially oil, is a very crucial raw material for the U.S. As mentioned above, more than two thirds of the world's oil reserves is located beneath this region. Apart from geopolitical importance of the Middle East as a part of Rimland, petroleum constitutes a substantial place in the policies of the U.S. toward the region. Actors such as U.S., EU, Russian Federation, China, India and Japan have been struggling over the energy resources and their market shares within the Greater Middle East geography.[18]

The global political approach of the U.S. to these global and regional issues seems very idealistic. Thus, the Greater Middle East Project with its rhetorical dimension has attracted attention. The project, as mentioned above, underlines a comprehensive social, economic, cultural, and political transformation for the Middle East. In this respect, democratization is the main target of this project to struggle against terrorism. There are two main methods to this project. The first is "soft power," which includes diplomacy, cooperation, media, human rights, NGOs, etc. The second approach is "hard power," which reflects military interventionism. Iraq invasion can be assessed in and be a model to this policy. With the Greater Middle East Project, the U.S. tries to deepen her control and legitimacy on one hand, and she wants to maintain her superiority on a global level and protect her hegemony as a global power on the other. As it is known, the "West" endeavored to build new political structure in the region, with military methods during World War I, and at the beginning of the Cold War, which created a great distance between the "West" and the Middle East. In the Cold War era, the U.S. preferred a remote control or special diplomatic method for the Middle East against the USSR. The end of Cold War has pushed the U.S. on the region in positioning for her global strategies. In this regard, the U.S. aims to eliminate the rival powers by means of the Greater Middle East Project. It might be argued that the most important rival of the U.S. at present is the EU, especially the Franco-German alliance. Although Schröder and Chirac who were against U.S. policies, replaced by Merkel and Sarkozy, who comply with the U.S., changed the picture and lessened the rivalry, the EU stands as a potential rival for the U.S. in spite of its problematic political and economic structure. On the other hand, strict statements of Putin against the U.S. on defense missiles, increased political tension, and China and Russia are still serious concerns for the U.S.[19]

Although there are some listed assumptions and aims of Greater Middle East Project, it has not been perceived in the same way by countries within the Greater Middle East region, by regional powers as well as global ones. The countries of the region, mostly ruled by authoritarian regimes, perceived the project as an instrument that would undermine their regimes. Egyptian President Mubarek, for instance, resisted the plan with these words: "We hear about these initiatives as if the region and its states do not exist, as if they had no sovereignty over their land."[20] Therefore, they almost unanimously reacted to the project negatively. Arab intellectuals were also skeptical about the project as they believed that the project should have been jointly developed with the participation of all parties concerned and not only by the U.S. In this reaction, the low opinion of the U.S. in the region played a determining role. Many believed that, although the goal of the project looked very impressive, in practice, the U.S. would try to legitimize her hegemonic designs through the Greater Middle East Project. Naturally, other global powers regarded the project as a new strategy of the U.S. to control the region and undermine their influence. However, the position of the EU was unique, as Western European powers were allies of the U.S. during the Cold War era and are still members of NATO.

European Union and Greater Middle East Project

The EU, as well as the members of the EU, regarded the Middle East as an important region for their interests. The main reasons for the EU's interest in the Middle East region was related to economic interests, security considerations, cultural, and social issues. The region is important for the EU since it is an easy access to energy resources. Xenophobia, which includes Islamophobia, cultural problems, illegal migration, drug trafficking, and terrorism, constitutes main political problems of the EU. Through the prevention of threats such as the proliferation of weapons of mass destruction, religious extremism, international terrorism and drug trafficking, the EU attempts to establish regional stability. This is mainly because, apart from geographic proximity, through Middle Eastern migrants living in EU countries, the EU worries that the problems from the Middle East will possibly spillover into the EU.

Because of its political, economic, cultural, and geopolitical concerns, the EU also gives importance to the Greater Middle East Project. The idea of following common policies among members of EU countries was formulated in Maastricht treaty and it was named as Common Foreign and Security Policy (CFSP). "The Maastricht Treaty, under the second pillar, title V and Article J, 'proudly proclaimed' the creation of the Common Foreign and Security Policy (CFSP), which was to cover all the areas of foreign and security policy."[21] Although the EU did not become a defense actor as a result of the Maastricht provisions, the taboo over discussing defense matters, which had existed since the 1950s, was broken. "The period starting in December 1998 with the Franco-British Summit in St. Malo—as usually referred to as the St. Malo process—witnessed the most significant challenge to the EU's vision of itself as a civilian power."[22] Formal launching of ESDP took place in the Cologne Summit in 1999 and efforts are taking place since that time to reach a common foreign and security policy.

After the establishment of common market and monetary union, attentions focused on common foreign and security policy in Europe. However, since the Maastricht treaty, the EU has not been able to reach a common foreign and security policy in practice. While analyzing and evaluating the position of the EU within the Greater Middle East Project, it must be remembered that the Common Foreign and Security Policy is still in the making and there are seriously different and contradicting opinions among member states of the EU. These contradicting opinions and handicaps of the common foreign and security policy directly affect the EU's relations with all actors in all regions and projects, including the Middle East and the Greater Middle East Project of the U.S.[23]

Despite some handicaps the EU displays regarding the CFSP, members of the EU have managed to act in accord in some cases. The 9/11 terrorist attacks have brought a new global security perception. The EU declared solidarity to struggle against terrorism. European leaders immediately displayed unlimited cooperation with America in the fight against international terrorism. Samuel P. Huntington, who has gained a great reputation with his Clash of Civilizations thesis, argued that the attacks on 9/11 gave back Europeans an identity which was lost. According to him, Europe and America would come together on the basis of common civilization interests.[24] In this supportive atmosphere, the U.S. has easily been able to invade Afghanistan. However, the EU has not demonstrated the same support for the U.S. for her invasion of Iraq. The desire of the U.S. to intervene in Iraq has influenced transatlantic relationships in a negative way. Kupchan has warned about the severity of the situation and claimed that if the division between the U.S. and the EU is not ended, the clash of civilizations will be seen "inside" the West, not between the West and the rest of the world.[25]

Europe, more correctly France and Germany ("old" Europe as Rumsfeld called it), did not join the U.S. in the 2003 Iraqi war. Unilateral Middle East policies of the U.S. created a tension in transatlantic relationships. In January, 2003, Xavier Solana confessed that although there are common values which connect them, the EU and the U.S. are gradually receding from each other. According to him, the disagreement between the two is dependent upon political, strategic and cultural differences. When the Cold War era ended, this historical difference came to light.[26] Discord between transatlantic parties also had attracted attention of Robert Kagan. This is why Kagan considered the U.S. as Mars and the EU as Venus in his work.[27] In his view, he tries to point out the difference between hard and soft powers.[28] In addition to this, Hubert Vedrine, former French Minister of Foreign Affairs, criticized U.S. policies conducted in the name of struggling against terrorism and he labeled this as a new threat.[29]

According to another important thinker Joseph Nye, disputes among the EU and the U.S. is related to the decrease of the U.S.'s soft power and its loss of image among the allies. He underlined that the unilateral and hegemonic approach of the Bush administration reflected a hard power, which was in contradiction with the EU choice to represent a soft power. Therefore, he emphasized that Europe and the U.S. should act together against new security threats by building up soft power again. In this sense, powerful military capacity of the EU is not a threat against the U.S. Also, return of the U.S. to the soft power would be a positive development in respect to its relationships with the EU and other states.[30]

During the Cold War era, there was a common threat perception and they were all agreed in war methods against the enemy. Post Cold War era, especially the 2003 Iraq invasion, revealed different perceptions and tendencies. 2003 Iraq War has become a war that affected political economy of the world directly. This war has also affected transatlantic relations negatively. Prior to the war, there were distinct political reflections of the U.S. and the EU countries. The U.S. seemed very hasty to start a military operation against Iraqi regime, without waiting to gain any international legal support. Unlike the U.S., the United Kingdom seemed ready to wait for a resolution from the UN. However, being a strategic partner of the U.S., the UK supported the U.S. with every pace. France and Germany, on the other hand, were against any possible military operation. According to them, diplomatic sanctions should have been lasting and permanent. France also played her veto right in the UN Security Council as a card against military operation. Upon this, the U.S. and the UK have considered the decision of the UN numbered 1441 as an authorization for the military operation.[31]

World leaders demonstrated a common view about the fight against international terrorism after 9/11. In this frame, the U.S. and the EU have not disagreed on military operations against terrorists in Afghanistan. Iraq discussions, however, removed all these common perspectives. The EU high representative for the common foreign and security policy, Javier Solana, and European commissioner for external relations, Chris Patten, stated that the EU defends diplomatic solutions on the Iraq issue. But these views were not shared by all members of the EU. Denmark, Italy, Portugal, Spain, and the United Kingdom supported the U.S. Belgium, France and Germany resisted a war so soon.[32] These developments demonstrated that there is a lack of common ideas about security and foreign policy, and for instance, Costas Simitis has regarded this situation as harmful for the EU.[33] On the other hand, Rumsfeld has made his well-known statement that categorizes the EU as the "New Europe" to point out the states which support the U.S. and the "Old Europe" to indicate the states which are against the unilateral military approach of the U.S.[34] President Chirac assessed this view of Rumsfeld as a lack of culture.[35]

The states guided by France and Germany kept on expressing that there was not considerable evidence for Iraq to be perceived as a military threat. What is more, according to the EU, it was difficult to construct a "model" democratic system in Iraq, above all trying to accomplish this through military methods was being perceived as a target which could not be attained.[36] Furthermore, following the September 11th attacks, the EU entered into collaboration with the U.S. firmly believing that peace and democracy would not come to the Middle East without finding a proper solution to Arab–Israel conflict and without effectively fighting against terrorism. Also, the result of the summit between Bush and Gerhard Schröder, the former Prime Minister of Germany, who was opposing the Iraqi war, is an indication of this. After the summit, a common declaration was announced, in which it was expressed that the parties were in consensus on underlining liberalization and democratization of the Middle East, enforcing the rule of law, and developing the economic and security infrastructure of the region. Moreover, following the summit, Schroeder pointed out that to reach Israeli and Palestinian peace, compromise was inevitable and parties must act according to this framework.[37] The EU did not change its attitude about the Greater Middle East Project during the NATO meeting held in January 2004 and, following the summit, some developments such as terrorist attacks in Madrid, Spain and in London, England occurred. Spain has withdrawn her soldiers from Iraq following the terrorist attacks. Also, during the NATO summit held in July 2004, France hindered NATO in assuming a great mission in Iraq. Another crucial view was shared by President Chirac at the International Strategic Studies Institute's lecture in 2004. In his speech, Chirac warned the U.S. to stop unilateral policies. According to him, the power centric approach could easily create conflict and crisis. Therefore, states should act interdependently for a fairer world and every one must approve the reality and importance of interdependency.[38]

The EU and the U.S. have different perspectives on some crucial issues: for instance, some EU members see a fundamentalist threat directed against the U.S., not the EU. These different perspectives can be seen in NATO discussions. Germany and France, especially during Chirac and Schroeder administrations, were not in accord with the U.S. Sarkozy and Merkel's periods seem more harmonious. Because of the lack of a common approach and policies, the EU is being criticized by some circles as follows:

The EU accuses the U.S. of wasting money in Iraq but doesn't mention its impact on the European economy. Meanwhile, European countries implicitly want the U.S. to secure Iraq. It is quite clear that a chaotic Middle East will produce more immigrants heading for Europe. Besides, no one knows how to realize reconstruction projects or to improve foreign investment if the chaos spreads. Before the war in Iraq, the U.S. had asked its Western allies if they wanted to support this action. Many EU member countries have promised to contribute in different ways. But when the U.S. faced serious problems on the ground, they all deserted the U.S., except the United Kingdom. As the latter has its own problems, it couldn't play its ally role as was expected. In brief, European countries left the U.S. to deal with its problem on its own. Whatever their reasons were, the price of this attitude has become unbearable.[39]

In the region, the ongoing conflicts, mainly the turmoil in Iraq and the Palestinian–Israeli dispute, the struggle against international terrorism, mainly the terrorist organizations based in this region and their possible sponsoring states, and finding the support for economic, social and political transformation of the region, have been main issues to be dealt with. Regarding these challenges, the EU has already developed a mixture of different tools and strategies ranking from Euro-Mediterranean Partnership/Barcelona Process[40] to the European Neighborhood Policy (ENP). The Euro-Mediterranean Partnership comprises 35 members, 25 EU Member States and 10 Mediterranean Partners (Algeria, Egypt, Israel, Jordan, Lebanon, Morocco, Palestinian Authority, Syria, Tunisia and Turkey). Libya has observer status since 1999.

The Barcelona Process is a unique and ambitious initiative which laid the foundations of a new regional relationship and which represents a turning point in Euro-Mediterranean relations. In the Barcelona Declaration, the Euro-Mediterranean partners established the three main objectives of the Partnership as follows:

1. The definition of a common area of peace and stability through the reinforcement of political and security dialogue (Political and Security Chapter).
2. The construction of a zone of shared prosperity through an economic and financial partnership and gradual establishment of a free-trade area (Economic and Financial Chapter).
3. The rapprochement between people through social, cultural and human partnership aimed at encouraging understanding

between cultures and exchanges between civil societies (Social, Cultural and Human Chapter)...[41]

On the other hand, the European Neighborhood Policy (ENP) was developed in 2004. In this policy, it is stated that "with the objective of avoiding the emergence of new dividing lines between the enlarged EU and our neighbors and instead strengthening the prosperity, stability and security of all concerned. In this way, it also addresses the strategic objectives set out in the December 2003 European Security Strategy."[42] The European Neighborhood Policy is referring to the EU's immediate neighbors by land or sea—Algeria, Armenia, Azerbaijan, Belarus, Egypt, Georgia, Israel, Jordan, Lebanon, Libya, Moldova, Morocco, the Palestinian Authority, Syria, Tunisia, and the Ukraine. On the other hand, although Russia is also a neighbor of the EU, the EU's relations are instead developed through a strategic partnership covering four "common spaces." The European Neighborhood Policy's central element is the bilateral ENP Action Plans agreed upon between the EU and each partner.

> These set out an agenda of political and economic reforms with short- and medium-term priorities. Implementation of the first seven ENP Action Plans (agreed in early 2005 with Israel, Jordan, Moldova, Morocco, the Palestinian Authority, Tunisia, and the Ukraine) is underway and that of the latest to be agreed (with Armenia, Azerbaijan and Georgia) is about to begin. Lebanon will follow shortly and the EU-Egypt ENP Action Plan is nearly agreed. Implementation is jointly promoted and monitored through sub-committees. Since the ENP builds upon existing agreements between the EU and the partner in question (Partnership and Cooperation Agreements, or Association Agreements in the framework of the Euro Mediterranean Partnership), the ENP is not yet 'activated' for Belarus, Libya or Syria since no such agreements are yet in force.[43]

The Middle East peace process is also another important concern of the EU's Middle East policy. The EU has also developed cooperation with the Gulf Cooperation Council (GCC) that involves Saudi Arabia, Kuwait, Bahrain, Qatar, United Arab Emirates, and Oman.[44] In a parallel way with the Greater Middle East Project, Barcelona Process and the European Neighborhood Policy, some EU countries are looking for their own project that underpins the Greater Middle East initiative as well as the EU's initiatives. For instance, French president Sarkozy put forward the project of Mediterranean Union and he pointed out that he is planning to realize the first meeting of the project in 2008. Sarkozy shared his idea of Mediterranean Union with Libya, Algeria, Tunisia, and Egypt, which is supported by Mubarak. For the project, the European Council, or G8, is taken as a model. Carrying the intentions of reaching a common migration policy, developing economy and trade, strengthening the rule of law in the region, protecting the environment and establishing a Mediterranean Investment Bank similar to European Investment Bank, the envisioned Union is thought to act in cooperation with the EU.[45]

As mentioned above, the EU is already cooperating with the countries of the region through its partnerships with the Mediterranean countries and countries of the Gulf Cooperation Council. On the other hand, apart from the Greater Middle East initiative, either through NATO or alone, the U.S. is also acting in the region. In Afghanistan, NATO had already taken over the UN mandate of international peace keeping force in August 2003. The alliance has also had Mediterranean Dialogue with Israel and six Arab states since 1994. It is a fact that although "there are some differences in threat perception and in strategic responses between the EU and the U.S., the problems that were specified as principal threats (international terrorism, weapons of mass destruction, and failed and corrupt states) in both the European Security Strategy and the September 2002 U.S. National Security Strategy are quite similar."[46] The main difference concerning the tools and strategies in dealing with these threats is the fact that the EU is a neighbor of the Middle East while the U.S. is not. Although the EU agrees with the targets of the Greater Middle East initiative, the EU and the U.S. seek different methods and approaches to reach these targets, which can be summarized as follows:

Firstly, the U.S. regards herself as the main security guarantor of the region and underlines the importance of the military action both as an instrument of preemptive action and as a means employed during crises. However, the EU emphasizes promotion of rule-based societies and institution and development of policies seeking to avoid more serious problems in the future as a major instrument of preemptive action.[47] In other words:

> Whereas, the U.S. tend to cite the democratic deficits of governments that oppose western interests in the region and threaten them with punitive measures, sanctions and maybe even the possibility of an externally imposed regime change, European policymakers will likely try to support reform-minded forces within the countries in questions and nudge existing regimes toward the path to reform through dialogue, material support and reforms of conditionality.[48]

Therefore, the EU's approach is similar to that of the Arabic world. The EU believes that democratic change and economic modernization must be driven from within the Arab societies themselves and quite sure these values cannot be imposed on these societies without any base in their home countries. Similarly, it is underlined that "democratization and human development in the region must spring from indigenous roots. Western democracies should not seek to impose any formula for democratic change. But they can and must help from the outside—morally, politically and materially."[49]

Secondly, in the EU's approach, there is no single size that fits all. Therefore, every country should be dealt with individually and national sentiments and identities of the region should definitely be taken into account. Experiments of the Barcelona Process revealed that it is good idea to mainly focus on principles like the rule of law, independence of the judiciary, transparency, accountability, and strengthening of civil society that constitute all necessary concepts of "democracy." This method will make it easier to take the elites of these countries along and create a common interest, rather than fears of externally enforced regime change. European policymakers may well be prepared to support even minor reform steps (education, administrative reform, or economic policies) in a country like Syria, even if the speed of political development in that country lags way behind what Europe would like to see, while criticizing countries like Tunisia, Palestine, Lebanon, or Israel for deficiencies of democratic development or human rights violations may be comparatively less serious.[50]

Thirdly, according to the EU's approach, a resolution to the Israeli–Palestinian conflict is key in achieving further progress in the region. In the European Security Strategy (2003), it is underlined that "Resolution of the Arab Israeli conflict is a strategic priority for Europe. Without this, there will be little chance of dealing with other problems in the Middle East."[51] The European Security Strategy regards a peaceful settlement for the Arab-Israeli conflict as the main ground for establishing firm political and economical development, and implementing a security policy in the region. In other words, European goals such as democratization and liberalization, establishing a regional economic cooperation, a free trade zone, and regional security cooperation will not likely be achieved unless Arab-Israeli conflict is solved. Because of this, the resolution of the Arab-Israel conflict is defined as "a strategic priority for Europe."[52]

Perceptions and approaches of the EU and the U.S. regarding the people of Palestine and Israel are different and the case also affects their policies differently. "Washington holds greater sway with Israel, while the Europeans enjoy greater credibility among the Palestinians. Israel trusts the U.S. but does not trust Europe. The EU, on the other hand, enjoys much more trust among the Palestinians."[53] Therefore, the U.S. is reluctant to press Israel for a solution while the EU emphasizes the importance of a peaceful settlement to the problem of attaining development in the region.

Fourthly, although attitudes of people changes from one country to another as will be seen below, the EU generally believes that Islam is a religion compatible with modernity. Islam is one of the factors that encourage the EU to deal with the Middle East. The EU believes in necessity of a modus Vivendi of Islam. Because of its large number of Muslim minorities, which is approximate to those in the Middle East, and due to the cultural and political relevance of the Mediterranean for the whole of Europe, Islam and Muslims are getting more significant for the EU's domestic as well as foreign policy. Europe borders the Islamic world and many Muslims live in Europe and many Muslims are Europeans. Furthermore, the overwhelmingly-Muslim populated Turkey is negotiating with the EU for full membership. Therefore, the Middle East in particular, and the Muslim world in general, is increasingly occupying a central focal point in the foreign and security policy discussions of the EU and its member states. This naturally has significant implications for the EU's attitude toward U.S. policies and strategic objectives. Therefore, EU policies and attitudes regarding U.S. objectives and actions in Afghanistan and Iraq and the 'war on terror' and the Greater Middle East initiative are, to some extent, influenced by the Islamic factor. However, there is a possibility this trend might turn the opposite direction and the EU might occupy a hostile position against the Muslim world. The Pew Survey reveals that the Western public believes that the Muslims in their countries want to remain distinct from their society, rather than adopt their nation's customs and lifestyles. There are especially worries over Islamic extremism in France, Spain, Germany, and Netherlands.[54]

Although there are some negative reactions to Muslims and the Muslim world in some EU countries, currently, the EU is interested in the Islamic world and believes in coexistence and dialogue. The U.S., on the other hand, recognizes the importance of Islam and tries to put forward the phenomenon of "moderate Islam" as a model for the rest of the Islamic world. Therefore, Turkey is regarded as a democratic partner[55] of the Greater Middle East initiative. In contrast to the general impression in the Muslim World, some circles, especially Serbs, however, criticize the U.S. for helping Muslims in Bosnia and Kosovo, for example.[56]

Fifthly, in general, the U.S. and the EU agree that a democratic transformation of the Greater Middle East, especially in the Arab world, is a goal that should be pursued.[57] However, it is usually argued that it would seem that, while the U.S. wants to concentrate more on military solutions and short-term effects, the EU prefers to base its strategy on the experience of the Barcelona Process. From the EU's perspective, "it is also necessary to build on what has already been achieved—like, for example, the Barcelona Process—instead of starting everything from scratch."[58] Therefore, from a

European point of view, what is needed is not a "forward strategy of freedom," but 'a common perspective for political, economical and social change in Europe's neighborhood that builds on the potentials in these countries and takes their societies on board, respects their dignity, and realizes the linkages that exist between political and economical underdevelopment, on one hand, and unresolved territorial conflict, on the other.'[59]

The U.S. launched the Middle East Partnership Initiative at the end of 2002, which resembles the Barcelona Process in many respects. The Middle East Partnership Initiative of the U.S. can be regarded as geographically more extensive, but less extensively funded and a more bilaterally inclined version of the Barcelona Process (Euro-Mediterranean Partnership) that has existed since 1995. Objectives of both projects are similar as well; the Middle East Partnership Initiative of the U.S. aims to promote political, economical, and educational reforms, women's rights, and supports activities of civil society.[60] While the EU criticizes the U.S. for not cooperating in her policies regarding the Middle East, it must be noted that some of the responsibility lies on the shoulders of the EU as well, as it discouraged the U.S. from taking part in its initiatives regarding the region.

> Admittedly, the fact that 'Barcelona' and Europe's experience with this long-term, multilateral and multidimensional process was barely acknowledged and responded to by Washington has partly to do with the fact that the EU has shown no interest in allowing the U.S., whose role as a security policy actor in the Mediterranean cannot be ignored, any form of participation, not even as an observer.[61]

Finally, it might be argued that there is a difference between policy styles of the EU and the U.S. While the U.S. usually focuses more on the persons in charge of dealing with the Middle East, as well as other regions, Europe generally puts more emphasis on institution-building. This might be an outcome of the difference between the U.S. political system and political systems assumed in Western Europe. In the U.S. presidential system, politics is much more personalized and the prime decision-makers is very important. On the other hand, with its complicated institutional structure and intricately institutionalized politics, individual personalities do not make a big difference in Europe. With regard to the Middle East region, a clear indication of these different approaches could be seen in the EU-U.S. debate over how to deal with the Palestinian president, Yasir Arafat. The U.S. and the EU policymakers may have had similar opinions about the personality of Mr. Arafat, in forming relations with him, however, the U.S. and the EU had demonstrated rather different policies. The U.S. administration decided to boycott him, while the EU maintained relations, stressing the importance of maintaining institutions which Europe and the U.S. have themselves helped create—notably, the Palestinian presidential elections in 1996 were supported and monitored by EU and U.S. officials. "Rather than demanding a change in Palestinian leadership, the EU concentrates on strengthening the Palestinian legislative branch and supports wide-ranging administrative reforms."[62] However, the EU has changed her attitude in the case of Hamas. Hamas was the victor in the 2006 general elections and won 76 seats, while El-Fetih won just 43 seats in Palestinian parliament. In this case, unlike its previous attitude, the EU acted in line with the U.S.[63]

Besides their different approaches and methods, the EU and the U.S. have many common grounds both in terms of substance and in appearance. An obvious example of this is that although migrations always occurred toward the U.S. (more correctly, toward the American continent) from different parts of the world since the discovery of the continent, probably the biggest, or at least the most influential portion of the present American population is comprised of people who had migrated there from Europe. Thus, in terms of ethnicity, culture, attitudes, behaviors, ideologies, philosophy, etc., European influence is outstanding. Therefore, in terms of foreign policy toward the Middle East, it is argued that:

> EU leaders should recognize the need for both greater European unity and for a closer alignment of U.S. and European views. It is trite but correct to claim that when the U.S. and Europe pull in the same direction they are often successful in tackling global problems. But when Europe and America are at odds, stalemate and failure nearly always follow. Both sides will have to adjust their policies to ensure a common transatlantic strategy on the Middle East, difficult though this.[64]

Although the EU has some idealistic approaches and policies regarding the Middle East, it also has some limitations that undermine these policies and weaken its approaches. Above all, the present shape of the Middle East was designed by Western European countries, especially Britain and France. Many problems that people of the region are facing today are rooted in the artificial design of the region shaped after World War I. Therefore, although the image of EU countries is better than that of the U.S. in the region, people of the region have doubts about the polices of the EU and some Western European countries, since they regard them as former colonizers.

As mentioned above, Common Foreign and Security Policy (CFSP) at the European level is still in the process of preparation and currently there is not a common policy. This means that, currently, to adopt and implement a common position is almost impossible. Rather than common policies, it is realistically more possible to talk about sometimes contradicting individual policies of member states. In this sense, for now, bilateral state relations are more influential than the relations that are held through the whole body of the EU.

Another handicap of the EU policy is having a common foreign policy which is still in the stage of preparation, and in parallel to this, the resource allocated for the activities of this foreign policy is very limited. Therefore, this limited resource should be used according to a list of priorities between various regions and various activities. Because of this lack of common policy, disagreements and even sometimes hostile disputes break out among the member states and they are not willing to provide the EU necessary financial resources. This deficiency of adequate amounts of resources causes handicaps for EU policies in the region.

Frustrated Arab states against the EU can also be regarded as one of the factors that hinder the EU's efficiency in the Middle East. Apart from the U.S. and the Soviet Union, the EU has also constituted a possible third option for Middle Eastern countries during the Cold War era. However, after the Cold War era ended, in the region, the EU has usually been regarded as an alternative to the U.S. hegemony. Thus, while the expectation of the region from the EU increased, the EU has not been able to meet these expectations because of its structural characteristics. This demonstrated that the competence of the EU is limited and it cannot balance out the U.S. in the region. Thus, the image of the EU in the region is being undermined.[65]

Conclusion

The U.S. was the victor of the Cold War era and with the dissolution of the USSR in 1991, the U.S. became a single super power. In order to maintain and strengthen her position, the U.S. has overtaken the role of safeguarding and furthermore, manipulated global as well as regional balances. In this regard, the Middle East is significant for the U.S. in several aspects such as the rich hydrocarbon reserves, geopolitical position, deficiency of democracy and human rights, poverty, illiteracy, artificial borders and artificial nations, rise of radicalism, and terrorist activities. The importance of the region encourages the U.S. to manipulate developments in the region and shape the region if possible according to her interests. In fact, the Greater Middle East Project was a product of this need and the U.S. has supported it.

The Greater Middle East Project aims to build a new economic, social and political structure that requires a reconstructing process. Naturally, by the countries of the Greater Middle East region, the project is not perceived in the same way as the global powers. Countries of the region, mostly having anti-democratic regimes, perceived the project as a new tool that will undermine their regimes. In the region, many believe that, although the goal of the project looks very impressive, in practice, the U.S. will try to legitimize her hegemonic designs through the Greater Middle East Project. Global powers, on the other hand, regard the project as a new strategy of the U.S. to control the region and undermine their influence. The position of the EU as a global actor is important as Western European powers were the allies of the U.S. during the Cold War era and are still members of NATO.

The EU believes that there are many social, political and economical problems in the Middle East. In order to deal with these problems, the EU formulated its own strategies and put forward the Euro-Mediterranean Partnership/Barcelona Process and the European Neighborhood Policy (ENP). The EU is also in cooperation with the Gulf Cooperation Council.

Although potential rivals, the U.S. and the EU usually agree on common threats such as international terrorism, weapons of mass destruction, and failed and corrupt states. Their main separation lies in the tools and strategies in dealing with these threats. The first basic difference between the American and European approaches is that, while the U.S. regards herself as the main security guarantor of the region and underlines the importance of the military action both as an instrument of preemptive action, which is employed during crises, the EU believes that democratic change and economic modernization must be driven into the Arab societies and that they cannot be imposed upon without any acceptable base in the home countries. The second is that, the EU criticizes the U.S.'s approach and argues that there is not a single size that fits all. Therefore, every country should be dealt with individually and national sentiments and identities of the region should definitely be taken into account. Third, according to the EU's approach, the resolution of the Israeli–Palestinian conflict is key in achieving further progress in the region. However, the U.S. is reluctant to push Israel for an immediate solution. Forth, because of some factors such as the large number of Muslim-populated EU countries, which is nearly as much as the Muslim population of the Middle East, and the cultural and political relevance of the Mediterranean to the whole of Europe, the EU is under the influence of Islam that affects EU polices regarding the Greater Middle East. In a global age, similar factors might influence the U.S. as well, but it will be in a different manner and to a limited degree. Fifth, it is usually argued that while the U.S. wants to concentrate more on military solutions and short-term effects, the EU prefers to base its strategy on the experience of the Barcelona Process. The EU advocates building on top of what has already been achieved, instead of starting everything over from scratch. Sixth, while the U.S. usually focuses more on the persons in charge of dealing with the Middle East, as well as other regions, Europe generally puts more emphasis on institution-building.

It might be argued that, if a serious rival power rises such as China or Russia, it is very likely the EU and the U.S. will cooperate as they did during the Cold War. If not, it is, in this case, very likely that we will observe some sort of rivalry between the U.S. and the EU. However, this depends upon whether or not the EU will be able to have a common foreign and security policy and complete its political integration successfully.

Although the U.S. and the EU agree on objectives of the Greater Middle East initiative, it is difficult to know to what extent the U.S. and the EU will be able to cooperate. However, if the Greater Middle East Project is implemented and successful, it should be related to some basic factors.[66] These include the following: First, the U.S. should be serious and sincere with this project and allocate enough resources to it, as she did in the case of the Marshal Plan.[67]

Second, a just solution for the Arab-Israeli problem that satisfies both sides is the key to the regional problems. In addition to Palestinians, Israel also should not use power, and must especially abstain from using excessively exaggerated power against Palestinians. This does not mean that Israel should not defend her people against terrorist attacks, but using excessive or unnecessary power is helping increase the number of radicals in the Arabic world and it is undermining the position of moderates as well as the credibility of the U.S. in the region. Overall, using power without a justly legitimized base will put the state using the power in an illegal position as the UN charter (legal defense, Article 51) and decision of UN Security Council (Article 42) forbids using power without exceptions.

Third, democratic, stable, model states should be established both in Iraq and in Afghanistan, just because the U.S. occupied these countries in the name of eradicating totalitarian regimes and creating democratic models. If this is managed successfully, these countries can influence the rest of the region and open the gate for new reforms. It seems, however, it will be very difficult for the U.S. to be able to attain this goal on her own.

Fourth, the opinion of the U.S. is very low in the region as well as in the whole Islamic world. The U.S. should gain the trust and support of Arabs as well as all Muslims in the world. To this end, Islamic sensitivities should be taken into account during the formulation and implementation of the policies, especially those regarding the region. A peaceful resolution to the Israeli-Arab conflict will especially help the U.S. gain public support in the region.

Fifth, the invasions of Afghanistan and Iraq showed that occupation is easy but to bring stability is difficult. Therefore, instead of 'revolution,' 'evolution' should be used as a strategy to change the region. For the success of any project, not solely states of the region, but NGOs and local people, should also participate in such regional efforts.[68]

Sixth, for the success of the initiative, the EU and the U.S. should cooperate rather than confront. Otherwise, this confrontation will handicap any project regarding the region.

Lastly, Turkey has close relations with the U.S. as well as the EU and she is, at the same time, a Middle Eastern country. Being the heir of an empire that ruled over this region for about four hundred years and having strong roots of tolerance and coexistence, Turkey, who is engaged in negotiating with the EU for membership, is a crucial country in the region. The Turkish way of understanding and practicing Islam (especially during the Ottomans) has always been very moderate and Turkey's experience in democratization and market economy is the highest in the region. Therefore, attaining a successful transformation for the region demands Turkish involvement in the project. With her rich experience and close cooperation with the countries of the region, she will strengthen the project in all aspects.[69]

---

[1] İdris Bal, "Turkey-USA Relations and Impacts of 2003 Iraq War," in Turkish Foreign Policy in Post Cold War Era, ed. İdris Bal (Boca Raton Florida: Brown Walker, 2004), pp. 119-125.

[2] Secretary Condoleezza Rice, "Special Briefing on Travel to the Middle East and Europe," Washington, DC. July 21, 2006. http://www.state.gov/secretary/rm/2006/69331.htm

[3] Eddie J. Girdner, "The Greater Middle East Initiative: Regime Change, Neo liberalism and US Global Hegemony," The Turkish Yearbook of International Relations, No.36, (2005), p. 38.

[4] Ibid., pp. 42-43.

[5] Richard G. Lugar, A New Partnership for The Greater Middle East: Combating Terrorism, Building Peace, (Washington, D.C.: The Brookings Institution).

[6] Girdner, The Greater Middle East Initiative: Regime Change, Neo liberalism and US Global Hegemony, p. 38.

[7] Gilbert Achcar, "Fantasy Of A Region That Doesn't Exist Greater Middle East: the U.S. plan," Le Monde diplomatique, April 2004, http://mondediplo.com/2004/04/04worl

[8] Benita Ferrero-Waldner, "The EU, the Mediterranean and the Middle East: APartnership for Reform," (The German World Bank Forum "Middle East & Germany: Change & Opportunities," Hamburg, 2 June 2006).

[9] Girdner, The Greater Middle East Initiative: Regime Change, Neo liberalism and U.S. Global Hegemony, pp. 42-43; http://www.al-bab.com/arab/docs/international/gmep2004.htm; See also Al-Hayat, 13 February, 2004.

[10] Çağrı Erhan, "Broader Middle East and North Africa Initiative and Beyond," Perceptions, Vol.X., No.3, (Autumn 2005), p. 159.

[11] İdris Bal and Ayfer Selamoğlu, "Büyük Ortadoğu Projesi: ABD, AB, Türkiye ve Bölge," in 21. Yüzyılda Türk Dış Politikası, ed. İdris Bal (Ankara: Lalezar Kitabevi, 2006), p. 196.

[12] Ibid.

[13] The factors that created instability in the Middle East see; İdris Bal, "Instability in the Middle East and the Relevant Role of the PKK," Turkish Foreign Policy in Post Cold War Era, ed. İdris Bal, (Boca Raton, Florida: Bro wn Walker Press, 2004), pp. 347-362.

[14] Hatipoğlu, "The European Union's Role in the Greater Middle East," p. 118.

15 See, Graham Evans, The Penguin Dictionary of International Relations, (London: Penguin Books, 1998), p. 219; Ramazan Özey, Dünya Denkleminde Ortadoğu Coğrafyası, (İstanbul: Aktif Yayınevi, 2004), s.23. Mackinder expressed his heartland theory in his work called "Democratic Ideals and Reality" (1919).
16 Bal, "Instability in the Middle East and the Relevant Role of the PKK," Turkish Foreign Policy in Post Cold War Era, p. 349.
17 Esra Hatipoğlu, "The European Union's Role in the Greater Middle East," http://www.fscpo.unict.it/EuroMed/EDRC5/euusamed01.pdf[17] Esra Hatipoğlu, "The European Union's Role in the Greater Middle East," [17] Esra Hatipoğlu, "The European Union's Role in the Greater Middle East," p. 118.
18 İdris Bal and Ayfer Selamoğlu, "Büyük Ortadoğu Projesi: ABD, AB, Türkiye ve Bölge," in 21. Yüzyılda Türk Dış Politikası, ed. İdris Bal (Ankara: Lalezar Kitabevi, 2006), p. 197.
19 Ibid.
20 Zambelis, The Strategic Implications of Political Liberalization and Democratication in the Middle East, p. 91.
21 Sinem A. Açıkmeşe, "The Underlying Dynamics of the European Security and Defence Policy," Perceptions, Vol. IX, No.1, (March-May 2004), pp. 123-129.
22 Ibid.
23 See, Esra Çayhan, "Avrupa Birliği'nde Ortak Dış Politika ve Güvenlik Politikası," Uluslararası Politikada Yeni Alanlar Yeni Bakışlar,ed. Faruk Sönmezoğlu (İstanbul: Der Yayınları, 1998), p. 351; Kamer Kasım, "NATO'ya ve ABD-AB İlişkilerine Etkisi Bakımından Ortak Avrupa Dış ve Güvenlik Politikası," Ankara Avrupa Çalışmaları Dergisi, Cilt.1. Sayı.2, (Bahar 2002), p. 88; Açıkmeşe, The Underlying Dynamics of the European Security and Defence Policy, pp. 123-124; For a source in Turkish about German foreign policy see, İbrahim S. Canbolat, Almanya ve Dış Politikası, (İstanbul, Alfa, (2003).
24 Jiri Sedivy and Marcin Zaborowski, "Old Europe, New Europe and Transatlantic Relations," European Security, No. 3, Vol.13, (2004): p. 190.
25 Charles A. Kupchan: "The End of the West," The Atlantic Monthly, November (2002), http://www.theatlantic.com/doc/prem/200211/kupchan
26 Ömer Taşpınar, "Transatlantik İlişkiler," Radikal, 21 Haziran 2004.
27 See, Robert Kagan, Of Paradise and Power America and Europe in the New World Order, (New York: Alfred A. Knopf Book, 2003).
28 Fuat Keyman, "Amerikan Yüzyılı ve Türkiye," Radikal 2, 13.07.2003.
29 "Atlantik Fırtına Yüklü," Radikal, 18.02.2002.
30 Sevilay Kahraman, "Avrupa Birliği ve Irak Krizi: Bölünmeden Yeniden Birleşmeye Uzun, İnce Bir Yol," Ankara Avrupa Çalışmaları Dergisi, Cilt.2, Sayı.4, (Bahar 2003), p. 156.
31 Bal, Turkey-USA Relations and Impacts of 2003 Iraq War, p. 132; Sir Timothy Garden, "In the Wake of Irak Rebuilding Relationships," NATO Review, (Summer 2003), http://www.nato.int/docu/review/2003/issue2/english/art1.html[31] Bal, Turkey-USA Relations and Impacts of 2003 Iraq War, p.132; Sir Timothy Garden, "In the Wake of Irak Rebuilding Relationships," NATO Review, (Summer 2003).
32 Garden, "In the Wake of Irak Rebuilding Relationships.

[33] Iraq split redraws the map of Europe Leaders' letter in support of war exposes increasingly deep continental rift By Stephen Castle, Andrew Grice and Andy McSmith in Madrid Published: 31 January 2003.
[34] Ibid.
[35] Bal and Selamoğlu, Büyük Ortadoğu Projesi: ABD, AB, Türkiye ve Bölge, p. 200; Radikal, 17.11.2004.
[36] Talha Ovet, "AB'nin Irak Savaşı'ndaki Politikası," Ankara Avrupa Çalışmaları Dergisi, Cilt.4, Sayı.2, (Bahar 2005), p. 67.
[37] Bal and Selamoğlu, Büyük Ortadoğu Projesi: ABD, AB, Türkiye ve Bölge, pp. 185-212; Radikal, 29.02.2004.
[38] Bal and Selamoğlu, Büyük Ortadoğu Projesi: ABD, AB, Türkiye ve Bölge, pp. 185-212; Radikal, 20.11.2004.
[39] Beril Dedeoğlu, "Europe's American impasse," Todayszaman, 24.02.2007, http://www.todayszaman.com/tz-web/yazarAd.do?kn=6
[40] The Euro-Mediterranean Conference of Ministers of Foreign Affairs, held in Barcelona on 27-28 November 1995, marked the starting point of the Euro-Mediterranean Partnership (Barcelona Process), a wide framework of political, economic and social relations between the Member States of the European Union and Partners of the Southern Mediterranean.
[41] http://ec.europa.eu/external_relations/gr/index.htm
[42] Ibid.
[43] http://ec.europa.eu/world/enp/policy_en.htm
[44] http://ec.europa.eu/external_relations/gr/index.htm; Esra Hatipoğlu, "The European Union's Role in the Greater Middle East," http://www.fscpo.unict.it/EuroMed/EDRC5/euusamed01.pdf, pp. 124-125.
[45] Zaman, 03 Ağustos 2007.
[46] Hatipoğlu, The European Union's Role in the Greater Middle East, p. 127.
[47] Ibid.
[48] Walker Perthes, "America's Greater Middle East and Europe," SWP Comments 3., German Institute of International and Security Affairs, (February 2004), p. 2.
[49] "Democracy and Human Development in the Broader Middle East: A Transatlantic Strategy for Partnership," (Istanbul Papers. 1, TESEV, Istanbul, Turkey, June 25 – 27, 2004).
[50] Perthes, America's Greater Middle East and Europe, p. 3.
[51] "A secure Europe in a Better World, European Security Strategy," Brussels, 12 December 2003, p. 9.
[52] Ibid.
[53] Perthes, America's Greater Middle East and Europe, p. 5.
[54] "Islamic Extremism: Common Concern for Muslim and Western Publics, Support for Terror Wanes Among Muslim Publics," Released: 07.14.05, http://pewglobal.org/reports/display.php?ReportID=248
[55] About Turkish model see, Bal, Turkey's Relations with the West and Turkic Republics: The Rise and Fall of the Turkish Model.
[56] For instance see, http://www.srpska-mreza.com/Bosnia/DevilTriangle.html
[57] Democratization and U.S. plans in the Middle East see, Chris Zambelis, "The Strategic Implications of Political Liberalization and Democratication in the Middle East," Parameters, (Autumn 2005).

[58] Esra Hatipoğlu, "The European Union's Role in the Greater Middle East," http://www.fscpo.unict.it/EuroMed/EDRC5/euusamed01.pdf, pp. 123-124, 127.
[59] Perthes, America's Greater Middle East and Europe, p. 2.
[60] Zambelis, The Strategic Implications of Political Liberalization and Democratication in the Middle East, p. 91.
[61] Perthes, America's Greater Middle East and Europe, p. 4.
[62] Ibid., p. 7.
[63] "Hamas celebrates election victory," Guardian, Thursday January 26, 2006; Ahmed Yusuf, "Fetih resmen darbe yaptı," Radikal, June 23, 2007; Akşam, January 27, 2006.
[64] Steven Everts, The EU and the Middle East: a call for action, (London: Centrte for European Reform Working Paper, Januaray 2003), p. 3.
[65] Hatipoğlu, The European Union's Role in the Greater Middle East, http://www.fscpo.unict.it/EuroMed/EDRC5/euusamed01.pdf, p.126.
[66] For initial version of these arguments see, Bal and Selamoğlu, Büyük Ortadoğu Projesi: ABD, AB, Türkiye ve Bölge, pp. 210-211.
[67] For similar arguments see, Mahdi Darius Nazemroaya, "Plans for Redrawing the Middle East: The Project for a "New Middle East," (November 18, 2006).
[68] For similar arguments see, François Heisbourg, "Beyond the U.S. initiative: Mideast democracy is a long-term, global project," International Herald Tribune, (Wednesday, March 24, 2004).
[69] About the role that Turkey play see for instance, Yakup Beris, Asli Gurkan, "Broader Middle East Initiative: Perceptions From Turkey," Turkey In Focus, Issue.7, (July 2004), TÜSİAD, Turkish Industrialists And Businessmen's Association, Washington Office.

Chapter 5
The Involvement of the European Union in the Middle East Peace Process

Umut UZER

In this article, I study the European Union involvement in the Middle East peace process. The institutional and conceptional strengths and weaknesses of the Union will be manifest as a result of this narrative.

I must first mention that the lack of a hegemonic or near-hegemonic European state and adoption of an all-European identity within the European continent are the two major deficiencies to the EU becoming a prospective candidate as a world power. Here, I first discuss European efforts to devise a pan-European foreign policy and its shortcomings, then I present major issues and developments related to the Middle East peace process. I conclude my study by analyzing the European involvement in the Middle East peace process. The argument below makes it clear that European engagement in the peacemaking process, be it at a financial or rhetorical level, has been limited rather than decisive.

One of the most compelling questions of the twenty first century is whether the EU will evolve into some sort of state. After all, the EU has most of the institutions and symbols of a state: an executive organ (the European Commission), a parliament (the European Parliament), a judiciary authority (European Court of Justice), a flag, a central bank, a currency, and an anthem. The decisions taken in Brussels, the headquarters of the EU, are binding on member states, albeit the decision-making process is achieved with contributions from all member states.

States possess a number of functions, among which foreign policy making is an important area for the external world. The EU is particularly weak in this sphere as the Common Foreign and Security Policy (CFSP) is not binding on member states and, as a consequence, they follow divergent paths in their respective foreign policies. In other words, member states follow their egotistic national interests as manifested in the 2003 American occupation of Iraq during which the United Kingdom was an ardent supporter and collaborator of the U.S., whereas France and Germany were highly critical of American policies. In sum, so far, there has not been an exclusive European foreign policy to discuss.

The EU is a novel project, which transcends the characteristics of an ordinary international organization. It would be more correct to label the EU as a supranational organization in which conflicting national projects compete with each other. Nation-states are members of the EU and comply with the decisions of the European Commission taken by the consent of all member states. It is not certain whether the EU will evolve in a state-like mechanism to be called the United States of Europe.

There are a number of possibilities for the future of international relations. American unipolarity can prevail for the long-run, a new multipolarity could emerge, or there could be, what Niall Ferguson calls, apolarity, meaning a world without great powers resulting in a chaotic international system. In the latter eventuality, the lack of "even *one* (sic) dominant imperial power" could arise from the possibility that potential great powers are too focused on domestic problems, and hence are disinclined to get involved in global crises.[1]

It remains to be seen whether the current unipolar world under American hegemony will be superceded by a multipolar world in which America is one of the major powers among which China, Japan, India, and possibly the EU occupy central positions. To emerge as a new pole, the EU needs to have a strong army thus complementing its economic prowess with military power. And an emergence of a European national identity over national and regional identities is also needed. Admittedly, numerous overlapping identities can cohabitate; but as it stands, we cannot detect a strong European identity during the first decade of the twenty first century.

It is only through the transformation of the EU into a state-like structure that it could have a more central role in the Middle East peace process. Otherwise, it cannot rival the overwhelming economic and military clout of the U.S. in the region.

Lacking the necessary tools, the EU could have played the role of a facilitator among the Israelis and the Palestinians, or presented venues for peace conferences, but without necessary material capabilities, it is quite unlikely that the EU will have an influential role in Middle East peace process. Unfortunately, former EU involvement in the peace process accentuate this fact.

A New Europe Between Old *raison d'etat* and a Novel Identity

The EU is an international organization with some supranational characteristics. Its supranational features can be observed from its delegation of significant levels of state sovereignty to the European Commission in Brussels. While the integrationists demand a U.S. of Europe, turning the present nation-states into units similar to the states in the U.S.[2] or *Länder* in Germany, the supporters of Europe of nation-states prefer to keep the EU pretty much the same way as it is today. For instance, at the Maastricht European Council summit in December 1991, the United Kingdom opposed the inclusion of the phrase "federal union" as an objective of the summit, so the goal was changed into "an ever closer union among the people of Europe."³

There are a number of European foreign policy objectives. Among those, promotion of regional cooperation and integration, democracy, and human rights can be enumerated. Furthermore, the EU is trying to prevent the spread of violence and crime.⁴ However, we should point out that these are quite general policies and there seems to be more coordination at the rhetorical, rather than implementation, level.

So it can be seen that member states of the EU prefer following their own foreign policies. As Europe lacks a strong military force, which is an essential part of power and does not have a strong European identity,⁵ prospects for a well-articulated and efficiently implemented foreign policy are rather dim.

Even though with the Single European Act in 1987, the EC decided to speak with one voice and preserve international peace and security,⁶ it would be correct to say that there is no full-fledged European foreign policy, and it is more "reactive" than "proactive." In the Gulf crisis of 1990-1991, EC passivity was amply demonstrated⁷ when the U.S. took the lead in the attempts to evict Iraq from Kuwait.

Once again, the Balkan crises of the 1990s depicted the EU not as a problem-solver, but rather as a contributor to upholding the peace already provided by the Americans. This is not to say the EU is incapable of resolving crises, at least in our case, in the Middle East; but to acknowledge the fact that American resolution has been and is essential for a peaceful solution of conflicts. Europe is able to be the junior partner in such endeavors, but not the key player, at least under the current circumstances.

The first effort to create a common foreign policy for the European nations was the *European Political Cooperation (EPC)*, which was a consultation and coordination process of the "foreign policy positions" of the six members of the EC. It was a "loose and voluntary arrangement," in which there would be common action "where possible." With the Single European Act, the EPC was characterized as the main instrument in the implementation of a truly "European foreign policy." With the Maastricht Treaty, however, EPC was replaced by the Common Foreign and Security Policy (CFSP); but in reality, there was very "little change in the practice of European foreign policy."⁸ The main difference between the EPC and CFSP was that the latter included defense matters, whereas the former lacked such a topic under its terms of reference.⁹

Furthermore, the CFSP envisaged the safeguarding of common values and independence of the Union. However, one should add that these principles are rather vague and how they will be implemented in specific policy areas are hard to determine.¹⁰

It would be an incomplete picture of European foreign liaisons without mentioning some of the strengths of the European countries. Two members of the EU, namely France and the United Kingdom, are permanent members of the United Nations Security Council. The President of the European Commission regularly attends the summits of the G7, among which four states are EU members. Furthermore, the European Commission has over 120 delegations and quasi-embassies all around the world.

The European Union might be suffering from the problem of collective action of large groups. In other words, as the number of member states in the Union increases, the ability of the EU to make important collective decisions diminishes. This negative correlation between the number of member states and the ability to take swift and decisive action might be a function of the difference between large and small groups. In a large group, members try to maximize their individual benefits, not their group interests. So, it follows that small groups can better preserve their interests by acting in a rational manner. This stems from the fact that in a single member country, public demands and interests push relative public good to be provided by the state, while, in a large group of states, on the other hand, members prefer to pursue a free ride and expect someone else to provide public good.[11]

Of course, this does not follow that the EU or the EEC as it was formerly known, did act more forcefully when it had only six members than today with its 27 members. However, the institutional capability of the community was rather weak at that period of time in history. Later in time, when the number of states within the Union rose, their national preferences and priorities also entered European politics. So it has become more difficult to reach decisions which satisfy all the member states. At this point, the accession of Cyprus in 2004 has been a case which negatively influenced the EU-Turkish relations.

Forming powerful institutions is another matter complementing this collective action problem. The EU does not lack institutions, in fact they are numerous, but what it needs is the creation of adequate instruments equipped with the full capacity of effective foreign policy making. For this, a consensus of the structural mechanisms of the Union is essential.

Europe's institutional identity defines the EU as a "normative and civilian power with a preference for multilateralism and international law." Implementing non-military solutions, which are mainly performed through diplomacy to resolve disputes and economic solutions to political problems, are the key elements of the EU's identity. The EU, together with the Council of Europe and OSCE, is the creator of liberal internationalist norms[12] and, as such, by redefining state sovereignty, it tries to replace power politics with the rule of law.[13]

As far as the peace process is concerned, I concur with the former American president Jimmy Carter who argued that the EC cannot act in unison as a challenger to the U.S. for bringing peace to the Middle East, since it lacks the necessary power or will for peacemaking in the region. It is only the U.S. that has the capability, interest and desire to help the Arabs and Jews reach peace.[14]

The Arab-Israeli Conflict and Efforts at its Resolution

The Middle East occupies a strategic location in the world. With its rich oil resources and the existence of numerous conflict areas, it is also a source of instability for the world at large.

The major conflict between the Arabs and Israelis is over territory and the right of Israel to exist as a legitimate state in the region. So, there are elements of territory, borders and two rival nationalisms between Arabs and Jews: that is Jewish nationalism, i.e. Zionism, opposed to Palestinian Arab nationalism and vice versa. It should be evident that the crux of the Arab-Israeli dispute is the Palestinian problem, as it is the existential matter for both Israelis and Palestinians. Israel's problems with Syria can be solved through the evacuation of Golan Heights. With the Palestinians, however, the strife is over a piece of territory known as *Eretz Yisrael* (the land of Israel) for the Jews or as Palestine for Arabs. The question is to find what sort of partition of this historic *Eretz Yisrael*/Palestine would satisfy both people occupying that small piece of territory.

Resolution 242 adopted by the UN Security Council on November 22, 1967, following the 1967 War, is considered to be the cornerstone for a Middle Eastern peace as it offered the formula of land for peace without specifically labelling its solution as such. 242 called Israel to withdraw "from territories occupied in the recent conflict" and, in return, end "all claims or states of belligerency" and to show respect to the right to exist of all states in the region. About the Palestinian problem, on the other hand, the Resolution only had this to say: there should be "a just settlement of the refugee problem."[15] It should be evident that resolution 242 did not adequately address the Palestinian problem. Moreover, Israelis argued that they were not required to withdraw from all the territories they occupied during the six-day war in 1967, but only to the extent they deemed not to detrimentally affect Israeli security. Regardless of these different interpretations, this resolution is considered the cornerstone for any Middle East peacemaking effort.

The peace process started with the disengagement agreements between Israel and Egypt and later between Israel and Syria in 1974 in the aftermath of the 1973 Yom Kippur/October War. The step-by-step approach was adopted in these talks supervised by the American Secretary of State, Henry Kissinger. As a consequence, Israel withdrew from the "Egyptian mainland and from the banks of the Suez Canal."[16] Thus the *status quo ante bellum* was restored to that of the 1967 war's borders. In other words, Israel preserved its conquests from the six-day war of 1967 but not its occupied territories from the 1973 October War.

Jimmy Carter's election victory in 1976 as the President of the U.S. was the harbinger of a new approach to the Middle East peacemaking process in the White House. Together with Middle East experts, Harold Saunders and William Quandt, the new administration, wanted a comprehensive solution to the Middle East conflict through an international conference and cooperation with the Soviet Union.[17]

One of the most important developments in the peace process was the Camp David Accords of 1978. Camp David is the presidential retreat of American presidents, located in the State of Maryland, not far from Washington. In 1978, President Jimmy Carter invited Egyptian President Anwar Sadat and Israeli Prime Minister Menachem Begin to Camp David to discuss the prospects for peace between Israel and Egypt. During the negotiations, Anwar Sadat explicitly said that he was ready to negotiate on every issue, except Egyptian sovereignty rights over Sinai. As a result of the talks between September 5 and September 17, 1978, a main framework for a peace agreement between the two countries as well as a self-rule plan for the Palestinians in the West Bank and Gaza was signed.[18]

The principles of the Camp David Accords were enshrined in the Egyptian-Israeli peace treaty of March 26, 1979. With this treaty, the state of war between Egypt and Israel was terminated and normal relations resumed. Israel was to withdraw to the international boundary between Egypt and the former mandated territory of Palestine.[19] In other words, Egypt was offering Israel peace in return for the territory it lost during the 1967 war, namely, the Sinai Peninsula.

The Preamble of the Treaty mentioned the necessity for all Arab states to join the peace process with Israel so as to establish "a just, comprehensive and lasting peace in the Middle East." Egypt and Israel would continue to discuss the future of the West Bank and Gaza Strip, and Jordan was invited to join the negotiations. The Palestinians could participate in the autonomy talks, provided they were in Jordanian and Egyptian delegations.[20]

The EEC, even though it verbally supported the Camp David, had a different approach than the piecemeal or step-by-step approach of the Camp David Accords. The European approach was such that a comprehensive resolution of the Arab-Israeli conflict was to be sought in a peace conference.[21]

It was fair to say that the Camp David did not adequately address the grievance of the Palestinians. That is why the European initiatives started. British Foreign Minister Lord Carrington called for the PLO to take part in the negotiations. French President Giscard d'Estaing repeated the same demand but he also asked for self-determination for the Palestinians.[22]

As the British wanted to amend 242 in a way that reflected Palestinian concerns, American President Jimmy Carter was adamant to protect resolution 242. Furthermore, he was worried that European efforts might unravel the Camp David Accords he brokered. He said that he was doing everything he could so that the EC could not interfere with the Camp David process.[23]

British Foreign Secretary Lord Carrington, as a response to all these statements, said that the U.S. involvement was necessary for the peace in the region and all they were doing was to try to complement the Camp David peace process.[24] Here, once again we detect the resurgence of the special relationship between the U.S. and the United Kingdom. In fact, the latter state played a balancing role between the U.S. and Europe, having close ties with both political entities.

Despite the fact there was a strong criticism in the Arab World against Egypt's separate peace with Israel, by the late 1980s, most Arab states, as well as the PLO, realized that it was logical for them to make peace with Israel in return for Israeli evacuation of the occupied territories it had acquired back in 1967. There were a number of efforts throughout the 1980s such as the Reagan Plan, the Fez Plan as well as Jordan's secret talks with Israel, but it was only after the Gulf Crisis/War of 1990-1991 that a meaningful peace process re-started.

Meanwhile in the U.S., initially, there was no great interest in the Middle East. Under George Bush Sr.'s tenure as president between 1988 and 1992, the Middle East experts were generally of the opinion that there should be no major plans to resolve the Arab-Israeli conflict. In fact, according to them, the situation was not ripe enough to seek a solution. People such as Dennis Ross and Richard Haas, preferred a gradual approach to the problem.[25] They were more interested in the dissolution of the Soviet Union and the challenges in the unipolar moment offered to America.

However on March 6, 1991, Bush addressed Congress and declared that a comprehensive peace should be reached through "the land for peace" formula. In a Middle East where the Arab-Israeli conflict ceased, Israel's security as well as Palestinian's legitimate rights would be recognized.[26] It seemed that a comprehensive peacemaking process was back on the agenda.

President Bush's speech was demonstrative of the fact that the U.S. administration was after a wholesale settlement of the conflict. As a consequence, Secretary of State James Baker flew to the Middle East and tried to convince the parties for a peace conference. The Israelis were particularly distant toward the UN or European participation in the conference. Baker pushed all parties hard to to attend the conference.[27] It was only after the defeat of Iraq in the Gulf War and its withdrawal from Kuwait that America was able to return its attention to the peace process. In fact, there was a linkage between the Palestine dispute and all other conflicts in the region—real or imagined. In other words, many people, from Saddam Hussein to Osama bin Laden, have presented the grievance of the Palestinians as an excuse for their aggressive behavior manifested in the occupation of Iraq and the attack on the World Trade Center and the Pentagon on September 11, 2001.

Hence, the U.S. initiated the convening of a peace conference in Spain. The Madrid Peace Conference was held in October 1991 to find a solution to the dispute between Arabs and Israelis. The dissolution of the Soviet Union was imminent at this point in history. This situation together with America's proven power in the Gulf War and Israel's unwillingness to continue to deal with the Palestinian *intifada*, which had been continuing since 1987, were all contributing factors to the beginning of this conference.[28]

The co-chairmen were President Bush and Soviet leader Gorbachov. Among the attendees were Israel, Syria, Lebanon, and a Jordanian-Palestinian delegation. European Community participated in these talks together with an additional thirty countries, which included the U.S., Russia, China, Japan, and India. Bilateral and multilateral talks were held between the Arabs and Israelis as a result of the Madrid Peace Conference. The EC was feeling that it was not given proper representation in both bilateral and multilateral talks. As a response to European complaints, Israel facilitated increased European involvement in the Committee for Arms Control.[29]

There was no clear achievement from the conference, but a willingness to continue the negotiations was displayed. The talks continued in different venues—first in Washington, then in Rome and afterwards in Moscow.[30]

After ten rounds of the Madrid peace talks from 1991 to 1993, a secret channel was pursued between Palestinians and Israelis. Shimon Peres was the first to articulate the Gaza-first approach in 1980. But as secret talks were underway in Norway, the Israeli government also offered the small West Bank town of Jericho, in addition to Gaza, so as to alleviate the feeling among Palestinian negotiators that Gaza would amount to Gaza only. In other words, to prove the Israeli government's willingness to evacuate some or most parts of the West Bank, the Jericho sweetener was offered to the Palestinians. Egyptians were particularly helpful throughout these negotiations.[31]

In early 1993 in Oslo, Norway, between Israeli academics Yair Hirschfeld and Ron Pundak, and high level PLO officials including Ahmed Qurei (Abu Ala) and Hassan Asfour, secret talks began. The groundwork for the secret talks were laid in 1992 between Israeli deputy foreign minister Yossi Beilin and Tarje Larsen, the head of FAFO, a peace research institute in Norway. They initiated the talks, which started between the above-mentioned individuals on January 20. The major difference between the official and secret negotiations was that the PLO was officially represented in the latter. That is why Arafat was more willing to compromise in the secret negotiations.[32]

Uri Savir, the director general of the Israeli Foreign Ministry, met Ahmed Qurei in Oslo, after first stopping in Paris and pretending never to have left the city. Hence, the secret talks started to have an official character, because besides the two independent scholars, now there was a high ranking official from the Israeli Foreign Ministry. They were joined with the two Israeli scholars, Hirschfeld and Pundak and Asfour who was a former PFLP member and the advisor of Mahmud Abbas. The Israelis were offering autonomy for Gaza and making it clear there could be no Palestinian administration in Jerusalem in the future as that city was central for Jewish national identity. Upon the orders of Arafat, the Palestinian delegation also demanded and received Jericho in the autonomy plan.[33] Talks continued until August 1993 and they were particularly intense in July, which culminated in the initialling of a draft agreement on August 20, 1993 under the presence of Israeli Foreign Minister Shimon Peres. The Declaration of Principles on Interim Self-Government entailed a step-by-step approach. According to this declaration, Israel was under obligation to withdraw from the Gaza Strip and Jericho within six months, civil authority was to be transferred to the Palestinian National Authority, which was to rule over these territories.[34]

The members of the peace delegation, including Hanan Ashrawi, were unaware of the Oslo process. Among the top leaders, only Arafat himself, Mahmud Abbas and Ahmed Querei were privy to the secret talks. Ashrawi was disturbed by major issues such as the status of Jerusalem and the condition of settlements in occupied territories to be discussed in the future.[35]

The secret talks, however, bore fruit; and in a ceremony in Washington on September 13, 1993, Yasser Arafat and Yitzhak Rabin signed the Declaration of Principles under American auspices.[36] This was a major psychological, as well as strategic, breakthrough. Two sworn enemies, Rabin and Arafat, were shaking hands in front of the world media.

A particularly interesting development was the donors' conference assembled in Washington two weeks after the signing of the Declaration of Principles on September 13, 1993. Israeli foreign minister, Shimon Peres, was instrumental in assembling this conference due to his desire to help the Palestinian economy, which would neutralize the radical elements in Palestinian society and make the region more open to peaceful measures. Furthermore, during his tenure as Foreign Minister, he initiated draft projects between his country and the PA, Jordan and Syria.[37] This clearly demonstrates the primacy of economics in Peres' world view.

The Palestinian National Authority was established in Gaza and Jericho in 1994. In May 1994, Yitzhak Rabin and Yasser Arafat signed the Gaza-Jericho agreement in Cairo. On May 25, 1995, Israel Defense Forces withdrew from the two territories and, on July 1, Arafat returned to Gaza[38] receiving a hero's welcome.

As a result of the signing of the Oslo II Agreement on September 28, 1995, Palestinian rule was extended to all major Palestinian cities except Hebron. According to this agreement, there were three categories of the territory in the West Bank and Gaza Strip. Area A, consisting of all the main cities except Hebron, would be under civil and security authority of the PA. Area B, which covered 450 villages, was going to be under PA's civilian authority, but was going to be militarily controlled by Israel's security forces. And the main roads and "thinly populated areas" of the Jewish settlements, which would be under Israeli domination, were labelled as Area C. There were going to be three further deployments from occupied territories on the part of Israel.[39] Thus, with the Oslo II Agreement and the January 1996 election, Arafat became the president of PNA and controlled all major Palestinian cities in Gaza and the West Bank with the exception of Hebron. Jerusalem was one of the topics of the final status talks, so it remained under the Israeli sovereignty. However, the fact that the Israeli Parliament, the *Knesset*, passed a Jerusalem law in 1980 declaring the city to be the eternal, indivisible capital of Israel, not only complicated the situation, but was also demonstrative of the fact that there was a consensus in Israel about a united Jerusalem as the capital of the state of Israel. In fact, the city has always remained the crux of the problem.

The period between 1992 and 1996, the golden age of the peace process, ended with the election of Binyamin Netanyahu as the Prime Minister of Israel in 1996. This caused a major setback in the peace process. Netanyahu was making statements implying that he would retain sovereignty over Golan Heights and that he was opposed to the establishment of a Palestinian state. In fact, he was following the line of Revisionist Zionism, opposing the withdrawal from any area of *Eretz Yisrael*, which encompassed present day Israel and the West Bank.[40]

However, despite his ideological orientation, Netanyahu finally decided on January 15, 1997, to withdraw from 80 percent of the city of Hebron; but Israel would be ruling over the Jewish sector in Hebron, as well as the nearby, Kiryat Arba.[41] This was a major compromise for the believers in Greater Israel. This agreement, together with the Wye River Agreement, comprised the two major breakthroughs during the tenure of Netanyahu.

On October 24, 1998, the Wye River agreement was signed in Washington. In a secluded area, at the Wye River Plantation in Maryland, there were talks between Americans, Israelis and Palestinians for nine days. Israel was to withdraw from 13 percent of the West Bank as part of further redeployment and hand these territories over to the Palestinians. This agreement was finally implemented in January 2000.[42]

In 1999, former chief of staff Ehud Barak was reincarnated as the leader of the Labor Party and he won the elections. The casualties were rising in south Lebanon, and Prime Minister Ehud Barak kept his campaign promise to unilaterally withdraw from south Lebanon, which was completed by May 24, 2000.[43]

The final attempt to reach a solution was tried in Camp David on July 11, 2000. President Clinton invited Arafat and Barak for the final solution of the Israeli-Palestinian dispute. Clinton, unlike Carter in the first Camp David talks, was not able to use strong tactics against the parties. In other words, he was much too lenient in expressing that the moment of truth had arrived to make a decision on the Arab-Israeli settlement. According to the agreements, Palestinians were to receive 85 percent of the West Bank. However, while Arafat demanded sovereignty over Jerusalem, Barak refused to give any concessions on the city. So the meeting adjourned on July 25 without accomplishing any breakthroughs.[44]

As a result of the rise and fall of the peace process, the second *intifada* started in September 2000 as a reaction to Israeli Prime Minister Ariel Sharon's visit to the al-Aqsa compound, known as the Temple Mount for the Jews. By the spring of 2002, Israel reoccupied most of the West Bank and as a consequence Arafat was kept isolated to his headquarters in Ramallah.[45]

There was another effort to resuscitate the peace process. Once again, it was an American initiative supported by the European nations and a number of other important actors in the world. American Secretary of State, Colin Powell, preferred diplomacy over military force, so he initiated the establishment of the Quartet, comprised of the U.S., Russia, UN, and the EU. As proposed by Bush in his June 2002 speech, forming a Palestinian State alongside Israel was discussed. A roadmap was prepared by the Quartet in which a two state solution, cessation of hostilities and the prevention of any return to the situation before September 28, 2000—the start of the second *intifada*—were deemed necessary. After the restoration of a ceasefire, an international conference was going to be held and a Palestinian state was going to be created. Ariel Sharon, the former hardliner, accepted the plan by saying that three and a half million Palestinians cannot be ruled indefinitely.[46]

Nevertheless, these efforts to solve the Israeli-Palestinian dispute also came to naught, as this plan was not implemented either. The death of the Palestinian leader in November 2004, election of Mahmud Abbas as the president of the PNA in January 2005, and Israel's unilateral withdrawal from the Gaza Strip in the fall of 2005, brought hope that the peace process could be re-started. However, the victory of Hamas in the January 2006 election isolated the PNA from the international community. It remains to be seen whether the dispute between Hamas and Fatah could be ended in conciliation and whether Hamas will recognize Israel and become a viable partner in the peace process.

There could be two alternatives in approaching the peace process. One could think of a gradual, step-by-step approach of the Oslo process or the problem could be addressed in a peace conference like the one held in Madrid in 1991.

Yitzhak Rabin always wanted the incrementalist approach when it came to peacemaking with the Arabs. This was the case in the 1970s as well as in the 1990s. He was not interested in comprehensive solutions to the dispute.[47]

One of the architects of the Camp David Accord, William Quandt, on the other hand, believes that America should play a major role in the peacemaking efforts. However, instead of "incrementalism," there needs to be an overall settlement of the conflict. While American involvement is the key in the peace process, the U.S. should pursue a more balanced approach between the Arabs and Israelis, which means jettisoning the pro-Israeli stance of American foreign policy. In this regard, moderate Arab states should be included in the Quartet and a Marshall Plan for the Middle East should be initiated.[48]

It is hard to determine which approach is better than the other. From 1993 onward, the gradual approach seemed to make sense. However, as time passed, it became evident that all major issues, such as Jerusalem, borders and Jewish settlements, were left for the final status talks and that is where the conflict seemed intractable.

In retrospect, the 1990s seem almost surreal. For instance, while members of Likud tried to lobby the American Congress to cut aid to the Palestinians, the Israeli ambassador in Washington talked to the members of Congress to convince them to give aid to the Palestinians.[49] Even though we can doubt whether the gradual approach to peacemaking was or is the right method to address the Arab-Israeli issue, this period of peacemaking attempts still remains as a golden age in Israeli-Palestinian relations, some of whose elements should be emulated for the resolution of the Arab-Israeli conflict.

Europe and the Middle East: Former Masters, Current Partners

European involvement in the Middle East peace process has not been very effective at all. With the establishment of the EEC, European member states, former colonial countries, tried to follow a more peaceful and stabilizing role in the region. However, even though they seemed to have somehow subsided, Arab countries continued to be suspicious toward Europeans and, in their judgement, the U.S. took the place of the British and the French is seen as a neo-colonial power.

In the aftermath of the World War II, especially after the 1956 Suez War, European, specifically British and French domination in the Middle East, came to an end. In fact, the two superpowers, the U.S. and the USSR, replaced the European powers in the Middle East. In fact, there have been historic ties between Europe and the Middle East. Actually, Europe's dependence on Middle Eastern oil only increased the strategic significance of the region to the Europeans. On the other hand, Europe was also dependent on the U.S. for its security.[50]

In sum, European supremacy in world affairs seemed to have passed its peak after WWII, particularly after the 1956 Suez War. As a reaction to this situation, Europeans tried to challenge the superpower monopoly in regional and global affairs. For instance, French Foreign Minister Michel Jobert, in one of his speeches given to the French National Assembly, stated that Europe was humiliated in the 1973 oil embargo crisis due to its lack of influence. Similarly, German Chancellor, Willy Brandt, called for a more active role for Europe in world politics by creating a more equal partnership in Alliance politics, namely between the U.S. and Europe. The 1973 crisis showed that the U.S. was no longer the guarantor of the free flow of oil from the Middle East to Europe, and hence, EPC was developed as an independent policy mechanism for the EEC.[51]

So far, European foreign policy proved to be inefficient during major Middle Eastern crises. For instance, during the 1967 six-day war, there was no European foreign policy cooperation. France, Britain and Italy took a pro-Arab stance, whereas Germany and the Netherlands were mainly pro-Israeli.[52] Due to the lack of a pan-European interest, we see this pattern of divergence in foreign policy matters throughout the EEC/EC/EU history.

In the December 1969 Hague summit, the European Political Cooperation (EPC) was established. It was stated that political unity of European countries was the aim of the EPC mechanism. Henceforth, the EC was to act as an independent actor by asserting the European identity common to all the people of the Community. The EPC was to be initiated with a report to be prepared a year later. Among the objectives of the Luxembourg report of 1970, one of the most ambitious EC statements prepared by Etienne Davignon, the creation of a united Europe and consultation on foreign policy decisions among member states in order to create a political union within the EC were included.[53] The first EPC meeting was held in November 1970 in Munich and the second one was held in 1971 in Paris. During the latter United Nations Security Council Resolution 242 was approved and the EEC expressed its willingness to contribute to the economic stability of the Middle East.[54] These were serious efforts to transform the EC into an influential player in the larger world scene; yet as this narrative will make it evident, strong policy coordination was never achieved among the European nations.

European engagement with Israeli territorial occupations can be seen in the Schuman document of May 13, 1971, which called Israel to withdraw from the occupied territories and accept internationalization of Jerusalem. Despite the dissatisfaction of Germany and the Netherlands with the pro-Arab tone of this document, these decisions were still made.[55]

The 1973 oil embargo imposed by the Arab states against these states, which were deemed to be unfriendly toward the Arabs, constituted a serious threat for Europe accessing the Middle East oil. From that time onward, Europe followed a more pro-Arab policy, which was immediately manifested in the November 6, 1973 EPC declaration. In this declaration, Israel was called to withdraw from the territories occupied in the 1967 six-day war, while at the same time, the sovereignty of all states in the region was reaffirmed. Last, the legitimate rights of the Palestinians were recognized,[56] which included the right to statehood, even though this point was not explicitly stated.

The November 6th declaration also indicated that peace in the Middle East could only be reached with resolutions 242 and 338 adopted by the UN Security Council in 1967 and 1973, respectively. As a result of this pro-Arab stance, the Organization of Arab Petroleum Exporting Countries (OAPEC) discontinued the 5 percent oil cutback against European countries.[57] In other words, European nations were rewarded by the Arabs for having adopted a pro-Arab policy. For Israelis, on the other hand, Europeans seemed as untrustworthy pragmatists who are ready to compromise the security of the state of Israel, if that served European interests.

The pro-Arab attitude of the Europeans can be attributed to a multiplicity of factors. First, the Arabs gained increased strength as a consequence of the oil tool they have diligently utilized in the 1973 oil embargo incident. Their need for Arab oil obliged the Europeans to court Arabs in their political causes, especially in the Palestinian dispute. Furthermore, with the rise of the radical left in the aftermath of the events of 1968, sympathy toward the Palestinians rose exponentially, as the PLO was perceived by the European left as part of the national liberation movements. This portrayal of the Palestinians as the underdog, together with the assertiveness of the Arab states toward this particular issue, made the Europeans more sympathetic toward the Arab cause. In other words, there were both material and ideational aspects of the European turning toward the Arabs.

One should also note that the Jews were no longer recognized as victims, but were rather seen as the oppressors in a world where decolonization, human rights and democracy were the mantra of the intellectuals. Palestinians gained a moral high ground, even though they resorted to terrorism against civilian targets.

Following the Algiers Summit of Arab countries in December 1973, on December 14 and 15, 1973, the EEC summit convened in the Danish city of Copenhagen. Foreign ministers of several Arab nations also attended this summit. So as a consequence, this summit was quite an important step in the start of the Euro-Arab dialog, which France had been advocating for some time. The EC was especially interested in negotiating with the oil producers to ameliorate the problematic situation of European energy needs.[58]

In its March 1974 summit, the EC decided to initiate the Euro-Arab dialog, which included the nine EEC countries plus 20 Arab League members. The Americans, who were not consulted, were opposed to this initiative, as they believed the Arabs wanted to politicize the forum. Rather, the U.S. wanted to establish a consumers' front to make a linkage between security and energy. The EC wanted the Euro-Arab dialog to address only economic and technical issues, but in fact it was "handled through the EPC," which was a political mechanism. Hence this constituted a clear contradiction.[59]

The Involvement of the European Union in the Middle East Peace Process

The Palestinian conflict was named as the central problem of the Arab-Israeli question in the Euro-Arab dialogue summit of December 1978 held in the Syrian capital, Damascus. What was symbolic about this meeting was that the EC was taking the side of the Arab rejectionist camp instead of Egypt, which was engaged in a peace process with Israel. In the March 1979 EPC declaration, the EC insisted on a comprehensive solution to the Middle East conflict and affirmed that a homeland was essential for a just solution to the Palestinian problem. And from this date until 1983, since Egypt was expelled from the Arab League, the Euro Arab Dialogue (EAD) was suspended.[60] At this stage, the majority of Arab states were reluctant to join the Egyptian bandwagon, and consequently, the Middle East peacemaking efforts. Up until the 1990s, Egypt remained the only Arab state to have made peace with the Jewish state.

As mentioned above, the EC procedures, like an international peace conference, might have been a more correct approach, but the Arabs were using the EAD as leverage against Israel not to make peace with this country. Meanwhile, Europe was not particularly helpful in furthering the Camp David Accords.

One of the most important declarations by the European Community on Middle Eastern affairs was the Venice Declaration. The European Council's Venice Declaration of June 13, 1980, urged all interested parties in the Middle East Conflict to find "a comprehensive solution to the Israeli-Arab conflict."[61] It should be reiterated that the EC was not very enthusiastic about the step-by-step approach of the Camp David and preferred an overall resolution to the Arab-Israeli dispute.

The Venice Declaration affirmed the security and the right of existence of all the states in the region, specifically naming Israel, so that the peace in the Middle East could be built upon the recognition of the state of Israel as a normal state. On the other hand, the Declaration also mentioned the legitimate rights of the Palestinian people. The most important one among these rights is, unquestionably, the right of self-determination. The Palestinians were to exercise their right of self-determination for a just solution for the Palestinian issue. The Venice Declaration was critical of United Nations Security Council Resolution 242 (without specifically mentioning 242), which had characterized the Palestinian problem as a refugee problem. Instead "a just solution must finally be found to the Palestinian problem which is not simply one of refugees."[62] The last phrase in particular demonstrates the EC's willingness to play a more active role in world affairs and shows that the Community has a different understanding of the Arab-Israeli Conflict than the United Nations or the U.S. Needless to say, the Europeans were openly critical of the 242.

The Palestinian Liberation Organization was enumerated among the parties of the conflict and the organization was expected to take part in the peace process negotiations[63] between the Arabs and Israelis.

The Nine, referring to the 9 members of the EC at the time, were also very sensitive toward the holy city of Jerusalem, whose status should remain unaltered in their judgment.⁶⁴ As a conclusion, the EC requested that Israel withdraw from all the territories it occupied in the 1967 six-day war. Furthermore, the EC characterized the Jewish settlements in the occupied territories, namely East Jerusalem, the West Bank, Golan Heights, and Gaza as obstacles to peace and contrary to international law.⁶⁵ So, the European Community was calling upon Israel to cease building any more settlements in the occupied territories and dismantling of most or all of them. Of course, the extent of the withdrawal was up to the Palestinians and Syrians, as the Palestinians had claims on East Jerusalem, the West Bank and Gaza, and the Syrians had claims on Golan Heights.

In sum, a comprehensive solution was envisaged for the Palestinian question, which was not commensurate with American, Egyptian and Israeli methods. At this point, the latter were preferring a step-by-step approach, tackling each issue separately and then moving on to the next issue. As was to be seen in the 1990s, this piecemeal approach seemed to have worked initially. However, as the big issues—such as Palestinian statehood, Jerusalem, settlements and final borders—were postponed for the final status talks, it became evident that when these issues were raised, they were actually the crux of the Israeli-Palestinian conflict, which are very hard to solve.

For the Likud government that was in power in Israel at the time and for most of mainstream Israelis, these calls were an anathema. The call for negotiations with the PLO was especially unacceptable, since it was perceived by the majority of Israelis as a terrorist organization. In fact, the PLO had not renounced terrorism nor accepted the state of Israel, so it was logical for Israel not to negotiate with an organization that did not recognize it. Hence, once the negotiations started, the PLO had to recognize Israel; otherwise it would have defied the logic to negotiate. However, to cut a long story short, Israeli political parties, especially the right wing party, Likud, under the leadership of Menachem Begin who was also the Prime Minister of the state of Israel, were not ready to negotiate with the Palestinians. By making peace with Egypt, the largest Arab country in the region, they had made their western front safe. So, they were in a very strong position vis-à-vis the Arab world.

As a result of all these considerations, Israel characterized the Venice Declaration as a "Munich surrender," which was the "second in their generation." By this, Israel tried to show that it knew how to defend itself.⁶⁶

The PLO, on the other hand, was expecting much more from the Europeans, hence, it was extremely disappointed. They were critical of the Venice declaration, because it did not recognize the PLO as the sole legitimate representative of the Palestinian people. They were also expecting the EC to reject 242⁶⁷ for its lack of reference to Palestinian problems, except that of the refugee issue.

Egypt welcomed the Venice Declaration, since the autonomy talks with Israelis for the West Bank and Gaza Strip were at a stalemate.[68] In fact, Israeli Prime Minister Menachem Begin was never interested in the autonomy talks with the Palestinians. He was more interested in getting the largest Arab state out of the way through a peace treaty, which he managed quite successfully.

It should be added that throughout the 1970s, the PLO gained larger legitimacy in European countries. For instance, in 1974, the PLO opened a liaison and information office in Paris and it also participated in the Euro-Arab dialog as part of the Arab League delegation. At the June 30, 1977 London summit, European countries called for the establishment of a homeland for the Palestinian people, for their legitimate rights to be recognized by Israel, and for the Arabs to recognize Israel's right to live in peace and security. Negotiations were offered for a just and lasting peace between the Arabs and Israelis to resolve their conflict. Israel rejected this statement[69] as it did not address Israeli security matters and they regarded negotiating with the PLO as an abomination during that time.

In the 1980s, the special relationship between America and Britain was reinforced because of the electoral victories of Ronald Reagan in the U.S. and Margaret Thatcher in the UK. In 1980, the EC sent Gaston Thorn as part of a contact mission to visit the Middle East, where he met the PLO Chief Yasser Arafat and Egyptian Foreign Minister Boutros Ghali. Thatcher was not supportive of new European initiatives in the Middle East, a state of affairs very much in line with the U.S. administration. Instead, she was emphasizing the special relationship between America and Great Britain, which entailed close cooperation between the two English-speaking countries. Even though Egypt was supportive of European openings, which was demonstrated by the speech of the Egyptian President Anwar Sadat at the European Parliament during which he called for mutual recognition between Israel and the PLO, the lack of British cooperation with its fellow members in the EC, made it apparent that the EC was not a strong international actor. Similarly, the French President perceived the Venice Declaration as leaning too much to the Arab side. He was sensitive to the needs of the Israelis.[70] With their attempts, France, Britain and other major European countries, were actually pursuing their own national policies rather than common European policies. Mitterrand wanted Egypt to return to the Arab camp from which it was ostracized after the Camp David Accords and to sign the Israel-Egypt peace treaty. The French Foreign Minister Cheysson was even clearer in his call for the establishment of a Palestinian state to solve the Palestinian question.[71]

France was trying to play an active and even-handed role in the region. Mitterand called for the establishment of a Palestinian state while becoming the first French president to visit Israel in March 1982. At the *Knesset*, he reiterated that a Palestinian state should be established in order to have peace in the region. Privately, he was telling the Israeli leaders that European initiatives were now over. Here, once again, we can observe that France was pursuing a national, not a European, foreign policy.[72] Because of these deficiencies, among the external powers, it was the Americans who mattered most in issues of war and peace in the Middle East.

The U.S. wanted European participation in the Multinational Force (MFO) to be deployed in the Sinai Peninsula between Egypt and Israel. So in 1981, American Secretary of State, Alexander Haig, approached the British Foreign Secretary, Lord Carrington. Carrington was first reluctant and European participation was not guaranteed until March 1982 when the MFO was finally deployed. The major problem about European involvement was that they wanted clarifications stating that they were sending troops based on their 1980 Venice Declaration. Israeli statesmen, including the Prime Minister, Menachem Begin, and the former Foreign Minister, Abba Eban, were critical about the European position and were reluctant to allow European participation particularly because, as Eban said, Europe ceased to be a viable partner in the peacemaking process. Still, Israeli government allowed European participation[73] and, as a result, there was an active participation on the part of EC members Britain, France, Italy and Holland in the Multinational Force. Contribution of peacekeepers to MFO, in a way, was surrender to the Camp David process. The fact of the matter was that there was no UN decision on this deployment of peacekeepers.[74]

In May 1981, Israeli Prime Minister Menachem Begin made a speech in which he swore that he would not abandon the West Bank, the Gaza Strip, and Golan Heights. This constituted a clear violation of the Camp David Accords, which provided self-rule for the Palestinians.[75] The Prime Minister was willing to make peace with Egypt only and to hold onto to the above-mentioned territories which, in his judgment, constituted the Biblical Land of Israel.

We can observe a positive European contribution in the crisis over Lebanon. In the aftermath of Israel's invasion of Lebanon in 1982, the EC called upon Israel to withdraw from Lebanon and threatened sanctions should Israel decide otherwise. This statement, however, was not very effective; nevertheless, the community supported the Habib plan for the evacuation of the PLO leadership from Lebanon. In fact, 800 American troops were supplemented by 800 French and 400 Italian soldiers.[76]

Israel was totally against any European involvement in the peace process. Even though occasionally it gave verbal support to certain European initiatives, such as the February 23, 1987 Brussels summit's call for a peace conference for the resolution of the Middle East conflict,[77] this proves to be only an exception. To this day, Israel has followed a unilateral approach toward Palestinians. Israel seemingly has more confidence in Americans, but still as a fact of the Zionist project, Israelis do not trust anyone but themselves, as they believe they can no longer allow any other state or international organization to make a decision over the fate of the Jews.

The Palestinian National Authority, on the other hand, expects a more active policy from the EU as far as the peace process is concerned.[78] The Palestinian spokesperson, Hanan Ashrawi, and the Palestinian leadership believed that Europe was more even-handed than the U.S., which was manifested in the Venice Declaration, and hoped that Europe could counterbalance "the pro-Israeli bias of the U.S. policy." However, she admits that due to the U.S. pressure, Europeans played a low-profile role, mainly succumbing to American policy initiatives.[79]

The EU pays special consideration to the resolution of the Arab-Israeli conflict. In fact "the achievement of lasting peace in the Middle East is a central aim of the EU." The Union envisages a two-state solution that would include Israel and a Palestinian state living in a peaceful coexistence in conformity with UN resolutions 242, 338 and 1402. The Europeans also believe that a "fair solution to the complex issue of Jerusalem" and a just and realistic solution should be found to the Palestinian refugees.[80]

About the situation in the Middle East, the EU calls for a freeze to the settlement activity of the Israelis in the occupied territories and believes that extra-judicial killings and collective punishments imposed on the Palestinians should cease. On the other hand, the EU condemns terrorism and includes Hamas and Islamic Jihad in its list of terrorist organizations.[81]

As part of its policy of regional cooperation, the EU tried to create a Mediterranean identity, but the Arab-Israeli conflict prevented the establishment of such an eventuality. The Euro-Mediterranean Partnership started with the 1995 Barcelona Conference between the EU and its Mediterranean neighbors, including Israel, Maghrab countries, Egypt, Jordan, the Palestinian Authority, Lebanon, Syria, Cyprus, Malta, and Turkey. Cyprus and Malta became members of the EU in 2004. In the Barcelona Declaration, a Euro-Mediterranean area of peace and stability established around the principles of human rights and democracy was envisaged and a free trade area was planned to be built by 2010. In this Euro-Mediterranean Partnership, there are currently 25 EU members and 12 Mediterranean partners.[82]

In relation to the EU-Israel relations, we must note that Israel was interested in an associate membership in the EEC ever since the 1960s. Interestingly, Germany was supportive of Israel's quest for membership, since a new relationship was emerging between Germany and Israel. France and Italy, however, were particularly reluctant about Israel's membership in the EEC because, among their other concerns, they also wanted to protect their agricultural products from Israeli competition. The reason Israel wanted to join the EEC was that, because of the common tariff between the EEC members as well as associate members such as Greece, Turkey and Spain, Israel was at a disadvantageous situation.[83]

In 2000, Israel finally obtained associate membership status in the EU. The Association Agreement had already been signed in 1995 in Brussels, and came into force five years later. This agreement superseded the 1975 Cooperation Agreement. According to this agreement, there would be a phased reduction of tariffs between the two parties.[84]

Trade between Israel and the EU is substantial, amounting to over 15 billion euros, which makes the EU Israel's "major trading partner." While exports to the EU constitute 33 percent of all Israel's exports, 40 percent of its imports are from the EU. The EU also pays between 5 and 10 million euros per year to support the Middle East peace process through its EU Partnership for Peace Program, in which the EU funds civil society initiatives.[85]

In April 2005, the EU also initiated the European Neighborhood Policy Action Plan with Israel and established 10 sub-committees to coordinate the details of the Action Plan. Political dialogue that entailed human rights dialogue, discussions about racism and anti-Semitism, are among the elements of cooperation between the EU and Israel. Topics like the Middle East peace process, non-proliferation of weapons and counter-terrorism, were also included for further consideration.

The EU has a long history of providing economic aid to the Palestinians, which dates back to 1971 when the EC helped the UN Relief and Works Agency for Palestinian Refugees in the Near East (UNRWA) and in 2004, the Palestinian Authority became part of the European Neighborhood Process. In 2005, the European Commission adopted a Communication: *EU-Palestinian cooperation beyond disengagement-toward a two state solution.* There were a number of recommendations and statements about the PA, among which included political viability and economic viability and ways to reach them. A special emphasis was given on the rule of law, protection of human rights and encouraging investment in the Palestinian territories.[86]

Ever since Hamas formed the government in March 2006, EU funds were channelled through the Temporary International Mechanism (TIM), so as to avoid giving aid to a Hamas-led Palestinian government. Despite this fact, the European aid to Palestinians increased in 2006 when compared to 2005.[87]

The EU showed interest in Palestinian affairs by also sending election observers for both the Palestinian presidential elections in January 2005 and the parliamentary elections in January 2006. However, as a result of the latter election in which Hamas obtained most of the seats in the Palestinian Legislative Council and hence formed the government, the EU stopped all political contacts with the PNA and terminated its economic aid, which was about 500 million euros.[88] The "long-term objective" of the EU assistance was to support the "creation of an independent democratic Palestinian state." In this vein, certain conditions were attached to the financial aid such as reforming "PA's public finances." The EU also provided training for

Palestinian judges and prosecutors and helped in the establishment of the Central Election Commission in October 2002.[89]

The two-state solution was re-emphasized at some of the recent summits. The Berlin Declaration of March 24, 1999 pointed out that a viable Palestinian state could ensure Israel's security. The Seville Declaration of June 22, 2002 reiterated the need for a democratic, viable Palestine within the 1967 borders, albeit with minor revisions living side-by-side with Israel for the emergence of a peaceful Middle East.[90]

However, European division resurfaced in the 2003 Gulf War when Britain, Spain and Italy gave support to the American War effort in Iraq, while France and Germany remained opposed to it. Hence, the EU was divided once again over foreign policy issues.

Another example of division within Europe over foreign policy priorities was in November 2006, when Spain, France and Italy prepared a peace initiative without consulting Britain. At the Spanish city of Girona, situated on the French border, Spanish Prime Minister, Jose Luis Zapatero, met with the French President, Jacques Chirac, and unveiled the peace initiative, which included the establishment of a national unity government in Palestine, the exchange of prisoners between Israel and PNA, the start of negotiations between Israeli Prime Minister, Ehud Olmert and Palestinian President, Mahmud Abbas, and the deployment of an international mission to Gaza to monitor the ceasefire. Britain and the three EU countries who prepared this initiative were at loggerheads regarding a UN Security Council resolution condemning the Israeli attack in Gaza, which resulted in the deaths of eighteen Palestinians. France voted for the resolution, but Britain abstained. The resolution was vetoed by the U.S.[91] These two incidents, once again, demonstrate the difficulties in pursuing a single European foreign policy in light of the conflicts in the Middle East and elsewhere in the world. Britain values its special relationship with the U.S. sometimes much more than its relations with the EU.

Having said that, however, Europe is still a magnet for people around the world. So, it still possesses significant amounts of soft power, defined as the "ability to get what you want through attraction," an ability that emanates from a country's culture, ideals and policies.[92] As an island of peace, prosperity and liberty, Europe is still a beacon for many people.

The Israeli Foreign Minister, Shimon Peres, for example, being one of the architects of the Oslo peace process that culminated in the 1993 Declaration of Principles and the mutual recognition between Israel and the PLO, has considered the EC as a model for the Middle East. According to him, economic cooperation between Middle Eastern countries could have the spill over effect into political problems,[93] just like the gradual transformation of the European Coal and Steel Community into the EEC and later to the EC and finally to the EU. Many European leaders, including the French President, Jacques Chirac; German Chancellor, Helmut Kohl; and the EC Commissioner, Jacques Delors were supportive of this modelling.[94] Peres envisaged creating a common market and institutions based on the EC model. This endeavor also necessitated democratization of the countries in the region, since this would rule out the possibility of war. This is because, as democratic peace theory projects, democratic countries do not fight each other; rather they solve their problems through mutual negotiations. Peres thought that such a regime change would lead to stability in the Middle East.[95] He actually met Jean Monnet in the 1950s and very much appreciated his ideas. The region needs a courageous approach based on Monnet to overcome war and poverty. The New Middle East would be found on cooperation projects on desalination of water, desert management, agriculture, and tourism. Turkey's peace pipeline proposal is also taken very seriously by Peres, as this plan purports to transfer water from Turkey to the Arab countries and Israel. As part of this initiative, disarmament would play a key role. All these endeavors would culminate in the signing of a "strategic pact" between Arabs and Israelis.[96] And, as a solution to the Palestinian problem and the question of its statehood, there could be a Jordanian-Palestinian confederation in political affairs on one hand, and a Jordanian-Palestinian-Israeli Benelux style economic arrangement, on the other.[97]

Peres believed that economic power has greater significance than military power. Hence, concepts such as strategic depth and holding onto territories were no longer held at this time due to the existence of long range missiles. He talked with EC officials, including Jacques Delors, former Dutch Foreign Minister, Hans van den Broek and also the French President, Mitterrand, so they would provide economic aid to the Middle East as a whole.[98] Syrian President, Hafiz al-Asad, on the other hand, perceived the New Middle East Concept as a plot to eradicate Arabism[99] in the Middle East and, hence, as a tool for Israeli expansionism.

So, it follows that the EU project still offers, or at least offered in the 1990s, for the people of the Middle East, and mostly to intellectuals of the region, a model of democracy and social state equipped with all necessary institutions they can emulate. However, realpolitik calculations, as well as national rivalries, seem to have restricted the EU from playing a more active role in the Middle East peace process. While European soft power cannot be denied, American hard power and also the mutual suspicions between Israelis and Arabs had the upper hand in preventing the successful completion of the peace process.

Conclusion

This article addressed the nature of the European Union's involvement in the Middle East peace process. While the EU has tried to play the role of the facilitator by giving foreign aid to the Palestinians and supporting the diplomatic initiatives of the U.S., the Europeans, however, lacked the political credibility among Israelis due to their past and present support of the Palestinians. Furthermore, the Israelis have always been suspicious of Europeans due to their complicity in the Holocaust. These factors diminished the leverage of the EU vis-à-vis the Middle East peace process.

Israelis characterized Europeans as taking a neutral stance in their hour of need. Criticisms of Europeans related to the unbalanced use of arms of Israel during the July 2006 war in Lebanon exacerbated their belief of the Europeans being no less than trustworthy states.[100] According to the Israeli understanding of this war, Hizbullah had kidnapped two Israeli soldiers and they were only trying to rescue them, whereas, the EU saw an infringement upon Lebanese territorial integrity by the Israelis. However, in all fairness, a number of EU members, including France and Germany, participated in the UNIFIL, which aimed at demilitarizing the Lebanese-Israeli border from non-Lebanese army elements, meaning the Hizbullah. So, the European contribution to peace efforts cannot be ruled out so easily.

Not all was sour in Israeli-European relations. In September 2006, a lobby organization, European Friends of Israel, among members of the Europeans' parliamentarians was established to improve relations between the two polities.[101] However, it should be evident that while economic relations between the EU and Israel are satisfactory, there is still a feeling of distrust in political arenas.

Of course, lack of influence in the Middle East peace process cannot be limited to Israel's reluctance. More importantly, the EU's lack of a strong foreign policy-making body and the fact that the Union does not act in unison are all important factors in its weakness to influence the affairs in the Middle East.

The U.S. is the only power which can put decisive pressure on the Jewish state to reach a comprehensive solution to the Palestine problem. More importantly, however, it is the parties themselves, Israelis and Palestinians, who should pass the ideological threshold and make the painful sacrifices about land and honor. Only then can a true peace be established in the Middle East.

---

[1] Niall Ferguson, *Colossus: The Rise and Fall of the American Empire* (London: Penguin, 2004), p. 298.
[2] John McCormick, *Understanding the European Union* (New York: Palgrave, 1999), pp. 3-5, 9.
[3] Ibid., p. 79.
[4] Karen Smith, *European Union Foreign Policy in a Changing World* (Cambridge: Polity, 2003), p. 2.
[5] Smith, European Union, pp. 3, 5.
[6] Ibid., p. 11.
[7] McCormick, Understanding the European Union, p. 79.

[8] Ibid., pp. 205-207 and Smith, European Union, p. 30. Another example of European weakness and American power in resolving international crises was the 1996 Imia/Kardak crisis between Turkey and Greece over an Aegean island during which the two countries came to the brink of war. American intervention was instrumental in solving the problem between the two NATO allies. See McCormick, Understanding the European Union, p. 207.
[9] Smith, *European Union*, p. 41.
[10] Ibid., p. 12.
[11] Mancur Olson, *The Logic of Collective Action: Public Goods and the Theory of groups* (Cambridge, Massachusetts: Harvard University Press, 1971), pp. 2, 44, 126.
[12] Smith, European Union, pp. 15, 20.
[13] Ibid., p. 199.
[14] Jimmy Carter, The *Blood of Abraham: Insights into the Middle East* (Boston: Houghton, 1985), p. 16.
[15] United Nations Security Council Resolution 242, November 22, 1967 in Carter, p. 219.
[16] Itamar Rabinovich, *Waging Peace: Israel and the Arabs at the End of the Century* (New York: FSG, 1999), pp. 21-22.
[17] Ibid., pp. 24-25. Also see William Quandt, *Peace Process: American Diplomacy and the Arab-Israeli Conflict since 1967*.(Washington: Brookings Institution Press, 2005), p. 184.
[18] Quandt, pp. 197-199.
[19] The Egyptian-Israeli Peace Treaty. March 26, 1979.
[20] Ibid.
[21] Panayiotis Ifestos, *European Political Cooperation: Towards a framework of Supranational Diplomacy?* (Aldeshot: Avebury, 1987), p. 444.
[22] Ibid., pp. 454-455.
[23] Ibid., pp. 457-458.
[24] Ibid., p. 462.
[25] Quandt, Peace Progress, pp. 293-294.
[26] Ibid., p. 306.
[27] Ibid.
[28] Rabinovitch, Waging, pp. 34-36.
[29] Shimon Peres, *The New Middle East* (New York: Henry Holt, 1993), pp. 10-11. Quandt, p. 310.
[30] Quandt, Peace Process, pp. 311-312.
[31] Peres, The New Middle East, pp. 20-23.
[32] Uri Savir,. *The Process: 1,1000 Days that changed the Middle East* (New York: Vintage, 1998), pp. 3-4.
[33] Ibid., pp. 9-19. It is not clear whether it was the Israelis or Palestinians who offered/demanded Jericho first.
[34] Ibid., pp. 57, 59.
[35] Hanan Ashrawi, This Side of Peace (New York: Touchstone, 1995), pp. 258, 260.
[36] Dennis Ross, *The Missing Peace.* (New York: FSG, 2005), pp. 119-121.
[37] Rabinovich, pp. 185-188.
[38] Savir, The Process, pp. 139-140.
[39] Rabinovich, Waging Peace, pp. 66-67.
[40] Ibid, pp. 26-27, 86, 94-95.

[41] Quandt, Peace Process, p. 346. This was "ideological heresy" for his followers, in Ross, Missing Peace, p. 426.
[42] Ross, pp. 361, 381, 458.
[43] Quandt, Peace Process, p. 364.
[44] Ibid., pp. 365-369.
[45] Ibid., p. 397.
[46] Ibid., p. 400, 402. EU's Special Envoy for the Middle East Peace Process is Marc Otte. See http://ec.europa.eu/comm/external_relations/israel/intro/index.htm
[47] Rabinovich, p. 183.
[48] Quandt, *Peace Process*, pp. x, 417-418, 426-427.
[49] Savir, The Process, p. 205.
[50] Ifestos, European Political, p. 379.
[51] Ibid., pp. 380, 383-384, 418.
[52] Ibid., p. 420.
[53] Ifestos, Panayiotis. *European Political Cooperation: Towards a framework of Supranational Diplomacy?* (Aldeshot: Avebury, 1987), pp. 149-152.
[54] Ibid., pp. 154-155.
[55] Ibid., pp. 420-421.
[56] Ibid., pp. 175-176.
[57] Ibid., pp. 426-428.
[58] Ibid., pp. 429, 431.
[59] Ibid., pp. 217, 432, 435.
[60] Ibid., pp. 437, 446-447 and Smith, p. 75.
[61] Walter Laqueur, and Barry Rubin. *The Israel-Arab Reader: A Documentary History of the Middle East Conflict* (New York: Penguin, 1984), p. 621.
[62] Ibid., pp. 621-622.
[63] Ibid., p. 622.
[64] Ibid.
[65] Ibid.
[66] Ibid., p. 463.
[67] Ibid., pp. 464-465.
[68] Ibid., p. 467.
[69] Ibid., pp. 436, 441-442.
[70] Ibid., pp. 471-475, 480, 485.
[71] Ibid., p. 488.
[72] Ibid., pp. 500-501.
[73] Boutros Boutros-Ghali,. *Egypt's Road to Jerusalem: A Diplomat's Story of the struggle for peace in the Middle East.*(New York: Random House, 1997), pp. 339-341.
[74] Ifestos, European Political, pp. 489, 494.
[75] Carter, Blood of Abraham, p. 45.
[76] Ifestos, pp. 505, 510.
[77] Ifestos, pp. 504, 527-528.
[78] Smith, p. 7.
[79] Hanan Ashrawi, *This Side of Peace* (New York: Touchstone, 1995), pp. 85-86.
[80] http://ec.europa.eu/comm/external_relations/mepp/index.htm
[81] http://ec.europa.eu/comm/external_relations/mepp/index.htm

[82] http://ec.europa.eu/comm/external_relations/israel/intro/index.htm and http://ec.europa.eu/comm/external_relations/gaza/intro/index.htm
[83] Howard Sachar, *A History of Israel: From the Rise of Zionism to our Time* (New York: Alfred Knopf, 1996), pp. 561, 572.
[84] http://ec.europa.eu/comm/external_relations/israel/intro/index.htm
[85] http://ec.europa.eu/comm/external_relations/israel/intro/index.htm
[86] http://ec.europa.eu/comm/external_relations/gaza/intro/index.htm
[87] Muriel Asseburg, , "The EU is wrong on the Palestinians" *Daily Star*, February 26, 2007.
[88] http://ec.europa.eu/comm/external_relations/gaza/intro/index.htm
[89] http://ec.europa.eu/comm/external_relations/gaza/intro/index.htm.My personal experience as an election oberserver for the 2005 presidential elections was that the CEC worked in a professional manner.
[90] http://ec.europa.eu/comm/external_relations/mepp/index.htm
[91] "European states offer Middle East peace plan without UK," *The Guardian*, November 17, 2006.
[92] Joseph Nye, *Soft Power: The means to success in world politics.* (New York: PA, 2004), pp. x, 2.
[93] Peres, The New, p. 11.
[94] Ibid., p. 12.
[95] Ibid., p. 62, 64. For the democratic peace theory see Bruce Russett. *Grasping the Democratic peace.* (Princeton: Princeton University Press, 1993).
[96] Ibid., The New, pp. 71-74, 85, 129.
[97] Ibid., p. 173.
[98] Ibid., pp. 30-31, vvc, 34-35.
[99] Rabinovich, Waging Peace, p. 197.
[100] Manfred Gerstenfeld "Europe's Mindset Toward Israel as Accentuated by the Lebanon War" http://www.jcpa.org/jl/vp547.htm.
[101] http://www.globalresearch.ca/index.php?context=viewArticle&code=20060914&articleId=3228

Chapter 6
The Euro-Mediterranean Partnership: On Good Intentions, Shopping Lists and à la carte Menus*

Zuhal Yeşilyurt-Gündüz

The Euro-Mediterranean Partnership, which was founded in 1995, is the broadest political, security, economic, and social agreement the European Union (EU) has ever signed with the countries situated at the southern shores of the Mediterranean Sea. The Partnership includes three chapters—the Political and Security Chapter, the Economic and Financial Chapter, and the Social, Cultural and Human Chapter—and therefore tries to realize an all-including advancement. The Political and Security Chapter and the Social, Cultural and Human Chapter are especially innovative, as they try to reach far beyond the conservative action line of just "trade and aid" for the Arab countries. Indeed, the Euro-Mediterranean Partnership is full of new ideas and good intentions. Evaluating the Partnership in political, economic, social, and cultural terms, this article tries to reveal whether or not the good intentions depicted in the Partnership are sincere.

The Euro-Mediterranean Partnership

The geographic proximity of Europe to the Middle East and the Mediterranean region enabled the EU to realize sensitive and durable advances to security and socio-economics in the region. The European Community (EC) started its Global Mediterranean Policy in 1972 with trade agreements between the EC and Iraq, Jordan, Lebanon, and Syria, which had a minor role in improving trade and development, and the Euro-Arab-Dialogue after the 1973 Arab oil embargo, which was, however, eclipsed by the Arab-Israeli conflict. After years of incessant endeavor, the European Union finally raised its status from "the 'payer' to the 'player,' i.e. from an observer status (Madrid Conference in 1991) to an equal partner in the so-called Quartet, promoting the Middle East Peace Process,"[1] standing equally next to the U.S., the Russian Federation and the United Nations.

The end of the Cold War ignited enormous geopolitical changes. It brought the division of the continent to an end—Europe was no longer split into the blocks of "East" and "West" anymore, it was now one whole continent. This brought the prospect of Eastern enlargement for the EU. This, at the same time, disturbed the Union's southern neighbours, as they felt more and more left outside the accession and enlargement process. The Mediterranean EU members reinforced the EU's relations with these neighbours, and the EU decided to deal with the complex economic (with per capita income as low as $ 2,000) and demographic (with still high population growth rates) situations of the Southern Mediterranean.[2] The perceived security "threats" stemming from the demographic and political developments of the Southern neighbours can be regarded as the most important factor that triggered the EU to deal with the Southern shore of the Mediterranean. Besides, worldwide trends of further regionalization enabled the EU to understand that an improvement in economic relations with the Mediterranean region was necessary. Moreover, following the Oslo Accords from 1993, it was also hoped that the region would finally find its peace, or at least regional détente. The deepening process of the European Community to the European Union in 1993 and institutional developments led to an improved and widened Common Foreign and Security Policy. Besides, the Mediterranean EU members hoped to balance the Union's future eastward enlargement with its enhanced relations with the South. By improving the situation on the Southern shore of the Mediterranean, the EU also expected to minimize the reasons for terrorism and illegal migration.

Security needs of the Southern Mediterranean countries, however, were different: they felt frightened from Europe's economic, political and military dominance and perceived threats to exclude their countries from EU markets. They hoped for economic and social improvements stemming from closer relations with the EU. In the end, a new demanding cooperation program was initiated, but, although it was called a "Partnership," which naturally should include equality and egalitarianism, it was clearly and undoubtedly dominated by the EU in all fields.[3]

On November 27 and 28, 1995, during her EU Presidency, Spain organized the Barcelona Conference which paved way to the Euro-Mediterranean Partnership, which is also called Euro-Med, EMP or the Barcelona Process, after the name of the city in which the event took place. This Partnership evolved from the Union's wish to reinforce relations with its Mediterranean neighbours in order to minimize sources of volatility in that region and to promote peace, prosperity and democracy. Indeed, the Barcelona Declaration set the objective "to turn the Mediterranean basin into an area of dialogue, exchange and co-operation granting peace, stability and prosperity."[4]

Acknowledging the enduring bond between both coasts of the Mediterranean, the EU and 12 Middle Eastern and North African countries—Algeria, Morocco, Tunisia, Egypt, Palestinian Authority, Israel, Lebanon, Jordan, Syria, and Turkey, as well as Southern Cyprus and Malta, who joined the EU on May 1, 2004—began the innovative Euro-Mediterranean Partnership.[5] It was founded on the values of human rights, peace and prosperity, and aimed to renovate the balance of relations and to support the advancement of the Southern Mediterranean countries. On the political side, it was also hoped that after the Oslo Accords from 1993, Euro-Med would bring about a political setting to integrate Israel with the region and a perspective for the building of the Palestinian state. The Association Agreements between the EU and the Mediterranean partners gave EMP a bilateral dimension, while the regional programs provided a multilateral aspect.

The Euro-Med Partnership is the broadest political, security, economic, and social accord that the EU has ever signed with Arab states. It has a different approach from former EU attempts to accomplish security by coalitions or economic interdependence and eliminates Europe's fixation with economics, as it affirms three baskets, or interconnected aims:[6]

1. The definition of a common area of peace and stability through the reinforcement of political and security dialogue (Political and Security Chapter).
2. The construction of a zone of shared prosperity through an economic and financial partnership and the gradual establishment of a free-trade area (Economic and Financial Chapter).
3. The rapprochement between people through a social, cultural and human partnership aimed at encouraging understanding between cultures and exchanges between civil societies (Social, Cultural and Human Chapter).

The Euro-Mediterranean Partnership revealed a connection between political and economic assistance, and an endorsement of democracy and human rights. Therefore, the partners believed that economic development depended on political stability and socio-economic equality, environmental protection and security. Besides, they assured that poverty reduction as well as internal stability relies on democratic institutions and democratic, pluralist, responsible, and transparent governments. The EU's aims were twofold: it intended to impede developments within its neighbours that could distress its own security and/or wealth and it tried to preserve, even expand, its weight in this region.[7]

With the Euro-Mediterranean Partnership, a new approach to development was embraced with three baskets, which went further than the conventional method of trade and aid. The Political and Security Partnership demanded a political dialogue to play a part for peaceful ending of conflicts, strengthening democracy and building the political environment essential for stable development. The Economic and Financial Partnership intended to generate a Euro-Mediterranean free trade area backed by amplified financial and technical support for capacity building. The Social, Cultural and Human Partnership, on the other hand, dealt with deficits in human development with the help of policies in fields like education and the realization of an inter-cultural dialogue.[8]

In order to realize its goals, a wide-ranging Work Program[9] was assigned to the Barcelona Declaration, the document that came out at the end of the ministerial meeting in Barcelona. This program included thirteen chapters linked to the Economic and Financial Partnership, eight chapters related to the Social, Cultural and Human Partnership, and only three chapters for the Political and Security Partnership, revealing openly and frankly the EU's economic emphasis on its relations with and perception of the region.

The annexed Work Program on "Political and Security Partnership: Establishing a common area of peace and stability" declared only to accomplish a political dialogue to find the most suitable instruments to initiate the principles of the Barcelona Declaration, and to bring workable suggestions for the next Euro-Mediterranean Meeting of Foreign Ministers. Besides, it was expected for foreign policy institutes in the region to launch a network for intense cooperation. This was all the Political Partnership should strive and work for.

Compare this with the huge working list in the "Economic and Financial Partnership: Building a zone of shared prosperity," which included fields like the cooperation in and final establishment of the Euro-Mediterranean Free Trade Area as "an essential element of the Euro-Mediterranean partnership," Investment, Industry, Agriculture, Transport, Energy, Telecommunications and Information Technology, Regional Planning, Tourism, Environment, Science and Technology, Water, and Fisheries. Most of these fields are part of the coverage of the EU's own internal "Common Policies." Therefore, it can be said that unlike the Political and Security Partnership, the Economic and Financial Partnership is very "EU-like," indicating, of course, that the EU is much more interested in economic rather than political cooperation with the Southern Mediterranean countries.

Certainly, with Euro-Med, the "first attempt in modern history to create strong and durable bonds based on peace and political and economic stability between the two shores of the Mediterranean"[10] was realized. It, nevertheless, was a bargain of diverse notions of the EU's identity which shape distinct advancements in the Mediterranean and, for sure, its securitization.[11] This is why real or perceived threats like (illegal) migration or terrorism is dealt with so widely within the EMP in general and especially in the Political and Security Partnership and—strange but true—in the Social, Cultural and Human Partnership.

Political Evaluation

Being in its twelfth year, so far the Euro-Med Partnership cannot be celebrated as a big success. On the political side, it has not been able to deeply change the authoritarian regimes of the Middle East and turn these countries into places where human rights, the rule of law and democracy are respected. The main reason for this failure was that Article 2 requiring suspension of the Association Agreements in case of violations of human rights and international law has not yet been put into force even once. So far, the reforms realized by the Southern Mediterranean countries have made only make-up effects, but not surgical corrections. When it came to ask for more reforms, the EU hesitated. The gap between the values expressed and hoped by the Partnership and the policies that had been put into practice has increased. The EMP was not able to contribute to the resolution of regional conflicts or help halting the failure of the Middle East peace process. Still, "security" sadly reigns over "peace."[12] And, as a gift of 9/11, "security" also reigns over "freedom."

Therefore, this basket can be called "a sleeping beauty,"[13] owing to structural deficiencies of the Barcelona Declaration and the Euro-Mediterranean Association Agreements, whose stipulations are unclear and imprecise, like a "loose shopping list of principles and declarations of (good) intent, and lacking any mention of concrete or at least potential implementation mechanisms."[14]

A look at the current situation in the Middle East openly reveals that the Euro-Mediterranean Partnership simply failed in creating a "common area of peace and stability," as spelled out in the Barcelona Declaration. The reason for this lies outside the EMP, namely in the failing of the Middle East peace process. Even so, the EMP has succeeded in building a trusting cooperation between the Northern and Southern shores of the Mediterranean. Notwithstanding the many crises it has faced so far, it has managed to survive, revealing an open interest of all participants in proceeding with the Partnership.[15] The "confidence building measures" realized so far, are hesitant steps in the right direction of region building. Besides, and even more importantly, Euro-Med is the sole organization where—besides the United Nations—Israel, the Palestinian Authority and the Arab states can, although this has not been so easy all the time, all come and work together. Within the EMP, the Palestinian Authority is being treated diplomatically as a quasi sovereign state and the EU's economic support has been helpful in the running of the Palestinian Authority.[16]

Due to a lack of an institutional framework of its own (Euro-Med neither has an independent Secretariat, nor a permanent locality), it depends totally on that of the EU, enabling the EU to dominate, direct the course of action and set the agenda; whereas the Southern Mediterranean countries solely follow.[17] Indeed, the ground-breaking expectation from the EMP picturing that the EU could indeed deal with the Southern Mediterranean countries on multilateral, equal and mutual grounds did not come true. In the end, the political dialogue could not bring along the domestic political reforms that were intended to be performed by the Southern Mediterranean partners.[18]

Euro-Med has succeeded in developing a framework for a trusting cooperation between Northern and Southern coastal neighbours. However,

Euro-Med needs to be developed further, particularly in the field of democratization, which has to reach beyond "cosmetic corrections."[19] The EMP showed the least amount of progress within the multilateral and the regional fields that were conceptionally innovative. The political and economic South-South integration has not been developed far, contrary to the success of the association agreements on bilateral level.[20] The EMP failed to create the promised area of peace, stability and common prosperity, also because of the failure of the Middle East peace process, for which the "Partnership" was not able to make the slightest contribution. At their 7th Conference, the Ministers of Foreign Affairs admitted this: "Political and security cooperation at official level has grown although the pace has been slower than hoped for. The partnership has not had any direct effect on the major unresolved conflicts in the region."[21] But nevertheless, it is an achievement that the EMP has continued. However, how further it will survive the substantial violent escalations in the Israeli-Palestinian conflict remains to be seen. Euro-Med has to further contribute to the relaxation between the conflicting parties and in the region itself by taking different measures of the three baskets, particularly by reviving the political dialogue, confidence building, and supporting the reform processes.[22]

Certainly, the term *"Barcelona Process"* reveals more openly the real potential of this regional project than the term "Euro-Mediterranean Partnership."[23]

Economic Evaluation

When it comes to economic relations, a clear asymmetry, which also influences aid relationships, has to be considered. Although there has been cooperation at some stages of the aid policy, the Southern partner governments were nearly barred and their civil societies were totally barred from aid management, since the EU tried to utilize its aid more proficiently and strategically. This, of course, alienated the Southern partners and could reduce the importance of aid policy as a political tool for change in the region. Definitely, this is a "contradiction in terms; while a 'partnership' implies equality; the EU clearly seeks a leadership role in the region."[24]

Nearly all agricultural products from the Southern Mediterranean that could compete with the EU products are restricted by the Union's Common Agricultural Policy (CAP) by trade tariffs or season calendars.[25] The statistics on trade and foreign direct investment (FDI) also do not show a lighter picture. Between 1993 and 2003, the EU's share in the total imports and exports of Southern countries fell constantly. In 2003, the level of FDI in all ten Southern partners was the same as in 1990, and this was just a little more than Poland's FDI alone in that year.[26] Between 1996 and 1999, the Middle East region was provided only less than ten million € per year from the EU's new democracy budget. Democracy aid still remains low, as only two to three percent of the EU's aid to the region goes to political reform.[27] What is more, within that time, the wealth gap between the North and the South increased enormously.

What disturbed the southern Mediterranean countries most is that they felt left out since the EU focused mainly on the eastward enlargement and devoted most of its financial aid to the then-future members. For example, in 2003, the EU gave €545 per capita, per year to these countries, while spending only €14 per capita, per year on the Euro-Med partners.[28] Besides, whereas Brussels employed the vision of EU membership to promote economic and political reforms in central and Eastern Europe, it was reluctant to use Euro-Med's influence to promote change in the South for trade, economic, and development aid, as the Partnership does not require the realization of political and human rights criteria like the Copenhagen Criteria for new EU members.[29]

While the EU wants to see trade liberalization and other reforms in Arab markets to increase economic relations, the Southern Mediterranean countries still consider their relations to be built on the traditional core-periphery model. Therefore, they will evaluate the accomplishments obtained by Euro-Med by the EU's dedication to economic and technological aid and especially by its motivation, to assume a more variable advance for a "partnership of equals."[30]

While it can be positively noted that infrastructure was developed and environmental issues are being discussed, cultural and human exchanges, however, have not been far-reaching due to the EU's security policy "marked by suspicion and closure"[31] that restricts the mobility of the people from the Southern Mediterranean. Moreover, the EU did not use all its capacity for political, economic and social development in the Middle East region either.

With no institutional frame for intra-regional free trade within Euro-Med, the Southern Mediterranean countries kept their high tariffs, and consequently, the intra-regional trade in the Southern Mediterranean was lower than 15 percent of the total. As necessary domestic structural reforms have not yet been materialized by these countries, they also still kept their outdated and inefficient economic models pervasively dominated by their governments; this of course did not help the economies to recover and refresh themselves. Indeed, although the Copenhagen economic criteria address these aspects specifically, and thereby help the acceding countries improve their economies with reforms and significant technical backing, nothing like this has been performed by the EU for their Southern Mediterranean "partners." This left the region in economic stagnancy. The Economic Partnership's main goal was the negotiations and finalizations of bilateral trade agreements. With Syria joining in as late as 2004, it took nearly ten years to finalize the last of the bilateral Association Agreements between the EU and the Southern partners. Besides, the trade agreements were not related or correlated to one another and could, therefore, not contribute to consistent markets and market circumstances. Although border tariffs were dealt with, technical barriers like harmonizing standards or rules of origin have not been touched. Moreover, liberalization remained just in the realm of industrial goods, not in services, investment or, what is especially important for the Southern Mediterranean countries, agriculture. This meant that the Southern shore of the Mediterranean opened markets to the Northern shore before they shaped and strengthened their peculiar integration.[32]

Unfortunately, some Arab governments misused the collapse of the Israeli-Palestinian peace route and the military confrontation and occupation of Afghanistan and Iraq by the U.S. as pretext and excuse for their sluggish performance in structural economic programs. Instead of establishing more and better democracy, and necessary political and economic reforms, they preferred to preserve and keep their regimes as they were and to strengthen and secure their domestic status.[33]

So far, the EMP has neither brought more foreign direct investments nor more prosperity to the Southern shore of the Mediterranean. Still, there is economic stagnation and a broadening of the human development deficit. Still, there is more bilateralism than the anticipated multicultural regionalism. Still, there is only insignificant South-South integration and negligible intra-regional trade in the Mediterranean area. All this diminishes the hopes for the in-time realization of the planned Euro-Mediterranean free trade area by 2010.[34] A clear asymmetry in economic power and capacity revealed itself especially in the Economic Partnership, with an accent on North-South integration and the opening of markets for EU goods and interests. There were no new initiatives for an innovative type of regional multilateralism and no institutional encouragement for the expansion of a regional Mediterranean market to promote intra-regional trade among the Southern Mediterranean countries and to bring in and increase foreign direct investment.[35]

Social, Cultural and Human Evaluation

The idea of including a Social, Cultural and Human basket in the Barcelona Declaration, is innovative, as it intends to show that mutual understanding and exchanges between the Southern and Northern shores of the Mediterranean are compulsory for political and economic programs that elevate democracy in the region. The Barcelona Declaration states that "dialogue between these cultures and exchanges at human, scientific and technological level are an essential factor in bringing their people closer, promoting understanding between them and improving their perception of each other." This indeed is laudable. However, it remains to be seen, "whether the EU can really cast of old, sometimes neo-colonial, attitudes and present-day fears"[36] and succeed in reaching this goal.

Cooperation in basket three reveals a tension between "freedom" and "security;" both require one another, but "more" of one can only be reached by "less" of the other. Instead, what would be necessary is a balance between both. This indeed cannot be seen in Euro-Med. On one side are the governments of the Southern Mediterranean shore who indeed give priority to security, but less priority to the security of their people, and more priority to the security of their own power. On the other side are the states of the Northern Mediterranean shore whose main concern is also mostly focused on security, even at the expense of freedom, revealing openly the well-known and disliked image of "Fortress Europe."[37]

Besides, there is an ambiguity in the third basket which makes it difficult to improve and deepen it. On the one hand, topics like socio-economic conditions in the Southern Mediterranean countries, cultural diversities between the Southern and the Northern shores, advanced ideas upon more comprehensive assistance and cooperation, are integrated in the third basket; these are all topics, which surely are not directly connected to the field of social, cultural and human affairs. On the other hand, subject matters which are not at all relevant to social and cultural cooperation are included, and this in a "rather harsh undertone" while bringing in "a-cultural issues"[38] like migration, terrorism, international crime, corruption, racism, xenophobia etc.

The reason for this is found in broadening the concept of security by the Copenhagen School to include not only national and military dimensions, but also social and human issues.[40] This, however, does not explain why these topics had to be included in basket three, after they had been discussed and dealt with in detail in basket one for the Political and Security Partnership.[41]

In March 2005, the first plenary meeting of the Euro-Mediterranean parliamentary assembly, which reviewed the progress of the Euro-Mediterranean Partnership, was held in Cairo. In order to reinforce civil society and its activities in the region, the EMP built the Anna Lindh Foundation for the Dialogue of Cultures in Alexandria aiming to expand partnership in social, cultural and human affairs.[42]

The EU politics did and still do contain many contradictions. On one hand, security and national security concerns prevail, and on the other, the Union allegedly tries to make borders more permeable. On one side lies the concept of free trade in the region, and on the other side is the protectionist Common Agricultural Policy that inhibits Southern Mediterranean countries to sell their agricultural products to their Northern neighbours. The EU's cooperation with authoritarian states is surely not in harmony with its values of democracy and human rights. Then again, an urged democracy imposed on these countries by force could lead to instability and volatility in the region. Undeniably, the Northern and the Southern partners found exit-options and excuses for their lacks in commitment, awareness, understanding, and interest whenever it fitted them. Besides, since the

Barcelona Declaration was the smallest common denominator of the 27 partners and their "rather diverging than overlapping governmental positions, the implementation path taken since 1995 to develop, launch and sustain the third basket is not a straight and coherent one."[43]

The Barcelona summit, which was held on November 27 and 28, 2005, was planned as an extraordinary occasion and as a "celebration" of the 10th anniversary of the Euro-Mediterranean Partnership. Notwithstanding this intention, its outcome was quite poor—solely a "Euro-Mediterranean Code of Conduct on Countering Terrorism,"[44] which does not even provide a common definition of terrorism, a condition that reduces its significance. Even so, for the first time ever, European and Arab states and Israel denounced terrorism together and offered recommendations for action. Out came the consent to be "united in the struggle against terrorism" and to "strengthen cooperation and coordination." The partners recognized "the links between peace, security, social, and economic development and human rights" and promised "to resolve conflict, end occupation, confront oppression, reduce poverty, promote good governance and human rights, improve intercultural understanding, and ensure respect for all religions." Moreover, a "Five-Year Work Program" was adopted (again, a new work program!), giving Euro-Med an extended time for its tasks. It reveals how "the political reform agenda ultimately tends to be sacrificed or relegated:"[45] Although education goals with defined deadlines and benchmarks were given *en masse* (e.g. halving the illiteracy rate by 2010, equal access to education by 2015), the specifications for economic reform were vague, with almost no deadlines, giving the possibility of exceptions instead. Even more ambiguous was the field of political cooperation, which reveals hardly any solid dedication and looks like "optional extras" to be discussed over and over again.

European Neighbourhood Policy (ENP)

In 2004, thanks to the insistence of the Mediterranean EU-members Spain, France and Italy, in keeping and reinforcing the balance of the EU's policy between the East and the South, Euro-Med was integrated into the EU's European Neighbourhood Policy (ENP) which, since 2003, aims to manage the Union's enlarged borders and intends to "strengthen the framework for the Union's relations with those neighbouring countries that do not currently have the perspective of membership of the EU."[46] Apart from Turkey, who has been a candidate since 1999 and started accession negotiations in October 2005, all Southern Mediterranean partners signed ENP agreements that encourage and definitely return to bilateral cooperation. The European Neighbourhood Policy rendered the Southern Mediterranean partners an opportunity to "participate in EU programmes and policies on the basis of the fulfilment of jointly agreed priorities, reflecting shared values and joint policy objectives."[47]

The Neighbourhood Policy contains benchmarking and action plans with lists of responsibilities and obligations to support common values like the rule of law and good governance.[48] As the action plans are produced in cooperation between the EU and each of its Southern Mediterranean partners, they deal with the situation of the concerned country and there is a hope that the EU's dominance can be limited and that the Southern Mediterranean countries will work more and in favor of the reform programs to which they contributed.[49] Therefore, there is no "common strategy" like in the Euro-Mediterranean Partnership, but there is a European strategy found on a distinguished, advanced approach with benchmarks and according to action plans. The EU's ENP partners have to realize political, social and economic reforms according to these benchmarks by gradually meeting the regulatory frames of the EU. The EU will then evaluate the situation and, in case of positive appraisal, will probably grant a more elaborate integration into its market. This means that the EU is not "'the driving force' in democratic change as it believes that lasting change in Arab countries must come from within."[50] Since the EU does not give the possibility of EU membership to its ENP partners, so far, the above mentioned prospects and fundraising are the EU's most important encouragements offered to its neighbours. Because the action plans take specific main concerns of the partners into account, the result is "a Neighbourhood *à la carte* that—with partial integration envisaged—is reminiscent of the all too familiar concept of Europe *à la* carte in a new context, i.e. Europe *à la carte* for non-members."[51]

The ENP is not a means for accession; it is more an alternative possibility for participation in the European integration for countries which have no perspective of accession in the near or far future. Therefore, the ENP tries to give a complementary offer, to decrease the "pressure" of enlargement and to provide a stable and prosperous region around the EU without the instrument of accession. However, this could mean that the ENP, although it was intended quite the opposite, creates and deepens a Europe of "insiders" and "outsiders" and, therefore, generates new division lines across the continent, just like during the Cold War years.

The European Neighbourhood Policy takes in nearly all of the EU's neighbour countries which have a land or a sea border with the Union. Since they have already launched binds with the EU that are much deeper than the ENP could ever realize, candidate countries (Turkey, Croatia, and Macedonia) and potential candidate countries (Albania, Bosnia and Herzegovina, Montenegro, and Serbia including Kosovo) are not included in the ENP. Neither Western European countries (Iceland, Norway and Switzerland), nor European micro-states (Andorra, Holy See, Liechtenstein, Monaco, and San Marino) are part of the European Neighbourhood Policy.[52]

Increasing the education budget by 50 percent for Southern partners, more than a third of whose populations are younger than 15, and initiating a dialogue with moderate Islamic religious groups are other changes that are planned or, to a degree, put into action. The 15 million Euro-budget allocated for the period between 2007 and 2013 comprises only 10 percent of the Union's budget for external activities and surely needs to be increased. What is more, Southern Mediterranean partners should also be able to define Euro-Med and the reform agenda at least as much as their Northern partners can.[53]

The ENP puts stress on security issues like preventing terrorist activities and managing migration flows, and tries to achieve a better governance and respect for human rights in those countries.

The drive behind the EU to realize the European Neighbourhood Policy is certainly geopolitical concerns. The EU tries to build a ring of states in its environment in order to shield itself and to influence others. The EU as a "regional centre intends to create—or maintain—a functioning semi-periphery (via its neighbours) in order to create a buffer-zone to the periphery (i.e. the neighbours' neighbours and beyond)."[54]

In ENP reports and declarations, the term "ring of friends" can often be found, revealing an emphasis on egalitarianism and equality. Conversely, "being funded by the EU and distribution of funds being mainly dependent on EU-satisfaction with the process, the equality exists rather on a rhetorical basis."[55]

The European Commission's "Wider Europe Communication" in point 4 "A Differentiated, Progressive, and Benchmarked Approach" openly conveys the hierarchy by explaining that prerequisites, laid down by the EU, have to be realized to gain from the policy: "The extension of the benefits [...], including increased financial assistance, should be conducted so as to encourage and reward reform—reforms which existing EU policies and incentives have so far not managed to elicit in all cases. Engagement should therefore be introduced **progressively**, and be **conditional on meeting agreed targets for reform.** New benefits should only be offered to reflect the progress made by the partner countries in political and economic reform. In the absence of progress, partners will not be offered these opportunities."[56]

This paragraph reveals an incongruity with other documents of the ENP, where the EU emphasizes that the "EU does not seek to impose priorities or conditions on its partners" and portrays the ENP as "an offer made by the EU to its partners."[57] Of course, the use of the above-mentioned term can also be seen positively, as a kind of "instrument to be adopted to defend EU credibility" which, for sure, could bring along "more effective EU support to democratic practices and human rights protection in third countries."[58] Nevertheless, it leaves a bad taste—as if the Northern shore of the Mediterranean had really solved all of its problems and as if it became a "wise teacher" for the "ignorant student," the Southern shore. However, one can hardly be the "student" *and* at the same time stand on equal footing with the "teacher," can they?

The change in strategy can be judged positively as a learning process of the EU. Successes of the acceding countries in realizing reforms and change, but a decade of failure within the Euro-Mediterranean Partnership revealed that processes of transformation cannot be imposed from outside without real and impulsive incentives. However, this new and important understanding is not really realized within the new concept of the European Neighbourhood Policy, as it misses obligatory and compulsory benchmarking in its action plans for domestic "political" reforms, which are included in detail for economic reforms and economic modernization. Considering that many authoritarian regimes in the Southern shores of the Mediterranean implement more and more economic reforms despite their application of stronger political oppression, the EU's hope for spill-over effects stemming from economic liberalization and spreading over to the political area does not seem to be very realistic.[59] What is worse, the perseverance on and priority of the economic cooperation and the neighbours' partaking in the EU market looks as if political cooperation is not considered as important as economic cooperation. The economic liberalization and the free market, therefore, give the impression to be of higher importance than human rights and democratic principles.[60]

The EU as *normative power?*

The EU's politics vis-à-vis the Southern Mediterranean countries and its desire to be a *"norm exporter"* reveal three main teething troubles. First, although the Barcelona Declaration is politically binding, judicially it is not, causing the partners to stick to the aims and projects whenever it fits them and leave it, when it does not. Devotion is deliberate as non-adherence to the Barcelona Declaration *acquis* is not sanctioned at all. This makes it hard for the EU to act as a normative power for its southern neighbours. A striking example for the opposite might be Turkey. A glance at Turkey reveals openly that the prospect of membership in the European Union (the "carrot" given by the EU) encouraged Turkey to start adopting the *acquis communautaire*, and to realize wide-ranging political, economic and judicial reforms. Of course it should not be forgotten that Turkey—very independently from the EU process—has been on the road of "Westernization" since the times of the Ottoman Empire, starting with the important legal reforms of *Tanzimat* (1839-1876) and continued with the Young Turks (1908-1918) up until Mustafa Kemal Atatürk's genius in building the Republic of Turkey (October 29, 1923) and reforming it according to the standards of "contemporary civilizations" (1923-1938). It should also not be forgotten that Turkey— unlike most Arab countries did not suffer a colonial history or colonialism by

European powers, which enabled her to take a more relaxed look at Europe than most Arab countries can or possibly ever will be able to. And who could blame them for this?

Nevertheless, it can be underlined that the political instruments the EU uses on various countries have, for sure, different influences on these countries. While the EU's promise and pledge for membership for Turkey induced Turkey to implement important political, economic and social reforms, the EU's instrument of Euro-Med for the Southern Mediterranean countries did not persuade these countries to change their political and economic models. As membership is excluded from the Euro-Mediterranean Partnership as well as from the European Neighbourhood Policy, there is simply minimal enticement for making changes and reforms. Moreover, as nonconformity with the EMP *acquis* is accepted, Southern Mediterranean governments are induced not to haste at all to implement important necessary reforms in time.[61]

The second problem for the EU as a normative power is caused by the EU's own institutions whose attitudes indeed reveal "a sort of institutional schizophrenia"[62] by showing diverse and dissimilar styles and methods toward the Southern Mediterranean countries. While the European Commission, with its inventive and innovative ideas and images, has the role of *"policy-entrepreneur,"* the European Parliament performs like a "critical watchdog" and criticizes lack of human rights in its meetings and yearly human rights reports. The European Council, on the other side, is quite pragmatically guided by concerns and reflections, causing it to comprehend, overlook and tolerate the difficulties of the Southern partners in carrying out political and democratic reforms, probably in order not to undermine the governments of these states, regardless of official declarations, claiming the opposite.

The third predicament is the fact that the EU's normative power is limited by the scarcity of funds which are desperately needed for the realization of the proclaimed goals. For the period between 2002 and 2004, only 25 million € out of a sum of 93 million € allocated for the MEDA regional support envelope was assigned for the development of good governance and the rule of law. This, of course, is far away from being enough to be helpful for the improvement of democratization in the region.[63] All this reveals that it is easier said than done for the EU to be active as a *norm exporter* in the Mediterranean region. On the other hand, **why** should the EU be a *norm exporter*? Are the EU's norms really simply the best? And, therefore, to be adopted by each and every country in the world in exactly the same manner?

Hélène Flautre, Chair of the European Parliament's Subcommittee on Human Rights, insists that the Europeans "must abandon the idea that the European Union is the 'teacher' in matters of democracy and avoid what borders on a neo-colonialist attitude."[64] It is important to understand that the

"West" has to be "modest about [its] ability to find the answers for other societies. Liberal democracy is the best form of government yet discovered. But if you rush to a multi-party election without first developing the underpinnings of liberal democracy—the rule of law, civil society, private property, independent media—you can end up with what Fareed Zakaria has called 'illiberal democracy.' We [i.e. Europe] can, and should, offer a toolbox of experiences in all aspects of transition, from how to write a constitution to how to deal with a difficult past. But then it's up to them [i.e. the Middle East]."[65]

Indeed, a look at history reveals that in order to legitimize colonialism, Europeans alleged to spread progress and modernity to the "inferior" and "barbarian" people, who had to be made alike and equal by "civilizing" them. While invading land in the Mediterranean, Europeans claimed to bring "civilization," "enlightenment," "prosperity," "law," and "social order." The imperial expansion was "justified" by their self-given task to disperse "civilization, commerce and Christianity." Thus, in the words of Michelle Pace, "This 'civilizing mission' philosophy still seems to be ingrained in the minds of European Union policymakers today."[66]

The imperialism started by the British, kept on and improved perfectly by the Americans, to build artificial states in the Middle East, hindered the formation of nation-states in the region, deterring the fostering of democratic thought. Since the newly-received independence was of no use and not felt by the people, and because the imperial powers worked hand in hand with monarchies who put down their own people, a democratic tradition could not emerge, radicalizing the region's populace, especially as "Western" states, neither stopped the bloodbath in Palestine, nor in Iraq, nor in Lebanon, nor elsewhere, neither then, nor today.[67]

It is a well-known fact that some "Western" states promoted Islamists and violent organizations for their own power calculations. Also after 9/11, "business as usual" continues. Neither the EU, nor, even less, the U.S., has realized a reorientation in this regard.[68]

Indeed, European states showed a distaste to support change even when the ruling regimes were known to be fraudulent and repressive, as this change might cause uncertainty or destabilizing outcomes in Europe's neighbourhood. European governments developed their relations with the mostly authoritarian regimes, and co-operated with those to hinder migrants from going to Europe or simply to sustain their energy needs, or for many other practical and pragmatic reasons.[69] Everyone who paid obtained what they had ordered, without being asked anything. Thus, Europe disqualified itself as the **partner** of the people. By co-operating with dictators rather than with their opposition, Europe, in the words of Rafik Schami, behaved "hypocritically"[70] toward the Southern Mediterranean countries. Therefore, the missing part was the humane offer of cooperation based on equality and equity which could have been enlightening and up-shaking for the common people. The Euro-Mediterranean "Partnership" definitely cannot be seen as this missing offer. Therefore, unfortunately, this offer is still deficient.

Concluding Remarks

The Euro-Mediterranean Partnership was innovative, holistic and full of good intentions. It was found on the values of human rights, peace and prosperity, and aimed to renovate the balance of relations and to support the advancement of the Southern Mediterranean countries. Its founding document—the Barcelona Declaration—set out the objective "to turn the Mediterranean basin into an area of dialogue, exchange and cooperation granting peace, stability and prosperity." However, it can be seen today, 12 years after the beginning of the Partnership, that there is still more misunderstanding than dialogue, more domination than exchange, more "civilizing" than cooperation, which reveals that the so-called "Partnership" was not so real. To be partners means to be equal, but there was simply no equality within Euro-Med—the EU unquestionably was superior—it decided who to trade with and whom to help out financially. The normative power of the EU was seen, heard and felt from the very beginning.

Perhaps most importantly, the southern shore of the Mediterranean still has not reached "peace, stability and prosperity." Still there are occupations, wars, suffering, and antagonism. Still there are people being killed, still there is more hatred than hope, and still there are more wars than peace. And still the author keeps on hoping for peace to come to the region, and stabililty and prosperity will follow peace.

---

* This article was finished in April 2007.
[1] Thomas Demmelhuber, "The Euro-Mediterranean Space as an Imagined (Geo-)political, Economic and Cultural Entity," Center for European Integration Studies, Discussion Paper C 159, 2006, p. 12.
[2] Ana Palacio Vallelersundi, "The Barcelona Process. A Euro-Mediterranean North-South Partnership," *Georgetown Journal of International Affairs*, Winter 2004, p. 146.
[3] Cilja Harders, "Europäische Mittelmeerpolitik aus arabischer Sicht," Aus Politik und Zeitgeschichte, B 45/2005, p. 15.
[4] For an overview see http://ec.europa.eu/comm/external_relations/Euro-Med/
[5] Ibid.
[6] Barcelona Declaration adopted at the Euro-Mediterranean Conference – 27-28.11.1995, http://ec.europa.eu/comm/external_relations/euromed/bd.htm
[7] Andreas Marchetti, "The European Neighbourhood Policy. Foreign Policy at the EU's Periphery," Center for European Integration Studies, Discussion Paper C 158 – 2006, p. 4.
[8] Brigid Gavin, "The Euro-Mediterranean Partnership. An Experiment in North-South-South Integration," *Intereconomics*, November/December 2005, p. 354.

[9] http://ec.europa.eu/comm/external_relations/euromed/bd.htm
[10] Sara Silvestri, "EU Relations with Islam in the Context of the EMP's Cultural Dialogue," *Mediterranean Politics*, Vol. 10, No. 3, November 2005, p. 386.
[11] Michelle Pace, "Conclusion: Cultural Democracy in Euro-Mediterranean Relations?," *Mediterranean Politics*, Vol. 10, No. 3, November 2005, p. 428.
[12] Ghislaine Glasson Deschaumes, "A Decade of Disenchantment," *cafebabel – European current affairs magazine*, 28.11.2005, http://www.cafebabel.com/en/article.asp?T=T&Id=5319
[13] Tobias Schumacher, "Introduction: The Study of Euro-Mediterranean Cultural and Social Co-operation in Perspective," *Mediterranean Politics*, Vol. 10, No. 3, November 2005, p. 282.
[14] Ibid., p. 282.
[15] Annette Jünemann, "Zehn Jahre Barcelona-Prozess: Eine gemischte Bilanz," *Aus Politik und Zeitgeschichte*, B 45/2005, pp. 13-14.
[16] Gavin, "The Euro-Mediterranean Partnership. An Experiment in North-South-South Integration," p. 357.
[17] Ibid., p. 354.
[18] Ibid., p. 360.
[19] Jünemann, "Zehn Jahre Barcelona-Prozess: Eine gemischte Bilanz," pp. 13-14.
[20] Harders, "Europäische Mittelmeerpolitik aus arabischer Sicht," p. 22.
[21] Conclusions for the VIIth Euro-Mediterranean Conference of Ministers of Foreign Affairs, Luxembourg, 30-31 May 2005.
[22] Isabel Schäfer, "Die Euro-Mediterrane Partnerschaft und der Nahostkonflikt," *Aus Politik und Zeitgeschichte*, B 45/2005, p. 29.
[23] Jünemann, "Zehn Jahre Barcelona-Prozess: Eine gemischte Bilanz," p. 14.
[24] Patrick Holden, "Partnership Lost? The EU's Mediterranean Aid Programmes", *Mediterranean Politics*, Vol. 10, No. 1, p. 19. See also pp. 34-35.
[25] Although the Common Agricultural Policy is one of the most hotly debated and criticised policies of the EU, eating up nearly half of the total Union budget, the hope for a real change in mind by EU countries is tiny.
[26] Kevin Byrne, "Euromed, an economic failure?," *cafebabel – European current affairs magazine*, 28.11.2005, http://www.cafebabel.com/en/article.asp?T=A&Id=1545
[27] Richard Youngs, "European Democracy Promotion in the Middle East," *Internationale Politik und Gesellschaft* 4/2004, pp. 112-113.
[28] Byrne, "Euromed, an economic failure?"
[29] Timothy M. Savage, "Europe and Islam: Crescent Waxing, Cultures Clashing," *The Washington Quarterly*, Summer 2004, Vol. 27, No. 3, pp. 40-41.
[30] Rory Miller and Ashraf Mishrif, "The Barcelona Process and Euro-Arab Economic Relations, 1995-2005," *Middle East Review of International Affairs*, Vol. 9, No. 2 (June 2005), pp. 105-106.
[31] Deschaumes, "A Decade of Disenchantment".
[32] Gavin, "The Euro-Mediterranean Partnership. An Experiment in North-South-South Integration," p. 356.
[33] Miller and Mishrif, "The Barcelona Process and Euro-Arab Economic Relations, 1995-2005," p. 105.

[34] Gavin, "The Euro-Mediterranean Partnership. An Experiment in North-South-South Integration," p. 360.
[35] Ibid., p. 355.
[36] Glenda G. Rosenthal, "Preface: The Importance of Conceptualizing Cultural and Social Co-operation in the Euro-Mediterranean Area," *Mediterranean Politics*, Vol. 10, No. 3, November 2005, pp. 279-280.
[37] Jünemann, "Zehn Jahre Barcelona-Prozess: Eine gemischte Bilanz," p. 9.
[38] Schumacher, "Introduction: The Study of Euro-Mediterranean Cultural and Social Co-operation in Perspective", p. 282.
[40] Barry Buzan, Ole Wæver and Jaap de Wilde: *Security. A New Framework For Analysis*, Boulder/London: Lynne Rienner, 1998.
[41] Schumacher, "Introduction: The Study of Euro-Mediterranean Cultural and Social Co-operation in Perspective," pp. 282-283.
[42] Sandra Lavenex and Frank Schimmelfennig, "Relations with the Wider Europe," *JCMS* 2006, Vol. 44, Annual Review, p. 148.
[43] Schumacher, "Introduction: The Study of Euro-Mediterranean Cultural and Social Co-operation in Perspective," p. 283.
[44] http://ec.europa.eu/comm/external_relations/Euro-Med/summit1105/terrorism.pdf
[45] Richard Gillespie, "Onward but not Upward: The Barcelona Conference of 2005," *Mediterranean Politics*, Vol. 11, No. 2, July 2006, pp. 274-275.
[46] http://europa.eu.int/eur-lex/lex/LexUriServ/LexUriServ.do?uri=CELEX:52003DC0104:EN:HTML
[47] Conclusions for the VIIth Euro-Mediterranean Conference of Ministers of Foreign Affairs, Luxembourg, 30-31 May 2005.
[48] Sarah Wolff, "Everybody needs good Neighbours," *cafebabel – European current affairs magazine*, 28.11.2005, http://www.cafebabel.com/en/article.asp?T=T&Id=5321
[49] Jünemann, "Zehn Jahre Barcelona-Prozess: Eine gemischte Bilanz," p. 12.
[50] Gavin, "The Euro-Mediterranean Partnership. An Experiment in North-South-South Integration," p. 358.
[51] Marchetti, "The European Neighbourhood Policy. Foreign Policy at the EU's Periphery," p. 13.
[52] Ibid., p. 6, Footnote 13.
[53] Wolff, "Everybody needs good Neighbours."
[54] Marchetti, "The European Neighbourhood Policy. Foreign Policy at the EU's Periphery," p. 16-17.
[55] Ibid., p. 15.
[56] Communication from the Commission to the Council and the European Parliament - Wider Europe - Neighbourhood: A New Framework for Relations with our Eastern and Southern Neighbours, http://eur-lex.europa.eu/smartapi/cgi/sga_doc?smartapi!celexplus!prod!DocNumber&type_doc=COMfinal&an_doc=2003&nu_doc=104&lg=en See also: http://europa.eu.int/comm/world/enp/pdf/com 03_104_en.pdf , p. 16 [bold type in original].
[57] Marchetti, "The European Neighbourhood Policy. Foreign Policy at the EU's Periphery," p. 15, Commission, *European Neighbourhood Policy strategy Paper*

COM(2004)373 final, http://europa.eu.int/comm./world/enp/pdf/strategy/Strategy_Paper_EN.pdf, p. 8.

[58] Stefania Panebianco and Rosa Rossi, "EU attempts to export norms of good governance to the Mediterranean and Western Balkan countries," Jean Monnet Centre Euro-Med, Working Paper No. 53, October 2004, p. 12.

[59] Jünemann, "Zehn Jahre Barcelona-Prozess: Eine gemischte Bilanz," p. 13.

[60] Panebianco and Rossi, "EU attempts to export norms of good governance to the Mediterranean and Western Balkan countries," p. 9.

[61] Ibid., pp. 2-3 and p. 8.

[62] Ibid., p. 12.

[63] Euro-Med Partnership, The Regional Strategy Paper 2002-2006 & Regional Indicative Programme, taken from Panebianco and Rossi, "EU attempts to export norms of good governance to the Mediterranean and Western Balkan countries," p. 12.

[64] Hélène Flautre, "The EU is not the teacher in terms of democracy," interview by Stéphane Carrara, Sarah Wolff and Vanessa Witkowski, *cafebabel – European current affairs magazine*, 28.11.2005, http://www.cafebabel.com/en/article.asp?T=T&Id=5315

[65] Timothy Garton Ash, "Free World: Why a Crisis of the West Reveals the Opportunity of Our Time," Penguin 2004, cited from Michelle Pace, "Imagining Co-presence in Euro-Mediterranean Relations: The Role of 'Dialogue'," *Mediterranean Politics*, Vol. 10, No. 3, November 2005, p. 297.

[66] Michelle Pace, "Conclusion: Cultural Democracy in Euro-Mediterranean Relations?," p. 428.

[67] Süleyman Seydi, "Batı'nın 'İslami Teröre' Yaklaşımı," *Stradigma*, No. 8, September 2003, http://www.stradigma.com/index.php?sayfa=yazdir_makale&no=24

[68] Sabine Riedel, "Der Islam als Faktor in der internationalen Politik," *Aus Politik und Zeitgeschichte*, B 37/2003, pp. 23-24.

[69] Savage, "Europe and Islam: Crescent Waxing, Cultures Clashing," p. 40.

[70] ["heuchlerisch"] Rafik Schami, "Ein arabisches Dilemma," *Aus Politik und Zeitgeschichte*, B 37 / 2003, p. 5.

Chapter 7
Limited Possibilities:
Defining the Interaction between the EU and the GCC

Christian Koch

The Gulf Cooperation Council (GCC) and the EU are close, geographical neighbours, yet their relationship has remained vague and not clearly defined. As stated in a strategy paper published by the Bertelsmann Foundation and the Center for Applied Policy Research: "The relationship between the EU and the GCC and its member countries has been of low intensity and reflects neither the geographic proximity nor the vital links in several fields existing between the two sides."[1] Certainly, when the Gulf Cooperation Council (GCC)—Bahrain, Kuwait, Oman, Qatar, Saudi Arabia, and the United Arab Emirates—was formed back in 1981, there was little indication about building up a working relationship with the EU, or the European Economic Community (EEC), as it was called back then. Overall, the formation of the GCC was an event that was probably hardly noticed in European capitals and in Brussels.

Moreover, what has complicated matters is that, from the outset, the GCC and the EU have represented very different institutions. The GCC was initially conceived as a security organization which was formed as a result of the turbulent years of 1979 and 1980 following the Iranian Revolution and the beginning of the Iran-Iraq War. Significantly, the GCC was formed after only three months of discussion among its constituent members, leading some to speculate that its formation was a "hasty reaction rather than a calculated initiative."[2] Others have argued that the establishment of the GCC was simply a reaction to external events and that, without the need to act; the individual Gulf countries would not have found it necessary to come closer together.[3] Overall, external factors would continue to play a role with regard to the development of the GCC.

Given the immediate threat to their own security, the GCC countries, from the outset, had to consider finding credible and effective means to deal with the challenge that both the Iranian Revolution and the implications of the Iran-Iraq War posed for the region at large. There was a feeling among the GCC leaders that the longer the six states waited, the more pressure and influence Iran and Iraq would exert to restrain them from putting forth a common position, or to force each of them to support the position of one vis-à-vis the other. In that context, security issues became significant with the GCC states which were clearly aware of the danger of inaction.

Although none of the initial committees set up as part of the GCC dealt exclusively with security as such, the final communiqué issued after the first summit meeting in May 1981, affirmed the will and the intention of the signatories to defend their security and independence and to keep the region free of international conflicts. Yet, the basic objectives of the GCC as outlined in Article 4 of the founding charter sought to go beyond the issue of security to vaguely define other potential areas of cooperation. Thus, it referred to:

- Achieving cooperation among the member states in all fields as a prelude to unity,
- Strengthening the links of cooperation among the people of the member states in different fields, and
- Stimulating scientific and technological progress in the fields of industry, mineralogy, agriculture, marine and animal resources, as well as encouraging cooperation of the private sector for the common good of the people of the member states.[4]

Given the fact that security cooperation also encroached on the more sensitive areas of sovereignty, the task of fostering economic integration took on increased importance as the GCC progressed. The bottom line here is that, despite many of its shortcomings, the GCC has emerged since its establishment as the only successful example of a functioning regional Arab organization. Among the leadership and populations of its member states, the GCC has become an accepted fact.

If one compares the formation of the GCC with that of the EU, one immediately notices the differences. Coming out of the ashes of the Second World War, European integration did not have to primarily concern itself with immediate security threats, but instead, considered the economic and social reconstruction of a shattered continent as its main priority. What the EU is today has thus originated from the very outset of almost solely economic issues and from the struggle of how to bring about cooperation in some of the key economic sectors of erstwhile enemies. Political and security-related issues and topics would only come much later; in fact, looking at the process of bringing about a common security and foreign policy, it is clear that European states are grappling with this dilemma even today.

We must also mention that the GCC and the EU are very different institutions in terms of their structure and set-up. While the GCC was set-up as an inter-governmental institution with the emphasis on cooperation rather than integration, the EU has been very much the opposite, always looking for ways in which actual integration can be fostered. Up until present day, the

the GCC represents an organization that does not enjoy any transfer of sovereignty from any of the individual GCC states. As a result, and as Gerd Nonneman has aptly noted: "The GCC Secretariat does not come anywhere near the functional equivalent of the European Commission."[5] Similarly, Abdulkhaleq Abdullah has argued that the GCC remains an institution that has all things for all people about which each member state has its own perception and expectations.[6]

This is further complicated by the prevailing top-down approach to decision-making, which continues to define the internal political set-up of the GCC countries where power remains concentrated in the hands of the few. While the EU is composed of a body of seasoned bureaucrats who daily engage in the formulation of the policy documents of the Union, the GCC remains dependent upon the willingness of the individual capitals and its ruling families to be able to construct policy positions and define the organization's overall direction. One analyst described this as the clashing systems of the EU with its rotating individuals and the GCC with the same people in the same positions over a long period.[7]

Given the above information, there are clear limitations to what can be achieved within the framework of an EU-GCC relationship. The question has also to be asked to what degree both sides are actually interested in and committed to broadening their ties and moving them beyond simple trade and exchange of goods. As this paper will try to define, there are obvious strategic reasons underlying the effort at cooperation, and moreover, those reasons will intensify in scope over the coming years. At the same time, it is important to recognize right at the beginning that there are things that can be expected from the GCC-EU relationship, but there are also issues that will likely remain unresolved, no matter how much cooperation is fostered. From an institutional perspective, the GCC does not fall under the European Union Neighbourhood Policy. Yet, neither the European Neighbourhood Policy nor the Euro-Mediterranean partnership has, until now, resulted in the establishment of a regional security structure or has sparked a widespread political reform process. As such, while it may be accurate to speak about a "notable gap" in terms of the development of EU-GCC relations, it may simply be a case of too many expectations, expected too soon.[8]

Unclear Direction: The GCC and the EU from 1980 until 2001

Originally, the GCC countries were part of the Euro-Arab Dialogue, which was initiated in 1974 following the first oil crisis. With this dialogue, however, which was effectively overshadowed by the Arab-Israeli conflict, very little was achieved in promoting closer Europe-Arab relations and even less in terms of a relationship between Europe and the Arab Gulf States. A first initial point of contact came in 1980 when then German Foreign

Minister Hans-Dietrich Genscher proposed to the European Council of Ministers the conclusion of bilateral agreements with all Arab Gulf States including Iraq. These agreements would cover the areas of energy and investment, as well as economic and technical cooperation.[9] Unfortunately, very little was achieved from this initiative, since both sides were skeptical of the actual value of a closer relationship. One Gulf representative actually characterized the European offer of bilateral agreements as merely short-term and driven purely by interests to secure stable oil supplies. Such a "cooperation would be forgotten as soon as the oil question had been resolved with some degree of certainty."[10]

Following the formation of the GCC, informal talks dominated the relationship with the EEC. Preparation for a formal cooperation agreement began in November 1984, which resulted in a ministerial meeting in October 1985 at which the two sides indicated their willingness to deepen and strengthen ties. A second ministerial meeting in June 1987 was followed by direct authorization from the European Council of Ministers for the Commission to begin talks of an official cooperation agreement. By this time, the numerous informal channels of discussion resulted in the major thorny issues being resolved, thereby, paving the way for the cooperation agreement to come about. On June 15, 1988, the agreement was signed by Hans-Dietrich Genscher as President of the Council of the European Communities, Claude Cheysson on behalf of the European Commission, Prince Saud al-Faisal al-Saud in his role as President of the Ministerial Council of the GCC, and Abdullah Bishara as GCC Secretary-General.[11]

The 1988 Cooperation Agreement, signed by both sides, stated the objective to be to help in "promoting overall cooperation between equal partners on mutually advantageous terms in all spheres between the two regions and further their economic development, taking into consideration the differences in levels of development of the parties."[12] While covering a wide array of issues from agriculture to industry, energy, investment, trade, and technology, the agreement served essentially to extend to the GCC-EEC relationship an institutional framework that had, until then, been missing. As a result, a Joint Cooperation Council was established with representatives of both sides and this council met on a yearly basis. From the start, the joint council sought to promote relations under the three main pillars stipulated by the Cooperation Agreement: political cooperation, undertaking negotiations toward a free trade agreement, and economic and technical cooperation. Yet, because the agreement was essentially a vague and generalized document that provided very little in terms of substance, cooperation remained limited. In addition, the development of mutually beneficial relations would soon be continuously thwarted by a combination of the incompatibility of institutional actors, the lack of political will, and the inability to conclude the free trade area negotiations. And while the joint council would meet annually,

Khader characterized the statements that have been issued every year as merely "a catalogue of niceties and politically correct statements."[13]

Abdullah Baabood attributes this lack of progress to the overall asymmetry between the two regional organizations, which, in his words, pits the deeper regionalism of the EU with its supranational bodies against the "shallow regionalism" of the GCC.[14] Certainly, it can be argued that there were difficulties from two perspectives in the EU's regional approach. First, since there had been little decision-making at the GCC level, there has always been the problem of having an actual coherent region to deal with. Without a centralized system through which an effective communication can be rendered, relations are proved to be cumbersome and largely reactive. Second, Europe itself was unsure about the level of priority it should accord to the Gulf region often arguing that a separate approach was not warranted, and also fearing that too much emphasis on the GCC would divert attention from other areas such as Europe's Mediterranean policy.[15] Consequently, the cooperation agreement was never pursued with urgency.

For the rest of the 1990s, only a little advancement was achieved. There was an effort in 1995 at the Granada EU-GCC Troika Ministerial meeting to assess the status of cooperation and attempt to give the relationship a renewed sense of purpose. Decisions taken at that meeting included strengthening the political dialogue, improving the framework for better energy relations and considering what was termed "de-centralized cooperation," (i.e. expanding ties between civil society organizations, business groups, as well as media and educational organizations). This was a hopeful sense of direction; but soon, it was proven once again that the overall environment was simply not ready to see many of these ideas implemented. Coinciding with the fact that economic relations also took a knock at the end of the 1990s with the GCC's recession severely impacting its exports to Europe, GCC-EU relations continued to languish at the lower end of the priority list for both sides. For example, the decision at the Granada meeting to open a European Commission office was not followed through. In fact, it was not until the beginning of 2004 that this actually occurred. Instead, it took dramatic changes in the external environment for the two sides to begin to see the benefits of better cooperation, and to find the focus necessary to move relations forward.

Rising Relevance: GCC-EU Relations Since 2001

The 10th joint council meeting, which was held in April 2001 in Manama, Bahrain, underlined the lack of movement that had characterized the previous decade. The council noted that negotiations for a free trade accord "had been ongoing for over ten years without much progress" and also that "the implementation of the Cooperation Agreement is monotonous and presents no tangible results."[16] In light of this assessment, the council meeting, however, again proved to be disappointing as it achieved very little in terms of putting forward suggestions of how to overcome the existing stalemate. If anything, the only positive outcome was that the parties admitted that expectations had not been met and, therefore, a new approach was necessary.

Within a year, the situation had changed dramatically. On the other hand, the events associated with September 11 acted as a catalyst as far as the relationship between Europe and the Gulf was concerned. In its aftermath, the regional realignment, in conjunction with the campaign against terrorism, as well as the previous hotspots of Iran and Iraq, focused the spotlight on the Gulf and moved the region into a more central position for European policymakers. Within a few years, the region's significance would increase with the U.S.-led invasion of Iraq and the concerns expressed over the Iranian nuclear issue. While Europe soon found itself playing catch-up with the rising strategic importance of the Gulf, it was also becoming clear that the region was no longer of interest from an energy and economic perspective alone. Instead, factors such as geography, culture and the political-strategic developments, all came together to underline the region's overall relevance.

Within began to emerge within European policy circles was the recognition that Europe had direct strategic interests in the Gulf, interests that it could ill afford to ignore. In addition, questions began to arise about the utility of allowing so-called Western interests to be protected and secured solely by the U.S.,which had been the main external actor defining the regional strategic environment for several decades. With regard to many issues, it became doubtful whether Europe could maintain its historical low profile and continue to concentrate only on economical interests while keeping political and strategic issues at bay. For one, GCC members alone made up 22.4 percent of total world oil production in 2005, a figure that is projected to increase to 33.0 percent by 2020. With energy security concerns on the rise, it became clear that the world's dependence on Gulf oil is going to increase. Second, given the problematic policies pursued by both Iran and Iraq, the GCC states became identified as islands of stability in a troublesome region. Despite many shortcomings on issues the EU considers important such as human rights, the autocratic forms of government of the Gulf monarchies, or the stringent forms of Islam, which were seen to be at the heart of extremism, the GCC states nevertheless were engaged in efforts to diversify their economies. They were working toward a greater regional integration, and also in varying degrees, moving in the direction of wider political participation and the opening-up of their political systems. In this respect, the transition taking place in the Gulf stood in contrast to the rest of the Middle East. In addition, as the first edition of the Gulf Strategy Paper of the Bertelsmann Stiftung and the Center for Applied Policy Research stated in 2002:

> The GCC countries have consistently supported the policies of the West and have never resorted to violent means for the resolution of conflicts. They have shown moderation with respect to Israel while at the same time upholding their position with respect to the need for a peace based on international law and UN resolutions. Thus, the GCC countries have proven to be an anchor of stability in a troubled environment where peace has been repeatedly challenged...[17]

The result was that the Gulf suddenly did not appear as far away as it used to. What also served as a further impetus to move the institutional relationship forward was the decision by the GCC summit meeting held in Muscat in December 2001 to implement a customs union as of January 2003 with a unified tariff of five percent. This movement had long been demanded by the European Commission as a prerequisite for the possible implementation of a Free Trade accord. With its decision, the GCC council signaled a willingness to break the deadlock that had prevented FTA negotiations from moving forward. Thus, in addition to the rapidly changing strategic environment, which necessitated a different view of the Gulf from Europe, there were also specific steps that allowed Europe to focus its strategies around particular issues where progress was actually possible.

What emerged as a response was an effort on behalf of the EU to broaden and strengthen relations and look beyond only economic and trade ties. Within this framework, the general notion that a higher degree of engagement was required gained acceptance in European political circles. On the side of the EU, there was an increasing awareness that the deteriorating security environment in the Gulf carried with it consequences affecting the proper security situation in Europe, and therefore, a closer engagement with the region was not only necessary but indispensable. In June 2004, in an ambitious attempt to integrate the GCC component, the EU formulated the 'EU Strategic Partnership with the Mediterranean and the Middle East' with the idea of having a complementary, yet distinct approach to the Gulf region, which is built on the already existing contractual relationship that has served as the basis for dialogue even on political and security issues. The Strategic Partnership document underlined that the "EU commits itself to advance its partnership with the countries of the Gulf" including considering bilateral political initiatives with those GCC members that display a desire to move forward more rapidly.

Specific aspects to be achieved include the intensification of a dialogue under relevant political instruments of the GCC, by establishing a framework for dialogue and confidence-building at the regional level, concluding and implementing the Free Trade Agreement, carrying out feasibility studies for technical assistance programs that will help to restructure the administrative frameworks in the Gulf, and finally, following youth exchange and university cooperation programs. As far as the EU was concerned, a dialogue with the GCC looked more promising than with any other part of the Middle East. Unlike the countries of the Euro-Mediterranean Partnership or the Arab League, the GCC represented a relatively unified bloc in terms of political systems, economic development, and social and religious background, which in turn made it easier for the EU to formulate its policies.

In addition to policy documents such as the European Security Strategy of 2003 and the 2004 Strategic Partnership with the Mediterranean and the Middle East, pronouncements by leading European officials also focused on broadening the relations between Europe and the Gulf States. For example, the decision of the European Council of Ministers on December 16, 2004 to begin accession talks with Turkey over possible membership broadened the EU's Middle Eastern geopolitical perspective. Even though Turkey's membership is at least over a decade away, since the actual accession negotiations are underway, it means that not only Middle Eastern, but also Gulf issues are finding prominence on the EU's agenda. If Turkey's membership occurs, the EU will have borders with two Gulf States, Iran and Iraq. Furthermore, during the 2005 Gulf Dialogue meeting which was organized by the London-based International Institute for Strategic Studies (IISS) in Manama, Bahrain, French Defense Minister, Michele Alliot-Marie, called for better strategic cooperation between Europe and the Gulf region arguing that Europe is an important political and security actor that has specific advantages and items to offer to the Gulf. She stated that Europe and the Gulf region share the same security concerns, and that Europe was, therefore, keen to expand its commercial and economic ties with the region into the fields of defense and security. Given the fact that troops from various European countries such as the United Kingdom, Poland, Italy, Germany, and the Netherlands had begun to serve in either Iraq or Afghanistan, there was also a domestic element that has catapulted the region into the consciousness of the average European and, hence, elevated Gulf issues to the list of priority concerns.

By the middle of 2007, it was clear that EU-GCC relations had already begun to make substantive progress. Whereas the long-awaited Free Trade Agreement (FTA) was still in the process of being negotiated, the final communiqué of the 17th session of the Joint Council between the European Community and the GCC states, which was held on May 8, 2007 in Riyadh, Saudi Arabia, noted that "important progress has been made" and that "the parties are getting closer to an agreement."[18] Clearly, the political will that had often been missing in the past became visible under the Germany'sEU presidency with an intense effort to move negotiations forward. This was underscored by the reference within the communiqué to strengthen their relations and deepen cooperation in "all areas" covered by the 1988

Cooperation Agreement and to focus where the relationship can be transformed into something "concrete" and "practical."

As such, the EU and the GCC held a number of expert meetings from the beginning of 2007 to look at specific fields of cooperation. This included a joint cooperation committee meeting in February, a regional director's meeting in March, an expert level dialogue on the effects of climate change in January, an energy expert group meeting at the end of April, as well as the fourth joint seminar on financing the combat against terrorism in May. The joint council meeting also agreed that a second economic dialogue meeting would be held in 2007.

Equally important was the fact that the concept of "decentralized cooperation" which was first mentioned following the 1995 Granada meeting, was revitalized with emphasis placed on promoting cooperation between universities in both regions, by creating a "Gulf window" within the EU's Erasmus Mundus program for students from the region and with the opening to GCC participation within the 7th EU Framework Research program in the fields of science and technology. Furthermore, there was an agreement on strengthening cultural dialogue between the two sides. In fact, the communiqué devoted an entire paragraph to this issue and the Alliance of Civilizations initiative.[19]

Factors Preventing a Closer Relationship

A review of the GCC-EU relationship since its inception thus reveals a mixed picture. On one hand, the cooperation remains below its actual potential and has certainly not met the expectations. On the other hand, the relationship has matured over the years and both sides now have a clearer vision in which closer ties are both warranted and possible. The nearly twenty year old Cooperation Agreement also underlined clear limitations of what can be expected within the GCC-EU framework: not only to work on the shortcomings, but more importantly, to define these limitations. It is precisely these boundaries that are making it difficult to define an implementable plan of action or agree on a concrete list of steps that can pave the way forward and make the relationship more productive, functional and institutional.

One of the key problem areas is that the project of a European Common Foreign and Security Policy (CFSP) remains very much a 'work in progress.' Efforts to establish the institutional framework of a European foreign ministry envisioned as part of the European constitution have been sidelined with the defeat of the constitution in a referendum in both France and the Netherlands. The result is that much of foreign policy remains in the hands of the individual European states. But it has also become much more difficult for the EU states to negotiate compromises among themselves and bring together diverging national interests into a consensus formula following its expansion to 25 and then 27 members. In that context, there are issues closer to home that continue to dominate respective agendas, thereby resulting in matters related to the Gulf being shifted down the priority list. After all, CFSP is only one of the many projects the EU is involved with. More pressing items, including issues like the concerns over enlargement and its impact, constitutional issues, the reform of the European treaties and an overall look at the development of the European idea have always been the first priority of the EU.

As far as the GCC states are concerned, the difficulty associated with the development of a Common Foreign and Security Policy is not the only obstacle. Bilateralism and partiality also dominate very much the European relations with the Gulf. The GCC countries are thus a primary example of why the CFSP had experienced such difficulties with countries such as France and the UK, having up until then refrained from what Bichara Khader refers to as "Europeanizing" their traditional ties with GCC states.[20] Here, the dictum that has been followed has been "what is good for an EU member state is good for the EU" and not the other way around. But instead of moving the EU toward a more common policy, the competition among EU member states has only increased as they tried to protect their interests in lucrative defense deals, for example.[21] The EU involvement as a collective unit is a very recent development. Even the Strategic Partnership document of 2004 refrains from calling for a relationship with the GCC as such and instead refers to considering "bilateral political engagement with the GCC members with a desire to move more rapidly on issues of concern."[22] It can be said that the Strategic Partnership is, therefore, an example of how, in fact, the inter-regional dialogue has been abandoned, or at the least, downgraded. Baabood and Edwards have characterized the Strategic Partnership document as merely a compensation for the GCC not being included in the EU's Neighborhood Policy and, as a result, "a paradox of Europe's strategic dependence and minimal EU presence."[23]

Another issue has always been the problem of what Helle Malmvig refers to as the lack of a "campaigner" within the EU (i.e. one prominent voice who will lead the way to greater EU involvement in the Gulf region).[24] Without such a unifier, it has not been possible to bring all the different interests and priorities of EU member states into sync to the point where an agreement about the level of importance of establishing deeper relations with the GCC countries exists. The same problem, however, also exists on the GCC side with a common argument coming out of EU policy circles that the GCC states have failed to engage in serious policy-making and have not acted in a manner that would warrant closer EU involvement. As mentioned at the outset of this paper, the different structural composition of the two institutions has certainly contributed to this difficulty; however, it would be unfair to say that while the EU represents many different interests, the GCC speaks in a more unified tone. Far from it, on a host of issues the GCC is as divided as ever and there is still the lack of an overall vision on what the GCC is and what it aspires to become.

In the meantime, another difficulty the GCC faced was identifying at what points Europe can add value, as it is a known fact that many of the problems for the region are directly associated with the region's volatile security environment. For the past few decades, direct threats to the security and stability of the GCC were caused by Iraq and Iran and transnational phenomena such as terrorism. These challenges required immediate answers and, in some way, necessitated a more direct security and defense relationship with the U.S. European political weight played only a secondary support role.

Curiously, regarding the GCC states, there has been a shifting emphasis in terms of the type of the relationship that is being envisioned. For the EU, ties with the Gulf, as aforementioned, were always primarily economy-related, and this specifically meant they were oil-driven. This, however, has not been the case for the GCC. In fact, initially, even prior to the Cooperation Agreement of 1988, Kuwait and Saudi Arabia argued against the possibility of an EEC-Gulf dialogue, initially proposed in January 1980, on the basis that the European approach failed to incorporate a short- as well as long-term strategic dimension that included the political and economic dimensions.

The dichotomy of political vs. economic considerations becomes the most obvious when considering the negotiations for a Free Trade Agreement between the GCC countries and the EU. As we mentioned earlier, while negotiations initiated back in 1990, the institutional mismatch between the GCC and the EU proved to be a significant obstacle in terms of moving the negotiations along. It was not until 1997, for example, the GCC received the negotiating mandate from its member states. Even then, prerequisites such as external tariff and customs unions were not established until 2001 and 2003, respectively. Thus, while the communiqué of the July 1995 Granada meeting called for an unlocking of the FTA negotiations, and while, as already mentioned, the 11th council communiqué of April 2001 mentioned that "negotiations have been ongoing for over 10 years without much progress" the limited political will that did exist was unable to overcome the basic economic and technical matters that prevented progress.

Yet, the GCC position of favoring a political dialogue clearly has its limits and is mainly directed at receiving the EU's support for crucial regional issues such as the GCC stance on the Arab-Israeli issue. Thus, the GCC has complained bitterly about the EU's insistence on claiming that the free trade area negotiations are also including the political and foreign policy issues. One example of this situation has been the inclusion of a human rights component, which entered into talks during the fifth joint ministerial meeting in 1994 and has been featured prominently ever since. This was given further impetus in the context of the post-September 11 environment when the EU decided to place greater emphasis on the issue of political reform based on the assessment that the region had been neglected in this regard.[25] The GCC viewed such tactics as domestic interference and an unnecessary distraction from the substance of the FTA. There was also the feeling among the GCC countries that the EU had presented a never-ending catalogue of requirements that unnecessarily prolonged the negotiations. The GCC Secretary-General Abdul Rahman al-Attiyah has, for example, stated: 'Unfortunately, from time to time European Union representatives come up with issues that are not really related to the formation of a GCC-EU Free Trade Area … human rights should not be an issue in economic negotiations because we are raising issues which have nothing to do with the economic cooperation and dialogue."[26] The EU's argument was that clauses on human rights and governance are standard parts of the EU's agreement, which are not perceived as valid by the GCC.

Finally, as evidenced by the early years of institutional cooperation, there is a gap between the official meetings that take place and official visits that are carried out at regular intervals, while the Gulf States, to a certain degree, have a poor image in the eye of not only the EU public but also the officials. The result is that, as Khader outlines, instead of "an effective complicity," a "perceived cultural distance" exists in between.[27] It may appear that this is a common problem which exists in the relationship between many different areas of the world and, therefore, it is certainly not unique to the EU's relations with the GCC countries. At the same time, given the rising importance of cultural issues and identity problems, it is clearly a factor that prevents the two sides from seeing particular items from a similar perspective.

Given the above-mentioned obstacles, it is, nevertheless, evident that the GCC-EU relationship has begun to take on a more substantive agenda. Thus, while economic and trade ties continue to predominate, items such as energy concerns, and broader political and strategic dimensions have gained greater importance. A closer look at each of these factors illustrates to what degree GCC-EU relations have broadened and where the direction for the future lies.

Economics Predominates

Economic relations between the Gulf and Europe are already strong and there is likely to be a continued expansion as this offers both sides numerous potential benefits. The EU is not only the principal trade partner of the Gulf, it is also the only region with which the GCC states run a trade deficit, which stood at 18 billion euros in 2006. Overall, the trade volume between the GCC and the EU, which has grown from 34.6 billion euros in 1996, to 54.4 billion euros in 2001, and reached over 91.0 billion euros by the end of 2006, was almost tripled in less than a decade. Hence, the GCC represents the sixth most important export market for the EU and their trade is equal to half the trade with the entire Arab world. The EU, on the other hand, is the largest trading partner of the GCC.

With the GCC states enjoying record income levels due to the high oil price environment that has been in place since 2002, the share of the EU as an import partner of the GCC, has witnessed a decline. But given the importance of the EU in transport equipment and development-related machinery, the Gulf represents an emerging market even outside the traditional economic base of energy and energy-related products. While about two-thirds of GCC energy exports go to Asia, exports from the GCC to the EU are more diversified than exports to other world regions. This is because the discovery of oil in the North Sea and increasing supplies from Africa and Russia made the EU rely more on energy resources closer to home than from the Gulf. At the same time, oil production in the North Sea peaked in 1999, and, together with European concerns about stable energy supplies from Russia, the GCC countries could once again enter the picture, resulting in rising energy exports to the EU.[28] This, in turn, would have a direct impact on the trade balance.

Another important area is cross-border investments. In recent years, Europe has become an important destination of portfolio and direct investments from the GCC to the point where Europe has emerged as a serious competitor for the still dominant dollar-based investments that make up the large majority of GCC foreign assets. Moreover, the GCC petrodollars have flocked increasingly into European security markets, and there have also been a number of well-diversified GCC investment deals in Europe, including: Kuwait-based MTC buying Dutch Celtel ($3.4 billion), the Saudi Basic Industries Corporation (SABIC) purchasing UK-based Huntsman Petrochemicals ($700 million), Abu Dhabi-based Mubadala buying 5 percent of Ferrari (about $2.8 billion), and Dubai International Capital buying two percent of DaimlerChrysler (about $1 billion).[29] The GCC has thus shown a clear disposition to invest in Europe. One obstacle to EU's investment in the GCC that remains to be overcome is the mindset among some European companies which sees the Gulf primarily as a risk area without seeing the promising economic potential. As a result, foreign direct investment patterns are subject to a high degree of fluctuation with the EU foreign direct investment (FDI) in the GCC picking up in 2005, following the years of decline between 2002 and 2004. The new investment patterns of the GCC already point toward a shift away from the U.S. and increased interdependence with Europe.

Table 7.1. Evolution of GCC-EU Trade 2000-2005 (billion euros)

		2000	2002	2003	2004	2005	2006
Bahrain	Exports	0.444	0.385	0.346	0.341	0.505	0.570
	Imports	0.900	0.944	0.956	1.195	1.153	1.433
Kuwait	Exports	3.211	1.812	1.930	2.262	3.195	4.040
	Imports	2.376	2.953	3.128	3.525	3.648	3.727
Oman	Exports	0.187	0.436	0.238	0.360	0.453	0.410
	Imports	1.141	1.388	1.296	1.672	1.759	1.734
Qatar	Exports	0.374	0.465	0.848	0.983	1.409	2.036
	Imports	1.351	1.907	2.221	3.358	3.088	5.085
Saudi Arabia	Exports	15.920	12.352	12.991	16.266	22.601	23.512
	Imports	12.143	14.246	13.578	12.588	15.584	17.574
UAE	Exports	2.518	2.914	3.912	5.325	9.855	5.778
	Imports	12.067	14.679	16.467	18.728	25.562	25.143
Total GCC	Exports	22.654	18.364	20.265	25.537	37.363	36.346
	Imports	29.978	36.117	37.646	41.066	50.373	54.696

Source: Eurostat, Official Statistics of the European Commission

With rising investment opportunities, the successful conclusion of the Free Trade Agreement between the EU and GCC should impact itself positively on overall economic relations and will most likely lead to a further increase in trade volume between the two sides. Being the largest importers of Gulf oil and representing the natural market for future Gulf energy exports, the GCC states have also moved quickly to conclude free trade accords with Asian countries such as India, China and Japan. In this context, however, the GCC continues to define the FTA negotiations as a litmus test for the EU's seriousness about bringing substantive issues to the table. Unlike the EU example, negotiations with Asian countries have not been sidetracked by having talks broadened to include such items as democracy, human rights and weapons proliferation.

Pending issues within the FTA negotiations with the EU include access to the service sector in GCC countries, further opening up of the energy sector, GCC petrochemical exports to the EU, transparency in GCC public procurement regulations, and the issue of rules of origin for exports coming out of GCC countries. Yet, the significance of the FTA lies beyond simply the promotion of better trade relations. As part of the negotiations toward a FTA, the EU aims to consolidate the GCC's own regional integration process as well as to direct the region's movement toward a rules-based framework. By promoting closer economic and trade ties, the EU sees increased levels of business contacts and mutual investments as important factors that contribute to stability, as there is likely to be an adverse reaction to any attempts to bring about a politically-motivated interruption of commerce. Furthermore, it is generally accepted that greater capital investments also contribute to the integration of service and capital markets.[30] Such a mechanism of economic development is thus a way to promote political reform at the same time.

The FTA is also significant because its successful conclusion will represent the first free trade area between two multilateral organizations. It is also not simply a goods-only agreement, but rather a comprehensive deal that includes such items as services, investment and public procurement issues. These points are usually not considered when criticism arises about the long period of negotiations. Although to be fair, for the majority at that time, at least for the first 12 years from 1990 to 2002, the technical conditions, such as customs union and WTO membership, were simply not there for considerable progress to be achieved.

Energy Security

Even under the precursor to the EU-GCC relationship, energy security has always been the main component of the Euro-Arab Dialogue. This dialogue began in the wake of the October 1973 oil crisis when oil shortages, for the first time, brought the notion of energy scarcity to the minds of official policymakers and the general public in Europe. As a result, the dialogue was an effort to ensure a regular supply chain of energy to Europe, the delivery of this energy at reasonable prices, and beyond that, to allow for Arab surplus petrodollars to be recycled in European financial markets.[31]

Recent developments in world energy markets have once again heightened both the consciousness about and concerns over energy security issues, marking the return of energy supply issues on the policy agendas of most countries. This is partly due to the phenomenal rise in oil prices which have sky-rocketed from an average price of $23.50 per barrel in 2002 to over $70 a barrel in June 2007. This was propelled by rising demand, in particular from Asia, and declining spare capacity of producing countries as well as their limited refinery capacities. Pundits agree that the age of cheap oil is over and that given present developments, specifically in the volatile oil-producing regions of the world, a price of over $100 a barrel can no longer be considered unrealistic.

Energy supply concerns are, however, not related only to oil prices. What is often missed in this equation is the fact that the issues of regional security and political stability are equally important factors for energy production and supply. Political issues as a whole are relevant as underlined by the crisis over Russian gas deliveries to the the Ukraine at the end of 2005, where it became blatantly obvious that consumer nations could easily be subject to a virtual state of blackmail solely because of their energy dependency. The crisis further showed that politics can stop the flow of energy and that even countries not directly involved in the dispute can be affected. The Russian energy conglomerate Gazprom, which was at the heart of the dispute, subsequently went a step further and stated that future supplies to Europe may be in jeopardy if the EU interfered with the company's expansion to the European market.

Security of supply is one of the core objectives around which the 2007 Green Paper of the European Commission on a European Energy Strategy is framed.[32] Given current trends and projections, there are concrete reasons for this emphasis. For one, European dependence on external sources of energy supplies increased as a result of declining production in traditional areas such as the North Sea and Norway. According to the *2006 Energy Review Report* released by the UK government, the country will move "from a position of virtual self-sufficiency to, by 2020, being 80-90 percent reliant on imports."[33] For Europe as a whole, import dependence in terms of energy supplies is set to increase from the current 50 percent to 70 percent in the next 20 to 30 years.

Europe's current reliance on Gulf energy supplies is limited and imports from the region have remained steady in recent years at approximately 22 percent. Yet, given its pre-programmed import dependence and the fact that stable Gulf supplies are essential for the maintenance of energy prices levels, Europe cannot afford to simply look past and ignore the security challenges the Gulf region is confronted with. For Europe, as well as for the other parts of the world, the equation remains the same in the issue of security and energy supplies cannot be seen in isolation from the issues and problems of general security facing the Gulf. Europe's energy policy thus has to be incorporated within the larger dimension of the external policies of the EU and within the context of the development of a common foreign and security policy.

Unfortunately, no high-level energy dialogue between the two sides exists and energy relations have not grown under the 1988 Cooperation Agreement. Furthermore, even prior to the agreement and ever since then, the issue of petrochemicals has been the core subject on which the two sides have found it most difficult to reach an agreement. Thus, energy issues and petrochemicals was not featured in the first two communiqués of the joint council meetings in 1990 and 1991.

It has only been with the joint council communiqué of May 2006 that the EU once again began to push for a Memorandum of Understanding on Energy with the GCC countries. As such, the concern over future energy supplies has translated into the need for diplomatic initiatives and an engagement that deals with instability and leads to a lessening in regional tensions. During the 2007 meeting, it was further agreed to reinforce cooperation in the field of energy following the holding of an Energy Expert Group at the end of April. It is likely that both sides will treat this dialogue with increased emphasis from this point forward.

The Political and Security Sphere

While progress on the economic front has been positive and beneficial to both sides, Europe and the Gulf have found it more difficult to expand their relations into the political, security and social spheres. However, it is a fact that Europe is becoming an increasingly political and security actor in the region and the notion that the GCC states present an anchor of stability in a highly volatile region has started to gain acceptance within various European policy circles. With the opening of a European Commission Office in Riyadh, the EU lent substance to this realization.

As a result of the events in Iraq, although the Gulf and Middle East region dominate the headlines, the most critical component has been the growing realization within both European and Gulf circles that a further deterioration in security and stability in the Gulf region is detrimental to both sides. Roberto Aliboni has noted that while the debate about a possible role for Europe in Gulf security matters is not new, the debate within Europe about the scope and prospects for such a role have certainly gained momentum.[34]

From the GCC perspective, there is a growing realization that the continued sole reliance on the U.S. as the guarantor for stability and security in the region is proving increasingly inadequate. The failure exhibited by the U.S. in efficiently handling the reconstruction process in Iraq, including its complete unwillingness to consider shortcomings in its policy approach to this country, led some states in the region to suggest alternative paths, including a greater degree of convergence with European partners. The statement given by Saud al-Faisal, the Foreign Minister of Saudi Arabia in December 2004, expressing that "security in the Gulf needs international guarantees which cannot be ensured by a single party, even by the sole superpower," should be seen in this context. In addition, the announcement of the U.S.-Middle East Partnership Initiative in December 2002 followed by the 'Partnership for Progress and a Common Future' for the broader Middle East and North Africa presented at the G-8 summit in June 2004, coupled with the Arab world's almost universal rejection of these initiatives, have led the GCC states to look for domestic political reform approaches other than the forceful approach used by the U.S.

Because the Gulf is seen as the primary area of influence for the U.S., Europe has not shown the will to adopt an independent policy in this region. In this context, there have been criticisms claiming that in fact Europe has benefited from the U.S.'s role to promote regional stability without having to bear any direct costs. Yet, it is important to point out that any potential European role in security affairs of the Gulf cannot be seen as a replacement for the one currently being played by the U.S. As Aliboni states:

> The EU is thus called upon to play a security role, beneficial to both the U.S. and the regional countries, in terms of more and bolder initiatives in the region. At the end of the day, all it has to do is to be more assertive and confident in renewing and enhancing its links with the GCC, setting out a substantive and consistent strategy towards the region…[35]

As explained above, the attempt by the EU to play such a strategic role as outlined by the 2004 Strategic Partnership has not resulted in any concrete outcomes. Neither is this likely to change in the near-term. The lack of consensus within the EU about what role it can assume is compounded by the existence of the extensive uncertainty about what exactly the GCC states seek from Europe when it comes to such a large strategic role.[36] Unless this contradiction is resolved, the discussion will, unfortunately, likely be prolonged and will result in continued dissatisfaction on both sides.

Prospective Outlook

Europe has started to look at the Gulf from a deeper strategic perspective, fully cognizant of the fact that turmoil and instability in the region also have direct relevance and implications. As Malmvig noted: "…the Gulf region will potentially emerge as the EU's new neighborhood, and this will make EU involvement in the Gulf increasingly unavoidable."[37] From a GCC perspective, Europe already represents what the region wants most: a system that enables both sides to overcome historical animosities and allow individual states to develop themselves while working for the common good of stability and prosperity.

The *Pax Americana* system that has so long been pre-dominant in the Gulf region is on the decline and thereby it has become possible for the EU to exert greater influence. Yet, Europe is not about to replace the predominant military power of the U.S. in the region. What Europe can do is continue to offer its services, pursue engagements that lead to greater regional interactions and offer mechanisms through which potential conflicts and issues can be dealt with constructively and peacefully. Europe, thus, can encourage the widening of institutional relations between the EU, NATO and the OSCE on one side, and the GCC on the other. The finalization of the Free Trade Agreement (FTA) would also be a strong message of the commitment of the EU and the GCC to move their relationship forward and look at areas beyond economy and trade. As the bloc pursues challenging economic projects such as the establishment of a common market in 2007 and a common currency in 2010, a FTA will not only be an important political signal, but it will also represent a clear statement of support for the intergovernmental structure of the GCC in particular. These projects need the EU's support, as it is also being considered a model.

Overall, the Gulf-Europe relations are bound to develop further and take on new qualitative aspects. Meanwhile, one should note that nobody should encounter disappointment from over-expectations. While the GCC and the EU share many similar interests and policies, there are still enormous institutional differences that will not be overcome by common ministerial statements or by reference to the need for greater cooperation. Furthermore, both the EU and the GCC continue to occupy only a secondary role when compared wth the primary interest of each organization. For the EU, the internal integration and consolidation process stands at the top of the list, even as concerns over regional stability on the EU's outskirts is rising. For GCC countries, the U.S. remains the only state that can provide the necessary guarantees for their national survival. Despite the economic gains that are being made and the overall development that is taking place, unlike EU countries, GCC states cannot be confident, in essence, that another regional war will not break out or that their own sovereignty will not become directly threatened. As a result, there is a heavy emphasis on hard security mechanisms the EU cannot and will not provide. Thus, accepting what the EU-GCC relationship can or cannot provide is the proper framework under which mutual ties should be examined.

---

[1] Bertelsmann Foundation and Center for Applied Policy Research, eds., *The EU and the GCC: A New Partnership*, March 2002, p. 3.
[2] Abdulkhaleq Abdullah, "The Gulf Cooperation Council: Nature, Origin and Process," in Michael C. Hudson, ed., Middle East Dilemma: The Politics and Economics of Arab Integration (New York: Columbia University Press, 1999), p. 154.
[3] Hassan Hamdan al-Alkim, The GCC States in an Unstable World: Foreign-Policy Dilemmas of Small States (London: Saqi Books, 1994), p. 162.
[4] The Charter Agreement is available on the website of the Gulf Cooperation Council under http://www.gcc-sg.org/CHARTER.html
[5] Gerd Nonneman, *EU-GCC Relations: Dynamics, Patterns and Perspectives* (Dubai: Gulf Research Center, 2006), p. 25.

⁶ Abdullah, "The Gulf Cooperation Council," p. 155.
⁷ Ana Echagüe, The European Union and the Gulf Cooperation Council, FRIDE (Fundación par alas Relaciones Internacionales y el Diálogo Exterior) Working Paper 39, May 2007, pp. 6-7.
⁸ The characterization of the "notable gap" is from a draft paper by Abdullah Baabood and Geoffrey Edwards entitled "Reinforcing Ambivalence: The Interaction of Gulf States and the European Union" presented at a workshop entitled "European Union-Gulf Cooperation Council Relations and Security Issues: Broadening the Horizon," and held within the framework of eighth Mediterranean Social and Political Research meeting, Florence – Montecatini Terme, March 21-25, 2007, p.1. The final version of the paper will be published in an edited volume by the Gulf Research Center by the fall of 2007.
⁹ For a broader discussion about the early developments of the Gulf-Europe relationship see Bogdan Szajkowski, "EU-GCC Relations in the Framework of the Euro-Arab Dialogue," in *Unfulfilled Potential: Exploring the GCC-EU Relationship*, ed. Christian Koch, (Dubai: Gulf Research Center, 2005), pp. 15-34.
¹⁰ Z, Wieczorek, "Report Drawn up on behalf of the Committee on External Economic Relations on Trade Relations between the EEC and the Gulf State," Working Documents (1980-1981), Second Edition, (European Parliament, Luxembourg), August 14, 1981 as listed in Szajkowski, ibid., p. 23.
¹¹ Szajkowski, "EU-GCC Relations," pp. 23-31. See also Bichara Khader, "EU-GCC Relations: A Concise Balance Sheet of the last 25 years," Paper presented at the workshop of the Istituto Affari Interazionali (IAI) and the Gulf Research Center (GRC) entitled *Fostering EU-Italy-GCC Cooperation* and held on December 13, 2006 in Rome, Italy, pp. 5-6.
¹² On the Euro-Arab Dialogue see Saleh Al-Mani and Salah Al-Shaikhly, *The Euro-Arab Dialogue: A Study in Associative Diplomacy* (London: Frances Pinter, 1983). The quote is from the preamble of the Cooperation Agreement between the European Economic Community and the GCC listed in the *Official Journal of the European Communities*, OJ No. L 54/3, February 25, 1989.
¹³ Khader, "EU-GCC Relations: A Concise Balance Sheet of the last 25 years," p. 25.
¹⁴ Abdullah Baabood, *EU-Gulf Political and Economic Relations: Assessment and Policy Recommendations* (Dubai: Gulf Research Center, September 2006), p. 30. This line of argument comes out in more detail in his doctoral dissertation entitled *EU-GCC Relations: A Study in Interregional Cooperation*, Gulf Theses (Dubai: Gulf Research Center, June 2006), in particular Chapter 5.
¹⁵ Echagüe, The European Union and the Gulf Cooperation Council, pp. 2, 3.
¹⁶ Khader, "EU-GCC Relations," p. 23.
¹⁷ Bertelsmann Foundation and Center for Applied Policy Research, eds., *The EU and the GCC: A New Partnership*, March 2002, p. 5.
¹⁸ Seventeenth EU-GCC Joint Council and Ministerial Meeting, Riyadh, May 8, 2007, Joint Communiqué available under http://www.consilium.europa.eu/ueDocs/cms_Data/docs/pressData/en/er/94036.pdf
¹⁹ The Alliance for Civilizations in an initiative of the Secretary-General of the United Nations and co-sponsored by the Prime Ministers of Spain and Turkey to "responds to a broad consensus across nations, cultures and religions that all societies are interdependent, bound together in their development and security, and

in their environmental, economic and financial well-being." Numerous high-level expert meetings have taken place and in April 2007, Jorge Sampaio, the former President of Portugal, as designated as the High Representative for the Alliance of Civilizations. Further information about the initiative can be taken from http://www.unaoc.org/

[20] Khader, "EU-GCC Relations," p. 25

[21] Luciani and Schumacher also mention in their paper that the UK and France "have not perceived a benefit in the Europeanization of relations with the GCC." As such, the GCC has been perceived as an area of competition rather than as a burden to be shared. See Giacomo Luciani and Tobias Schumacher, GCC-EU Relations: Past Record and Promises for the Future (Dubai: Gulf Research Center, 2004), p. 10.

[22] Baabood and Edwards, "Reinforcing Ambivalence".

[23] Ibid., Echagüe refers to the 2004 Strategic Partnership document as a "shallow framework." See Echagüe, op.cit., p. 4.

[24] Helle Malmvig, "An unlikely match or a marriage in the making? EU-GCC relations in a changing security environment," Danish Institute for International Studies (DIIS) Brief, November 2006, p. 5.

[25] Richard Youngs argues that lack of progress in the Free Trade Area negotiations in 2004 was due to the desire by the Saudi ruling family "to limit the reach and pace of political change." See Richard Youngs, *Europe and the Middle East: In the Shadows of September 11* (Boulder: Lynne Rienner Publishers, 2006), p. 186.

[26] http://www.vegamedia.com/new/interviews/al-attiyah.html

[27] Khader, "EU-GCC Relations," p. 27.

[28] Eckart Woertz, "Overlooked and Understated: EU-GCC Economic Cooperation," *Gulf Monitor*, June 2006.

[29] Ibid.

[30] Echagüe, The European Union and the Gulf Cooperation Council.

[31] Khader, op.cit.

[32] "Fueling our future: The European Commission sets out its vision for an Energy Strategy for Europe," Brussels, Press Release IP/06/282, March 8, 2006 available under www.europa.eu.int/rapid

[33] UK Department of Trade and Industry, *The Energy Challenge*, Energy Review Report 2006, p. 77.

[34] Roberto Aliboni, *Europe's Role in the Gulf: A Transatlantic Perspective* (Dubai: Gulf Research Center, 2006), p. 9

[35] Ibid., p. 29.

[36] Nonneman, EU-GCC relations, op.cit., p. 15.

[37] Malmvig, "An unlikely match or a marriage in the making?" p. 13.

Chapter 8
Europe's Role in Iran's Quest for Nuclear Power*

Mustafa Kibaroğlu

Iran's nuclear program has become a highly controversial issue in international politics, especially since the unveiling of the uranium enrichment facility in August 2002 that was built clandestinely in Natanz since 1984 with the support of China.[1] While American and especially Israeli officials and experts assert that Iran has secret plans to use its nuclear infrastructure to develop nuclear weapons, Iranian officials, on the other hand, deny such allegations and claim that they will use their nuclear capacity exclusively for peaceful purposes.[2] Notwithstanding the official rhetoric, many Iranian scholars, intellectuals, civil, and military officials argue that Iran should seriously consider developing nuclear weapons as well, given the fact they have the necessary skills and capabilities, and the reasons to do so.[3]

With respect to weapons development, there are two basic views. One view, which is supported by a minor group, suggests that Iran should definitely have nuclear technology and even weapons. These are mostly the bureaucrats and scientists who have been involved in the nuclear projects for many years, as well as others who are well entrenched in the state structure. The other view, which is supported by a majority of people, holds that, as a regional power with great ambitions, Iran must have nuclear capabilities. A proportion of those who are against nuclear weapons development are in opposition because of the timing. They argue that international conjuncture is not suitable and suggest waiting. The statements made by the U.S. and Israeli officials about military strikes strengthen the views of those who endorse nuclear weapons development. Weaponization of Iran's capabilities will depend on the political decision of the leadership.

Whether or not the Iranian leadership will give the critical decision of weaponization of their nuclear capabilities, the size of Iran's existing nuclear infrastructure, and more to be developed in time, together with the achievements of Iranian scientists and technicians who claim to have developed indigenous capabilities, may very well elevate Iran soon to the status of a "nuclear power" and even to the position of a "nuclear-weapons-capable state." Whether this is a thing to be proud of, as many Iranians from all walks of life obviously are, or something that may have adverse consequences for Iran ultimately, as it goes in this direction, remains unclear. What is clear, however, is that, for a variety of reasons, this issue will continue to be a top priority item on the agenda of all the states concerned, both from inside and outside the region.

Therefore, it is worth understanding how Iran managed to develop a considerable technological infrastructure and to accumulate valuable scientific expertise in the nuclear field under the rule of two diverse leaders, namely the Shah Pahlavi and the Imam Khomeini. It is also worth knowing why Iran's capabilities became the locus of scholarly interest and an issue of hot political debate, especially in the last ten years. Hence, this chapter aims to discuss the background of Iran's decade-long efforts to develop the nuclear infrastructure and the scientific accumulation that it has today, and that it is planned to be further expanded. Iran's achievements in the nuclear field couldn't be studied in isolation from a multitude of factors that contributed, in one way or another, to its efforts to build elaborate nuclear capabilities. In this context, the role of leading European countries such as France and Germany will be particularly emphasized.

A series of developments that took place in the world in the 1960s and 70s, which resulted in a fierce competition among the Western European nations as well as the U.S., Canada and Japan, in marketing their nuclear technologies to developing states, including Iran, deserve mentioning. Because the lack of coherence in the policies of these countries in the implementation of the basic principles and norms of the nuclear non-proliferation regime, due to their diverging national interests and differing threat perceptions, contributed, directly or indirectly, to the spread of sensitive technologies and scientific knowledge throughout the world under the guise of peaceful exploitation of nuclear technology. The repercussions of these policies were later seen in the form of nuclearization of a good deal of countries like Israel, India, South Africa, Pakistan, and more recently North Korea, as well as others like Argentina, Brazil, Libya, Iraq, and Iran, all of which have come close to the threshold.[4]

It is interesting to note that a number of factors that drove Iran and Western European nations toward cooperation in the nuclear field in the 1970s under the Shah's monarchic regime—such as national security or national pride issues for Iranians, and economic benefits or the challenge of the U.S.' supremacy upon Europeans—are observed to still be present in their relations under the Imam's theocratic regime. In other words, in all these years, there is a continuity, as well as change, in the respective positions of Iran and the European nations, which is believed to be worthy of exploring, in order to see if they may potentially hint at some ways and means to help resolve the conflict.

European Nuclear Export Policies and Iran's Nuclear Program

The role played by France and especially West Germany (hereafter Germany) in the expansion of its nuclear infrastructure, as well as raising a cadre of Iranian professionals and scientists, cannot be underestimated.[5]

For instance, in 1974, Iran signed contracts with the French company Framatome to build two 950 MW(e) pressurized water reactors and the site preparation work began in Darkhovin on the Kharoon River near Ahvaz, the southern tip of the border with Iraq. In 1975, Iran purchased a ten percent share in Eurodif, a joint venture uranium enrichment company of France, Belgium, Spain, and Italy. Iran's contract with Eurodif envisaged supply of about 270 tons of uranium enriched to three percent in U-235.[6] It was estimated that the Iranian share in this large enrichment plant at Tricastin in France would provide Iran with sufficient quantities of low enriched uranium (LEU) fuel that was required for its national program at least until the mid-1990s.[7] In connection with these contracts, a significant number of Iranian students, scientists and technicians have gone to France to advance their skills and knowledge in nuclear engineering, nuclear physics and other related branches.

On the other hand, Germany and Iran reached an agreement in 1976 for the establishment of six nuclear power reactors in Iran, the first two of which would be built by German Kraftwerk Union (KWU) in Bushehr, each housing Siemens 1,300 MW(e) reactors. In the same year, Iran also concluded nuclear fuel contracts with Germany and in 1977, with France.[8] There were also negotiations between Germany and Iran for selling uranium enrichment technology to Iran.[9] Aside from cooperation in the technology transfer, there was also a huge program of training Iranian nuclear scientists in Germany. According to Prof. Erwin Haeckel, senior researcher in the German Council on Foreign Relations, "as of the late 1970s, there were hundreds of Iranian students in German universities studying nuclear physics, and nuclear engineering."[10] Hence, Prof. Haeckel argued, "if Iran is regarded to be able to carry out a massive nuclear program, there is a heavy footprint of German cooperation. We cannot gauge easily what contribution we made, but a heavy legacy has to be taken into account."[11]

Lack of Coherence in European Nonproliferation and Export Control Policies

In the 1970s, due to a lack of coherence in the nuclear non-proliferation strategies of the West, and the disharmony in their export control policies, a number of aspiring states like Pakistan, South Africa, Argentina, Brazil, Iran, and Libya have exploited most of the opportunity to have access to sensitive technologies. There were a number of reasons for such an outcome that have ultimately led to nuclearization of a good deal of these countries. One was the decision of the Nixon administration in July 1974 to suspend the supply of low enriched uranium (LEU) that would mean literally cutting off the supply of fuel for nearly all light water reactors (LWR) in the world outside communist countries. The U.S. was making an official statement that it could no longer be counted as a reliable fuel supplier for the burgeoning civilian nuclear power industry it had promoted globally.[12]

One consequence of this U.S. action was to give new impetus to Western Europe's and Japan's programs for developing their own fuel producing technologies and merchandising them abroad. These technologically advanced states were already undertaking projects for construction of nuclear plant enrichment as well as reprocessing. Reasons behind building reprocessing spent reactor fuel facilities was to more fully utilize the energy value of LEU and to extend the life of natural uranium resources; and moving forward toward commercialization of the light metal fast breeder reactors (LMFBR), which promised eventual self-sufficiency and an end to dependence on external sources of natural uranium as well as enrichment services. The Commercial incentive to find customers abroad was powerful. It sharpened the competitive edge of the challenge to the dominant U.S. reactor manufacturers. Europeans showed themselves ready to sell sensitive enrichment and reprocessing technologies to sweeten the terms of reactor deals, or simply to satisfy consumer wants. Within the next few months in early 1975, France revealed plans to sell reprocessing plants to South Korea and Pakistan; and Germany entered into a massive deal with Brazil for the transfer of enrichment as well as reprocessing technology. These transactions disturbed the U.S. because of the seeming reluctance of European suppliers to impose strict conditions of sale, especially the requirements that all of the recipients' nuclear facilities be placed under safeguards.[13]

In the late 1970s, the U.S. government launched an International Nuclear Fuel Cycle Evaluation (INFCE) to devise measures which could "minimize the danger of proliferation without jeopardizing energy supplies or the development of nuclear energy for peaceful purposes." The hope was that some alternative to a plutonium-producing fuel cycle could be found. However, in 1980, INFCE concluded that although certain measures could make misuse of the fuel cycle more difficult, there was no technical way to produce nuclear energy without using or producing materials that could be used in nuclear weapons at the same time.[14]

From Germany's standpoint as a non-nuclear weapons state (NNWS), the Social Democrats in power had insisted that it was allowed to develop, produce and operate technologies encompassing the whole nuclear cycle. Nevertheless, there was a conflict between the U.S. and Germany over the nuclear export policies. The U.S. was able to establish a new standard requiring any further transfers of sensitive technologies like enrichment and reprocessing be discussed in advance within the newly established Nuclear

Suppliers Group (NSG).[15] But Germany was producing cutting-edge nuclear technologies and was anxious to sell to whoever might be suitable.[16] According to Prof. Krause, Director of the Institute for Security Studies at the University of Kiel, there was a general sense that the transfer of such technologies by Germany, Japan and France could lead to an erosion of the Nuclear Non-Proliferation Treaty.[17] The German ambition of mastering and controlling the whole nuclear cycle paved the way to the establishment of the joint URENCO enrichment plant in the Dutch city of Almelo by Germany, Britain and the Netherlands.[18]

The conflict with the U.S. over nuclear exports was debated in the scholarly and political circles in Germany primarily as a case of a transatlantic dispute that was reflecting the growing maturity and self-assertiveness of Germany. For the first time, German government had openly defied the U.S. and it seemed that nuclear non-proliferation policy and nuclear export controls were areas where Germany was ready to invest political capital.[19]

On the other hand, the behavior exhibited by France in the nuclear non-proliferation was ambivalent. France had not taken part in the negotiations of the NPT, nor did it sign when opened to signatures in 1968, but declared that it would behave as if it had signed the Treaty. Yet, France refused to take part in the meetings of the Zangger Committee[20] set up by NPT parties to spell out the list of materials and equipment that, under Article III of the Treaty, could only be supplied under safeguards to non-nuclear weapons states. Prof. Bertrand Goldschmidt, one of the founders of the French Atomic Energy Agency, said that although the French attitude toward nuclear non-proliferation moved closer to that of other major industrial powers by agreeing to EURATOM[21] inspections, the French policy of abstention from the NPT and the development of an independent nuclear force won a broad national consensus in the late 1970s. The problem of horizontal proliferation and the dangers for world stability have never taken the same importance nor caused the same deep anxiety for the French public, official circles, or media as it has in countries like the U.S., Canada and Sweden. Being satisfied with their policy of nuclear exports conformed to the NPT, the French public never queried the official decision not to sign the Treaty.[22]

Divergence of Views Between Western Europe and the U.S.

Americans viewed the Western Europeans' record of non-proliferation policies as doubtful. They believed that the Western Europeans were the major stumbling block on the road to a successful conclusion of the NPT. In the same vein, the Europeans were also viewed by Americans as continually subordinating non-proliferation to narrow vested interest since the 1970s, such as the German-Brazilian deal, and Belgium's negotiations with Libya. Americans also believed that it was the Europeans who prevented an agreement on a water-tight export policy among supplier nations that would have restricted exports to countries that accept to implement full-scope safeguards and put a total ban on the transfer of sensitive technologies.[23]

But, when looking at the same issues from the European perspective, an explanation comes from Prof. Harald Müller, Director of Peace Research Institute Frankfurt, stating that "two categories of states were affected by non-proliferation: the superpowers trying to maintain world order, and those countries in or very close to the proliferating region. Western Europe fell in neither category."[24] It was far enough from the nearest possible proliferation spot (i.e., the Middle East), and it was dependent on world trade for its welfare. The higher dependence on exports and imports has led Europeans always to embrace a more comprehensive understanding of security than its Atlantic partner did. For Europe, economic security, as one component of national security, was (and still is) as important as the military one. Unless proliferation presented a challenge to world order, Europeans, who are the trading nations, would not share a deep interest in its limitation.[25]

Hence, Prof. Müller argues that, basically, "the problem was the fears of Western European countries and eventually the European Community, about their position in the world politics," and the question of whether Europe could "meet the American challenge and remain the first-rate economic power in the world economy, or would the NPT emerge as an instrument as well as a sign of Europe's second-rate status, except for France and the United Kingdom as nuclear-weapons states? Because, trade for Europe was not only instrumental in promoting their economic welfare, but also a key tool in fostering foreign policy goals, far more would be at stake than pure economics."[26]

Islamic Revolution and its Impact on Iran's Nuclear Program

The Shah Reza Pahlavi's nuclear power projects undertaken by Western European and American firms, which had just taken off, had to make an emergency landing due to turbulence created by the Islamic Revolution in the spring of 1979 under the leadership of the Imam Khomeini. The immediate impact of the Revolution and the Imam's takeover of power from the Shah was the need to consolidate the new order in the country as well as to fight a war against forces of Saddam Hussein, who launched a large-scale offensive in September 1980. The Revolution also caused a dramatic change in Iran's disposition in the world political arena vis-à-vis the foreign and security policy matters.

Revolutionary Iran adopted the Imam Khomeini's slogan "*Na Sharq, Na Gharb, Faqat Jumhuri-ye Islami*," which means "neither East, nor West, only the Islamic Republic [of Iran]" as the fundamental guiding principle of its foreign policy.[27] Hence, in the early years of the Revolution, almost anything that was

Western was rejected, and the nuclear projects were no exception to such an attitude. According to Dr. Vaziri, "Ayatollah Khomeini's return from exile to Tehran on February 1, 1979 ushered in a brief but intense *anti-modernization* phase in Iran's domestic and foreign policies. The clerics rejected the Shah's plans to finance the rapid modernization of the civilian and military infrastructures with Iran's oil revenues. In fact, they reduced oil exports, allowed much of the American military hardware purchased by the Shah to fall into disrepair, purged the armed forces of suspected opponents, and did not impede the flight of many scientists who had worked on Iran's nuclear projects." Vaziri also notes that, during the 'Cultural Revolution' of spring 1980, the nascent nuclear infrastructure constructed under the Shah was languished, and the work on the Bushehr nuclear reactors and the Darkhovin nuclear reactor site was halted in 1979.[28] On the same issue, the president of the Atomic Energy Organization of Iran (AEOI) under the Shah's regime, Dr. Akbar Etemad notes, "as regards the AEOI, there was a tendency to destroy everything within it, and many people—professional and otherwise-had a say in the matter. The destructive forces of the Revolution inside and outside the AEOI succeeded in bringing nearly all the projects to a halt; all the major projects were cancelled or left dormant."[29]

Iran's Attempts to Resume the Nuclear Program

Once the dust of the chaotic revolutionary internal dynamics scattered, Iranian clergy attempted to resume the nuclear projects which had come to a halt with the regime change. There were a number of reasons for the clerical leadership to see the nuclear projects from a different, but certainly more positive perspective. One of the reasons was the Iraqi offensives against Iran, especially those involving massive air strikes on ports and oil refineries in the Persian Gulf. The initial trauma of Iraq's attack and subsequent brutality of combat led the clerics to learn the hard way that modern military technology, and especially weapons of mass destruction, could make a decisive difference in war.[30]

Another reason for the Iranian top clergy to change their attitude toward nuclear power projects was, according to Dr. Etemad, the severe energy crisis experienced after the Revolution. Hence, a high degree of priority was again given to the construction of power plants. The clerics have also "realized that they had killed the goose which laid the golden egg" by destroying the AEOI.[31] They then decided to pull its staff together with a new president to revive the Organization as well as to settle the nuclear projects with the German Kraftwerk Union in order to resume the building of the Bushehr nuclear power plant.

In the early 1980s, President Ali Akbar Hashemi Rafsanjani first got the blessing of the Imam Khomeini to endorse the nuclear projects. Initially Khomeini had strong reservations against the nuclear projects on the grounds that they would make Iran dependent on foreign technology. Then, Rafsanjani asked the French and the German companies to resume working in their construction of nuclear power plants. The German firm KWU, that used to build the Bushehr power plant, did not agree to resume construction, most possibly due to the pressure of the U.S. administration that was deeply at odds with Iran, especially since the "hostage crisis" at the U.S. Embassy in Tehran.[32]

The French company Framatome, too, denied resuming work at the Darkhovin site, which was chosen for a nuclear power plant to host two 950 MW(e) reactors and the construction of the Esfahan Nuclear Research Center. President Hashemi Rafsanjani recalls "in those days [they] realized the West was not going to give the sensitive technology to Iran."[33] Hence, Iran turned its face to other potential suppliers of nuclear technology such as Pakistan, Argentina, Spain, Czechoslovakia, China, and the Soviet Union, in order to resume work in the Bushehr nuclear plant and also to expand the scope of its nuclear infrastructure.

In the midst of the war with Iraq, the Esfahan Nuclear Research Center was opened in 1984, which could be seen as Islamic regime's determination to pursue its nuclear aspirations inherited from the previous monarchic regime. Thanks to the Chinese assistance, fuel fabrication and conversion facilities, which are crucial for uranium enrichment, were also built in Esfahan.[34] With Pakistan, a nuclear cooperation agreement was signed in 1987, according to which, 39 Iranian nuclear scientists and technicians would advance their skills in Pakistani nuclear facilities, reactors and laboratories.[35] That same year in May, Iran signed a $5.5 million agreement with Argentina for the supply of uranium enriched to 20 percent and for the training of Iranian scientists at the Jose Balaserio Nuclear Institute. In February 1990, a Spanish paper reported that Associated Enterprises of Spain was negotiating the completion of the two nuclear power reactors at Bushehr with the help of another Spanish firm called ENUSA (National Uranium Enterprises) that was to provide the fuel. In another effort, Iran sought assistance of Skoda from Czechoslovakia for the import of a reactor.[36] Moreover, benefiting from an active economic relationship with Sweden, Iranians have approached Swedish firms to see what role they might be willing to play in the completion of the Bushehr power plant. Similarly, Iran had maintained active political and economic relations with India and asked their assistance in various fields, including the completion of the Bushehr power plant.

Despite Iran's relentless efforts to resume work at the nuclear sites that were under construction prior to the Islamic Revolution, it rendered no fruit.[37] In the meantime, the Iraqi air force attacked the Bushehr site several times causing serious structural damage.[38] Then, China and Russia looked like promising alternatives and Iran wanted to exploit its chances in these countries. Of these, the cooperation agreement with the Russian Federation bore more fruit for the Iranian nuclear program.

Russia-Iran "Deal of the Century"

After almost a decade-long effort to revitalize the long-stalled nuclear power projects, as well as to expand the scope of scientific and technological infrastructure, Iran was left with Russia as the potential major supplier country. As was the case with China, Iran had prior talks with Russia in the late 1980s and even agreed in principle to cooperate in the nuclear field. President Hashemi Rafsanjani remembers "[he] took the initiative and talked with Michael Gorbachev for the completion of the Bushehr power plant." However, dramatic changes in the Soviet Union that led to the collapse of the socialist regime and Boris Yeltsin to come to power as the President of the Russian Federation, caused delays in the implementation of the agreement between Rafsanjani and Gorbachev. After the settling of the new regime in Russia, Iranian authorities brought the issue to the table again in the talks with their Russian counterparts. President Rafsanjani recalls, "Russia would support Iran to finish Bushehr in six years and the Russian authorities said they would start from scratch, and [the Iranian authorities] said OK."[39] Hence, during a visit from Viktor Mikhailov, the Minister of Atomic Energy (Minatom) of the Russian Federation, at the request of Dr. Reza Amrollahi, the President of the Atomic Energy Organization of Iran, a Nuclear Cooperation Accord was signed by the Russian firm, Zarubezhatomenergostroy and the AEOI on January 8, 1995, in Tehran. Accordingly, Russia and Iran agreed:

> To cooperate in the completion of the construction of Block No. 1 at the Bushehr nuclear power plant; to utilize Iranian personnel as much as possible; to subsequently deliver the fuel at world prices; and to submit a proposal for the training of the Iranian personnel so that after a preliminary period of operation, Block No.1 at Bushehr can be run exclusively by Iranian personnel... Russia and Iran also agreed to prepare and sign: in three months a contract for delivery of a light water reactor for research with a power 30-50 MW(th) from Russia; in the first quarter of 1995, a contract for the delivery of 2000 tons of natural uranium from Russia; in the first quarter of 1995, a contract for the preparation and training for AEOI's scientific personnel, 10-20 graduate students and Ph.D.s annually at Russian academic institutions; within six months, a contract for the construction of a uranium mine in Iran after which negotiations will be conducted for the construction of a centrifuge plant for enrichment of uranium... The parties further agreed: to cooperate in the construction of low power reactor, less than 1 MW(th), in Iran for instructional purposes; to examine the issue of cooperation

on the construction of a desalination plant; and to carry out meetings no less frequently than once a year.[40]

The nuclear deal would cost a little less than $1 billion, and the first of the two Russian-designed VVER-1000 reactors would become operational by 2001. However, the U.S. administration strongly reacted to the Russians and asked them not to go ahead with the construction and other activities related to the centrifuge plant that would give Iran the capability to produce weapons-grade uranium that could be used to manufacture atomic bombs. Eventually, although the U.S. failed to convince Russia to cancel the deal as a whole, especially after this issue came before the Gore-Chernomyrdin Commission that was discussing a host of issues between Russia and the U.S., the Russians agreed to call off the negotiations on the centrifuge plant, as well as the sophisticated arms sales, including missiles, to Iran.[41]

Iran's Current Nuclear Capabilities

An analysis of Iran's negotiations with potential nuclear suppliers, whether they bore fruit or not, indicates that almost without exception, Iranians requested training of their scientists and technicians in the scientifically and technologically more advanced countries, as well as the establishment of uranium enrichment (i.e., HEU production) and spent fuel reprocessing (i.e., plutonium separation) facilities. These can be seen as clear indications that Iran, under the regimes of both the Shah and the Imam, always wanted to have a complete nuclear fuel cycle which would elevate the country to a nuclear power status. It seems that Iran has managed to achieve its goal to a significant extent. [42] On the account of Iran's nuclear facilities, Dr. Ali Ashgar Soltanieh, from the Iranian Ministry of Foreign Affairs, notes:

> To a great extent, Iran's nuclear activities in uranium ore processing, uranium conversion and enrichment as well as heavy water production, research reactor designing and manufacturing centrifuge machines are the result of research and development and experiences gradually gained during the last three decades. All these are achieved during the period of sanctions and lack of cooperation by industrial countries in the area of peaceful uses of nuclear energy.[43]

On the same subject, Dr. Mohammad Ghannadi from the AEOI states that:

> Oone third of [Iran] is under exploration; in 200 km south of Yazd and 600 km south of Tehran one of the holes [mines] was done by Chinese and the other by Iranians; annual production

of yellowcake capacity in Yazd is 67 tons; uranium conversion capacity is 296 tons natural uranium; 34 tons slightly enriched uranium; 11.3 tons natural uranium for heavy water research reactor which started in operation in spring 2004; Iran ranks the 8th country in the world with its 200 tons of Uranium Hexafluoride production capability; the enrichment capacity [envisaged] is 150 tons (for 54,000 centrifuge machines); zirconium production capacity is 50 tons/year; for waste management there is a near surface repository in Yazd and Esfahan. Except reprocessing, [Iran has] all elements of nuclear fuel cycle.[44]

Also, Ayatollah Hasan Rohani, the Secretary of the Supreme National Security Council of Iran, argues that a "40 MW(th) heavy water reactor which is expected to enter into operation in 2008, is being built in Arak province fully with the technical and scientific skills of Iranian scientists and technicians as well as the technological parts designed and produced in Iran."[45] Additionally, Dr. Asadullah Sabouri from the AEOI indicated that:

> The first reactor at the Bushehr nuclear power plant will start operation in December 2006; there are 300 Iranian engineers as well as 400 technicians who will run the reactor; Iran's regulatory infrastructure is enhanced, thanks to the close cooperation with Russia and the IAEA in the areas of reviewing safety reports, seismic hazard evaluation, reviewing design documents, establishment of quality management systems, and the physical protection of the plant." Moreover, Dr. Sabouri notes "a decision is taken at the state level to have a 10-20 percent share of nuclear energy in overall electricity generation by installing a 7,000 MW(e) capacity by the year 2021." He also says that "there is the approval for the construction of a nuclear power plant and site selection studies for 5,000 MW(e) reactors."[46]

As for the level of education in the nuclear field in Iran, Dr. Mahmood Reza Aghamiri from the Shahid Behesti University states that:

> At present, there are 45 departments in Iranian universities in the nuclear area and there are plans to have 80 departments in the medium- to long-term; there are eight nuclear research centers, with plans to expand to 15 in the future; and there are 450 post-graduate students (mostly engineers) in the nuclear field, and this number is expected to reach 1,500 in the future.[47]

Iran's Position in the Nuclear Puzzle

In general terms, Iranian authorities consistently claim to have the right to obtain peaceful applications of nuclear energy as a State Party to the NPT since the beginning of its entry into force.[48] They specifically refer to Article IV of the Treaty, which reads as follows (in two paragraphs):

> 1. Nothing in this Treaty shall be interpreted as affecting the inalienable right of all the Parties to the Treaty to develop research, production and use of nuclear energy for peaceful purposes without discrimination and in conformity with articles I and II of this Treaty.
> 2. All the Parties to the Treaty undertake to facilitate, and have the right to participate in, the fullest possible exchange of equipment, materials and scientific and technological information for the peaceful uses of nuclear energy. Parties to the Treaty in a position to do so shall also cooperate in contributing alone or together with other States or international organizations to the further development of the applications of nuclear energy for peaceful purposes, especially in the territories of non-nuclear-weapon States Party to the Treaty, with due consideration for the needs of the developing areas of the world.

Hence, Iranian authorities, who repeatedly claim to run a nuclear program "for exclusively peaceful purposes," expect to be treated like other non-nuclear weapons states, such as Argentina or Brazil, that have enrichment as well as reprocessing capabilities, but they are not subject to accusations of developing nuclear weapons.[49]

Regardless of the rejection of such accusations by Iranian authorities, the Americans especially assert that Iran indeed has a secret nuclear weapons development program. With the capabilities it has developed over the years, particularly the uranium enrichment facility that may enable Iran to produce weapons-grade uranium for making atomic bombs, Americans argue that Iran may soon become a *de facto* nuclear weapons-state. They base their policy of denial and their request from Iran to give up uranium enrichment program on the spirit and the letter of Article II of the NPT, which reads as follows:

> Each non-nuclear-weapon State Party to the Treaty undertakes not to receive the transfer from any transferor whatsoever of nuclear weapons or other nuclear explosive devices or of control over such weapons or explosive devices directly, or indirectly; not to manufacture or otherwise acquire nuclear weapons or other nuclear explosive devices; and not to seek or

receive any assistance in the manufacture of nuclear weapons or other nuclear explosive devices.

The essence of American argument draws on the fact that, according to the Treaty, "each non-nuclear-weapon State Party to the Treaty undertakes not to...seek...manufacture of nuclear weapons." Given the revelations about Iran's uranium enrichment facility in Natanz that was built clandestinely without timely IAEA notification as part of its obligations under the Safeguards Agreement with the Agency, the U.S. considers such an attitude as an indication of having secret intentions to develop weapons that contradicts the undertakings of non-nuclear weapons states like Iran under Article II of the NPT.[50]

As a counter argument, Iranian authorities claim that the IAEA certified that the non-notification of Natanz was a "failure" rather than a "violation" of Iran's safeguards obligations. They also gave lengthy explanations as to how "internal bureaucratic dynamics in Iran have played a role in the failure to provide the IAEA with the design information and all other related data about the facility."[51] However, some of them also say in private that, "they had no other alternative but to build the facility secretly" arguing that "had they notified the IAEA that they had plans to build a uranium enrichment facility, the U.S. would have definitely prevented [them] from finalizing the project."[52]

The Position of the European Union

The EU has played a crucial role in this whole process since the historic visit of the Foreign Ministers of three leading members of the Union, namely the UK, France and Germany to Iran in October 2003, on the eve of the "deadline" set by the IAEA, to Director General Mohamed El Baradei for Iran to sign the Additional Protocol.[53] Then, these three EU countries, dubbed the "EU Trio" or "EU-3" and Iran have gathered together to sort out a workable solution to the claims of Iran on one hand, and the U.S. on the other, as well as to satisfy the expectations of the Europeans.[54] As such, the EU behaved true to its longstanding and ever-improving policy of "using diplomacy as a means of finding solutions to international problems" rather than resorting to use of military force, at least in the early stages of any conflict.

Such an approach is usually seen as "a waste of time" by the American administration that criticized Europeans about buying Iran time to do whatever it may be doing secretly (i.e., building nuclear weapons). Nevertheless, the EU's engagement with Iran also played into the hands of the U.S., mainly in two respects. On one hand, it kept Iran under considerable pressure and scrutiny that at least caused delays in its nuclear projects while the U.S. couldn't effectively focus on that country due to its state building efforts in Iraq, which absorbed a huge amount of resources (human and otherwise) of the Bush Administration. On the other hand, the U.S. gave the EU the opportunity to prove the "merits" of its "diplomatic approach" to solve the problem that may also satisfy the Americans. Moreover, in connection with the second, the U.S. was also relieved from the burden of being accused—as was the case prior to the invasion of Iraq—of not giving a chance to diplomacy.

Even though the governments of the European countries, either in their individual capacities or as a whole, have been spending genuine effort to find a way out of the conflicting situation, the chances seem to be weak for several reasons. First, the positions of Iran and the U.S. are so widely apart from each other that it looks like only a magic formula may bring the sides together. Moreover, Iranian officials claim "[they] have made it crystal clear to the Europeans that permanent cessation of uranium enrichment would be out of consideration, and that, only in this condition that the negotiations could be pursued."[55] Hence, Iranians are seemingly frustrated with the Europeans because they think that, during their talks with the U.S., they may have given the Americans a different impression about Iran's stance vis-à-vis the uranium enrichment issue, which is repeatedly said to be "non-negotiable."

Second, even if an agreement could be reached, Europeans might not deliver what they may have suggested to deliver in terms of economic benefits and technological assistance. Therefore, clerical leaders have harshly criticized Iranian officials who have agreed to temporarily suspend the uranium enrichment and asked them "what did they get in return for such a gesture."[56] It is clear from the stance of the Iranian officials that they look to the U.S. who is, indeed, their real counterpart in this debate, over the Europeans. "If a deal will ever be cut, it should be between Iran and the U.S. without intermediaries [like the EU]" said Iranian officials.[57] However, due to the present political climate, the chances to gather the Americans and Iranian officials around a negotiation table are not high, unless there is a "second track diplomacy" going on somewhere, which is quite likely.

No doubt, Europeans are also aware of their limitations. However, it is still in their interest to keep the negotiations going. This is because, the alternative to this is the high probability of another hot confrontation in the Middle East, a region that is strategically important for Europeans due to their economic (e.g., oil) and security (e.g., stability) considerations. Hence, so long as the Iran's nuclear program is on the negotiations table, the likelihood of such a confrontation is thought to be lower than it might be otherwise.

A third reason why the chances of finding a workable solution to the nuclear puzzle at hand, through the EU-Iran talks, is the perceived degree of threat to the Europeans, which, however, differs considerably from that of the Americans, not to mention the Israelis. Europeans' threat perception seemingly does not put an unbearable pressure on their shoulders. Although countries like Germany and France, who have helped Iran to develop its nuclear program, have expressed their concerns with the possible military implications of Iran's evolving nuclear capabilities, they have also limited their political stance—and their relations with Iran—to staying on the legal grounds as prescribed by the nuclear non-proliferation regime, particularly the NPT articles. One important factor, among others, that must have influenced the stance of these countries was (and still is) the way they interpret the motivations and intentions of Iran for developing a complete fuel cycle. For instance, Prof. Harald Müller argues, "Germany believes that Iranian WMD programs are principally of a defensive/deterrent character. While the extension of the range of Iranian missiles is seen with discomfort and as a security *concern*, it is not really rated as a major *threat* to European, and German security because of the lack of aggressive and offensive motivations."[58]

Conclusion

Notwithstanding these rather discouraging elements in the stance of the EU in the middle of the nuclear debate, Iran cannot afford to underestimate the value of the Europeans, not only in this context, but also as a long-term partner in many fields. Iran's geographic proximity to the EU and the potential of the trade between the parties is so significant that no soberminded Iranian decision-maker would be able to turn his back to the Europeans, and *vice versa*. Considering that Iran's nuclear dossier has been transferred to the UNSC, the political stance of the UK and France in particular, being the veto powers, as well as the European public opinion in general will be of crucial importance in Iran getting through the process without suffering seriously. Therefore, just like the Europeans who need to get concessions from Iran in order to strengthen their hands before the Americans, who are seemingly adopting a nonchalant behavior toward them, Iran as well, should feel urged to make further concessions, to the extent possible, to have the EU on its side. Creativity of the diplomats on both sides should be further exploited so as to mitigate the fears of the Americans and particularly the Israelis, stemming from the scenarios depicting a nuclear-weapons-capable Iran whose leaders have a rich track record of making threatening statements targeting Israel and the U.S.

---

[*] Parts of this chapter are excerpted from the author's previous research on the subject during his sabbatical fellowship at the Belfer Center of the J. F. Kennedy School of Government at Harvard University during the 2004-2005 academic year, which have been published in the Spring 2006 issue of *Middle East Journal* and the March 2007 issue of *Middle Eastern Studies* cited below.

1 Natanz is located between Esfahan and Kashan in central Iran south of Tehran. The uranium enrichment facility is some 100 miles north of Esfahan.

2 Mustafa Kibaroglu, "Good for the Shah, Banned for the Mullahs: The West and Iran's Quest for Nuclear Power," *Middle East Journal* 60, no. 2, (2006): pp. 207-232.

3 The author had the opportunity to conduct formal interviews as well as informal conversations with Iranian scholars, experts, intellectuals and officials from various branches of the state bureaucracy during his two visits to Tehran in December 2004 and March 2005. The views expressed during these interviews and the minutes of the lengthy conversations will be mentioned throughout the text, where appropriate. Some of those talked to the author only on the condition of non-attribution; therefore, they will not be cited in the text, while some others didn't mind being quoted or cited.

4 Nuclearization of each of these countries has been possible in their peculiar conditions whose study is certainly beyond the scope of this paper. There is, however, a very rich body of literature to learn more about each of these cases, such as: Leonard Spector, *Nuclear Proliferation Today: the Spread of Nuclear Weapons 1984* (New York: Random House, 1984); Seymour Hersh, *The Samson Option: Israel, America and the Bomb*, (London: Faber & Faber, 1991); Shyam Bhatia, *India's Nuclear Bomb* (New Delhi: Vikas, 1979); Ziba Moshaver, *Nuclear Weapons Proliferation in the Sub-Continent* (New York: St. Martin's, 1991); William C. Potter, *International Nuclear Trade and Non-Proliferation: The Challenge of Emerging Suppliers* (Lexington, MA.: Lexington Books, 1990); David Albright, Frans Berkhout and William Walker *World Inventory of Plutonium and Highly Enriched Uranium* (New York: Oxford University Press, 1992); David Fischer, *Towards 1995: The Prospects for Ending the Proliferation of Nuclear Weapons* (Dartmouth: UNIDIR, 1993); Mitchell Reiss and Robert S. Litwak, eds., *Nuclear Proliferation After the Cold War* (Baltimore: Johns Hopkins University Press, 1994); Shai Feldman, *Nuclear Weapons and Arms Control in the Middle East* (Cambridge, MA.: The MIT Press, 1997); Harald Müller, David Fischer, and Wolfgang Kotter, *Nuclear Non-Proliferation and Global Order* (London: Oxford University Press, 1994). Others are cited throughout the chapter.

5 Mustafa Kibaroglu, "Iran's Nuclear Ambitions from a Historical Perspective," *Middle Eastern Studies* 43, no. 2, (2007): pp. 223 - 245.

6 Frank Barnaby, *How Nuclear Weapons Spread: Nuclear-Weapon Proliferation in the 1990s* (London: Routledge, 1993), pp. 114-117.

7 Akbar Etemad, "Iran," in *A European Non-Proliferation Policy*, ed. Harald Müller (Oxford: Oxford University Press, 1987), pp. 203-227. Akbar Etemad, a native of Iran, studied electrical and nuclear engineering in Switzerland and France, and served from 1974 to 1978 as the first President of the Atomic Energy Organization of Iran (AEOI).

8 Haleh Vaziri, "Iran's Nuclear Quest: Motivations and Consequences," in *The Nuclear Non-Proliferation Regime*, ed. Raju G. C. Thomas (Princeton, NJ: Princeton University Press, 1986), p. 311.

9 Barnaby, *How Nuclear Weapons Spread*, p. 114

10 Interview with Prof. Erwin Haeckel on the sidelines of the Conference on "Germany and Nuclear Nonproliferation" held in Berlin, Germany, February 25-27, 2005.

11 Interview with Prof. Erwin Haeckel, Berlin, Germany, February 26, 2005.

[12] Michael J. Brenner, *Nuclear Power and Non-Proliferation: The Remaking of U.S. Policy* (Cambridge: Cambridge University Press, 1981), p. 14.
[13] Ibid., pp. 13-16.
[14] Jozef Goldblat, *Nuclear Non-Proliferation: A Guide to the Debate* (London: Taylor & Francis, 1985), p. 9.
[15] The Nuclear Supplier Group has reproduced a set of guidelines that most of the suppliers of nuclear plants and materials agreed to in London on September 21, 1977. That's why this group is equally known as the London Club. This set of guidelines is also attached to communication addressed on January 11, 1978 to the Director-General of the IAEA. These guidelines for nuclear transfer are also labeled as INFCIRC/254. The initial signatories of the guidelines are; Belgium, Canada, Czechoslovakia, France, the former German Democratic Republic and the Federal Republic of Germany, Italy, Japan, the Netherlands, Poland, Sweden, Switzerland, UK, U.S., and the USSR.
[16] Joachim Krause, "German Nuclear Export Policy and the Proliferation of Nuclear Weapons – Another *Sonderweg?*" paper presented at the conference on "Germany and Nuclear Nonproliferation," Berlin, Germany, February 25-27, 2005, p. 1.
[17] In coming to such a conclusion, Prof. Krause referred to a number of American scholars and their works some of whom are: Albert Wohlstetter, "Spreading the Bomb Without Quite Breaking the Rules," *Foreign Affairs*, no. 25 (1976), pp. 88-96; Ted Greenwood, Harold A. Feiveson and Theodore B. Taylor, *Nuclear Proliferation: Motivations, Capabilities, and Strategies for Control* (New York: McGraw Hill, 1977).
[18] The facility employed the Pakistani nuclear scientist Abdel Qader Khan, who was later known for being responsible of proliferation of the then poorly guarded enrichment technology of URENCO to Pakistan and South Africa, as well as to Libya and Iran more recently. Ibid., p. 3.
[19] Ibid.
[20] The Zangger Committee named for its Swiss chair Prof. Claude Zangger, and the Nuclear Suppliers Group shared in common the purpose of limiting the transfer of significant material and technology to states that are suspected of being engaged in clandestine nuclear weapons manufacturing. The Committee started to meet as early as 1970.
[21] For a comprehensive study on the emergence and evolution of EURATOM, see Darryl A. Howlett, *EURATOM and Nuclear Safeguards* (London: MacMillan Press, 1990).
[22] Bertrand Goldschmidt, "Proliferation and Non-Proliferation in Western Europe: A Historical Survey," in *A European Non-Proliferation Policy: Prospects and Problems*, ed. Harald Müller, (Oxford: Clarendon Press, 1987), pp. 24-25.
[23] For a comprehensive account of divergences between Europe and the U.S. on proliferation matters in the 1970s see Harald Müller, "Non-Proliferation Policy in Western Europe: Structural Aspects," in *A European Non-Proliferation Policy: Prospects and Problems*, Harald Müller (Oxford: Clarendon Press, 1987), pp. 71-97.
[24] Ibid., pp. 72-74.
[25] Ibid.
[26] Ibid., p. 86.

[27] Persian translation of the slogan is borrowed from Haleh Vaziri, an Iranian scholar. See her chapter on "Iran's Nuclear Quest," p. 314.
[28] Ibid.
[29] Etemad, "Iran," p. 214.
[30] According to Dr. Vaziri, "the first four or five years of the Iran-Iraq War shocked the clerics into realizing the value of modern military technology. The use of such technology –and perhaps even a nuclear weapons capability- would have deterred Iraq's initial aggression against the Islamic Republic and resort to violations of the international laws of war conduct. From the perspective of the clerics, the Reagan administration not only had opposed their hegemonic aspirations, but also allied with Iraqi Ba'ath in the effort to defeat Iran. Had the Islamic republic possessed a nuclear weapons capability, the U.S. may have thought twice about interjecting its navy into the Persian Gulf and about engaging Iranians.". See Vaziri, "Iran's Nuclear Quest," p. 316.
[31] Dr. Akbar Etemad notes, "some government officials even explicitly blamed those who had decided to cancel the Bushehr nuclear power plant project. It was said that one of the causes of the shortages of power was the failure of government to implement the project," which was estimated to become operational in the early 1980s. See Etemad, "Iran," p. 214.
[32] On November 4, 1979, Iranian militants and students stormed the U.S. Embassy in Tehran and held hostage some 70 diplomats and citizens of the U.S. This act triggered the most profound crisis of the Carter presidency. For details see Jimmy Carter Library & Museum accessible online at http://www.jimmycarterlibrary.org/documents/hostages.phtml. President Carter applied economic pressure by halting oil imports from Iran and freezing Iranian assets in the U.S.. At the same time, he began several diplomatic initiatives to free the hostages, all of which proved fruitless. On April 24, 1980, the U.S. attempted a rescue mission that failed. After three of eight helicopters were damaged in a sandstorm, the operation was aborted; eight persons were killed during the evacuation. Secretary of State Cyrus Vance, who had opposed the action, resigned after the mission's failure. In the U.S., failure to resolve the crisis contributed to Ronald Reagan's defeat of Carter in the presidential election. After the election, with the assistance of Algerian intermediaries, successful negotiations began. On January 20, 1981, the day of President Reagan's inauguration, the U.S. released almost $8 billion in Iranian assets and the hostages were freed after 444 days in Iranian detention; the agreement gave Iran immunity from lawsuits arising from the incident. Further information is also available at http://www.bartleby.com/65/ir/Iranhost.html.
[33] Rafsanjani made this statement during his address to the closing session of the "International Conference on Nuclear Technologies and Sustainable Development" convened in Tehran, Iran, on March 6, 2005.
[34] On this matter, Prof. Steven Miller notes, "Chinese labels and tags on almost every single piece that were used during the construction of the facility in Esfahan, including the screw drivers, do still remain intact." Prof. Miller made this statement while he shared his observations about his visit to Esfahan facility, in a seminar as part of the Managing the Atom Project at the Belfer Center for Science and International Affairs in Harvard University on April 13, 2005, Cambridge, Massachusetts, U.S..

35 Vaziri, "Iran's Nuclear Quest," p. 318.
36 Anthony H. Cordesman, *Iran and Nuclear Weapons* (Washington, D.C.: Center for Strategic and International Studies, 2000), p. 8.
37 Etemad, "Iran," p. 216.
38 The Iraqi bombings occurred on March 24, 1984; February 12, 1985; March 4, 1985; July 12, 1986; November 17, 1987, November 19, 1987; and July 19, 1988. See Cordesman, *Iran and Nuclear Weapons*, p. 7.
39 Rafsanjani's address to the Nuclear Technologies conference in Tehran, Iran on March 6, 2005.
40 English translation of the full text of the Nuclear Cooperation Accord can be found in Michael Eisenstadt, *Iranian Military Power: Capabilities and Intentions*, (Washington, D.C.: The Washington Institute for Near East Policy, 1996), pp. 106-107.
41 At their summit meeting in Vancouver, Canada in April 1993, President Clinton and President Yeltsin created the U.S.-Russian Joint Commission on Economic and Technological Cooperation. Since then it has become known as the Gore-Chernomyrdin Commission after its co-chairmen, U.S. Vice President Al Gore and Russian Prime Minister Viktor Chernomyrdin. The Commission's original mandate was to support cooperation between the U.S. and Russia in the areas of space, energy, and high technology. However, as of July 1996 the Gore-Chernomyrdin Commission had been expanded to include eight different committees: Space, Business Development, Energy Policy, Defense Conversion, Science and Technology, Environment, Health, and Agribusiness. The Commission formally convened about twice a year in either Washington or Moscow. For more on this subject see, for instance, the website of *Nuclear Threat Initiative* available online at http://www.nti.org/db/nisprofs/russia/forasst/otherusg/gcc.htm.
42 On the issue of Iran's nuclear capabilities, there exists a vast literature consisting of books, journal articles, reports, policy papers, and op-eds, most of which, however, refer to secondary sources or Western (i.e., European, American and Israeli) intelligence reports. For a detailed documentation of Iran's nuclear facilities that have become almost a common knowledge, the reader is suggested to see, for instance, a compilation by Andrew Koch and Jeanette Wolf, *Iran's Nuclear Facilities: A Profile* (Monterey, CA: Center for Nonproliferation Studies, 1998). For a more up-to-date information including satellite imageries of some of the facilities in Iran, visit http://www.GlobalSecurity.org.
43 Dr. Soltanieh, Deputy Director General at the Foreign Ministry, made this statement during the International Conference on Nuclear Technologies and Sustainable Development convened in Tehran, Iran, on March 5, 2005.
44 Author's notes from the presentation of Dr. Ghannadi in a panel on "Iran's Peaceful Nuclear Program: Requirements and Imperatives," during the International Conference on Nuclear Technologies and Sustainable Development in Tehran, Iran on March 5, 2005.
45 Ayatollah Rohani made this statement, among others, during his opening address to the International Conference on Nuclear Technologies and Sustainable Development convened in Tehran, Iran, on March 5, 2005.

⁴⁶ Author's notes from the presentation of Dr. Sabouri in a panel on "Iran's Peaceful Nuclear Program: Requirements and Imperatives," during the International Conference on Nuclear Technologies and Sustainable Development in Tehran, Iran on March 5, 2005.

⁴⁷ Author's notes from the presentation of Dr. Aghamiri in a panel on "Iran's Peaceful Nuclear Program: Requirements and Imperatives," during the International Conference on Nuclear Technologies and Sustainable Development in Tehran, Iran on March 5, 2005.

⁴⁸ Among many such statements made by Iranian officials, here and there, time and again, compact and comprehensive coverage of the essential points representing Iran's official position can be found in a journal published by the Tehran-based Center for Strategic Research. See "Peaceful Nuclear Activity and Our Constructive Interaction with the World: An Interview with Dr. Hassan Rohani," *National Interest* 1, no. 1 (2005): pp. 5-21.

⁴⁹ Both Argentina and Brazil were under the spotlights of the nuclear nonproliferation community for their engagements in nuclear weapons programs, which hopefully have been dismantled in the early 1990s with the democratization of these countries. Argentina and Brazil, then long time "hold outs" have formed the Argentine-Brazilian Agency for Accounting and Control of Nuclear Materials (ABACC) in July 1991 and joined the NPT. Accordingly, in December 1991, the Quadripartite Agreement was signed by Argentina, Brazil, ABACC, and the IAEA. This Agreement provides the application of *full-scope safeguards* by the IAEA in cooperation with ABACC, to all nuclear materials and installations subject to bilateral and international agreements. In practice, the Quadripartite Agreement is modeled on the EURATOM-IAEA safeguards agreement, and is therefore equivalent to verification under the NPT. Mustafa Kibaroglu, "EURATOM & ABACC: Safeguard Models for the Middle East?" in *A Zone Free of Weapons of Mass Destruction in the Middle East*, ed. Jan Prawitz and James F. Leonard (New York, Geneva: United Nations Institute for Disarmament Research, 1996), pp. 93-123.

⁵⁰ Iran signed a comprehensive Safeguards Agreement (INFCIRC/214) with the IAEA in 1974.

⁵¹ These and other similar views were expressed by many Iranians during the Nuclear Technologies conference in Tehran on March 5-6, 2005. The most elaborate explanations came from Dr. Ali Asghar Soltanieh, from the Iranian Ministry of Foreign Affairs, who was apparently in charge of devising Iran's nuclear diplomacy.

⁵² Conversations with Iranian officials and scholars, on the sidelines of the conferences in Tehran in March 2005 who wished not to be identified.

⁵³ The experience gained from the thorough inspections of the IAEA in Iraq following that country's defeat in the hands of the Coalition Forces mandated to liberate Kuwait revealed unequivocally the weaknesses of the verification mechanism under the framework of the NPT. The IAEA Board of Governors thus initiated in 1993 a study called 'Programme 93+2' which aimed at drawing lessons from the UNSCOM experience as well as the dismantlement of South Africa's nuclear weapons capabilities, with a view to strengthening the NPT's verification mechanism. The study that was terminated in December 1995 was adopted by the IAEA as INFCIRC/540 also known as Additional Protocol. Unlike the Model Protocol INFCIRC/153 that was drafted in 1971 and which must be adopted by

every Non-Nuclear-Weapons States Parties to the NPT in order to conclude a Safeguards Agreement with the IAEA, the very same States Parties are not legally bound to adopt the new and strengthened inspections procedures of the Additional Protocol. For an eloquent discussion on the Additional Protocol and its implications in the context of Iran's nuclear program see Chen Zak, *Iran's Nuclear Policy and the IAEA: An Evaluation of Program 93+2* (Washington D.C.: The Washington Institute for Near East Policy, 2002). Also see Theodore Hirsch, "The IAEA Additional Protocol: What It Is and Why It Matters," *The Nonproliferation Review* 11, no. 3 (2004): pp. 140-166.

[54] Although the EU-3 is usually acknowledged as representing the 27-member European Union, there are also resentments among the Europeans scholars and intellectuals who argue that the EU-3 do not necessarily represent the position of their respective countries. Views along these lines were abundant among the European participants of the conferences convened in Tehran in March 2005.

[55] Conversations with Dr. Mousavian, a former leading member of the Iranian team negotiating with the Europeans, March 4, 2005, Tehran, Iran.

[56] Conversations with Dr. Mousavian.

[57] Conversations with Dr. Mousavian.

[58] Harald Müller, "Germany and WMD Proliferation," *The Nonproliferation Review* 10, no. 2 (2003): p. 7. Prof. Müller also argues "Germany believes that political dialogues with both Iran and North Korea, and possibly with Libya, offer better prospects for the resolution of potential conflicts." See Herald Müller, "Germany hopes it will go away," *The Bulletin of the Atomic Scientists* 57, no. 6 (2001): pp. 31-33. Considering the weight of Germany in the making of the common foreign and security policy of the European Union (which is indeed still in the making) it wouldn't be wrong to argue that this is pretty much the position of most, if not all, of the EU members in the Iranian nuclear puzzle.

PART III
RUSSIA and COMMONWEALTH of INDEPENDENT STATES

Chapter 9
The South Caucasus in the European Periphery[1]

Vít Stříteský

During the last 15 years, the EU has allocated much more than one billion euros to the South Caucasus region. Many good opportunities that have been actualized by these resources show that they are not wasted. These results, on the other hand, cannot be considered as very impressive. One of the particular reasons of this is that the EU, for a long time, behaved as a generous donor who, however, does not want to be disturbed any further. Until recently, the EU was not visible in the region which corresponded to its bad reputation. To an extent, the situation has improved with the appointment of the EU Special Representative for the South Caucasus, and with the inclusion of Armenia, Azerbaijan and Georgia into the European Neighborhood Policy.[2]

This chapter first briefly describes some recent geopolitical dynamics and key regional problems that complicate the realization of any challenging policy. I then try to evaluate the EU's previous engagements and specify its weak points. The chapter is concluded by addressing the process of the ENP negotiation, as well as its prospects and understandings. Some recommendations are also given throughout the text.

The Changing Dynamics of Caspian Geopolitics

The South Caucasus has always been a geopolitically important area. While the contending powers and their characteristics change throughout the course of history, being situated on the clash of divergent regional cultures, the strategic value of this place bridging two continents continues. Hence, stressing something rather apparent, geopolitics must be taken into serious consideration and should be kept under constant observation. This is now even more important, as the whole region has been changing substantially during the past fifteen years and is also emerging as a particularly dynamic region.

To clearly depict the geopolitical trends, I will divide the post-Soviet history of the region into three periods. Meanwhile, we will show that the EU's engagement also has some general geopolitical predispositions.

The South Caucasus as the Post-Soviet Periphery

The period after the disintegration of the Soviet Union was marked with unconditional political and economic dependency on its former center. In this period of time, Moscow was substantially able to fulfil its geopolitical goals.

Most importantly, the support of the Ossetian and mainly Abkhazian separatism led to the creation of the Russian military bases on Georgian soil.[3] However, it should also be noted that a similar strategy did not turn out so successful in the case of the war over Nagorno Karabakh. The new geopolitical impetus also attracted another two regional powers, Turkey and Iran, even if their impact proved to be considerably limited. The European powers and the U.S., although extremely reluctant, responded to Georgian and Azerbaijani calls to the West and almost did not express any interest in regional affairs. These attitudes were in response mainly to not wanting to provoke any deeper Russian intervention and further complicate relations with Moscow on these sensitive issues. Furthermore, the inner instability of nearly disfunctional states constituted a principal hurdle for any Western interest.

The Period of the Great Game

The situation changed dramatically after September 20, 1994, when the Contract of the Century was signed.[4] During this period, shortly after the official end of the war in Nagorno Karabakh, the geostrategic importance of the region fundamentally increased, and U.S. officials were unhesitant to embrace the region to fold vital U.S. interests.

The reasoning of the Great Game followed the thoughts originally formulated by Zbigniew Brzezinski,[5] according to whom the potential adverse developments in Russia, which will possibly expand into the former Soviet republics, could be restrained by the creation of a stable corridor while supporting bordering countries. The choice of the Baku-Tbilisi-Ceyhan pipeline can be understood as the objectification of this strategy. This is why the U.S., regardless of uncertain economic prospects,[6] has chosen the Western way of transit through the BTC pipeline.[7] Russia's geopolitical counter-strategy and strength was based on attempts to destabilize the region by monopolizing the conflict management and freezing the conflicts in Abkhazia, South Ossetia and Nagorno Karabakh, hence, increasing the investment risk. The blockage of the agreement on the status of the Caspian Sea also became part of the strategy, since, according to a Russian perspective, the Caspian resources were insignificant, and would have needed too huge of an investment to be exploited.[8]

Thus, the nature of the situation implied that the realization of the Caspian projects would be endangered as long as Russia dominated the region. In other words, the military and political presence of the U.S. in the region was widely understood as the sign of successful achievement of these goals. This relatively pessimistic view changed as a result of the events following 9/11.

The Geopolitics in the War Against Terrorism

The terrorist attacks on U.S. cities brought in new incentives to American strategy regarding the Caucasian-Central Asian region. The planned operation in Afghanistan motivated Americans to ensure a military base within northern Afghan borders. In October 2001, such a base was placed in Khanabad in southern Uzbekistan. This was the first time that a NATO member had established a military presence in the former Soviet area. The base in Khanabad was followed by the NATO airbase in Bishkek in Kyrgyzstan.[9] The obviously particular circumstances of these moves basically precluded any Russian protests and forced Moscow to accept it.

The new conditions of the "War on Terror" prompted not only the U.S., but also the EU, to deal seriously with the problem of the diversification of the strategic resources. The definite approval of the BTC pipeline also came in October 2001. Moreover, Americans substantially intensified the efforts to reach an agreement with Kazakhstan to build the trans-Caspian pipeline, which would transport an extensive proportion of Kazakhi oil (probably from the Karachaganak and Kashagan fields) on the bed of the Caspian to Baku where it would be connected to the BTC pipeline. And finally, since the spring of 2002, the U.S., under the pretext of the conditions of the war against terrorism, started extensive military cooperation with the crucial transition point—Georgia. Fortunately, the last political and geopolitical changes also "awakened" the EU who, for a long time, had marginalized the importance of this region.[10] In the summer of 2003, a Special Representative for the South Caucasus was appointed to the region.[11] The European Commission also employed a Rapid Reaction Mechanism to support democratization processes in Georgia after the Velvet Revolution, as well as allocating 32 million euros for economic development and confidence building programs. Finally, in June 2004, in order to conclude this geopolitical attempt, the EU corrected the mistake made in March 2003 by incorporating Armenia, Azerbaijan, and Georgia into the ENP.

The South Caucasus – A Difficult Space for the EU's Engagement

I have already noted that the EU has only slowly been recognizing the strategic importance of the region. The South Caucasus is a peripheral region which does not offer much as a region of production nor as a consumer market. However, the EU's interests should be prompted by at least one positive and various negative aspects. As for the former, we should mention the energy resources and their transportation, which can create a significant possibility of a needful diversification of these resources. The negative side implies the understanding that, even while constituting a European periphery[12], the South Caucasus may become a threat to European security. This issue is not only connected with the unresolved conflicts that have the potential to ignite wars in the European neighborhood, but even more importantly with international crime and trafficking.[13]

First and foremost, the general situation in the South Caucasus is complicated by the mutually impaired bilateral relations between the states of the region and regional powers. Tense relations naturally prevailed between Armenia and Azerbaijan due to the unresolved conflict over Nagorno Karabakh. After the ceasefire in May 1994, Azerbaijan lost about one sixth of its former territory while the number of Internally Displaced Persons (IDP) reached almost 1 million. Additionally, for more than a decade, constant negotiations brought practically no result, and even further complicated the path to reach a prospect of an imminent solution. The Karabakh issue also substantially affects relations with regional powers. Most importantly, it also hinders relations between Turkey and Armenia, which have already been burdened by historical animosities.[14] The openly expressed Azerbaijani Western strategic orientation has naturally created damnatory reactions in Moscow. Finally, Azerbaijan has complicated relations with its Southern neighbor, Iran. The problems are created by the separatist activity of the Azerbaijani minority living in the region bordering Iran, and by the Iranian support provided to the Islamist forces in Azerbaijan.

Georgia always remained neutral in the conflict over Nagorno Karabakh. Yet, even if the unresolved conflicts in Abkhazia and South Ossetia are internal Georgian problems, their effects and circumstances fundamentally poisoned its relations with Russia. The last current Russian attempt to complicate the export of Georgian wine and mineral water was another expression of a long-term mutual lack of trust and misperception.[15] The problem with the Russian military bases on Georgian soil could soon be solved, but the most painful issue with the Russian engagement in the separatist regions of Abkhazia and South Ossetia still remains. It has been reported that Russia has provided military assistance to South Ossetian authorities, but most evidently, Moscow offered Russian citizenship to the populations of these provinces. Russia also controls some strategic resource supplies—especially gas—which became "obvious" during the energy cutbacks, which markedly coincided with the negotiations over military bases. In general, it can be concluded that Russian strategy still counts on substantial influence in the former Southern Soviets. This view is also present in the Russian National Security Concept according to which any weakening of integrationist ties in the CIS is seen as a threat. Also, the creation of a common economic space and joint participation in the protection of the external borders of the CIS is viewed as necessary.[16]

The entire problematic complexity of security, and of political and economic relations, has basically paralyzed any regional cooperation that could be based on shared interests. This is a situation related both to the regional and interstate problems and also to the international relations. The countries of the South Caucasus have virtually never established any common framework to deal with regional and world powers, or international organizations such as the EU or NATO. This situation has led some analysts to conclude that, even if theoretically the South Caucasus displays some typical regional characteristics, in reality, it does not make sense to consider it as a region in terms of security. From this point, South Caucasian states renounce the strategic advantage which has lately been proven many times to be profitable by e.g., the Central European states.

Crucial Problem – Frozen Conflicts

It is more than obvious that in the possible security, political and economic developments, the unresolved conflicts over the former Soviet autonomies constitute the most pressing issues. Although they tamper with all three countries, they naturally pose the most serious challenge for Georgia which could, in the case of successful separation, lose a substantial part of its territory. Moreover, Abkhazia is, without doubt, a place with a solid strategic and economic potential and South Ossetia borders with the heart of the Georgian historical statehood. Both conflicts also have the potential to destabilize the whole country and possibly the entire region. One should also be reminded that the BTC pipeline spans most of the Georgian territory. From this perspective it becomes clear why Georgia seems to be in the center of the U.S. Eurasian strategy as well as appearing to be in the main focus of the EU's regional engagement.

Ajaria

The new ambitious Georgian president Mikheil Saakashvili, after his accession, proclaimed the unification of the country as his top priority. He became successful in the first instance when he managed to supersede the regional monarch of Ajaria, Aslan Abashidze, from his prominent seat in Batumi. Abashidze's power was previously built on gains from the control of trans-border trading with Turkey, warm relations with the leading officers of the military base in Batumi, and neutrality in the Abkhazian and Ossetian conflicts.[17] The unspoken agreement with former Georgian president Eduard Shevardnadze, according to which Abashidze did not challenge Georgian territorial integrity in return for considerable financial autonomy, came to an end with the Velvet Revolution. The situation escalated further during the election campaign of March 2004, but the definite fall of Abashidze came after the May parliamentary election. Although Abashidze's party won the election in Ajaria, on an all-Georgian scale it ended up below the percentage rate needed to enter the parliament. Abashidze was then finally defeated by the official Russian unwillingness to back him. Although the restoration of central control over Ajaria was evidently the least challenging of Georgian objectives, it heavily boosted Saakashvili's self-confidence.

South Ossetia

The endeavors of Tbilisi's government then turned to South Ossetia which, unlike Ajaria and Abkhazia, was not a favored region during Soviet times. The strategic importance of the place is, however, evident in several facts. First, the region is formed by three valleys which also bypass the Caucasus range and thus provide possible transit points on the Georgian—the Russian border. Second, its kin region North Ossetia/Alania is located on the Russian side of the border, which naturally intensifies separatist tendencies. Finally, as already noted, South Ossetia is situated close to the Georgian historical center.[18]

Since the end of the war, central government has not established yet its full control over the region. On the other hand, with the exception of those in Abkhazia, most of the Georgian IDPs were allowed to return to their homes[19] and the border remained generally open. Nevertheless, the Ossetian leadership still refused any autonomist proposals which did not reflect the post-war *de facto* independence. Long-term Ossetian president Eduard Kokoity also rejected similar suggestions offered by Saakashvili after the end of the Ajar crisis. The Georgian government decided to create an economic pressure on this defiant region while establishing strong controls on the internal borders. These controls were meant to spoil the contraband trade which makes up the core of the South Ossetian economy. This Georgian attempt also gave rise to the strong protests from Moscow in favor of guarding South Ossetian "independence."[20] The entire situation gradually escalated with increasing numbers of troops on both sides.

Some speculation about weakening Russian support then appeared during the Ljubljana summit of OSCE in December 2005, where Russia surprisingly did not veto the document which precisely mentioned the need to find a peaceful solution to the Ossetian problem while keeping Georgian territorial integrity.[21] At the same time, however, Russian interests were aimed at the maintenance of the composition of the Joint Control Commission[22] which should, according to Georgians, also include the EU and U.S. representatives. Indeed, as I will argue later, South Ossetia really does provide some possibilities for deeper EU engagement.

Abkhazia

The Abkhazian matter could be considered the most sensitive issue. Having formerly been regarded by many people as one of the most beautiful spots within the whole USSR, this place witnessed the bloodiest post-Soviet war at the beginning of the 1990s. Moreover, approximately 200,000 IDPs serve, particularly in big Georgian cities, as a very visible painful memento.[23]

In reflection of South Ossetia, Abkhazia also ended up being *de facto* independent after the war of the early 1990s. Additionally, Abkhazians, according to a well-founded estimation, also won a reasonable ethnic majority in Abkhazia, where ethnic Abkhazians control the region. Abkhazian representation has taken similar attitudes to the Ossetians and refused any efforts to forge an agreement on a federal basis. Also, Abkhazian elites had above-standard relations with officials in Moscow. For example, the founder of the independent Abkhazia, Vladimir Ardzinba, who served as president until the election of 2004/2005, had friendly relations with the then-Russian Minister of Foreign Affairs, Yevgeny Primakov and Anatoly Lukyanov, who became known as the ideologue of the August coup in 1991.

The void between the regimes in Tbilisi and Sukhumi seems to be even deeper than in the case of South Ossetia. In fact, Saakashvili, too objectively, has not even tried to challenge Abkhazian independence. On the other hand, although the tension in South Ossetia has recently escalated several times to limited exchanges of fire, the situation in Abkhazia has been calmer for a while, as the last serious tensions only appeared around the return of the group of Georgian IDPs into the predominantly Georgian-populated Gali region, in May 1998.

From a more recent perspective, the most fundamental event was the vacation of Vladislav Ardzinba from the presidential office. His successor, Raul Khadjimba, who was determined in advance as the "Abkhazian Putin," and whose Soviet career was connected with the secret services, was also openly backed by his former colleague in the Kremlin. Surprisingly, however, he was beaten by Sergey Bagapsh, who showed a greater reservation in his attitudes against Moscow and was paradoxically more open to negotiations with Tbilisi. Although any breakthrough in Georgian-Abkhazian relations has not taken place since the beginning of 2005, and the solution of the problem is still immense, it should be noted that at least communication between Tbilisi and Sukhumi has improved.

The conflict over Nagorno Karabakh displays a geopolitically more complex problem than the conflicts in Georgia. It should be considered a regional problem, since, besides Armenia, Azerbaijan and Russia, it also somehow involves Turkey and Iran.[24] Armenia is also widely seen as the only Russian ally in the South Caucasus, which further diminishes the space for any Azerbaijani manoeuvring.

Similarly, as occurred in Georgia, the Nagorno Karabakh conflict was frozen at the stage where Azerbaijan cannot accept any solution that would challenge its territorial integrity, while Armenia, on the other hand does not want to abandon the advantage and reality of a war victory. However, it should also be stressed that this interstate conflict is also often used in internal politics. While the position of Ilham Aliyev in Azerbaijan is naturally strong, this can be particularly important for Armenian President, Robert Kocharian, who allegedly raises the Karabakh issue when he faces potent oppositional attacks.

South Caucasus and the EU

As opposed to other European Neighborhoods, the South Caucasus has the misfortune of not having a traditional advocate or proponent inside the EU. This problem became obvious, for example, during the beginning of the ENP's first wave of negotiations. Indeed, although Armenia, Azerbaijan and Georgia had already been members of the Council of Europe and signed the Partnership for Peace, their voices were not loud enough and they were excluded from the first wave of the ENP.

In this respect, another observation can also be considered in relation to this problem. While revising the most positive moves of the EU concerning the Caucasus region, it can clearly be seen that small EU countries have been the most accommodating. The most assertive changes occurred during the presidencies of Holland, Finland, Greece and Sweden. There is also a particular hope that the Scandinavian and new EU members from the Central and East Europe, in particular, could accept the role of the advocates and proponents of South Caucasian countries' interests.[25]

Similarly, as I have also noted in the introduction, the EU has a somewhat impaired image in the South Caucasus. It is also one of the main messages of this text, which will be more precisely addressed later, that the reason for its worsened reputation lies particularly in the fact that the EU has only very limited capacities to respond to the most damaging regional issues. From this perspective, it should be noted that the fall of the European Constitutional Treaty project was also observed by the regional elites, probably rightly so, as applying the brakes on the further accession process and, more importantly, as the danger for the deeper development of the Common Foreign and Security Policy.

The position of the EU, not only throughout the 1990s, but also in the first years of this millennium, could be characterized as the invisible donor. Even if the amounts allocated from European sources have been significant, they are still substantially lower than those provided by the U.S. Roughly speaking, the overall allocations reached nearly 500 million euros for each state. The Technical Assistance for the Commonwealth of Independent States (TACIS) national allocations between 1992 and 2004 reached about 100 million euros for each country, while other resources came also from the European Agricultural Guidance and Guarantee Fund (EAGGF).[26] It is certainly important that the EU is not a marginal trading partner for all three countries. Approximately one third of exports and two thirds of imports of Azerbaijan are carried out with EU members. In the case of Armenia, these figures total about 45 percent and 35 percent respectively. Quite interestingly, Georgia still trades predominantly with post-Soviet countries and Turkey. Its exports with EU member states reach roughly 20 percent and imports 25 percent.[27]

During the 1990s the EU's approach toward the South Caucasus did not differ from that applied to other post-Soviet countries. The most significant tools became the Partnership and Cooperation Agreements which were signed in 1996.[28] The rather technical and economy-based agreements were also supported by the implementation of the almost cash-starved TACIS programs. The 'technical' approach was broadened later when the Commission prepared Country Strategy Papers for the period of 2002-2006. These documents also identified some priority areas such as the rule of law, human rights, poverty reduction, or conflict resolution, and prevention. Due to political changes, the Georgian Strategy Paper was revised in 2003 and became the most carefully formulated as well as the most ambitious document.[29]

Even if the previous lines reveal that the EU did not show any endeavor of a more precise and subtle approach based on differentiation; it still reflected the distinct political situation in all the three countries. Most importantly, in the cases of Armenia and Azerbaijan, the EU overlooked the problematic issues concerning human rights, civil society development and judiciary reform, as well as reform of the law enforcement sector.[30] This time, the EU had to seriously take diverse expectations of these countries into account. Briefly reviewed, the highest expectations and statements of dissatisfaction came often from Georgia, which pushed the EU for more active engagement in security issues. Armenia took a rather pragmatic position by demanding help, especially for its economic, technical and trading problems. Azerbaijan could be considered as the most ambitious country with regard to mutual importance or complementarities while naturally building its stance on energy resources. What has become more and more obvious, however, was the improvement of the EU's engagement to be heavily dependent on a more active involvement in conflict prevention and resolution. Yet, these are exactly the areas in which the EU displays a particular weakness, while feeling much better in a peace-building role and post-conflict reconciliation. I will now briefly summarize its activities in the above-mentioned conflict places.

The negotiation over the conflict in Abkhazia, the so-called Geneva Process, is primarily UN-sponsored and the EU stands outside of it. However, the EU has functioned as a generous donor there. In various programs supporting mainly the economic stability and institutional development, the EU has held a strict depoliticizing strategy.[31] With this attitude, while the EU has taken part in the process of project-related decision-making, it, at the same time, has kept itself clear from engaging in the Georgian-Abkhaz struggle. On the other hand, this approach also confirms that the EU has also given up carrying out any attempt for resolution in the region. This strategy, however, may help to improve social, political and economic conditions without touching primary conflict resolution fields such as demobilization, disarmament and reintegration. The EU is actually working around, rather than on, the conflict. As a result, the projects are again donor driven, still operating largely from outside, and perhaps most importantly, do not imply the strategy of conditionality.[32]

Some weaknesses and difficulties exhibited for the engagement in Abkhazia were not shown in the case of South Ossetia. The EU has managed to tie its project to the negotiation process and agreement in the Joint Control Commission while participating at least in its expert groups. From this perspective, the EU should exert pressure to gain a full-fledged seat in the JCC for the EU Special Representative (EUSR). Although the strategy of conditionality has partly been at work in South Ossetia, the projects, which are mostly focused on economic and infrastructural development, could certainly be performed on more effective fields, if conditioned by the EUSR directly in the JCC.

Seeing the case of Nagorno Karabakh from this perspective, the analysis seems to be rather easy. It is a matter of fact that, after the peace agreement signed in 1994, the EU has not established any considerable supporting program. Yet, it should also be immediately noted that both Armenia, and especially Azerbaijan, strictly refused any EU engagement. Recently, both countries have somewhat mitigated their position after pressure coming primarily from the Council of Europe. It is also obvious that the situation in Karabakh is far from being ripe for the implementation of any support program. Such conditions would require a significant change in the relations between Armenia and Azerbaijan. Accordingly, however, this situation could provide a space for the EU to promote the processes of reconciliation and confidence building.

As I have already mentioned, one of the important strategic decisions which opened the way for a closer cooperation between the EU and the South Caucasus, was already given before the incorporation of the countries into the ENP. During the Greek presidency, the EU decided to implement an originally German proposal and appointed an EU Special Representative to the South Caucasus (EUSR). In fact, it was the first attempt of the EU to implement a common strategy for Armenia, Azerbaijan, and Georgia. The position of the EUSR has naturally been complicated by many factors which were already mentioned previously in the text. First of all, from the perspective of cooperation potential, the South Caucasus does not really work as a region. Secondly, the political performance of the EUSR has to be very sensible, since it virtually implies dealing with significant neighbors—Russia, Iran, and Turkey—and, at the same time, becoming part of a framework of several international organizations currently engaging in the region, which is not yet fully coordinated. Finally, the EUSR has been responsible for interposing the common standpoint of the EU, which obviously requires the unification of the positions of EU members, as well as of the institutions already involved in the area. This is mostly the case for

France, Germany and the UK, who serve as the Group of Friends supporting the Special Representative of the UN Secretary-General in Abkhazia, and for France who, together with Russia and the U.S., co-chairs the Minsk Group mediating on the Nagorno Karabakh conflict.[33]

The first EUSR Finnish diplomat Heikke Talvitie was replaced in February 2006 by Swedish Peter Semneby. The change on the post also allowed for some recapitulation. Despite Talvitie's very active engagement, experience has shown that the EUSR should be more visible in the region as well as in Brussels. Talvitie travelled extensively throughout the region; however, he was naturally more focused on Georgia. Moreover, his main office was still based in Helsinki. It is, hence, perhaps a good decision that his successor decided to stay officially near the Commission in Brussels.[34] Nevertheless, the fundamental problem lies in the mandate the EUSR obtains from the Commission, especially in the sensitive but crucial area of conflict resolution. We must note that, the position of the first EUSR was generally considered as weak in the region.

ENP and the Key Issues in the South Caucasus

Countries' expectations, which have been outlined above, became obvious during the beginning of the ENP Action Plans negotiations. Both, Armenia and Georgia, submitted their own "Framework Proposals for Action Plan" in June 2005. Armenia then, after several rounds of negotiation with the EU representatives, accepted the result. The negotiation process with Azerbaijan had been complicated by the completely unrelated conflict with Cyprus[35]; however the content of the document seems to have been agreed upon. It should be noted that both countries, Armenia and Azerbaijan, yielded consent to the EU's intention to support the OSCE Minsk group's endeavor to find a solution to the conflict in Nagorno Karabakh. The commission also expressed its view that both countries should reach a consensus on the exact wording of the part concerning the conflict resolution. This could be seen as the lessening of the former Armenian attitudes; however with such an acquisition the question about validity of the chapter seems to be in place. Being always the most active of the countries when it comes to the relation with the West, Georgia became highly dissatisfied with the result of the negotiation process. Quite unsurprisingly, Georgian representatives were dissatisfied with the level of the security commitments planned to be taken by the EU which is supposed to counter Russian influence. The most problematic point from the Georgian perspective, however, is related to the EU's unwillingness to take more measures for conflict resolution from the European Security and Defense Policy (ESDP) toolbox.[36]

In September 2006, final negotiations on the ENP Action Plans for Armenia, Azerbaijan and Georgia took place. Although both general and public reflections of these events are particularly low in these countries, I will try to indicate some key issues entering the rudiments of the debates in Armenia and Georgia.

Armenia has been highlighting its problems with a successful performance which, from the European perspective, seems to be conditioned by the progress in democratic reforms. The implementation should also enable some possibilities for its European aspirations to be targeted mostly to the EU internal market. Other significant problems, which should be touched by the Action Plan, are related to poverty reduction and the fight against corruption. In this regard, Armenia should also benefit from extensive technical and financial support and an extension of the European Investment Bank (EIB) mandate, as well as from the mechanisms such as Technical Assistance and Information Exchange (TAIEX) or Twinning.[37] I have already mentioned that question marks still remain in the case of the actual wording of the Nagorno Karabakh chapter.

Armenians appear to view the ENP initiative as very much security-driven. Indeed, they understand the EU's motivation to secure a stable and predictable neighborhood, which will also be prone to European values. In relation to this, it is noticeable that Armenia still has not adopted its security strategy and hence lacks a coherent document in which its security interests would be clearly defined. Obviously, mostly for political reasons, security discussions in Armenia have been centered on the conflict over Nagorno Karabakh, so far. Hence, quite interestingly, there is a certain possibility that the EN could also become a useful tool for promoting a security doctrine. According to Armenian analysts, besides the issue of Nagorno Karabakh, the EU document should also address the danger of Armenian isolation, which is evidently connected to the geopolitical realities presented earlier. In correlation to this, the Armenians are also concerned about cultural security that implies the demolition of Armenian heritage outside Armenia, as well as a certain armenophobia, which has been on the increase.[38]

In Georgia the political, economic, and social reforming process had already started after the Rose Revolution.[39] I have also mentioned earlier that the revolution events in fact prompted several EU supporting mechanisms. Georgia has also expressed its willingness several times to cooperate closely with the EU, and has acted very actively during the negotiation processes. Indeed, Georgia has particularly struggled for the EU's deeper engagement in the solution of the regional conflicts. In general, Georgia has experienced the most developed debate on the European issues, as well as being under the gaze of many foreign analysts.

Besides, the breaking of the unpleasant status quo in Abkhazia and South Ossetia, another significant Georgian challenge has been the strengthening of the state. Concerning this problem, the ENP Action Plan should suggest some specific steps to be taken in juridical reform, which should generally become an implementation of the previous Rule of Law

Mission in 2004-2005. The problem of law enforcement has also been a priority for the Georgian government, since the insufficient progress in this area seriously undermines the possible positive impact of the reforms. The EU could also use the potential of the EUSR's team on this issue. Nevertheless, the second EUSR has also obtained a new and wider mandate enabling him to play a more active role in seeking the settlement of Georgian conflicts. The ENP Action Plan should steer Georgia toward opening up the conflict zones, as well as taking some pragmatic steps that could promote the interest of the regional leaderships in entering into negotiations with Tbilisi. The EU should then exceed its already increasing involvement in rehabilitation and reconstruction activities, and support this endeavor materially and financially. The question remains about the possibility the Action Plan could include a chapter on shared border management. The Georgian government expressed its interests after the withdrawal of the OSCE border mission and subsequent crises on the Georgian-Russian border. It should also be noted that the EUSR has received a special mandate in this area. With regard to this problem, the EU could provide Georgia with managerial and training support. Moreover, there have also been considerations about the deployment of the EU Border Assistance Mission, which could operate on the ground-plan already exercised in the Moldovan-Ukrainian border in the end of 2005.[40]

Future of the Caucasian European Neighborhood through the ENP Lenses

The ENP has been interpreted and understood in several ways. Indeed, according to Petr Kratochvíl, the greatest obstacle of the ENP lies in the vagueness of the policy producing a number of clashing interpretations, which are supported by different players from both within and outside the EU.[41] The ENP is interpreted as an enlargement substitute, a pre-enlargement policy, an instrument to widen the zone of influence, or as a reenvisioned version of the Barcelona Process. All these interpretations are also relevant to the South Caucasus. As part of the conclusion, I will now briefly explain their relation to the situation in the South Caucasus, particularly Armenia and Georgia.

I have already mentioned that in the South Caucasus, the EU's motivation to be engaged in the region has been widely understood as the attempt to build a stable and predictable neighborhood.[42] Other aspects, such as the energy resource diversification, have been presented mainly by international observers. The EU officials have been particularly diligent in pontificating on the future of the EU-South Caucasian relations and they have never openly expressed the possibility of full membership for Armenia, Azerbaijan or Georgia. The former European Commission President, Romano Prodi, before his visit to the region in September 2004, stated:

> This first-ever visit by a European Commission President highlights the EU's interest in the region following the inclusion of all three countries in the European Neighborhood Policy. My visit is intended to send the important message that the EU is fully committed to supporting the Southern Caucasus countries as they work to build stable societies based on democratic values and to affording these countries real prospects of strong ties with the European Union that bind them into Europe.[43]

More recently, the Commissioner for External Relations, Benita Ferrero-Waldner, during a visit to the region in February 2006, expressed the EU's view in similar terms while stating that:

> [By] including the countries of the South Caucasus in the ENP we have opened a new chapter in our relations with these countries. I hope that we can swiftly conclude our work together with Armenia, Azerbaijan and Georgia on the Action Plans so that these relationships can intensify further. I also hope that in 2006 we can see good progress on the peaceful settlement of the conflicts in the region. During my visit I will be explaining how we can support the countries on their way to a more stable, prosperous and democratic future. This process not only supports Armenia, Azerbaijan, and Georgia individually, but brings benefits for the South Caucasus region as a whole.[44]

Obviously, the top EU officials never mention possible membership, and similarly, the latest ENP Country Reports strictly talk about 'partnership.'[45] Hence, from the EU's perspective, the ENP appears to serve as a clear alternative to the enlargement process.

The issue gets more complicated when it comes to the application of the zone of influence hypothesis. This view is definitely promoted by the former regional hegemon—Russia.[46] However, it should be stressed that this Russian attitude does not only reflect historical geopolitical experience, but also deeper fundamentals of the Russian foreign policy. Yet, as Kratochvíl also notes, this interpretation, in general, implies the non-cooperative nature of policies and relations, which is in complete contrast to the one behind the European policies. Viewing the issue from this perspective, I would argue that part of the relational problem with Russia is rightly the fact that the EU will not have intended entering into such a game with this particular nation.

Although particularly Georgian officials have taken very pro-European stances, they also appear to remain realistic about possible full membership. Most recently, the Georgian Minister of Foreign Affairs Gela Bezhuashvili talked in Brussels about the 'reinforcement of Georgia's relations with the European Union..'[47] His governmental colleague, Minister of European and Euro-Atlantic Integration, Giorgi Baramidze, responded to the question about possible membership with these words: 'First of all, I have to tell you that at this stage we are not even talking about membership, because we are realistic. We know that we are not ready, Europe is not ready. We don't want to be anybody's headache. We want to be good neighbors and good partners of Europe.' [48] He further remarked that Georgia is happy about the new framework of the ENP and will be building its relationship with the EU on the basis of the ENP while also expecting a new structural document, which will define these relations. Baramidze did not forget to mention that German endeavors were to strengthen the ENP toward the "ENP-Plus."[49]

It should also be held in consideration that Georgian diplomacy has currently been more down-to-earth, focusing mainly on obtaining an invitation to enter NATO. We could conclude that, although Georgian officials do not openly deny possible membership to the EU, they also realistically interpret the ENP, with regard to the situation inside the EU, basically as the enlargement substitute.

I have already mentioned that the discussion in Armenia, due to its internal political situation, has not developed in such a way as in Georgia. Quite importantly, however, the ENP process has recently prompted a potentially fruitful discussion about the concept of national security. The document already quoted "European Neighborhood: Policy and Security," and interestingly, it mentions a working document called 'Benchmarks of Armenian Security,' which is now discussed in academic as well as political communities.[50] It is certainly not without interest that according to the authors of the aforementioned Benchmarks document, which could become a foundation for the future security conception, this includes a statement that Armenia does not intend to apply for a NATO membership, as well as not containing a single word indicating that Armenian should become an EU member.[51] Armenia has lately been the closest ally of Russia in the South Caucasus, and therefore, the contingency is that Armenians will view the EU's activities through the Russian geopolitical lenses, presupposing that the EU has attempts to extend its zone of influence. Notwithstanding this, I would also argue that the more realistic streams in Armenian politics would, in all probability, interpret the ENP rather as an enlargement substitute.

Despite the fact that the EU has generally never been a strong topic in Azerbaijan, it should be mentioned that Azerbaijani political and public debates, to a certain extent, are mainly reflected on the issue of Turkish-EU relations. The interest on the Azerbaijani side was driven not only by the natural deep ties between Azerbaijan and Turkey, but also, recalling the character of the debate in Europe, by the very concern of wondering whether the EU would ever be open for a non-Christian state.[52] Generally the Azerbaijani position could be considered as rather pragmatic. The representatives of this energy resources-rich country would usually welcome any kind of the EU's engagement which could help to settle the Azerbaijani territorial disputes. On the other hand, while stressing the developing cooperative relations, they tend to hope the EU will condone the weak democratic record this Caspian country has been showing in the post-Soviet era. It should be noted that, however, the EU officials do not appreciate only the economic potential of Azerbaijan, but also its balanced position within the region and especially the character of its relations with Russia.[53] Generally, Azerbaijani elites have never considered the EU membership as a realistic option, and hence, fully perceive the ENP as an alternative for enlargement.

Conclusion

This chapter intended to highlight several problems. Firstly, I have tried to recall the role played by the geopolitical conditions of the region. The first part shows that the South Caucasus is geopolitically a very dynamic region and that any player that is trying to become involved in this region should be aware of its geopolitical realities. Secondly, my aim was to indicate some key problems the region faces, observe their recent developments and to define them for possible EU engagement. I have also correspondingly mentioned the marred image of the EU in the region. Although the situation has been improving, it should be stressed that the image of the EU may only be altered, if the EU starts to deal with the most pressing issues that are on top of the political and security agendas. It should also be noted that there is a significant space for more active engagement on the part of the EU, which has also been praised by countries in the region. In other words, there are good reasons for the EU to be involved in Caucasian issues and furthermore, for the countries of the region to continue to lay their hopes and trust in this kind of progress. From this perspective, the deployment of the ENP could be seen as a good step forward.

---

[1] This chapter includes some revised parts which have been originally published in my chapter *The EU and Its Neighbourhood: Policies, Problems, Priorities*, ed. Petr Kratochvíl, (Prague: Institute of International Relations, 2006)

[2] According to recent surveys, about 80 percent of Georgians and Armenians are in favor of European Union accession. For more see, *Conflict Resolution in the South Caucasus: The EU's role*, International Crisis Group, March 2006, p. 3

[3] The bases were situated in Batumi (Adjaria), Akhalkalaki (Armenian-populated province of Dzhavakheti), Gudauta (Abkhazia), and Vaziani (near the capital Tbilisi). Although some of the bases have been liquidated recently in accordance with the Istanbul Agreements signed in 1999, the issues around the Russian military bases still

remains highly controversial and even more complicates the Georgian-Russian relations.
4 This contract was originally signed between Azerbaijani national agency SOCAR and Western Oil Consortium comprising British Petroleum (GB), Amoco (U.S.), Lukoil (Russia), Pennzoil (U.S.), Unocal (U.S.), Statoil (Norway), Mc Dermott International (U.S.), Ramco (Scotland), Turkish State Oil Company (Turkey), Delta-Nimir (Saudi Arabia)
5 See, please, Zbigniew Brzezinski, *The Grand Chessboard: American Primacy and Its Geostrategic Imperatives*, (New York: Basic Books, 1997)
6 For detailed analysis see, for instance, Ryan Baum, *Timeframes, Markets and Government Influence: An Economic-Based Look at Pipeline Routes for Caspian Sea Oil*, Princeton University, 1998, http://www.wws.princeton.edu/wws401c/1998/ryan.pdf, Ronald Soligo, and Amy, M. Jaffe, *Unlocking the Assets: Energy and the Future of Central and the Caucasus*, Baker Institute Study, Rice University, 1998, http://www.bakerinstitute.org/Publication_List.cfm?PY=1998, and Thomas, R., Stauffer, "Caspian Fantasy: The Economics of Political Pipelines," *The Brown Journal of World Affairs*, Vol. VII, Number, Issue 2, Summer/fall 2000, http://watsoninstitute.org/bjwa/archive/7.2/Oil/Stauffer.pdf
7 The crucial transit point for the Azerbaijani and possibly Kazakh and Turkmen oil is Georgia, since it has no alternative after the rejection of the transit through Armenia, Iran, and Russia.
8 More recently, however, Russia has on the background of rapprochement with Turkey, reconsidered her attitude towards the BTC while Russian state companies have even speculated about an active involvement.
9 The base in Uzbekistan was closed down in November 2005
10 For the deeper analysis, please, see, Bruno, Coppieters, "Special Representative to a new periphery," The South Caucasus: a challenge for the EU, *Chaillot Papers*, no.65, 2003, Dov, Lynch, "The EU: towards a strategy," The South Caucasus: a challenge for the EU, *Chaillot Papers*, no.65, 2003
11 The first Special Representative, Finnish diplomat Heikki Talvitie, was in February 2006 substituted by Swedish diplomat Peter Semneby.
12 See, Bruno, Coppieters, "Georgia in Europe," in *Commonwealth and Independence in Post-Soviet Euroasia*, eds. Bruno Coppieters, Alexei Zverev and Dmitri Trenin, , (London: Frank Cass, 1998), pp. 44-68
13 see, for instance, Svante, E., Cornell, "The Growing Threat of Transnational Crime,"The South Caucasus: a challenge for the EU, *Chaillot Papers*, no.65, 2003
14 The issue of the genocide of 1915 is particularly vivid in Armenia. See http://www.armenian-genocide.org/
15 See, for example, RFE/RL Caucasus Report, 11 April 2006, http://www.rferl.org/reports/caucasus-report/2006/04/12-110406.asp
16 See David Darchiashvili, "Georgian Security Problems and Policies," The South Caucasus: a challenge for the EU, *Chaillot Papers*, no.65, 2003 pp. 109-110. It should also be noted that Georgia already left the Council of Defense Ministers of CIS in February 2006 because of her NATO membership aspirations.
17 See, for example, Giorgi, M., Derlugian, "The Tale of Two Resorts: Abkhazia and Ajaria before and since the Soviet Collapse," in *The Myth of Ethnic Conflict*, eds. Beverly, Crawford and Ronnie, D., Lipschutz, (Berkeley: University of

California, International and Area Studies Research Series, 1998) or Monica, Toft, "Two-Way Mirror Nationalism: The Case of Ajaria," in The Politics of the Caspian, eds. Moshe, Gammer, and Monica, Toft, (London: Frank Cass Publishers, 2004)

[18] For more see, for instance, Julian, Birch, "Ossetia: A Caucasian Bosnia in Microcosm," *Central Asian Survey*, vol. 14, no. 1, (1995), or Nicola, Cvetkovski, "The Georgian-South Ossetian Conflict," (Danish Association for Research on the Caucasus, 2002)

[19] The return was not such a sensitive issue as in the case of Abkhazia since Ossetians dominated the autonomy already before the war.

[20] Ossetians have several times expressed a will to become members of the Russian federation

[21] See http://www.osce.org/documents/html/pdftohtml/17369_en.pdf.html

[22] The Joint Control Commission was established in Dagomys peace agreement signed in June 1992 to monitor joint peace-keeping troops.

[23] On Abkhazia see, for instance, Svante, E., Cornell, Small Nations Great Powers, (London: RoutledgeCurzon, 2003), Derlugian, *The Tale of Two Resorts*, and "The Forgotten Abkhazia: Anatomy of Post-Socialist Ethnic War," *PONARS Memo 163*, 2000, George, Hewitt, *The Abkhazians*, (London: RoutledgeCurzon, 1999, Ghia, Nodia, "The Conflict in Abkhazia: National Projects and Political Circumstances," http://www.abkhazia-georgia.parliament.ge/Publications/Georgian/ghia_nodia_1.htm, Per, Normark, "Abkhazia – Time for Conflict Resolution," paper prepared for the Second METU Conference on International Relations, Ankara 2003, Gueorgui, Otyrba, "War in Abkhazia: The Regional Significance of the Georgian-Abkhazian Conflict," in *National Identity and Ethnicity in Russia and the New States of Euroasia*, ed. Roman, Szporluk, (New York: M.E. Sharpe, 1994)

[24] For more see, for example, Svante, E. Cornell, "Undeclared War: The Nagorno-Karabakh Conflict Reconsidered," *Journal of South Asian and Middle Eastern Studies*, vol. 20 no. 4 (1997)

[25] See, for example, Arkady, Moshes, "The Eastern Neighbours of the European Union as an Opportunity for Nordic Actors," Danish Institute for International Studies, *Working Paper* 12/2006

[26] The TACIS allocations amounted 99 million euro in Armenia, 111 million euro in Georgia, and 123 million euro in Azerbaijan. From EAGGF 65 million euros was sent to Azerbaijan, 62 million to Georgia, and 50 million to Armenia.

[27] These figures are certainly rounded and reflect the average for the last years.

[28] All three PCAs can be found at http://ec.europa.eu/comm/external_relations/ceeca/pca/index.htm

[29] The Country Strategy Papers can be found at http://ec.europa.eu/comm/external_relations/sp/index.htm

[30] Recently the Commission has designed and covered a project supporting juridical environment in Azerbaijan.

[31] The most significant is The Economic Rehabilitation Program for Georgia/Abkhazia promulgated this year by the Commission. The Program will last three years during which 4 million euros will be provided.

[32] See, *Conflict Resolution in the South Caucasus: The EU's role*, pp. 17-18

[33] For more see, Bruno, Coppieters, "Special Representative to a new periphery," The South Caucasus: a challenge for the EU, *Chaillot Papers no.65*, 2003, Dov, Lynch, "Sharpening EU Policy towards Georgia," http://www.iss-eu.org/new/analysis/analy135.pdf#search=%22Sharpening%20Lynch%22

[34] See, *Conflict Resolution in the South Caucasus: The EU's role*, p. 23

[35] The controversy followed after the Azerbaijani decision to establish commercial and air links with Northern Cyprus and subsequent reaction of the Cyprian Greek government.

[36] See, draft proposal for ENP Action Plan at http://www.eu-integration.gov.ge/pdfs/ENPActionPlanENG.pdf and other corresponding documents at http://www.eu-integration.gov.ge/eng/

[37] See, ENP Armenia Action Plan Summary, at http://www.armeniaforeignministry.com/pr_06/060202-action_plan.doc

[38] See, European Neighborhood Policy and Security, http://www.ichd.org/files/pdf/21_ENP5.pdf#search=%2221_ENP5%22

[39] For an overview and some critical points see, Pamela Jawad, "Democratic Consolidation on Georgia after the Rose Revolution," *PRIF Report No. 73*, 2005, Robert, Legvold and Bruno, Coppieters (eds.), *Statehood and Security: Georgia after the Rose Revolution*, (American Academy of Arts and Sciences: MIT Press, 2005)

[40] This paragraph draws particularly on Lynch, *Sharpening EU Policy towards Georgia*, see also, *Conflict Resolution in the South Caucasus: The EU's role*, and Damien Helly, and Giorgi Gogia, "Georgian Security and the Role of the West," in Coppieters and Legvold, *Statehood and Security*, pp. 271-307

[41] See, Petr Kratochvíl, "The European Neighborhood Policy: The Clash of Incompatible Interpretations," in *The EU and Its Neighborhood: Policies, Problems, and Priorities*, ed. Petr Kratochvíl, (Prague: Institute of International Relations, 2006)

[42] For a rather sceptical view on the positive influence of the ENP see, please, Jaba Devdariani, "Europe Remains Ambiguous in its South Caucasus Neighborhood," *Central Asia – Caucasus Analyst*, 2004, http://www.cacianalyst.org/view_article.php?articleid=2527

[43] See, http://ec.europa.eu/comm/external_relations/ceeca/news/ip04_1104.htm

[44] See, http://europa.eu/rapid/pressReleasesAction.do?reference=IP/06/161&format=HTML&aged=0&language=EN&guiLanguage=en

[45] All three ENP Country Reports can be found here http://ec.europa.eu/world/enp/documents_en.htm#2

[46] See, for example, Nadia, Arbatova, "Europe: How wide? How deep? - A Russian View," *European Policy Centre*, 2004, http://www.theepc.be/en/ce.asp?TYP=CE&LV=177&see=y&t=42&PG=CE/EN/detail&l=3&AI=396

[47] See, Comment of the Minister of Foreign Affairs of Georgia on the results of his visit to Brussels on September 15 2006, http://www.mfa.gov.ge/index.php?lang_id=ENG&sec_id=35&info_id=2144

[48] See, http://www.rferl.org/reports/caucasus-report/2006/09/32-220906.asp

[49] See, *Ibid*

[50] As far as I know it is impossible to get another then Armenian version.

[51] See, European Neighborhood Policy and Security, http://www.ichd.org/files/pdf/21_ENP5.pdf#search=%2221_ENP5%22

[52] Leila, Alieva, "EU and South Caucasus," *CAP Discussion Paper*, Bertelsmann Group for Policy Research, 2006, p. 7
[53] Ahto, Lobjakas Ahto, "Azerbaijan: EU Taking Note on Baku's Strength," *RFE/RL, November 7*, 2006, http://www.rferl.org/features/features_Article.aspx?m=11&y=2006&id=0F418E0F-3F21-4AE3-8F3E-BCEEB1C4BE40 2006

Chapter 10
EU Policy toward Central Asia

Yelda Demirağ

Located between the Pamir Mountains and the Caspian Sea, Central Asia, where many civilizations emerged, has seen the rise and the fall of so many great empires and states built by Mongolians, Persians, Ottomans, Russians, and the Soviets. After the dissolution of the Union of Soviet Socialist Republics (USSR), the importance of the former soviet members in the region, who have now gained their independence, remained high for Russia who, for centuries, controlled the region's contact with the outside world. However, the region has become pivotal for countries such as the U.S., Turkey, Iran, China, India, and Pakistan, as well as for Russia after independence.

In the twenty-first century, international relations are becoming more intertwined in the sphere of economics, and balance of interests, as well as new strategies of economic cooperation, are gaining importance. From this point of view, the material richness of the region in raw materials, and especially in energy resources, attracts great powers' interest into this area. Energy is now the driving force of the global economy and, in the next century, it will most likely continue to be the main drive for economic and social developments. The demand for energy reinforces economic growth and, therefore, causes a dramatic increase in population growth in the long-term. In this context, Central Asia is becoming more and more important with its potential of petroleum and natural gas reserves. Kazakhstan has the Caspian Sea region's largest recoverable crude oil reserves and its production accounts for almost two-thirds of the roughly two million barrels per day (bbl/d) of crude oil that is currently being produced in the region. In 2005, Kazakhstan produced approximately 1.29 million barrels of oil per day (bbl/d) and consumed 222,000 bbl/d, resulting in net exports of over one million bbl/d. The Kazakhi government hopes to increase production levels to around 3.5 million bbl/d by 2015.[1] Between 1999 and 2004, having nearly the doubled the amount of its oil production, Kazakhstan grew its oil producing capacity by 15 percent every year.[2]

In 2004, the petroleum production in the Caspian basin was 1.6 billion barrels, as much as is produced in Brazil, the second largest producer of South America. The 2010 predictions foresee a daily production rate of three to five million barrels a day. This amount surpasses the production of Venezuela. The amount of the region's natural gas potential equals the total natural gas production of South America, Central America and Mexico combined. The regional production is estimated to reach 8.8 trillion cubic feet by 2010. This would equal the total natural gas production of the Middle East[3]. According to the data from International Energy Agency, Turkmenistan's known natural gas reserves vary between 6.7 and 9.2 trillion cubic meters and it also has an extra reserve of eight trillion cubic meters[4]. This amounts to approximately 6 percent of world's natural gas reserves.[5] In addition to the use of the regional resources, the attempts at carrying these into global markets lead to a rise in the hopes for economic development and prosperity; however, it also increases competition and threatens regional security, since there is a belief that those who would control transit petroleum transportation would control not only Central Asia, but also an increasing number of people around the world.

In addition to the countries mentioned above, another actor interested in the region is the EU. The EU started diplomatic links with these countries right after their independence, and has supported radical economic and political reform movements in the region. In this study, we focus on the Central Asian policy of the EU. We try to answer questions like: to what extent the EU has influence over the region; how it can make its presence felt next to the other actors; to what extent EU policies toward the region respond the problems of the region; and how successful the EU is in solving these problems. In this respect, in the first part of this study, we examine the problems that Central Asian countries have been facing since their independence, and in the second part, we analyze the general interest toward the region and the role played by the EU, in this context. In the third part, we take the aims of the EU under consideration. In the fourth part of the study, we evaluate the projects and the programs that the EU is using to reach its goals. And, in the final part, is a discussion of how influential the EU policies have been so far and whether there is a need for new strategies and policies.

The Structure and Problems of the Region

The Central Asian countries have gained their independence at an unexpected time, and therefore, were devoid of social, political and economic measures and preparations in order to live completely independent of the former Soviet center. The region did not experience the rise of destructive nationalism, as did the Balkans or in the Caucasus. However, the key threats that the European Security Strategy outlines,[6] including terrorism, regional conflicts, state failure, and organized crime, are all relevant to Central Asia.[7] Even though the countries of the region each have their own problems, the problems they are facing may be categorized under four general headings as political, social, economical, and security-related matters.

In some countries in the region, the former Communist Party Secretaries are still in power. Governments often use means of war under cover of combating terror and strengthening national security as a cloak to consolidate their power and to target vulnerable groups. In these countries, decisions concerning the country's future are taken without counseling the opposition, solely based on personal interests. Consequently, democratization works slowly. Issues related to human rights are also generally left unsolved. Respect for freedoms of thought, conscience and religion is not at a desired level, and there is censorship over mass media and other means of communication. Dissidents, activists and journalists have been subject to arbitrary detention. In 2006, for instance, RFE/RL correspondent, Ogulsapar Muradova, died in jail under suspicious circumstances after a trial that was internationally viewed as failing to reach international standards of fair proceedings.[8] According to the report of Amnesty International, in some Central Asian countries, human rights violations are being committed with virtual impunity. According to the report, torture, arbitrary detentions, harassment, and jailing of oppositionists still continue in the region. Also, it is stated that in the region, corrupt law-enforcement officers are rarely called for account, despite the fact that thousands of people routinely claim to have been ill-treated in order to extract confessions of guilt.[9]

In Central Asian countries, the joy of political independence has been replaced with the struggles of gaining economic independence. These countries which moved swiftly toward free market economy began to face problems in terms of financing, applying new technology and raising qualified labor force, even if they had great potential in terms of energy and agricultural production. The most prominent among the economic problems is the troubles caused by the transition from the Soviet-inherited central economy and reliance to Russia, into a market economy. During the Soviet era, major raw materials such as natural gas, petroleum, coal, aluminum, and cotton were sent to Russia for processing and the region was condemned to monoculture. Furthermore, Central Asian populations were more often used in the agricultural fields and located at centers of agriculture, while the Russian minority, who constituted the qualified workforce, was located in towns. After gaining independence, regional countries had to struggle to stand on their own feet and change this structure so they could survive within the international system. Also, while the exportation of natural resources enrich the countries and create an increase in GDP, since their incomes are shared by a small group of elites, the socio-economic level of large masses decreases. In a country such as Uzbekistan, where the minimum wage is $9 a week and the pension is $18 to $20 a month, macroeconomic signs are meaningless to large masses. Hence, with the exception of Turkmenistan, Central Asian countries were in a lower position in 2005 in terms of levels of underdevelopment than in 1992 according to the UN

Development Program data.[10] Economic problems also bring about social problems. Economic decline caused a decrease in public spending on health and education, caused an increase in epidemics, and a related rise in fatality in mothers and babies. In the same manner, the decrease in expenditures allocated to education causes the quality of education to suffer, as well as a decrease in the number of pupils enrolling in educational institutions. The low incomes in the education sector force teachers to moonlight. There is also a very widespread mechanism of bribery which is also infecting educational institutions through which students receive pass reports and diplomas without attending school.[11]

Widespread poverty aggravates the risk of ethnic and social conflicts. Symbolic practice of legal amendments on market economy, unequal distribution of income and unemployment may also be counted in further problems faced by these countries. The increasing unemployment forces a rising number of people to migrate to Russia or elsewhere as migrant workers.[12] *Table 10.1* gives general indicators of the situation in Central Asian countries.

Table 10.1. Indicators 2004

	Kazakhstan	Kyrgyzstan	Tajikistan	Turkmenistan	Uzbekistan
Area (min.km2)	2.7	0.19	0.14	0.49	0.45
Population (millions)	15.185.844 (July 2005 est)	5.146,281 (July 2005 est)	7.163.506	6.5	26.0
GDP per capita (U.S. $)	7,436	1,931	1,200	5,326	1,867
GDP Growth (percent)	9.4	-0.6	8.0	7.0	4.0
Inflation (percent)	6.8	4.9	7.9	10.5	10.0
Foreign Direct Investment (U.S. $ millions)	2,700	83	40	330	250
Population growth rate	0.3percent (2005 est)	1.29 percent	2.1 percent	1.89 percent	2.34 percent
Life expectancy at birth	66.55 (UN,2005)	68.16	65.22	66.01	64.44

Source: EBRD Transition Report 2006

The security of the region is mainly threatened by terrorism and radical Islamic movements. The underlying reasons for the emergence of fundamentalism or radical Islam are complex. The movements fed by religious extremism or militant Islamism are not the cause, but the consequence of deeper and more complex problems. Inner belligerent feelings and the growing dissatisfaction of various population groups with their negative socio-economic conditions—unemployment, poverty, and little prospects of social advancement—use religious sensitivities as channels to spew out personal and social protest feelings.[13] In the region, terrorists and their support groups operate in close liaison with transnational crime networks, drug and arms smugglers, and human traffickers. The incapacity of Central Asian states to control their territories and enforce their laws is worsened with the overall low economic situation, and has also made the region an ideal venue for the emergence and flourishing of transnational criminal activities. The region is a major transhipment area for drugs destined for Europe.[14] The problem of drug trafficking in the region is aggravated by the geographical closeness of the Central Asian countries to West Asian drug zones and it shows up in different forms within the region.[15] In fact, the most threatening aspect for all Central Asia is the illegal drug production in Afghanistan. Since Tajikistan has a 1,000 kilometer border with Afghanistan,[16] in the post-independence period, this region has become a route through which the heroin produced in Afghanistan is transferred to Europe by smugglers.[17]

Another threat to regional security is the weapons of mass destruction (WMD) that have been produced and stored in the region during the Soviet rule. Even though these weapons were returned to the Russian Federation after the disintegration of the Soviet Union,[18] at present, the know-how resources and technology needed for creating these weapons are readily available in the region. From this perspective, Kazakhstan is the main Central Asian country that emerges in the forefront.[19] As an additional problem, the records of the materials used in making nuclear, chemical and biological weapons have not been kept in an orderly fashion. For the world's peace and stability, the strict control of these materials is crucial. Even if international pressure is applied to this matter, frailties like the weak border crossings between Central Asian countries, feeble security where these materials are stored, the lack of technical and electronic equipment that could strengthen these places, and the undeveloped security culture in the region, seriously aggravate the situation. Suitable geographical and socio-cultural conditions in the region for transferring WMDs to the outside world are a major threat to international peace and stability.[20]

In addition to their common problems, the countries in the region also have some geographical problems peculiar to themselves. Kazakhstan, for instance, has a limited population despite its large surface area. In other words, Kazakhstan's security depends on the goodwill of its neighbors.[21] Turkmenistan, on the other hand, has a water shortage problem. To supply its water demand, the country mostly depends on the Amu-Darya River, which is also shared by Uzbekistan, and there is a possibility of conflict that may arise from using the rights of this water supply.

In sum, there are many problems in the region and the lack of opposition within the system, as in the examples of Uzbekistan and Turkmenistan that lead to radical, out-of-the-system movements. While lack of democracy, a pluralist political system and the rule of law during the communist regime led to the overthrow of this authoritarian regime through revolutionary means, as happened in Kyrgyzstan, the post-revolutionary period became one of chaos where stability virtually disappeared.

International Interest toward the Region

The rise in interest toward the region in the post-independence period was seen as a replay of the great power-game between Russia and Britain[22] under twenty-first century conditions.[23] Nevertheless, the major difference that separates the second great game from the first is the increase in the number of players and the intensification of economic, political and strategic dimensions of the competition among the actors involved. In this new power game, the U.S., China and Russia appear as primary actors, while Turkey, Iran, Pakistan, India, the EU, and Japan take roles of potential players. Moreover, this time, not only governments, but also national and multinational companies participate in the game.[24]

Russia, which had to deal with its internal problems right after the dismemberment of the USSR, started pursuing an active policy in the region once again. The interest toward the region, mainly from Turkey, the U.S. and Iran, and the political weakness of the Central Asian countries, led Russia to interfere with domestic affairs of these republics.[25] In addition to this, the presence of rich petroleum and natural gas resources in the region has provoked Russian intervention in the regional affairs. As a combination of all these cases, Russia began to consider objectives for a new foreign policy. For its new foreign policy related to Central Asian and Caucasian republics, Russia describes this "near abroad" as its "backyard" and tries to prevent outside powers from gaining influence over the region.[26] To control the American and Turkish activity in the region and prevent NATO's enlargement toward the East, Russia tried to find strategic allies, and in that moment, Iran, with its regime against the U.S. and the West, has become the most natural and important ally.[27] Its interests in the region have even led the Russian Federation to cooperate with its traditional adversary, China, through Shanghai Cooperation Organization.[28]

In the wake of 9/11, Russian foreign policy has gone through some changes. In this period, President Vladimir Putin, who began to pursue a more realist foreign policy, declared a comprehensive cooperation with the U.S. in Washington's anti-terrorist campaign. He also declared that Russia would assist the U.S.'s anti-terrorist campaign by providing information to the U.S. about terrorist bases, allowing the use of Russian airspace for humanitarian flights in areas of anti-terrorist operations, accepting the Central Asian airfields to be used by the U.S. for anti-terrorist operations, and supporting and arming the Northern Alliance in Afghanistan.[29]

In this context, one can observe that the U.S. began to pursue a more intensive policy in the region. In early 1990s, Washington was not keen on asserting its influence in the region, acknowledging it as Russia's sphere of influence.[30] In the meantime, the U.S. limited its policy to espousing the Turkish model for the Muslim states emerging from the Soviet Union. It can be claimed that the American policy toward the region began to change from 1997 onward and it became more directly interested in the region. On the other hand, Stuart Eizenstat, the deputy director of Economic Affairs in the U.S. State Department, claimed in a speech he made in the U.S. Congress in September 1997, that the U.S. policy toward the region was based on the following five principles: 1) preservation of the independence and hegemony of the Caucasian countries and development of their economies and democracy; 2) following stronger and swifter approaches so that the conflicts among these countries are solved; 3) using regional resources for production in order to supply world energy needs; 4) encouraging U.S. firms to invest in the region; and 5) continuing the pressure against Iran.

Nevertheless, until 9/11, American involvement in the Caspian Sea basin and Central Asia had largely been restricted to economic and diplomatic efforts, accompanied by a number of military aid agreements. The attacks on September 11 and the operation in Afghanistan that followed have made the American policy toward Eurasia come to life. The U.S. has understood that, in order to continue its global hegemony, it had to control Eurasia.[31] In that point, we can see that the key point in the U.S. policy vis-a-vis Eurasia is Afghanistan. Through Afghanistan, the U.S. obtained important bases in Central Asia, and hence, managed to settle right in the core of Eurasia.[32]

In the region, increased activities of Russia, China, Iran, and the emergence of Shanghai Cooperation Organization are further developments that raised American interest in the region.[33] Against China and Russia, who secured their presence in the region through the issues of security and terrorism, the U.S. entered into the region with the very same excuse, that is, terrorism. The security and stability of Afghanistan mattered not only because of the general interests over the region, but also in order to take region's resources of petroleum and natural gas under U.S. control. The major priority of the U.S. was to keep Iran and Russia away from these resources.

As mentioned above, the Afghanistan operation was not limited to teach a lesson to Usama Bin Laden or the Taleban. The main target was possibly to gain a strong base in Afghanistan and, from this country, to expand further into the region. Yet, the U.S. had more to gain. For instance, by this means, Chinese expansion toward Central Asia might be prevented; Iran might be kept under control; Putin's ability to operate in his near abroad would be diminished; the impact of the Taleban over Central Asian countries would be prevented; and the Shanghai Cooperation Organization would be daunted. So, at the beginning, the U.S. began to use the Uzbek, Kyrgyz and Tajik airspace. Then, the airports at Termiz and Hanabad in Uzbekistan, Manas in Kyrgyzstan, and Kulyab, Kurgan-Tyube, and Hokand in Tajikistan were opened to U.S. airplanes. 3,000 U.S. soldiers were located in Kyrgyzstan and 1,000 more were sent to Uzbekistan.[34]

However, the U.S. presence and its strong strategic significance in the region in the wake of 9/11 began to change from 2005 onward. The regional governments began to declare their distress about the American presence in the region, as they began to believe the revolutionary regime changes were covertly supported and arranged by the U.S. The Uzbek government decided that the U.S. should evacuate the Hanabad military base within six months; this was soon followed by Kyrgyzstan'sdeclaration at the July 2005 meeting of Shanghai Cooperation Organization, in which he stated that the U.S. military presence in Manas was no longer necessary. These were the first two important signs of the changing situation for the U.S. in the region. In addition, the first official visit of the new Kyrgyz President Bakıyev to Moscow in September 2005 can be observed as an inclination in the balance of power favoring Russia and China.[35] After shortly analyzing the role of major actors in the region, it is also necessary to assess the role of the EU alongside these actors.

EU's Targets Concerning the Region and the Importance of the Region for the EU

The main goals of the EU for the region are defined as installing democratic principles and rule of law, attaining respect for human rights and strengthening market economy. In addition to these aims, establishment of regional stability, settlement of disputes, sustainability of independence, and unification with the international economy are the further goals to be achieved.

The presence of the EU began to be felt right after the disintegration of the Soviet Union and important projects regarding the region were started. However, a clear policy was only established in 1995 with the *Common Foreign and Security Policy* (CFSP) of the EU and accordingly, relations of individual member countries with the regional states were incorporated within the CFSP and, with a common consensus, it was decided that the EU has important geopolitical and economic interests in the region. Although with the 9/11 attacks and the operation in Afghanistan, the EU interest in the region began to increase, it can still be said that the region is not yet among the major interests of the EU.

Presently, however, the EU aspires to make its engagement in Central Asia more strategic. The burgeoning political role of the Council in the region, the appointment of the EU Special Representative (EUSR) and elaboration of the new Regional Strategy for 2007-2013 by the EC created a momentum to reflect over the past and develop a comprehensive future policy.[36]

The region is important for the EU for three reasons: European security; the increasing European dependency to foreign energy resources and its willingness to improve its choice for energy resources; and, finally, the potential of the region as a market for European products.

It can be said that the EU sees the presence of a political and economic zone of stability in neighboring areas as a requirement for EU security and, in relation to this perspective, it tries to create a secure zone in the Middle East and Africa, the nearest two regions to the Union's borders. With the enlargement of May 1, 2004, the EU had new member states.[37] The enlarged EU naturally had new borders. These new borders also brought a new immediacy to EU thinking about the states situated on its periphery and upon the policies that should be adopted in response to potential and actual threats emerging from these regions.[38] The EU, to the present day, also prepared foreign policies for possible candidate countries; it, however, appears drifting from its mainstream policies. The Commission's Wider Europe Communication reflects an attempt to develop policies for states with whom the EU has significant interest, but for whom membership is not in current perspective. In this context, for South Caucasus, the Council appointed Heikki Talvitie as the European Union Special Representative (EUSR) on July 7, 2003.[39] Also, on June 14, 2004, the EC decided to include Georgia, Armenia and Azerbaijan in the European Neighborhood Policy (ENP), which is a sign that, not only the economic, but also the political profile of the EU is increasing in the region. However, one cannot claim that the EU chose to be politically active until the very recent developments in Central Asia.

Energy is an issue with a strong strategic importance for the EU. The EU is the world's biggest importer and the second most intensive user of energy right after the U.S. Fifty percent of its present energy consumption is imported. This will be 70 percent in 2030. Plausible assumptions about European rates of economic growth, energy prices, environmental regulations, and other factors over the coming two decades lead to projections of increasing dependence on energy imports.[40]

With its 25 member states, in the year 2005, the EU consumed about 493 billion square meters of natural gas. Twenty-four percent of the EU's energy consumption is constituted by natural gas, 42 percent of which is produced by the EU itself; 24 percent is imported from Russia; 14 percent from Norway; 11 percent from Algeria; and the remaining 9 percent is imported from Egypt, Gulf countries, Libya, Nigeria, and Qatar.[41] From 1986 to date, the EU is in a delicate position in terms of supplying its energy needs, especially petroleum and natural gas, and now has to import around half of its required energy. According to the International Energy Agency, this dependency is likely to grow in time. The increasing need for energy in Europe, as well as its dependency to outside sources creates a deep concern within the EU. This concern can be clearly seen in the *Green Paper* that the EC announced in November 2000.[42] There are three prominent regions which can supply the EU's energy needs: the Russian Federation, Gulf countries, and the Middle East and North Africa. The EU refrains from being dependent solely on the Middle East and North Africa due to the ongoing instability in these regions, and is very sensitive about not being tied to Russia either.[43] In fact, the fear created by the Russian blockage of natural gas flow to the Ukraine in the winter of 2006 has led the EU to try and find alternatives to Russian energy provision, and at the June 15 and 16, 2006 EU Summit, the need for alternative pipelines that would link the EU to the Caspian and Central Asian fields bypassing Russia became part of the agenda.[44] Moreover, during the official visit of the Russian President Vladimir Putin to Beijing on March 21, 2006, agreements between Rosneft, Gasprom and Chinese National Petroleum Company (CNPC) were concluded. It was decided that until 2011, with the pipelines from East Siberia to the Pacific Ocean, 1.6 billion barrels of petroleum were to be sent to Japan and China. In the wake of these developments, Semyon Vaynshot, the CEO of Transneft, the Russian monopoly on pipelines, threatened that "after the completion of the Pacific shore pipeline, Russia will cease its oil tranfer to Europe."[45] In sum, the EU wants a diversification in the supply of its energy needs, and in this respect, gives extra importance to the Caspian basin. However, the infrastructure of the system to be used to transfer the resources from the Caspian region to Europe has to be improved. New developments have been achieved in this aspect, as well. For example, the foundations of the Caspian Pipeline Consortium (CPC) that would enable the Kazakhi petroleum to be transported to Europe were laid in 2001. The first flow of petroleum in the Baku-Tbilisi-Ceyhan Pipeline that would carry the Azerbaijani petroleum to Ceyhan in Turkey and then to Europe was performed in June 2005.[46]

On the other hand, Central Asia is also important as a market for European countries. The wish for integration of the region into the global economy and its potential of becoming a market for European goods, influence EU policies on the region dramatically. One of the major motives of the TRACECA program is the incorporation of the Central Asian countries into the global market through Europe.[47]

Table 10.2. Trade indicators 2004-2005 (min Euro)

	Kazakhstan		Kyrgztan		Tajikistan		Turkmenistan		Uzbekistan	
	2004	2005	2004	2005	2004	2005	2004	2005	2004	2005
Exports	16668	22419	565	553	736	732	3065	3934	2019	4362
Exports to EC	6355	9138	25	16	186	88	520	774	605	520
Imports	11874	14032	1078	899	958	1072	2200	2934	2526	3299
Imports from EC	3229	3606	96	109	64	87	412	327	464	560

Source: Eurostat/Comext,2006.

EU Assistance in the Region

After identifying the importance of the region for the EU and the EU's goals concerning the region, we need to analyze the means used to guarantee the achievement of these goals. The EU has started a series of projects concerning the region in the wake of the independence. The most important and the first among these is the TACIS Program accepted at the Rome Summit of December 1990. After the June 28-29, 1991 Luxembourg, the December 9-10, 1991 Maastricht, and the June 25-27, 1992 Lisbon summits, more importance was given to the improvement of mutual relations with the former Soviet republics, and with the Madrid Summit of December 1995, a common political agenda toward the region was set in accordance with the CFSP. The TACIS (Technical Assistance to the Commonwealth of Independent States) is an aid program that has been in motion since 1991 and is aimed at supporting the economic and political transformation in the twelve new states established after the disintegration of the USSR and Mongolia. Fund for TACIS is allocated through various programs. In this respect, some national country programs followed by some regional programs and a limited number of small projects have been put into practice. The TACIS Program has three major aims to actualize: transition to a market economy and democracy; strengthening of bilateral ties; and integration to the global economy for the countries within the scope of the program. According to this program, the mutual relations of any member state in the region would be incorporated into the common EU foreign policy. With a common decision, the EU has shown that it had strong geopolitical and economic interests in the region. The Agenda-2000 Report of the EC foresaw the improvement of relations with regional states. Moreover, to ensure the improvement of these relations on legal grounds, partnership and cooperation treaties were signed between the EU and Central Asian republics.[48] In addition to technical aid, within the ECHO project, about €153.5 million was transferred to the region for humanitarian aid.[49] As a result of these programs over the last 15 years, the EU has laid the foundation for an active and comprehensive long-term partnership with Central Asian countries. In particular, the EU has provided substantial assistance to the region. The 2000-2006 budget of the TACIS was 3.238 billion euros.[50]

Since its beginning in 1991, the TACIS program has been focused on energy, transportation, education, building industrial and commercial institutions, and production and distribution of food. In 2002, new arrangements were made for the program, which included defining preferential areas and determining strategy documents for these new regions.[51] The terrorist attacks in the U.S. on September 11th and the subsequent war in Afghanistan have caused the EU to revise its policies regarding Central Asia. In 2002, the EU Troika visited Central Asia at the ministerial level and, on December 10, 2001, the General Affairs Council decided to strengthen bilateral relations between Central Asian states and the EU.[52] The Council discussed ways to invigorate the relations between the EU and countries of Central Asia. The Council agreed to further develop the relations between the EU and Central Asian countries through bilateral agreements and treaties, and on finding solutions to the region's problems in order to create stability.[53]

In the period between 2002 and 2006, a wider range of practices was fulfilled on the basis of the experience gained from previous TACIS projects and an allocation of €50 million per year was reserved to this end. Moreover, with Article 18 of the Amsterdam Treaty concluded on November 2, 1997, EU Special Envoys have been appointed to carry out special works in particular regions and countries. From February 28, 2007 onward, Pierre Morel took over this duty from Jan Kubis, who had fulfilled this task since July 18, 2005. Mr. Morel's mandate includes furthering the following EU policy objectives in the Central Asia:

- Promoting good and close relations with Central Asian countries on the basis of common values and interests as set out in relevant agreements;
- Contributing to strengthening stability and cooperation between the countries in the region;
- Contributing to strengthening democracy, rule of law, just and stable governance, and respect for human rights and fundamental freedoms in Central Asia;
- Addressing key threats, especially specific problems with direct implications for Europe; and
- Enhancing the EU's effectiveness and visibility in the region through also establishing closer coordination with other relevant partners and international organizations, such as the OSCE.[54]

In 1993, in a meeting of Central Asian and Caucasian ministers and the EU held in Brussels, The TRACECA (Transport Corridor Europe-Caucasus-

Asia) Project was agreed upon. As a first step, the conference proposed creating an unbroken rail corridor from Western Europe to China via the Black Sea, South Caucasus, Caspian Sea, and Central Asia to be financed as a global EU strategy with four goals: strengthening the political and economic sovereignty of CIS countries in the TRACECA region to enable their effective participation in the world economy; supporting regional cooperation between TRACECA countries; promoting regional investment by international and private financial resources; and linking the Eurasian transport corridor with European and world transport systems. The first inventors to join the Project were the European Bank for Reconstruction and Development (EBRD) and the World Bank (WB), and were later joined by the Islam Development Bank (IDB) and the Asian Development Bank (ADB). Japan is participating in the Project implementation through the ADB.[55] It is, in fact, the revitalization of the ancient Silk Road. The project is strategically significant, as it is an alternative to Moscow and, hence, creates an alternative transport route for Europe. The global interest toward TRACECA as a transport corridor is increasing day by day. The TRACECA projects that have been fulfilled to date include providing technical assistance, constructing land roads and railroads, and enlivening sea transport. Below, the projects that the Central Asian countries are part of are shown in Table 3:

Table 10.3. TRACECA Projects Aimed For Central Asia

Railroad Projects	Budget	Beginning and Ending Dates	Countries Involved
Railroad Infrastructure Maintenance	1.200.000	March 1996-1997	Five Central Asian states
Trans-Caucasia Railroad Common	2.000.000	July 1996-1997	Five Central Asian states
Feasibility project for the Fergana Valley-Bishkek-Kashgar railroad project	1.500.000	November 2001-2002	Kyrgyzstan, Uzbekistan, Tajikistan
Motorway Projects	**Budget**	**Beginning and Ending Dates**	**Countries Involved**
Project Dolphin	475.000	August 1995-Ekim 1997	Uzbekistan, Turkmenistan
Motorway Transport projects	700.000	March 1996-Ekim 1997	Five Central Asian states
Investment Projects	**Budget**	**Beginning and Ending Dates**	**Countries Involved**
Bukhara Cotton Export Distribution Center	2.000.000	February 1998-February 1999	Uzbekistan

Source: http://www.traceca.org/rep/broschure/broshure.pdf

The INOGATE (Interstate Oil and Gas Transport to Europe) program was started in 1995 with an increase in the Union's interest in energy resources in the region and continues through collaborations with global financial institutions. The Program's goals include rehabilitation and modernization of production of crude oil and natural gas in the region; creation of new alternatives for the transportation of petrol from the region to the West; and improvements in regional trade on energy-related products.[56] In 1999, the first INOGATE Summit was held in Kiev with the 13 participating nations and an umbrella treaty was concluded. The INOGATE Umbrella Agreement is an interstate agreement that sets out an institutional system designed to rationalize and facilitate the development of interstate oil and gas transportation systems, and to attract the investments necessary for their construction and operation. Since it came into effect on February 17, 2001, the agreement has been signed by twenty countries.[57] Within the INOGATE framework, the energy resources of especially Kazakhstan and Turkmenistan are prioritized and projects were started in relation to these resources.[58]

The legal framework of the EU's relations with Central Asian countries is set by Partnership and Cooperation Agreements (PCAs). This partnership pursues the following goals: establishing a framework that will help to improve mutual political relations; providing support for regional countries in the fields of economic development and transition into democracy and a free market economy; and cooperating in fields of science, technology and culture.[59] PCAs ability to act as a guide for the EU's strategy of political engagement and development within the present circumstances is limited. This is actually an *ad hoc* situation and is mainly an issue which is based on engagement [60] A great part of the documents is devoted to technical measures that are supposed to be taken by the EU and the economic exchange that are supposed to be facilitated by partner states. In contrast, discussions over political and other objectives of the agreements are minimal.[61]

Table 10.4. EU total assistance to Central Asia 1991-2001 (min Euro)

Kazakhstan	Kyrgyztan	Tajikistan	Turkmenistan	Uzbekistan	Total
159.5	228.5	400.0	89.3	177.1	1332.3

Source: *www.delkaz.cee.eu.int*

The Scorecard of the EU in the Central Asia

Since the independence of the Central Asian countries, the EU has been trying to increase the economic prosperity of these countries, facilitate their transition into a market economy, increase stability and prosperity in the region, and establish European values such as democracy, human rights and rule of law. Another reason for the EU's interest in the region is its rich petroleum and natural gas resources.

Up until today, despite several projects implemented by the EU complying with these goals, the majority of these projects tend to be economic and technical in nature. Especially until 2001, no comprehensive agenda or strategy was developed and, therefore, the EU has remained in a secondary role in comparison with the other actors that are active in the region.[62] Meanwhile, the EU's profile in the region has been shadowed by the facts such as: activities of other actors in the region, Russian perception about the region seeing it as its backyard, increased American involvement in the wake of 9/11, the geographical distance of the region from Europe, hardly manageable political partnerships, and the lack of a pressure group that lobbies for Central Asia within EU structures.

Evaluating the situation that is reached today, we can say that there has been little movement on the fields of the rule of law, human rights and democratization. There has been little progress in integrating the economies of this region into broader European markets, except the energy sector. The privatization process has been deeply corrupt. Consequently, it cannot be said that the EU managed to completely realize all its aims planned for the region. These goals were not reached because of reasons emanating from both the EU itself and the region's characteristics. From the EU's perspective, there appears to be difficulties of putting the projects into practice due to several technical limitations. For instance, distribution of financial resources committed to the TACIS program requires applications which take long processing periods. Another limitation stems from the cultural and political composition of the region. Generally speaking, the administrators of the region's countries do not put investments to efficient use and exploit them according to their own benefits. The aid provided by several companies, international aid organizations and states since the independence of the regional countries has not been fully transferred to the people. Most people are either unemployed or work for very limited salaries. Economic problems raise social problems and trigger illegal activities, hence increasing the crime rate. Beyond the state, relations among the people living in the region are mainly based upon patrimonial, kinship, ethnical, and regional links. What appears to be corruption to us may appear to those engaged in the practice as serving the needs of their community. This impedes the development of the civic nation and civil society the EU aims to establish.[63]

In sum, the EU should pursue a strategy that focuses more on these countries and projects that promote their development and especially give Kyrgyzstan's impoverished economy a helping hand. The death of Niyazov opens up a window of opportunity to encourage the unsettled Turkmen leaders to institute reforms. All the countries in the region need a bridge to the West even more than the West needs them. Without the EU, they would be forced to enter into reluctant dependency on China and Russia.

In conclusion, the Central Asian region ranks very low when compared to other priorities of the EU such as problems of EU enlargement, the EU

Constitution and the agricultural policy. However, the limited nature of EU activities in the region does not mean that its efforts in the region were in vain or lack value. For instance, the TRACECA program enabled access to financial resources allocated to energy and transport sectors. Furthermore, the activities of the EU with regard to preventing illegal drug trafficking in the region has led to positive developments in legal and domestic affairs of these countries.[64] The economic presence of the EU in the region has accelerated reforms.

Factors like terrorism, organized crime, illegal migration, unsuccessful and corrupt administrations that are causing instability and, therefore, perceived as threats by the EU, are still teeming in the region. The EU has refrained from playing the role of pioneer in the resolution of political disputes and instability in the region, and selected the choice of supporting international initiatives on these issues. The EU has, in fact, the potential to pursue a much more active policy in the region. Under these circumstances, new policy approaches are needed for stabilizing the potentially risky situation. The appointment of an EU Representative to the region in 2005 can be seen as a sign that a new strategy toward the region may have been initiated.

During his visit to Central Asian countries between October 31st and November 4th, 2006, German Foreign Minister, Frank-Walter Steinmeier, said, "The EU wants to develop a new EU strategy for Central Asia."[65] Also, in the last week of March 2006, the EU delegation headed by the EU's term president, Frank-Walter Steinmeier, paid a visit to Astana for two days. During this visit, the delegation held several meetings with Central Asian foreign ministers. Steinmeir underlined the importance of this meeting as being the first of its kind among foreign ministers. He also said that the time has arrived to start an "all-inclusive and strategic partnership" between the EU and Central Asian republics, and he also mentioned that the common problems related to security and international terrorism have made it necessary to form a strategic partnership.[66] As mentioned above, European interest in Central Asia has three strands. One is the desire to secure a share in the region's oil and gas resources, since natural resources of Caspian Sea could help secure Europe's long-term energy needs. In this respect, the EU identified Uzbekistan, along with Kazakhstan and Turkmenistan, as key engagement targets in its efforts to reduce energy dependence on Russia. The Soviet-era pipeline network has had a virtual monopoly on the transport of oil and gas deposits. The newly completed oil pipeline that runs from Baku to the Turkish Mediterranean coast represents a challenge to Russia's pipeline dominance over Central Asia's natural resources. The other strand is the aim of promoting the establishment of democratic governments and providing stability in the region. Thirdly, the region is located in the immediate vicinity of instability caused by tensions in or around Afghanistan, Pakistan and Iran.

The EU intended to demonstrate the growing significance of relations with Central Asia by more than doubling assistance to the region during the period of time between 2007 and 2013, with a total of 750 million euros. Moreover, Benita Ferrero-Waldner, who attended the EU-Central Asia ministerial Troika on March 28th, expressed that: "EU enlargement has brought us closer to Central Asia and the time is ripe for a more intensive engagement with the Central Asian countries. That is why the Commission is contributing to the development of a new EU Strategy for relations with the region. According to his statement, in the next four years, poverty reduction will continue to be the key priority for the EC assistance. The second main focus will be the promoting good governance, strengthening public institutions, improving the investment climate and other trade policy reforms. The content of all programs will be tailored to the specific needs of each country. Energy and trade relations are increasingly important areas of cooperation between the EU and Central Asia."

In sum, Central Asia, which has become one of the favorite regions of the global power struggle, is also becoming a scene for new actors in search for new activities. The EU, which appears to be included in the power struggle among the U.S., Russian Federation and China, is on the way to make dramatic changes in its Central Asian policy. The EU, under the German presidency, gives away the signals that it will redesign its Central Asian policy "from scratch and as needed." The primary goal of the EU, which has remained an outsider to regional developments, is to be seen as a global actor in Central Asia. The EU intends not to be left outside of the global geopolitical game. The region, which has a vital role for Russia, China, India, and Iran, also provides one of the bases of the American global-scale policies. It is possible that the new EU policies, which the Union designed seemingly in accord with the needs of the regional countries, appear to be more "pragmatic" and free from direct criticisms aimed at the regional countries, especially Uzbekistan. It is hard to predict the short-and-medium-term effects of this approach and what it will yield in the long-term.

Conclusion

The dense interest and diplomatic traffic from the EU toward the region is striking. As stated by Benita Ferrero-Waldner, the EU commissar responsible for foreign relations, a kind of "historical" process has begun for both the EU and the Central Asia. The statements of both sides expressing that they will meet more often to determine a common strategy and the €750 million budget that is foreseen by the EU for the time period until 2013, are both signs indicating the EU has a long-term interest in building cooperation with the region. Central Asia has not experienced such a spotlight since 1991. In spite of the projects and economic aid programs for the region, there has been no detailed agenda concerning it. In sum, we can say that "the

EU showed an interest towards the region, but did not produce effective policies regarding the needs and facts of the region."

During the visit of the EU commission to Almaty in the last week of March, 2007, under the leadership of EU president Frank Steinmeier, Foreign Minister of Germany, it was expressed that the time for strategic partnership had come. Both the rising energy needs of the EU and Russia's devious approach toward the matter have been influential in this change of EU policy toward the region. Drug trafficking, migration and environmental problems are the other important factors. The worsening situation in Afghanistan, unwanted outcomes that may trigger instability for the EU's energy security, the rising interest and influence of both China and the U.S. in the region, are all factors that disturb the EU and force it to focus more closely on the region. In conclusion, the EU, the "latecomer actor" of the region, seems now to be pursuing a more focused and active policy.

On the other hand, it can be perceived that regional countries are positive about the EU's increasing interest by which they wish to balance the rising Russian, American and Chinese activities in the region. Furthermore, the anxiety they feel due to the threat emerging from Afghanistan and their wish to gain the most from the competition by increasing the number of actors interested in the region may also be counted as further causes for the regional countries' positive attitude toward the engagement with the EU. Only time will tell to what extent the mutual expectations of the sides shall be realized.

---

[1] Country Analysis Brief, Kazakhstan Energy Data, Statistics and Analysis, www.eia-doc.gov/emev/cabs/Kazakhstan/pdf.
[2] For figures in this subject see, EIA , Int'l Petroleum Monthly. Forecast: Short Term Energy Outlook.
[3] http://www.stat.U.S..gov *Caspian Sea Region: Key Oil and Gas Statistics*, August 2003.
[4] http://www.iea.org/textbase/nppdf/free/1990/caspian_oil_gas98.pdf
[5] Fiona Hill, "The Great Game: The 2020 Edition". *The Globalist*, July 12, 2002, p. 14.
[6] Javier Solana, "A Secure Europe in a Better World," *European Council*, June 20, 2003, p. 4-8.
[7] Anna Matveeva, "EU stakes in Central Asia," *Chaillot Papers*, no.91, (2006): p. 2.
[8] Joshua Kucera, "Turkmenistan takes terror to new level," *Eurasia Insight*, September 22, 2006, p. 9.
[9] Breffni O'Rourke, "Central Asia: Rights Groups Highlight Region's Problems," *RFE/RL*, March 27, 2007.
[10] http://www.undp.org
[11] Information based on interviews with pupils and students while visiting the region.

[12] For instance, in Kyrgyzstan, the unemployment rose from 1,792 people in 1992 to 12,614 in 1994, 50,405 in 1995, 77,198 in 1998, and this last figure doubled in 2003. *International Labor Organization* (ILO) Bureau of Statistics, 2004. http://www.ilo.org

[13] Poonam Mann, "Religious Extremism in Central Asia," *Strategic Analysis*, 25, no.9, (2001):p.12; for the emergence of radical Islam and its development see.; Askar Aytmatov, "The Shade of Extremism over Central Asia," *Perceptions*, 36, no.3, (2001):p.11; *ICG Asia Report*, no.59, Central Asia: Islam and the State, 10 July 2003; *ICG Asia Report* no.72, Is Radical Islam Inevitable in Central Asia? Priorities for Engagemant, 22 December 2003, Anna Matveeva, "The Islamist Challenge in Post-Soviet Eurasia," in *Political Islam and Conflicts in Russia and Central Asia*, ed. Lena Johnson & Murad Esenov, (Utrikespolitiska Institutet: Sweden 1999).Ahmed Rashid, *Jihad: The Rise of Militant Islam in Central Asia*, (New Haven: Yale University Press, 2002), p. 41.

[14] S.Neil MacFarlane, "Caucasus and Central Asia: Towards a Non-Strategy," in *EU Foreign and Security Policy: Towards a Neighbourhood Strategy*, ed. Roland Danrauther (London:Routledge, 2004), p. 123.

[15] For drugs use and trafficking in the region, see: *International Narcotics Control Strategy Report 2002*:http://www.state.gov.documents/organization/8692.pdf, *Global Illicit Drug Trends 2002*, New York, United Nations Publications, 2002.

[16] "Central Asian Experts Praise Tajik President," RFE/RL, October 27, 2006, see also; Nadir Devlet, "Crisis Sources in Caucasus, Central Asia, South and East Asia and Affectes on Turkey's Security," *Studies in the Politics, History and Culture of Turkic Peoples*, (İstanbul: Yeditepe Üniversitesi Yayınları, 2005), p. 26.

[17] "Islamic Movement of Uzbekistan Controls Drug Traffic to Central Asia, Special Services Say," *Pravda*, May 30, 2001; (http://english.pravda.ru/cis/2001/05/30/6301.html)

[18] On 21 December 1991, Kazakhstan has agreed with the Alma-Ata Declaration to transfer all nuclear missiles it had to the Russian Federation by July 1992.

[19] Mustafa Kibaroğlu, "Orta Asya'da Kitle İmha Silahları ve Silahsızlanma," in *Küresel Politikada Orta Asya: Avrasya Üçlemesi I*, ed.Mustafa Aydın (Ankara: Nobel Yayıncılık, 2005), p. 320.

[20] Ibid. p.325.

[21] Nadir Devlet, "Crisis Sources in Caucasus, Central Asia, South and East Asia and Affectes on Turkey's Security," *Studies in the Politics, History and Culture of Turkic people*, (İstanbul: Yeditepe University Yayınları,2005), p. 27.

[22] For information on the new great game, see: Rajor Menon, "The New Great Game in Central Asia," *Survival*, 45, no.2, (2002); p. 11.

[23] For competition between Britain and Russia in the 19th century, see: Yelda Demirağ, "Büyük Oyun":19.Yüzyılda Rusya ve İngiltere'nin Orta Asya'da Rekabeti, in *Geçmişten Günümüze Dönüşen Orta Asya ve Kafkasya*, ed. Yelda Demirağ and Cem Karadeli (Ankara: Palme Yayınları, 2006), pp. 1-17.

[24] Mustafa Aydın, "Büyük Oyun ve İkinci Büyük Oyun'un Ayırt Edici Özellikleri" , *Türk Dış Politikası Kurtuluş Savaşından Günümüze Olgular, Belgeler, Yorumlar*, ed. Baskın Oran, (İstanbul:İletişim Yayınları, 2002), p. 392

[25] Ronald Grigor Suny, *The Soviet Experiment Russia, the USSR and the Successor States*, (New York: Oxford University Press, 1998), pp. 1-21.

26 For the first phase of Russian policy on Central Asia and Caucasia, see: Lena Johnson, *Russia and Central Asia: A New Web of Relations*, (London: Royal Institute of International Affairs, 1998).

27 The economic and military relations between Russia and Iran developed in 1997 with reports of the Russian sale of equipment to Iran, which was valued at over U.S. $4bn, and in which there are possible clauses that foresaw Iran had to see to its economic duties as Iran had a weak economy from sufffering petrol prices. Viktor Vishniakov, "Russian-Iranian Relations and Regional Stability," *International Affairs*, 45, no.1, (1999), pp.143-153. See also; Shahram Chubin, "Iran's Strategic Predicament," *Middle East Journal*, 54, no.1, (2000), pp.10-24.

28 There are political and cultural factors in addition to the fact that the region is the nearest possible area to reach for its energy needs in China's interest in Central Asia and its rapprochement with the Russian Federation. China is also very keen on the preservation of stability in Central Asia due to its fear of Muslim separatist movements in its own region of Xingiang. Beyond these reasons, the most important factor for the Sino-Russian rapprochement is the increasing geostrategic and military presence of the U.S. in the region.

29 Leszek Buzsynski, "Russia and The Commonwealth of Independent States in 2002: Going Seperate Ways," *Asian Survey*, 43, no.1, (2003),pp.15-24.

30 For the U.S. policy toward the region before September 11, see: Stephen Blank, "The U.S. and Central Asia," in *Central Asian Security: The New International Context*, ed.Roy Allison and Lena Johnson (London:Royal Institute of International Affairs, 2001); Boris Rumer, "The Powers of Central Asia," *Survival*, 44, no.3, (2002); Çağrı Erhan, "ABD'nin Orta Asya Politikası ve 11 September," in *Küresel Politikada Orta Asya*, ed. Mustafa Aydın (Ankara: Nobel Yayınları, 2005).

31 As Z. Brezinski clearly states, the power which dominates Eurasia would be controlling two of the three most developed and economically viable regions of the world. Round 75 percent of Earth's population live in Eurasia and most of the world's physical richness in terms of economic enterprises and subterranean substances. Eurasia holds 60 percent of world GDP and three quarters of world's known energy sources. It is also the domain of the world's politically most ambitious and dynamic states. Zbigniew Brzezinski, *Grand Chessboard: American Primacy and Its Geosatrategic Imperatives*, (Basic Books, 1997), p. 74.

32 The Vaziani base in Georgia has been planned to hold training for special forces till May 2004. Tajikistan has allowed the U.S. to use ex-Soviet airforce bases in the country in November 2001 in exchange for support to the "Operation for Sustainable Freedom." The agreement was announced on 10 June 2003, during the talks between U.S. Secretary of Defense Donald Rumsfeld and the Tajik Foreign Minister Talbak Nazarov in Dushanbe. David Isenberg, "ABD Ordusunun Gittikçe Büyüyen Ayak İzleri," *Asia Times*, June 10, 2003.

33 This organization established in 1996 between Russia, China, Kazakhstan, Kyrgyzstan and Tajikistan and then named as the Shanghai Five, has changed its name to Shanghai Cooperation Organization later on with the participation of Uzbekistan. This organization which at first aimed at solving border disputes developed to include work on security. Pakistan, South Korea, and North Korea are preparing to become members while India is enjoying the status of observer.Turkey

has concluded cooperation agreements with each member state on a one-on-one basis.

34 Charles William Maynes, "America Discovers Central Asia," *Foreign Affairs*, 82, no.2, (2003), p. 121.
35 Vladimir Socor, "Moscow Hardens Tone to Washington on Central Asia," *Eurasia Daily Monitor*, July 19, 2005.
36 Anna Matveeva, "EU stakes in Central Asia," Paris: Institute for Security Studies, European Union, *Chaillot Papers*, no.91, (2006): p. 5.
37 Cyprus, the Czech Republic, Estonia, Hungary, Latvia, Lithuania, Malta, Poland, Slovakia, and Slovenia.
38 Dov Lynch, "The EU:towards a Strategy," in *The South Caucasus: A Challenge for the EU*, ed.Dov Lynch, Chaillot Papers, no.65, (2003): p.32.
39 Council Joint Action 2003/496/CFSP; http://ue.eu.int/pesc/envoye/cv/talvitie/ 1_16920030708en00740075.pdf (accessed July 17, 2007)
40 John Gault, "The European Union: Energy Security and Periphery," in *EU Foreign and Security Policy: Towards a Neighborhood Strategy*, ed. R. Dannreuter (Edinburgh: Taylor & Francis, 2003), p. 129.
41 http://www.europa.eu.int/scadplus/lrg/en/lvb/127047.html (accessed July 19, 2007)
42 *Green Paper: Towards a European strategy for security of energy supply*, Brussels, November 29,2000, Document COM(2000) (accessed July 21, 2007).
43 John Gault, "The European Union: Energy Security and Periphery," in *EU Foreign and Security Policy: Towards a Neighborhood Strategy*, ed. R.Dannreuter (Edinburgh: Taylor & Francis, 2003), p. 126.
44 Brussels European Council- 15/16 June 2006 Presidency Conclusions 17/7/2006 Nr.10633/106.(accessed July 21, 2007).
45 Yazar "Transneft Threatens to Cut Oil Supplies to Overfed Europe," *RFE/RL*, March 22, 2006.
46 *Hürriyet*, May 25, 2005; *Wall Street Journal*, May 25, 2005; *The Independent*, May 25, 2005.
47 Ali Resul Usul, " Avrupa Birliği'nin Orta Asya Politikaları: Sessiz ve Derinden," in *Küresel Politikada Orta Asya: Avrasya Üçlemesi I*, ed. Mustafa Aydın (Ankara:Nobel Yayıncılık, 2005), pp. 187-213.
48 Cees Wittebrood, "Caucasus and Central Asia: The Eurasian Region - Towards a More Comprehensive EU policy," in *Economic Developments and Reforms in Cooperation Partner Countries* ed. Patrick Hardouin, Reiner Weichhardt & Peter Sutcliffe (Brussels: NATO, 2001), pp. 259-266.
49 http://www.europa.eu.int/comm/ezternal_relations/tacis/intro/tacis_leaf_uk.pdf. (accessed July 19, 2007).
50 John P.Bonin, "Europe and Central Asia after the May 2004 EU enlargement: A brief synthesis," *Economic Systems*, 29 (2005), pp.1-5.
51 Strategy Paper 2002-2006 & Indicative program 2002-2004 for Central Asia http://www.ec.europa.eu/comm/external_relations/ceeca/rsp2/02_06_en.pdf (accessed July 19, 2007)
52 Esra Çayhan, "The European Union's Central Asia Strategy," *bilig*, no.26, (2003), pp. 22-23.

[53] For further information see; 2397th European Council Meeting General Affairs: Central Asia Conclusions, 15078/01(Presse 460), 10.12.2001.(accessed July 19, 2007). http://ue.eu.int/newsroom/up.asp?MAX=1&BID=71&DID=69077&File=/press Data/en/gena/DOC.69077.pdf&LANG=1

[54] Press Releases, Council appoints new EU special representative for Central Asia, PRES/06/277, October 06, 2007. (accessed July 19, 2007).

[55] Teimuraz Gorshkov & George Bagaturia, "TRACECA: Restoration of Silk Route," *Japan Railway & Transport Review*, no.28, (2005), pp. 50-55.

[56] The European Union Inogate Program, *INOGATE Newsletter*, no:1, (1998), p.1.(accessed August 14, 2007).

[57] Türkiye, Turkmenistan, Tajikistan, Slovakia, Rumenia, Moldova, Greece, Macedonia, Kyrgyzstan, Kazakhstan, Latvia, Georgia, Armenia, Bulgaria, Belarus, Azerbaijcan, Federal Republic of Yugoslavia, Uzbekistan, the Ukraine, and Albania.

[58] For Inogate Projects see; http://www.inogate.org/html/resource/resource7.html. (accessed August 15, 2007).

[59] Partnership and Cooperation Agreement between the European Communities and their Member States, Official Journal L 246, 17/09/1999, p. 31-37. (accessed August 16, 2007).

[60] Anna Matveeva, "EU stakes in Central Asia," Paris: Institute for Security Studies, European Union, *Chaillot Papers*, no.91, (2006), p. 5.

[61] S.Neil MacFarlane, "Caucasus and Central Asia: Towards a Non-Strategy," in *EU Foreign and Security Policy: Towards a Neighborhood Strategy* ed. Roland Dannreuter (London:Routledge, 2004), p. 127.

[62] Alexander Rahr, "Europe in the New Central Asia," in *The New Central Asia in Search of Stability*, eds. Sherman W.Garnett, Alexander Rahr and Koji Watarebe (New York: The Trilateral Comission, 2000), p. 50.

[63] S.Neil MacFarlane, "Caucasus and Central Asia: Towards a Non-Strategy," in *EU Foreign and Security Policy: Towards a Neighborhood Strategy*, ed. Roland Dannreuter (London:Routledge, 2004), p. 123.

[64] Havva Kök, "Avrupa Birliği ve Orta Asya," *Avrasya Dosyası*, 11, no.1, (2005):p. 14.

[65] Ahto Lobjakas, "EU: German Presidency's Focus on Central Asia, Black Sea, Russia," *RFE/RL*, December 19, 2006. "Central Asia: German Foreign Minister Seeks EU-Wide Policy," *RFE/RL*, November 3, 2006.

[66] Mehmet Seyfettin Erol, "EU's new Central Asia Policy and its Energy Dimension," *The Journal of Turkish Weekly*, April 2, 2007.

Chapter 11
Inner-Caspian Neighborhood Challenge for the EU: Significance and Characteristics of an Emerging Energy Hub

Mert Bilgin

The neighborhood concept of Europe drastically changed in the aftermath of the Soviet disintegration, which created new republics that are now trying to transform themselves according to the necessities of the global market. The EU supports this transformation, because liberal and democratic Eurasian neighbors can contribute to the EU's intention of sustaining a more secure environment enriched with opportunities of economic cooperation. This interaction necessitates deeper analysis of the Eurasian neighborhood, which, in turn, calls for new scopes that are appropriate for comparative studies. Within this perspective, this section: 1) brings out how the EU categorizes Eurasian neighbors; 2) suggests that actual conceptualization fails to match geopolitical significance of the Caspian Sea region and its gas and oil resources; 3) introduces a new cluster of country groups; and 4) elaborates the political and economic characteristics of three states, in order to offer a further understanding of transitional structures of these selected countries.

The EU categorizes its Eurasian neighbors by clustering their similarities. Yet, more needs to be done, because these clusters are generally based on conventional geographic criteria and lack the significance of other factors, such as energy sources, as in the case of Azerbaijan, Kazakhstan and Turkmenistan (AKT, henceforth). In fact, the EU follows literal tradition, and while it considers Azerbaijan within the context of Caucasus, regards Kazakhstan and Turkmenistan as parts of Central Asia.[1] The categorization and the neighborhood policy based upon this consideration is clearly defined in various cases such as security initiatives that are carried out by the Organization for Security and Cooperation in Europe (OSCE), and economic cooperation initiatives activated by Technical Aid to CIS (TACIS) and Transport Corridor Europe-Caucasus-Asia (TRACECA) programs. OSCE activities and TACIS and TRACECA projects are developed, budgeted, implemented, and assessed on conventional geographic connotation of Caucasus and Central Asia. There are at least two points open to criticism arising from conventional geographical clusters depicted by the EU. First of all, despite a certain amount of attention (obvious in OSCE,

TACIS and TRACECA initiatives), the EU has not attributed enough significance to the Caspian Sea shored by Russia, Azerbaijan, Kazakhstan, Turkmenistan, and Iran. Secondly, although AKT takes place within ten Eurasian countries, with which the EU has already signed "Partnership and Cooperation Agreements (PCAs),"[2] the EU does not fully transform the special significance of these countries into concrete policies, which might help meeting its energy demand.

Within this perspective, this paper groups AKT within inner-Caspian Region, which deserves to be carefully considered within the EU's neighborhood policy, in terms of energy supply and security concerns. The first section describes why AKT shall be considered as part of the inner-Caspian Region and then shows the significance of this region as an energy hub. The following sections include country analysis, with an emphasis on the states, in order to offer highlights that may help intertwining the EU's security and energy supply policies in this region.

External Dynamics of Inner-Caspian vis-à-vis the EU
The Meaning of Inner-Caspian *Neighborhood for the EU*

Although the Caspian is geographically far away from the EU, the interest in this region has began increasing due to the concerns of security and energy supply.

Regarding security aspect; the EU enlargement and current developments in post-Soviet region increased the significance of geopolitical movements and caused European democratic criteria to lean more toward security concerns.[3] Within this sense, OSCE, which originally goes back to Helsinki Final Act in 1975, clearly expresses how the EU perceives democratization and stability as a matter of security in its wider neighborhood.[4] The rise of OSCE as an organization, that seeks democratic means to sustain security, gained impetus right after its 1994 Budapest meeting, which indicated further will of Europe to combine humanitarian concern with democracy and security through a sort of *Europeanization* in the neighborhood.[5]

The EU's concern in developing democracies within and around Europe, with the aim of ensuring the security of its member countries, has now reached the inner-Caspian region composed of AKT. These countries were inescapably parts of the post-Soviet region facing the security dilemmas of transforming into national entities.[6] The September 11 attacks increased the significance of this region, which is neighbored by Afghanistan and Iran, and consequently, made the U.S. attribute financial assistance programs of $42 million to so-called Central Asian countries.[7]

At the mean time, the EU expressed a strong commitment to construction of stability and democracy within this region in order not to be challenged by contingent radical transformations.[8] Although difficulties related to intangibility and relativity of "support for democracy" programs enabled certain critiques,⁹ it may be suggested that the EU managed to achieve a certain degree of success. For this purpose, the EU signed Partnership and Cooperation Agreements with Azerbaijan and Kazakhstan on July 1, 1999 and with Turkmenistan in May 1998, which is not yet in force.¹⁰ The EU developed interactive relations with Azerbaijan, a certain amount of cooperation with Kazakhstan and very weak relations with Turkmenistan. In fact, the EU has been concerned with Azerbaijan more than the other two, in political terms. For instance, its security concerns led the EU to form the Minsk group in March 24, 1992, in order to reconcile political problems between Azerbaijan and Armenia. The Minsk Group, composed of Azerbaijan, Armenia, Russia, Byelorussia, the U.S., Germany, France, Italy, Sweden, the Czech Republic, and Slovakia, has been influential for attaining ceasefire between Azerbaijan and Armenia a year after the hard clashes arose from Nagorno Karabakh conflict.¹¹ The 1994 Budapest meeting created a more effective OSCE in Eurasia. Currently, in addition to its activities to contribute to the rise of sound democracies, OSCE established offices in Azerbaijan,¹² Kazakhstan¹³ and Turkmenistan.¹⁴ OSCE considers Azerbaijan within its Caucasus branch, whereas Kazakhstan and Turkmenistan are positioned within Central Asia. This categorization fits geographic locations that match certain security concerns,¹⁵ yet it does not meet the significance of AKT as a coherent energy hub.

Regarding energy aspect; it must, first of all, be emphasized that the EU needs to re-consider AKT within its close neighborhood in order to diversify its dependence on energy imports. The EU's enlargement is not only motivated by the great potential of a population of about 485 million people, but also by the EU's energy consumption, which is more than 1,745 million tons of oil equivalent (mtoe) per annum, half of which is satisfied through imports. The figures referring to the EU's dependence on oil and gas are even worse, because imports reach as high as 76.6 percent of oil and 50 percent of total gas consumption.¹⁶ Meanwhile, AKT have attained the chance of trading their rich hydrocarbon reserves in world markets at fair prices, after a very long time of Russian domination. Post-Soviet development of energy infrastructure, in conjunction with TACIS and TRACECA to a certain extent, has enabled Azerbaijan to transport its hydrocarbon reserves through Baku-Tbilisi-Ceyhan (BTC) oil and Baku-Tbilisi-Erzurum (BTE) gas pipelines. Meanwhile, Kazakhstan and Turkmenistan have remained out of the Western energy transportation corridor through Turkey because trans-Caspian pipelines, which could extend these countries to Baku by passing through Caspian, have been delayed up until now.¹⁷

As a matter of fact, this region is significant for the EU in terms of geopolitical and economic terms.¹⁸ Geopolitically, the locations of these countries are very critical, because they are situated in the middle of three important regional powers (Russia, Iran and Turkey), each of which, with different concerns, engage in diverse expansions in terms of security. Russia aims to dominate these countries by trying to perpetuate the former characteristics of the metropolis-satellite relations.[19] Iran, on the other hand, aims to broaden her influence over AKT by using their Islamic characteristics.[20] Naturally, Turkey wants to develop close relations with these Turkic countries with whom she shares cultural and linguistic affinities. Moreover, neighboring countries such as Georgia and Armenia, as well as other international actors such as the U.S. and China, devote special attention to the inner-Caspian region.

Economically, when the hydrocarbon reserves of AKT are analyzed, it may be suggested that the natural resources of these republics accentuate their geopolitical importance.[21] Proven oil reserves for the entire Caspian Sea region are estimated at 16–32 billion barrels, which is comparable to those in the U.S. (22 billion barrels) and in the North Sea (17–33 billion barrels). Proven gas reserves in the Caspian region, on the other hand, are estimated to be at 236–337 trillion cubic feet (tcf), which is comparable to 300 tcf North American reserves, but somewhat larger than Western Europe's (168–242 tcf).[22] According to the moderate estimations of the U.S. Energy Information Administration, the oil reserve of Azerbaijan is between 31 and 40 billion barrels. The reserves are somewhere between 95 and 103 billion barrels for Kazakhstan and about 34 billion barrels for Turkmenistan. Azerbaijan's gas reserves are about 35 tcf and Kazakhstan's are 88 tcf, whereas Turkmenistan is the richest in its gas reserves with a figure reaching up to 159 tcf.[23]

AKT deserves a closer look within the context of European neighborhood challenge. Under the influence of the Soviet legacy of strong centralization, it is of utmost significance to understand the idiosyncratic characteristics of these states. This analysis is aimed to highlight further research upon the inner-Caspian region by putting forward that democratization in AKT promises to serve for European interests, both in terms of security and in energy supply issues. Vice versa, when inner-Caspian energy hub becomes connected to the EU markets through the Western energy corridor via Turkey, AKT will probably accelerate their democratization processes. Therefore, the EU needs to attribute special significance to Azeri oil and gas, Kazakhi oil and Turkmen gas, which all involve initiatives to activate trans-Caspian pipelines routed to the West. This will unite the inner-Caspian with the European markets as a coherent energy system.

Highlights of Inner-Caspian Neighborhood for the EU

The EU has not been able to prove an ultimate success regarding the geopolitical aspects and importance of Caspian energy. Its approach somehow remained only in moral terms and skipped the significance of the Caspian region.²⁴ In the meantime, the achievements of the U.S. and Russia are remarkable, along with multinational companies, which have acquired significant production sharing agreements from Azerbaijan and Kazakhstan. Russia managed to develop its existing oil transportation system especially in the case of Kazakhstan. Russia also managed to perpetuate the former characteristic of its gas trade with Turkmenistan, which was based on Turkmenistan's full dependence on Gazprom's pipelines. Furthermore, Turkey managed to activate BTC and now is about to import Shahdeniz gas from Azerbaijan, which is expected to flow through BTE in 2007. Iran benefited from being a Caspian littoral and started swaps with Azerbaijan and Turkmenistan.

Where is the EU's place in this structure? In a nutshell, the EU has remained outside the scene up until now. Actually, it seems as if the EU will benefit partially from BTE gas pipeline aiming to bring Azeri gas to Europe via Georgia and Turkey. Nevertheless, this gas pipeline cannot fully satisfy growing European energy needs. In other words, the EU needs to activate trans-Caspian oil and gas pipelines carrying Kazakhi oil and Turkmen gas through the Western energy corridor via Turkey.

The last five years, characterized by hiking energy prices, have shown how Caspian region was geopolitically significant for the EU and how energy issues tended to become a political tool jeopardizing its security initiatives built on neighborhood policies. The EU lately became aware of this trend right after the gas shortages created by Russia, which was using energy as a political tool in the case of the Russian-Ukrainian crisis, in late 2006 and early 2007. "However, the instruments and actions taken to achieve the stated objectives were flawed in the sense that they did not address some structural inefficiencies of EU external energy links, which is true especially in regards to the management of the EU-Russia energy dialogue inaugurated in 2000."²⁵

In fact, the EU began focusing on Caspian energy issues in 2004. On November 13, 2004, the EU, along with partner countries in the Black Sea and Caspian region, participated in the Energy Ministerial Conference in Baku, which would be known as the Baku Initiative thereafter. On November 30, 2006, the EU and the Black Sea and Caspian Sea regions agreed on a common energy strategy at the Energy Ministerial Conference in Astana, Kazakhstan, which is also known as the continuation of the Baku Initiative.²⁶ The European Commission and Governments of Armenia, Azerbaijan, Belarus, Georgia, Kazakhstan, Kyrgyzstan, Moldova, Tajikistan, Turkey, the Ukraine, Uzbekistan, and the Russian Federation (as an observer) accepted a new Energy Road Map for enhanced energy cooperation to reach a comprehensive legal and regulatory framework governing an integrated "EU-Black Sea-Caspian Sea" common energy market based on EU acquits.²⁷ Through these initiatives, the EU showed it was currently aware of the Caspian region as an alternative energy supplier. Meanwhile, Russia did not show as much concern as it had furiously exhibited previously against the TRACECA and INOGATE programs, thinking they may change political landscape in the Caucasus and Central Asia.[28] Russia's current calmer attitude can also be read as she now had acquired what she wanted, especially from Kazakhstan and Turkmenistan. Nevertheless, it must also be emphasized that recent oil discoveries in Kazakhstan, such as Kashagan oil, and in the period after the Turkmenbashi's death in December 2006, a new milieu of geopolitical maneuvers was formed which demanded the alertness of the EU. Economic cooperation initiatives carried out by the TACIS and TRACECA might satisfy the EU's security concerns by also diversifying its energy supplies while the inner-Caspian becomes a part of the Western energy corridor. Therefore, the EU needs to exert more effort to embrace inner-Caspian region at least as an energy supplier and to also include Kazakhstan and Turkmenistan in the Western energy corridor.

Azerbaijan and Kazakhstan have been involved in rapprochement with global energy markets by the virtue of their cooperation with multinational companies due to their close relations with concerned countries, including Russia, on one hand, and the U.S. on the other. Meanwhile, Turkmenistan has remained out of global energy markets. The EU might benefit from new opportunities if it manages to combine Turkmenistan with European markets; an achievement which will definitely lead to activating the inner-Caspian region as a coherent energy system.

The EU's security concerns are currently being amalgamated within a broader neighborhood policy that combines political and economic factors through the rise of civil society and democracy. These factors are also clear in its initiatives embracing AKT and accentuating the significance of internal dynamics of the inner-Caspian region. Nevertheless, as stated earlier, the EU fails to understand how these three inner-Caspian countries deviate from other Caucasian, Central Asian and Caspian countries due to their strategic significance as emerging energy hubs. The EU shall definitely consider the influence of external factors related to energy geopolitics upon internal transformation of the inner-Caspian countries. The political and economic structure of these countries indicates how they can detour from existing democratization experiences, since they still carry-over members of the former Communist Party (CP) who are now very eager to benefit from the rising oil and gas trade.

Finding ways of acculturating the inner-Caspian region into the global energy markets constitutes a key concern for the EU's neighborhood policy.[29] First, there is a positive correlation between the acculturation of inner-Caspian countries into global energy markets and their liberal transformation. This is why Azerbaijan and Kazakhstan, two well acculturated countries in global energy markets, indicate higher rates of liberalization when compared to Turkmenistan, which is completely dependent on Russia's Gazprom and thus remains democratically untransformed. Secondly, the inner-Caspian region still offers opportunities to the EU, especially in terms of natural gas. The EU will be able to diversify its energy supplies and strengthen security issues if Turkmenistan becomes involved in the Western energy corridor along with Azerbaijan and, if possible, with Kazakhstan. On the contrary, if Turkmenistan remains excluded from the Western energy corridor, it will intensify its relations alternatively with Russia, China and Iran.[30] This option will not only deprive the EU of natural gas at favorable prices, but also contradict with its security concerns.

Internal Dynamics of Inner Caspian
Political Characteristics in Retrospect

When geopolitical and economic significance of AKT are matched with the security concerns of the EU, one reaches an inevitable conclusion: Political structures of AKT are highly crucial, because the states in the inner-Caspian region are the main instruments in determining both security and energy policies. When both factors are considered together, the potency of the political aspect increases. This shows that the regimes of these countries are vital for meeting security and energy supply concerns of the EU. In the aftermath of the disintegration of the USSR, the governing elite of the Soviet era has turned into the national governors of AKT and led to fraudulent referenda and rigged elections in almost all cases.[31] Consequently, all of these countries stumble between the transition to democracy and the patronage relations of those people who hold political power by virtue of their communist background. If democratization and civil society are the two main pillars that constitute the cornerstones of the EU's security policy *vis-à-vis* Eurasia, then characteristics of the states of AKT deserve deeper attention.

Azerbaijan: The disintegration of the USSR created a political triumph for the carry-over of the former Communist Party (CP), with partial exception of the ex-president Abulfeyz Elchibey, since they had occupied strategic positions in the post-Soviet Azeri state. Changing hands of power from Elchibey, who was a renowned activist with no strict affiliation to the CP, to Haydar Aliyev, who was a renowned, high ranking leader in the former CP, proves how being a member of *Nomenklatura* is a vital criterion for reaching the highest levels of political mobility. "Elchibey, who had been the leader of the Azerbaijani Popular Front at the time of his election, was typical of the first generation of post-communist leaders in the former Soviet Union, many of whom were idealistic former dissidents, who ultimately proved to be unskilled and naive as politicians."[32] Elchibey's "The Popular

Front" gained an electoral victory by authorizing his presidency one year after the declaration of independence by the Azeri Parliament in 1991. Following the presidential elections, various parties such as the "National Independence Party", "the Musavat Party" and "the Social Democratic Party" came to life and competed with "the Popular Front." Elchibey's presidency did not last long, not only because he was not a *Nomenklatura* member, but also due to his ignorant economic policies that exacerbated the tough situation that came into being during the clashes with Armenians.

From the beginning, it must be remembered that Elchibey was an activist who was imprisoned for three years for anti-communist activities at Baku University in 1974 when Haydar Aliyev was the first secretary of the Azerbaijan CP. This was more than a coincidence. In fact, Elchibey confronted H. Aliyev's political power obtained out of the CP once more, almost 20 years after this incident. On June 18, 1993, H. Aliyev replaced Elchibey after a process of *coup d'État* allegedly supported by Russia. After the coup, H. Aliyev's power was a great success, since Russia was backing the pro-Russian ex-president Ayaz Muttalibov, who was supposed to move from Moscow back to Azerbaijan. H. Aliyev continued his success as a president. He successfully dealt with every issue at which Elchibey had failed. First, he signed production sharing agreements with multinational oil companies. Second, he somehow continued ceasefire with Armenia although the Nagorno Karabakh conflict remained unresolved. Finally, he perpetuated a balance among Russian interests, multinational demands and other external pressures such as those of the U.S. and Turkey.[33] Aliyev, as a former member of the CP and ex-chief of the former KGB of Azerbaijan, sustained his political power until his death. Throughout his life, he built the cornerstones of contemporary Azeri politics.

To summarize the post-Soviet Azeri politics, we must explain first how the president increased his power. Presidential change followed in 1995 in the elections for *Milli Mejlis* (November 12 and 26), which resulted in the New Azerbaijan Party (NAP) government. Allies attained 115 seats, the opposition attained seats as follows: APF (4), PNIA (3), Musavat Party (1), and two seats remained vacant.[34] The change of presidency was very critical for Azerbaijan's neighborhood because constitutional and practical capabilities of H. Aliyev would affect the political economy of the whole Caucasus. The president attained enormous power due to his executive superiority over the government. Although the president was being elected by popular vote for a five-year term, the fact that the prime minister and the first deputy prime ministers were being appointed by the president, after the confirmation of the National Assembly, donned him with extensive powers.

On October 11, 1998, H. Aliyev gained the overwhelming majority (77.6 percent) of popular votes for presidency.[35] The National Assembly elections, which were held on November 4, 2000, strengthened H. Aliyev's positioning as his New Azerbaijan Party gained 108 seats by cooperating with allies, where other seats were partitioned by Azerbaijan Popular Front (6), Civic Solidarity Party (3), Party for National Independence of Azerbaijan (2), Musavat Party (2), Communist Party of Azerbaijan (2), APF (1), and Compatriot Party (1). In other words, H. Aliyev proved to be the leader of the country with no other alternative.[36]

Nevertheless, his health problems cut short his presidency. On October 15, 2003, Azerbaijan held presidential elections during which H. Aliyev's son, Ilham Aliyev, obtained 76.84 percent of the votes and became the new president. The election was controversial because of the clashes between the police and supporters of the opposition who accused the government of rigging the election. The OSCE International Election Observation Mission in Azerbaijan reported a number of irregularities throughout the electoral process and stated that government resources were used for supporting Ilham Aliyev's campaign, and the elections enabled him to hold the presidential office. H. Aliyev's death at age 80 (one month after the elections, due to heart and kidney problems) did not encounter drastic opposition as his son had already become his successor, sustaining stability by benefiting from extensive presidential authority.[37]

The EU was a part of this process in its political sense. The Council of Europe increased its pressures to make the new president cautious on human rights issues, which became a delicate issue after the incidents in the October 2003 elections, whereby the police had arrested prominent opposition members. Consequently, Ilham Aliyev approved their release in March 2005, prior to his political move to become the chairman of the New Azerbaijan Party holding the government. Indeed, just like his father, he would be elected as the party chairman, despite discontentment of the opposition suggesting that the president should not be involved in an affiliation with a political party, according to laws. Anyhow, this was a shrewd political movement, as government elections were to be held the following November. The plan succeeded. New Azerbaijan Party won absolute majority and gained most of the seats in the parliament right after the elections held on November 6, 2005 (next to be held in November 2010).[38] The demonstration carried out by the opposition on November 9, 2005 did not transform into a civic revolution similar to those that occurred in the the Ukraine, Georgia and Kyrgyzstan and this strengthened Ilham Aliyev's presidential status.[39]

Despite all these facts, Azerbaijan was willing to attain rapprochement with the EU, not only through energy trade but also by launching political and economic liberalization programs. Nevertheless, this intention was jeopardized by its territorial problems with Armenia, as 20 percent of Azerbaijan is still under Armenian occupation. If the Minsk group manages to become more active at rehabilitating Azerbaijan's problems with Armenia, this will not only consolidate security in Caucasus, but also expand new economic opportunities including transportation of Caspian hydrocarbons to Europe.

Kazakhstan: Being a former member, the CP is still influential at shaping the post-Soviet political structure in Kazakhstan. Current president, Nursultan A. Nazarbayev, was renowned for his ardent support for the continuation of the Soviet Union.[40] This was interesting because it was *Mikhail Gorbachev* who had appointed him as the leader of the Kazakhstan CP in late 1988. Nazarbayev was the former chairperson of the Supreme Soviet when Gorbachev's *Glasnost* and *Perestroika* were creating a deep impact upon existing institutions. Unlike Gorbachev, Nazarbayev consolidated his power in the aftermath of the disintegration of the USSR. The national elections of Kazakhstan, held on December 1, 1991, made Nazarbayev the first and probably the longest-lasting president of Kazakhstan.

Nazarbayev gained the 81.7 percent of the votes in the following presidential elections held on January 10, 1999 (organized one year earlier than scheduled) and obtained the chance to consolidate power for another seven years until 2006.[41] Nazarbayev used this chance by passing presidential decrees that extended his authority to make constitutional amendments, appoint and dismiss the government, the administrative heads of regions and cities, as well as to dissolve the government.[42] Nazarbayev appointed not only the Prime Minister Kazymzhomart Tokayev, but also the cabinet formed by the Council of Ministers and gained enormous power over the Senate and the Majilis constituting the bicameral Parliament. Nazarbayev is still above the parliament and he directly appoints seven of the 47 senators.[43] Following the Meijlis elections in 2004, the last presidential election was held on December 4, 2005 (next to be held in 2012). Nazarbayev won 91.1 percent of the votes against Zharmakhan A. Tuyakbai (6.6 percent) and Alikhan M. Baimenov (1.6 percent).[44] Senate elections were also held in December 2005 (next to be held in 2011), the results of which allowed the president to strengthen his positioning.[45]

The political evolution of Kazakhstan indicated that the president was increased his power despite liberal economic policies.[46] Liberalization of Kazakhstan should be analyzed in terms of two aspects. On one hand, the state consolidated power by the operational capabilities of the president through presidential decrees and constitutional amendments on behalf of his office. Meanwhile, an ardent liberalization program in harmony with the IMF was launched. This program created extensive privatization and reconstructed of the financial system including the banks.[47] There are severe differences between the levels and essences of political and economic liberalizations. This contrasting situation is a consequence of the government's concern to sustain equilibrium between the Soviet tradition and liberal pressures. The state adopted neo-liberal policies in order to attract foreign direct investments, especially in the energy sector, but referred to the

Soviet tradition to consolidate political power and sustain viability. This was a compulsory formulation to compromise the demands of diverse actors, while guaranteeing the power of the traditional governing elite in an emerging country where issues of hydrocarbons have started to be effective in almost every aspect of politics as well as the economy.[48] Even though the autocratic aspect of Kazakhstan does not fully respond to European security concerns, one thing is clear—Kazakhstan's economic liberalization and its integration to the European energy system promises to facilitate a smooth transformation to liberal democracy, as presumed in the EU standards. Moreover, Kazakhstan has a very strategic significance, which might offer highlights to extend the EU's security through the democratization approach throughout Central Asia.[49] In fact, just like the Azeri case, the more the EU manages to link Kazakhstan to its energy supply infrastructure, the more likely it helps the democratization process in this region.

Turkmenistan: Turkmenistan adopted an authoritarian political system right after it gained its independence. This authoritarianism had historical reasons, such as the tribal structure, which offered a very appropriate basis for presidential supremacy.[50] Consequently, Turkmenistan's post-Soviet political structure was shaped by the personal cult of Saparmurad Niyazov or Turkmenbashi so to use his latest name meaning "the leader of Turkmens," as attributed to him by the Parliament. This personal cult started in 1991 and ended on December 21, 2006 when he died from heart failure.

Raised in a Soviet orphanage, Niyazov graduated from Polytechnical Institute of Leningrad (St. Petersburg) as an energy engineer and became a member of the CP in 1962. He later became the first secretary of the Turkmenistan CP. His communist years and experience in energy issues would make him the most stubborn leader of the post-Soviet region, especially because of his hard bargains with Russia on gas prices which were well beyond market levels. To start the story from his presidential career, it may worth emphasizing how he gained almost all the votes. He obtained 98.3 percent of the votes in the presidential elections of Turkmenistan held on October 27, 1990. He appeared to be the legal and natural leader when Turkmenistan proclaimed its independence from the Soviet Union on October 27, 1991.[51] Following the elections, formal reports reflected 100 percent support for him. He gained 99.5 percent of the votes in the next elections held on June 21, 1992. His presidential authority was very influential as he was appointing the Prime Minister, Council of Ministers and deputy chairmen of the cabinet of ministers. On December 28, 1999, the Assembly (Majlis) approved him as President for life during a session of the People's Council (Halk Maslahaty).[52]

Turkmenbashi's presidency lasted until his death on December 21, 2006. His former deputy, Gurbanguly Berdymukhammedov, replaced him after the elections held on February 13, 2007. To the extent the next elections for legislature would be held in 2008, Berdymukhammedov expressed his will to launch a certain amount of liberalization programs in order not to confront severe political discontentment and harsh opposition.

Turkmenistan's meaning for the EU may be analyzed in terms of periods of Turkmenbashi and post-Turkmenbashi. The CP tradition and the tribal norms and regional values have offered Turkmenbashi the chance to consolidate his power. Furthermore, Turkmenistan's gas became a very significant tool for sustaining his absolute authority by benefiting from the trade with Russia.[53] Unlike Azerbaijan and Kazakhstan, Turkmenistan did not cooperate with multinational companies due to Turkmenbashi's choice not to share natural resources with other actors. The state has been committed to becoming a *rentier state* by the will of Turkmenbashi, who considered this transformation a step toward a self-sufficient, prosperous country. Turkmenbashi's choice kept Turkmenistan out of European sight, although its rich gas reserves might be of utmost significance for European rising gas demand.[54] Within this sense, post-Turkmenbashi's period is very crucial. Berdymukhammedov, as the new President, might enable transporting Turkmen gas by a trans-Caspian pipeline passing through Georgia and Turkey.[55] This is a major drive for the EU to consider Turkmenistan within its near neighborhood and include initiatives to convince Turkmenistan to reach European markets.

Economic Characteristics in Retrospect

AKT face difficulties of transformation, which refers to replacement of Soviet structures by liberal terms appropriate for integration with the global economy. Just like anywhere else in the post-Soviet region, this transformation is still a very thorny issue for at least two reasons. First of all, remnants of the CP cadres are still in charge and shape the transition. Secondly, mutual dependency between republics is very high as the Soviet Russia deliberately created strict specialization to strengthen the integrity among the republics. What makes AKT economies different from others is the impact of their oil and gas trade.

The post-Soviet era created two general effects upon the transitions of these countries through homogeneous and heterogeneous paths. This arose from the fact that the political structure in post-Soviet countries was determined by their concerns and challenges of survival in the post-communist rubble; whereas the policy responses adopted by political leaders diversified priorities and capacities.[56] Within this context, there were two common factors which drastically affected post-Soviet transformation of inner-Caspian countries.[57]

Table 11.1. Inner-Caspian Countries in Retrospective (2006)

Basic Economic Indicators	Azerbaijan	Kazakhstan	Turkmenistan
Population, total (millions)	8.4	15.1	4.8
Population growth (annual percent)	1.0	0.9	1.4
Life expectancy at birth, female (years)	75.2	71.1	67.1
Life expectancy at birth, male (years)	69.6	60.1	58.6
GDP (current US$) (billions)	12.56	56.09	6.77
GDP growth (annual percent)	26.2	9.4	NA
Inflation, consumer prices (annual percent)	6.7	7.6	NA
Foreign direct investment, net inflows (percent of GDP)	41	9.5	NA
Unemployment, total (percent of total labor force)	N.A.	8.8	NA
Time required to start a business (days)	115	24	NA
Internet users (per 1,000 people)	49	27	8

Source: World Development Indicators (2006)

First of all, these countries started to commercialize their oil and gas reserves independently, which led to an increased revenue impact on their social and economic structures. This fact, too, had two aspects. On one hand, the rapid influx of oil and gas revenues created the pressures of Dutch disease, which can roughly be defined as over-valued national money, increasing imports and expanding energy sector that are detrimental to the growth of agriculture and non-energy industries.[58] The influx of oil and gas revenues, on the other hand, tends to generate rentier states, which allocate their oil revenues to the political dynasty of certain groups. In any case, inner-Caspian countries need to effectively use the revenues from their natural resources, allocate them for supporting non-energy sectors and become well acculturated to the global economy if they want to harmonize prosperity with development.[59]

Secondly, as these countries are deprived of technology for oil and gas production and need partners for transportation, they have to confront various types of dependencies. The way they chose to commercialize their hydrocarbons directly affected the characteristics of their dependencies. Azerbaijan and Kazakhstan were involved in production sharing agreements with multinational companies. Azerbaijan managed to build a new transportation system out of the traditional Soviet structure with the help of the BTC and BTE. Meanwhile, Kazakhstan improved its existing infrastructure and continued cooperation with Russia throughout the transportation process.[60] Meanwhile, attempts of Turkmenistan to contribute to Western markets through Turkey remained unsuccessful, due to political problems between Turkmenistan, Azerbaijan and Turkey.

Being countries of the inner-Caspian region, AKT have similar aspects, but they differ from each other in the policy options made by their political leaders in commercializing their oil and gas. These countries are perhaps different in terms of their ways of adaptation to the new era, their economic growth rates and qualities, and socio-economic tendencies, but they all exhibit a positive correlation between acculturation into the global energy markets and their level of economic liberalization. In fact, Kazakhstan proved to be the most liberal inner-Caspian country, followed by Azerbaijan, with its accelerating liberalization, while Turkmenistan remained untransformed.

To elaborate on Azerbaijan, it must be emphasized that the Nagorno Karabakh conflict created drastic deterioration in its economic structure. Azerbaijan's GDP diminished 60 percent between 1990 and 1995. 1995 can be considered as the beginning of a new era, not only due to the positive impetus gained after ceasefire with Armenia, but also by the entry of multinational oil companies, which rapidly increased oil production.[61] An average annual growth rate of 12 percent was sustained since 2001 mainly by virtue of oil and gas revenues.[62] Since the activation of foreign projects, especially the BTC pipeline, foreign direct investments peaked in 2004 reaching $2.3 billion, which expanded Azerbaijan's GDP by as much as 26 percent corresponding to $13 billion in 2005.[63] The current trend indicates that Azerbaijan will continue its rapid economic growth rate with the help of the BTC and possibly BTE, which is expected to start functioning in 2008.

Kazakhstan, on the other hand, can be considered the most successful inner-Caspian country in terms of its achievements in liberalization throughout 1990s.[64] Having liberalized its trade regime, Kazakhstan managed to attract enormous direct foreign investments, especially in its energy sector, which led to annual growth rates more than nine percent since 2001. Although, the period between 1996 and 2003 witnessed the move of real exchange rates supporting the national currency, Tenge, Kazakhstan gave signals that it could prevent negative externalities of the oil boom.[65] As of 2006, high oil prices enabled Kazakhstan to hoard more than $24 billion in a fund to be used for coping with pressures that might lead to Dutch Disease.[66] Nevertheless, regional inequalities[67] and sectoral dysfunctions are still significant as they constitute barriers in front of further development.[68]

Turkmenistan faced Dutch disease more severely when compared with Azerbaijan and Kazakhstan. This desert country is a mono-culture which was formerly dependent on cotton and gas exports to Soviet Russia. The independence allowed the country to use its gas revenues freely. However, Turkmenistan did not have many transport alternatives, so it had to continue its gas trade with Russia. Unlike Azerbaijan and Kazakhstan, both of which built alternative transport routes by cooperating with multinational actors,

Turkmenistan remained completely dependent on Russian gas infrastructure. Russia was paying $66 for a thousand cubic meters when she was selling this gas at about $200 to third countries. Nevertheless, Turkmenistan benefited from high oil prices and increased its total exports by an average of 15 percent per year between 2003 and 2006.[69] In 2006, Turkmenistan managed to increase gas export price to Russia, from $66 per thousand cubic meters to $100. At the same time, Turkmenistan's aim of becoming self sufficient in basic agricultural products, failed.[70] Furthermore, poor cotton harvests decreased the total production about 50 percent. So, in other words, Turkmenistan has remained untransformed with its deteriorating economic structure, while high oil prices and favorable gas trade terms with Russia enabled the state to consolidate political power. The death of Turkmenbashi on December 21, 2006 can be considered the start of a new era, which might lead to liberalization in both political and economic terms.[71] If the new president, Berdymukhammedov, manages to launch successful liberalization programs, Turkmenistan may cope with Dutch disease pressures. If, on the contrary, he prefers to benefit from high oil prices and more favorable gas export prices to Russia, this country may soon turn into a rentier state, greatly suffering from Dutch Disease.

Conclusion

This chapter indicated that the EU's neighborhood policy upon Caspian region confronts three impediments. First of all, the EU makes a geographical differentiation between Caucasus (including Azerbaijan, Georgia and Armenia) and Central Asia (including Kazakhstan, Uzbekistan, Turkmenistan, Kyrgyzstan, and Tajikistan). This geographical clustering, which works well for programs such as TACIS, TRACECA and OSCE initiatives, cannot fully comprehend the importance of the Caspian region for security and energy concerns of the EU. Consequently, and secondly, the EU skips the strategic significance of the inner-Caspian region as an energy hub, despite its promise to decrease the EU's dependence on energy imports from Russia. Thirdly, although TACIS, TRACECA and OSCE initiatives seem to coincide with the EU's security and democracy parameters, policies implemented up until now seem to neglect the interaction between energy and security issues and unique political structures of AKT.

Further analysis showed that the EU became aware of the dangers that might arise from not diversifying energy supplies. Nevertheless, the EU continues to suffer from regional conceptualizations that are too broad, such as its recent movement for energy cooperation through the Baku Initiative. This is extensively due to the EU's insistence on the extended multilateral partnership approach placing all partners from Eurasia including the Black Sea, Caucasus and Central Asia on the same footing.

In response to these problems, this paper showed that AKT must be considered distinctly as a coherent region that deserves a special neighborhood policy. These three countries not only share similar historical background, Soviet legacy and a recent post-Soviet transformation, but also possess at least 80 percent of Caspian hydrocarbons. Having emphasized the significance of the inner-Caspian as a hydrocarbon hub, this paper examined parameters of energy, security and political regimes together by giving details of political and economic transformations of AKT. We explained that the transformation in Azerbaijan was moderate, gradual in Kazakhstan and very slow in Turkmenistan.

It seems that after the death of Turkmenbashi, a new era, in which the U.S., Russia and China will involve new geopolitical maneuvers, may begin in Turkmenistan. The EU, however, needs to develop relevant and effective strategies in order to benefit from Caspian hydrocarbons. The EU has to intertwine energy, security and democratization issues not only through TACIS, TRACECA and OSCE initiatives, but also by launching new initiatives that might accelerate the rise of the Western energy corridor that transports inner-Caspian hydrocarbons to Europe. This necessitates good relations with the existing political elite, which might involve closer relations with Russian leaders who can endanger the activation of the Western energy corridor if they feel politically jeopardized. This is where the inner-Caspian neighborhood puts a challenge in front of the EU for its security and energy concerns, along with its search of democratic regimes in Eurasia.

---

[1] EU Commission External Relations, *The EU's relationship with the countries of Eastern Europe & Central Asia*, http://ec.europa.eu/comm/external_relations/ceeca/index.htm.
[2] These countries are: Armenia, Azerbaijan, Belarus, Georgia, Kazakhstan, Kyrgyzstan, Moldova, Mongolia, Russia, Turkmenistan, the Ukraine and Uzbekistan.
[3] Michael J. Heffernan, *The Meaning of Europe: Geography and Geopolitics*, New York, Oxford University Press, 1998.
[4] Organization for Security and Cooperation in Europe, OSCE 2004, *What is the OSCE?* http://www.osce.org/publications/sg/2004/11/13554_53_en.pdf.
[5] Attila Ágh, "Processes of democratization in the East Central European and Balkan states: sovereignty-related conflicts in the context of Europeanization," *Communist and Post-Communist Studies*, Vol. 32, No. 3, September 1999, pp. 263-279.
[6] Ronald Grigor Suny, "Provisional Stabilities: The Politics of Identities in Post-Soviet Eurasia," *International Security*, Vol. 24, No. 3, Winter 1999, pp. 139-178.
[7] "Security Assistance Bonanza after September 11," *Middle East Report*, No. 222, Spring 2002, p. 11.
[8] The rise of civil societies in post-Soviet region strengthens the possibility of democratic stability, which in turn coincides with the EU's neighborhood intentions. See, Andrew T. Green, "Comparative Development of Post-Communist Civil Societies," *Europe-Asia Studies*, Vol. 54, No. 3, May 2002, pp. 455-471.

⁹ Ronald Inglehart, "How Solid Is Mass Support for Democracy: And How Can We Measure It?" *Political Science and Politics*, Vol. 36, No. 1, January 2003, pp. 51-57.
¹⁰ EU Commission External Relations.
¹¹ See, Graham Usher, "Thee Fate of Small Nations: The Karabagh Conflict Ten Years Later," *Middle East Report*, Winter 1999, pp. 19-22.
¹² OSCE Office in Baku, http://www.osce.org/baku/.
¹³ OSCE Centre in Almaty, http://www.osce.org/almaty/.
¹⁴ OSCE Centre in Ashgabad, http://www.osce.org/ashgabad/.
¹⁵ For instance, see, Rafis Abazov, "Kazakhstan's Security Challenges in a Changing World," *Contributions to Conflict Management, Peace Economics and Development*, Vol. 1, 2004, pp. 229-242.
¹⁶ European Commission Staff Working Document, *Annex to the Green Paper: A European Strategy for Sustainable, Competitive and Secure Energy, What is at stake*, Background document, Brussels, SEC(2006) 317/2, p. 8.
¹⁷ Mert Bilgin, *Avrasya Enerji Savaşları*, İstanbul, IQ Yayınları, 2005, pp. 79-82.
¹⁸ At this point it may be suggested that the EU has not fully contemplated the geopolitical significance of this region in terms of oil and gas. In fact, the EU remained outside of the geopolitical maneuvers mainly carried out by the U.S., Britain and Russia. See, Lutz Kleveman, *The New Great Game: Blood and Oil in Central Asia*, New York, Grove Atlantic, 2003.
¹⁹ Russia's influence in this region dates back almost about 140 years. See, Edward Allworth (ed.), *Central Asia: 120 Years of Russian Rule*. Durham, Duke University Press, 1989.
²⁰ Islam lies deep inside different segments of society along with Russian and Soviet influence. See, Ahmed Akbar and David Hart (eds.), *Islam in Tribal Societies*, London, Routledge, 1984.
²¹ Mert Bilgin, "The Emerging Caspian Energy Regime and Turkey's New Role," *The Turkish Yearbook of International Relations*, No. 34, 2003, pp. 1-22.
²² Igor Effimoff, "The oil and gas resource base of the Caspian region," *Journal of Petroleum Science and Engineering*, Vol. 28, No. 4, December 2000, pp. 157-159.
²³ U.S. Energy Information Administration, *EIA Caspian 2007*, http://www.eia.doe.gov/emeu/cabs/caspian.html.
²⁴ Svante E. Cornell, "Commentary: So far, Europe's approach to central Asia has been moralistic and counterproductive," *Europe's World*, Spring 2007, pp. 17-21 at 17.
²⁵ "The EU wants to build an energy strategy in the Caspian region," *KavkazCenter*, 11 January 2007, http://www.kavkazcenter.com/eng/content/2007/01/11/7137.shtml.
²⁶ "The EU and the countries of the Black Sea and Caspian Sea regions agree on a common energy strategy," *EU Press Release*, Brussels, 30 November 2006, http://europa.eu/rapid/pressReleasesAction.do?reference=IP/06/1657&format=HTML&aged=0&language=EN.
²⁷ Ibid.
²⁸ Alessandro Vitale, "The EU wants to build an energy strategy in the Caspian region," *CaucazEuropeNews*, 09/01/2007, http://www.caucaz.com/home_eng/breve_contenu.php?id=293.
²⁹ This issue is very interesting in the sense that it combines security and energy concerns of the EU. It is likely to witness relatively more democratic systems, when

the economies of these countries are well acculturated with the global economy. Otherwise, natural resource revenues might generate the rise of authoritarian regimes inclined to manipulate sociological factors, such as religion and ethnicity, to sustain their positions. For similar cases see, Leonard Wantchekon, "Why do Resource Dependent Countries Have Authoritarian Governments?" *Journal of African Finance and Economic Development*, Vol. 5, No. 2, 2002, pp. 57-77.

[30] For China's ardent initiatives around Caspian, see, Philip Andrews-Speed and Sergei Vinogradov, "China's Involvement in Central Asian Petroleum: Convergent or Divergent Interests?" *Asian Survey*, Vol. 40, No. 2, March 2000, pp. 377-397.

[31] M. Steven Fish, "Postcommunist Subversion: Social Science and Democratization in East Europe and Eurasia," *Slavic Review*, Vol. 58, No. 4, Winter 1999, pp. 794-823 at 795.

[32] Leila Aliyeva, "Political Leadership Strategies in Azerbaijan," *Contemporary Caucasus Newsletter*, Vol. 1, No. 1, Winter 1995, pp. 14-16 at 14.

[33] Penetration of Western oil industry in Azerbaijan took place with a liberalization process generating democratic development. See, Daniel Heradstveit, "Democratic development in Azerbaijan and the role of the Western oil industry," *Central Asian Survey*, Vol. 20, No. 3, September 2001, pp. 261-288.

[34] Legislative branch is unicameral composed of National Assembly or *Milli Mejlis* (125 seats; members serve five year terms).

[35] Sub-Committee on NATO Enlargement and the New Democracies *Secretariat, Visit to Baku, January 22 - 24 October 1998, Trip Report*, March 1999, http://www.nato-pa.int/archivedpub/trip/as65pced-baku.asp.

[36] See, European Commission External Relations, *The EU's relations with Azerbaijan, 2007*, http://ec.europa.eu/comm/external_relations/azerbaidjan/intro/index.htm.

[37] "Former Azerbaijan president dies," *BBC News*, 12 December 2003. http://news.bbc.co.uk/2/hi/europe/3315081.stm.

[38] NAP 58, Azadliq coalition 8, CSP 2, YES 2, Motherland 2, single seat parties 7, independents 42, undetermined 4. See, CIA, World Fact Book Azerbaijan 2007, https://www.cia.gov/cia/publications/factbook/geos/aj.html.

[39] "Azerbaijan President Says Revolution Impossible," *RFERL*, 13 November 2005, http://www.rferl.org/featuresarticle/2005/11/143553B3-71F5-4B5C-9E67-267F5B55731B.html.

[40] Kazakhstan is relatively liberal country in its economic sense. Nevertheless, politically it can be found authoritarian. See, Sally N. Cummings, "Kazakhstan: an Uneasy Relationship - Power and Authority in the Nazarbayev Regime," in S. Cummings (ed.), *Power and Change in Central Asia*, London, Routledge, 2002, pp. 59-73.

[41] Rafis Abazov, "The 1999 Presidential Elections in Kazakhstan," *Electoral Studies*, Vol. 20, No. 2, June 2001, pp. 313-321.

[42] Meanwhile, reports from Kazakhstan indicate significant violations of democracy and human rights. See, Joma Nazpary, *Post-Soviet Chaos: Violence and Dispossession in Kazakhstan*, Sterling, Pluto Press, 2002.

[43] CIA The World Factbook, *Kazakhstan Country Report*, 8 February 2007, https://www.cia.gov/cia/publications/factbook/geos/kz.html.

[44] Donnacha Ó Beacháin, "Parliamentary elections in Kazakhstan, September and October 2004," *Electoral Studies*, Vol. 24, No. 4, December 2005, pp. 762-769.

45 CIA.

46 International efforts to flourish a civil society by supporting non-governmental organizations did not reach at its aims in Kazakhstan. For the Kazakh case, see, Pauline Jones Luong and Erika Weinthal, "The NGO Paradox: Democratic Goals and Non-Democratic Outcomes in Kazakhstan," *Europe-Asia Studies*, Vol. 51, No. 7, November 1999, pp. 1267-1284

47 Peter Bofinger, "The economics of orthodox money-based stabilizations (OMBS): The recent experience of Kazakhstan, Russia and the the Ukraine," *European Economic Review*, Vol. 40, No. 3-5, April 1996, pp. 663-671.

48 Mert Bilgin, *Hazar'da Son Darbe*, İstanbul, IQ Yayınları, 2005, pp. 188-238.

49 For the strategic significance of Kazakhstan see, Robert Legvold (ed.), *Thinking strategically: the major powers, Kazakhstan and the Central Asian nexus*, Cambridge, MIT Press, 2003.

50 John Anderson, "Authoritarian Political Development in Central Asia: The Case of Turkmenistan," *Central Asian Survey*, Vol. 14, No. 4, 1995, pp. 509-528.

51 Ibid.

52 "Turkmenistan's Leader is Voted President for Life," *The New York Times*, 29 December 1999, p. 10.

53 Mert Bilgin, *Hazar'da Son Darbe*, İstanbul, IQ Yayınları, 2005, pp. 242-286.

54 If Turkmenistan liberalizes its energy laws, this would offer significant investment opportunities to multinationals, as well as facilitate the plan of the EU to diversify its gas supplies. See, Jonathan Hines and James B. Varanese, "Turkmenistan's Oil and Gas Sector: Overview of the Legal Regime for Foreign Investment," *Journal of Energy & Natural Resources Law*, Vol. 19, No. 1, 2001, pp. 44-63.

55 Integration of Turkmenistan with EU's pipeline infrastructure promises to decrease extremist occurrences arising from its isolation thus far. For extremism in the region see, Christina M. Kelly, "The U.S. and Turkmenistan: Striking a Balance Between Promoting Religious Freedom and Fighting the War Against Terrorism," *Pace International Law Review*, No. 15, 2003, p. 481.

56 Anna Matveeva, "Democratization, Legitimacy and Political Change in Central Asia," *International Affairs*, Vol. 75, No. 1, January 1999, pp. 23-44 at 24.

57 It may even be suggested that the Soviet heritage and national responses to it played the most significant role in determining current economic structures. See, Pamela Blackmon, "Back to the USSR: why the past does matter in explaining differences in the economic reform processes of Kazakhstan and Uzbekistan," *Central Asian Survey*, Vol. 24, No. 4, December 2002, pp. 391-404.

58 See, Christine Ebrahim-Zadeh, "Dutch Disease: Too Much Wealth Managed Unwisely," *Finance and Development*, Vol. 40, No. 1, 2003, pp. 50-51.

59 Erling Roed Larsen, "Escaping the resource curse and the Dutch disease? When and why Norway caught up with and forged ahead of its neighbors," *The American Journal of Economics and Sociology*, Vol. 65, No. 3, 2006, pp. 605-636.

60 Some analysis put emphasis on natural cooperation opportunities among Central Asia, Russia and China. See, Shiping Tang, "Eonomic Integration in Central Asia: The Russian and Chinese Relationship," *Asian Survey*, Vol. 40, No. 2, March, 2000, pp. 360-376. If inner-Caspian's European neighborhood can be sustained through trans-Caspian pipelines passing through Western energy corridor, AKT will definitely have more options beyond geographical means.

[61] See, World Bank, *Azerbaijan Country Brief 2006*, http://web.worldbank.org/WBSITE/EXTERNAL/COUNTRIES/ECAEXT/AZERBAIJANEXTN/0,menuPK:301923~pagePK:141132~piPK:141107~theSitePK:301914,00.html.
[62] World Bank.
[63] EIA, *Azerbaijan 2007*, http://www.eia.doe.gov/emeu/cabs/Azerbaijan/Background.html.
[64] Yelena Kalyuzhnova, *The Kazakhstani Economy: Independence and Transition*, London, Macmillan, 1998.
[65] Ali M. Kutan and Michael Louis Wyzan, "Explaining the real exchange rate in Kazakhstan, 1996-2003: Is Kazakhstan vulnerable to the Dutch disease?" *Economic Systems*, Vol. 29, No. 2, 2005, pp. 242-255.
[66] EIA, *Kazakhstan 2007*, http://www.eia.doe.gov/emeu/cabs/Kazakhstan/Background.html.
[67] Regional inequalities match Kazakhstan's traditional tribal structure. See, Martha Brill Olcott, *Kazakhstan: Unfulfilled Promise*, Washington DC, Carnegie Endowment for International Peace, 2002, pp. 197-203.
[68] UNDP, *Poverty in Kazakhstan: Causes and Cures*, Almaty, Kazakhstan, 2002.
[69] CIA, *World Fact Book Turkmenistan 2007*, https://www.cia.gov/cia/publications/factbook/geos/tx.html.
[70] Scott Rozelle and Johan F. M. Swinnen, "Success and Failure of Reform: Insights from the Transition of Agriculture," *Journal of Economic Literature*, Vol. 42, No. 2, June 2004, pp. 404-456 at 408.
[71] Natalia Antelava, "Leader's death leaves uncertain future," *BBC News*, 22 December 2006, http://news.bbc.co.uk/2/hi/asia-pacific/6202215.stm.

Chapter 12
Opportunities and Challenges for Cooperation in the Black Sea Region: The EU and the BSEC

Emel G. Oktay

By memberships of Romania and Bulgaria in January 2007, the borders of the European Union (EU) now extend to the Black Sea. The second batch of the fifth[1] and the latest enlargement has also enabled the EU to become a Black Sea power, which is both capable to influence and vulnerable to the developments in the region. However, the EU has, so far, shown little interest in the Black Sea as a region and in dealing with the Organization of the Black Sea Economic Cooperation (BSEC) as an institutional entity. Although the EU's new policy is presented as expanding the zone of prosperity, stability and security beyond its borders,[2] it has not been exhibiting all its potential in the Black Sea region as a 'civilian force.'

The Black Sea region was initially described as including the littoral states of the Black Sea (Bulgaria, Romania, Turkey, the Ukraine, Russia, and Georgia) plus Moldova and the two other countries situated in the Southern Caucasus, Armenia and Azerbaijan. The later change of the term making it a 'wider Black Sea area' which added Western Balkans, is now commonly accepted.[3] Although the region has delineated borders, it has been steadily gaining importance since the collapse of the Soviet Union and the end of the Cold War. Terrorist attacks first on the U.S. and then on several European cities that are believed to be emanating from the 'Greater Middle East' induced a further attention to be paid on the region which is at present considered as 'The New Near East.'[4]

For the last fifteen years, the Black Sea region has emerged both as a boundary and a bridge to new challenges and opportunities for Western institutions. It is a major crossroad for energy and commerce, as well as for criminal and terrorist activities.[5] In the final analysis, besides being a barrier to many transnational threats, it is increasingly becoming important for Europe as a major east-west energy supply conduit. Since the great majority of EU member states are not energy producers, the security of energy supplies is becoming more and more important for the EU.[6]

Considering the geopolitical significance of the Black Sea area, regarding the region, rather than having no policy at all, the EU preferred forming a complex web of relations defined by several policies. In this context, the EU initiated three strategies: the enlargement process (Croatia, Former Yugoslav Republic of Macedonia and Turkey are the candidate states), the European

Neighborhood Policy (based on bilateral action plans with Moldova, the Ukraine and southern Caucasian countries) and the Agreement on 'four common spaces' with Russia.[7] The common characteristic of these separate strategies is their reliance on bilateral relations. Although the EU has developed complementary regional policies in its relations with all of its neighboring regions such as the Northern Dimension, the Stability and Association Process and the Euro-Mediterranean Partnership, it left the Black Sea area out of this concern. Despite the fact the BSEC is the only indigenous, longstanding and highly institutionalized organization in the region, the EU always kept itself at distance from this organization.

In this study, we have two purposes. First, by examining the European Security Strategy (ESS), we look at the main challenges and prospects that the Black Sea area poses for the EU as a strategically important neighborhood area. Then, we examine the EU's approach toward the region mainly on a bilateral and regional basis. In this context, we analyze the European Neighborhood Policy (ENP) and the attitude of the EU as a much more powerful and deep-rooted regional integration project vis-a-vis the indigenous BSEC. The study will conclude by reaching the point showing that the EU needs to close the gap among its policies by adopting a more constructive and comprehensive approach toward the BSEC. As initial engagements with the BSEC, region-wide projects and financial instruments that will provide support on energy, transport and environment can be commenced.

Challenges and Prospects Posed by the Black Sea Area for the EU

Since the end of the Cold War, the international context in which Europe has been operating has dramatically changed. Termination of the Soviet threat and the bipolar division, unification of Germany, expansion of the EU and NATO toward the East, all drove the context of political, economic and security issues to be altered. Since the collapse of communism more than 15 years ago, most of the time and political energy of the Euro-Atlantic community was spent on the task of anchoring and integrating Central and Eastern Europe, stopping the Balkan wars and putting these countries back on the track leading to the European integration and finally, trying to establish a new and cooperative relationship with Russia.[8]

Constituting a 'civilizational black hole' in western historical consciousness,[9] the Black Sea area, for most of the post-Cold War period, was not on the immediate agenda of the West. Then the terrorist attacks on major Western cities and the interest in safe and stable flow of energy through the region, shifted the EU's attention to the Black Sea area. The region is usually referred to as the "Euro-Asian energy corridor" linking the

Euro-Atlantic system with Caspian sea energy supplies and the states of Central Asia.

The Black Sea countries, today, are part of the wider European security system. The accession of Romania and Bulgaria first to NATO in April 2004, and then to the EU in January 2007, confirmed the link between the stability of the Black Sea region and European security. Similarly, with its northern coast covering the entire southern shore of the Black Sea, Turkey has been guarding NATO's southern flank for more than half a century and, in 2005, it started accession negotiations with the EU. Meanwhile, both the the Ukraine and Georgia, closely followed by Moldova, are also pursuing NATO and EU membership.

Although acknowledging the challenges and prospects posed by the Black Sea region as a strategically important neighborhood area for its security, the EU gives first priority to the need for completing the job of consolidating peace and democracy in Europe.[10] European Security Strategy (ESS), as announced by Javier Solana, sets the task as 'to promote a ring of well-governed countries to the East of the EU and on the borders of the Mediterranean with whom we can enjoy close and cooperative relations.'[11]

The security challenges and opportunities faced by the Black Sea as a strategic neighborhood can be assessed clearly by examining the ESS, which was adopted in December 2003 by the Council. The ESS specifies five key threats: terrorism, proliferation of weapons of mass destruction (WMDs), regional conflicts, state failure, and organized crime.[12] All these threats are directly relevant to the Black Sea region. As clarified in the ESS, active or frozen regional conflicts (Trans-Dniester, Abkhazia, South Ossetia and Karabakh) can lead to 'extremism, terrorism and state failure' as well as provide 'opportunities for organized crime,' of which Europe is the 'prime target.' One of the challenges mentioned in the Strategy is the energy dependence considered as a 'special concern for Europe,' which means taking a stronger and more active interest in the problems of the Southern Caucasus is also acknowledged as strategic priority.[13]

The ESS underlines the need for the EU to build security in 'its neighborhood' indicating that geography is still important in 'an era of globalization.'[14] With the goal of preventing new dividing lines and conflicts spreading into Europe, the delicate neighborhood is clearly demarcated from the Balkans to the Southern Caucasus and from the Middle East to the Mediterranean (all are included in the ENP, except the Balkans where the countries have Stability and Association Agreements with the EU). In pursuing strategic objectives, the EU is encouraged to be more active and deploy a full spectrum of instruments for crisis management and conflict prevention at its disposal, including robust intervention when necessary.[15]

Because of its comprehensive approach to security, the ESS has the potential to serve as a reference framework and driving force for policies in all fields of external action, from trade to development to the Common Foreign and Security Policy (CFSP) and European Security and Defense Policy (ESDP). Biscop points out that the recognition of interdependence between all dimensions of the security—political, socio-economic, cultural, environmental, and military—and the need of formulating integrated policies for these dimensions has initialized this comprehensive security understanding.[16] With regard to establishing security in its Neighborhood, the EU itself will assume a leading role. The same approach is also applied in the following two levels: Establishing dialogue, cooperation and partnership in all fields of external action, and utilizing the whole range of instruments at the disposal of the EU.[17] In this context, being the EU's strategic neighborhood, the Black Sea receives the full attention and obviously the EU realized that, despite being a powerful global economic actor, it must project its European might to a regional context that involves full range of capabilities in the fields of economy, politics, diplomacy, and military.[18]

EU's Approach Toward the Region

Until most of the work for the accession of ten new member states to the EU was completed, the Black Sea area had not been able to gain a place on the EU's overcrowded policy agenda. For a long period of time, the EU involvement and commitment was minimal. Countries in Eastern and Central Europe (Moldova, Russia, the Ukraine, Armenia, Azerbaijan, and Georgia in the Black Sea region) signed Partnership and Cooperation Agreements (PCAs) with the EU and received minor levels of assistance under transition support programs such as TACIS.[19] According to the EU perspective, a decade of transition in the region has resulted impoverishment of society, de-industrialization and the rise of oligarchic power structures.[20] Belarus, the Ukraine and Moldova were struggling with the transition problems at every aspect of governance. In direct investment and trade matters, the Black Sea did not carry a particular importance for the Union.

The immediate impact of the EU's big bang enlargement that was completed in May 2004 was felt in the Black Sea area. When the borders of the EU reached Belarus, Moldova and the Ukraine, tremendous security challenges arose ranging from Justice and Home Affairs (JHA) questions of organized crime and international terrorism, to Common Foreign and Security Policy (CFSP), from non-proliferation of weapons of mass destruction (WMD) and conflict settlement, to wider questions of corruption and sustainable development.[21]

Facing these challenges, the EU felt the urgency to upgrade the monitoring and security of its external borders through stricter control of the flow of goods and people, which actually meant stringently closing its external borders. At the same time, however, the EU had to remain engaged with its neighbors and foster ties across borders for a wide range of exchanges. On the eve of the enlargement, balancing exclusiveness and inclusiveness was the most important challenge faced by the EU.[22] The Commission policy paper dated March 2003, on the ENP titled "Wider Europe-Neighborhood: A New Framework for Relations with our Eastern and Southern Neighbors," answered a sizeable demand. When, in June 2004, the Council endorsed the European Neighborhood Strategy Paper, it was obvious that the objectives of the ENP served the broader goals of the ESS, which had been adopted six months prior.

Overall, the main argument of the new policy is that, as a post-modern force, rather than as a modern power, the EU exercises influence and shapes its environment through 'what it is,' rather than 'what it does.'[23] The gravitational pull the EU exerts in international relations is based on the weight of its markets, capital and technological resources, as well as on the attractiveness of the European way of life.[24] Therefore, the Black Sea is the place where, as a civilian force, the EU's normative power is going to be put to test. Whether the EU is going to enhance its strategic role by increasing its normative power and influence or not will depend upon its success in bringing peace and prosperity to its immediate neighborhood.

At present, as mentioned by several analysts,[25] the EU has three separate strategies toward the Black Sea region: the enlargement strategy (Croatia, Macedonia and Turkey are the candidate states and Western Balkans are in the Stabilization and Association Process), the European Neighborhood Policy (based on bilateral Action Plans) and the Agreement on 'four common spaces' with Russia. Reliance on bilateral relations is the common characteristic of these separate strategies.

Regional sectoral initiatives and programs in key areas run by the EU in cooperation with the regional countries (by-passing the BSEC) to promote its interests can also be counted in these strategies. INOGATE (the 1995 Interstate Oil and Gas Transport to Europe), which was implemented to promote the regional integration of pipeline systems; TRACECA (Transport Corridor Europe-Caucasus-Asia); PETrA (part of TRACECA), which aims to improve transport infrastructure; and DANBLAS (Danube-Black Sea Environmental Task Force), which was initiated to try to establish cooperation for the protection of water and eco-system of the wider Black Sea region, are all included in these programs.[26] Although there is ample room for cooperation with the BSEC in the above mentioned areas and the legal and institutional framework is already in place, the EU, so far, has preferred the do-it-yourself method.

The European Neighborhood Policy (ENP) and the Black Sea Area

Carrying the purpose of influencing internal and external policies of regarded countries, the ENP focuses on developing bilateral relations between the EU and each of these individual countries.[27] In the Black Sea area, countries included in the ENP are Belarus, Moldova, the Ukraine, and Southern Caucasus (Armenia, Azerbaijan and Georgia). The EU-Russia relations have been developing along on a separate track upon Russia's will.[28] The self-exclusion of Russia from the ENP framework leaves a large hole in the center of the policy.[29] Since the aim of this article is not to concentrate upon the pros and cons of the ENP for the individual countries of the Black Sea area, we will mainly try to make an overall assessment on the nature of this bilateral approach.

Through the Neighborhood strategy, the Union's policy is to use the pre-accession processes including plans (Action Plans), targets, conditionality, and regular monitoring in order to achieve a high level of integration, a strengthened cooperation on border management and common management of cross-border and regional issues. If only the partners could fulfill their commitments to strengthen the rule of law, democracy and respect for human rights; promote market-oriented economic reforms; and cooperate on key foreign policy objectives such as counter-terrorism and non-proliferation of weapons of mass destruction, the EU could offer an ever-deeper relationship.[30]

The Action Plans are one of the key instruments for the implementation of the ENP and, although the content of each individual Action Plan is said to be specially tailored for a particular partner country, their structures are generally similar to each other. All of the action plans commonly contain chapters on political dialogue and reform, economic and social cooperation and development, trade-related issues, market and regulatory reform, cooperation in justice, liberty and security issues (Justice and Home Affairs), sectoral issues (e.g. transport, energy, information, society, environment, research, and development), and human dimension (people to people contacts, civil society, education, and public health).

Funding of the ENP is provided by a new European Neighborhood and Partnership Instrument (ENPI), which will replace existing funds (TACIS, MEDA and others such as the European Initiative for Democracy and Human Rights-EIDHR) and include a cross-border cooperation component. Under the cross-border module, 'joint programs' that will bring together regions of member states and partner countries sharing a common border, will be co-financed by the European Regional Development Fund (ERDF). The Commission proposed that funding for the next budget cycle, between 2007 and 2013, should be significantly increased to match the political priority given to the ENP partners plus Russia.[31]

Weaknesses of the ENP as a Bilateral Approach in the Black Sea Region

It is far from evident that the ENP, as currently constructed, will be able to act as an instrument of the EU's ambitions for promoting its 'transformational influence' and strengthening its claim as regional and international actor. The ENP is going to face some internal challenges such as some weak points of the ENP and some institutional problems as they emerge from tensions concerning competences about external relations that occur within the EU, and some external challenges posed mainly by the U.S. and Russia, which have their own agendas in these regions.

Although the ENP shifts toward a more diversified approach and includes a great variety of countries in its policy framework, it is still counterproductive for those that are genuinely seeking a firm engagement within the EU. As Dannreuther comments "There is a problem of distinct vagueness, similar to that of the eventual 'prize' to be offered, of how multiple targets are to be prioritized, the time-scale for completion, and the exact benefits gained by their fulfilment."[32] In fact, despite all the statements of hard work put into them, for three reasons, it is difficult to see how the Action Plans can provide a real incentive for making reforms: Sometimes it is not clear who (the EU or the neighbor) is carrying the action; even if it is clear that the neighbor is supposed to take the action, the details and procedures of the progress are then not clear; and a definite time span for attaining particular objectives is not given, as there are no clear benchmarks, either.[33]

Overall, as it is very apparent in the case of the Ukraine and Moldova, the ENP is not seen as a viable, coherent alternative to the enlargement. Basically, Ukrainians are furious about being treated in the same basket with North African and Middle Eastern countries. In addition, the ENP is not expected to offer credible tools to the EU in dealing with security challenges in the Black Sea area. The EU is often oscillating between activity and inactivity, where it issues declarations on political developments in neighboring countries, but meanwhile, the member states do not have the will to push for concerted action at the EU level. There are important problems of consistency and cross-pillar coherence when it comes to important political issues and the ENP has no remedy for this.[34]

The EU claims to foster a friendly atmosphere for neighbors by the new tools provided by the ENP. However, it is not clear whether these extra tools are sufficient to promote fundamental economic and political reform for the neighbors and enable them to tackle the perceived problems posed by their geographical proximity to the enlarged EU. The task the EU set for itself is formidable: overcoming the 'welfare division' between the enlarged EU and its neighbors. On the political side, this division is even greater. The majority of the countries in the region is either authoritarian or has weakly institutionalized democracies. Closely related to this situation is the presence of long-standing ethno-nationalist, religious or communal conflicts.[35]

In addition, the pre-eminence of political objectives (such as respect for human rights and democratic principles, cooperation in the fight against terrorism and non-proliferation of weapons of mass destruction) and the EU's attitude of mostly protecting its own interests concerning the issues of migration and energy that it exhibits during promoting its internal and external security agenda, give neighboring countries an unpleasant taste about the true nature of the ENP.[36] On the side of incentives, despite the talks about cross-border cooperation, EU member states are hesitant to take actual steps in visa facilitation, establishing local border traffic regimes or allowing border area populations to maintain traditional contacts, all of which mean blurring outer borders.[37] In addition, the trade incentives offered for agricultural products is far from being satisfactory. The EU continues to be protective of its internal market. Although, the Commission policy paper on the ENP, "Wider Europe-Neighborhood: A New Framework for Relations with our Eastern and Southern Neighbors" dated March 2003, included granting four freedoms (including free movement of persons) to partner states, these are not mentioned in the final Strategy Paper dated May 2004.[38]

Last but not least, the EU is still lacking the instruments to deal with either the countries of concern (such as Belarus) or the conflicts in the Black Sea Neighborhood (Moldova, Armenia, Azerbaijan, and Georgia). Conflict resolution in the neighborhood is considered something the ENP should contribute to by 'facilitating pragmatic advances on the ground,' even between countries divided by conflicts, through an emphasis on bilateral aspects of relations and on differentiation and sub-regional cooperation. However, it is not clearly put forward what kind of pragmatic advances were actually meant or, put to it more simply, "what does the term 'pragmatic advances' mean?" The only explanation provided for this is a statement saying that the ENP Action Plans 'takes into account of special circumstances and include certain actions directed at confidence building.' The assumption is, through its reform agenda, the ENP would serve to support more specific actions carried out in the context of CFSP.[39] The issue stems mainly from the tensions in the 'gray areas' that fall in between the Community and the Common Foreign and Security Policy.[40]

As Bretherton and Vogler frame it: 'In new areas of policy, where practices and understandings have yet to be constructed, cross-pillar tensions continue to arise.'[41] The formal responsibility for the ENP lies with the Commission, the policy links economic development with security concerns, cross-border crime, democratization and human rights. Although, the link between the ENP and the EU's Special Representatives in conflict areas is formulated as 'the ENP Country Reports and Action Plans are developed by the European Commission, working in close cooperation with the EU's High Representative for the Common Foreign and Security Policy Javier Solana on matters related to political cooperation and the CFSP and where there are EU Special Representatives (paragraph 5), as in the Southern Caucasus or Moldova (Transdnistria) or in the Middle East, the Commission also works closely with them on the development and implementation of the political aspects of the relevant ENP Action Plans,' in practice, however, the case is totally different.

In March 2005, for example, the appointment of a CFSP Special Representative to Moldova, primarily regarding the conflict over Transnistria, was conditioned with the Commission's insistence that the appointed person not be involved in the implementation of Moldova's recently agreed ENP Action Plan. The issue was resolved through negotiation of a compromise mandate, which stated that the Special Representative would deal only with the 'relevant aspects' of the ENP.[42] Considering that the coordination problems in each political issue probably had to be resolved by separate negotiations for every ENP country with a different Action Plan, we can say that the ENP may not be able to serve in specific actions that are being carried out within the context of CFSP.

BSEC as an Indigenous Regional Organization

With the Summit meeting held in Istanbul in 1992 that brought together six Black Sea littoral states (Bulgaria, Georgia, Romania, Russia, Turkey, and the Ukraine) and five neghbouring countries (Albania, Armenia, Azerbaijan, Greece, Moldova), the BSEC was established under the initiative of Turkey, to 'turn the Black Sea basin into a haven of peace, stability and prosperity.'[43] When its Charter came into force in May 1999, the BSEC became a 'regional economic organization' holding an international legal entity. Serbia and Montenegro joined the organization in 2004. BSEC represents a region of some 350 millon people with an area of nearly 20 million square kilometers, which is also the second-largest source of oil and natural gas, after the Persian Gulf region.[44]

The BSEC has been an organization for economic, rather than political, cooperation.[45] Its involvement in political and security matters in the region is limited to matters such as conflict resolution, peace building and peacekeeping, arms control and disarmament. Nevertheless, ten years after its establishment, most member countries acknowledged the fact that "without a viable security dimension and solution to the region's many problems, the organization could not move ahead" and the difficulty in security cooperation with the BSEC was on the agenda at the Decennial Summit of Istanbul.[46] In terms of cooperating on soft security matters such as organized crime, environmental protection and illegal immigration, the BSEC has already provided a forum for multilateral dialogue encouraging member states for more action.

Over the years, the BSEC has developed a coherent set of institutional structures, functional mechanisms and policy instruments. It constitutes main, subsidiary and related bodies. At the highest level, Heads of States and Governments irregularly meet to set policy guidelines and decide about

BSEC's strategic direction. As an intergovernmental organization, the Council of Ministers of Foreign Affairs (CMFA) is the decision-making authority regularly meeting in ordinary sessions to debate over policy issues and to adopt resolutions, decisions and recommendations that are binding on the Member States and the BSEC institutions. As in the EU mechanism, every six months, the Council meetings mark the end of the term of the Chairmanship-in-Office (CiO) of the organization which rotates in alphabetical order. The chairmanship is also assisted by the troika mechanism including the former and subsequent CiO.

A Committee of Senior Officials (CSO) prepares the Council meetings and during the periods between the Council meetings, it represents the Council. The BSEC Permanent International Secretariat (BSEC PERMIS) headed by the Secretary General, operates under the authority of the Chair-in-Office, which was established in Istanbul to assume executive and administrative responsibilities. PERMIS has its own budget and does not have legal authority. It coordinates the activities of the Working Groups,[47] covering different sectors under the guidance of a Country coordinator appointed for a two-year term. Project Development Fund (PDF) was created in 2002 with the purpose of facilitating the elaboration and promotion of projects with high regional cooperation and development impact in the BSEC region in the early stages of their conception.

The intergovernmental structure is supported by four related bodies which is non-governmental in character: the Parliamentary Assembly of the Black Sea Economic Cooperation (PABSEC) with an international secretariat based in Istanbul, the Business Council (BSEC BC) based in Istanbul, the Black Sea Trade and Development Bank (BSTDB) based in Thessaloniki, and the International Center for Black Sea Studies (ICBSS) based in Athens.

In fifteen years, the BSEC was successful in gathering most of the activities the member countries consider to correspond to their shared interests within one institutional network. It contributed to the establishment of a cooperation culture in the region in many ways and laid the groundwork for more ambitious steps forward. As the most institutionalized organization in the region, the BSEC was ready to undertake concrete responsibilities and agreements that have been concluded in areas like combatting organized crime, including terrorism, or emergency assistance in cases of natural or man-made disasters.[48] The organization gradually enhanced its project-oriented character by generating concrete proposals for regional undertakings (such as interconnection of electric grids, identification of obstacles to trade) and by creating functional networks (like liaison officers for combatting organized crime and for emergency situations). As examples of region-wide multilateral projects, two memoranda of understanding were completed and opened for signature in 2006, one on a Black Sea Highway Ring and the other, on the Motorways of the sea. In addition, two regional projects on the increase of intra-regional trade, as well as investment promotion, were agreed upon to be implemented in cooperation with the UNDP and OECD respectively.[49]

BSEC sets its priority areas as follows: "defining the key areas of cooperation (such as transport, energy, trade and investment, cross-border cooperation, environment, good-governance, combatting organized crimes); reforming itself to improve its efficiency and to enhance its capacity and finally developing a regional framework of cooperation with the EU."[50]

The EU and The BSEC: Is Regional Partnership on the Horizon?

The BSEC, so far, has not been the target of a specific EU regional initiative. The EU's presence in the Black Sea region in the early 1990s was characterized by bilateralism, which imposed certain constraints on the EU's relations with the Black Sea region as a whole. The need for greater engagement was not recognized until the late 1990s. As the importance of the region, in terms of the access it provided to Caspian and Central Asian energy resources, increased, modernization of the regional infrastructure in energy and transportation facilites attained priority in the EU's emerging strategy toward the Black Sea region.

In 1997, the European Commission in its Report to the Council stated that "The EU has a major interest in promoting political stability and economic prosperity in the Black Sea region and stimulating the development links both within the region and with the EU."[51] Based on this Communication, the EU Council included in its Conclusions (19 December 1997) a section on the Black Sea region, highlighting its strategic importance for the EU, the role the BSEC could play in this respect and possible priority objectives for cooperation. Apart from the energy, transport and communication facilities connecting the Black Sea to Europe, regional commercial cooperation and the creation of favorable conditions to attract the EU and foreign investments, providing well-sustained development, environmental protection, and nuclear safety areas are emphasized as priorities. Also in 'Agenda 2000: For a Stronger and Wider Union' released in December 1997, the Commission listed the BSEC among the regional initiatives that "it welcomed and supported."[52]

Since 1997, the EU representatives have been participating in BSEC meetings (sectoral Ministerial Meetings, BSEC Working Groups and Workshops especially on transport, energy and institutional renewal issues) in 'official guest' status by sending officials or representatives at the expert level. Although the EU's cooperation with the BSEC in regional matters has been on the agenda for the last ten years, there have been no institutional links until now. Moreover, the BSEC's reply to the EC's communication with the adoption of the 'Platform for Cooperation between BSEC and the

EU' in 1999, did not receive any response from the EU, and the BSEC's invitation in early 2001 to establish an observer status was also rejected.

The reason for the cautious reply might be related to the complexity of the EU's existing set of bilateral relations with BSEC countries:

- Greece, Bulgaria and Romania are EU member states,
- Turkey is engaged in pre-accession negotiations,
- Serbia-Montenegro and Albania are involved in the Stabilization and Association Process (SAP) for the Western Balkans,
- The Ukraine, Moldova, Armenia, Azerbaijan, and Georgia are in the ENP process and signed Action Plans, and
- Russia has a special status of being 'strategic partner,' and signed the Agreement on 'Four Spaces.'

These different types of relations with the EU means 'different operating procedures and programs, legal bases and financial instruments causing exhausting administrative and legal complications.'[53] As Manoli expresses, 'the BSEC-EU relations will always reflect certain aspects of the state of affairs in bilateral relations acounting for a certain degree of diversification.'[54] Therefore, before developing a strategic approach about the EU-BSEC partnership, 'concrete modalities of interaction with the BSEC has to be considered first by the BSEC member states and institutions.'[55]

In a recent Communication on 'stregthening the European Neighborhood Policy,' the Commission considered enhancing regional cooperation as an essential part of the EU's neighborhood policy. In this context, the Black Sea region was mentioned as 'offering a great potential for dialogue and cooperation at the regional level.' Indicating the lack of will for any sort of 'partnership,' the EU sees the role of the Black Sea Economic Cooperation Organization (BSEC) as 'providing a useful platform for our dialogue and cooperation with the region as a whole.' The Commission has also been examining the possibility of establishing closer contacts with the BSEC, including observer status. At most, 'establishment of regular dialogue with the BSEC at Foreign Minister level, which would help implementing and further developing the Union's Black Sea regional policy' was considered as useful. Finally, the Commission announced its intention to further address the question of strengthened Black Sea dialogue in a separate communication in 2007.[56]

In the Communication, emphasis was given to the new cooperation instruments 'both around the Mediterranean and the Black Sea,' such as the 'new cross-border cooperation programs' that are established under the ENPI. The Commission believes in the efficiency of these programs 'offering a real possibility of promoting grass-roots cooperation among local and regional authorities and addressing issues of common concern—such as the environment, transport and communications, maritime safety, the marine environment, regional economic development, tourism, and socio-cultural exchanges' coinciding with the areas on which the BSEC members have already been focusing.

On the BSEC side, after a series of meetings and several modifications with inputs from member states, on January 17, 2007, a document titled 'BSEC-EU Interaction: The BSEC Approach' was endorsed by the Committee of Senior Officials and presented for the consideration of EU institutions during the preparation of the forthcoming European Commission Communication on strengthening the Black Sea dialogue. The message to the EU was the 'establishment of an *open and regular dialogue, development of a balanced, mutually beneficial and result oriented relationship* with the Organization of the BSEC as a representative regional organization in an institutionalized format' (emphasis added). In doing so, it was believed that the implementation of the region-wide projects of mutual interest would be greatly facilitated. With an effort to make the offer more plausible, the BSEC put the emphasis on the more effective use of available programs and funds rendering a new cost-effective and mutually advantageous partnership.[57]

Compared to the current country-by-country arrangements, closer BSEC-EU integration among many sectors could bring an added value, especially if priority is given to development of synergies and implementation of economic and related capacity-building projects in a regional format.[58] The suggested policy fields and sectoral objectives where closer BSEC-EU integration can yield advantages are listed as follows:[59]

- Development of infrastructure, including transport, energy and telecommunications,
- Carrying out trade and economic activities, including cross-border cooperation, especially facilitating favorable conditions for trading and investment,
- Providing environmental protection and sustainable development,
- Cooperating in combat against organized crime and providing emergency assistance,
- Establishing institutional and social sectors, and
- Performing common works in science and technology.

It is also suggested that a variety of legal, policy and financial instruments that are already operating at the bilateral level be tailored for the successful implementation in the region-wide projects. As mentioned above, the ENPI was launched as a main source of EU financing in the Black Sea region, which 'focuses on cross-border issues, promote regional and sub-regional cooperation and sustainable development on the Eastern border.'[60] Besides the cross-border cooperation, which is bilateral in character, the ENPI, as well as the preparation of multi-annual programs for 'single borders or groups of borders,' is also supposed to provide 'more flexible support' for multilateral programs that will be established especially 'over those maritime crossings where distance and other factors do not allow for efficient bilateral cross-border cooperation.' Matters of environment, energy, transport, and telecommunication networks, public health and the fight against crime can be categorized within these programs.[61] Effective use of the ENPI, as a new financial instrument for region-wide projects, would also depend on the nature of cooperation between the BSEC and the EU.

Black Sea Synergy - A New Regional Cooperation Initiative of the EU

The recent Commission Communication titled "Black Sea Synergy-A New Regional Cooperation Initiative" was released on April 11, 2007 and endorsed the need for a Regional Policy in the Black Sea.[62] Besides, completing the chain of regional cooperation framework around the EU, the Black Sea Synergy complements the 'ENP plus' initiative of German Presidency of the EU that aims to strengthen the relations with the Eastern neighbors, namely, the Ukraine, Moldova and Belarus.[63] Emphasizing the coordinated action at regional level on key sectors such as energy, transport, environment, movement, and security, the Black Sea Synergy reveals the EU's intention to be involved more intensely in defining further regional cooperation priorities and mechanisms. However, the BSS also clearly indicated that the regional cooperation is only complementary to already existing bilateral relations and the establishment of new institutional or bureaucratic structures is not considered.

Adding little to the present status of relations between the EU and the BSEC, the Black Sea Synergy just sees the wide membership opportunities of the BSEC, since Russia and Turkey are the founding members, an advantage that may contribute to its own success.[64] EU-BSEC links, including meetings between senior officials who have perspectives of more effectively coordinated concrete projects, are expected to serve primarily *for a dialogue* at the regional level.[65] As a meager step, responding to the BSEC's initiative, the Commission declared its intention to seek observer status and to support EU Member States' application for observer status.[66] Another proposition for the EU-BSEC cooperation is that the Black Sea Synergy can offer new possibilities, including the development of mechanisms for joint financing, benefitting the experience gained from the schemes like the Northern Dimension partnerships.[67]

Conclusion

Although the BSEC repeatedly expressed political will to cooperate with the EU institutions on a regular basis, the EU had shown little interest in the Black Sea as a region and in dealing with the Organization of the Black Sea Economic Cooperation (BSEC) as a regional partner. Given the increasing importance to the Black Sea as a strategic neighborhood area and assuming the role of a new regional player, the EU now decided it cannot ignore the region any further. Struggling with the problems of post-enlargement adjustment and internal consitutional dispute, the EU could not allocate adequate energy to the region. EU policies toward the region such as further enlargement, ENP and 'common spaces' with Russia are necessary, but not sufficient, in dealing with the challenges and opportunities posed by the Black Sea as a strategic neighborhood. In terms of enhancing relations between the EU and the BSEC, the latest Commission document on Black Sea Synergy has flattened the expectations in terms of offering new possibilities for more comprehensive and concrete cooperation between the EU and the BSEC.

Although the need for a fresh look on the potential benefits of an elevated role for the EU in the Black Sea regional cooperation was acknowledged by the Commission, the opportunity for the achievement of strengthened Black Sea dialogue with the BSEC has still not been achieved. As the recent Black Sea Synergy proves, the ongoing tendency within the EU is to keep the relationship with the BSEC at a minimum level without disrupting the diversified nature of the bilateral relations with the countries in the region. Although, at present, this approach might seem the most convenient, given the proximity and the strategic importance of the region and the urgency of the matters to be addressed, it is wiser for the EU to seek a multilateral framework for coordination and establish a comprehensive partnership with the Organization of BSEC. Since Turkey and Russia, as the founding members of the BSEC, are more prone to use the BSEC framework for cooperation, especially in energy and security matters, it is more profitable for the EU to seek cooperation under the BSEC framework for region-wide projects and provide financial and institutional support for the implementation of these projects.

---

[1] According to the official website of the European Commission (http://ec.europa.eu/enlargement/index_en.htm), the signature of the Accession Treaty of Romania and Bulgaria *"marks the completion of the fifth enlargement of the EU"*. Consequently, the enlargement in 2004 was only the first part of the *Fifth Enlargement*. Also, recently Elmar Brok, a German member of the European Parliament and the chairman of the EP Committee on Foreign Affairs, added "We do not think that Croatia is a part of the future wave of the (European Union) enlargement. Croatia is the last part of the ongoing process of the enlargement according to the formula 10 plus two plus one."
http://www.vlada.hr/default.asp?gl=200608250000011
[2] Benito Ferrero-Waldner, "The European Neighborhood Policy: The EU's Newest Foreign Policy Instrument," *European Foreign Affairs Review* 11, (2006): p. 139.
[3] As mentioned by Asmus and Jackson there is also a greater Black Sea system infiltrating into East and Central Europe even deeper into Germany, through great commercial rivers that flow into the Black Sea: the Danube, Dniester, and the Dnieper. Ronald D. Asmus and Bruce P. Jackson, "The Black Sea and Frontiers of

Freedom," in *A New Euro-Atlantic Strategy for the Black Sea Region*, eds. Ronald D. Asmus, Konstantin Dimitrov and Joerg Forbrig (Washington D.C.: German Marshall Fund, 2004), pp. 19-20.
[4] Charles King, "The New Near East," *Survival* 43, no. 2, (2001).
[5] Eugene. B. Rumer and Jeffrey Simon, *Toward a Euro-Atlantic Strategy for the Black Sea Region*, Institute for National Strategic Studies, *Occasional Paper* 2, (Washington D.C.: National Defense University Press, April 2006).
[6] Michael Emerson and Marius Vahl, "Europe's Black Sea Dimension- Model European Nationalism, Prét-a-Porter," in *Europe's Black Sea Dimension*, eds. Terry Adams, Michael Emerson, Laurence Mee and Marius Vahl (Brussels: Centre for European Policy Studies (CEPS) and Athens: International Center for Black Sea Studies (ICBSS), 2002), pp. 15-16)
[7] Marius Vahl, *The EU and the Black Sea Regional Cooperation: Some Challenges for BSEC* (Brussels: CEPS, 15 April 2005).
[8] Ronald D. Asmus and Bruce P. Jackson, "The Black Sea and Frontiers of Freedom," in *A New Euro-Atlantic Strategy for the Black Sea Region*, eds. Ronald D. Asmus, Konstantin Dimitrov and Joerg Forbrig (Washington D.C.: German Marshall Fund, 2004), p. 18
[9] The term is used by Asmus and Jackson, Ibid.
[10] Ibid., p. 21.
[11] European Council, *A Secure Europe in a Better World: European Security Strategy* (Brussels 2003).
[12] Ibid., pp. 3-5.
[13] Ibid., pp. 5, 10.
[14] Ibid., p, 7.
[15] Ibid., p. 11.
[16] Sven Biscop "The European Security Strategy and the Neighborhood Policy: A New Starting Point for A Europe-Mediterranean Security Partnership," in *European Neighborhood Policy: Political, Economic and Social Issues*, ed. F. Attina amd R. Rossi (Catania: Centro Jean Monnet "Euro-Med," 2004), p. 25.
[17] Ibid., pp. 25-6.
[18] Ronald Dannreuther, "Developing Alternatives to Enlargement: The European Neighborhood Policy," *European Foreign Affairs Review* 11, (2006): p. 184.
[19] PCAs are legal frameworks, based on the respect of democratic principles and human rights, setting out the political, economic and trade relationship between the EU and its partner countries. Each PCA is a ten-year bilateral treaty signed and ratified by the EU and the each individual state. For detailed account of PCAs, see http://ec.europa.eu/comm/external_relations/ceeca/pca/index.htm
[20] Dov Lynch, "The Security Dimension of the European Neighborhood Policy," *The International Spectator* 1, (2005): p. 34.
[21] Ibid.
[22] The concepts of exclusiveness and inclusiveness is explained in Charlotte Bretherton and John Vogler, *The European Union as a Global Actor*, (London and New York: Routledge, 2006), pp. 56-59.
[23] Bjorn Moller, *The EU as a Security Actor, Security by Doing and Security by Being*, DISS Report 12, 2005.

24 Hans W. Maull, "Europe and New Balance of Global Order," *International Affairs* 81, no. 4, (2005): pp. 778-779.
25 Marius Vahl and Sergiu Celac, "Ready for a Breakthrough: Elements for a European Union Strategy Towards the Black Sea Region," *South East European and Black Sea Studies* 6, no. 2, (2006): p. 170.
26 Ibid., pp. 181-184.
27 Karen E. Smith, "The Outsiders: The European Neighborhood Policy," *International Affairs* 81, no. 4, (2005): p. 762.
28 From the very beginning, Russia made it clear that it preferred to develop a strategic partnership and to be recognized as equal, not restrained by what is offered to itself by the EU alongside very diverse countries extending from Moldova to Morocco.
29 Michael Leigh, "The EU's Neighborhood Policy," in *The Strategic Implications of European Union Enlargement*, ed. Esther Brimmer and Stefan Fröhlich (Washington D.C.: Center for Transatlantic Relations, Johns Hopkins University), pp. 101-125.
30 Ferrero-Waldner, "The European Neighborhood Policy," p. 140.
31 In December 2004, it was announced that the Commission would seek a budget of 14.9 billion euros for the ENPI for the period between 2007 and 2013 which would represent a significant increase from the 8.5 billion euros allocated to TACIS and MEDA from 2000-2006. This amount includes the funds also allocated to Russia.
32 Dannreuther, "Developing Alternatives to Enlargement," p. 191.
33 Smith, "The Outsiders," pp. 764-765.
34 For issues of consistency and coherence in the EU, see Bretherton and Vogler, *The European Union as a Global Actor*, pp. 174-178.
35 Roberto Aliboni, "The Geopolitical Implications of the European Neighborhood Strategy, *European Foreign Affairs Review* 10, (2005): pp. 3-11.
36 The exception is the Israel's action plan reflecting a more equal partnership document.
37 Judy Batt, *The EU's New Borderlands*, CER *Working Paper* (London: Center for European Reform, October 2003).
38 See Communication from the Commission, 'European Neighborhood Policy' *Strategy Paper*, COM (2004) 373 Final, Brussels, 12.5.2004.
39 http://ec.europa.eu/world/enp
40 Simon Duke, "Areas of Gray: Tensions in EU External Relations Competences," EIPAScope 1, (2006).
41 Bretherton and Vogler, *The European Union as a Global Actor*, p. 176.
42 Ibid., pp. 176-177.
43 The idea of creation of a 'Black Sea Coopeation' originally belongs to a Turkish Ambassador (retired) Sükrü Elekdag. See, Sukru Elekdag, 'Karadeniz Isbirligi ve Refah Bolgesi (Karadeniz Cooperation and Prosperity Region), *Cumhuriyet*, 20 February 1990.
44 http://www.bsec-organization.org
45 The BSEC Charter sees the priority areas as trade and economic development, banking and finance, communications, energy, transport, agriculture and agro-industry, health care and pharmaceuticals, environmental protection, tourism, science and technology, exchange of statistical data and economic information,

collaboration between customs and other border authorities, human contacts, combating organized crime, illicit trafficking of drugs, weapons and radioactive materials, all acts of terrorism and illegal migration (BSEC Charter). The intention to create a 'free trade zone' among the BSEC members was proved impossible due to pre-existing obligations of some member states in other organizations (for example the commitment of EU member states to the single market).

[46] Mustafa Aydin, *Europe's next shore: The Black Sea Region after EU enlargement*, Occasional Paper 53, (Paris: Institute for Security Studies, June 2004), p. 23.

[47] Working Groups are subsidiary organs and are established according to the priority areas mentioned in the Charter (see above Footnote). By the end of 2006, there were 17 permanent Working Groups with responsibilities in agriculture and agro industry, banking and finance, combating crime and terrorism, cultural affairs, education, emergency assistance, energy, environment, exchange of statistical data and economic information, health care and pharmaceutics, information and communication technologies, institutional renewal and good governance, science and technology, small and medium enterprises, tourism, trade and economic development and transport.

[48] Vahl and Celac, "Ready for a Breakthrough," pp. 174-175. Further action is expected in areas such as education and culture, environment, information and communication technologies, institutional renewal and good governance, science and technology, tourism.

[49] See *BSEC-EU Interaction: the BSEC Approach*, BSEC Document, 17 January 2007, pp. 5-6.

[50] L. Chrysanthopoulos, *BSEC: 14 Years of Regional Cooperation*, Statement at the ICBSS Annual Conference "The Black Sea Region: Quo Vadis? Rhodes, 7-8 July 2006.

[51] Commission of the European Communities, *Communication from the Commission to the Council: Regional Cooperation in the Black Sea Area: State of Play, Perspectives for EU Action Encouraging Its Development*, Brussels, COM(97) 597 final, 14 November 1997.

[52] Commission of the European Communities, *Communication from the Commission to the Council: Agenda 2000: For a Stronger and Wider Union*, Brussels, COM(97) 659 final, December 1997.

[53] Emerson and Vahl, "Europe's Black Sea Dimension," pp. 19-20.

[54] Panayota Manoli, 'Bringing the Black Sea Economic Cooperation and the European Union Closer,' Editorial, *Southeast European and Black Sea Studies* 5, no. 2 (2005), pp. 168.

[55] Ibid.

[56] Commission of the European Communities, *Communication from the Commission to the Council and the European Parliament, on Strengthening the European Neighborhood Policy*, Brussels, COM(2006) 726 final, 4 December 2006.

[57] *BSEC-EU Interaction: the BSEC Approach*, p. 3.

[58] *BSEC-EU Interaction: the BSEC Approach*, p. 8.

[59] *BSEC-EU Interaction: the BSEC Approach*, pp. 8-11.

[60] Communication from the Commission, *'European Neighborhood Policy' Strategy Paper*, COM (2004) 373 Final, Brussels, 12.5.2004, p. 14, 18, 25-26.

[61] Ibid., p. 27.

[62] Commission of the European Communities, *Communication from the Commission to the Council and the European Parliament, on Black Sea Synergy-A New Regional Cooperation Initiative*, Brussels, COM(2007) 160 final, 11 April 2007.
[63] For the ENP Plus initiative of the German Presidency see Franz-Walter Steinmeier, 'Interaction and Integration-A New Phase of Ostpolitik: globalization demands interaction, not isolationism', *Internationale Politik*, Spring 2007, DGAP, Berlin.
[64] Commission Communication, *on Black Sea Synergy-A New Regional Cooperation Initiative*, p. 9.
[65] Ibid.
[66] Ibid., At present seven EU member states (The Czech Republic, Germany, France, Italy, Austria, Poland and Slovakia) have observer status with the BSEC.
[67] Ibid., p. 10.

Chapter 13
EU Security Involvement in the Greater Black Sea Area: A Romanian Perspective

Cristina Romila[*]

The Greater Black Sea Area (GBSA) and the evolution of its regional security environment, after the end of the Cold War, became only recently an independent topic of research. The GBSA concept was launched in a study titled "The Black Sea and the Frontiers of Freedom,"[1] which was written by the American researchers Ronald D. Asmus and Bruce P. Jackson who are inspired by similar concepts like the Greater Middle East. It refers to several countries that are considered to belong to different geographical areas: Armenia, Azerbaijan, Bulgaria, Georgia, Moldova, Romania, Russia, the Ukraine, and Turkey.

The GBSA highlights a complex regional security environment mainly characterized by the important geostrategic position of certain states for the transit of oil and natural gas from Caucasus and Central Asia to Europe. While the countries of the region exhibit differences in their relations with the EU, NATO and U.S., encompassing membership in NATO, integration into the EU, as well as skepticism concerning close relations with the U.S. and Russia; they also have some similar characteristics like the persistency of "frozen conflicts," local separatism, active networks of terrorism, transnational organized crime, illegal migration, smuggling, proliferation of weapons of mass destruction, incipient democratization and modernization, weak governance, and environmental threats.

The European Community has been present in the region ever since the demise of the Soviet Union. Following the terrorist attacks of September 11, the geopolitical and geostrategic role of the GBSA was reconsidered by the EU under the issues of combat against terrorism and the subsequent evolution of the Greater Middle East and Iraq. All of the above mentioned security aspects, alongside the integration of Romania and Bulgaria into the EU, turned the GBSA into the EU's Eastern frontier necessitating the EU to define a strategy for the region. The EU already took a significant step in this direction in April 2007 when the EC presented the communication, "Black Sea Synergy - A New Regional Cooperation Initiative."[2]

Relying on a larger concept of security, the present study represents an effort to identify counter-arguments to the possible impediments about defining an EU strategy for the GBSA in order to prove that such an endeavor is not only necessary, but also feasible.

EU's Current Stage of Involvement in the GBSA-A General Perspective

The demise of the USSR brought about a security vacuum in the GBSA that international actors such as the EU, NATO and the U.S. assumed the responsibility to deal with. The EC has been present in the region since the beginning of the 90s when it developed the TACIS program.

The EU has acted through significant financial support to promote stabilization and boost regional democratization and development. Therefore, the EU's involvement refers to stimulating economic security and political dialogue within the framework of the Common Foreign Security Policy, (CFSP) rather than within the European Security and Defense Policy (ESDP). However, the new unconventional risks and threats, that are surfaced in the new security environment after the end of the Cold War, became new challenging matters for EU security. Currently, the EU member states work closely with GBSA countries on implementing programs mainly related to border security and combating organized crime.

Within the framework of the CFSP and also the EU's first pillar, the EU's institutionalized involvement in the GBSA is based on both a bilateral approach that involves establishment of relations with each of the states in the region and, to a much more limited extent, on a regional cooperation (EU initiated TACIS: Technical Assistance to the Community of Independent States, TRACECA: Transport Corridor Europe-Caucasus-Asia, INOGATE: Interstate Oil and Gas Transport to Europe, and established relations with BSEC). Within the framework of ESDP, the EU developed two civilian operations: a border assistance mission at the frontier between Moldova and the Ukraine and a law enforcement mission in Georgia both of which will be briefly presented below.

The EU mainly defines its actions in the Black Sea region within the framework of the European Neighborhood Policy (ENP) that was launched in 2003-2004 and is designed to promote peace, stability, economic prosperity, and democracy in the neighboring areas. The EU, in its relations with each of the ENP countries, including those in the GBSA (Armenia, Azerbaijan, Belarus, Georgia, Moldova, and the Ukraine), set several instruments of cooperation and assistance, such as "common strategies," partnership and cooperation agreements (PCA), the TACIS Program, and, most recently, the ENP Instrument.

The TACIS program, initiated in 1991, within the context of the demise of the Soviet Union, aims to provide financial and technical assistance to the ex-Soviet space and also to encourage the rapprochement of the ex-Soviet countries to the EU. One of its most important achievements was the development of INOGATE, connecting the CIS (Community of Independent States) to Europe in the field of energy. Since 1991, the EU assistance under TACIS to the former USSR member states[3] amounts to about 500 million euros per year[4].

TRACECA was established in 1993 to address problems and deficiencies seen in trade and transport systems of the region. It also aims to provide assistance[5] for political and economic sustainability of the member states[6] by attracting loans from international financial institutions and private investors, and promoting integration with Trans-European Networks.

The EU also developed bilateral relations with BSEC which are amplified by the proximity of the memberships of Romania and Bulgaria into the EU. Moreover, BSEC carried out several initiatives in the areas of high interest for the EU, such as visa facilitation, transport and communication networks, and fighting against organized crime.

Finally, within the framework of ESDP, the first operation undertaken by the EU in the GBSA was EUJUST Themis (July 2004 – June 2005), which provided assistance to Georgian authorities for the judiciary sector reform. The border assistance mission for Moldova and the Ukraine (initiated on December 1, 2005), which aims to boost cooperation between the two states in the field of border security on the Transnistrian sector, was the second operation performed by the EU.

In conclusion, one can note that the current involvement of the EU in the GBSA mainly refers to the following issues: using tools of economic security such as aids and development programs; settling political dialogue with each of the states in the region; supporting the democratization process, particularly through economic means and by providing assistance to the process of reform in the judiciary field; supporting national authorities for increased efficiency in the field of border security and combating organized crime. It mainly addresses modernization problems perceived as threats to the security of the states in the region. As a matter of fact, the communication rendered by the *Black Sea Synergy* identifies several cooperative objectives the EU should promote for the states in the region, such as establishing a strong democracy and good governance, addressing migration issues, dealing with frozen conflicts, providing energy security, solving environmental problems, transport networks, trade and maritime issues, promoting research works, education, and regional development.

Impediments to an EU Security Strategy for the GBSA

According to the general view, there are several factors that could impede the defining of an EU security strategy for the GBSA, which include:

1) The Russian factor and the EU's increased energy dependency on Russia. It can be argued that it should not be considered an insurmountable impediment; rather it could be perceived within the framework of cooperative relations that are advantageous for both partners. Moreover,

later in the study, we will point out that the EU has alternatives to this situation.

2) The Turkish factor and the EU's slow pace toward integrating Turkey. This paper assesses that, on the contrary to the fears of some circles within the EU, the Turkish factor should boost a regional strategy that will be defined by the EU, due to some significant geostrategic and geopolitical reasons as follows: Turkey has a geostrategic position which gives it an important role in the transport of oil and natural gas from the Caspian region to Europe that bypasses Russia; Turkey's geopolitical proximity to the Middle East that will be the EU's direct neighbor once the GBSA becomes the EU's Eastern frontier, is the other main reason necessitating Turkey's integration.

3) The EU's reluctance in being a more assertive actor in resolving "frozen conflicts."

4) The heterogeneity of political, economic and security profiles of the GBSA's states. Despite this fact, however, most of them face similar problems like inferior levels of modernization, political and economical instability etc."

5) EU member states' favoring their national foreign and security agendas to the detriment of the CFSP. In this study, we consider that the lack of political will and unitary vision constitute an important impediment in defining an EU strategy for the GBSA.

This study focuses on analyzing three of the above mentioned impediments from a policy-oriented perspective: the Russian factor and the energy dependency, the Turkish factor, and EU reluctance to increase its level of involvement in the resolution process of "frozen conflicts."

The Russian Factor and the Energy Issue

Russia and the EU signed a Partnership and Cooperation Agreement that came into force in 1997, and embarked on an ambitious multi-leveled process of cooperation and political dialogue. According to this Agreement, the EU-Russia relations were planned to evolve in the creation of four common spaces:[7] a common economic space; a common space of freedom, security and justice; cooperation in the field of external security; and a space of research and education. Since 1991, the EU allocated to Russia more than 2.6 billion euros under the TACIS program, to promote its transition to a market economy and reinforce democracy and the rule of law. However, Russia refused to participate in the EU's ENP, stressing that relations should be considered within the framework of a strategic partnership and Russia should be treated as a strategic partner.[8]

Due to the increased concerns over internal problems, partnership relations had secondary priority both for Russia and the EU's foreign policies. The war in Chechnya and the domestic modernization process were at the core of Russia's preoccupations, while the EU, on the other hand, expanded to ten other countries along with simultaneous internal integration reforms. This situation changed when the Ukrainian-Russian gas dispute brought Russian energy policy to the attention of European public opinion and policymakers.

The EU still carries serious interests in cooperating with Russia in terms of economic security (the energy issue[9]) as well as taking its geographical proximity into consideration. With its oil production of 9.3 million barrels a day and natural gas production of 1.6 billion barrels a day, Russia is the most important oil and natural gas supplier of the G8 countries.[10] It also has the biggest natural gas reserve in the world.[11]

Roughly 35 percent of Europe's natural gas supplies and oil imports are from Russia. The energy dependency on Russia is estimated to reach 70 percent by 2020.[12] Currently, France, Germany, and Italy's dependency on Gazprom gas supplies have reached about 30 percent, while that of the new EU members of Central and Eastern Europe have increased to more than 90 percent. At the same time, alternative energy resources (solar, wind, hydropower, and geothermal power) will not likely solve this problem in the short- or medium-term, since they cover only 6 percent of the EU's energy consumption.[13].

Considering Russia has strong geostrategic arguments in the region in which to be involved, under the fact of the above data, one wonders to what extent the EU can get involved in the GBSA in order for relations with Russia not to be affected. Still being influential in the former Soviet space,[14] its interests regarding the energy sources in the Caspian region and transportation of the natural resources of the Caspian region to Europe can be listed among the most obvious arguments of Russia.

Complex Relations Between the EU, Russia and GBSA States

The relations of the states in the Black Sea region with the EU are complex and complicated in regard to both the EU's tools of action, and the states' objectives of foreign and security policies. As presented in the first chapter, the ENP remains to be the EU's main tool of action.

The ENP may be considered[15] quite risky because of its ambiguity that encourages false expectations of membership[16] and its unilateralist approach according to which the EU sets the conditions for the relations with neighbors. Consequently, it promotes a binding way of action without offering in exchange a specific motivation, such as the perspective of integration into the EU.

Although this overview may look pessimistic, we must accept that, due to their previous integration and dependency upon the USSR, the promising objectives offered by the ENP, like the eventual economic integration of these states in the Single Market, are too ambitious to be reached by these states. In a longer-term, these attempts can also be perceived as challenges against Russia's interests. Despite these acts being based on a bilateral form, the ENP, nevertheless, provides a holistic approach to the region by clearly addressing the problems and using the right instruments.

Referring to the ENP framework and existing instruments of cooperation with countries in the region, the EC's communication on the *Black Sea Synergy* of April 2007 supports a balanced regional approach to the problems affecting this region in which a comprehensive perspective of actions is defined. The communication of the EC—*A Strong European Neighborhood Policy*—highlights the conceptual principles of the ENP, which are: differentiation (bilateral relations, but holistic approach), ownership (the partner countries are supposed to "co-determine their path in the ENP"), and regional processes (the bilateral relations do not impede that the ENP interlinks with regional cooperation arrangements). The document also refers to the EU's measures of paving ways toward further economic integration of ENP countries, increasing their mobility and ability to deal with regional conflicts, realizing sector reform and modernization, participating with their partner countries in community programs and agencies, and establishing financial cooperation.[17]

Meanwhile, intense efforts are being spent to find a convenient formula for the states in the region who are in a predicament of rapproaching the EU and, at the same time, maintaining good relations with Russia. Countries in the region are participating in several regional cooperation arrangements, some of which are initiated by Russia (Commonwealth of Independent States – CIS), some subsequent initiatives within the CIS (the Treaty on Collective Security), some of them align themselves to the plans of building a single economic space while others establish alliances with the implicit purpose of counterbalancing Russia (GUAM, Georgia and the Ukraine's initiative of an "alliance of democracies").

In recent years, relations with Russia have been firmly and publicly questioned. In May 2006, a regional tendency of distancing from Moscow had surfaced, when intentions of leaving the CIS were publicly announced in Georgia, the Ukraine and Moldova. However, the Moldovan Parliament rejected this option and it is unlikely for the Ukraine to take such a radical step in its relations with Russia[18]..

All these issues are to be taken into consideration by the EU when defining a security strategy for the GBSA.

The facts presented above demonstrate that both Russia and the EU have pragmatic reasons and also opportunities that could favor cooperation, rather than competition, in the GBSA. EU relations with Russia in the GBSA could develop into a partnership based on equality[19] that would practically translate into the so-called "joint management of overlapping near – abroads."[20] It is aimed to prevent Russia to perceive the ENP and the EU's actions in the region as motivated by intrusive reasons. "[A] policy that essentially cedes the Black Sea to Russian influence[21]" would be harmful for Russia itself and would not render an advantage for anybody, since it is likely to retard the democratization of Russia. On the contrary, Russia should be encouraged to "shed its age-old zero-sum approach to geopolitics[22]," since its interests in the region could be better achieved through a secure and stable neighborhood.

This scenario seems to be supported by some voices from the EU, too. Andris Piebalgs, the European energy commissioner, stressed that the Energy Policy for Europe (EPE) should rely on the foreign policy objective of exporting the European market economy values to Russia and the Middle East: "A market economy is not imaginable without democracy, without human rights or without freedom of expression (…)[23]."

However, in the longer-term, the EU's growing role of being a prominent regional actor may direct Russia to increasingly use the EU's energy dependency as a foreign policy instrument. Besides, as a reflection of Russia's energy policy toward countries in the region, we know that Gazprom stated it intends to re-direct its gas supplies from the EU to North America or even China, while Transneft hinted to do the same with crude oil by building the Eastern Siberia-Pacific Ocean pipeline.[24]

One can also note that Russia's strategy of offereng alternatives to the transportation routes that certain countries in the region plan to build with EU support is also part of this policy. For example, the Russian initiative *South Stream* strongly competes with the Nabucco pipeline project. Moreover, by agreement with Central Asian countries rich in natural resources, Russia plans to reinvigorate the *Central Asia Center*, a Soviet inherited system evaluating ways to boost gas exports from Turkmenistan to Russia via Kazakhstan, which would strengthen Russia's position in the Caspian-Black Sea region.

In order to prevent the monopoly on the European energy market and, implicitly, Russia's increased influence in this respect, the EC issued a document that contains a series of proposals, most important of which is that a single company cannot simultaneously extract, control the production, and distribute gas. It is even stated that "by bringing national markets together, the Commission foresees more potential for member states to assist one another in the face of energy supply threats."[25]

Despite the realistic concerns regarding this perspective, one can argue that the Russian factor can also be understood within the framework of cooperation advantageous to both partners.

Besides, being a technology know-how provider, the EU has become a customer that would be difficult to replace in the longer run. Therefore, one can assess that public statements of Russian companies claiming to redirect their market interests toward the East are not a solution for Russia in the short- or medium-terms, also because of the oil production and transport capacity of this area are still limited.

The Turkish Factor and the Issue of Finding Alternatives to the EU's Energy Dependency on Russia

The EU energy paper, "An external policy to serve Europe's energy interests," stresses the need for the EU to support the building of pipelines bypassing Russia, although it continues to be considered a major energy partner. The development of oil pipelines from the Caspian region and Central Asia via Turkey to the EU should constitute a priority for the EU.[26]

The Caspian region could represent an energy alternative for the EU and, in this case, the Black Sea region would become a highly important geostrategic area for the transport of oil and natural gas.[27] Currently, the pipelines transporting oil from the Caspian Sea do not directly reach the Western countries, but they pass through Russia.[28] Therefore, the Black Sea region provides an alternative oil transportation route[29] that will bypass Russia.

It is estimated that in 2015, a total of 150 million tons of oil from the Caspian Sea region will be transported through the Black Sea, and 90 million tons of this quantity will be carried by ships to Romania and Bulgaria from where they will take the route to Western countries through pipelines.[30] From this perspective, Turkey's strategic position will become increasingly important for Europe.

However, Turkey is generally perceived as a regional actor that would not easily accept a change in the regional status-quo by admitting the presence of several international actors such as the EU and NATO, along with the subsequent promotion of closer relations with Russia. Russia being her second-largest trading partner, Turkey carries interests in cooperating with Russia at various levels, the most important of which is keeping the Montreux Convention of 1936 in force[31] and enhancing mutual economic relations.

Moreover, since Russia obviously plans to be the main supplier of Caspian gas to the EU, a new pipeline should be built to transit Azerbaijan, Georgia and Turkey. It could eventually boost the evolution of Russia-Turkey relations into an influential regional partnership both in the region and in Europe.

One should keep in mind that the EU taking advantage of Turkey's geostrategic position seems politically dependent on speeding up Turkey's integration. EU relations with Turkey have, at times, been stressed, and negotiations are not expected to conclude soon. Turkey is also highly concerned that the EU might favor the membership aspirations of the Ukraine and Moldova, the two ENP countries, and therefore, its integration may become an even more remote perspective. As strengthening its relations with Turkey is a long-term interest of the EU, Turkey should be reassured about her membership and she must be prevented from distancing herself from the Euro-Atlantic community.[32]

The EU's Role Within the Framework of International Efforts to Deal With "Frozen Conflicts"

One of the main conventional threats to the GBSA's security is the persistence of the so-called "frozen conflicts" in Abkhazia and South Ossetia, Nagorno-Karabakh, and Transnistria. All are ethno-territorially motivated, affect inter-state relations in the region and have a trans-border impact with a significant risk of propagation. International efforts to solve these conflicts are seen insufficient and ineffective in terms of both means and political will of getting involved. The difficulties in dealing with these problems are listed as follows: Unwillingness of each participant in the conflicts to support and apply the proposed solutions; radical nature of their requests, which make negotiations difficult or even impossible; in the case of the EU, procedural difficulties of implementing actions that support the democratization process which is a tool of the EU's foreign policy[33]; involvement of third parts in the conflicts, as it is the case with Russia; and last, but not least, inefficient reactions of the international community due to a mixture of lack of interest, political will and reticence in dealing with Russia.

A recent report of the International Crisis Group[34] shows that the EU's contribution to crisis resolution in the South Caucasus region has been insignificant. It has not directly participated in negotiations over conflict areas, neither focused on the political and security dimensions of the resolution process, but has so far preferred acting all around the conflicts. The EC's communication on the *Black Sea Synergy* confirms this point of view. Similarly, the more recent EC's communication, *A Strong European Neighborhood Policy,* underlines that "the EU can make an important contribution by working around the conflict issues, promoting similar reforms on both sides of the boundary lines, to foster convergence between political, economic and legal systems, enabling greater social inclusion and contributing to confidence building."[35]

Although it has the most interest from the Europe due to its geographical proximity to the future EU Eastern frontier, until recently, the Transnistrian conflict seems to have been brushed aside. The EU involvement highlights the following characteristics and ways of action: supporting OSCE's plans of conflict resolution; setting of a border assistance mission at the Moldavian-Ukrainian frontier; appointment of a Special Representative that participates as an observer to the negotiations process according to the Yushcenko plan; preparing a thesis of a regional democratization as a solution to the conflict; and perceiving that the settlement of the conflict depends on all participants who are in close cooperation with Russia.

These facts exemplify that a dual action is being carried out on behalf of the EU. On one hand, the initiatives developed until now hint that the EU is willing to effectively engage in conflict solving process. On the other hand, when the EU initiatives such as the border assistance mission are examined closely, it can be seen that, despite some recent European declarations criticizing Russia's partisan approach that supports the Transnistrian side, it has no intention of directly acting in the resolution of the conflict apart from preventing the spread of unconventional risks from the East to the West, such as organized crime, smuggling, etc.

However, the discourse of certain European institutions is now changing. As a case in point, on July 10, 2007, the European Parliament issued a resolution that underlines "the EU's firm commitment to the territorial integrity of Moldova," and the implementation of the Istanbul OSCE Summit declaration of 1999. It also "calls for greater involvement of the EU in solving this conflict (…), including the enhancement of the EU's status to that of a negotiating partner."

One can assume that the EU has been highly reluctant to address the Transnistrian issue, for fear of challenging Russia. However, one should also take into account that, besides the energy dependency and the general relations that might be lying behind the EU's attitude, there is also the fact that the Russian minority is the largest in the EU (6 million people),[36] which means a substantial Russian penetration occured into the EU through a large Russian speaking population.

A general assessment of the presented facts leads us to conclude that the EU has been highly reluctant in get directly involved in the resolution process of the GBSA's "frozen conflicts." This may be explained by two main factors: the lack of capabilities adaptable to the profile of each conflict and the lack of political will and strategic motivation.

The ENP's instruments and programs implemented in the embattled areas have not been adequate for a serious EU engagement. Without a more assertive attitude toward the parties involved, particularly directed at Russia's questionable actions, EU involvement will continue to be considered inefficient. This may lead to a loss of credibility in the GBSA countries affected by conflicts, thus delaying the entire democratization process.

A Romanian Perspective on the GBSA and the EU Involvement in This Region: Analytical Comments

Considering the modernization progress it recorded so far, Romania reconsidered its objectives of foreign and security policies toward an enhanced engagement in the GBSA and the Balkan region and has, so far, acted as a regional security provider.

Romania defines the GBSA as a bridge between Central Asia, the Middle East and Europe. It also established close relations with the Caucasus region which was referred to as the Black Sea-Caucasus region by the Romanian President.[37]

Romania's policy regarding the GBSA can be considered under the following components: supporting an enhanced regional cooperation; focusing on a broader agenda of regional cooperation (political, economic, NGOs network, academic, military, environmental etc.); building regional cooperation on existing regional arrangements and, where necessary, building new ones; supporting the internationalization of the Black Sea by considering the involvement of outside actors in the region, such as NATO, EU and the U.S., as essential for the stabilization of the region; revising certain agreements, like the Montreux Convention; preventing the rising of a regional leader; and engaging Russia in the regional cooperation arrangements.

Romania's actions aim to enhance regional confidence-building, promoting stability and spreading the democratization process and good governance to the entire region through direct cooperation with democratic international actors. The project of the new Romanian security strategy of April 2006[38] stresses the importance of acting on the basis of these principles.

They were defined by taking into account two scenarios referring to possible evolutions in the region. The first involves maintaining the current status quo, with exclusive responsibility resting upon the regional actors in dealing with their problems (the "regional ownership" view). The other alternative is internationalization of the GBSA, which stresses the need for having the EU, NATO and the U.S. to be involved also in security matters and defining a Euro-Atlantic strategy for the GBSA.

Romania intends to act according to the second perception on the future of the region and remains committed to boosting regional stability and thereby, closely cooperating with regional organizations and arrangements. Romania also ambitiously initiated new arrangements such as the *Black Sea Forum on Partnership and Dialogue*,[39] which brings together regional experts, decision-makers, civil society representatives, businessmen, and representatives of international and Euro-Atlantic institutions in order to create a regional network aimed to improve regional communication. Within this framework, the *Black Sea Fund* was created in September 2006. It is also worth mentioning that in March 2006, during the Romanian Presidency of the Council of Europe Ministerial Committee, the *Black Sea Euro-region* initiative was launched.

Romania has lobbied for an EU regional approach toward the states in the GBSA arguing that, through Romania's and Bulgaria's integration, the Black Sea became the Eastern frontier of Europe. It would inevitably engage the EU, both in terms of dealing with regional threats and taking advantage of regional benefits, particularly of alternative energy transportation routes.

From this point of view, the EU should engage in close connection with the NATO and avoid duplication. It can use existing arrangements and also participate in regional security arrangements. Romania's security strategy project specifies that international actors, including the NATO and the EU, who have interests in the region, should benefit from an equal treatment.

It is well known that the EU's contribution in dealing with unconventional threats has been substantial. However, it could be eventually linked to GBSA's arrangements such as the *Black Sea border security initiative*.[40] The EU's contributions should be extended to address the conventional ones, too, and become a direct party to negotiations for solving the "frozen conflicts" in cooperation with NATO and OSCE.[41] The need for addressing the "frozen conflicts" together with outside actors has been one of the core elements of Romania's regional policy. President Basescu named them "black holes," pointing to the threats they pose to Europe's security "because of proliferation of organized crime, human trafficking and weapon smuggling, as well as increasing threat of international terrorism."[42]

When defining its security strategy, Romania followed the principles and risk assessment values of the EU. In accordance with this, terrorism, proliferation of WMD, regional conflicts and organized crime are considered the highest threats and risks to national and regional security.

A Euro-Atlantic strategy for the GBSA is regarded as a solution to the above mentioned threats and risks. Experiences gained by the NATO and the EU within the framework of their concerted approach to the Balkans region will obviously be very useful in this initiative. We must, however, note that it is critical for all the states in the region to be encouraged to participate in this initiative and the EU, NATO and the U.S. should have a sincere and decisive commitment to the regional process of stabilization.[43]

It is also important to underline that Romania does not intend to acquire any status of a regional leadership in its attempts. By boosting regional cooperation and dialogue, Romania aims to bring the region closer to the Euro-Atlantic community's system of values and to overcome the perceptions and ways of action that are reminiscent of the Cold War.

Arguments in Favor of an EU Security Strategy for the GBSA: Conclusions and Recommendations

"…with the expected membership of Bulgaria and Romania, and eventually Turkey, the EU will truly become a Black Sea power, accounting for half of its coastline, and all the non-EU Black Sea countries will border at least one EU member state."[44] The EU has strong reasons to define a security strategy for the GBSA. Most importantly, to the ever increasing dependency and Russia's exploitation of this need, the energy issue should certainly trigger the EU to undertake such an endeavor. Secondly, it is the urgent objective to deal with trans-border unconventional threats that have become a menace to each of the EU's members. Thirdly, although the EU has been reluctant to participate in the "frozen conflicts" resolution process, these disputes, because of the spread of unconventional threats such as proliferation and organized crime, are perceived as problems affecting not only the parties involved, but the entire European security. It is widely accepted that, after Romania and Bulgaria joined the EU in January 2007 and Turkey's eventual integration was taken into the enlargement program, the GBSA became the EU's eastern frontier, closer to the Middle East, and close also to all of its problems.

There are two main scenarios to be considered in the event a decision is taken in this regard. The first one relies on the assumption that the strategy will be simply applied to the region with a unitary and comprehensive approach by putting together the EU's current tools of action. In this approach, sensitive issues, such as taking concrete measures to act upon to solve "frozen conflicts" problem, are not addressed, and only unconventional threats, environmental issues and border security matters will be dealt with. This approach can yield benefit as it will be perceived unobtrusive and can be considered an economical effort, since it does not likely necessitate any extra political and financial instruments.

Here, main objectives can be listed as boosting regional cooperation; stabilizing the region through economic development; and defining a potential role for the ESDP in the GBSA. The tools of action, however, would remain the same as the aid development programs, increased political dialogue, etc. According to this approach, relations with Russia and the negotiation process with Turkey will not suffer any major changes.

The second scenario is based on a more assertive strategy for the GBSA and a close cooperation with the NATO[45] in which both conventional and unconventional threats will be addressed. In this strategy, which also includes solving the problems of "frozen conflicts," a deeper involvement at different levels, serious crisis management and more active political participation during the negotiations are considered. This scenario also includes an energy strategy that offers alternative solutions to the dependency on Russia.

This strategy refers to the EU's participation at the decision-making process of regional cooperation organizations. As a matter of fact, the EU will be able to link its tools of regional action to certain regional cooperation arrangements that are already in effect.

On the other hand, although a certain level of tension will be inevitable, relations with Russia, which will be profitable for both the EU and Russia itself, are going to change in accordance with the level of pragmatism of the interaction of the two parties. Meanwhile, relations with Turkey may jump onto a much more positive course and Turkey's integration into the EU will be accelerated.

There are several recommendations suggesting that the second scenario should be taken into consideration:

- *Inclusiveness*, which means that a strategy of the EU prepared for the GBSA should refer to all the countries in the region;
- *A bottom-up approach*. The EU should build cooperation with and get involved in the GBSA within the framework of already existing cooperation arrangements that could eventually be adjusted to new requests. The EU's involvement should be linked to regional organizations that developed initiatives that might be of interest for the EU, such as BSEC, SECI, Black Sea Border Security Initiative, and even the Black Sea Harmony, given its importance in combating unconventional threats in the Black Sea and in the event that the other regional countries become members of it;
- *A step-by-step approach* that should, first of all, boost regional cooperation in fields that are of common interest and not on sensitive issues of regional states, such as the fields of combating unconventional threats, environment protection, transport, telecommunication, and border security. These should be addressed before dealing with more sensitive issues, such as solving the "frozen conflicts";
- *Broadening the maritime policy of the EU to a regional dimension*;
- *Making use of the "structured cooperation" principle*. Recognizing the difficulty to reach an agreement on a GBSA strategy inside the EU, the so-called "structured cooperation" option should be taken into consideration to bring together the states that have interests in the region in which Romania and Bulgaria, the new EU members, are included to lobby in favor of such an endeavor;
- *Extending the conditionality-based economic aid* to the countries in the region in order to advance further the inter-state cooperation both at regional and sub-regional levels, according to the principles of cooperative security. This, however, is more feasible at sub-regional levels;
- *Coordinated actions between the EU and the NATO*. The institutionalized relations between NATO and the EU should be extended also to the GBSA. As a matter of fact, the EU could successfully collaborate with NATO in reforming the security sector where NATO is already involved through its PfP instruments. Moreover, the EU should reconsider the way it acted together with NATO in stabilizing the Balkans region;
- *Improving the existing democratization tools* so that an increased support to civil society of the regional countries, and even to the already existing GBSA network of NGOs, will be provided;
- *A more realistic approach* to the region is considering that a policy based on the premise of boosting regional economic development to facilitate regional stability might fail, since the regional actors are

viewed from a perspective of "rational choice." It ignores the ethnic drives and aspirations of certain actors who are mainly motivated by memories of an ancient status to become regional leaders;
- *Increased EU assertiveness directed at solving the Transnistrian conflict* by demanding to play a major role in negotiations, as a near- and medium-term strategy;
- *A bolder policy toward Russia*. The EU will continue to approach Russia as a strategic partner, given the level of complexity reached by the EU-Russia relations, but it should use a more assertive policy when addressing sensitive issues;
- *Acting toward strengthening relations with Turkey;*
- *Increasing support in building new alternative routes for energy transport.*

The EC's communication on the *Black Sea Synergy* also refers to the need of considering some of the above mentioned recommendations, such as those related to energy security, dealing with "frozen" conflicts and promoting democracy. However, this is not intended to be formed into a formal EU strategy, but rather an initiative that would complement the existing regional cooperation framework, mainly referring to the BSEC. It aims to boost cooperation in the area covering a wide range of issues from economic and environmental problems to security matters.

It is a significant step forward to define a comprehensive approach to the region. Nevertheless, it seems to be rather a declaration of intentions, since it does not refer to concrete measures applicable in all the mentioned fields of interest.

This study tried to argue that Romania can support establishing a deeper EU involvement in the region that will use the existing cooperation framework and, when necessary, developing new regional arrangements. A Romanian perspective pleads for the EU to play a direct role in the process of resolution of "frozen" conflicts, in cooperation with other international actors. The energy security is another aspect on which a regional EU strategy should focus. Moreover, under the guidance of some particular recommendations for defining a regional strategy, this study emphasized that there are no serious impediments in front of such an endeavor, except the lack of political will and of a concerted foreign policy agenda of the member states.

We did not mean to reflect an exhaustive approach, but we tried to draw attention on a particular way that this topic is perceived at least by an academic of a regional state that became a member of both NATO and the EU.

* At the time this study was written, she was a research assistant with the Institute for Political Studies of Defense and Military History (Romanian Ministry of Defense). The opinions expressed in this study are the author's only and do not reflect an official point of view.

[1] Ronald D. Asmus and Bruce P. Jackson, "The Black Sea and the Frontiers of Freedom," *Policy Review*, June 2004.

[2] Commission of the European Communities, "Black Sea Synergy - A New Regional Cooperation Initiative," COM(2007) 160 final, http://ec.europa.eu/world/enp/pdf/com07_160_en.pdf.

[3] However, the program has been criticized by European officials who pointed to the ineffective way in which it was implemented. As a case in point, they proved that in Russia there were undertaken 29 projects financed through TACIS and only 9 of them attained the assumed objectives. See Anthony Browne, "Gone East: how 7 billion euros EU cash melted away with the Cold War," *The Times*, April 21, 2006.

[4] The total TACIS aid program amounts to 7 billion euros by now.

[5] 39 technical assistance projects and 14 investment projects for the rehabilitation of infrastructure were financed.

[6] The member states are Turkey, Moldova, Uzbekistan, Azerbaijan, the Ukraine, Armenia, Bulgaria, Georgia, Kazakhstan, Kyrgyz Republic, Tajikistan, Turkmenistan.

[7] Decision adopted at the Russia-EU summit in Sankt Petersburg, of May 2003.

[8] Sergei Lavrov, Russian Foreign Minister, suggested in 2005 that it would be necessary to establish an EU-Russia Council that should function in a similar way to the NATO-Russia Council. EU is currently designing a strategic partnership treaty with Russia to be signed in 2007 that will also refer to the energy and security issues.

[9] EU-Russia energy relations are the object of the *Energy Charter Treaty*, drafted in 1991, but not ratified up to present. It would allow the EU to make use of Russian pipelines to transport gas and oil from Central Asia.

[10] Laurentiu Constantiniu, "Frate, frate, dar…gazu-i pe bani" (translation from Romanian, "We are brothers, but...the gas is not free"), *Cadran Politic*, anul III, nr 32-33, December 2005-January 2006.

[11] As a matter of fact, Moscow adopted in May 2003, a strategy that aims to "position" Russia as a leader in the world's energy markets. By 2020 Russia intends to increase its production of crude oil to 450-520 million tons/year and its production of natural gas to 700 billion cubic meters/year, see Sergei Blagov, "Russia pledges to uphold global energy security," *Eurasia Daily Monitor*, May 2, 2006, the Jamestown Foundation.

[12] Because of this reason, several European countries even consider boosting the nuclear energy option.

[13] "Erneuerbare Energien in Zahlen- nationale und internationale Entwicklung". Internet-Update. Bundesministerium fur Umwelt, Naturschutz und Reaktorsicherheit. Berlin 2005, referred to in Martin Malek, "Security Challenges in the South Caucasus. Ethno-territorial Conflicts, the Access to Energy Resources and the Russian Factor," *Monitor Strategic*, no 1/2006, IPSDMH, Bucharest.

[14] As noticed by the political analyst Dmitri Trenin, "For Russia to take an interest in neighbouring countries is not only natural but imperative," in Dmitri Trenin, "Russia, the EU and the common neighbourhood," Centre for European Reform, September 2005.

15 See Fabrizio Tassinari, "Security and Integration in the EU Neighbourhood. The case for Regionalism," *CEPS Working Document*, no 226/July 2005, Centre for European Policy Studies.

16 See Javier Solana, interview by Celia Chauffour "The European Neighbourhood Policy is not a policy aimed at EU enlargement; it neither foresees it nor excludes it." September 4, 2005 www.caucaz.com
The membership would be an option feasible in the long term. Reactions on behalf of certain EU's member states indicate remote perspectives of membership for GBSA's countries in favor of "privileged partnerships." http://www.caucaz.com/home_eng/breve_contenu.php?id=204.

17 A Strong European Neighbourhood Policy, COM (2007) 774 final, Brussels, December 5, 2007 http://ec.europa.eu/world/enp/pdf/com07_774_en.pdf.

18 The Ukraine's energy infrastructure is shared with Russia and 60 percent of Ukrainian foreign trade remains with Moscow. For more details, see Graeme P. Herd and Fotios Moustakis, "Black Sea Geopolitics: a Litmus Test for the European Security Order?" *Mediterranean Politics*, Vol. 5, No.3, Autumn 2000.

19 In case of dealing with regional crisis, it should promote the joint assessment of a situation and joint planning and command and control. See Dov Lynch in "The Russia-EU Partnership and Shared Neighborhood," report presented to the "Eastern Europe and Central Asia" Working Group (COEST), the Hague, July 2004.

20 Ambassador Sergiu Celac, "Five reasons why the West should become more involved in the Black Sea region" Ronald D. Asmus (editor), *A New Euro-Atlantic Strategy for the Black Sea Region*, Washington; The German Marshall Fund of the U.S., 2004.

21 Ronald D. Asmus, Bruce P. Jackson, op.cit.

22 Ronald D. Asmus and Bruce P. Jackson, op.cit.; the same idea is backed by Dmitri Trenin "The best that Russia could do for its smaller neighbours would be to become more stable, prosperous and at peace with itself. This (…) would give Russia considerable "soft power"-the ability to convince rather than coerce-in the region," in "Russia, the EU and the common neighbourhood," Centre for European Reform, September 2005.

23 Andris Piebalgs quoted in Andrew Rettman, "Europeanization of Russia needed for EU energy security, Piebalgs says," *EUobserver*, March 28, 2006.

24 Elmar Brok, German conservative member of the European Parliament even described this situation as "the announcement of a Cold War with new methods," quoted in Mark Beunderman, "Russian energy chief advocates EU oil supply cut," *EUobserver*, April 25, 2006. See also Russian President Vladimir Putin's declarations at the Sochi EU-Russia summit (on the Black Sea coast), May 2006. (for a briefing see Andrew Rettman, "No energy deal at mild-mannered EU-Russia summit," in *EUobserver*, May 26, 2006).

25 *The EU Electricity & Gas markets: third legislative package*, September 2007, http://ec.europa.eu/energy/electricity/package_2007/index_en.htm

26 See Mark Beunderman, "New energy paper seeks less EU reliance on Moscow," *EUobserver*, June 2, 2006.

27 EU actually does not at all refer to the Black Sea area, while the Caspian basin is only mentioned twice. See European Commission, "A European Strategy for

Sustainable, Competitive, and Secure Energy," *Green Paper*, Brussels, March 2006, http://ec.europa.eu/energy/green-paper-energy/doc/2006_03_08_gp_document_en.pdf. For a more detailed analysis, see Vladimir Socor, "European Union's Energy Paper: A Muffled Call to a Slow Wakeup," *Eurasia Daily Monitor*, May 2, 2006, the Jamestown Foundation.

[28] In the Black Sea region there were built the pipelines Baku-Novorossiyk (Russia); Tengiz-Novorossiyk; Baku-Mohackale-Novorossiyk all transferring Kazakh and Azeri oil.

[29] In the project phase, there are the pipelines: Burgaz (Bulgaria)-Dedeagac (Greece); Burgaz-Vlore (Albania); Baku-Supsa (Georgia), NABUCCO Project (Turkey-Bulgaria-Romania-Hungary-Austria) and the Baku-Tbilisi-Ceyhan (1730 km with a 50 million tons capacity). For details, see Michael Cohen, "Energy Security in the Black Sea area," *Monitor Strategic*, no1/2006 (under publication), IPSDMH.

[30] See Ali Kulebi, "Eurasian Energy lines and Turkey," *The New Anatolian*, March 15-16, 2006.

[31] The Montreux Convention (July 20, 1936), published as *Convention regarding the Regime of the Straits signed at Montreux*. It settled the re-militarizing of the Straits; forbid the flights surveillance undertaken by military planes as well as the circulation of submarines. It also limits and even forbids the free circulation of military navies in time of war, should Turkey be neutral. http://www.turkishpilots.org.tr/ingilizce dernek/DOCUMENTS/montro.html.

[32] The Turkish Foreign Minister Abdullah Gül pointed to rising anti-Europe and anti-U.S. views even among "moderate liberal people" who previously backed Ankara's pro-western orientation., in Lucia Kubosova "Ankara warns of rising anti-EU sentiment among Turks," *EUobserver*, July 20, 2006.

[33] Differently from the U.S., EU needs the approval of the authorities of the states on the territory of which these kinds of actions are to be developed. See Andrew Rettman, "EU moving to U.S. model on pro-democracy funding," *EUobserver*, April 19, 2006

[34] "Conflict Resolution in the South Caucasus: The EU's Role," *Europe Report* no 173, March 20, 2006 http://www.crisisgroup.org/library/documents/europe/ caucasus/173_conflict_resolution_south_caucasus.pdf.

[35] A Strong European Neighbourhood Policy, COM (2007) 774 final, Brussels, December 5, 2007 http://ec.europa.eu/world/enp/pdf/com07_774_en.pdf.

[36] Leftist groups of the Baltic countries even created a political party "the EU's Russian Party," see Dan Dungaciu, "Moldova ante portas," Ed. TRITONIC, Bucharest, 2005.

[37] Romanian President Traian Basescu's speech at the Council of Foreign Relations, Washington D.C., U.S., of March the 10th 2005, http://www.presidency.ro/ ?_RID=det&tb=date&id=6035&_PRID=ag.

[38] See the text of the strategy project on http://www.presidency.ro/dsdp/ docs/phpMQabHR.pdf.

[39] The launching reunion took place in Bucharest on June the 5th-6th 2006, www.blackseaforum.org.

[40] Launched in Bucharest, Romania, in 2004.

[41] Romanian President Traian Basescu's speech at the Council of Foreign Relations, Washington D.C., U.S., of March the 10th 2005, http://www.presidency.ro/?_RID=det&tb=date&id=6035&_PRID=ag.
See also Romanian President Traian Basescu's speech at the Palace of Cotroceni conference, Bucharest, April the 20th 2005 http://www.presidency.ro/?_RID=det&tb=date&id=6173&_PRID=ag.
[42] Romanian President Traian Basescu's speech at the Council of Foreign Relations, Washington D.C., U.S., of March the 10th 2005, http://www.presidency.ro/?_RID=det&tb=date&id=6035&_PRID=ag.
[43] *Romania's security strategy*, (project) http://www.presidency.ro/dsdp/docs/phpMQabHR.pdf (in Romanian).
[44] Mustafa Aydin, "Europe's next shore: the Black Sea region after EU enlargement," Occasional Paper no 53, June 2004, EU's Institute for Security Studies.
[45] For more details, see Eugene B. Rumer and Jeffrey Simon, *Toward a Euro-Atlantic Strategy for the Black Sea Region*, Occasional Paper 3, April 2006, Institute for National Strategic Studies, National Defense University, Washington, D.C.

Chapter 14
European Union's Neighborhood Relations with Eastern Europe and Russia: Values, Interests and Future Challenges for EU Foreign Policy

Giselle Bosse

> Most importantly, we confirmed that the EU-Russia relationship is based on common values, including respect for human rights and democracy, the rule of law and a free market economy. These values must guide us as we turn to implementation.[1]

In 2002, the EU began to develop a new policy toward its neighboring countries in order to avoid new lines of division on the European continent following the 2004 Eastward enlargement and to meet the challenges arising from the new borders created with the Ukraine, Belarus and Moldova. The initial drafts for the 'Wider Europe' initiative included a strong emphasis on shared 'European values' as the precondition for enhanced relations with the three countries in Eastern Europe. Never before had the EU foreign policy toward Eastern Europe placed such an emphasis on democratic values as a condition for future cooperation and without offering the prospect of imminent accession.

More significantly still, the Russian Federation[2] was included into the initial drafts of the emerging neighborhood policy, much to the dismay of several of the larger member states, as well as the Russian President, Vladimir Putin. At stake was not only the 'Russia First' approach that had characterized European policy toward Russia in the past. The emphasis on 'shared values' in the neighborhood policy was also little appreciated by the Russian government. In May 2003, Russia refused to participate in the European Neighborhood Policy (ENP) and instead, developed a 'strategic partnership' with the EU within the framework of the Four Common Spaces Roadmap.

The following article aims to analyze this relationship between the EU, its 'new' Eastern neighbors and Russia, with an emphasis in particular on the role of values, interests and institutions. The role of values in internal EU policies has been subject to a number of academic enquiries in the recent past.[3] Values, however, are now also increasingly part of the EU's foreign policy agenda.[4] The emphasis on 'European values' in EU policy is, in turn, often associated with ambitious normative agendas of EU institutions, such as the Commission and the Council Secretariat.[5] Institutionalists have long pointed to the increasing role of the EU institutions in the conduct of the Union's foreign affairs and the gradual emergence of value-based EU foreign policy.[6]

In the past, EU foreign policies toward neighboring countries, specifically vis-à-vis Russia, have been driven predominantly by the interests of individual EU member states, rather than the Union's institutions.[7] This raised the question of whether or not, or to what extent, the ENP and the Four Spaces Roadmap reinforce this old 'state-centric' EU foreign policy paradigm or if they reflect a value-based EU foreign policy.

In the first part, the article closely examines the role and importance of 'European values' in previous EU policies toward Russia and its other neighbors in the East and tries to find an answer to the following question: Did common values matter in these policies, or was the relationship driven solely by traditional member state interests? In the second part, the article revisits the formulation process of the ENP, explains why and how the Russian Federation was initially included in the policy and discusses the extent to which decision-making was linked to shared European values (as opposed to traditional member state and/or geopolitical interests). The third part analyzes similarities and differences between the ENP (case study Moldova) and the Four Common Spaces Roadmap in respect to the importance and emphasis on 'European values.' By way of conclusion, I examine the future role and prospects of a value-based EU policy toward its neighbors, especially in light of the ongoing negotiations of the EU-Russia Agreement in November 2007.

European Values in EU Relations With its Neighborhood and Russia Prior to the ENP

Following the end of the Cold War, the EU's relations with neighboring states in the East went through several stages: from the Partnership and Cooperation Agreements (PCA) concluded with Russia, Moldova, the Ukraine and Belarus between 1994 and 1995, to the Common Strategy with Russia in 1999 and the parallel development of the European Neighborhood Policy and the Four Common Spaces in 2003/2004. Over this period of time, the role of values in EU neighborhood policies has considerably changed.

The PCAs with Russia and other Eastern neighboring countries mainly focused on trade matters and contain few references to European values.[8] One of the key objectives of the PCAs is to support efforts for the consolidation of democracy and the transition into market economies.[9] The PCA with Moldova, for example, lays down the general principles of the agreement, including respect for democracy, principles of international law and human rights as well as the principles of a market economy.[10] Most provisions of the PCAs, however, do not explicitly refer to 'shared values' and instead focus on trade relations.

In 1999, the EU drew up a Common Strategy (CS) for Russia which served as a background for the EU policy until 2004. The EU outlined the strategic goals of the partnership in which the EU 'welcomed Russia's return to its rightful place in the European family' on the basis of 'shared values enshrined in the common heritage of European civilization.'[11] In general, the document gives equal weight to the consolidation of democracy and the rule of law besides areas of action to integrate Russia into a common European economical and social space.[12]

The implementation of the PCAs with Eastern European neighbors and Russia is supported by the EU's TACIS financial instrument. TACIS is geared toward supporting the private sector and economic development. Only a small fraction of the instrument went into projects related to civil society and human rights.[13]

In other words, provisions for 'shared values' in the context of the PCAs, the 1999 CS with Russia and the EU's financial assistance to Eastern European neighbors and Russia were indeterminate and predominantly focused on the principles of economic liberalization and the creation of market economies, rather than democratic norms and values.

The Inclusion and Self-exclusion of Russia from the ENP: EU Institutions, Values and 'State-centric' Reactions

Faced with the prospect of enlargement toward Central and Eastern Europe, toward the end of 2002, the EU decided to take the first steps to formulate a response to those countries in Eastern Europe which would soon border the Union. The original aim was to avoid new dividing lines in Europe and, at the same time, to tackle the challenges arising from the newly created borders of the Union in the East.

The first initiatives toward a wider Europe appeared rather randomly on the EU agenda and varied in their definitions of the geographical scope of the new policy. A proposal by the UK in June 2002 stressed the need to solely focus on the three new Eastern neighbors of the EU, namely the Ukraine, Moldova and Belarus.[14]

Shortly afterward, the Swedish government produced a document on Wider Europe stressing the importance of an all-embracing and inclusive policy toward the Union's neighborhood, including the partners in the Mediterranean as well as Russia.[15]

By the end of 2002, a consensus appeared to be emerging in EU institutions (the Commission and the Council Secretariat) that the new policy should not just focus exclusively on the Ukraine, Moldova and Belarus, but also on Russia. This view was taken forward especially by the High Representative of the CFSP, Javier Solana, and Christopher Patten, the Commissioner for External Relations at the time. In a letter to the Danish Presidency in August 2002, they stressed that there was a '(...) need also to consider how Russia might be linked to, or fall within, a new neighborhood policy.'[16] The reason for the inclusion of Russia was primarily linked to the substance of the basic objectives of the Union toward the Ukraine, Moldova, Belarus, and Russia; the aim to foster stability and prosperity through gradual political reform based on shared European values. The letter states that 'in the end, Russia is an indivisible part of the region—it is difficult to envisaged strengthened regional cooperation without Russia.'[17]

In September 2002, the General Affairs and External Relations Council (GAERC) recognized all proposals but appeared to arrive at the preliminary conclusion that the Ukraine, Moldova and Belarus alone should be part of any future neighborhood initiative.[18] Still, the European Council in Copenhagen (here the decision was made on the date for the conclusion of accession negotiations and the accession of the CEECs to the EU in May 2004) confirmed the inclusive approach for the EU neighborhood policy, including strengthened relations not only with Russia, but also with southern Mediterranean countries. The Council then tasked the Commission and the High Representative to bring forward further proposals for the Wider Europe initiative.[19]

The end of 2002 and the beginning of 2003 were clearly marked by the Union's desire to renew its relations with the Russian Federation. It aimed at revising its Common Strategy on Russia, creating a Common European Social Area and promoting the EU-Russia Energy dialogue. At the same time, Russia was interested in pushing forward its accession to the World Trade Organization, for which it needed the support of the EU. The EU-Russia summit in May 2003 was regarded as a major step toward such an enhanced relationship.[20]

Heavily occupied with the preparations and institutional reforms for the upcoming enlargement, including the development of a Constitution for Europe, only few member states paid attention to the further development of the ENP. The Commission, therefore, took center stage during the further formulation of the neighborhood initiative. Its Communication on 'Wider Europe' in March 2003 presented the first serious attempt to clearly define the content and scope of the new neighborhood policy.[21] In the second paragraph of the Communication, the Commission clearly defines the scope of the new policy, including Russia, the Western NIS and the Southern Mediterranean.[22] With respect to Russia, the Communication stresses that the new neighborhood policy will only constitute one pillar for the overall EU-Russia strategic partnership but does nevertheless aim for the full inclusion of the country into the policy.[23]

This 'one single size fits all' approach was partly the result of some last minute changes that the Commission was forced to apply to its Communication following the high level intervention by the then-Commission President, Romano Prodi, to include the Southern Mediterranean in the framework (which was not anticipated by the Directorate General (DG) of the External Relations responsible for much of the text in the Communication).[24] Still, the inclusion of Russia into the new policy was a clear intention of the Commission right from the start of the formulation process, as was the clear emphasis on 'shared European values.'

In April, the Council of General Affairs and External Relations (GAERC) confirmed the general direction of the neighborhood initiative outlined in the Commission Communication, but did not further comment on its general scope. The EU-Russia relations are discussed separately, but the need to reinforce the relations with Russia in view of the forthcoming EU-Russia Cooperation Council on April 15, 2003 and the EU-Russia summit on May 31, 2003 was re-emphasized.[25]

In June 2003, the GAERC largely endorsed the Commission Communication on Wider Europe. In terms of geographical scope of the policy, however, only the Ukraine, Moldova, Belarus, and the Mediterranean partners were mentioned.[26] Russia was not referred to at all. Indeed, from mid-2003 onward, Russia has never appeared again as a partner in the ENP, other than as a recipient of the financial instrument that was designed later as part of the formulation process of the ENP to support the new policy. What has happened?

Very little consultation took place between the EC and the Russian government on the contents and geographical scope of the ENP. Indeed, the inclusion of Russia into the new policy was largely a unilateral act on the part of the Commission. As soon as the Communication was published, President Vladimir Putin rejected the proposal and subsequent negotiations with the EU on an Action Plan within the framework of the ENP. Instead, at the St. Petersburg Summit in May 2003, the EU and Russia agreed to reinforce their cooperation by creating the four 'Common Spaces' (economy; freedom, security and justice; external security, research and education) within the scope of their 'strategic partnership.'

The Russian government found its inclusion into the ENP patronizing, because of the unilateral action by the Commission as well as the focus on 'European values' in the ENP.[27] Indeed, Russian officials made it very clear to the Commission that its Communication had been inadequate.[28]

The inclusion of Russia in the ENP was driven forward not only by Solana and Patten, but also the respective country desks within DG External Relations, who favored a more conditional (and values-based) EU policy toward Russia in the past and saw a chance to exercise greater influence over EU-Russia relations through the framework of the neighborhood policy.[29]

Member states were largely left unaware of the precise details of the March Commission Communication prior to its publication. Especially the German and Italian governments later regretted not having been sufficiently involved in the early formulation of the Wider Europe initiative.[30] In other words and to conclude, the inclusion of Russia into the EU's new neighborhood policy was of a short duration and reflected the concerns of EU institutions rather than member state interests.

From the outset, the Four Common Spaces appear very similar to the structure of the ENP. The 'strategic partnership' of the Four Common Spaces is, therefore, often interpreted as a purely symbolic framework that puts Russia in a more important position compared to its neighbors, which are included in the ENP.[31]

If this is the case, one could indeed speak of a major turn in EU relations with its neighborhood. Moreover, the ENP suggests a 'normative turn' in EU relations with its neighbors in general. If the contents of the ENP related to democratic values match those of the Common Spaces,[32] the interests of EU institutions would have left a major imprint also on EU-Russian relations. Both developments taken together would lend strong support to the theoretical expectations linked to an emergent institutionalized system of EU Foreign Policy based on norms and values. The next section of the article, therefore, looks at the role and significance of 'European values' in the two EU policies toward neighboring states: the ENP toward Eastern Europe and the Four Common Spaces with Russia.

Values vs. Interests: Changing Emphases on Values in the ENP and the Four Common Spaces

> The four common spaces are now a weaker and fuzzier still derivative of the neighborhood policy, giving only token attention to democracy and excluding explicit reference to EU norms as the reference for Russian-EU convergence. As a result the roadmaps do not really inform us about where the EU and Russia are heading.[33]

Concluding the PCAs, the EU has only just begun to discuss the meaning of Europe and its common values. The Treaty on the European Union did not yet contain explicit references to values.[34] In the course of the following decade, however, the EU gradually established a list of common values; as manifested in successive treaty revisions[35] and, most recently, in the Constitution for Europe which devotes an entire article on 'The Union's values.'[36] The prospect of enlargement served as a 'trigger' for such development. With the EU's decision to offer membership to some Central and East European Countries (CEECs) in 1993, the Copenhagen European Council had to agree on membership criteria which would condition eventual accession. The 'Copenhagen criteria' were not linked explicitly to the concept of 'shared values' but included political criteria such as stable institutions, guarantee of democracy, the rule of law, respect for human rights and minority rights.[37] This catalogue of 'European values' was then directly 'transferred' to the ENP as a condition for enhanced relations with the Union.[38]

Early drafts of the ENP map out a very ambitious agenda in respect to the values upon which the enhanced relations with the 'new' neighbors should be based. In its Communication on the ENP Strategy Paper, the Commission enumerates the following aspects of European values, this time under the explicit heading of the 'Commitment to Shared Values,' including:

- Strengthening of democracy and rule of law, reform of the judiciary and fight against corruption and organized crime,
- Respect for human rights and fundamental freedoms, including freedom of media and expression, rights of minorities and children, gender equality, trade union rights and other core labor standards, the fight against the practice of torture, and prevention of ill-treatment,
- Support for the development of civil society,
- Cooperation with the ICC, and
- Commitments required to essential aspects of EU external action, such as the fight against terrorism and proliferation of weapons of mass destruction, as well as abidance by the international law and efforts to achieve conflict resolution.[39]

In its ENP Country Report on Moldova, for example, the European Commission broadly examines the current state of these commitments.[40] The report starts with a reinterpretation of the significance of 'values' within the former PCA, and then underlines the importance of development of political institutions based on these values—democracy, the rule of law and human rights.[41]

The Commission Report also highlights various deficiencies in the commitment to the shared values. 'Democracy and the rule of law' require improvements, specifically with a view on democratic elections, laws on political parties and socio-political organizations, powers of local government, an independent judicial system, and criminal procedure codes to fight corruption.[42] The human rights situation in Transdniestria is highlighted and heavily criticized by the Commission.[43]

The ENP, therefore, establishes an extensive framework on the nature and content of shared values. Still, this discourse of common values is neither coherent nor consistent, partly because of the *ad hoc* nature of the

ENP, and also due to the bilateral nature of negotiations of the ENP Action Plans (APs).⁴⁴

Most Action Plans miss the rigour and detail in which value gaps were identified in the initial Country Reports. The Action Plan on Moldova, for example, shifts the emphasis from the 'commitment to shared values' and value gaps, to cooperation on Justice and Home Affairs, such as border management or the combat against terrorism.⁴⁵ With regard to the Transdniestria conflict, the human rights situation is not mentioned, except for a brief elaboration on 'efforts towards a settlement (…) guaranteeing respect for democracy, the rule of law and human rights.'⁴⁶

The clash between EU institutions' ambitions to construct a set of coherent and detailed European values and the reality of bilateral intergovernmental relations is most evident in the dialogue with Russia. The concept of the 'Four Common Spaces' foresaw enhanced relations between the two parties toward a Common Economic Space, a Common Space of Freedom, Security and Justice, and Common Spaces of External Security and Research and Education.⁴⁷ In May 2005, these spaces were further defined in terms of concrete objectives and measures, so-called *Road Maps*, at the EU-Russia summit in Moscow.⁴⁸ What is striking in these documents is the general lack of reference to 'common values,' in particular when compared to respective provisions in the ENP Action Plans. Values as such are only loosely mentioned on few occasions.

Enhanced cooperation in the area of freedom, security and justice, for example, is to be carried out on the basis of common values. These are interpreted as the implementation of international commitments, respect for the principle of non-discrimination, respect for the rights of individuals in the EU member states and in Russia (including immigrants and persons belonging to minorities), and respect for fundamental rights and liberties as set out in international conventions.⁴⁹ Concrete measures to establish the common space, however, are dominated almost exclusively by the objective to fight terrorism and various forms of organized crime.

From an overall view, we can say that the roadmaps provide few interpretations of common values and even fewer concrete references to these values which were not sufficiently 'shared' by Russia. This marks a stark difference to the ENP Strategy Papers and Action Plans with other neighboring countries.

The eventual Common Spaces framework also differs substantially from internal documents formulated by EU institutions, and the EU Commission in particular. In its Communication in February 2004, the Commission directly refers to the 'weakening of the values to which the EU and Russia (…) are committed' in the four years of Putin's presidency.⁵⁰ The conduct of the 2003 Duma elections, continuous conflict in Chechnya and selective application of the law are cited as key examples. For the Commission, this suggests a discriminatory application of the law or lack of respect to human rights which 'should be raised vigorously and coherently by the EU and its Member States.'[51] Similarly, the EP has consistently raised concerns over Russia's commitment to 'shared values,' calling for its Strategic Partnership with the EU to be based on 'the same values as the ENP,' and criticizing the lack of results in the implementation of existing EU policies.[52] Although European institutions have evidently less influence on the definition of shared values in bilateral intergovernmental relations with neighboring states, their role in the design and implementation of the financial assistance for future neighborhood policies is (potentially) considerable.

In 2007, the European Neighborhood and Partnership Instrument (ENPI) replaced the existing EU financial assistance to all neighboring states participating in the ENP, including Russia. The new instrument succeeds TACIS for both Russia and Eastern ENP partner states. The objectives of the ENPI are based on existing agreements, and the Commission Communications and Council Conclusions sets out the overall strategy of the Union vis-à-vis neighboring countries, including the ENP Action Plans, where they apply.[53] In the case of Russia, priorities are defined in light of roadmaps on the Four Common Spaces.[54]

Overall, the ENPI aims to support partner countries' commitment to common values and principles.[55] More specifically, the Commission proposes a wide range of objectives covering most aspects of the ENP: The promotion of social development and gender equality, employment and social protection, and core labor standards; the protection of human rights and fundamental freedoms, and support for democratization; and fostering the development of civil society.[56] The ENPI thus places a fairly equal emphasis on the 'shared values' dimension of the ENP, in addition to, for example, measures connected to the promotion of a market economy or secure border management. It is not, however, clear from the ENPI provisions, whether or not, and indeed how the measures concerned with shared values will be applied to Russia. Furthermore, Russia will receive less assistance from the EU in the future (implying less support for the promotion of shared European values).[57]

The analysis of the role and importance of shared European values in the EU's policies toward Moldova and Russia has led to the following preliminary conclusions. Early drafts of the ENP placed a clear and pronounced emphasis on democratic values, an emphasis which is not replicated in the framework of the Four Common Spaces. Even the later policy documents on the ENP and the Action Plans in particular, lack significant details regarding the 'commitment to shared values.' This clearly demonstrates that EU institutions not only lost influence over the formulation process of the Four Common Spaces toward Russia, but also vis-à-vis neighboring states, as the example of the Action Plan with Moldova has highlighted.

In other words, roadmaps of neither the ENP nor the Common Spaces reflect the level of commitment to shared values to be expected from a coherent and robust EU foreign policy based on norms and values. Nevertheless, the emphasis on "European values" remains strong in the ENP financial instrument, which now serves to support the implementation of the Four Common Spaces.

Conclusions and Prospects for a More Value-based EU Foreign Policy

What does the future hold for the role of European values in EU-Russian relations? Following the introduction of the Four Common Spaces and the Roadmaps, the London Summit in October 2005, focused on the practical implementation of the Roadmaps, but progress (on all issues, not to mention democratic values) to date has been very slow, at least due to discord in JHA and CFSP/ESDP issues.[58]

At the EU-Russia Summit in Sochi in May 2006, agreements were signed on visa-facilitation and readmission. EU Readmission Agreements have been heavily criticized for lacking sufficient references to the protection of refugees and asylum seekers and to international human rights standards in general.[59] The EU-Russia Readmission Agreement is no different in this respect and reveals the prime concern of EU member states for their own internal security rather than 'shared European values.'[60]

In Sochi, leaders also agreed to develop a new EU-Russia agreement to replace the PCA which reached the end of its initial ten-year period on November 30, 2007. The Commission is suggesting that the new agreement covers the vast area of cooperation built in the intervening years, notably set out in the common spaces roadmaps adopted at the summit in May 2005. Such an agreement would, just like the PCA, finally endow a legal basis to the Common Spaces framework and, as such, make its provisions legally binding for both partners.

The Commission wants the new agreement to be based on recognition of common values, including democracy, human rights and the rule of law. Some of the larger EU member states (France, Italy and Germany) are opposing a heavy emphasis on shared values in the new agreement.[61]

However, the Union's relationship with Russia has become an increasingly contentious issue, not just between EU institutions and member states, but also among the member states. Many of the new member states have been highly supportive of the tougher line toward Russia, which was taken by Council Secretariat and Commission from 2002 onward. In other words, the calls with a greater emphasis on adherence to common values as a precondition for future EU-Russia cooperation have become more pronounced. This development may be significant in terms of the importance of shared values in the new agreement.

Will future cooperation between the EU and its Eastern neighboring states and Russia be more values-based in the future? This is difficult to predict. The formulation process of the ENP Action Plans and the Common Spaces Framework was marked by bilateral intergovernmental negotiations and, hence, interests of the EU member states and neighbor states' governments feature very clearly in the final policy texts. Provisions on 'shared values' are either absent or very vague.[62] The implementation of the Action Plans in the next few years will eventually provide a more comprehensive picture of the importance of 'European values' in the ENP.

Negotiations for the new agreement with Russia were still ongoing in November 2007. The EU-Russia summit in Mafra in October failed to reach an agreement on a number of key strategic issues, including the liberalization of energy and relations with the 'common neighborhood.'[63] The human rights situation in Russia has not disappeared completely from the negotiation talks,[64] but it is clear that the core disagreements between the Union and Russia stem from differences in traditional geopolitical interests and concerns.

At the same time, it must not be forgotten that not all EU institutions share the same values-based agenda with regard to external relations. DG External Relations usually follows a political agenda that is geared toward the enhancement of relations to neighboring states, but its officials do not necessarily prioritize their adherence to 'European values.' The commitment to values in the form of democratic reforms or 'good governance' has been promoted by former DG Enlargement officials, some of whom were/are involved in the ENP. DG Trade or DG JLS have much less interest in the 'value-dimension' of EU relations with neighboring countries.[65]

The ENP and the Common Spaces Framework do not represent a sustained commitment to an agreement on 'European values' on behalf of the EU, its institutions and member states. Hence, the tension between interests and values in EU foreign policy is likely to continue.

> We still maintain the fiction that nothing but the love of peace actuates our foreign policy. A certain amount of hypocrisy which varies between honest self-deception and conscious dishonesty characterizes the life of every nation (...) We make simple moral judgments, remain unconscious of the self-interest which colours them, support them with an enthusiasm which derives from our waning but still influential evangelical piety, and are surprised that our contemporaries will not accept us as saviours of the world.[66]

[1] B. Ferrero-Waldner, EU Commissioner for External Relations and European Neighborhood Policy, *EU-Russia Relations*, Speech to the European Parliament, May 25, 2005.
[2] From here onward referred to "Russia."
[3] T. Christiansen, K. JØrgensen and A. Wiener, eds., *The Social Construction of Europe*, (London: Sage, 2001); M. Merlingen, C. Mudde and U. Sedelmeier, "The Right and the Righteous? European Norms, Domestic Politics and the Sanctions against Austria," *Journal of Common Market Studies*, Vol. 39, No. 1, (2001): pp. 59-77; C. Leconte, "The Fragility of the EU as a "Community of Values: Lessons from the Haider Affair," *West European Politics*, Vol. 28, No. 3, (2005): pp. 620-49.
[4] See for example: R. Schuette, "E.U.-Russia Relations: Interests and Values – A European Perspective," *Carnegie Papers*, No. 54, (December 2004).
[5] M. E. Smith, *Europe's Foreign and Security Policy: The Institutionalisation of Cooperation* (Cambridge: Cambridge University Press, 2004).
[6] K. Smith, *The Making of EU Foreign Policy: The Case of Eastern Europe*, 2nd ed. (Basingstoke, Palgrave: MacMillan, 2004); M. E. Smith, "Institutionalization, Policy Adoption and European Foreign Policy Cooperation," *European Journal of International Relations*, 10, 1, (2004): pp. 95-136.
[7] See for example, R. Dannreuther, ed., *European Union Foreign and Security Policy: Towards a Neighborhood Strategy* (London: Routledge, 2004; W. Wallace, "Looking after the Neighborhood: Responsibilities for the EU-25," *Notre Europe Policy Papers*, no. 4, (2003)
[8] See A. Misseroli, "The EU and its Changing Neighborhood: Stabilization, Integration and Partnership," in *European Union Foreign and Security Policy: Towards a Neighborhood Strategy*, ed. R. Dannreuther (London: Routledge, 2004), pp. 12-26.
[9] Agreement on Partnership and Cooperation between the EU and the Republic of Moldova, November 28, 1994, pp. 1-3.
[10] Ibid., p. 6.
[11] *Common Strategy* of the European Union on Russia, June 4, 1999, 1999/414/CFSP.
[12] Ibid.
[13] Moldova Action Program 2003, based on Council Regulation 99/2000 of December 29, 1999 concerning the provision of assistance to the partner states in Eastern Europe and Central Asia.
[14] Letter from Jack Straw to Josep Piqué (Foreign Minister of Spain), Foreign and Commonwealth Office, London, January 28, 2002, and letter from the Swedish Minister of Foreign Affairs and Minister of International Trade to Josep Piqué, Regeringskansliet, Stockholm, March 8, 2002.
[15] Ibid.
[16] C. Patten and J. Solana, Letter to P. S. Möller (Danish Presidency) on 'Wider Europe', August 7, 2002.
[17] Ibid.
[18] General Affairs and External Relations Council, Brussels, September 30, 2006: 12134/2.
[19] *Presidency Conclusions*, Copenhagen European Council 12 and 13 December 2002, Brussels, January 29, 2003, 15917/02, p. 7.
[20] See for example: The Priorities of the Greek Presidency 2003, 'Our Europe: Sharing the Future Community of Values,' p. 25.

²¹ Commission of the European Communities, *Communication* 'Wider Europe – Neighborhood: A New Framework for Relations with our Eastern and Southern Neighbours, Brussels, March 11, 2003, COM (2003) 104 final.
²² Ibid., p. 3.
²³ Ibid., p. 5.
²⁴ Interview, Commission Official, Brussels, June 2006.
²⁵ GAERC Council Meeting, Luxembourg, April 14, 2003, 8220/03.
²⁶ GAERC Council Meeting, Luxembourg, June 16, 2003, 10369/03.
²⁷ For further details, see: G. Bogutcaia, G. Bosse and A. Schmidt-Felzmann "Lost in Translation? Political Elites and the Interpretative Values Gap in the EU's Neighborhood Policies," *Contemporary Politics*, 12, 2, (2006): pp. 117-137.
²⁸ Interview Commission Official, Brussels, May 2006.
²⁹ Interview Commission Official, Brussels, June 2006.
³⁰ Ibid.
³¹ See for example: S. Müller-Kraenner, "The European Neighborhood Policy," (Heinrich Böll Stiftung: 2004), http://www.boell.de/downloads/ aussen/European_ Neighborhood_Policy_smk.pdf#search=%22ENP%20Russia%20rejection%22 (accessed October 15, 2005).
³² Differences between the ENP and the Common Spaces have also been examined in respect to economic issues, see: M. Vahl, "A Privileged Partnership? EU-Russian Relations in a Comparative Perspective," *DIIS Working Paper*, 3, (2006): p. 13.
³³ M. Emerson, "EU-Russia: Four Common Spaces and the Proliferation of the Fuzzy," *CEPS Policy Brief* (Centre for European Policy Studies: Brussels, 2005).
³⁴ Treaty on European Union, *Official Journal of the European Communities*, C 191, July 29, 1992: the only reference to values is found in Article J.1 on the objectives of the common foreign and security policy, one of which is 'to safeguard the common values, fundamental interests and independence of the Union.'
³⁵ With the Treaty of Amsterdam, Article F was amended to include: 'The Union is founded on the principles of liberty, democracy, respect for human rights and fundamental freedoms, and the rule of law, principles which are common to the Member States', *Official Journal of the European Communities*, C 340, November 10, 1997.
³⁶ Treaty Establishing A Constitution for Europe, *Official Journal of the European Union*, C 310/11C, December 16, 2004.
³⁷ European Council, *Presidency Conclusions*, Copenhagen European Council June 21-22, 1993, http://www.europarl.eu.int/enlargement_new/europeancouncil/pdf/cop _en.pdf (accessed January 25, 2006).
³⁸ Interview Commission Official, Brussels, June 2006.
³⁹ Commission of the European Communities, Communication for the Commission, European Neighborhood Policy, *Strategy Paper*, Brussels, May 12, 2004, COM (2004) 373 final, pp. 12-13.
⁴⁰ Moldova was chosen because it was one of the first three neighboring countries to be included into the ENP together with the Ukraine and Belarus. It is therefore a good case study to trace changes in the use of values in the ENP from the very beginning of the formulation process of the policy.
⁴¹ Commission of the European Communities, *Staff Working Paper*, European Neighbourhood Policy, Country Report, Moldova, May 12, 2004, SEC (2004) 567.

[42] Ibid., pp. 6-8.
[43] Ibid., pp. 10-11.
[44] E. Baracani, "From the EMP to the ENP: A New European Pressure for Democratisation in the Southern Mediterranean? The Case of Morocco," in: *Europeanisation and Democratisation: Institutional Adaptation, Conditionality and Democratisation in the EU's Neighbour Countries*, ed. R. Di Quirico (Florence: EPAP, 2005), pp. 261-80; R. Del Sarto and T. Schumacher, "From EMP to ENP: What's at Stake with the European Neighbourhood Policy towards the Southern Mediterranean," *European Foreign Affairs Review*, No. 10, (2005): pp. 17-38.
[45] ENP Action Plan, EU-Moldova, December 9, 2004.
[46] Ibid., pp. 8-9.
[47] EU-Russia Summit, *Joint Statement*, St Petersburg, May 31, 2003, http://europa.eu.int/comm/external_relations/russia/sum05_03/js.htm (accessed January 15, 2006).
[48] EU-Russia Summit, *Summit Conclusions*, Moscow, May 10, 2005, Road Maps, Annex 1-4, http://europa.eu.int/comm/external_relations/russia/summit_05_05/finalroadmaps.pdf#ces (accessed January 15, 2006).
[49] Ibid., Annex 2.
[50] Commission of the European Communities, *Communication from the Commission* on Relations with Russia, Brussels, February 9, 2004, COM (2004) 106, p. 2.
[51] Ibid.
[52] European Parliament, *Resolution* on the European Neighbourhood Policy (Provisional Edition), January 19, 2006, Strasbourg, 2004/2166 (INI).
[53] Commission of the European Communities, *Proposal* for a Regulation of the European Parliament and of the Council laying down general provisions establishing a European Neighbourhood and Partnership Instrument, Brussels, September 29, 2004, COM (2004) 628 final, pp. 3-4.
[54] Ibid., p. 4.
[55] Commission of the European Communities, *Proposal* for a Regulation of the European Parliament and the Council of the European Union: 2004/0219 (COD), p. 12.
[56] Ibid., p. 15.
[57] Ibid., pp. 36-37. For Russia's likely relative and absolute share of EU external assistance, see: M. Vahl, A Privileged Partnership? EU-Russian Relations in a Comparative Perspective, *DIIS Working Paper*, 3, (2006), p. 16.
[58] Vahl, *A Priviledged Partnership?* p. 16.
[59] See for example: S. Peers "Readmission Agreements and EC External Migration Law," *Statewatch Analysis*, 17 (2003).
[60] Agreement between the Russian Federation and the European Community on Readmission (2006), available online: http://www.delrus.ec.europa.eu/en/images/pText_pict/509/Readmission_agreement_EN.doc (accessed March 24, 2006).
[61] CEPS European Neighbourhood Watch, (Brussels: Centre for European Policy Studies, July 31, 2006), p. 8.
[62] For details of the process, see for example: G. Bosse, "The European Neighbourhood Policy and the Problem of Coherence in EU Conflict Prevention and Crisis Management" (paper presented at the EUCPCM Workshop, UACES

Research Group on European Conflict Prevention and Crisis Management Policies, Loughborough University, UK, June 16, 2006).

[63] Portuguese *Presidency of the EU* on the 20th EU-Russia Summit in Mafra, *Press Release*, October 26, 2007.

[64] During the Mafra EU-Russia Summit in October 2007 Vladimir Putting made a controversial effort to counter criticism of Russia's human rights situation. He suggested the creation of an institute to promote human rights and democracy in the EU. See: 'No breakthroughs in EU-Russia talks', *EurActiv.com*, 29 October 2007, available online: http://www.euractiv.com/en/foreign-affairs/breakthroughs-eu-russia-talks/article-167973?_print (accessed November 15, 2007).

[65] Interview Commission Official, Brussels, July 2006.

[66] R. Niebuhr, "Awkward imperialists," *The Atlantic Monthly* (May 1930), quote found in: J. Fallows, "In Praise of Hypocrisy: The Role of Values in Foreign Policy," *Perspectives*, (Sydney, Australia: Lowy Institute for International Policy, May 2006), p. 8.

Chapter 15
The EU's Policies Toward the Ukraine

Sergiy Glebov

Although the EU-Ukraine relationship is not a key factor for global and regional transformations yet, it has the capacity to become such in the near future in case the Ukraine is able to achieve its strategic goal—to join the EU as a full member. Meanwhile, the new political configuration for Europe and Eurasia is seen as an important step for constructing a multipolar world. This goal is a corner-stone and sometimes even a trouble for current EU-Ukraine relations. From the very beginning, during the bilateral relations, the Ukraine has always been willing, at least on the official level, to acquire a full membership in the EU. More importantly, in accordance with the Copenhagen criteria, the Ukraine is, in principle, eligible to join the EU. This applies strong obligations not only on the Ukraine to conform itself to the criteria in order to start negotiations for accession, but also on the EU to define a clear strategy for the Ukraine. Moreover, a consolidated position for the Ukraine is a must for its perspective to become a part of the united European community. This is why it is necessary to stress that analyzing the EU's policies toward the Ukraine can be understandable and rational only in case, when these policies are defined under the perspective of possible full membership of the Ukraine in this organization.

Strategic Factors of the EU Policies toward the Ukraine

For the last five years, two main factors have influenced EU policies toward the Ukraine; the first one of which originates from within the EU, and the second one comes from inside the Ukraine. Both factors are influencing the way the bilateral relations are formulated and reflecting the complexity faced by the EU when developing its policy toward the Ukraine.

The first factor to be examined is the EU's lack of a Euro-integrative perspective for the Ukraine. This is an acute problem due to the uncertainty inside the EU related to the future level of relations with the Ukraine. As there are advocates of full membership of the Ukraine in the EU, there are also member-states, which doubt or directly oppose the Ukraine's ability to become a part of the EU. The discourse on new members is crossed by the hot dispute on the necessity of future enlargement in particular and the EU's ability to manage it in general. Acute problems inside the EU, which are going much further than just discourse on the European Constitution, are showing that the future membership of the Ukraine in the EU is under question. This is not only because of political reasons or geopolitical choice of "widening," but because of the concrete parameters of "deepening:" economic, financial, market, labor, social and foreign policy complications. The perspective of the next round of the EU enlargement with some Balkan states and Turkey is not resolved either. So, the the Ukraine's Euro-integrative perspective is facing a hard discussion which may be resolved while answering three interconnected questions: Is the EU willing to be enlarged more in principle? Is the EU interested to continue its enlargement through the Western Newly Independent States (NIS)? Is the EU ready to consider the Ukraine as a potential candidate to be included in the Union? The complexity of finding answers to each of these questions influences not only the dynamics of the current policy of the EU toward the Ukraine, but also ignites a painful reaction, or even irritation, in some EU officials, especially when they are asked about the Ukraine joining the EU.

The second factor is the paradoxical and dramatic situation inside the Ukraine, whose internal and external policies send different, sometimes even opposing signals to the EU and the rest of the world. The dramatic, even absurd situation has been worsened because of the fact that the Ukraine clearly stated its strategic goal to be a member of the EU in 1998 and NATO in 2002 and reconfirmed it several times. Nevertheless, the ambivalent foreign policy of the Ukraine reflects highly contested discourse on where the Ukraine should pose, within integrated Europe and Euro-Atlantic structures of security, or stay by the side of Russia and keep having Russian-led integrative political, economic and military institutions.[1] Additionally, there is no consensus inside Ukrainian ruling elites and society on which way to go either. Western Ukraine is supporting pro-European vector while Eastern Ukraine advocates a pro-Russian direction. All this misunderstanding has finally led to the most destructive foreign policy crisis on the level of a decision-making mechanism in the contemporary history of the Ukraine. Occasionally, the Ukraine was balanced on the edge of political crisis because of such different approaches toward the foreign policy, but the actual crash-point took place in December 2006. This happened when at the end of 2006, the mentioned contradiction fired an open political battle between pro-Western President, Minister of Foreign Affairs and pro-Russian Prime Minister with the political majority in the Government and Parliament. Due to these clashes in political interests, this political crisis ended wtih dramatic events in April-June 2007, which almost inspired a second "orange revolution" in the Ukraine. This situation has not been any clearer, even after Prime-Minister Viktor Yanukovych, who was himself actually a pro-Russian politician, assured European partners in late June 2007 that there was no alternative to the European course of the Ukraine integrating into the EU.[2] Another problem to be overcome by both sides is that European politicians do not trust Ukrainian politicians, since they sometimes do not even know who is responsible from the Ukrainian side to conduct negotiations and who holds the last word in formulating the Ukrainian strategy before the EU.

"Geopolitical Razors" of the Ukraine as a Test for the EU

The task is getting even tougher when some particular specifications of the Ukraine vis-a-vis the EU are taken into account. The Ukraine, at least theoretically, may be accepted as the number one candidate from the Commonwealth of Independent States' (CIS) zone to become a member of the EU in future. On the part of the EU, on the other hand, there is a chance to integrate the first former USSR republic, which is also part of the CIS. Another important point to mention is that the strategic partnership between the Ukraine and the EU can be developed and studied even without any limitation of concrete dates and terms, because once the political decision to start the negotiations on accession is accepted, the dramatic mechanism of geopolitical changes will be activated. This may be compared to the 1991 dissolution of the USSR to some extent. In terms of geopolitics, the indicated CIS space is the one that is strongly connected to the sphere of Russian vital interests and influence where the Russian Federation is trying to remain as a super-power. Even from this point of view, we can say that losing three Baltic States has caused almost no serious harm to Russian interests compared to what Russia might lose when the Ukraine integrates with the EU. When we are talking about losing, we must, first of all, mention that the political influence of the official Kyiv has a tremendous effect on the global and regional security architecture, as well as on the new format of economic relations in the region of Eastern Europe in pan-European format. At the same time, however, there is no need to overestimate or underestimate the Russian factor in the EU-Ukraine relations.

The EU policymakers, while defining the strategy and tactics toward the Ukraine, are well aware that in a wide theoretical sense, the Ukraine falls into the conceptual model of Borderland Europe, meaning the territories that lie between the enlarging EU and Russia, or of their overlapping peripheries. Such an approach was underlined in Michael Emerson's "The Elephant and the Bear," in 2001. According to this, the regions of Borderland Europe fall into several categories: integrating peripheries, or states that aspire to integrate with one or the other of the two empires; divided peripheries, or states that are divided between Western and Eastern orientations and are looking toward both empires at the same time; and overlapping peripheries, which is when a community from one of the empires finds itself marooned or enclaved within the other empire.[3] The peculiar situation with the Ukraine shows that it has been absorbing all three categories at the same time, which gives its foreign and domestic policies a lack of strategy and clearness in future development. On the conceptual level of Borderland Europe, which may also be identified as a "gray zone," the Ukraine at the moment is a divided periphery which looks for the status of integrating periphery by overcoming the syndrome of overlapping periphery. As long as the Ukraine is in the process of choosing an appropriate model of development, in any case its strategic aim must be to resolve the problem of changing the status from "periphery" to the integrated "center." That will be possible only if the Ukraine is able to integrate into a democratic conglomerate of equal partners, where the meaning of "periphery" and "center" also exists, but in a comparative-technical paradigm where it loses the negative empire-colonial meaning. Looking at the current model of integrating Europe within the EU, it is not hard to predict, that the Ukraine may be interested in pursuing the European vector. In practice, however, the scene is not that clear especially if the Ukraine will remain as a divided periphery.

For both the Ukraine and the EU, even theoretical assumptions of full integration are a strong challenge compared with their potential to develop in the future. Present EU-Ukraine relations can be accepted as a current test for both sides. For the EU, it is necessary to check whether it has geopolitical ambitions supported by an adequate ability to proceed with the enlargement to cover the whole CIS space and to guarantee a solid lifelong undisturbed living status in accordance with the Copenhagen criteria. For the Ukraine, on the other hand, full integration with the EU means not only taking a crucial step in its state building, but also becoming a successful European state. This reveals that the Ukraine is able to secure its independence, sovereignty and integrity, as well as to build its own democracy and market economy with a satisfactory level of living, in order to prevent and escape from permanent social crises and to guarantee personal and collective security measures. However, this is a test that is still to be passed and, frankly, sounds too optimistic. Presently, much more pragmatic problems are hampering this optimistic scenario.

The EU and the Ukraine: "Uneasy" Rapprochement

Despite that the Ukraine has proclaimed its strategy to become the member of the EU in 1998, its march "into Europe" has not been only slow, but it has also been one step forward, two steps backward. On the bilateral level there is no strongly awaited breakthrough and immediate shift from the unclear dialog into more concrete steps, as the direction of accession negotiations are still held under the shadow of uncertainty. Nevertheless, since the beginning of the late 1990s, fundamental geopolitical changes have been inevitably pushing the EU toward the Ukraine. As a result, the EU has been sharing a common border with the Ukraine since May 1, 2004. For international organizations, the ability to enlarge by means of integrating new members is an essential part of their appropriate functioning and development. In this sense, it was not hard to predict that the EU would appear on the stage, when Brussels would be forced to pay attention to the

Ukraine as the new EU neighbor after the 2004 enlargement. Moreover, for the Ukraine the EU is a center of power and pole of attraction and this pushes Kyiv now not only toward Brussels, but also toward capital cities of each EU country neighboring the Ukraine. Does this mean that EU countries share a common strategy toward the Ukraine? No doubt, the strategy of Poland, Slovakia, Hungary, and Romania are differing from those that are on the west of Warsaw, Bratislava, Budapest, and Bucharest. Sometimes, because of the Ukraine, some minor contradictions even occur between the new EU members—states bordering the Ukraine—and the old members—states not sharing a border with the Ukraine. Nevertheless, the Ukraine became a part of the EU strategy some time ago and since then, we have been witnessing its uneasy evolution.

The rapprochement of the Ukraine is still continuing in many directions on different levels by the use of various tools. This rapprochement is performed through both institutional and personal initiatives, depending on the political wills of the EU and the Ukraine. Is has been a two-way street, for which, however, the most strategic initiatives always came from the side of the EU. It has been possible to start the rapprochement thanks to two main factors: the dissolution of the USSR which was followed by the appearance of Newly Independent States, and the firm strategic decision of the EU to enlarge toward the East. Both factors are interconnected, but the crucial step forward was taken by the EU after the European Economic Community was transformed into the EU following the 1993 Maastricht Treaty and the decision to integrate new democracies from Central and Eastern Europe was taken.

The EU, where we can find four G8 members and two out of five constant UN Security Council members, is the largest integrative community in the world with a perspective of federalization. From the very beginning of the post-bipolar period, it was doomed to play a super-active role in the process of political transformation in geographical Europe, including Western NIS. The most powerful instrument that may bring Brussels and Kyiv closer is the EU's enlargement toward the East. As we already mentioned, the Ukraine is not a subject of any enlargement strategy adopted in the EU. Meanwhile, the Ukraine has a chance to show why the European choice for the Ukraine may be the most effective way to defend its national interests in a short- and long-term perspective. This can be carried out by means of taking an active part in the processes of European integration and by proving why the EU must be interested in integrating the Ukraine. The concept of "integration of the Ukraine with the EU" should be considered from a much wider perspective than just obtaining a full EU membership, since the Ukraine, not only politically, but also technically (bureaucratically) will not be able to join the EU within the next 10-15 years. At the same time, this reality does not weaken the European choice of the Ukraine, because for the Ukraine, European integration is seen as a process for the full-scale political and economic transformation to democracy and market economy, and the perspective of joining the EU as a full member is actually an instrument that will push the Ukraine to perform the transformation successfully.

The EU-Ukraine Relations as a Need for the Ukraine

As a pre-condition to full membership, the Ukraine has to follow the idea of internal Europeanization based on the "Strategy of Integration of the Ukraine with the EU," adopted by the Ukrainian President, Leonid Kuchma on June 11, 1998.[4] The Strategy corresponds to the national interests of the Ukraine and has to assist the Ukraine "in integration to the European political, security, information, economic, and judicial space." The Ukraine has to share the attitudes and approaches approved in the EU to achieve (or, at least to approach at the beginning) some certain standards of social life as well as economic goals by transforming itself into a well-established democracy. Hence, the main interest of the Ukraine in integrating into the EU is associated with the interest in re-emerging a firm political will from the Ukrainian post-communist political elite to become a modern (in some spheres post-modern), integral and consolidated community which shares European values, like respect for human rights, rule of law, market economy, and guarantees its citizens' individual and social security, and economic prosperity on the basis of social justice. To achieve such a desirable model of a state system will only be possible when the Ukraine will not only take the EU as a lighthouse for its internal and external policies, but also be ready to treat the EU as an undisputed contributor to, assistant to and facilitator for Ukrainian reforms. Such assistance must be accompanied by a permanent monitoring and constant consultations between Kyiv and Brussels on the way, on which all potential candidates reach an official candidate-state status, which includes a standard action plan process. Such an intensive tutelage must be considered as a logic and idea partaking upon pan-European affairs and "acknowledged interference" of the Ukraine into the process of the European integration and Europeanization and must never be regarded as a direct interference of the EU into the internal affairs of the Ukraine.

Democracy and legitimacy are the two principal ideas that need to be adopted during the contemporary discourse about the European integration. The debate about democracy in the EU is based on the twin assumption that the Union, although partly-formed, is a polity and that it impinges to a growing extent on the institutions and practices of national democracies.[5] Despite this fact, there is still a great necessity to focus on a high level of democracy through which current political (and consequently economic and judicial) diseases of the Ukraine can be healed. The EU has the capacity to improve the Ukraine for the better. At this point, another matter is that whether the Ukraine is ready and wishes to become a modern European state, will work hard on reforms, demolish corruption, and apply high European standards even without necessarily obtaining the full membership in the end.

The EU-Ukraine Relationship Basis: The Art of Possible

Nevertheless, EU policies toward the Ukraine are now developing out of the question of whether the Ukraine is going to be an EU member or not. The EU relations with the Ukraine are based on the Partnership and Cooperation Agreement (PCA), which entered into force in 1998 (for an initial ten year period renewable by consent of the parties). A Protocol to the PCA was signed by the EU and the Ukraine on March 30, 2004 to extend the application of the agreement in full to the 10 new EU Member States that joined the EU on May 1, 2004. A further protocol to the PCA extending its application to Bulgaria and Romania has been agreed to. A joint EU-Ukraine Action Plan is based on PCA and was endorsed by the EU-Ukraine Cooperation Council on February 21, 2005. The Action Plan, which has been concluded for a period of three years, provides a comprehensive and ambitious framework for working with the Ukraine, identifying all the key areas of reform. The Ukraine is considered a priority partner country within the European Neighborhood Policy (ENP). The institutional framework of bilateral relations is based on the main bilateral structures that are established by the PCA, which include: bilateral Summit meetings (annual) between the Presidents of the Ukraine and the EU Presidency together with the President of the Commission and the EU's High Representative, Cooperation Councils, Cooperation Committees, and Sub-Committees.

Following enlargement, the EU has become the Ukraine's largest trading partner accounting for about 32 percent of the Ukraine's total trade (for example, in 2005 the Ukraine's exports to the EU-25 amounted to €7.7 billion, and imports €13.0 billion).[6] The Ukraine, at its turn, constitutes less than 1 percent of total EU trade.[7] Trade with the Ukraine is on a Most Favored Nation treatment conducted under the PCA, which allows trading of goods without any quantitative restrictions, except for in the steel sector, which is currently governed by a separate agreement providing for export quotas to the EU. Funding under the national TACIS programs, which has been the framework for technical assistance for the Ukraine since the early 1990s, has been substantially increased from €47 million in 2002 to €88 million in 2005 and €100 million in 2006.[8] The European Neighborhood and Partnership Instrument (ENPI) are set to replace TACIS in 2007.

The Ukraine is seeking to accede to the WTO, and for this aim, in March 2003, it signed its bilateral market access protocol with the EC. The Ukraine is now working to become capable to meet all the multilateral rules of the WTO and the EU is supporting the Ukraine in this process. In December

2005, the EU granted to the Ukraine Market Economy Status, which is particularly relevant for trade defense investigations.

A perspective for a future a Free Trade Area is also contained in the PCA. The establishment of a Free Trade Area between the Ukraine and the EU will be accelerated with a view to enable an early start of negotiations once the Ukraine has joined the World Trade Organization.

Nowadays, the EU is preparing for the negotiations of a comprehensive New Enhanced Agreement with the Ukraine, as a successor to the Partnership and Cooperation Agreement. With the EU Council Conclusions of February 2005, the EU took a political commitment to start early consultations on an Enhanced Agreement with the Ukraine that would outline when the political priorities of the Action Plan were to be fulfilled.

On September 13, 2006 the EC proposed negotiating directives for a new Enhanced Agreement with the Ukraine. The Commission proposed that the new agreement should be a comprehensive agreement covering all areas of the EU-Ukraine interaction which can reach all possible areas that are beyond the existing Partnership and Cooperation Agreement. It should include provisions on common values, enhanced cooperation on justice, freedom and security, extensive specifications on energy, and cooperation in a broad range of areas such as transport and environment. A Free Trade Area should be one of the main elements, for which negotiations could start once the Ukraine has completed its WTO accession process. Negotiation of the new agreement most likely will continue to build upon the positive progress that has already been established through the implementation of the EU-Ukraine Action Plan.

The recent constitutional crisis in the Ukraine, which took place right after the March 26, 2006 Parliamentary elections, which were claimed to be democratic, hampered the negotiations on the Enhanced Agreement. Currently, the Ukraine is still under the concern of the EU as a European Neighbor and is a subject of the ENP, which does not foresee future membership. Meanwhile, as seen by proponents of Ukrainian membership in the EU, the definition of the ENP as it realtes to the Ukraine is not correct in principle, because this title for a policy indicates that it covers the neighbors around Europe, while the Ukraine is in Europe). Benita Ferrera-Waldner, the EU Commissioner for External Relations and ENP, once again made clear in June 2007, that the question of the the Ukraine's membership in the EU remains opened, but is a question of the future.[9]

"The Border" Dimension of the EU Security Policy toward the Ukraine

Nowadays, while the strategic issues are still in question, some concrete bilateral topics continue to be negotiated by Brussels and Kyiv. The EU openly expresses its interest and concern for some security issues which threaten the security of both the Ukraine and the EU. One of these issues is the "frontier issue." With its Common Foreign and Security Policy, the Union has been exerting pressure on the security measures, especially after the last enlargements. The EU appeared to be even more dramatic contributor to the security situation in Central and Eastern Europe than NATO. It is the EU, not NATO, which constituted new boundaries in Eastern Europe during the process of the May 1, 2004 enlargement and closed the borders between the new EU members and the new EU neighbors, including the Ukraine. A security concern of the EU toward the Ukraine is natural. They are not just members, but both share the common border on the Poland-Romania axis. Any border, even within the process of European integration should be protected and such a protection is among the top priority concerns of the EU countries, especially when security agendas are connected to someone, who is on the other side of a border.

The scope of problems connected to "soft" or non-strategic security issues seems to be among the current priorities of the EU's defensive policy and the Department of Justice and Home Affairs. It is not accidental that one of the main features of the new security initiatives in Europe is to strengthen the borders militarily, financially and institutionally. Strong attention is given to the issue of combating corruption on the borders to ban illegal migration and illegal goods trafficking (in April 2004, for example, 23 Polish frontier-guards were arrested for the bribing on the Peremyshl section of Poland-Ukraine border).[10] The EU is even ready to give additional funds to EU neighbors to strengthen their borders all around its territory.

The most evident regional problem related to the issue of border protection is the situation in Moldova and Transnistria. The EU is interested in peaceful resolution of the conflict between Chisinau and Tiraspol, though at the same time Brussels is highly concerned with the protection of its boundaries in the Southeast part of Europe. In this respect, the foreign policy of Romania toward Moldova may be crucial in identifying future EU-Ukraine relations in the whole region, including the Black Sea. The European Union Border Assistance Mission to Moldova and the Ukraine (EUBAM), launched on November 30, 2005 with its headquarters in Odessa, might become a key promoter of the EU policy in the Northwest part of the Black Sea region. Under the EU's Neighborhood Policy, the EU is reaching out to its neighbors in order to promote prosperity, common values and security, as well as to help breaking down trade barriers. EUBAM is one of the vital instruments to support such an agenda. The actual appearance of this EU institution itself shows that the EU has a strong intention to be involved in a long-term regional cooperation in the security field with the Ukraine and other Western NIS.

Naturally, this impact caused by the EU will constantly increase. The new EU countries of Central and Eastern Europe do not want to border a "gray zone." This is also true and applicable for Poland, Hungary, Slovakia, Baltic States, Finland, Romania, and Turkey. These countries themselves will be the actual actors which will aggressively promote the development of multilateral trans-border cooperation in security fields on the East of their own boundaries. It is understandable when Moldova, Belarus and the Ukraine, countries that are bordering the Russian Federation, are connecting their own security with that of the countries they border.

For the Ukraine, it is essential that the EU's border protection process develop in a way that it will not construct a new curtain in Eastern Europe. This means that the EU, as well as OSCE, Council of Europe and other European institutions should be interested in keeping their involvement in post-Soviet space. If Brussels decides to and completes the integration after 2007, the EU will still be interested in contributing to regional security as a peace moderator and crisis manager for a number of reasons. The Ukraine only strengthens its partnership with the EU in this sense. This is why the decision taken by the European Council in June 2007 to extend a mandate for the EUBAM to Moldova and the Ukraine for the next two years sounds reasonable and timely.

The EU Foreign and Security Policy toward the Ukraine: the Factor of NATO

In the post-Cold War era the EU has been carrying the next long-term coordination for its security strategies closely with NATO, whether the EU wants to decrease the influence of the U.S., or not. The EU and NATO appeared to be on the vanguard of international processes shaping the Europe's future. At the same time, tactical approaches to the eastern borders of both the EU and NATO, and toward the Ukraine are interpreted slightly differently in the headquarters of the two institutions in Brussels. In the Ukraine and in many other countries, NATO and the EU are generally accepted as one homogeneous body even at points where NATO has military, the EU has economic priorities. At the same time, however, there is a key difference between NATO and the EU with respect to relations with the Ukraine: NATO, to which military and geopolitical issues are fundamental concerns, is more pro-Ukrainian because of the global position of the U.S. on one hand, and the Russian factor on the other; the EU, however, has its own privileged position free from the need of any aid from the U.S. and this is why the EU is more inbound and less pro-Ukrainian because of its own high-standard, economic top-interests and its dependence on Russian energy and common military neighborhood. Moreover, the issue of the Ukraine and relations between the U.S. and the EU, the issue of the Ukraine became part of a contradicting a never-ending story on European Eurocentrism and European Atlantism (though, this is what also resembles and reminds us of the case of Turkey in relations with NATO, the U.S. and the EEC/EU).

Taking this difference into consideration and tactically it is easier to get a full NATO membership for the Ukraine than to join the EU. At the same time, a NATO membership may be seen as a key step for the Ukraine that may facilitate its entrance to the EU. The European integration is sometimes seen as a continuation and integral part of the Euro-Atlantic integration. This is true for some Central and Eastern European countries that first became NATO members. They were then granted membership status. But this is not true for Turkey, which became a NATO member a number of decades ago and desperately has been waiting for EU membership almost the same period of time. Of course, there were different international situations— "Cold War" and "Post-Cold War" periods—when the decisions on NATO and EU enlargements were made. But still, the two organizations are so close to each other that, for the outsiders, there is almost no conceptual difference between tactical membership in the EU and membership in NATO on the way to strategically aim at being a part of democratic and stable Europe.

Naturally, there is an institutional difference for those European countries that are NATO members, but not EU members, and vice versa, but no actual difference for those that are outside of both organizations—even for the neutral countries, such as Austria or Sweden, for whom there is no urgent need to be part of NATO. NATO will most likely remain indifferent to any military threat to these countries. They, however, are already inside NATO's zone of responsibility, even without a membership status. Moreover, Finland, another neutral EU member, is now planning to reconsider its status and discuss the option of joining NATO. The same can also be said for the Ukraine: to remain neutral, but to continue its course toward the EU by building its own Europe inside its frontiers. Whereas for the Ukraine today, to join NATO within the next 4-5 years is much more realistic than to join the EU within the next 15-20 years. What's really important for the Ukraine at present is to take all crucial steps leading to democratic European space by means of NATO membership which also requires not only military, but also political obligations to develop democracy and a market economy.

This is why the question of the Ukraine attracts more attention inside NATO and is regarded more realistically than the the Ukraine question discussed inside the EU. It is because of the same reason that the issue of the Ukraine in NATO seems so painful for Russia from many points of view. But the most disturbing fact is that the Ukraine may join NATO and slip away from the Russian zone of influence. Russia is more flexible and relaxed when talking about the Ukraine and the EU, because it has nothing to panic about, since the EU does not open itself institutionally to the Ukraine now, nor in the foreseeable future. It would also be interesting to witness how Russian foreign policy will react to the Ukraine at the time, when the issues of the Ukraine's membership to the EU become real. It will also be interesting to see the reaction of the EU when the Ukraine appears among NATO members…

The Energy Security and EU-Ukraine-Russia Triangle as a Factor of the EU Policy Toward the Ukraine

Recently, the security discourse in Europe has significantly shifted toward the sphere of energy security where the future role of the Ukraine is getting special attention. The dependence of the EU on Russian oil and gas, and the dependence of Russia on the EU's financial resources make both sides important partners to each other for a long time. At this point, the Ukraine plays a key role in connecting Russian gas to the European market. The gas transit crisis that broke out between Russia and the Ukraine at the end of 2005 and at the beginning of 2006 has disclosed the existence of a deep threat for the energy security of Europe and this raised some sympathy toward the Ukraine against the Russian "energetic" blackmailing. The shock of this temporal instability in the gas supply made the EU reflect more upon securing its energy needs and finding alternative energy resources. This matter gained even more significance especially during a time when it is quite hard to find alternative sources while, at the same time, knowing that the energy consumption will be constantly increasing in the future. In this case, the EU is interested in supplying stable transit of Russian gas through Unkrainian territory in the future.

Obviously, giving secondary importance to its non-economic interests in its relations with Russia and the other NIS, the EU will naturally be interested in negotiating directly with Russia. Lack of geopolitical ambitions and the economic pragmatism may lead to the most unpleasant scenario for the Ukraine in which the EU, trying not to intervene in Russian-Ukrainian relations, may promise Russia not to grant the Ukraine a membership perspective, and may "close its eyes" to the low democracy level in the Ukraine. Russia, on the other hand, guarantees stable transport of Russian gas through the Ukraine. Any weakening in the "democratic pressure" exerted by the EU upon the Ukraine may create perfect outside conditions to aggravate the non-democratic sides of any Ukrainian regime, which, under this scenario, can make the Ukraine untouchable to both the EU and Russia. The Ukraine generally plays on the side of Russian international interests. In this respect, when the EU will guarantee its energy needs, it will not need to be bothered by any Ukrainian claims for membership anymore and Russia will continue keeping the Ukraine under its influence, especially in sharing and privatizing Ukrainian gas and oil transport systems. Pragmatically, a non-democratic Ukrainian regime can carry out its business under cover both with the EU and Russia.

Such a scenario is not favored by the democracy-oriented Ukrainian society and by Ukrainian Euro-optimists who are not at all keen to see the Ukraine as a passive object of closed negotiations between the EU and Russia that sacrifice the freedom and democracy for the material stability of post-Soviet oligarchs and, at any price, gain energy security of the EU in return. This scenario seems very likely to come true in the near future. There also is a possibility that the competition between the EU and Russia in the energy sector will be tied. The Odessa-Brody-Plotsk (Gdansk) pipeline project is another energy link which is planned to connect the EU to the Black Sea through the Ukraine. Poland, as well as the EU, is also interested in this project. In regard to this project, the press release issued by the European Commission to the Ukraine and Belarus on August 8, 2005, noted: "The construction of the Black Sea-Ukraine-Poland oil transportation corridor is a crucial infrastructure project in the context of EU and Ukrainian policies for security of oil supplies."[11] Considering that the EU is heavily dependent upon the unstable energy resources of Russia, it is quite reasonable to ask the question: "Have no alternative routes been considered in the past, and if there were, why were they rejected?"[12]

The Odessa-Brody pipeline, the first phase of which was put into operation in 2002, is still working, despite having now pumped Russian oil to Odessa, instead of pumping Kazakhi oil in the northern direction and the pipeline is still a valuable alternative route for Caspian oil to reach Europe. Predicting that the EU's middle-term strategy about the Ukraine will be partly focused on the Odessa-Brody-Plotsk pipeline project, it will be rational for the EU to try to achieve three main objectives. First, and the most challenging, is to make it clear and convince its members that this project is so vitally important for the EU that it is ready to lobby for the flow of oil to be restored back toward the North, even if it has to confront Russian and Ukrainian Presidents' resistance. The second one is to raise necessary funds to stretch the pipeline from Ukrainian Brody to Polish Plotsk. The third objective is to convince itself that it is ready to regard the Ukraine as a long-term, strategic collaborator that has integrative potential. Will the EU use this opportunity and overtake the necessary responsibility in a long-lasting geopolitical and energy security game in the Black Sea region under such circumstances? The question may seem quite rhetorical, but it is vital for all involved parties, especially the Ukraine. Although the current situation is not in favor of this project, that can change in the future. This is the reason that triggers Poland and the Ukraine to try their best to promote the project.

Some "Ukrainian Reflections" on the EU's Cautious Steps Toward the Ukraine at the Beginning of the 21st Century

Just as the EU is trying to see concrete European steps taken by the Ukraine, the Ukraine is also expecting an adequate response from the West in return. How a cautious policy of the EU toward the Ukraine can correct Ukrainian foreign policy was seen on the eve of the dramatic Presidential elections in the Ukraine in late 2004. The Ukraine's strategic aim to join NATO and the EU, to establish a close relationship with NATO, to support the antiterrorist coalition in Iraq, to ensure the Odessa-Brody-Poland pipeline-project is aimed to serve the EU, and even the conflict over Tuzla with Russia in 2003, all showed Brussels and Washington that the Ukraine was waiting for concrete steps to be taken by its Western partners. Ukrainian Euro-optimists have been waiting for real integration steps to be taken by Brussels, and criticizes it for being passive toward Kyiv. Actually, intense negotiations held by the EU with the Ukraine about the Chernobyl problem, shows that the EU can establish quite concrete relations with the Ukraine if it feels the necessity.

Due to various reasons, the Ukraine changed some of its foreign-policy priorities in order to build closer relations with Russia in 2003-2004. In 2004, political and economic benefits in establishing closer relations with Russia were more attractive for the government in Kyiv than the unclear, "Western" future of the Ukraine. From among these uncertainties, we can list some crucial ones. On September 19, 2003, a decision to join the Single Economic Space was taken. The President and the Prime-Minister of the Ukraine stated in summer 2004 that the Ukraine was not ready to discuss a concrete date of the NATO accession.[13] In the new military doctrine adopted on July 15, 2004, the aim of the Ukraine to join NATO was excluded. The Odessa-Brody pipeline, officially on July 5 and technically in September 2004, redirected the Russian oil toward Brody-Odessa. On the eve of the 2004 elections, the "ruling political party" was supporting pro-Russian candidate for Presidency who was competing with a pro-Western candidate. This caused different repercussions to be raised from neighboring states. Polish Vice-Prime-Minister Hausner, for example, stated that Poland assessed the decision of the Ukrainian government to reverse the flow of the Odessa-Brody pipeline as the Ukrainians' denial to join the European integration.[14] The EU was really disturbed about the Ukrainian integration into the Single Economic Market with Russia, Belarus and Kazakhstan, which was considered in Brussels as a real obstacle on the way to the European integration.[15] From the perspective of the Ukraine, however, this did not mean that the Ukraine had given up its "Western" vector. In fact, the Ukraine was always interested in the cooperative security system in Europe to prevent a new iron curtain from being formed and to eliminate current and future contradictions, like the one between NATO and Russia. Thus, the Ukraine could be saved from playing the difficult role of regional counterbalancing under pressure from both sides, especially in a situation when the Ukraine can change its priorities in favor of European and Euro-Atlantic integration. This was actually what had happened in 2005.

We have to outline that the Ukraine, with its political ambiguity, does not ignore the logistics of the current security and political situation both in Europe and in the world. While trying to squeeze out maximum benefit from "multi-vector" policy through strengthening integral cooperation on all possible "Western" and "Eastern" directions, it also pushes both sides to just "mention" the Ukraine on the political map from time to time. This approach causes the Ukraine's respondents to address their own interests while, at the same time, mentioning how important the Ukraine is for them. This example was not only seen in the case of Russia when the Ukraine turned toward NATO in 2002. The political and economic rapprochement of Russia and the Ukraine in 2003-2004 forced the West to speak about the strategic importance of the Ukraine. After the cold statements of Romano Prodi, which were mainly addressed to the Ukrainian EU perspectives,[16] the former Austrian foreign minister Benita-Maria Ferrero-Waldner (anticipating one of the top positions in the European Commission on that time), stated in October 2004 that the EU must be interested at least in holding the Ukraine on its side not to appear in the Russian sphere of influence, because Russia is going back in terms of democracy.[17] The U.S. expressed its concern as well. During his visit to Poland in October 2004, Paul Wolfowitz stated that the aim of the U.S. and its allies comprising a united Europe would not be completed until the Ukraine joined the NATO. He also stated that the U.S. should pay more attention to the Ukraine and that "NATO needs to give the hand to the Ukraine and at the end to admit it as a full member."[18] This view was naturally supported by Poland, which is strongly advocating and pushing Ukrainian interests in the EU and NATO. At the meeting on October 10, 2004, Poland and ten other EU members asked the EU to give the Ukraine a European perspective to keep it closer to the EU.[19] Here we must mention Brzezinski's thesis. Unfortunately, some positive signs of pro-Ukrainian interests were seen from the side of the West when the Ukraine was moving closer to Russia and the voice of the Ukraine was hardly heard when it tried to talk to the West directly.

The Ukraine's EU Membership: To Be or Not To Be? If "To Be," then "When"?

After the "Orange Revolution," the EU has tried to find an adequate approach regarding its future relations with the Ukraine. At this point, the issue of the Ukraine's possible membership remains the corner-stone of the EU strategy as to the Ukraine when filling the content on the current stage of relations. Strategically, the proclaimed aim to join the EU was the top priority for the new Ukrainian government in 2005, which was strongly associated with the pro-European former Ukrainian Minister of Foreign Affairs, Boris Tarasiuk. Unexpectedly, some radical talks emerged inside the Ukraine about EU membership perspectives that somehow even frightened the EU. The EU accession talks with the Ukraine, which were unreal during President Kuchma and were almost impossible with the pro-Russian candidate, Prime Minister Yanykovich before 2005, suddenly were placed on the agenda by the EU. The EU had to either react fast in order to instill European foreign policy priorities into the Ukraine, or just calm the situation down strategically and leave the Ukraine with the status of "only a neighbor of the EU."

After a short period of idealistic, even romantic inspirations between the EU and the Ukraine in 2005, while President Yushchenko was the most welcomed Ukrainian politician in the EU since the beginning of 1990s and hoped to start negotiations on accession in 2008, Brussels faced disappointment at the end of 2006 and the beginning of 2007. The unfinished democratic revolution in 2004 that hampered democratic reforms caused constant political crisis in the Ukraine. The accession perspective, however, is strongly connected to what the Ukraine will be able to achieve on its way to the united Europe. Consequently, the EU reacted quite clearly to such a situation when the talks about reform in general did not lead them to any factual outcome. For example, while speaking at an EU-Ukraine summit meeting in Helsinki, Finland, in October 2006, the European Commission president, José Manuel Barroso, said the Ukraine had not enacted sufficient economic and political reforms to make it a contender for EU membership. "The Ukraine is not ready, and we are not ready," he said.[20] Barroso added at a joint news conference with Yushchenko that his comments should not be construed as a "negative signal" for the Ukraine, but were calculated to encourage the country to press ahead with difficult reforms.[21] The issue was that what had been proclaimed did not match what had been achieved in practice.

As a result, the Ukraine found itself stuck in an irresolute manner. As it was written in Frankfurter Allgemeine Zeitung in March 2007, "After the year 2004 in the Ukraine a paradoxical process of accession without an accession perspective has started."[22] Meanwhile, it is quite natural that Boris Tarasiuk, today out of office but remaining as one of the most active pro-European politicians in the Ukraine, is convinced that the EU must make a political decision as to the future membership of the Ukraine as it was made to all European countries in the beginning of 1990s.[23] At the same time, in May 2007, Andre Sewerin, one of the members of the European Parliament, stated that on the current stage of the EU-Ukraine relations, not only emotions, but also the rule of law and European values must play their roles.[24] He concluded that only under such conditions will the Ukraine have a membership perspective.[25] It is natural that the EU is waiting not on the Ukraine's regular political surprises, but on real social changes that will identify future relations of the Ukraine with the EU.

The possibility of membership of the Ukraine, on the other hand, is strongly connected to the perspectives of further enlargement of the EU in principal. On the background of pessimism inside the EU, during the EU Summit in December 2006 in Brussels, Barroso, the President of the European Commission, Barroso, confirmed that the enlargement would carry on and the doors would be kept open.[26] Obviously, all countries, which are not EU members, have to respect the requirements of the EU, but the EU in its turn, if these countries fulfill all requirements, cannot refuse them membership.[27] The EU's enlargement process is a matter to be developed under three "C"s—communication, consolidation and conditionality.[28] Chancellor Angela Merkel outlined her thoughts on partnerships with non-member states while preparing for Germany's EU presidency before January 1, 2007. Speaking in the Bundestag before the EU summit in December 2006, she said Europe must develop privileged partnerships with non-members irrespective of any on-going entry talks.[29] "It involves the Ukraine, countries around the Black Sea and indeed others," she said. "That is why we need to have policies that are attractive to our neighbors. That way, we can bring the EU closer to countries that can't become members."[30]

One possible solution regarding the cooperation with the Ukraine is suggested by Peter Sain ley Berry, a famous British expert and former European Commission's official. He proposed to form a temporal "club of candidates" by the countries that are willing to join the EU, but have yet to receive an invitation. He suggested "that the Western Balkans and other potential EU candidates should not compete over accession to the EU, racing against each other to slip in under a closing door; they should cooperate. As the EU seeks increasing involvement with the Western Balkans, Turkey, the Ukraine and the Caucasus, these countries should respond by working together to address issues of reform and development that they need to tackle in any case before accession. One way of doing this would be by forming a community of their own, with common institutions paralleling those of the EU. This entire community might then adhere to the EU as a bloc."[31] The proposed mechanism is quite challenging and to some extent radical. Even though it sounds very optimistic and opens "European perspective" to the Ukraine, there is at least one very serious negative in the idea.

The idea to be regarded "as one whole group" is irrational when all potential candidate countries are having their own particular problems, because it can cause a hindrance to others on the way into the EU. In this sense, the "adherence as a bloc" may never happen. The domestic problems, which each country faces to overcome in order to approach the EU standards and criteria, will be multiplied by the number of "alien" obstacles. Moreover, the integration strategy must be followed individually, not collectively. Collective movement is possible for some countries in certain parts of Europe that show relatively similar levels of development. On the other hand, it is hard to combine all candidate countries in one set; we cannot, for example, place Georgia, which suffers from military threats, on the same level as the advanced state of Croatia. Moreover, the rest of the European countries will most likely develop their relations with the EU on the basis of individual strategy and agreements. The combination of twosome-threesome sets of countries may be designed in order not to accept anyone. Recently, Turkey and the Ukraine are seen as the two countries that are running toward the EU in tandem. From the perspective of the Ukraine, this can be seen as a good sign since it is kind of an honor to be combined with a country that has been knocking on the European door for almost forty years and is very mcuh on its way to Europeanization. For Turkey, however, it is perhaps not a promising sign for these reasons for the Ukraine to be counted in the European integration. The worst scenario is depicted in a famous joke as follows: "When will Turkey become a member of the EU? Never. When will the Ukraine become a member of the EU? Right after Turkey."

Meanwhile, the issue of concrete dates is becoming more and more acute even when discussing the possibility of the EU membership in principle. The current Ukrainian Minister of Foreign Affairs Arseniy Yatsenuk stated in late June 2007, that the Ukraine needs now to see concrete signs that indicate "physical" grounds, or evidence of the Ukraine's integration[32] The real breakthrough in indicating concrete dates for accession was achieved during the Yalta European Strategy (YES) Forth Annual Summit on June 29-30, 2007. Ex-President of Poland, Aleksandr Kvasnewsky, stated that accession of the Ukraine will become real by 2020.[33]

This date was also supported by Marek Siwets, Vice-President of the European Parliament, who indicated that this term may even be shorter. We have already mentioned how painful obtaining concrete dates and the issue of terms have been in bilateral EU-Ukraine relations. The factual announcement of the possible date itself can be seen as upgrading the level of bilateral relations. In this regard, such a step shows a main, but currently still weak pillar of the EU's future strategy toward the Ukraine. The explanation of the stated approach by Marek Siwets is timely and important: "The announcement of such date was kind of a provocation one year ago. Then it was noted, that without concrete term it was impossible to continue further discussion about the Ukraine's membership in the EU. Following this, last year I asked international observers to create positive scenario for the Ukraine. And this date was introduced, which is quite good. But nobody liked it… But I saw, that someone took this date as a real one. So did I."[34]

Still not everybody is pleased about this date. Ambassador of Germany to the Ukraine, Reinhard Sheffers, was quite skeptical and confirmed that currently there was no question discussed about the accession of the Ukraine. "The year of 2020 no one accepted as a goal," he concluded.[35] Rainer Lindner, German expert from the Association for Science and Politics, also stated that the EU has two concrete tasks as to the Ukraine in

2007 namely, joining WTO, what could become a sign as to the ability of the state to reform, and beginning the negotiations for a free trade zone with the EU. He thinks that for the development of the Ukraine, such aims are more important than any statement on a possible date of accession to the EU.[36]

What Next? (In Lieu of a Conclusion)

As it mentioned above, the EU is preparing to negotiate a comprehensive New Enhanced Agreement with the Ukraine to start the new strategic era of relations from 2008. The main agenda of the bilateral relations for the second half of 2007 comprises the discussions over the content of the long-awaited Agreement. Basically, there is at least one cornerstone position which may hamper the negotiations and cause a split inside the EU about its common strategy toward the Ukraine which is: to mention or not to mention the secret word of "membership." In January 2007, the EU Council of Ministers stressed that the New Enhanced Agreement with the Ukraine, which has been under elaboration since the beginning of 2008, does not need to define any concrete parameters or to design the future development of the bilateral relations. As also mentioned earlier, the Enhanced Agreement includes the goal of furthering the rapprochement, economic integration and political cooperation between the EU and the Ukraine. However, it includes neither a condition implying the possibility of the Ukraine's membership in the EU, nor any condition indicating the impossibility of such a membership.[37] France is one of the foremost opposing countries against the Ukraine's European perspectives. During its discussions in March 2007, France excluded all points hinting accession perspectives for the Ukraine, from the draft of the future agreement.[38]

On the other hand, in July 2007, during the following session held in Strasbourg, support for the Ukraine's future accession to the EU was discussed in the European Parliament. This impulse was given by Mikhal Tomasz Kaminsky, a Polish member of the European Parliament, in his Report, which was approved by Committee on Foreign Affairs on June 5, 2007, and by the majority of MPs on July 12. Even though the European Parliament has only a counseling voice on the issues of external policies, principal decisions are being taken by the Council of Foreign Affairs Ministers or by the EU Council. Here, we can still find a crucial recommendation: "Parliament called on the Council to consider giving the Ukraine a clear European perspective; the New Enhanced Agreement should in this context create an appropriate and effective framework for the gradual integration of the Ukraine with the EU and open the way to its membership of the EU."[39] It seems that the advocates of the Ukraine within the European Parliament are looking in a much deeper way and think more strategically. Irzhi Byzek, MP from Poland, for example, stated that "After three years from "Orange Revolution" we may still not be satisfied with the level of democracy and market economy development. But those, who passed through the experience of the USSR know how hard it is to get rid of all the previous problems."[40] Anna Ibrizazhich, MP from Sweden supported the idea by saying, "We have to help the Ukraine to heal from that Soviet past."[41]

Even if the EU Council will not take the recommendation of the European Parliament into consideration, the fulfillment of the New Enhanced Agreement itself could trigger the Ukraine to make itself prepared to join the EU in the end, since the conditions of a free trade zone between the EU and the Ukraine can place the Ukraine in a position similar to that of Norway or Switzerland.

The splash of EU policy toward the Ukraine in June-July 2007 was not accidental because some people in the EU wanted to support pro-European oriented political forces in the Ukraine on the eve of the Ukraine's Parliamentary elections on September 30, 2007. Other good news for Euro-optimists in the Ukraine, as well as for other European non-EU countries, was announced in June 2007. The EU Council agreed to make changes in the EU Treaty which opens the way for further enlargement of the EU.[42] Some flexible conditions on accession for new members were also introduced. Moreover, the fulfillment of Copenhagen criteria will not be a necessary condition for accession.

Good news for the Ukraine was issued on June 18, 2007. Within the framework of the EU-Ukraine Cooperation Council, which took place on this date, the EU and the Ukraine were expected to take a concrete step forward in their bilateral relations by signing two agreements on visa facilitation and readmission. The signature of these agreements followed the official start of the negotiations on a new Enhanced Agreement reflecting the strategic importance of developing EU-Ukraine relations. Regarding the agreements, Vice-President Frattini, Commissioner responsible for the Justice, Freedom and Security portfolio, stated, "I was very pleased that the agreements on visa and readmission had been signed—this means that Ukrainians will now be able to travel more easily while maintaining the efforts to clamp down on illegal migration."[43] He also added that: "The EU and the Ukraine can aspire to a qualitatively higher level in their relationship, and these agreements are particularly important in this perspective: facilitating people-to-people contacts can greatly help in increasing mutual understanding and improving our relations in all fields."[44]

Despite the fear of many European countries to add another big country like the Ukraine, with a population of about 47 million, because they think it would cause a hindrance to the effectiveness of the bloc, more than 55 percent of the citizens of the EU support the Ukraine's accession to the EU whenever it fulfills all the necessary conditions.[45] Moreover, in the Ukraine, Europeans can find not only problems, but also opportunities. One of the problems in shaping the EU's strategy particular to the Ukraine is the constant political crises occurring in the Ukraine. Persistent political instability threatens the Ukrainian integration into the European Community. Due to this fact, European partners do not understand the real intensions of the Ukraine and cannot estimate how serious the Ukraine's political rhetoric of obtaining EU membership is. The European strategy regarding the Ukraine, on the other hand, is also full of doubt. Nevertheless, Europeans considered the parliamentary elections held on September 30, 2007 in the Ukraine as a new turning point in bilateral relations, which may bring stability to the internal political life of the Ukraine and clarity to its foreign policy. Only on this basis will further democratic transformations in the Ukraine become possible and in the light of European values, European perspective may turn into reality.

---

[1] On political ambiguity of the Ukraine as of a natural factor and integral part of Global and European security see Sergiy Glebov, "Security Policy of the the Ukraine in a Globalising World," in *Security Under Global Pressure*, ed. Istvan Tarrosy (Hungary, Pecs: Europe Center PBC, 2005), pp. 59-70.

[2] Янукович не ограничится соседством с ЕС (Yanukovych will not be limited by neighboring with the EU), June 27, 2007, http://www.korrespondent.net/main/196548/

[3] Michael Emerson, *"The Elephant and the Bear." The European Union, Russia and their Near Abroad* (Brussels: Center for European Policy Studies, 2001), p. 3.

[4] "Strategy of Integration of the Ukraine with the EU, adopted by the Ukrainian President Leonid Kuchma on June 11, 1998," Ministry of Foreign Affairs of the Ukraine, http://www.mfa.gov.ua/mfa/ua/publication/content/2990.htm

[5] Brigid Laffan, "Democracy and the European Union," in Developments *in the European Union*, ed. Laura Cram, Desmond Dinan and Neill Nugent (New York: St. Martin's Press, 1999), p. 330.

[6] European Commission. The EU – the Ukraine Relations, http://ec.europa.eu/external_relations/ukraine/intro/index.htm

[7] Ibid.

[8] Ibid.

[9] Комиссар Евросоюза сказала правду о будущем Украины (The EU Commissioner said truth about the Ukraine's future), June 14, 2007, http://www.korrespondent.net/main/194626/

[10] International news. April 16, 2004, www.podrobnosti.com.ua

[11] The European Commission starts project on the extension of the Odessa-Brody oil pipeline to Poland, http://www.delukr.ec.europa.eu/page35926.html

[12] Roman Kupchinsky, "the Ukraine: Odesa-Brody Pipeline Potential Still Unused," *RFL/RL*, January 12, 2007, http://www.rferl.com/featuresarticle/2007/01/a93dfee7-ec31-4862-af51-fddb54c2ca95.html

[13] Экономика Украины не позволяет ей назвать дату вступления в НАТО, (the Ukraine's economy does not allow the Ukraine to determine the NATO accession

date), July 27, 2004, http://www.rambler.ru/db/news/msg.html?mid=4846859&s=6

[14] Реверс евроинтеграции (Reverse of the Eurointegration), International news, July 11, 2004, http://www.podrobnosti.com.ua

[15] "European Parliament, Wider Europe - Neighborhood: A new framework for relations with our Eastern and Southern Neighbours. Committee on Foreign Affairs, resolution." Pay attention to page 51 concerning the future of Ukraine-EU relations in terms of the Ukraine's participation in the Single Economic Space, Euro-Atlantic Cooperation Institute, Kyiv, the Ukraine, http://ieac.org.ua/pics/content/15/1068458394_ans.pdf

[16] See, for example, "Романо Проди не видит перспектив Украины в ЕС" ("Romano Prodi does not see EU perspectives for the Ukraine"), May 5, 2004, http://www.tribuna.com.ua/news/2004/05/05/8299.html

[17] Будущий комиссар ЕС по международным отношениям Бенита Ферреро-Вальднер заявила о том, что Европейский Союз должен хотя бы удержать на своей стороне Украину (Future EU commissar in International relations Benita Ferrero-Waldner stated, that the European Union should at least keep the Ukraine on its side), International news, October 5, 2004, http://www.korrespondent.net

[18] Замглавы Пентагона: Украина должна быть в НАТО (Pentagon deputy head: the Ukraine must be in NATO), International news, October 6, 2004, http://www.korrespondent.net

[19] ЕС согласился дать Украине "европейскую перспективу" (EU agreed to give the Ukraine "European perspective"), International news, October 11, 2004, http://www.korrespondent.net/main/103983

[20] Dan Bilefsky, "EU "not ready" to invite the Ukraine to join the bloc. Caution accompanies expansion fatigue," *International Herald Tribune*, October 27, 2006, http://www.iht.com/articles/2006/10/27/news/ukraine.php

[21] Ibid.

[22] Украина лишилась европерспективы из-за Франции (the Ukraine lost European perspective because of France), March 6, 2007, http://www.korrespondent.net/main/181731

[23] Тарасюк: ЕС предложил Украине политику, неправильную по определению (Tarasiuk: The EU proposed to the Ukraine politics, which is wrong in the core), March 6, 2007, http://www.korrespondent.net/main/181780

[24] Європа грюкне дверима перед Україною, якщо порушать компроміс (Europe will shut the door in front of the Ukraine in case compromise failed), May 31, 2007, http://www.pravda.com.ua/news/2007/5/31/59691.htm

[25] Ibid.

[26] Членство в ЕС Украине пока не светит (the Ukraine has not been admitted to join the EU yet), January 22, 2007, http://www.korrespondent.net/main/176347/

[27] Ibid.

[28] Україні запропонують політику трьох "С" (the Ukraine will be proposed to follow three "C" politics), December 15, 2006, http://www.pravda.com.ua/news/2006/12/15/52345.htm

[29] German Chancellor's foreign policies under fire at home, http://euronews.net/create_html.php?page=detail_info&article=396080&lng=1

[30] Ibid.

[31] Peter Sain ley Berry, "The Balkans Needs to Form its Own Union. With early EU entry for Balkans states unlikely, they should consider forming a union of their own," *Balkan Insight*, November 9, 2006, http://www.iwpr.net/?p=brn&s=f&o=325437&apc_state=henh

[32] Яценюк чекає від Європи знаків (Yatsenuk is looking for signs from Europe), June 29, 2007, http://www.pravda.com.ua/news/2007/6/29/60940.htm

[33] Україну побачили в ЄС через 13 років (the Ukraine is seen in the EU in 13 years), June 29, 2007, http://www.pravda.com.ua/news/2007/6/29/60936.htm 29.06.2007

[34] В Европарламенте назвали реальную дату вступления Украины в ЕС (The real date of the Ukraine's accession to the EU was proclaimed in the European Parliament), July 2, 2007, http://www.korrespondent.net/main/196942/ 02

[35] Посол Германии: Вопрос вступления Украины в ЕС не стоит (German Ambassador: there is no question posed as to the the Ukraine's accession to the EU), July 4, 2007, http://www.korrespondent.net/main/197343

[36] Німеччину цікавлять прагнення України (Germany is concerned by Ukrainian aspirations), February 26, 2007, http://www.bbc.co.uk/ukrainian/indepth/story/2007/02/070226_lindner_int.shtml

[37] Членство в ЕС Украине пока не светит (the Ukraine has not been admitted to join the EU yet), January 22, 2007, http://www.korrespondent.net/main/176347/

[38] Украина лишилась европерспективы из-за Франции (the Ukraine lost European perspective because of France), March 6, 2007, http://www.korrespondent.net/main/181731

[39] "Report with a proposal for a European Parliament recommendation to the Council on a negotiation mandate for a new enhanced agreement between the European Community and its Member States of the one part and the Ukraine of the other part. Rapporteur: Michał Tomasz Kamiński, 8 June 2007. Committee on Foreign Affairs. PE 384.482v03-00. A6-0217/2007," European Parliament, http://www.europarl.europa.eu/sidesSearch/sipadeMapUrl.do?PROG=REPORT&L=EN&SORT_ORDER=D&S_REF_A=%25&LEG_ID=6&COM_ID=808#

[40] Євродепутати підтримали майбутнє приєднання України до ЄС (Members of the European Parliament supported future accession of the Ukraine to the EU), July 12, 2007, http://www.pravda.com.ua/news/2007/7/12/61424.htm

[41] Ibid.

[42] Вступити до ЄС стане легше (To join the EU will be more easier), June 23, 2007, http://www.pravda.com.ua/news/2007/6/23/60710.htm

[43] Further strengthening EU-the Ukraine bilateral relations: visa facilitation and readmission agreements are signed today, June 18, 2007, http://www.delukr.ec.europa.eu/page43515.html

[44] Ibid.

[45] Більша частина ЄС кличе Україну до себе (The majority of the EU is calling the Ukraine to the EU), June 2, 2007, http://www.pravda.com.ua/news/2007/6/2/59818.htm

Chapter 16
The European Union and Uzbekistan Relations since its Independence

Havva Kök

The European Union (EU) is one of the major players trying to be influential in Central Asia. Most of the studies carried out on post-Soviet Central Asia focused on roles of major powers like the U.S., Russia and China, while they, until recently, paid relatively less attention to Western Europe. This essay seeks to review the EU's policy, giving a better understanding of these policies in the region, and to define EU priorities and interests. Uzbekistan will constitute our main focal point. Uzbekistan has a fast growing population of over 24 million, and it is a prominent center of economy and culture in the region. Situated amidst Russia, China and the Muslim world, Uzbekistan is/can be an important partner for the EU. In this study, we seek answers to the following questions: How did the EU policy toward Uzbekistan develop? What are the turning points? Why should the EU pay serious attention to Uzbekistan? What is the framework of the EU's relations with Uzbekistan? What assistance does the EU provide for Uzbekistan? What are the main aims of this assistance? What is the level of the EU's trading relationship with Uzbekistan? What is the scope of the EU's political engagement with Uzbekistan? What can the EU and Uzbekistan do to strengthen their relations with each other?

Reasons for Uzbekistan's Importance to the EU

The EU has only recently come to recognize its interest in Central Asia. The European Security Strategy defines the key threats to Europe as "terrorism, regional conflicts, state failure, and organized crime"[1] which are, in one way or the other, relevant to Central Asia. Therefore, the EU wants to increase its engagement in Central Asia based on more strategic grounds. In this respect, the appointment of a new EU Special Representative (EUSR) for the region, on July 18, 2005, is significant.[2]

Uzbekistan, with a total area of 447.400 km2 and over 27 million inhabitants, occupies a key strategic position in Central Asia. It borders all the Central Asian countries and Afghanistan. Thus, any state that holds influence in Uzbekistan would also be able to influence neighboring republics. Uzbekistan has half the population of Central Asia and large Uzbek minorities live in neighboring states.[3] Uzbeks are Turkic-speaking, sunni-muslim people. Uzbekistan possesses the region's largest and best-equipped armed forces. It has also rich energy—especially gas—reserves. Its economy is largely based on cotton.

Uzbekistan matters for the EU for three reasons: its strategic importance in terms of instability risks in the region; being an important base for the war in neighboring Afghanistan; and its key energy resources that could lessen Europe's dependence on Russia.

Instability Risks and Uzbekistan

Although the EU sees no direct security threat from Uzbekistan, it is concerned that any regime changes in the country may stimulate a radical religious extremism or an aggressive Russian intervention in the region, both of which would significantly affect Western interests.

Looking at the general structure of Central Asia, it can be said that the greatest threat to stability in the region comes from the cooperation networks between extremist, terrorist and criminal groups that are active within Central Asia. Trans-border crime and terrorism is encouraged and aggravated by poverty, inequality and frustration by state policies.

Political Instability Risks

A general outlook at Central Asia's situation is helpful in understanding Uzbekistan's importance in terms of instability risks. Since they gained their independence, the states of Central Asia have experienced periodic violent conflicts between different ethnic and religious groups.

Tajikistan was engulfed in a civil war from 1992 to 1997 which left severe scars on the country's economic and social fabric.[4] In 2005, the Kyrgyz Republic underwent a change of government in the aftermath of prolonged popular uprising against the flawed results of earlier elections.[5] The central government in Kyrgyzstan is still under the threat of losing control of both institutions and territory. In Uzbekistan, the growing harassment of civil society and religious groups after the bloody intervention of security forces in Andijan (May 2005) has exacerbated existing discontent among much of the population.[6]

Thus, examples in Kyrgyzstan, Tajikistan and Uzbekistan so far have demonstrated that unstable social and economic conditions, if handled in an authoritarian manner, might bring about widespread protests and threaten to destabilize the Central Asian countries, as seen in Andijan in 2005.

Since borders in the region are poorly demarcated, it is difficult to prevent people or groups from crossing illegally. Therefore, any restlessness occuring in any Central Asian country can have disastrous consequences for the entire region. Serious instability in one state may cause huge refugee flows, which can suddenly overwhelm the response capacity of neighboring countries. Furthermore, such a crisis may also have severe economic consequences for third parties, since the infrastructure of the region is still closely interdependent.

Events in Afghanistan, Iraq and elsewhere show that unstable regions are ideal havens for terrorist and criminal groups. As any instability in Central Asia can disturb the member states of the EU, it can also turn Europe into an attraction for potential refugees. "There is a global interest in stability in this region. Central Asia is anonymous in the West because it's been relatively stable. If it becomes unstable, it will no longer be anonymous, and people will ask why we weren't interested earlier," commented a European observer.[7] This is particularly so with Uzbekistan. As mentioned earlier, Uzbekistan is a key country to keep under observation with regard to future prospects for conflict and stability. Karimov's dictatorship is looking increasingly fragile and serious thought should be given to facing the serious consequences of its ultimate collapse in neighboring states, particularly in Kyrgyzstan and Tajikistan. These two are the weakest states in the region whose infrastructures are closely linked with that of Uzbekistan. Additionally, "the potential arrival on their territories of refugees fleeing unrest could pose major political and humanitarian challenges, as shown by the crisis provoked by a mere 500 refugees in Kyrgyzstan in the spring of 2005."[8]

Hence, Uzbekistan presents the greatest risk of serious instability in the region. Due to exploitative economic policies and the overt brutality of President Islam Karimov's regime, through which millions have been struggling to survive, people have been left in frustration and anger. The years lasting authoritarian rule and the presence of rich resources in Uzbekistan mean that Karimov eventually leaving the scene might bring about a potential violent successive struggle. The danger of further instability in the short- to medium-term is high.[9]

In May 2005, Uzbek security forces suppressed an uprising in the eastern city of Andijan and killed hundreds of unarmed civilians. Since then, the government has suppressed independent journalists, human rights activists and civil society. While relations with the West were severed, relations with Russia and China have never been closer.[10]

Radicalism and Terrorism

Anger over repression, corruption and poor governance has caused some radical Islamist groups to find support in Central Asia.[11] Two of them are the most widely known: Hizb ut-Tahrir (the "Party of Liberation") and the Islamic Movement of Uzbekistan (IMU). The former seeks to unite all Muslims in a single worldwide caliphate by peaceful means;[12] and the latter is an armed militant organization that emerged out of Karimov's oppression on Islamist opposition in Ferghana Valley in the 1990s. Supporters of both Hizb ut-Tahrir and IMU insist that their movement seeks to achieve its goals through wholly nonviolent means.[13] Indeed, while in recent years, an overall upsurging activity of Hizb ut-Tahrir and violent incidents attributed to the IMU or its allies have been witnessed throughout the region, it is still difficult to justify the measures taken by the Karimov government against independent religious figures of all colors in Uzbekistan. Furthermore, no violence that is attributed to extremist organizations has specifically targeted Europeans or European interests.[14]

Hizb ut-Tahrir movement, which has been active at least since the mid-1990s, has been most harshly suppressed in Uzbekistan where accused members of this organization face long-term imprisonment.[15] Arrests and trials of alleged Hizb ut-Tahrir supporters still continue.[16] The Uzbek government's accusation, of which the IMU still is considered a serious terrorist threat, is unclear and reliable information is hard to find. Karimov is inclined to exaggerate the terrorist threat to justify his brutal suppression.[17] Nonetheless, the political environment—weak state institutions, corruption, disillusionment with mainstream religious institutions, heavy-handed law enforcement, and, to varying degrees, limitations on legitimate dissent—create a suitable environment in which radical groups of all types, terrorist or otherwise, can expect to find recruits. Thus, without addressing the underlying issues, radicalism cannot be suppressed by force alone.

The real problem comes from the fact that the regime has, for a long time, been suppressing all secular democratic opposition, a situation which leaves the only way of expressing opposition open to radical Islamist movements. A clear distinction must be made between religious Muslims and radical Islamists. Uzbek people need to find a way to express frustration by legitimate means. The more Karimov's government continues to suppress all forms of opposition with the same level of severity, the more radical groups will gain ground among Uzbek people, which can have a destabilizing effect on the entire region. It is vital to be aware of the dangers of the Uzbek regime, undeniably one of the most repressive ones in Central Asia, which puts the whole region at risk.[18]

It should also be noted that most radical Islamists in Uzbekistan who advocate armed struggle were trained and armed in Afghanistan. In order to escape the Uzbek security forces, they find refuge in Afghanistan and Tajikistan by crossing the border, enabling them subsequently to carry out operations targeting Uzbekistan.

Afghanistan

In the post-9/11 world, Afghanistan has become a major European priority. Central Asia's proximity to Afghanistan is one of the main reasons for the EU's interest in the region and, being a neighbor to Afghanistan, especially Uzbekistan. Therefore, Central Asia's stability is crucial because stability in Afghanistan requires stable neighbors and their cooperation.

As a result, NATO forces maintain airbases in Uzbekistan; France has had a small base at Dushanbe's international airport since 2001,[19] and Germany has had some 300 troops at the southern city of Termez since 2003 to support NATO's International Security Assistance Force (ISAF) in Afghanistan. Germany is currently the only NATO country with troops in Uzbekistan. The U.S. was ordered to abandon the "Qarshi Khanabad" airbase in July 2005.

Germany, along with the U.S., is also the only country permitted to use Uzbek airspace.[20] In January 2006, Uzbek authorities accused the Germans of allowing other NATO forces to travel to Afghanistan via the base and demanded more payment.[21] As for Germany, "(it) does not want to be used by the Uzbek authorities to split NATO," and the German military would probably withdraw from Central Asia if the U.S. did so," stated Alexander Rahr of the German Council on Foreign Relations.[22] Contrary to this expectation however, Germany has held onto its military base in Termez, which Berlin sees as important to the operations it is performing as part of the NATO force in neighboring Afghanistan.

But any military value in having a base near, but safely, across the border from Afghanistan should certainly be weighed against the tremendous damage the regime does in the wider struggle against jihadi extremism. When it comes to combating terrorism, the Uzbek government, far from proving itself a valuable ally in this international effort, continues to create repressive conditions in which popular support for radical Islam will only grow.[23] During the early stages of independence, Uzbekistan's relative socioeconomic and political stability was attributed to President Islam Karimov's authoritarian government. As a result, despite the country's terrible human rights record and increasingly repressed regime, most international financial assistance (including security aid) has continued to flow. Ironically, looking at the past, the international community has helped create exactly the conditions it has always feared the most regarding Islamist radicalism in the region by ignoring the Karimov government's human rights abuses. Moreover, growing political repression together with poverty provide a fertile ground for violence and instability.

The European Union's Energy Security

The EU's interest in reducing its dependence on external sources of energy and diversifying its energy supply has increased Brussels' interest in stabilizing Central Asia, and widening access to the region's abundant energy reserves. With its significant hydrocarbon resources and favorable geographical location for transport routes to European markets, Central Asia will play an important role in ensuring the EU's energy supplies. Together with Russia, Kazakhstan, Turkmenistan, and Uzbekistan, Central Asia possesses the world's second largest reserves of oil and gas. Kazakhstan alone has double the oil reserves of the North Sea (with government figures estimating total reserves to be three times higher), while gas reserves of Turkmenistan and Uzbekistan are believed to be the 5th and 8th highest in the world, respectively.[24]

The EU's Growing Energy Vulnerability

The EU is one of the world's largest importers of oil, gas and coal. Its external dependence on imports, particularly gas, is significant and forecasted to grow steadily.[25] Currently, the EU imports around half of its energy requirements. According to the Commission's Green Paper[26] on security of energy supply (November 2000), if no action is taken, by 2030, it is estimated that the EU will import 94 percent of its oil and 84 percent of its gas.[27] The Green Paper determined the options to reach "sustainable, competitive and secure" energy supplies for Europe.[28]

From this perspective, the EU reliance on Russian energy is also significant; 46 percent of EU gas imports come from Russia.[29] Russia is the only gas supplier to Estonia, Latvia, Lithuania, Slovakia, and Finland and the major supplier to Hungary, Austria, Poland, the Czech Republic, Greece, and Bulgaria.[30] Moreover, Russia's energy sector influence is growing through acquisition of production and transportation infrastructure in Eastern Europe and the Caucasus, signing an agreement with Germany to construct a gas pipeline under the Baltic Sea, and controlling Central Asian energy export routes.[31]

Since the the Ukraine-Russia gas dispute in January 2006, energy security has risen to the forefront in the EU's international political agenda.[32] Hence, diversifying the EU's gas supply, as opposed to oil, has become the key challenge, and EU states are trying to reduce over-reliance on Russia. In connection with this, the EU has begun to realize that Central Asia is an important economic and energy partner. Central Asian oil and gas reserves, if linked directly to Europe via the South Caucasus and Turkey, are regarded as an important energy supply diversification alternative.

Central Asian Energy Potential

Three of the five Central Asian states have significant energy reserves. Kazakhstan, Turkmenistan and Uzbekistan, together with Russia, possess the world's second largest reserves of oil and gas.[33] Kazakhstan oil reserves are in the global top ten and gas in the top fifteen. Turkmenistan has large, unexplored gas reserves. Uzbekistan is also a significant gas producer.[34] However, almost all Central Asian gas export has been monopolized by Russia. Turkmenistan, Uzbekistan and Kazakhstan pumped over 50 billion cubic metres[35] of gas in 2005, which is 10 percent more than Russian consumption.[36] Apart from a little amount of Turkmen gas, most of the gas exports from the region go northward through Uzbekistan and Kazakhstan to Russia, where one part continues to flow to the Ukraine through Russian-controlled pipelines. Kazakhi gas is also mostly shipped to Russia. Uzbek gas is primarily consumed in the region, but a significant quantity is also exported to Russia. "This is due to the north-south axis of the pipeline infrastructure left over from the Soviet Union, designed to bring Central Asian energy to Russia's industrial core. With Russia controlling the transport, the countries have little negotiating clout and are forced to sell the gas at well below market prices."[37]

Central Asian gas is a primary source for Russian domestic use and European export. Experts say that Russia is unlikely to have the storage or spare production capacity to maintain domestic and international supply during even a short disruption.[38] In case of any sudden disruption, Russia would then have to cut off either domestic consumers or neighbors. As for the EU member states, they do not generally keep strategic gas reserves (gas reserves, unlike oil reserves, are not a common practice), and so they would be at risk of a critical shortage if Central Asian instability disrupted their supply.

In addition to the EU and Russia, a number of other countries (i.e. the U.S. and China) are interested in acquiring Central Asian gas. A U.S.-backed Afghan pipeline proposal from Turkmenistan across Afghanistan to markets in Pakistan and India is under discussion.[39] China, which has an oil pipeline connecting to Kazakhstan, has also negotiated with Turkmenistan about importing natural gas and recently signed an agreement to invest $600 million in gas production in Uzbekistan.[40]

In short, the EU member states face a challenge to import gas from a region homes some of the world's most repressive states that are also strategically important. On the other hand, issues of transparency and good governance are also needed for effective delivery of energy, regional stability and economic cooperation. In any case, if the EU is to have influence over the development of Central Asian energy and associated export routes, it must be far more active in the region than it has been to date.

EU Energy Needs and Uzbekistan's Gas Reserves

Uzbekistan's natural gas reserves are predicted to be 1.86 trillion cubic metres, which is enough to power the whole of the EU for four years.[41] Some analysts, however, are skeptical about both the size of Uzbekistan's gas reserves and its willingness to meet EU needs. "Everyone in the region is laughing at the EU, because all Uzbek gas has already been sold to Gazprom," said a Turkish petroleum expert.[42] In 2006, Uzbekistan concluded $2 billion agreements with Russian companies Gazprom and Lukoil for the development of the Uzbek gas sector.[43] Since the beginning of 2007, new production sharing agreements have been signed between Kremlin-controlled firms and Uzbekistan.[44]

Uzbekistan gas exports amount annually about 12.6 billion cubic meters, about 9 billion cubic meters of which goes into Russia's Gazprom system from where it heads toward west. The rest is sold to Kazakhstan, Tajikistan and Kyrgyzstan, countries that are heavily dependent on Uzbek energy. 9 billion cubic meters is about 11 percent of Germany's annual consumption.[45]

Framework for the EU's Relations with Uzbekistan
General Political Framework

With the collapse of the former Soviet Union, the EU decided to support the countries of Eastern Europe and Central Asia in their transition process toward a market economy and democracy. Thus, since the beginning of the 1990s, the EU has developed a much more formal and political relationship with 13 countries of the region. The overall aim is to foster enduring political, economic and cultural links, so as to ensure peace and security by building strong trading links.[46]

The EU's eastward enlargement progress from the year 2000 has sharply increased the number of EU countries sharing a border with the partner countries. Together with the events of 9/11, this has influenced the dialogue between the EU and countries from Eastern Europe and Central Asia. In order to safeguard its political, economic and strategic interests in Central Asia—and in Uzbekistan—the EU has planned to extend the European Neighborhood Policy[47] to Central Asia, under the German EU presidency. The policy, which was presented by the European Commission in May 2004, aims reinforcing ties with neighboring and partner countries, through an array of new forms of cooperation and assistance.

The European Commission has developed a representative network in the countries of Eastern Europe and Central Asia, constituted of seven EC Delegations, including Almaty, Kiev, Moscow, and Tbilisi, as well as Bishkek, Dushanbe and Yerevan (the last three having a non-resident Head of Delegation). In addition, the Commission has established "Europa Houses" in Baku and Tashkent that constitute a central point of reference in the country for information about the program of technical assistance (TACIS) and other programs.

Economic Engagement

After diplomatic relations were established between the republic of Uzbekistan and the EU in September 1994, economic relations have developed in two main directions. The first is directly associated with the signing of the Partnership and Cooperation Agreement (PCA) between Uzbekistan and the EU. The second relates to the benefits from the program of technical assistance (TACIS) that involves support for the implementation of economic reforms.

The Partnership and Cooperation Agreement (PCA)

The EU's relations with Uzbekistan, as with other former republics of the Soviet Union, are based on the Partnership and Cooperation Agreement (PCA) signed on June 21, 1996. The aim of this Agreement was to facilitate Uzbekistan's political, economic, commercial, and cultural integration with the EU.[48] It was based on the 1989 Trade and Cooperation Agreement, signed with the former Soviet Union. The PCA provided a framework for wide-ranging cooperation in the areas of political dialogue, trade and investment, and economic, legislative and cultural cooperation.[49]

This bilateral dialogue, however, was temporarily interrupted after the Uzbek government refused to give sanction to an independent inquiry to be carried out about the events that broke out in Andijan. In November 2005, the EU announced a partial suspension of the PCA meetings and an indefinite suspension of the Cooperation Committee.[50] A year-long visa ban upon 12 Uzbek officials and an arms embargo have been imposed. Nevertheless, on November 13, 2006, the Council of the EU, while renewing sanctions, welcomed the readiness of Uzbekistan to strengthen without delay a bilateral dialogue on human rights and decided to reinstate the technical meetings within the PCA.

At present, the EU has no delegation presence in Tashkent, but a Europa House, a technical office providing details of EU-assisted projects in Uzbekistan, has been established in the capital under the TACIS program (Technical Assistance to the Commonwealth of Independent States). Since its establishment, Europa House has succeeded in the development of various initiatives with the government of Uzbekistan in the country as well as on regional levels in a variety of sectors.

EU Assistance to Uzbekistan: TACIS

The TACIS program has been the main instrument within strategic development cooperation with countries of Eastern Europe and Central Asia, which include both national and regional programs in areas such as nuclear safety, cross-border cooperation and regional cooperation. Launched by the EC in 1991, the TACIS Program has provided grant-financed technical assistance to 12 countries of Eastern Europe and Central Asia (Armenia, Azerbaijan, Belarus, Georgia, Kazakhstan, Kyrgyzstan, Moldova, Russia, Tajikistan, Turkmenistan, the Ukraine, and Uzbekistan), and mainly aimed to enhance the transition process in these countries.[51]

The TACIS Program for Uzbekistan has mainly been directed to support the implementation of economic reforms. In January 1994, the Uzbek Bureau of Commission of European Union (UzBureauCEU) was opened in Tashkent in order to actualize this program. It defined a set of priorities to be: "concerning the restructuring of state enterprises and private sector development, reforms in public administration, education, agriculture, energy, transport and the rational use of labor resources."[52]

Since 1992, Uzbekistan has benefited from assistance through the TACIS program. (A total of €161.85 million has been disbursed through the end of 2005). Table 1 shows the composition of EU Assistance to Uzbekistan for the period 2002-2005—Almost 195 projects have been carried out that cost 160 million euros.

TACIS has been active in Uzbekistan in a variety of areas from macro-financial assistance to humanitarian aid (ECHO) and assistance provided through the Food Security Program, from public administration to energy sector, from health and agriculture, to environment protection and education.[53] Tempus, for example, is an EU's program aimed to cooperate in the field of higher education, which is thought to be the largest international program for higher education reform in Uzbekistan.[54] Some regional programs like BOMCA-CADAP (Border Management and Drug Action Program for Central Asia) covered all five Central Asian republics including Uzbekistan.[55]

Beyond TACIS

In the context of its enlargement, the EU has required a simplified political and administrative framework for delivering the cooperation programs. Consequently, the EU decided to stop a variety of assistance initiatives from the spring of 2007, among them was the TACIS Program. "Out of six remaining instruments, the European Union's Cooperation and Economic Cooperation Instrument is foreseen, inter alia, for Uzbekistan."[56] In addition to the traditional frame of technical assistance, the European Union's Cooperation and Economic Cooperation Instrument offers "program and project financing, budgetary support, subsidies, direct investments, capital investments, pool financing, etc."[57]

Thus, after expiry of the TACIS Regulation in 2007, assistance to Central Asia will be provided by the new EU financial Development and Cooperation Instruments (DCI).[58] The European Commission has proposed budgets for the 2007 – 2013 period as follows:[59]

Stability Instrument	4.5 billion euros
Humanitarian Instrument	6.3 billion euros
Macro-financial Instrument	1.2 billion euros
Pre Accession Instrument	14.6 billion euros
European Neighborhood Instrument	14.9 billion euros
Development Cooperation and Economic Cooperation	44.2 billion euros

Table 16.1. EC Assistance to Uzbekistan 2002-2005(million euros)[60]

	Programs / Projects	2002	2003	2004	2005
1	Support for the implementation of the EU/assistance		1,5		1,0 (preparationmulti component / sectoral strategies/pgs
2	Support to the Accounts Chamber			1,0	
3	Public Finance Management				1,5
4	Support to the reform of Official Statistics	0,45	0,5	0,5	0.750
7	Development Uz standards			1,25	1,0 metrology equipments
10	Training Penitentiary				1.0
13	Land Registration 3 phase		2,0		
14	Support to the modernization of the Oliy Majlis (Parliament of Uzbekistan) 2 pha	1,0			
15	Policy Advice Program	1,5	1,2	1,2	1.0
	Customs	**1**	**1**	**1**	
	Development and modernization of efficient Central Asian Custom Administrations	1	1,0	1,0	
	Education	**4,9**	**1,7**	**4,1**	
1	NIS Managers' Training Program	1,4		1,5	
2	Tempus Program III	2,5	1,7	2,6	2.0
3	Social partnership in education and training	1,0		1,25	
	IBPP				
	IBPP-Support to Civil Society and Local Initiatives	1,45	0,8	0,9	1.0
Track 3	Ferghana valley -enclaves	1,0	1,0	1,0	2,0
	Total	11,3	9,7	11,0	11,250

The 2007-2010 Central Asia Indicative Program focuses on EC bilateral cooperation "on the promotion and strengthening of civil society/social partners and rule of law."[61] Rural development schemes for direct assistance to local populations in the context of poverty reduction and raising living standards, focusing on the Ferghana Valley, will also continue.[62] Europa House is considered to be an essential element for facilitating current and future EU-Uzbek cooperation.[63] Future relations are principally linked to visible progress in implementing the PCA and the continuation of domestic reforms in Uzbekistan.

Other Assistance Programs

In addition to TACIS mainstream initiatives, the EU's assistance to Uzbekistan has comprised other TACIS-related programs, such as "IBPP (Institution Building Partnership Program—designed to support the development of non-profit organizations from civil society, local & regional authorities and public institutions) and MTP (Management Training Program —with an overall aim to support the development of CIS economies by assisting in the training of managers)."[64]

Bilateral Trade Relations

Uzbekistan is the EU's second largest trading partner in the region after Kazakhstan. In 2004, the EU imported €605 million of goods and services from Uzbekistan, and exported some €464 million, placing it second only to Russia in terms of the total volume of bilateral trade (€1,069 million). Uzbekistan's primary exports to the EU are precious stones and metals, agricultural products, textiles and clothing, while it primarily imports machinery, electrical equipment and chemicals. In 2005, the bilateral trade balance changed in favor of the EU (from -€141 million in 2004 to €92 million last year), with imports from Uzbekistan declining to €474 million and EU exports to the country increasing to €566 million.[65]

Political Engagement after Andijan
EU Sanctions

On December 14, 2005, after the Uzbek security forces violently oppressed a demonstration and killed hundreds of civilians in Andijan in May 2005, the EU decided to prohibit the sale of weapons to Uzbekistan and the travel of high ranking Uzbek officials to EU countries. Moreover, the EU announced the suspension of the Partnership and Cooperation Agreement (PCA) with Uzbekistan. The sanctions were imposed for "indiscriminate use of force" during the suppression of the uprising in Andijan and prevention of independent investigation of the events.[66]

In November 2006, a year after the EU sanctions against Uzbekistan came into force on November 14, 2005, the EU-Uzbekistan Cooperation Council held a meeting in Brussels. As a result of this meeting, on November 13, 2006, the 25 EU ministers agreed to extend the arms embargo for another 12 months and the visa ban for another six months, while resuming low-level talks by acknowledging some moves by President Islam Karimov to address concerns over his policies.[67] In an EU statement, it was said that: "it was profoundly concerned by the human rights situation" in Uzbekistan and added that the EU "urges Uzbekistan to implement fully its international obligations related to human rights and fundamental freedoms."[68]

But Germany defended that the sanctions achieved nothing in the wya of improving the human rights situation in Uzbekistan and simply pushed the country closer to Russia. France and Poland supported Germany's view. The UK and several Scandinavian countries, along with the U.S., took a firmer line. "That's the only leverage we have. It would be the wrong political signal at the wrong time," a British diplomat said.[69] The Belgium-based International Crisis Group urged the EU not only to renew sanctions, but also to extend the visa ban to include the President Karimov and his family. They asserted that the human rights situation in the country had gotten worse rather than improved since Andijan.[70]

The U.S. welcomed the EU's decision to renew sanctions on Uzbekistan because of its human rights situation. The State Department Spokesman, Sean McCormack, said, "We share the European Union's concern about the human rights situation in Uzbekistan, and we will continue to cooperate closely with it directly and through the United Nations. Respect and dignity for human rights is essential for the future prosperity of the Uzbek people, and a necessary element of successful democratic reform."[71]

Germany's EU Presidency and Uzbekistan

Before its presidency, Germany ignored the travel ban for selected Uzbek officials and allowed Zakirjan Almatov, the Uzbek interior minister responsible for the Andijan massacre, to enter Germany in late 2005 to receive cancer treatment in Hannover.[72] Although the "Almatov affair" has damaged its credibility within the EU, Germany defends its position to seek "dialogue" and "engagement" over punitive actions.[73]

Unlike other EU states, Germany accepted only a few refugees after Andijan events. In April 2006, Craig Murray, the former UK Ambassador to Taskent, told an investigatory commission of the European Parliament that "Germany's intelligence agencies also cooperated with Tashkent and benefited from the information extracted from prisoners through torture."[74] German human rights official Günter Nooke went to Tashkent in June 2006. After Nooke's visit, the German parliament declared that human rights principles were "not impaired," and that the "human rights organizations operating in Uzbekistan" had even "expressly welcomed" the Germans' presence.[75] In October 2006, two separate German delegations visited Uzbekistan, being the first EU contacts with Uzbekistan since December 2005. In the beginning of November 2006, German Foreign Minister Frank-Walter Steinmeier visited Tashkent expressed openly a desire to see the sanctions lifted. With the trade turnover around $330 million in 2006 between the two countries, Steinmeier said they were particularly interested in diversifying economic activities in the areas of education, medicine, industry, and tourism, as well as various new investment projects. "We discussed issues that are important for both of our countries, and I am sure they will effectively serve to strengthen the partnership," said Steinmeier. "This is also the opinion of all those who are here as part of the representative delegation."[76]

Experts support the view that Germany's Uzbekistan diplomacy is motivated by a desire to keep the German military base outside the Uzbek city of Termez from where Germany supplies its forces to Afghanistan.[77] Roy Allison, a specialist in Central Asia at the London School of Economics, said, "It is unsurprising that Germany has called for a softer stance on Uzbekistan. Germany as an individual state has some significant trade ties as well as a large diplomatic presence in Central Asia. Whether Germany can carry out a shift of policy in the EU is another story because human rights issues remain a high priority for some countries." [78]

In accordance with this, the Uzbek government has refrained from shutting down the German base, and from expelling German non-governmental organizations working in Uzbekistan. By the end of 2006, Berlin spent more than €17 million in Termez.[79] However, German officials have strongly denied that Germany's Uzbekistan diplomacy had anything to do with the military base in Termez.[80]

On the other hand, there were reports in late January 2006 that the Uzbek Ministry of Foreign Affairs was threatening to close the German airbase at Termez, accusing Germany of allowing U.S., Danish and Hungarian troops to pass through en route to Afghanistan.[81] The Uzbek government also demanded that Germany invest some €20 million in the local development. (Berlin had already spent €12 million on renovating and modernizing the airbase, and currently pays a monthly rent of €240,000).[82]

On the contrary, relations with some EU members have become particularly tense. Shortly after Andijan, the Uzbek government expelled the foreign media accusing of supporting terrorism, and organizing and financing the events. Particular pressure was on the British Broadcasting Corporation (BBC), Radio Free Europe-Radio Liberty (RFE/RL), and the Institute for War and Peace Reporting (IWPR). BBC Central Asia correspondent Monica Whitlock left Uzbekistan after the Uzbek ministry of foreign affairs accused the local BBC office of supporting terrorism. However, none of these accusations were backed up with any evidence.[83]

After Presidency

German Foreign Minister Frank-Walter Steinmeier announced that one of Berlin's top priorities during its EU presidency was to focus on further developing the European Neighborhood Policy (ENP)[84] and thus to come up with an initiative for Central Asia. For this aim, there have been many visits by German parliamentarians and also by German government officials to Central Asia. Regarding this initiative, German Foreign Minister Frank-

Walter Steinmeier said: "We need to have a good look at the effectiveness of a neighborhood policy. Time is right for this," And he explained that "in conjunction with the Portuguese presidency during the second half of 2007, the ENP will be reviewed and further developed in order to guarantee stability and growth in the neighboring regions of Europe."[85]

Hence, following Germany's EU presidency, Steinmeier emphasized the importance of Central Asia and stressed three truths to be acknowledged in order to develop a successful strategy toward the region:

- The region is directly to the north of the crisis area, the arch between Pakistan, Afghanistan and Iran and struggling not to be drawn into the crisis;
- It is a region that had to defend itself against the efforts of fundamentalists, and;
- It is important because of its abundance of raw materials, especially in energy sources.[86]

Steinmeier said that it was, therefore, "necessary to develop a European initiative and promote the rule of law and democracy" in the region. Accordingly, at a summit held in June 2007, the Council of the EU decided to adopt the new EU strategy on Central Asia.[87] From this perspective, Germany believes that Uzbekistan's regional weight makes it a key to Berlin's plan to extend the ENP. An enhanced EU political and economic integration package to Central Asia under the German EU presidency is yet to be seen.[88]

Conclusion

Uzbekistan is a key country to be watched with regard to Central Asia. It is the most populous country in the region and borders each of the four other Central Asian states. Therefore, any change in the country would affect the entire region.

Europe sees no direct security threat from Uzbekistan; however, it is vigilant that any regime change might significantly affect Western security interests. Uzbekistan matters for the EU for three reasons: it has strategic importance in terms of instability risks in the region; it is an important base for the war in neighboring Afghanistan; and it holds key energy resources that could decrease Europe's energy dependence on Russia.

Instability risks in Uzbekistan include political instability and terrorism. Karimov's suppressive regime is looking increasingly fragile, and any medium- to long-term regime change might have serious consequences on other fragile states in Central Asia such as Kyrgyzstan.

There are more direct security concerns for the EU as well. In the post-9/11 world, with Afghanistan now being a major European priority, Central Asia can hardly be overlooked. Thus, Uzbekistan's proximity to Central Asia and its neighborhood to Afghanistan is one of the main reasons for the EU's interest in the region. Quite simply, stability in Afghanistan requires stable neighbors. Moreover, events in Afghanistan, Iraq, and elsewhere indicate that unstable regions are ideal havens for terrorist and criminal groups.

Another reason for the EU's interest in Central Asia, thus Uzbekistan, is to reduce its dependence on external sources of energy and to diversify its energy supply. Russia, Kazakhstan, Turkmenistan, and Uzbekistan, all together, possess the world's second largest reserves of oil and gas. Uzbekistan is thought to have 1.86 trillion cubic metres of natural gas reserves—sufficient to power all the EU countries for four years.

Relations between Uzbekistan and the EU have developed in two main directions. The first is directly associated with the signing of the Partnership and Cooperation Agreement (PCA) between Uzbekistan and the EU. The second relates to the benefits from the program of technical assistance (TACIS) which supports the implementation of economic reforms. The PCA provides a framework for wide-ranging cooperation in the areas of political dialogue, trade, investment, economy, legislation, and cultural cooperation. After the expiry of the TACIS Regulation in 2007, which was the main instrument for the strategic development cooperation with the Central Asian countries, assistance to Central Asia began to be provided by the new EU Financial Development and Cooperation Instruments.

What can the EU and Uzbekistan do to strengthen its relations with the EU? The EU can and should take a more active role in the region and especially, in Uzbekistan. Its political involvement is limited largely to meetings of the PCA signed with Uzbekistan. The lack of proper EU political representation in Tashkent has hindered a real and more active EU engagement.

During the German presidency, the EU focused on developing further the European Neighborhood Policy (ENP) and normalizing relations with Uzbekistan and started an initiative for Central Asia. Accordingly, at a summit held in June 2007, the EU Council adopted a new EU strategy on Central Asia. A more enhanced EU political and economic integration package to Central Asia is waiting to be actualized under the German EU presidency.

In short, in formulating a new policy and discussing its future involvement in Central Asia, under the German presidency, the EU is dealing with a vast number of engagements and critical issues, such as Turkey, the Balkans and Iran. The EU is aware of the fact that it has other pressing priorities, and the EU's influence is likely to be secondary to that of the U.S., Russia and China. Thus, the geopolitical impact the EU can exert upon the region should not be overestimated.

The overall EU objective in Central Asia is to secure stability and regional integration. However, as long as Uzbekistan is under Karimov's dictatorship there is risk of possible unrest, which sets up the possibility for intimidation of its weaker neighbors, the EU's objective will remain idle.

Therefore, the international community must consider creative short-term and long-term strategies for dealing with Uzbekistan and the region.

In the short-term, firstly, current arms sale sanctions and visa bans can be accompanied with an effective cotton policy. Western cotton buyers should curtail their business with the Uzbek cotton companies that have links to the security services that rely largely on income from cotton sales. Secondly, any strategy dealing with Uzbekistan must take also Russia and China into account, because the EU has limited opportunities to influence the region. Yet, this new strategy/relationship still remains unclear as it is not yet put in a precise form. The logic of events is driving all sides—the EU, Central Asia, the U.S., Russia, and China, to find new forms of strategic cooperation. Thirdly, no international policy should cause any ordinary Uzbek citizen pay for their government's mal-policies. Therefore, the EU should particularly engage with the Uzbek government to improve the living conditions of the majority of the most vulnerable citizens, particularly rural women and children, and labor migrant policies. Nevertheless, the EU should currently acknowledge that it has almost no influence on the Karimov government in the short-term. The emphasis should rather be made on longer-term measures, essentially on maintaining political activities, activities of civil society and educational opportunities, expecting a change that may occur in the future.

Last, but not least, any strategy should serve in two aspects: First, it should open the way to Uzbekistan's capacity for a peaceful regime change that can strengthen stability in Uzbekistan. Second, it should expand the capacity of neighboring states to resist Uzbekistan's economic and political pressures and help them in crisis management, handling refugee flows, and improving policing and border security.

---

[1] "A Secure Europe in a Better World," *European Security Strategy*, December 12, 2003, http://www.consilium.europa.eu/uedocs/cmsUpload/78367.pdf.

[2] The EUSR contributed to the implementation of the EU's policy objectives in the region, which include promoting good and close relations between the countries of Central Asia and the EU, contributing to strengthening of democracy, rule of law, good governance and respect for human rights and fundamental freedoms in Central Asia as well as enhancing EU's effectiveness in the region, including closer coordination with other relevant partners and international organizations, such as the OSCE. Joint Action 2005/588/CFSP, OJ L 199, July 29, 2005, Joint Action 2006/118/CFSP,OJ L 49 of February 21, 2006. http://consilium.europa.eu/cms3_fo/showPage.asp?id=442&lang=en, http://www.europa-eu-un.org/articles/en/article_6775_en.htm.

[3] Large numbers of Uzbeks were deliberately left out of the newly created Uzbek Socialist Republic, when the borders of the Soviet republics were drawn in the 1920s and 1930s. This Soviet policy aimed that a major hot issue would remain in place for

the purpose of distracting the local populations of Central Asia from any existing problems.

4 "Tajikistan: An Uncertain Peace," *Crisis Group Asia Report*, No:30, December 24, 2001.

5 The new government has proved to be ineffective, public confidence in the administration and law enforcement is slipping whilst the influence of criminal circles is increasing. The country was on the brink of chaos and President Bakiyev has just signed a new constitution under pressure from the opposition and street demonstrations on November 9, 2006. The compromise obtained is incomplete and fragile. *CNN International*, November 9, 2006.

6 For Kazakhstan see Gulmira Arabaeva, "Murder widens political gulf in Kazakhstan," *IWPR Reporting Central Asia*, No. 436, February 24, 2006, http://www.iwpr.net/?p=rca&s=f&o=259857&apc_state=henprca; for Kyrgyzstan see Crisis Group Asia Report No:81, "Political Transition in Kyrgyzstan: Problems and Prospects," Crisis Group Asia Report No:37, August 11, 2004, "Kyrgyzstan's Political Crisis: An Exit Strategy" Crisis Group Asia Report No:22, August 20, 2002, "Kyrgyzstan at Ten: Trouble in the "Island of Democracy," Crisis Group Asia Report No:109, August 28, 2001, "Kyrgyzstan: A Faltering State," Crisis Group Asia Report No:97, December 16, 2005; for Tajikistan see "Tajikistan's Politics: Confrontation or Consolidation?" Crisis Group Asia Briefing No:33, May 19, 2004; "Tajikistan: A Roadmap for Development," Crisis Group Asia Report No:51, April 24, 2003; for Turkmenistan see "Repression and Regression in Turkmenistan: A New International Strategy," Crisis Group Asia Report No:85, November 4, 2004, "Cracks in the Marble: Turkmenistan's Failing Dictatorship," Crisis Group Asia Report No:44, January 17, 2003.

7 Interwiew with an European expert at the European Union Secretariat in Ankara, July 5, 2006.

8 Ibid.

9 For more, see "The Failure of Reform in Uzbekistan: Ways Forward for the International Community," *Crisis Group Asia Report*, No:76, March 11, 2004; *Crisis Group Asia Report*, No:46, "Uzbekistan's Reform Program: Illusion or Reality," *Crisis Group Asia Report*, No:21, February 18, 2003.

10 "Central Asia: What Role for the European Union?," *Crisis Group Asia Report*, No:113, April 10, 2006, p. 3.

11 "Is Radical Islam Inevitable in Central Asia? Priorities for Engagement," *Asia Report*, No:72, December 22, 2003; "Central Asia: Islam and the State," *Asia Report*, No:59, June 10, 2003; "Radical Islam in Central Asia: Responding to Hizb ut-Tahrir," *Asia Report* No:58, July 10, 2003.

12 For more information, see "Radical Islam in Central Asia: Responding to Hizb ut-Tahrir," *Crisis Group Asia Report*, No:58, June 30, 2003.

13 Interview with an Hizb ut-Tahrir supporter in Tashkent, October 11, 2003.

14 http://fergana.akipress.org/, March 31, 006.

15 See Gulnoza Saidazimova, "Central Asia: Hizb ut-Tahrir's Calls for Islamic State Find Support," *Radio Free Europe/Radio Liberty*, January 17, 2006, http://www.rferl.org/featuresarticle/2006/01/e73441be-0bd5-4e98-8046-4eba329d890c.html.

16 "Uzbekistan: oglashen prigovor po delu trekh obviniaemykh v chlenstve partii 'Khizb ut-Takhrira'," http://www.fergana.ru, September 19, 2006; "V Uzbekistane nachalsia sud nad predpologaemym liderom tashkentskogo otdeleniia organizatsii 'Khizb ut-Takhrira'," http://www.fergana.ru, September 22, 2006.
17 "Central Asia: What Role for the European Union?," *Crisis Group Asia Report*, No:113, April 10, 2006, pp. 7-8.
18 Josette Durrieu, *Security and Stability in Central Asia*, Assembly of Western European Union The Interparliamentary European Security and Defense Assembly, Document A/1952, http://assembly.weu.int, December 19, 2006, p. 20.
19 See Crisis Group Briefing, "Uzbekistan: In for the Long Haul," http://www.crisisgroup.org/library/documents/asia/central_asia/b045_uzbekistan_in_for_the_long_haul.pdf.
20 Ibid.
21 It has been speculated that Germany was permitted to keep its base in Termez, because it let Interior Minister Zokirjon Almatov to receive medical treatment in Hannover despite an EU visa ban. Crisis Group Briefing, "Uzbekistan: In for the Long Haul," op. cit.
22 "Uzbekistan: Germany Likely To Leave Uzbek Base," *Radio Free Europe/Radio Liberty* February 21, 2006.
23 Andrew Stroehlein, "Uzbekistan: Beyond Sanctions," *Transitions Online*, November 22, 2006, http://www.crisisgroup.org/home/index.cfm?id=4519&l=1.
24 See *World Energy Outlook 2005*, International Energy Agency, and *Statistical Review of World Energy*, BP, June 2005.
25 See Ibid.
26 A new European Commission Green Paper on energy strategy was published on 8 March 2006, and it was reported that it was extensively revised after Russia cut off gas to the Ukraine. See "Call for EU to boost energy security," *Financial Times*, February 20, 2006. The Green Paper is available at http://europa.eu.int/comm/energy/green-paper-energy/index_en.htm.
27 See "A European Strategy for Sustainable, Competitive and Secure Energy," *Annex to the European Commission Green Paper*, at http://europa.eu.int/comm/energy/green-paperenergy/doc/2006_03_08_gp_working_document_en.pdf.
28 The bilateral energy dialogue between the EU and Russia was launched in October 2000. It aimed at securing Europe's access to Russia's huge oil and gas reserves (Russia has one third of the world's gas reserves). The dialogue assumes that interdependence between the EU and Russia will increase, since the EU has to to secure the supply of its needs, and Russia has to secure its foreign investments and facilitate its access to the EU and world markets (over half of Russia's trade turnover is carried out through the EU). Currently, however, a breakthrough on the Energy Dialogue is pending.
Meanwhile, bilateral deals between Russia and separate EU states continue to prevail over a specific EU approach. "A European Strategy for Sustainable, Competitive and Secure Energy," at http://europa.eu.int/comm/energy/green-paperenergy/doc/2006_03_08_gp_working_document_en.pdf.
29 Ibid.
30 See *World Energy Outlook 2005*, International Energy Agency, and *Statistical Review of World Energy*, BP, June 2005.

[31] See Crisis Group Briefing, "Uzbekistan: In for the Long Haul," op. cit.
[32] The largest oil and gas reserves around the globe are situated in politically or economically insecure regions (Middle-East, Russia). North Sea oil and gas fields have already been exploited beyond their peak, leaving Europe dependent on non-EU countries for future supply, unevenly distributed "Geopolitics of EU energy supply," July 18, 2005, http://groupsites.ius.edu/physics/E/Reserves.html.
[33] Statistics on reserves and production and export levels are available in the *Statistical Review of World Energy*, op. cit. See also the U.S. Energy Information Agency, www.eia.doe.gov.
[34] Ibid.
[35] This includes gas imported by the Ukraine through Russian pipelines and comprises approximately 37bcm from Turkmenistan, 8bcm from Uzbekistan, and 6bcm from Kazakhstan.
[36] For comparison, this is equivalent to 10 percent of EU consumption: the EU consumed 467bcm in 2004.
[37] "Central Asia: What Role for the European Union?," *Crisis Group Asia Report*, No:113, April 10, 2006, p. 4.
[38] Interview with a senior expert from BOTAS, Turkish Pipeline Company, March 17, 2007.
[39] Continued instability in Afghanistan and growing insurgency in Baluchistan must be overcome before this pipeline is built. It also requires significant investment in production in Turkmenistan and infrastructure in Pakistan.
[40] "China-Kazakhstan pipeline starts to pump oil," December 15, 2005, http://www.chinadaily.com.cn/english/doc/2005-12/15/content_503709.htm; "China's Role in the World: Is China a Responsible Stakeholder?," http://www.uscc.gov/hearings/2006hearings/transcripts/aug_3_4/06_08_3_4_trans.pdf.
[41] *World Energy Outlook 2005*, op.cit and *Statistical Review of World Energy*,op.cit.
[42] Interview with a petroleum expert in Ankara, April 11, 2007.
[43] Andrew Stroehlein,"Uzbekistan: Beyond Sanctions," *Transitions Online*, November 22, 2006, http://www.crisisgroup.org/home/index.cfm?id=4519&l=1.
[44] Sergei Blagov, "Uzbekistan Harbors Energy Development Plans; Russia Ready to Help" 15 February 2007, http://www.eurasianet.org/departments/insight/articles/eav021507a.shtml.
[45] Over the past few years, small increases in Uzbek gas exports have been realized not by increasing output, but by the Karimov regime's literally turning off the taps to poor people in certain towns. In fact, this was one of the main reasons behind the protests in Andijan in May 2005.
[46] *European Community Regional Strategy Paper for Central Asia for the period 2007-2013*, Draft, p.5, http://www.delkaz.cec.eu.int/upload/download_files/PCAKazakhstan.pdf.
[47] http://www.eu.int/comm/world/enp/index_en.htm, April 14, 2007.
[48] See "The Partnership and Cooperation Agreement between the EU and the Republic of Uzbekistan," http://www.eu.int/comm/external_relations/ceeca/pca_uzbekistan.pdf.
[49] http://www.europahouse.uz/en/stat/index.htm.

⁵⁰ See the conclusion to the General Affairs and External Relations Council meeting on 3 October 2005, http://ue.eu.int/ueDocs/cms_Data/docs/pressData/en/gena/86441.pdf.
⁵¹ http://www.europahouse.uz/en/stat/index.htm. Mongolia was also covered by the TACIS program from 1991 to 2003, but is now covered by the ALA program.
⁵² http://www.europahouse.uz/en/stat/index.htm. European Commission External Relations' website http://europe.eu.int/comm/external_relations/ceeca/index.htm, http://europe.eu.int/comm/external_relations/uzbekistan/intro/index.htm. http://europe.eu.int/comm/external_relations/delegations/intro/web.htm.
⁵³ The long list of TACIS projects successfully implemented in Uzbekistan, among others, is as follows: "Support to the Committee of Economic Reforms under the Oliy Majlis, Support to the State Property Committee in Policy Development for Privatization, Support to the Academy of State and Social Construction, Support to the Banking Association, Strengthening the Public Administration and Assistance to the Civil Service Reform." Europe House Uzbekistan website http://www.europahouse.uz/en/stat/index.htm, February 17, 2007.
⁵⁴ Ibid.
⁵⁵ Ibid.
⁵⁶ *European Community Regional Strategy Paper for Central Asia for the period 2007-2013*, Draft, p.5, http://www.delkaz.cec.eu.int/upload/download_files/PCAKazakhstan.pdf; Also see http://www.europahouse.uz/en/stat/index.htm.
⁵⁷ Ibid. For the scope of DCECI see European Commission External Relations web page.
⁵⁸ The Central Asia Indicative Program (CA IP) 2007-2010 defines the interventions of the new instruments for the five Central Asian republics during this four year period. a) "Promotion of Central Asian regional cooperation and good neighbourly relations (Regional Projects), b) Poverty reduction and increasing living standards Good governance and market economic reform." *European Community Regional Strategy Paper for Central Asia for the period 2007-2013*, Draft, p.18, http://www.delkaz.cec.eu.int/upload/download_files/PCAKazakhstan.pdf.
⁵⁹ Ibid.
⁶⁰ http://www.europahouse.uz/en/stat/index.htm.
⁶¹ Ibid.
⁶² *Central Asia Indicative Program (2007 – 2010)*, Country/Region: Central Asia, Budget Years: 2007-2010, Programming Service: DG External Relations E/3, June 15, 2006.
⁶³ Europa House Tashkent website, http://www.europahouse.uz/en/stat/index.htm, 14 March 2007. *Other TACIS initiatives in Central Asia:* The European Union's TACIS program for Eastern Europe, the Caucasus and Central Asia supports a communications project called 'TACIS Information and Communications Activities' (TICA). "This project aims to raise the level of knowledge and awareness in both EU and beneficiary countries of EU activity within the framework of the TACIS program." For List of all TACIS projects in Uzbekistan see http://www.europaid-tacis.tv/centralasia.html; In the field of energy, the EU launched the INOGATE Program in 1995, "a TACIS line of finance aimed at addressing some supply security issues in participating INOGATE countries such as infrastructural deficiencies, regulatory standard requirements and possibly the improvement of the investment framework especially, for downstream

projects." http://www.eu.int/comm/world/enp/index_en.htm, March 14, 2007. European Neighborhood and Partnership Instrument for the 2007-2013 period is aimed to broaden the competencies of the INOGATE. Though conceived solely as an energy technical assistance tool, it has enabled environment to support regional cooperation in trading and consumption between European countries and their Caspian partners.

64 Europe House Uzbekistan website http://www.europahouse.uz/en/stat/index.htm, February 17, 2007.

65 For a more details for the composition of bilateral trade between the EU and Uzbekistan see the Commission's Trade website: http://www.trade.cec.eu.int/intra/intradoclib/intradoclib_995.xls

66 "Uzbekistan Looks East for New Friends," *RFE/RL*, November 25, 2005; Simon Tisdall, "Russia: Putin Defends Ties With Uzbekistan, Belarus, Iran," *The Guardian*, January 31, 2006; Daniel Kimmage, "Military Component Between East And West," *RFE/RL*, November 17, 2005; "Playing Russia Against The West," *RFE/RL*, January 25, 2006; Ahto Lobjakas, "EU Commissioner Criticizes Moscow's Assertive Policy Toward Neighboring States," *RFE/RL*, January 26, 2005.

67 "EU renews Uzbekistan sanctions," *BBC News Asia-Pacific*, November 13, 2006.

68 "The EU's relations with Uzbekistan," http://ec.europa.eu/external_relations/uzbekistan/intro/index.htm.

69 "EU likely to roll back Uzbekistan sanctions," November 9, 2006, http://euobserver.com/9/22775.

70 Penny Spiller, "Europe's Uzbekistan Dilemma," *BBC News Asia-Pacific*, November 13, 2006.

71 U.S. Department of State Office's Press Statement, November 13, 2006, 2006/1032, The U.S. Mission to the European Union http://useu.usmission.gov.

72 On December 12, 2005, victims of human rights violations urged the German government to arrest Almatov for crimes against humanity. "Germany: Uzbek security chief accused of crimes against humanity," *Human Rigths Watch*, http://www.hrw.org, December 15, 2005. Their call was supported by Manfred Nowak, the UN special rapporteur on torture. See the December 16, 2005 press release of the Special Rapporteur, available online at http://www.unhchr.ch/. But before any action was taken, Almatov left Germany. "Controversial Uzbek interior minister resigns," *RFE/RL*, December 22, 2005, http://www.rferl.org/featuresarticle/2005/12/4BDD6821-CBD1-4ED0-B714-CA0E3C431AED.html, "Germany: Challenge to Ruling on Uzbek Ex-Minister," June 22, 2006, http://www.hrw.org/english/docs/2006/06/20/german13552.htm

73 Interview with the EU diplomats in Ankara, November 2, 2006.

74 "Germany's dialogue with the Uzbek regime: a disgrace for German democracy," http://craigmurray.co.uk:/archives/2006/04/germanys_dialog.html; See also Christian Neef, "Germany's Favorite Despot," Spiegel Online August 16, 2006. http://service.spiegel.de/cache/international/spiegel/0,1518,42912,00.html.

75 Ibid.

76 http://www.uzbekistan.org, November 2, 2006.

77 The Germans have had a military base in Termez since February 2002. It has 300 military staff, six transport aircraft and seven helicopters. It serves as a hub for supplying Germany's contingent to the NATO-led International Security Assistance

Force (ISAF) in Afghanistan. Christian Neef, "Germany's Favorite Despot," in *Spiegel Online* August 16, 2006. http://service.spiegel.de/cache/international/spiegel/0,1518,42912,00.html. See also "Germany's dialogue with the Uzbek regime: a disgrace for German democracy," http://craigmurray.co.uk:/archives/2006/04/germanys_dialog.html.

[78] Roger McDermott, *Eurasia Daily Monitor*, Vol. 3, No: 2006, November 7, 2006, http://www.jamestown.org.

[79] The Americans were asked to quit Uzbekistan in 2005 fall. For four years, they kept a large air base at Karshi-Khanabad, 270 kilometers northwest of Termez. Currently Washington, like most NATO states, is even prohibited from using Uzbek air space. Karimov's lack of action toward Germany sharply contrasts with Uzbek moves against the U.S., considering even the closure of virtually all American-affiliated NGOs in the country.

[80] German and European officials justified waiving the visa ban by humanitarian concerns. "This is not just a 'diplomatic illness' –this really is cancer," one official said.See *RFE/RL Newsline*, December 12, 2005.

[81] Agence France-Presse, November 11, 2005.

[82] "Uzbekistan obiavil o vozmozhnom prekrashchenii dogovora arendy bazy FRG v Termeze," http://news.ferghana.ru/detail.php?id=2217&mode=snews, February 1, 2006.

[83] See Galima Bukharbaeva's article "Witness to a Massacre: An Uzbek reporter risked her life to tell the world of Andijan assault," *Dangerous Assignments*, fall/winter 2005, at http://www.cpj.org/Briefings/2005/DA_fall05/galima/galima_DA_fall 05.html, and "Uzbekistan: Where journalism is branded terrorism," *International Herald Tribune*, September 21, 2005. Bukharbaeva received an International Press Freedom award from the Committee to Protect Journalists (CPJ) in November 2005.)

[84]http://europe.eu.int/comm/external_relations/delegations/intro/web.htmThomas Nehls, *RFE/RL*, February 21, 2006.

[85] Ibid.

[86] Ibid.

[87] Thomas Nehls, *DW Turkish Service*, March 28, 2007

[88] Roger McDermott, *Eurasia Daily Monitor*, Vol. 3, No: 2006, November 7, 2006, http://www.jamestown.org.

PART IV
TURKEY: BRIDGE TO NEIGHBORHOOD?

Chapter 17
Linking Turkey's EU Accession Process and the ENP Regional Initiative: Necessary Cross-Border Cooperation with South Caucasus

Burcu Gültekin-Punsmann

The European Neighborhood Policy (ENP) stems from the imperative to develop a strategy toward bordering states and regions. Enlargement has been a key tool on projecting stability across the European continent, as successive enlargements are making a reality of the vision of a united and peaceful continent. The extension of the zone of security through the promotion of better governance and economic and social development in the European vicinity becomes a burning issue.

The policy objectives underlying the ENP are inextricably linked to the nature and function of EU borders. In theory, the essence of the ENP is that of allowing the EU to devise an alternative to enlargement while preventing future EU borders from becoming hard exclusionary boundaries and, instead, developing into integrated borderlands. The ultimate and ideal aim is the extension of the "European governance" area by applying the acquis beyond the EU's external border.

The European Commission's recommendation for the opening of accession negotiations with Turkey is a long awaited awareness of Turkey's capacity to contribute to stability, security and prosperity in its region. Turkey's accession to the EU would present a sizeable challenge in terms of border management. The external border of the EU would be significantly lengthened. However, border management actions should not transform Turkey's external borders into security fences.

The EU's and Turkey's neighborhoods are increasingly overlapping. This is particularly true for the Black Sea region and the Caucasus, fully fledged partners in the ENP. Only the linkage between Turkey's EU accession process and the ENP would transform the latter into a sound strategy, and make it an efficient tool supporting sub-regional integrations and efforts aimed at conflict resolution.

It is equally important that the cross-border program of the European Neighborhood and Partnership Instrument (ENPI) for the Black Sea basin allows or indeed encourages the funding of cross-border projects between Turkey and the South Caucasus. Turkey is part of the Black Sea cross-border initiative. However, Turkey's participation should not be sought only in maritime programs, but also in the South Caucasian initiatives. The issue of the opening of the Turkish-Armenian border, remnant of the Iron Curtain, becomes, therefore, a pressing issue.

Cross-Border Regionalism at the Heart of the European Integration is the Driving Force of the European Neighborhood Policy

Borders have both material and symbolic uses. They can have a very obvious physical presence even though they are visually indistinct, and they are typically the bearers of a wider symbolism as the material embodiment of history. They are often seen as encapsulating a history of struggle against outside forces and as marking the limits of the community or society. Borders are filters with highly variable degrees of permeability or porosity. Borders look inwards and outwards: they simultaneously unify and divide, include and exclude.

When the border is intended as an area of demarcation, separation or division, by political geographers, it has been commonly referred to as a frontier or a boundary. The border marks the line separating spaces of territorially defined sovereignty; it may act as a barrier to human, economic, cultural and social exchange, and movement, or in the most dramatic instances, it can mark the interface of political or military confrontation. Alternatively, a border can be translated into terms such as borderlands or border-region; acquires a diametrically opposite meaning. The border, far from being a line of division between the inside and the outside, between the self and the other, becomes an area of exchange, interaction and integration. In this case, the border tends to be geographically wider, politically inclusive, economically active and a space in which hyphenated identities are allowed to exist and encouraged to flourish. Borderland elites and people do help to shape cross-border relations while interacting with external factors and the wider geopolitical environment. Borders are reproduced in everyday transactions in ways which express but also modify the interstate and geopolitical influences on border regions.

Cross-border regions, straddling state borders, have grown in number and importance in Europe, initially with the encouragement of the Council of Europe, and more recently with the EU's promotion of the Single Market. Cross-border regionalism has flourished over the past two decades, beginning in the heartlands along the western border of Germany, and taking a new step in the 1990's when, in response to the opening of the Iron Curtain, Euroregions were set up from the Finno-Russian border down to Austria, Slovakia, Hungary and Slovenia. Euroregions involve concrete cooperation between regional and local authorities on both sides of the borders, which can in time lead to substantial and effective links across the borders. They can promote common interests and thus strengthen civil society and local democracy as well as having beneficial effects on the local economy.

Cross-border regionalism can be seen as part of a process of political regulation, operating at different spatial scales and describing a spatially integrated approach to problem-solving, involving actors from local, regional and central levels. In a normative sense, it implies the achievement of a higher level of interstate cooperation, contributing to the development of new forms of regional governance above and beyond traditional administrative and nationally-oriented frameworks. Cross-border regionalism manifests itself not only as systems of governance but also as interests and development priorities articulated in the form of strategies that guide cooperative action. Basically speaking, these strategies reflect local problems and development contexts as well as opportunistic behavior in securing support from European and national sources.

The European strategy for developing an area of good "neighborliness" has been based on cross-border cooperation. In the past fifteen years, Europe's North has undergone an intense process of multi-dimensional and multi-level regional cooperation. This has contributed to guiding the transition of Poland and the Baltic states toward EU membership; it has pursued the inclusion of Russia in cooperative efforts, and it has encouraged the participation of non-state grassroots actors in the regional framework. On the Eastern external border of the Union, regional economic cooperation is already quite strong. The Northern Dimension initiative, aiming to address trans-national and cross-border issues along the EU-Russian border and problems related to uneven regional development, was launched in 1998. This initiative had been promoted by Finland since 1997, and was devoted to adding value to EU foreign and security policy by enhancing regional cooperation in the European North and by actively integrating Russia in different policy sectors. In 1999, the government of Poland, at that time still an applicant country, called for a new Eastern policy of the Union. In 2002, the pressure became more consistent as Great Britain and Sweden urged the European Commission to think of a more substantial strategy toward EU prospective neighbors. It was in 2003 when the Commission put forward some concrete proposals for a new approach of the Union toward its prospective neighborhood, which resulted in the establishment of the EPN.

The financial instrument introduced in 2007 and covering the period 2007-2013, the EPNI is particularly adapted to respond to the specificity of cooperation across external EU border. The instrument aims at supporting cross-border cooperation between partner countries and the Member States bringing substantial efficiency gains operating through a single management mechanism.

The ENPI regulation highlights the need for the removal of obstacles to effective cross-border cooperation along the external borders of the EU in order to avoid the creation of new dividing lines. It has been stated that "cross-border cooperation should contribute to integrated and sustainable regional development between neighboring border regions and harmonious territorial integration across the Community and with neighboring countries."

The linkage between regional development and cross-border cooperation is widely acknowledged. The European Regional Development Fund (ERDF) will contribute to cross-border cooperation programs established and implemented under the provisions of the ENPI by financing the part of Member States.

The ENPI will cover all the borders between EU Member States on one side and countries covered by the ENP on the other side. It will also support trans-national cooperation involving beneficiaries in at least one Member State and one partner country and replace existing internal and external cross-border programs in Member States and partner country regions adjacent to the future EU external border.

The strategy paper(s) for Cross-Border Cooperation (CBC) will be mainly aimed at establishing the list of joint cross-border programs. The eligible territorial units of Member States and partner countries have been defined as all NUTS-III level regions along land borders and sea crossings of significant importance and all NUTS-II maritime regions facing a common sea basin. These programs should normally be bilateral across land borders or sea crossings of significant importance and multilateral for maritime regions. Cross-border programs are providing support mainly to projects such as the following:

- Related to economic development, which are expected to support the economic contacts of neighboring regions by encouraging initiatives for entrepreneurship and cooperation between the institutions of the partner countries;
- Environment problems of the neighboring regions, including issues such as river basin management, flood protection and fire prevention, are expected to be addressed;
- Cultural resources of the border region are expected to be protected and promoted; and
- Cooperation networks and people to people contacts will be established.

The Extension of the European Neighborhood Policy to South Caucasus

Originally limited to the four Western Newly Independent States and ten Mediterranean Countries[1], the coverage area of the ENP was extended, following the Brussels European Council decision of June 17-18, 2004, to include the three countries of the Southern Caucasus. The appointment of the EU Special Representative for the South Caucasus on July 7, 2003 was the first sign of the shift in the European approach toward the South Caucasus, brought on the international agenda after the Roses' Revolution in Georgia and the increasing attention paid to the Black Sea region. The European Security Strategy of December 12, 2003, clearly stated that the EU "should *now* take a stronger and more active interest in the problems of the Southern Caucasus, which will in due course also be a neighboring region." The European Parliament accepted a resolution on February 26, 2004 on "EU's Policy towards the South Caucasus." The fact that the South Caucasus countries share with the candidate countries, Romania, Bulgaria and Turkey, either a sea or a land border is also underlined.

The inclusion of Armenia, Azerbaijan and Georgia in the ENP in June, 2004 was indeed publicized as a significant step forward in the Union's engagement with the South Caucasus region. The South Caucasus was included in the ENP in 2004, as it could not be de-linked from the challenges the EU faces in its neighborhood. The conflicts of Abkhazia, South Ossetia and Nagorno-Karabagh are being perceived as serious impediments against the prospects of stabilization and integration in the EU's close neighborhood. The efficiency of the role of the Union in the South Caucasus will depend on its ability to establish a true partnership particularly in the area of conflict resolution, political and economic reform, and intra-regional cooperation.

The EU signed the ENP Action Plans with the three South Caucasus countries on November 14, 2006, stressing the importance of the regional scope of the initiative. Regional cooperation carries the potential to impact positively the settlement of conflicts. The South Caucasus Republics have been invited by the EU to enter into an enhanced regional and cross-border cooperation, and share responsibility in conflict prevention and resolution. It has been acknowledged that the peaceful solution of the Nagorno-Karabakh conflict and Georgia's conflicts are essential for stability in the EU neighborhood. The cross-border programs in the South Caucasus should be seen as tool for conflict transformation and peace-building, they should promote confidence-building across ceasefire lines and increase engagement with non-recognized republics. In its communication "Black Sea Synergy-A New Regional Cooperation Initiative," the Commission advocates a more active EU role through increased political involvement in ongoing efforts to address the conflicts: "a special attention must be paid to promoting confidence-building measures in the regions affected, including cooperation programs specifically designed to bring the otherwise divided countries together."

The European Commission is the largest international donor in both the South Ossetia and Abkhazia conflict zones. Since 2002, the European Commission has allocated a total of €11 million in humanitarian assistance to the most vulnerable populations affected by the unresolved conflict in Georgia and approved on December 14, 2006 an additional aid package of €2 million.

The economic dimension of the political settlement of conflicts should not be underestimated. Border openings and the establishment of official trade relations carry the potential to foster new dynamics to defreeze conflicts by questioning the status quo, rather than recognize the facts on the ground. The possibility of introducing a "Euroregion" cooperation model in the Southern Caucasus, mentioned in the Actions Plans, apparently out of reach in the short-run, can be the guiding objective of the regional and cross-border initiatives.

EU's Borderlands in the Perspective of Turkey's EU Accession Process

The European Commission's recommendation for the opening of accession negotiations with Turkey is a long awaited awareness of Turkey's capacity to contribute to stability, security and prosperity in its region. The Commission's paper on *"Issues arising from Turkey's Membership Perspective"*[2] depicts Turkey's neighborhood as traditionally being characterized by instability and tensions. Turkey's accession will raise expectations regarding EU policies toward the Middle East and the Caucasus. Indeed, Turkey could be a factor for enhancing stability and the role of the EU in the region, but its membership would present challenges as well as opportunities in the field of foreign affairs. Much will depend on how the EU itself will take on the challenge to become a fully fledged foreign policy player.

The external border of the EU would be significantly lengthened. The borders with Bulgaria and Greece will be internal; the external land border would be extended to Georgia (276 km), Armenia (328 km), Azerbaijan (18 km), Iraq (384 km), Iran (560 km), and Syria (911 km). To this new external land border of 2,477 km should be added the Black Sea blue border which runs for 1,762 km, and the Aegean and Mediterranean blue border which runs for 4,768 km. The paper acknowledged that Turkey already devotes considerable resources to border management in order to ensure its own security and stresses that Turkey would, through accession, and in particular after the possible lifting of internal borders, become responsible for ensuring an efficient protection of the new external border, and hence, have to play a key role in ensuring the security of the Union itself.

Border management issues on Turkey's Eastern and Southern borders are among major priorities of the Turkey's accession process. Turkey's inclusion in the Schengen-zone and the lifting of internal borders will depend on the evaluation of its border management practices. Consequently, Turkey adopted the National Action Plan to implement the Integrated Border Management Strategy in 2003. Important steps have been taken to align with the EU Visa Negative List. By May 2003, 75 percent alignment with the said list was achieved.³ Turkey will adapt her visa stickers to the norms of the EU and the International Civil Aviation Organization (ICAO). More dramatically, Turkey has to stop issuing visas at its borders.

The National Action Plan for alignment with the acquis on migration and asylum was adopted in March 2005. In May 2005, Turkey opened negotiations with the EU concerning a readmission agreement.

Cross-border cooperation programs are only now being implemented on Turkey's Western borders, the current EU external border. The Instrument for Pre-Accession Assistance will address both the current Candidate Countries (i.e. Turkey, Croatia, FYROM[4]) as well as the potential future candidate countries (Albania, Bosnia & Herzegovina, Serbia, Montenegro). One focus of the new instrument will be on cross-border cooperation between the current EU Member States on one hand, and the (potential) candidate countries on the other.

Consequently, cross-border programs are operating on Turkey's Western borders, namely between provinces on the Turkish-Greek and Turkish-Bulgarian borders. Theoretically, a cross-border program between Turkey and the Republic of Cyprus is now under consideration. While small scale cross-border programs have already started between Turkey and Bulgaria, they were also initiated between Turkey and Greece. The Commission decided to address the EU's 2007 external border immediately after the October 2003 amendment of the Phare-CBC regulation, to include the external borders of Romania and Bulgaria. Nowadays, the Turkey-Bulgaria Cross-Border Cooperation Program is supported by the 2003 Pre-accession Financial Assistance Program. A Joint Programming Document for 2004-2006 has also been prepared.

The Multi-Annual Financial Framework[5] (MIPD) for Turkey established an indicative allocation of funds for cross-border cooperation. The MIPD has allocated EUR 24.8 million for cross-border cooperation programs for 2007-2009. Amounts allocated to Turkey-Bulgaria, Turkey-Greece and Turkey-Cyprus are respectively EUR 5.025 million, EUR 8.391million and EUR 0.835 million.

The challenge of Turkey's border management has to be addressed by Turkey's efforts to improve and deepen its relations with the neighboring countries coordinated with a sound European strategy toward its new periphery. Cross-border cooperation initiatives will also contribute to securing Turkey's borders with her non-EU member neighbors, by avoiding transforming them in security fences.

The Black Sea Cross-Border Cooperation Program and Turkey

Since 2007, the Black Sea has formed one of the borders of the Union, bringing the expectation of, a strengthened regional approach to become an essential part of the neighborhood policy. The communication of the European Commission "Black Sea Synergy-A New Regional Cooperation Initiative," which was issued on April 11, 2007, aims to increase the EU's involvement in further defining priorities and mechanisms at the regional level, in order to address the "significant opportunities and challenges in the Black Sea area." The Turkey-EU pre-accession strategy together with the ENP and the Strategic Partnership with Russia will form one of the pillars of the EU Black Sea strategy. Being an all inclusive structure, the Organization of the Black Sea Economic Cooperation (BSEC), with Turkey and Russia being the founding members, is expected to contribute to the success of the EU's Black Sea strategy. Additionally, the Council of Europe has recently made the first step toward the establishment of a Black Sea Euro-region, at a meeting held in Samsun in the fall of 2006.

The Black Sea cross-border cooperation program established under the ENPI will, for the first time, offers a real possibility of promoting grass-roots cooperation among local and regional authorities and addressing issues of common concern in the Black Sea region, such as the environment, transport and communications, maritime safety, the marine environment, regional economic development, tourism, and socio-cultural exchanges. This sea basin program on Black Sea coastal areas aims at facilitating further development of contacts between Black Sea towns and communities. Bulgarian-Romanian and Turkish-Bulgarian cross-border projects proposing to enhance the development of links and cooperation along the western coast of the Black Sea will also be financed[6].

However, it is equally important that the ENPI's cross-border program for the Black Sea basin allows or indeed encourages the funding of cross-border projects between Turkey and the South Caucasus. Turkey's participation should not be sought only in maritime programs, but also in the South Caucasian initiatives. This would considerably increase the positive impact capacity of the Black Sea cross-border cooperation program in the conflict areas.

Neighborhoods of the EU and Turkey are increasingly overlapping. This is particularly true for the Black Sea region and the Caucasus, fully fledged partners in the ENP. Only the linkage between Turkey's EU accession process and the ENP would transform the latter into a sound strategy, and make it an efficient tool supporting sub-regional integrations and efforts intending to resolve conflicts. Being integrated into the enlargement process, Turkey can play a pivotal role in framing and implementing the ENP. Cross-border cooperation applied to Turkey's external border will contribute tremendously to the creation of an area of good-neighborhood and shared prosperity at the European periphery. Turkey's eastern border, separating Anatolia from the Caucasus, ancient frontier with the USSR, is as important as the border between the enlarged Union and Russia, for the stability of the European continent.

The Remaining Iron Curtain on Turkish-Caucasian Borderland

The Turkish-Caucasian border had been the traditional frontline between Turkey and Russia: these borderlands at the edges of the Russian and Ottoman Empires had most of the time been battlefields. Turkey's Caucasian border was part of the Iron Curtain during the Cold War and became NATO's South Eastern border at the end of the bipolar system. Turkey, along with Norway, was one of the two flanking states of NATO that shared a land border with the USSR. The former Turkish-Soviet border stretches over 619 km. The demarcation of the Turkish-Soviet border in the 1920s ran through the village of Sarp/Sarpi. Until 1937, peasants were able to freely cross the border to tend to their farms or visit their relatives, but after an uprising on the Soviet side, it was sealed by a barbed-wire fence and the local leaders of Turkish origin were sent to Siberia. It used to take two to three months to send a letter from Sarp to Sarpi. To visit one another, villagers had to make an arduous two-day journey through the Doğu Kapı border crossing, if permission was granted. Sarpi was considered as the most sensitive borders of the USSR.

In the early 1990s, the days of Turkey sharing a land border with the USSR ended. Turkey discovered in her vicinity a new world that had been separated by an *"Oriental iron curtain"* for 70 years. Turkey shares a 276 km long border with Georgia, a 325 km long border with Armenia and a 18 km long border with Azerbaijan, the Autonomous Republic of Nakhitchevan.

Turkey 'discovered' her new neighbor, Georgia, with the opening of Sarp/Sarpi border gate in 1988, and the opening of a second gate at Türkgözü at Posof/Vale in 1994. The opening of Dilucu crossing in 1993 created links between Iğdır and the Azeri enclave of Nakhitchevan. The opening of the Sarpi border crossing in 1988 was a historical event. The Adjarians still remember the 17 km long queue starting from the Gogno Fortress to Sarpi, and people all over the Soviet Union gathering to Batumi to go into Turkey. Batumi, for the first time in history, was being integrated with Turkey. Today, the Turkish consulate is issuing an average of 200 visas per day, with a minimum of 70 visas.

In the meantime, the Turkish-Armenian border was sealed in the context of an escalation of the Upper Karabagh conflict. On March 28, 1993, Armenian forces launched a new offensive action to establish a second corridor between Armenia and Upper Karabagh through the town of Kelbajar, north of Lachin, causing a new flood of Azeri refugees. On April 10, 1993, following the Armenian attack against the Azerbaijani city of Kelbajar, the Turkish Government retaliated by stopping the supply of wheat across the Turkish territory to Armenia and sealed the Turkish-Armenian border post; a decision that also ended direct communication between the two countries. Since that day, opening the border has been directly linked to the resolution of the Upper Karabakh issue. After the official closure of Doğu Kapı/Akhourian in 1993, direct land communications with Armenia were severed and a proposal to open a second gate at Alican/Makara, near Iğdır, was postponed.

Since the beginning of Turkey's accession process to the EU, the closed Turkish-Armenian border has been attracting increased attention. The issue of whether a candidate might integrate the EU with a sealed border has been raised. The issue of the opening of the Turkish-Armenian border has never been among the Copenhagen political criteria that Turkey has to comply with. The European Commission, since 2000, in its successive Regular Reports on Turkey's Progress toward Accession, has been highlighting that the Turkish-Armenian border remains closed and welcomes efforts, both at intergovernmental and NGO levels, aimed to change the status quo. However, the Commission has not made an explicit call in any of its written documents for the border to be opened and did not describe the situation as a blockade. The theoretical debate about whether a closed border can be an obstacle for the accession has lost relevance with the accession of a divided island, Cyprus. Nevertheless, preserving hermetical borders contradicts the European philosophy. Efforts at reducing the barrier functions of borders and transforming borderlands into an area of opportunity have been one of the major achievements of the European integration. However, the Turkish-Armenian border has been brought on the Turkey-EU political agenda, and therefore, constitutes a significant strain, exacerbated by the campaigns of EU-based Armenian lobbies.

On September 27, 2006, in its resolution on Turkey's progress toward accession, the European Parliament called on Turkey to establish "good neighborly relations" with Armenia, which is a member of the EPN and lift its *'blockade'* on the country. The resolution states that the "unjustifiable blockade against Armenia (...) threatens the stability of the region, hampers good-neighborly regional development and breaches the priorities of the revised Accession Partnership and the requirements of the Negotiation Framework, Democracy and the rule of law." In short, the EP, whose decisions have no binding effect on Turkey's accession process, urges Turkey to take the necessary steps, without preconditions, to establish diplomatic and good neighborly relations with Armenia, to withdraw the economic *'blockade'* and to open the land border as soon as possible.

While commenting on the newly-signed EU neighborhood agreements with the South Caucasus countries, the EU High Commissioner for Foreign and Security Policy, Javier Solana, highlighted the importance of the opening of the Turkish-Armenian border by stressing; "We don't defend in any case closed borders, we defend open borders and movement of trade, people, goods. This is very important in today's global world where you cannot be closed; you have to be open by definition. We would like very much to see

Armenia and Turkey cooperate. History is history; we have to look into the future, not to the past."⁷

Although Turkey's problematic relations with Armenia have not become a major issue in its EU agenda, since it is overshadowed by other serious problems in current Turkish-EU relations, the opening of the border will eventually become more prominent during Turkey's accession process.

Turkish Accession and Regional Cooperation in the Caucasus

Likewise, Turkey can significantly enhance its international standing and foreign policy goals through the establishment of full and normal relations with Armenia. Turkey's major foreign policy goal is to become a member of the EU. The issue of the opening of the Turkish-Armenian border is not among the Copenhagen political criteria but the European Commission underlines the importance of the normalization of relations. Since 2000, the European Commission, in its successive Regular Reports on Turkey's progress toward accession, has underlined that the Turkish-Armenian border is closed and welcomed efforts both at intergovernmental and NGO levels to change the status quo.⁸ The 2004 Regular Report on Turkey's Progress toward Accession scrutinizes Turkey's relations with its Caucasian neighbors, with a particular focus on cross-border relations: "Turkey's border with Armenia is still closed. However, there seems to be raising public awareness of the benefits of reopening the border and making preparations for enabling goods transit from third countries. Charter service started in October 2003 to provide air transportation from Istanbul to Yerevan. In February 2004, the Turkish Minister of Communications stated that the reopening of the railway between the two countries would benefit the eastern Anatolian economy. A trilateral meeting took place for the first time at the level of foreign ministers between Turkey, Armenia and Azerbaijan, in the margins of the NATO summit held in Istanbul in June 2004. Turkey has made a positive contribution to regional stability in the Southern Caucasia by its attitude towards the political changes in Georgia as well as the situation in Adjaria."

However, the Turkish-Armenian border that has been brought on the Turkey-EU political agenda therefore constitutes a significant strain, exacerbated by the campaigns of the EU based Armenian lobbies. On September 27, 2006, the European Parliament, in its resolution on Turkey's progress toward accession, called on Turkey to establish "good neighborly relations" with Armenia, which is a member of the ENP and to lift its *'blockade'* on the country. The resolution states that the "unjustifiable blockade against Armenia (...) threatens the stability of the region, hampers good-neighborly regional development and breaches the priorities of the revised Accession Partnership and the requirements of the Negotiation

Framework, Democracy and the rule of law." In short, the EP, whose decisions have no binding effect on Turkey's accession process, urges Turkey to take necessary steps without any preconditions, to establish diplomatic and good neighborly relations with Armenia, to withdraw the economic *'blockade'* and to open the land border as soon as possible.

The report of the European Commission, analyzing issues arising from Turkey's membership perspective, considers that the extension of its borders to Armenia, Azerbaijan and Georgia, will give the EU the capacity, through Turkey, to have a stabilizing influence in Southern Caucasus, provided that Turkey is willing to try to solve conflicts with its neighbors during its accession process. Turkey's potential contribution to easing tensions between Azerbaijan and Armenia in the dispute concerning Nagorno-Karabakh is highlighted.

In this regard, with the establishment of diplomatic relations and the opening of the land border, the need for the normalization of its relations with Armenia becomes more pressing issue for Turkey. In this respect, the opening of the border will increase the sense of security on both sides. The perception of a potential threat stemming from the border will vanish with emerging trade ties and human interactions. Foreseeing the lifting of this political barrier, the EU has great potential to play a constructive role in the region as a civil power with experience in successfully employing economic incentives linked to political and diplomatic initiatives. The EU needs to conduct a dialogue with Turkey on policies and actions vis-à-vis the region. Additional support through instruments such as technical assistance and twinning will boost further development of various forms of cross-border cooperation involving local and regional authorities, non-governmental actors, and business communities.

Eastern Anatolian region is the less developed region of Turkey. The share in the GDP of the Eastern Anatolian region is 4.14 percent and the GDP per capita is 841 TRY while the national GDP per capita is 1837 TRY.[9] According to the socio-economic development index of the State Planning Organization issued in 2003, Muş and Ağrı are the least developed provinces in Turkey.[10] Their remoteness from political and economic centers is the main reason for the underdevelopment. Kars is located 1,800 km from Istanbul, and a half an hour distance from the Armenian city, Gyumri. The Turkish authorities have so far refrained from assessing the cost of maintaining the closed border, but former President Süleyman Demirel hinted at the prevailing official opinion when he stated that 'Turkey cannot take the risk of displeasing her Azeri brothers in order to allow a few to make some profit' in the 1990's. Although, Armenia would represent a relatively low percentage of Turkey's total foreign trade and economy, these recent changes reveal that Armenia could become a considerable economic partner and a noteworthy market for Eastern Anatolia.

For decades, Kars was a gate to the Caucasus and the Soviet Union because of its railway connection, and its cultural and historical proximity to the region. The city is situated 70 km away from the border gate at Doğu Kapı, which was an official border crossing between Turkey and the Soviet Union. Despite problems of compatibility between Turkish and Soviet railway networks, the opening of the border gate and the construction of the railway network permitted traders in Kars to export toward the Soviet Union during the Cold War era. In the early 1990's, the flow of goods also began between the province of Kars and the young Republic of Armenia. Daily railway connections allowed Armenian businessmen to travel to Kars relatively easily. However, the closure of the Doğu Kapı border gate condemned Kars to isolation. In 2005, there were only five exporters in Kars.[11] The local customs department had at that time been transferred to Erzurum, where the Union of Exporters' of the Eastern Anatolian Region is also based. In the meantime, Ardahan and Iğdır, which were former districts of Kars, separated from the administrative territory of Kars and were granted their own provincial administrations. In addition, the opening of the Posof/Vale border crossing permitted Ardahan to become a gateway to Georgia and the Dilucu border crossing linked Iğdır to the Azerbaijani enclave of Nakhichevan.

The closure of the border crossing and the condemnation of the railway increased the feeling of isolation in Kars. For local authorities, the closure of the border gate is even more difficult to understand, since Istanbul and the Black Sea Coast are fully authorized to maintain economic and human relations with Armenia. In this regard, many local politicians from Kars argue that the powerful Black Sea lobby supports the closure of the Doğu Kapı border gate. The feeling of being deprived of new opportunities is widespread in this part of Anatolia.

The re-opening of the Doğukapı/Akhourian border crossing is likely to yield significant benefit for the local population. The municipality of Kars has been striving hard to develop relations with Armenia by establishing more cross-border contacts.

The Commission should ensure that EU budgets allocated to regional development in Turkey's Eastern region promote cross-border cooperation as well. A sound regional development strategy for the Turkish Eastern Anatolian region cannot be elaborated without sustained cross-border cooperation. In due course, however, the EU would be well advised to ensure that the opening of the Turkish-Armenian border is fully integrated in the region's development strategy.

The promotion of infrastructure interconnections and modernization in the field of transport and energy is an important task. The rehabilitation of the railway connection between the Turkish city of Kars and the Armenian city of Gyumri, integrated into the TRACECA transport corridor in

December 2001, will be tremendously beneficial for the whole region, carrying the potential to foster new dynamics to defreeze conflicts by questioning the status quo and boosting the integration of production and distribution networks.

Preparing the Border Opening and Addressing Technically Neighborhood Issues

The political impact of the creation of Turkish-Armenian technical commissions shouldn't be underestimated. The work that will be carried out within each of these commissions will be issue based. The aim is to set up a few joint task forces gathering state officials (diplomats and state experts) who will work in close interaction with academics, NGO workers and local officials. The socialization process among Armenian and Turkish officials will foster in return the determination and impact on the formation of the political will. The existence of an official framework for intergovernmental will positively affect the normalization process. Frequent meetings among state experts will sustain the process.

The neighborhood notion has to be the guiding principle of the technical intergovernmental commissions. The mission of these commissions will go well beyond the normalizations of political relations. Their work will be valuable even in the context where the two sides maintain normal state-to-state relations. The aim will be to establish an infrastructure for bilateral track-two diplomacy projects, today limited to separate and ad hoc initiatives mostly financed by international donors. The Europeanization process in which Armenia and Turkey are both engaged can boost the efficiency of the work of the technical commissions set on the intergovernmental level.

Technical Commission on Customs

The commission will gather state experts from each Customs administration. The Turkish customs regime has undergone an in-depth modernization process necessary for the full completion of the Turkey-EC Customs Union. In this respect, many Turkish customs officials have been in charge of training sessions in regional organizations. This technical commission should constitute the framework that will allow Turkish Customs experts to provide a technical training to their Armenian colleagues. Turkish Customs Administration has already organized training seminars and study visits for Customs officers within the Economic Cooperation Organization. Alternatively, the regional framework of the Black Sea Economic Cooperation can be used to establish cooperation on customs between Turkey and her Caucasian neighbors, including Armenia. The improvement of the transit transportation requires cooperation on border crossings formalities. The commission will address the issues of the harmonization of regulations and their uniform implementation, effective tax collection and selective but more effective customs control.

Technical Commission for the Development of the Border Trade

In 2003, the Turkish Under secretariat for Foreign Trade decided to create centers for border trade in Eastern and Southeastern Anatolian border provinces.[12] The aim of the initiative is to regulate border trade and promote cross-border economic contacts. The provinces of Artvin, Ardahan, Kars, Iğdır, Ağrı, Van, Hakkari, Şırnak, Mardin, Şanlıurfa, Kilis, Gaziantep, and Hatay are within the coverage area of this initiative. A center for border trade will be opened near Artvin on the Turkish-Georgian border. The Turkish-Armenian technical commission for the development of border trade, while preparing for the opening of the border, can initially work on establishing a regulatory mechanism for future cross-border trade.

Technical Commission for Border Management,

Border management issues are among major priorities in Turkey's accession process. Turkey's inclusion in the Schengen-zone and the lifting of internal borders will depend on the evaluation of its border management practices. Improvements in the capacity of public administration to develop effective border management in line with the *acquis* and the best practices of the EU is listed in the short- and medium-term priorities in the 2003 Accession Partnership. The full implementation of Schengen, which will affect Turkey's relations with its non-European neighbors, is also among the medium-term priorities of the partnership. A National Action Plan to implement the Integrated Border Management Strategy was adopted in 2003. The Turkish-Armenian border management commission, together with commissions established by Georgia and Azerbaijan, will support the national effort undertaken within the EU accession process on a regional level.

Joint Monitoring of the Medzamor Power Plant

A Turkish-Armenian team has to be set for the joint monitoring of the Medzamor nuclear plant, which is situated at a distance of 28 kilometres from the center of Yerevan near the Turkish-Armenian border. The power plant was first closed on environmental grounds in 1989 in the wake of the Spitak earthquake. In the 1990s, however, the supply of gas from Azerbaijan and Georgia became irregular, resulting in power shortages that deepened the severity of the economic crisis. Consequently, the earlier closure of the power plant was reversed. Unit 2 of Medzamor was reopened in 1995, subject to regular monitoring of the International Atomic Energy Agency.

Today, nuclear energy constitutes 36 percent of electricity production in Armenia. The Medzamor plant is financially managed and fueled by the Unified Energy System of Russia. Its closure, planned for 2004, as part of a broader agreement with the EU, was deferred in the face of lacking viable alternatives. The Medzamor power plant is, therefore, not only a primary source of energy for Armenia, but also perceived to be a great concern for its security and that of its neighbors. An accident will affect equally Gyumri, Yerevan, as well as Kars and Iğdır.

Conclusion

The challenge in management of the new longer external borders of the EU has to be addressed by Turkey's efforts to improve and deepen its relations with neighboring countries coordinated with a sound European strategy toward its new periphery. Cross-border cooperation applied to Turkey's external border will contribute tremendously to the creation of an area of good-neighborhood and shared prosperity at the European periphery. Turkey's eastern border, separating Anatolia from the Caucasus, ancient frontier with the USSR, is as important as the border between the enlarged Union and Russia, for the stability of the European continent.

Cross-Border Cooperation practices have played an important role in stabilizing Eastern Europe. Mindful of Europe's history of shifting borders, the EU, during the 1990s, set an accession to the pre-condition requiring that the borders were sacrosanct and non-negotiable. *Border change* refers to changing the symbolic meanings and the material functions of existing borders in situ. This was important for the security of the continent, but made harmonious relations in border regions even more of a necessity, especially in formerly disputed, sensitive regions. Lessons learned should also be applied eastward.

---

[1] In the communication of the European Commission on "Wider Europe-Neighborhood: A New Framework for Relations with our Eastern and Southern Neighbours," the South Caucasus is only mentioned in a footnote stating "Given their location, the Southern Caucasus, therefore, also fall outside the geographical scope of this initiative for the time being." Commission of the European Communities, "Wider Europe-Neighborhood: A New Framework for Relations with our Eastern and Southern Neighbours," *Communication from the Commission to the Council and the European Parliament*, COM (2003) 104 Final, March 11, 2003, p. 4.

[2] "Issues Arising from Turkey's Membership Perspective," *Commission Staff Working Document*, {COM(2004) 656 final}, SEC(2004) 1202, October 6, 2004.

[3] As a first step, Turkey introduced visa requirements for six Gulf countries (Bahrain, Qatar, Kuwait, Oman, Saudi Arabia and United Arab Emirates) which the EU subjects to visa requirements, as of September 1st 2002. As a second step, thirteen countries (Indonesia, Republic of South Africa, Kenya, Bahamas, Maldives, Barbados, Seychelles, Jamaica, Belize, Fiji, Mauritius, Grenada, and Santa Lucia) have

been listed for visa requirements, and these entered into force between May and July, 2003.

[4] Turkey recognizes the Republic of Macedonia with its constitutional name.

[5] This Multi-annual Indicative Planning Document (MIPD) is the strategic document for IPA. It is established for a three-year rolling period, with annual reviews. It follows the Multi Annual Indicative Financial Framework (MIFF) which indicatively allocates funds per beneficiary and per component. It draws on the pre-established Instrument for Pre-Accession Assistance (IPA) components.

[6] For the possible participation of Turkey in the ENPI Black Sea multilateral Sea Basin program, the ENPI Mediterranean multilateral Sea Basin program and the relevant ERDF trans-national programs (Europe South–East program and Mediterranean program), the following indicative amount of funds have been earmarked: 2007: 3.449 million Euro, 2008: 3.518 million Euro, 2009: 3.588 million Euro. The share of funds to be allocated for the participation of Turkey in the ENPI Black Sea multilateral Sea Basin program should be of the order of 20–25 percent of the total amount.

[7] "Neighbourhood agreement with EU will benefit Armenia greatly," *RFE/RL Caucasus Report*, Vol. 9, No. 39, 16, November 16, 2006.

[8] The European Commission in its 2005 Regular Report on Turkey's progress towards accession, states "Turkey's border with Armenia remains closed. However, the bilateral dialogue process between Turkey and Armenia continues on various levels, including the Ministers of Foreign Affairs. Within the framework of this process, nine meetings were held by officials. There has been an official exchange of letters between the Turkish Prime Minister and the Armenian President. In his letter dated April 2005, the Turkish PM proposed to set up a joint commission composed of independent historians and other international experts with unconditional access to all relevant archives with a view to discuss the tragic events of 1915. In his response the Armenian President pointed out that, instead of employing historians, both governments should rather establish diplomatic relations first and create a joint government commission dealing with all critical questions of the relationship, including closed borders. Both leaders were due to meet in Warsaw in the margin of the Council of Europe Summit, but the meeting did not take place. Direct flights from several Turkish cities to Yerevan continue. In the wake of the 90th anniversary of the tragic events of 1915, Turkish academics participated in conferences in Yerevan. Armenian Parliamentarians made an official visit to Turkey. In September 2005 a conference entitled 'Ottoman Armenians during the collapse of the Empire: Scientific Responsibility and Issues of Democracy' took place in Istanbul. As regards relations with the Southern Caucasus, Turkey indicated full support for the European Neighborhood Policy." 2005 Progress Report, COM (2005) 561 final.
The Commission in its 2006 Progress Report states that "since the official exchange of letters between the Turkish Prime Minister and the Armenian President in April 2005, there have been no significant developments in relations with Armenia. Turkey has not opened its border with this country. This would be an important step forward in the establishment of good neighbourly relations. It would be beneficial to both sides, in particular with respect to trade.," COM (2006) 649 final.

[9] Data of the Turkish National Statistics Institute based on the census of 2000.

[10] State Planning Organization, Regional Development data.

[11] Data provided by the Undersecretariat of the Prime Minister for Foreign Trade. According to the data of 2000, exports per capita in Kars are 7 USD, 84 USD in the Eastern Anatolian Region, and 2249 USD on a national level.
[12] Government decree on the establishment of border trade centers, 2003/5408

Chapter 18
Turkey Between the Middle East and the EU: Boundaries and Bridges

Bezen Balamir-Coşkun

Since the establishment of the Republic of Turkey in 1923, Turkish foreign policymakers have underlined the primacy of 'West' in Turkish foreign policy. During its Western orientation, the Republic of Turkey never realized that she was being alienated from the Middle Eastern affairs. 1,673 kilometer-long borders with Iran, Iraq and Syria, 90 percent Muslim population, ongoing conflict with Kurdish separatist groups, and the certain historical and cultural ties with the regional states and societies make Turkey's involvement in regional affairs inevitable.

Traditionally, Turkish foreign policymaking has revolved around two basic principles; maintaining the nation's independence and sustaining security, and preserving the status quo, which involves the country's modernist, secularist and national regime. Only after the 1990s did the framework of Turkey's foreign policy change in parallel to a chain of internal changes. This development has created more maneuver area for Ankara's foreign policy, particularly for its Middle East policy. With the Justice and Development Party (AKP) government, which came to power in November 2002, Turkey's ruling elite has gained self-confidence in adopting an active and constructive role in the Middle East. Furthermore, Turkish state elite found themselves role-searching between Europe and the Middle East.

Turkey's current Middle East policy is not just important for its regional vision and security needs, but also extremely important in terms of Turkey's relations with the West in general and with the EU in particular. The objective of this chapter is to discuss the Turkish Middle East policy with references to its relations with the EU. In the first section, the evolution of Turkish foreign policy toward the Middle East will be discussed. In the second section, the 22nd Turkish government's Middle East policy under the influence of the developments in its relations with the EU will be examined. The last section will analyze Turkey's current claim of constituting a bridge between Europe and the Middle East in light of its international and domestic repercussions. This section includes some suggestions for the improvement of Turkey's strategic position between the EU and the Middle East.

The Evolution of Turkey's Middle East Policy (1920s – 1990s)

During the formation years of the Republic of Turkey (1920s-1930s), Turkey followed a nonalignment policy in international era since it was a war-torn country desperate for an internal reconstruction literally from scratch, which made seeking peace a necessity. Thus, Mustafa Kemal Ataturk, the founder and the first president of the Republic of Turkey, followed two foreign policy goals: to create a strong state which could defend its territorial integrity and political independence; and to make Turkey a full, equal member of the European community of Western nations. Consequently, analyses of past policies of Turkish Republic prove that Turkish foreign policy has always given priority to relations with the West rather than the Middle East. For a long time, Turkish foreign policy toward the Middle East has been considered an extension of its Western-oriented foreign policy. Throughout the history of the Republic of Turkey, Western orientation has remained one of the indispensable fundamentals of Turkish foreign policy.[1] In regard to the concern over the Middle East, on the other hand, Turkey has always been linked to the Middle East "through sub-systems, but not by an overarching foreign policy emphasis which is reserved for the West."[2]

Avoiding any interference in regional affairs has been the main principle for Turkey's policies toward the Middle East. Although bilateral relations with regional states have been established, the main idea was to leave the Arabs alone. The 1937 Sadabad Pact, which was concluded with Iraq, Iran, and Afghanistan, was a good example of how Kemalist foreign policy distanced itself from the Middle East. Rather than being an example of regional cooperation, the Sadabad Pact underlined the signatory countries' affirmation of non-interference in each others' affairs. Thus, the roots of Turkish foreign policy toward the Middle East were laid in an era when Turkish foreign policymakers tended to avoid involvement in Middle East affairs.

As was pointed out by Kemal Karpat, from the 1940s onward, objectives of the Turkish foreign policy over the Middle East were based on first ensuring the national security, second attaining economic benefits, and third, expanding her influence in the area.[3] In this sense, the Turkish policy toward the Middle East became an extension of Turkey's pro-Western foreign policy. None of these objectives were adopted for the sake of strengthening relations with regional states, but rather as a result of Turkish attempts to prove herself to the West as a cooperative partner in regional affairs. Until the 1960s, Turkey's core foreign policy objectives remained the same. Regarding the Middle East, Turkey was not very interested in the political structure and objectives of their Middle Eastern neighbors.

During the 1960s, Turkey attempted to establish a rapprochement with the Middle East, again not for her own sake, but in order to strengthen her position vis-à-vis the West. The mistakes committed during the 1950s paved the way to a new Turkish foreign policy, drafted in the mid-1960s. It was expected to correct previous mistakes that were blamed for the deterioration of relations with the Middle East which caused Turkey to be isolated in the region and alienated within the UN due to the Cyprus case. The most prominent feature of the so-called new Turkish foreign policy of 1960s and 1970s was her emphasis on multi-faceted policy making. Applied to the Middle East context, such a policy required less cooperation with the U.S., and a more balanced attitude toward the Arab-Israeli dispute. Turkey pursued balanced policies during the 1973 Yom Kippur War. Within this context Turkey insisted on that the military bases in Turkey were not to be used to aid Israel during the 1967 and 1973 Arab—Israeli wars. In the case of Palestinian Liberation Organization (PLO), led by Yasser Arafat, claiming international recognition from the international community, Turkey voted in favor of PLO to obtain an observer status in the United Nations. But this was not an indication of a complete reversal in Turkish foreign policy.

Turkey's foreign policy during the 1960s was defined by the following principles: not interfering in the domestic affairs of Middle Eastern countries; maintaining diplomatic relations with Israel on one side and giving political support for the Arab cause, on the other; preserving her close ties with the West in regard to their impact on Turkey's relations with the Middle East; and developing bilateral relations in the region. Throughout 1990s, Turkish foreign policymakers have been guided generally by these principles. During the Gulf Crisis, however, the Turkish foreign policy deviated from its traditional Middle Eastern policy which focused on non-involvement in Middle Eastern conflicts. According to Philip Robins "...in a changing world, especially one which has altered so profoundly on the cusp of the new decade, there will be modifying pressures on even the most basic principles of foreign policy. Iraq's invasion of Kuwait...provided a new challenge to the principles of Turkish policy on the Middle East."[4]

The Gulf Crisis of 1990-1991 brought a degree of change to Turkish foreign policy in which Turkey had to involve in an inter-Arab dispute; something had been avoided since the foundation of the Turkish Republic. The profundity of the change in the external environment, the twin revolutions which came along with the ending of the Cold War era and further integration of Europe, leads analysts to conclude that Turkey automatically responded to these changes by adapting its foreign policy. Turkey's foreign policy transformation, however, has been gradual and intertwined with the internal developments.

Turkey has always been cautious against the Middle East. Ongoing turmoil and instability in the region, lack of a democratic tradition and the continuous flow of arms into the region accompanied with hostile regimes have always heightened Ankara's anxieties. After the end of the Cold War, international and local developments particularly overlapped those related to the Middle East. The revival of the 'Greater Middle East' idea in international era posed a challenge for Turkey both externally and internally. According to Dietrich Jung and Wolfango Piccoli, the idea of 'Greater Middle East' has caused the revival of the neglected Ottoman heritage and confronted the state elite with challenges and opportunities for which the Kemalist power bloc was not ready to face.[5] Kurdish nationalism, Islamic internationalism and pan-Turkist revivalism has become a matter of bilateral relations and confronted the Kemalist elite whose existing political instruments which are composed of—an authoritarian decision-making, a notion of a narrow territorial and unitary state; neglecting all social, ethnic and religious divisions; viewing national security only in military terms- have remained inadequate to respond these internal and external challenges.[6] Domestic conflicts caused by social changes were allegedly associated with foreign intervention. This tendency was seen clearly in Turkey's relations with its Middle Eastern neighbors throughout the 1990s. Turkey's relations with Syria, Iraq and Iran during the 1990s are the best illustration of this tendency. The disagreement between Syria and Turkey over the distribution of water overlapped with the Kurdish problem and developed into a dangerous conflict that brought two neighbors to the brink of war. In response to the Operation Provide Comfort which handed over Kurds a Kurdish sanctuary in the Northern Iraq, Turkish officials declared their determination to protect integrity of the Iraqi state and their objection to the creation of a Kurdish state in the Northern Iraq. The period was marked by Turkish Military Forces' regular interventions into the Northern Iraq. Last but not least of examples is the Iran case for which some Turkish officials and journalists has tended to attribute the rise of political Islam in Turkey to foreign —mainly Iran's- intervention. Besides Pan-Turkism and Kurdish nationalism, this attribution has also been possible sources of tension between Iran and Turkey throughout 1990s.

Since the 1950s, Turkey has been dragged into Middle Eastern politics even though it does not conceive itself as part of the region. Turkish governments adopted a cautious policy in its attitudes toward the Middle Eastern crises as a result of pragmatic choices. The development of Turkey as a regional power, both militarily and economically, weakened its ability to stay away from the Middle East whose security complex has become more interwoven with the Turkish one. Thus, the guiding principles of last decades, such as non-interference in internal affairs and preference of limited bilateral relations with Middle Eastern states became less sustainable. At the beginning of the twenty-first century, Turkish state elite found themselves at a crossroad as a result of new regional and international environment.

Since the 1990s, Turkey has undergone a serious internal reform process that has changed the framework of its foreign policy. This development has created more room for maneuvering for Ankara's general foreign policy, particularly for its Middle East policy. Turkey's new orientation seems more flexible and adaptive to the challenges in the region. Throughout the 1990s and at the beginning of the millennium, Turkey's ruling elite has showed self-confidence that it can play a constructive role in the Middle East independently.

Transformation of Turkey's Middle East Policy: Operation Iraqi Freedom and Beyond (2002 – 2006)

The region is extremely important for Turkish foreign and military affairs since most of the issues that threaten Turkish security originate from the Middle East. Particularly, the political developments in Iraq and the internal clashes among different ethnic and religious elements within the Iraqi society have become one of the most important issues of Turkish foreign and security policy.

As far as Turkey's Middle East policy is concerned, we can say that it can be analyzed within the classical framework of power politics, linking political action to material capabilities and geo-strategic limitations. Within this context, William Hale defined Turkey as a *middle power*. According to Hale, Turkey has a limited chance for independent action within international system and has often been shadowed by the penetration of the allied great power into the regional affairs.[7] This position has been particularly effective on Turkey's Middle East policy orientation. Since 2003, Turkey has been sharing border with the U.S., the greatest power of the new world order, and consequently not just her policies toward Iraq, but also her relations with Syria and Iran have caused tensions with the U.S.

The general transformation that has realized in Turkish foreign policy after the 1990s has also reflected in its Middle Eastern policy. Previously, Turkey's relations with Arab states particularly with Syria were hurt by its relatively good relations and military alliance with Israel. Recently, Turkish government has succeeded in balancing its relations both with the Arab states and Israel.

After the November 2002 parliamentary elections, a brand new party—Justice and Development Party (AKP)—emerged as the largest single party in the 550-member Turkish Grand National Assembly. It was quite unusual to have a single-party government with 363 deputies for Turkey that has been ruled by coalition governments for many decades. Even though the AKP is one of the successor parties to an Islamic party (Virtue Party –Fazilet Partisi in Turkish) which had been closed down because of its openly Islamist character, both the party leader Recep Tayyip Erdoğan and the Prime Minister Abdullah Gül signaled that Turkey's foreign policy orientation to Europe and the West, the perennial priorities of the country's Kemalist elite, would not change under their leadership.

The re-emergence of conflict between Iraq and the U.S. was a watershed for the new government. The uneasiness among public and political elite was exacerbated by deep economic problems of the country, and the scenario of renewed Kurdish refugee flows to Turkey in case of a war in Iraq. It was widely assumed that Turkey would join U.S.-led 'coalition of the willing' even though the public opinion was overwhelmingly against the war. Turkey's need for continuing external aid and strategic urge by the country's military elite to be part of a coalition led by the world only superpower clashed with the public opinion. On the other hand, messages given by the EU throughout the Iraqi crisis hurt Turkish national indignity. Thus, the ghosts of early 1920s began to awaken, so-called Sevres Syndrome,[8] a Turkish preoccupation with renewed attempts by the great powers to reshape the Middle East to Turkey's disadvantage.

Considering the sensitivity among Turkish public regarding revival of the Sevres Syndrome, Recep Tayyip Erdoğan, who was not yet the PM then, began to speak about the need for Turkey to consider different policy options toward its Middle Eastern neighbors. Consequently, in January 2003, the AKP initiated a new opening to the Middle East. It was an attempt by the AKP to manage the Iraq issue and to find a sustainable regional policy. Within this context, considering the economic and humanitarian crisis Iraq's neighbors faced during and after the Gulf War, Turkey launched a neighborhood initiative prior to the U.S.-led military intervention in Iraq. Through the *'Neighbors Forum'* Turkey has attempted to promote consultations between Iraq and the neighboring countries. Moreover, a *Special Envoy* was appointed to coordinate Turkey's national and international endeavors vis-à-vis Iraq. Turkey has also designated a high level *Special Coordinator for Reconstruction and Humanitarian Assistance* in order to mobilize Turkey's assistance to Iraq.

As protests across the world against the war in Iraq proliferated, the AKP took refuge in the assumption that war could be prevented. As was stated by Robins, "having won a popular mandate just three months before, it was reluctant to go against a public opinion so obviously against war, and a support base that would frown upon."[9] In March 2003, absolute majority of the Turkish Grand National Assembly voted in favor of the motion 264 to 251, but it was lost on a technical ground. This was a shock for international community, particularly for the U.S. who expected an unconditional support from the Turkish government. In three months between December 2002 and March 2003, Turkey has undergone an extraordinary reversal in its foreign policy. Since then, Turkey's privileged relationship with the U.S. has been undermined and the underemphasized relations with the Middle East have been prioritized.

Since 2003, Turkey has developed a *'proactive peace policy'* toward Iraq, which aims at developing relations with different segments of Iraqi society regardless of ethnic and sectarian differences. Within this context, before the elections, major Sunni opposition figures and envoys from the U.S. were invited to Ankara to ensure Sunni participation in the Iraqi national elections. Through proactive communication with different Iraqi groups, Turkish diplomats aimed to prevent conflicts in Iraq:

> Turkey thus naturally continues to support the political process and remains firmly committed to assisting Iraq in its search for security, peace and stability. Aware of the vital importance of rebuilding Iraq's national security network and capabilities, Turkey has been contributing to NATO's Training Mission in Iraq. Turkey's contributions as a transit hub for humanitarian assistance, essential goods and services to Iraq are crucial for its reconstruction.[10]

In general, the recent Turkish Middle East policy has been developed vis-à-vis the EU's and individual member states' contradictory claims and increasing demands from Turkey. Furthermore, the increasing 'Islamophobia' in Europe as a result of so-called Islamist terror organizations' attacks to the U.S. and its allies, the cartoon crisis,[11] the initiation of discriminatory measures toward the Muslims in several European countries have caused resentment toward the Europe among Turkish public. In order to ease the domestic tensions, the AKP government has developed new foreign policy rhetoric: Turkey being a bridge between the East and the West, between the Middle East and Europe, and between civilizations. Both the government and Turkish state elite has underlined the Turkey's role as 'bridge' between two worlds.

Turkey between the Europe and the Middle East: Boundary or Bridge?

Regional security complex theory suggests that the international system divided into regional security complexes in which security interactions either conflicting or co-operative that are more intense among its members than between its members and those of other security complexes.[12] Between such complexes, lies an insulator that maintains security interactions with all neighboring complexes. Normally the role of the insulator is to provide stability by preventing the security interactions from one complex to the other. In their 1999 article, Barry Buzan and Thomas Diez argued that Turkey "plays the role of an insulator [between European and the Middle Eastern security complexes], a peripheral actor in all of the security regions surrounding it. ... [I]ts main function, in practice, is separate other regional security dynamics from each other."[13]

According to Diez, while Turkey is active in Europe through its membership in the NATO and its association with the EU, it has also interlinked with the Middle Eastern regional security complex as a result of its military links with Israel, and disputes over water resources with Iraq and Syria.¹⁴ However, Turkey has not been able to fully integrate into any of the regional security complexes. In this sense, Turkey constitutes an unusual insulation as a result of her active security relations with both complexes. Turkey's candidacy to the EU membership brings Turkey closer to the European security complex which resulted in the European and the Middle Eastern complexes directly bordering each other. Consequently, Turkey's buffering position as an insulator has become debatable.

Since the end of 1990s, Turkey has realized its key position between the two regional security complexes. Within this context, Turkish governments and foreign policymakers have decided to underline Turkey's position as a 'bridge' between two regional complexes even between 'civilizations.' According to Ersin Kalaycıoğlu "a multifarious economic, cultural, and diplomatic role of extending Europe's values and norms into the "Greater Middle East"…seems to be developing for Turkey."¹⁵ Both Turkish society and the Government has embraced Turkey's this role which underlines the self-image of Turkey as a bridge over troubled land and connecting cultures.¹⁶

Considering the background given in the first section, the 'bridge' rhetoric is not a totally novel idea. This rhetoric has rooted in multi-faceted policy making, which had dominated Turkish foreign policy rhetoric after 1960s. As a reflection of this rhetoric, Turkey kicked off *'Alliance for Civilizations'* initiative together with Spain in order to develop mutual understanding between Islamic world and the Christian world. Furthermore, Turkey has intensified its good relations with its Middle Eastern partners as well as Western partners. Besides the ongoing economic and financial ties with the EU, Turkey signed a trade agreement with Syria in 2004 and opened its financial markets to Arab capital as well as Western capital.

As another reflection of the 'bridge' rhetoric, since 2004, Turkey has expressed its readiness to facilitate negotiations between Israel and Palestine. Turkey is well placed to get involved together with Europe in the resolution of Israeli—Palestinian conflict as it was equidistant between both sides. Turkey has played a balanced diplomacy toward both sides of the conflict in order to contribute reconciliation. As an indication of her intention to become a mediator between Israel and Palestinian Authority, in November 2007, Turkey invited the leaders of both sides to meet in Ankara prior to their historical meeting in Annapolis.

The question is how these two geographies/cultures perceive Turkey's role to bridge them to each other? It is agreed that Turkey's accession in the EU would contribute to security and stability in a wide geographic framework that would make the EU a real global power. The European Security Strategy had underlined the EU's intention to play a role in the region outside of Europe, and Turkey could effectively contribute to this goal both within the Europe and elsewhere. It is believed that only a country like Turkey carrying mixture of characteristics from both East and West could make the European Security and Defense Policy (ESDP) a real and a potent multi-cultural power can contribute the stability, dialogue and cooperation outside Europe as well as inside. Furthermore, Turkey's geo-strategic position as a transit route of transportation, communication and trade with the Caucasus, Asia and the Middle East and its position in the Baku—Tbilisi—Ceyhan oil pipeline increased Turkey's strategic importance for the EU.

Turkey's strategic decision in 2003 regarding its involvement in the U.S.-led Iraq operation brought Turkey closer to the EU's soft power/multilateral approach in international affairs. Turkish foreign and security policy is already within the European mainstream, and far closer to European than American approaches on particular issues like Iran, Iraq and the Middle East process. Turkey's new positioning vis-à-vis the U.S. is actually a reflection of new regional dynamic in the Middle East. Particularly, as a result of Turkish Parliament's refusal of the deployment of U.S. troops for the second front in Northern Iraq, Turkey's relations with the Middle East became warmer as well as its relations with the Arab world. Its involvement in peace keeping operation in Lebanon, prioritizing her role as regional broker in conflicts occur in the Middle East, urging active diplomacy and her approach of 'proactive peace' in Iraq have made Turkey's position stronger in the eyes of both European and Middle Eastern states. Turkey has actively played broker role in recent diplomatic crisis between the West and Syria and between the West and Iran. However, it is extremely important that Turkish Ministry of Foreign Affairs has to initiate an effective public relations campaign for promoting Turkey's role to bridge Europe to the Middle East at the international level. Within this context, the discourses and actions of Ministry of Foreign Affairs, Military Forces and the Government must be coherent and consistent.

Recently, the U.S. is investing in promoting a 'coalition of moderate states' in the region. Together with her European partners, the U.S. is promoting diplomacy instead of military solutions to regional conflicts. Within this context, it is believed that regional powers could play the conflict-broker role. In this sense, Saudi Arabia's diplomatic initiation in March 2007 to resolve internal clashes between Fatah and Hamas in Palestine was particularly important. Moreover, recent Saudi-Iranian rapprochement has kindled optimism in the region. Iranian President Ahmedinejad's official visit to Saudi Arabia raised hopes for cooperation between the two regional powers to resolve regional conflicts. In this regard, Turkey also has to place herself in this regional diplomatic initiation in order to prove herself as a regional broker for the Middle Eastern conflicts. The planned meeting of foreign ministers, that was part of Iraq's *Neighbors Forum*, was an important step for Turkey. Through this meeting, Turkey succeeded in bringing Syrian and Iranian foreign ministers and the American foreign minister to the same table. This sort of diplomatic initiative will strengthen Turkey's claimed position bridging the West to the Middle East.

On the other hand, Middle Eastern counterparts have had prejudices against Turkey and could not totally trust Turkey. From the 19th century onward, Turk—Arab relations began to deteriorate and the relations between Turks and Arabs were haunted by the memories of the rift during the World War I. Since the foundation of the Republic of Turkey, the relationship between Turkey and the Arab regimes of the region had been shadowed by a legacy of historical resentments and mutual suspicions. Unfortunately, 'the terrible Turk' discourse which was developed by Arabs during Young Turk movement of 1900 was still alive until recently and it was one of the denominators of Arab political thought vis-à-vis Turkey. Yet, Arabs had not overcome and forgiven to be labeled as 'back-stabber' or 'traitor' by Turks, and Turkey's strategic alliance with Israel and the U.S. against Arabs. In this regard, positive improvements have been attained. Recently Turkish intelligentsia has initiated a 'reconciliation with the Ottoman legacy' movement, which coincided with a growing nostalgia toward Ottoman rule among Arabs. In this sense, both sides have come to a conclusion that the incidents which placed Arabs in opposition to Turks were just part of historical conjuncture and have nothing to do with contemporary states and communities. Consequently, both Turks and Arabs have been experiencing a mind-set change toward their Ottoman roots, which led to improving relations between Arabs and Turks. For Turkey, this was a chance "to reclaim the muscle of its Ottoman forebears as a force in the Middle East."[17] This mind-set change accompanied with the AKP government's Middle Eastern turn has immensely contributed in changing Arab perceptions about Turkey and Turks. Furthermore, Turkey's independent foreign policy making eased the Arab perception of Turkey as the 'lackey of the West' or 'servant of the U.S..' Now, most of the Middle Eastern states admire Turkey as democratic, secular and liberal state who is respected by the international community.

Another important issue to be taken into consideration is the Turkish public's role in Turkish foreign policy making. Even though Turkey's new orientation in foreign policymaking seems more flexible and adaptive to the international development it is getting more and more attentive toward domestic sensibilities. Consequently, the Turkish Government has found itself playing a *two-level-game* regarding its policies toward the Middle East and the EU. It is obvious that Turkey's current Middle East policy aims to balance domestic sensitivities and international requirements.

Turkish public opinion is sensitive to both European and Muslim concerns like Palestinian aspirations. This situation has been seriously taken into consideration by the Recep Tayyip Erdoğan Government who guaranteed the public support for a second term. Turkish government has been considering Turkish public's sensitivities regarding the foreign policy and security issues in general. The Turkish Parliament's rejection to participate in the U.S.-led operation in Iraq clearly illustrates the Turkish Government's efforts to satisfy its constituencies. Since the beginning of its political term, AKP plays Robert Putnam's *'two-level game'*[18] in order to balance internal dynamics and external requirements. The Iraq war and the anti-Muslim policies of the American Administration after the 9/11 attacks fueled the anti-American sentiments among Turkish public. This period was marked by tensions between the U.S. administration and the Turkish Government and improvement in Turkish Government's relations with the Middle Eastern states. During this period, AKP Government tried hard to balance internal pressures that were against its participation in American-led 'war on terror' and the external pressures for its participation in the 'coalition of willing.' Furthermore, the government has tried to provide relief for the uneasiness of the Turkish public regarding the Greater Middle East Project of the U.S. which fired old flames of the Sevres Syndrome.

On the other hand, following October 17, 2005, the date when the EU officially approved to start negotiations with Turkey, the incidents such as the EU's interventions to Turkey's sovereignty issues in the name of conditionality have raised an anti-EU tendency among the Turkish public. According to the 2007 Transatlantic Trends Survey conducted by German Marhall Fund, 56 percent of European respondents stated that it is likely that Turkey will join the EU compared with only 26 percent of Turkish respondents believed that Turkey will become an EU member. According to same survey majority of Turkish respondents (54 percent) also viewed EU leadership in the world undesirable.[19] It is highly probable that the increasing numbers of Euro skeptics among Turkish people will be effective in Turkish foreign policy making. Therefore, Turkish Government needs to make a serious effort to improve their management of public opinion.

Recently Turkish Middle East policy has been developed vis-à-vis the contradictory claims of the EU and individual member states and increasing demands from within Turkey. Despite the enthusiasm exhibited by the Turkish Government, requirements of the EU, particularly those related to the issues of Turkish 'sovereignty,' have touched the nerves of Turkish public and military elite. The Euro skeptic circle in Turkey has increasingly outnumbered and started to criticize the AKP government's position of *'to do whatever they want for the sake of membership'* and demanded more independent and "honorable" foreign policy vis-à-vis European demands. On the other hand, AKP government's openness policy toward the Arab world has attracted secularist Turks' critiques and caused tensions between the Government and the secularists. In order to balance Euro skeptic and secularist demands, Turkish Government has been working on the 'bridge' rhetoric.

Conclusion

With the demise of the Soviet Union and the subsequent end of bipolarity many states and their respective foreign policy experts have been confronting with uncertainties related to the actualization of the new world order, and the question where to find an adequate place in this emerging new order. This scenario fits particularly for Turkey that is often characterized by its geo-strategic position that requires a careful balance between Europe and the Middle East. During 1990s Turkey sought for its role in post-Cold War era. In the meantime Turkey developed self-confidence in managing her foreign affairs. The majority Government of the AKP coincided with Iraqi crisis and this coincidence posed a watershed for the Turkish foreign policy in general and the Middle East policy in particular. Since then, Turkish foreign policymakers have underlined Turkey's role as a bridge between the West and the Middle East. In spite of the eagerness of both the Turkish Government and the Turkish community to play the role of bridging two geographies and cultures, this path will evidently not be smooth. The success of this transformation from bordering the Europe to bridging Europe to the Middle East is now a matter of time to wait and see. Both the reluctance of Europeans for Turkey's integration into the EU, and the unpredictability of the Middle Eastern politics and regional instability might hinder Turkey's claimed position.

---

[1] Oral Sander, "Turkish Foreign Policy: Forces of Continuity and Change," *Turkish Review* Winter Issue, (1993), p. 31.
[2] Leonard Stone, "Turkish Foreign Policy: Four Pillars of Tradition," *Perceptions* VI/2, (1993), p. 1.
[3] Kemal Karpat et al., *Turkish Foreign Policy in Transition*, (Leiden: E.J. Brill, 1975), p. 115.
[4] Philip Robins (1999) *Turkish Foreign Policy*, Ramat Gan: The Begin Sadat Center for Strategic Studies
[5] Dietrich Jung and Wolfango Piccoli, *Turkey at the Crossroads: Ottoman Legacies and the Greater Middle East*, (London: Zed Books, 2000), p. 106.
[6] Ibid.
[7] William Hale, *Turkish Foreign Policy 1774 – 2000* (London: Frank Cass, 2000), pp. 7-8.
[8] The perception of being encircled by enemies attempting destruction of the Turkish state has remained a feature of the social habit of the Kemalist elite in Turkey.
[9] Phillip Robins, "Confusion at Home, Confusion Abroad: Turkey between Copenhagen and Iraq," *International Affairs* 79/3, (2003): p. 564.

[10] Republic of Turkey - Ministry of Foreign Affairs, *Synopsis of the Turkish Foreign Policy*. http://www.mfa.gov.tr/MFA/ForeignPolicy/Synopsis/SYNOPSIS.htm

[11] One of the Danish newspapers published a number of cartoons of Prophet Mohamed. These cartoons were considered as humiliation by the Islamic circles and after re-publishing of these cartoons by several European newspapers caused anger among the Muslims all over the world

[12] Barry Buzan and Ole Wæver, *Regions and Powers: The Structure of International Security*, (Cambridge: Cambridge University Press, 2003)

[13] Barry Buzan and Thomas Diez, "The European Union and Turkey," *Survival* 41/1, (1999): p. 47.

[14] Thomas Diez, "Turkey, the European Union and Security Complexes Revisited," *Mediterranean Politics*, 10/2, (2005): p. 172.

[15] Ersin Kalaycıoğlu, *Turkish Dynamics: Bridge across Troubled Lands*, (Hampshire: Palgrave MacMillan, 2005), p. 200.

[16] Ibid.

[17] "Turkey's Foreign Policy: An Eminence Grise," *Economist.com*, November 15, 2007

[18] In Putnam's metaphor, statesmen are strategically positioned between both levels: domestic and international: At the national level, domestic groups pursue their interests by pressuring the government to adopt favorable policies, and politicians seek power by constructing coalitions among those groups. At the international level, national governments seek to maximize their own ability to satisfy domestic pressures, while minimizing the adverse consequences of foreign developments. Robert D. Putnam, "Appendix I: Diplomacy and Domestic Politics: The Logic of Two-level Games," in *Double-Edged Diplomacy: International Bargaining and Domestic Politics*, eds. Peter B. Evans, Harold K. Jacobson and Robert D. Putnam, (Berkeley and Los Angeles: University of California Press, 1993), p. 435.

[19] The German Marshall Fund of the U.S., *Transatlantic Trends Key Findings 2007*, p. 22

CONCLUSION

Conclusion:
The EU's Neighborhood Challenge

Bezen Balamir-Coşkun

International politics and security is intimately linked to geography, since political communities are intended to be defined in terms of geographical borders. The issue of drawing/protecting borders determines the given political community's relations with its neighbourhood, which is inherently linked with the notion of collective security for the given political community. Even though the notions of borders and neighborhoods have been blurred in a highly interconnected world, the political communities still tend to prioritize the security challenges coming from immediate neighborhoods. The European Union case provides a remarkable account of the intrinsic relation between the neighborhood and security. In the 2003 European Security Strategy Report, it is stated that large-scale aggression against any Member State is improbable, but Europe faces new threats such as terrorism, proliferation of weapons of mass destruction, regional conflicts, state failure, and organized crime, all of which are firmly connected with the security and stability of the EU's neighborhood regions.

The enlargement in 2004 brought a number of challenges to the EU. The most significant of these is the neighborhood that dramatically changed due to the enlargement. New neighbors and different relations with the third states have been added to the EU agenda. Therefore, the need for a strategy to organize the new neighborhood has risen. For the EU, the responsibility of engaging in political and economic stabilization of the neighborhood regions has been assumed as more than necessary. Thus, the neighborhood dimension of European foreign and security policy has gained a new impetus. The EU's engagement in its immediate neighborhood, which is a broad geographical area from the Commonwealth of Independent States (CIS) to the Middle East and North Africa, presents a genuine challenge for foreign and security policy. In this edition, the authors discuss the crucial link between neighborhood and security in the EU context. The contributors have explored the challenges that its neighborhood poses and the EU's policies to deal with the neighborhood challenge. The analyses covered different aspects of the EU's relations with its neighbors.

In general, the EU divides its neighborhood into three regional groupings: the Mediterranean, including many of the Middle East states; the Western Balkans; Russia and the other eastern neighbors. Hence, the volume dealt with the EU's neighborhood by dividing the book into three parts based on these defined geographical groupings: Western Balkans, Russia and the CIS, and the Middle East. The contributors covered the EU's neighborhood challenge through chapters that are focused on regional, country-specific or thematic issues. Irrespective of the chosen level of analysis, almost all the chapters underlined the neighborhood dimension of European security either in terms of soft security or hard security issues.

In order to engage in its immediate neighborhood, the EU aimed to combine the formula of *'stabilization through cooperation'* with its attempts to export European security model based on democracy and liberal economy. However, as shown by different authors, the main objective of the EU in promoting cooperation and stability models in its neighborhood is to provide security for the EU itself and its citizens. Juncos' chapter on the EU's approach to organized crime in Bosnia Herzegovina, and Kibaroglu's chapter on the EU's approach toward Iran's nuclear capacity, clearly show how the EU links its internal security concerns, like organized crime and energy security, with its claims vis-à-vis the neighborhood. It is the EU's overt prioritization of its own interests and security before the objectives listed in policy documents regarding the promotion of economic development and political stabilization of neighborhood regions that has caused disappointment in its neighbors. As discussed by Yesilyurt, the EU's underestimation of the neighbors' expectations from the partnership with the EU has caused failure in implementing the Barcelona Process.

On the other hand, Bosse raised the question of the role of values in the EU's foreign policymaking toward its eastern neighborhood. Besides Russia, the Ukraine and Moldova cases, which were discussed by Bosse, tensions also exist between the normative fundamentals and the strategic objectives of the EU in the Middle East. While both the value logic and the security logic are present in the official discourse, the latest developments raise questions about whether the EU's norm export in the wider neighborhood is compatible with the EU's interests in ensuring the cooperation of neighboring states on hard and soft security matters.

Another issue raised by several authors is the EU's insistence on defining the expected relations with the neighbors based on the concepts of *'interdependence'* and *'partnership.'* The power imbalances between the EU and many of its neighbors have created unequal, one-sided dependencies. Except in the Russia case, the EU's relations with its neighbors inevitably create dependency instead of independence. Even the Neighborhood Policy is based on this inequality. As was intended by the ENP, in return for progress in demonstrating shared values and reform, partner countries will be offered benefits from closer economic integration. The ENP offers benefits from the internal market. That is to say, the possibility of benefiting more from the partnership with the EU depends on the neighbors' fulfilment of action plans prepared by the EU.

The contributors of the volume have also agreed on that, in spite of the challenges, its new neighborhood gives the EU the ability to turn the situation in its favor and contribute to stability and security of the neighborhood as well as of the Union. There are several suggestions made by the authors throughout the chapters. The authors made a wide range of suggestions, such as making use of the structured cooperation principle; extending the conditionality-based economic aid; coordinated actions between the EU and NATO, and between the EU and the U.S.; developing the existing democratization tools; increased EU assertiveness directed at conflict resolution in neighborhood regions; increased support to building new alternative energy transport routes; and developing inter-regional relations with existing regional organizations in the neighborhood.

As far as the Middle East is concerned, as was underlined by Koch, Kibaroglu, Uzer, Bal, Yeşilyurt, and Gündüz, the EU has to look at the Middle East region from a deeper strategic perspective, fully recognizing the fact that turmoil and instability in the region also have direct relevance and implications for it. The American domination in the region is on the decline, and therefore, it has become possible for the EU to exert greater influence. Yet, Europe is not about to replace the U.S. as the predominant military power in the region. In his chapter, Koch argues that what Europe can do is "to continue to offer its services, pursue engagements that lead to greater regional interactions and offer mechanisms through which potential conflicts and issues can be dealt with constructively and peacefully."

Last but not least, in the last part of the edition, Gültekin-Punsmann and Balamir-Coşkun suggest that the EU's neighborhood challenge could be eased by linking Turkey's efforts to improve and deepen its relations with the neighboring countries with a sound European strategy toward its new periphery.

Throughout the chapters, contributors discussed the different aspects of the EU's neighborhood challenge. Due to the fact that the enlarged EU is surrounded by politically and economically challenged regions, the Union's policies regarding its neighborhood is becoming more and more important regarding the security of the EU. Besides their security implications, the EU's policies regarding its neighborhood are also among the main indicators of the EU's global reach. As most of the cases analyzed here show, in spite of its claim to be a global actor, until recently, the EU has focused on the internal security dimension of its relations with its neighbors and undermined its claimed global role. Hence, it has fallen short in satisfying its neighbors' expectations from the Union as a global power that could contribute to the security and stability of its neighborhood regions. The authors argued that the EU is on its way to becoming a global actor, but still far from actually being one. To this end, the EU needs to pursue a more active, action-oriented approach and it needs to take more risks. It is argued that the EU has the potential to actively engage in its neighborhood and become successful in contributing stability and security of its neighbors. But it has to take a global perspective instead of remaining internally-focused and internal security-oriented.

Index

A

Abkhazia, 45, 212, 214, 215, 216, 217, 219, 220, 221, 222, 226, 227, 228, 275, 301, 383
accession, 24, 25, 26, 28, 32, 45, 60, 82, 83, 90, 122, 146, 154, 155, 172, 215, 218, 226, 275, 276, 278, 284, 313, 316, 319, 329, 331, 332, 336, 342, 344, 345, 346, 347, 348, 349, 351, 379, 384, 385, 386, 388, 389, 390, 393, 394, 395, 404
Action Plan, 24, 28, 53, 105, 138, 221, 222, 224, 229, 277, 278, 279, 280, 281, 284, 317, 320, 321, 323, 326, 335, 336, 383, 384, 385, 393
Afghanistan, 52, 86, 95, 96, 101, 102, 106, 108, 113, 152, 172, 213, 235, 237, 238, 242, 246, 248, 254, 353, 354, 355, 356, 357, 359, 366, 367, 372, 375, 398
Ajaria, 215, 216, 227
Albania, 31, 32, 37, 39, 67, 69, 74, 80, 87, 155, 252, 281, 284, 310, 385
Algeria, 104, 105, 106, 146, 239
Aliyev, Haydar, 259, 260
Aliyev, Ilham, 217, 261
Amsterdam Treaty, 81, 242
Arab
   -Israeli conflict, 107, 124, 125, 130, 137, 145, 167
   League, 132, 133, 135, 172
Argentina, 188, 189, 194, 198, 206
Armenia, 105, 211, 213, 214, 217, 218, 219, 220, 221, 222, 223, 224, 225, 227, 228, 229, 239, 252, 255, 256, 257, 260, 261, 266, 267, 268, 273, 276, 278, 280, 281, 284, 293, 294, 308, 361, 383, 384, 387, 388, 389, 390, 391, 392, 394, 395
Austria, 291, 310, 324, 339, 358, 380
Azerbaijan, xix, xx, xxi, 45, 105, 211, 213, 214, 217, 218, 219, 220, 221, 223, 224, 225, 228, 230, 239, 253, 255, 256, 257, 258, 259, 260, 261, 264, 265, 266, 267, 268, 270, 272, 273, 276, 278, 280, 281, 284, 293, 294, 300, 308, 361, 383, 384, 387, 389, 390, 393

B

Bahrain, 105, 165, 169, 172, 178, 394
Balkans, ix, xxi, 24, 25, 26, 31, 32, 33, 34, 35, 36, 37, 38, 39, 40, 41, 42, 43, 44, 45, 48, 49, 51, 52, 53, 54, 59, 60, 62, 64, 66, 67, 69, 75, 80, 81, 82, 83, 84, 86, 87, 88, 89, 90, 232, 273, 275, 277, 284, 304, 306, 345, 351, 368, 414
Baltic, 310, 331, 338, 358, 381
Barcelona Process, 27, 104, 105, 107, 108, 109, 112, 116, 146, 150, 160, 161, 223, 414
Belarus, 105, 252, 257, 268, 276, 278, 280, 286, 294, 313, 314, 315, 316, 317, 325, 338, 341, 342, 361, 374
Belgium, 79, 102, 189, 191, 203, 365
Black Sea
   synergy, 295, 298, 301, 307
Border
   management, 384, 393
Brazil, 188, 189, 190, 198, 206, 231
Britain, xvii, 76, 81, 110, 131, 135, 136, 139, 191, 236, 249, 269, 381
Bulgaria, 33, 80, 252, 273, 275, 281, 284, 287, 293, 295, 300, 303, 304, 306, 308, 310, 335, 358, 383, 384, 385

C

Canada, xv, 80, 188, 191, 203, 205
Caspian Sea, 212, 227, 231, 237, 243, 246, 248, 253, 254, 256, 257, 269, 300
Caucasus
   South Caucasus, x, xv, xvii, 45, 211, 213, 214, 217, 218, 219,

220, 221, 223, 224, 225, 226, 227, 228, 229, 230, 239, 243, 251, 301, 308, 310, 358, 379, 382, 383, 386, 388, 394
Central Asia, x, xiv, xvi, 27, 28, 95, 98, 212, 228, 229, 231, 232, 233, 234, 235, 236, 237, 238, 239, 240, 241, 242, 243, 244, 245, 246, 247, 248, 249, 250, 251, 252, 253, 254, 255, 258, 263, 267, 268, 269, 270, 271, 275, 283, 293, 299, 300, 302, 308, 309, 324, 353, 354, 355, 356, 357, 358, 359, 360, 361, 362, 363, 366, 367, 368, 369, 370, 371, 372, 373
Chechnya, 296, 320
China, 99, 112, 120, 126, 178, 187, 194, 195, 231, 236, 237, 238, 240, 243, 245, 247, 248, 250, 256, 259, 268, 270, 271, 299, 353, 355, 359, 368, 369, 372
civil society, 32, 37, 41, 53, 58, 80, 107, 109, 138, 150, 153, 159, 169, 219, 245, 258, 259, 271, 278, 303, 306, 315, 319, 321, 354, 355, 363, 364, 369, 381
civilian power, 71, 72, 88, 101, 122
Cold War, 23, 24, 49, 69, 71, 75, 95, 99, 100, 101, 102, 111, 112, 113, 114, 115, 145, 155, 202, 273, 274, 293, 294, 304, 308, 309, 314, 338, 387, 391, 399, 408
Common Strategy, xix, 314, 315, 316, 324
Community Assistance for Reconstruction, xix, 32, 84
Conditionality, 326
conflict, xv, xvii, 23, 25, 26, 31, 35, 36, 37, 44, 54, 69, 70, 74, 75, 77, 78, 80, 81, 82, 86, 87, 103, 107, 109, 112, 113, 121, 123, 124, 125, 129, 130, 133, 134, 135, 136, 137, 139, 145, 150, 154, 167, 188, 190, 191, 199, 212, 214, 217, 219, 221, 222, 223, 236,븣255, 260, 266, 275, 276, 280, 281, 301, 302, 307, 310, 319, 320, 337, 342, 355, 379,

383, 386, 387, 397, 400, 402, 404, 405, 415
Contact Group, 70, 78, 84, 89
Copenhagen Criteria, 151
corruption, 41, 53, 54, 55, 58, 65, 153, 222, 245, 276, 319, 335, 337, 355, 356
crisis management, 61, 82, 275, 305, 369
Croatia, 32, 33, 36, 37, 39, 70, 75, 77, 80, 85, 155, 273, 277, 287, 385
cross-border cooperation, xv, 283, 284, 285, 361, 381, 382, 385, 386, 390, 391
Cyprus, xvii, 39, 85, 122, 137, 146, 221, 229, 251, 385, 388, 399
Czech Republic, 251, 255, 291, 358
Czechoslovakia, 71, 194, 203

D

Dayton Agreement, 54, 55, 74
democracy, 32, 36, 58, 96, 98, 103, 107, 111, 117, 121, 132, 137, 140, 146, 147, 148, 150, 152, 153, 158, 163, 178, 236, 237, 241, 242, 244, 254, 258, 259, 263, 267, 270, 275, 278, 294, 295, 296, 299, 307, 310, 313, 314, 315, 318, 319, 320, 322, 325, 327, 332, 334,븣339, 340, 341, 343, 348, 360, 367, 369, 374, 375, 381, 414
democratization, 27, 32, 38, 80, 96, 97, 99, 103, 107, 114, 140, 150, 158, 206, 213, 233, 245, 254, 256, 258, 259, 263, 268, 280, 293, 294, 295, 299, 301, 302, 303, 306, 321, 415

E

Egypt, 104, 105, 106, 123, 124, 125, 133, 134, 135, 136, 137, 143, 146, 239
energy, xiii, xv, 26, 27, 38, 45, 99, 100, 132, 159, 168, 169, 170, 173, 176, 177, 178, 179, 180, 181, 190, 193, 196, 197, 198, 205, 213, 219,

223, 226, 231, 233, 237, 239, 242, 243, 245, 246, 248, 250, 251, 253, 254, 255, 256, 257, 258, 259, 261, 262, 263, 265,틀266, 267, 268, 269, 271, 273, 274, 275, 278, 280, 283, 285, 286, 287, 289, 290, 294, 295, 296, 297, 299, 300, 302, 303, 304, 305, 307, 308, 309, 310, 323, 336, 338, 340, 341, 354, 357, 358, 359, 360, 362, 367, 368, 371, 372, 373, 391, 394, 414, 415

enlargement, 24, 25, 41, 43, 44, 45, 48, 49, 54, 58, 59, 60, 63, 69, 82, 83, 90, 145, 151, 155, 174, 223, 224, 225, 226, 236, 239, 245, 247, 251, 254, 255, 273, 276, 277, 279, 287, 290, 309, 311, 313, 315, 316, 318, 325, 329, 332, 333, 335, 337, 344, 348, 360, 362, 379, 386, 413

Eurasia, 237, 248, 249, 250, 251, 255, 259, 267, 268, 270, 308, 310, 375

Euro-Arab Dialogue, xix, 167, 179, 184

European
  Court of Justice, 119
  identity, 37, 119, 120, 121, 131
  Parliament, xvi, 43, 119, 135, 158, 162, 184, 287, 290, 291, 302, 309, 324, 326, 344, 346, 347, 348, 350, 351, 365, 383, 388, 389, 394

Europeanization, xv, 39, 42, 43, 185, 254, 268, 334, 392

F

Finland, 338, 339, 344, 358, 381
Fortress Europe, 59, 153
France, 39, 76, 78, 79, 81, 89, 101, 102, 103, 108, 110, 119, 122, 131, 132, 135, 136, 137, 139, 141, 154, 173, 174, 185, 188, 189, 190, 191, 192, 199, 201, 202, 203, 221, 255, 291, 297, 322, 347, 350, 351, 357, 365, 375

G

Geneva Process, 219
Georgia, xv, xvii, xx, 82, 96, 105, 211, 213, 214, 215, 217, 218, 219, 220, 221, 222, 223, 224, 225, 227, 228, 229, 239, 250, 252, 256, 257, 261, 264, 267, 268, 273, 275, 276, 278, 280, 281, 284, 293, 294, 298, 300, 308, 310, 361, 383, 384, 387, 389, 390, 391, 393
Germany, xvi, xviii, 75, 78, 79, 88, 89, 91, 101, 102, 103, 108, 114, 119, 120, 131, 137, 139, 141, 172, 188, 189, 190, 191, 199, 201, 202, 203, 207, 221, 248, 255, 274, 287, 291, 297, 322, 346, 351, 357, 358, 360, 365, 366, 367, 371, 374, 375, 380
global player, 69, 87
globalization, 275, 291
governance, 25, 37, 38, 49, 154, 155, 156, 158, 162, 163, 176, 242, 247, 276, 283, 290, 293, 295, 303, 323, 355, 359, 369, 373, 379, 381
Great Game, 212, 248, 249, 269
Greater Middle East
  and North African Project, 95
  Project, 27, 95, 96, 99, 100, 101, 105, 111, 112, 407
Greece, xvii, 33, 39, 45, 85, 137, 142, 252, 281, 284, 310, 358, 384, 385
Green Paper, 180, 240, 251, 269, 310, 358, 371
Gulf Crisis, 75, 125, 399

H

hard security, 56, 57, 61, 183, 414
Helsinki Final Act, 254
human rights, 25, 32, 37, 38, 55, 77, 80, 99, 107, 111, 121, 132, 137, 138, 146, 147, 148, 151, 153, 154, 156, 157, 158, 160, 170, 175, 178, 219, 233, 238, 242, 244, 245, 261, 270, 278, 279, 280, 288, 299, 313, 315, 319, 320, 321, 322, 323, 325, 327, 334, 355, 357, 361, 365, 366, 369, 374

Hungary, xxi, 39, 251, 310, 333, 338, 349, 358, 380

I

Iceland, 155
India, 99, 120, 126, 178, 188, 194, 202, 231, 236, 247, 250, 359
Iraq
    War is, xvi, 102, 114, 115, 165, 204
Islam, xx, 98, 108, 112, 114, 160, 161, 163, 170, 234, 243, 249, 269, 355, 357, 364, 370, 400
Islamophobia, 100, 403
Israel, 95, 96, 103, 104, 105, 106, 107, 112, 113, 123, 124, 125, 126, 127, 128, 129, 131, 132, 133, 134, 135, 136, 137, 138, 139, 141, 142, 143, 144, 146, 149, 154, 171, 187, 188, 201, 202, 289, 399, 401, 404, 406

J

Japan, 71, 80, 88, 99, 120, 126, 178, 188, 190, 191, 203, 236, 240, 243, 252
Jordan, 104, 105, 124, 125, 127, 137, 145, 146

K

Kazakhstan, xix, 28, 213, 231, 234, 235, 241, 244, 246, 248, 249, 250, 252, 253, 255, 256, 257, 258, 262, 264, 265, 266, 267, 268, 269, 270, 271, 272, 299, 308, 342, 357, 358, 359, 360, 361, 364, 368, 370, 372
Kuwait, 105, 121, 125, 165, 175, 177, 178, 206, 394, 399
Kyrgyzstan, 213, 234, 236, 238, 243, 245, 249, 250, 252, 257, 261, 267, 268, 354, 355, 360, 361, 367, 370

L

Lebanon, xxii, 104, 105, 107, 126, 128, 136, 137, 141, 144, 145, 146, 159, 405

Libya, 104, 105, 106, 188, 189, 191, 203, 207, 239

M

Maastricht Treaty, 48, 64, 75, 100, 121, 333
Malta, 137, 146, 251
Marshall Plan, 130
Mediterranean, ix, xv, xix, xxi, 24, 27, 96, 104, 105, 106, 108, 109, 112, 114, 116, 137, 145, 146, 147, 148, 149, 150, 151, 152, 153, 154, 155, 156, 157, 158, 159, 160, 161, 162, 163, 167, 169, 171, 172, 184, 246, 274, 275, 284, 288, 309, 315, 316, 317, 326, 382, 384,본395, 409, 413
Mexico, 232
Middle East
    peace process, 27, 119, 120, 130, 138, 140, 141, 149, 150
migration, 49, 57, 97, 98, 100, 106, 146, 148, 153, 156, 246, 248, 280, 290, 293, 295, 337, 348, 385
Minsk Group, 221, 255
Moldova, xv, xx, 80, 105, 252, 257, 268, 273, 274, 275, 276, 278, 279, 280, 281, 284, 286, 289, 293, 294, 295, 298, 300, 302, 308, 310, 313, 314, 315, 316, 317, 319, 320, 321, 324, 325, 326, 337, 338, 361, 414
Montenegro, 32, 33, 34, 40, 43, 67, 80, 84, 85, 155, 281, 284, 385
Morocco, 104, 105, 146, 289, 326
Muslim, 54, 76, 108, 112, 116, 237, 250, 353, 397, 407

N

Nagorno Karabakh, 212, 214, 217, 220, 221, 222, 255, 260, 266
Nakhitchevan, 387
neighbor, 25, 105, 106, 155, 279, 333, 356
neighborhood, 24, 25, 26, 72, 109, 159, 182, 253, 254, 255, 256, 257, 258, 260, 264, 267, 268, 271, 274, 275, 276, 277, 280, 284, 286, 299,

Index

313, 314, 315, 316, 317, 318, 321, 323, 338, 383, 384, 386, 388, 402, 413, 414, 415
Netherlands, xiii, xvii, 79, 108, 131, 172, 173, 191, 203
Nigeria, 239
normative power, 27, 72, 88, 157, 158, 160, 277
North Korea, 188, 207, 250
Norway, 80, 126, 155, 180, 227, 239, 271, 348, 387
nuclear weapons, 71, 187, 190, 191, 198, 199, 203, 204, 206

O

oil, 54, 75, 96, 98, 99, 123, 130, 131, 132, 145, 167, 170, 175, 177, 178, 179, 180, 193, 200, 204, 213, 227, 231, 244, 246, 248, 253, 255, 256, 257, 258, 260, 264, 265, 266, 267, 269, 270, 281, 293, 296, 297, 299, 300, 308, 309, 310, 340, 341, 342, 349, 357, 358, 359, 368, 371, 372, 405
Oman, 105, 165, 178, 394
organized crime, 26, 41, 47, 48, 49, 50, 51, 52, 53, 54, 55, 56, 57, 58, 59, 60, 61, 62, 63, 64, 65, 66, 81, 232, 246, 275, 276, 281, 282, 285, 290, 293, 294, 295, 302, 304, 305, 319, 320, 413, 414
Ottoman, xiv, 73, 157, 387, 395, 400, 406, 408

P

Pakistan, 95, 96, 188, 189, 190, 194, 203, 231, 236, 246, 250, 359, 367, 372
Palestine, 82, 107, 123, 124, 125, 138, 139, 141, 159, 404, 405
PCA, xxi, 288, 294, 314, 319, 335, 336, 360, 361, 363, 364, 368
Petersberg tasks, 82
Poland, xxi, 150, 172, 203, 251, 291, 333, 337, 338, 341, 342, 346, 349, 358, 365, 381

Q

Qatar, 105, 165, 178, 239, 394

R

reform, 24, 32, 36, 38, 43, 54, 57, 58, 60, 63, 66, 106, 107, 150, 151, 154, 155, 156, 167, 174, 176, 179, 219, 222, 232, 271, 278, 279, 280, 295, 298, 316, 319, 335, 345, 347, 362, 363, 365, 373, 383, 400, 414
refugees, 26, 32, 34, 38, 39, 79, 81, 133, 137, 322, 355, 365, 387
Romania, xv, xvii, 33, 80, 85, 273, 275, 281, 284, 287, 293, 295, 300, 302, 303, 304, 306, 307, 310, 311, 333, 335, 337, 338, 383, 385
rule of law, 25, 32, 49, 53, 61, 85, 103, 106, 107, 122, 138, 148, 155, 158, 159, 219, 236, 238, 242, 244, 245, 278, 296, 313, 315, 319, 320, 322, 325, 334, 344, 363, 367, 369, 388, 390
Russia, x, xiv, xv, xvi, 24, 26, 27, 28, 49, 75, 79, 80, 84, 89, 99, 105, 112, 126, 129, 177, 194, 195, 196, 197, 205, 212, 214, 216, 217, 220, 224, 225, 226, 227, 228, 231, 233, 234, 236, 237, 238, 239, 245, 246, 247, 248, 249, 250, 252, 254, 255, 256, 257, 258, 259, 260, 263, 264, 265, 266, 268, 269, 271, 273, 274, 276, 277, 278, 279, 281, 284, 286, 287, 289, 293, 295, 296, 297, 298, 299, 300, 301, 302, 303, 304, 305, 307, 308, 309, 310, 313, 314, 315, 316, 317, 318, 320, 321, 322, 323, 324, 325, 326, 327, 330, 331, 340, 341, 342, 349, 353, 354, 355, 357, 358, 359, 360, 361, 364, 365, 367, 368, 369, 371, 372, 374, 381, 386, 387, 394, 413, 414

S

Saudi Arabia, 105, 165, 172, 175, 178, 181, 227, 394, 405

securitization, 26, 48, 51, 52, 54, 57, 58, 59, 60, 62, 63, 148
self-determination, 26, 39, 74, 86, 124, 133
Slovakia, 39, 85, 251, 252, 255, 291, 333, 338, 358, 380
Slovenia, 33, 55, 70, 75, 77, 85, 251, 380
soft power, 81, 86, 99, 102, 139, 140, 309, 405
South Africa, 188, 189, 203, 206, 394
South Ossetia, 45, 212, 214, 215, 216, 217, 220, 222, 228, 275, 301, 383
sovereignty, 26, 43, 71, 100, 120, 122, 128, 129, 131, 166, 167, 183, 243, 268, 332, 380, 407
Soviet Union, 75, 111, 124, 125, 126, 194, 195, 211, 235, 237, 238, 259, 262, 263, 273, 293, 294, 359, 360, 361, 387, 391, 408
Spain, xvii, 39, 79, 85, 102, 103, 108, 126, 137, 139, 146, 154, 184, 189, 194, 324, 404
Stability Pact for Southeastern Europe, 80, 82, 90
superpower, 44, 70, 71, 72, 87, 130, 181, 402
Sweden, xvii, 191, 194, 203, 249, 255, 339, 348, 381
Switzerland, 80, 155, 202, 203, 348
Syria, 104, 105, 107, 123, 126, 127, 137, 145, 146, 151, 384, 397, 400, 401, 404, 405

T

Tajikistan, 234, 235, 238, 241, 243, 244, 250, 252, 257, 267, 308, 354, 355, 356, 360, 361, 370
terrorism, xiii, xvii, 25, 48, 49, 50, 53, 60, 65, 96, 97, 98, 99, 100, 101, 102, 103, 104, 106, 112, 132, 134, 137, 138, 146, 148, 153, 154, 162, 170, 173, 175, 213, 232, 234, 237, 246, 275, 276, 278, 280, 282, 290, 293, 304, 319, 320, 353, 354, 357, 366, 367, 375, 413
Thessaloniki Summit, 33, 82

Transdniestria, 319, 320
Tunisia, 104, 105, 106, 107, 146
Turkey, x, xi, xiii, xv, xvii, xviii, 28, 80, 95, 96, 104, 108, 114, 115, 116, 117, 137, 140, 142, 146, 154, 155, 157, 158, 172, 184, 212, 214, 215, 217, 218, 220, 225, 227, 231, 236, 240, 249, 250, 255, 256, 257, 260, 264, 266, 269, 273, 275, 277, 281, 284, 286, 287, 293, 296, 300, 304, 305, 307, 308, 310, 330, 338, 339, 345, 346, 358, 368, 379, 383, 384, 385, 386, 387, 388, 389, 390, 391, 392, 393, 394, 395, 397, 398, 399, 400, 401, 402, 403, 404, 405, 406, 407, 408, 409, 415
Turkmenistan, xix, 232, 233, 234, 235, 236, 241, 243, 244, 246, 248, 252, 253, 255, 256, 257, 258, 259, 263, 264, 265, 266, 267, 268, 271, 272, 299, 308, 357, 358, 359, 361, 368, 370, 372

U

Ukraine, x, xiv, xx, 28, 105, 180, 240, 252, 257, 261, 268, 271, 273, 274, 275, 276, 278, 279, 281, 284, 286, 293, 294, 295, 298, 300, 308, 309, 313, 314, 315, 316, 317, 325, 329, 330, 331, 332, 333, 334, 335, 336, 337, 338, 339, 340, 341, 342, 343, 344, 345, 346, 347, 348, 349, 350, 351, 358, 359, 361, 371, 372, 414
Uzbekistan, x, xx, 213, 227, 233, 234, 236, 238, 241, 243, 244, 246, 247, 249, 250, 252, 257, 267, 268, 271, 308, 353, 354, 355, 356, 357, 358, 359, 360, 361, 362, 363, 364, 365, 366, 367, 368, 369, 370, 371, 372, 373, 374, 375

V

Venice Declaration, 133, 134, 135, 136, 137
Vojvodina, 40, 72

W

war, 23, 26, 32, 33, 34, 36, 37, 44, 53, 54, 55, 72, 74, 75, 76, 77, 80, 95, 96, 101, 102, 103, 104, 108, 116, 123, 124, 131, 133, 134, 136, 139, 140, 141, 142, 183, 192, 193, 194, 204, 212, 213, 216, 217, 228, 233, 242, 293, 296, 310, 339, 354, 367, 398, 400, 402, 407

Western Balkans, ix, xxi, 24, 25, 26, 31, 32, 33, 34, 35, 36, 37, 38, 40, 41, 42, 43, 44, 45, 46, 49, 51, 52, 53, 59, 60, 62, 64, 65, 66, 67, 69, 80, 82, 83, 86, 87, 90, 273, 277, 284, 345, 413

Wider Europe, 67, 156, 162, 239, 277, 280, 313, 315, 316, 317, 318, 324, 325, 350, 394

World Bank, 80, 114, 243, 272

X

xenophobia, 44, 153

Y

Yugoslavia, xx, 31, 34, 40, 69, 72, 73, 74, 75, 77, 78, 83, 85, 88, 89, 252

Z

Zakaria, Fareed, 161
Zapatero, Jose Luis, 139